THE LIBRARY
ST. MARY'S COLLEGE OF MARYLAND
ST. MARY'S CITY, MARY

D1593481

THE YOUNG HEIDEGGER

S T U D I E S   I N   C O N T I N E N T A L   T H O U G H T

John Sallis, *general editor*

Consulting Editors

Robert Bernasconi

Rudolf Bernet

John D. Caputo

David Carr

Edward S. Casey

Hubert L. Dreyfus

Don Ihde

David Farrell Krell

Lenore Langsdorf

Alphonso Lingis

William L. McBride

J. N. Mohanty

Mary Rawlinson

Tom Rockmore

Calvin O. Schrag

Charles E. Scott

Thomas Sheehan

Robert Sokolowski

Bruce W. Wilshire

David Wood

THE
YOUNG
HEIDEGGER
Rumor of the Hidden King

John van Buren

Indiana University Press

Bloomington and Indianapolis

© 1994 by John van Buren

All rights reserved

No part of this book may be reproduced or utilized in any form
or by any means, electronic or mechanical, including photocopy-
ing and recording, or by any information storage and retrieval
system, without permission in writing from the publisher. The
Association of American University Presses' Resolution on
Permissions constitutes the only exception to this prohibition.

The paper used in this publication meets the minimum require-
ments of American National Standard for Information Sciences—
Permanence of Paper for Printed Library Materials, ANSI
Z39.48-1984.

Manufactured in the United States of America

Library of Congress Cataloging-in-Publication Data

Van Buren, John, date
    The young Heidegger : rumor of the hidden king / John Van Buren.
      p. cm. — (Studies in Continental thought)
    Includes bibliographical references and index.
    ISBN 0-253-36202-4 (alk. paper)
    1. Heidegger, Martin, 1889-1976. 2. Philosophers—Germany—
Biography. I. Title. II. Series.
B3279.H49V28 1994
193—dc20
[B]   94-4292

    2 3 4 5 00 99 98 97 96

*In memory of
my brothers*

*Tom
and
Robbie*

*who remain
a time to come*

Contents

14 The Mystery of All Life   295

15 Indications of Ethics   319

16 Reinscribing Heidegger   362

      Notes   399
      Index   409

Acknowledgments

I WOULD LIKE to thank the following journals and publishers for permission to use portions of my previously published essays: "The Young Heidegger: Rumor of a Hidden King (1919-1926)," *Philosophy Today* 33 (1989): 99-109; "The Young Heidegger and Phenomenology," *Man and World* 23 (1990): 239-72; "The Young Heidegger, Aristotle, Ethics," in Arleen A. Dallery and Charles E. Scott (eds.), *Ethics and Danger: Essays on Heidegger and Continental Thought* (Albany: State University of New York Press, 1992), pp. 169-85; "Stories of Being," in Arleen A. Dallery and Stephen Watson (eds.), *Transitions in Continental Philosophy* (Albany: State University of New York Press, 1994); "Martin Heidegger, Martin Luther," in Theodore Kisiel and John van Buren (eds.), *Reading Heidegger from the Start: Essays in His Earliest Thought* (Albany: State University of New York Press, 1994); "Heidegger's Autobiographies," *Journal of the British Society for Phenomenology* 23 (1992): 201-21; "Heidegger's *Sache*: A Family Portrait," *Research in Phenomenology* 22 (1992): 161-85; "Heidegger's Early Freiburg Lecture Courses," *Research in Phenomenology* 23 (1993): 132-52.

I would also like to thank Samuel IJsseling, Director of the Husserl Archive in Louvain, Belgium, for permission to cite from Husserl's letters to Heidegger from May 27, 1916 onward (LH); and Frithjof Rodi and Friedrich Hogemann at the Archiv der Dilthey-Forschungsstelle, Ruhr-Universität, Bochum, Germany, for permissions to cite from Walter Bröcker's transcript of Heidegger's 1925 lecture series, "Wilhelm Diltheys Forschungsarbeit und der Kampf um eine historische Weltanschauung" (WDF), and from Franz-Josef Brecht's transcript of Heidegger's SS 1920 lecture course, "Phänomenologie der Anschauung und des Ausdrucks (Theorie der philosophischen Begriffsbildung)" (PAA).

I am especially grateful to John Caputo and Theodore Kisiel for their remarks on the present text.

I wish to acknowledge Gary Madison, Jakob Amstutz, Kenneth Dorter, and Sam Ajzenstat for reading an earlier draft begun in 1985 and completed in 1989.

My thanks to Janet Rabinowitch, senior sponsoring editor at Indiana University Press, and the series editor, John Sallis, for their interest in my text, as well as to Robert Bernasconi on the editorial board and my reader Thomas Sheehan.

To the numerous others who offered comments and assistance, I also express my appreciation.

Thanks to my colleagues in the philosophy department at Fordham University for their support.

To Daniel and Annette Ahern, the "housefriends," I am thankful for the *Gelassenheit* of our conversations.

To my mother and father, and brothers and sisters, I remain ever grateful for their love and support.

To my wife, Eileen, I am eternally beholden for lending her loving hand during the time of final editing.

Abbreviations

REFERENCES ARE GIVEN to texts in the original language and to the published English translation; the two are separated by a slash. In the body of my text, I have often modified published translations. References within the text are often grouped either in a note or in parentheses at the end of the paragraph. Heidegger's *Gesamtausgabe* (Frankfurt: Klostermann, 1976ff.) is abbreviated below as "G," with the volume number immediately following and the year of publication given in parentheses.

Texts of Heidegger

BCP "On the Being and Conception of *Physis* in Aristotle's Physics B, 1," tr. Thomas Sheehan, *Man and World* 9 (1976): 219–70.

BL "Drei Briefe Martin Heideggers an Karl Löwith," in Dietrich Papenfuss and Otto Pöggeler (eds.), *Zur philosophischen Aktualität Heideggers*, Vol. 2: *Im Gespräch der Zeit* (Frankfurt: Klostermann, 1990), pp. 27–39.

BW *Martin Heidegger: Basic Writings*, ed. David Farrell Krell (New York: Harper & Row, 1977).

BZ *Der Begriff der Zeit* (Tübingen: Max Niemeyer, 1989)/*The Concept of Time*, tr. William McNeill (New York: Basil Blackwell, 1992).

CA "Contributions to *Der Akademiker*, 1910–1913" (German and English), tr. John Protevi, *Graduate Faculty Philosophy Journal* 14–15 (1991): 486–519.

CT "The Concept of Time in the Science of History," tr. Harry S. Taylor and Hans W. Uffelmann, *Journal of the British Society for Phenomenology* 9 (1978): 3–10.

DT *Discourse on Thinking*, tr. John M. Anderson and E. Hans Freund (New York: Harper & Row, 1966).

DW Transcript of "Dasein und Wahrsein nach Aristoteles (Interpretationen von Buch VI Nik. Ethik)," lecture given on December 2, 1924, in Cologne.

EB *Existence and Being*, tr. Werner Brock (South Bend, Indiana: Regnery/Gateway, 1979).

EGT   *Early Greek Thinking*, tr. David Farrell Krell and Frank A. Capuzzi (New York: Harper & Row, 1975).

EP   *The End of Philosophy*, tr. Joan Stambaugh (New York: Harper & Row, 1973).

EPR   *Einleitung in die Phänomenologie der Religion*, lecture course WS 1920–21, transcript by Fritz Kaufmann.

ER   *On the Essence of Reasons*, tr. Terrence Malick (Evanston: Northwestern University Press, 1969).

G1   *Frühe Schriften* (1978). Heidegger's dissertation on Duns Scotus contained in this volume has been translated in Harold J. Robbins, "Duns Scotus's Theory of the Categories and of Meaning by Martin Heidegger" (Ph.D. Diss., De Paul University, 1978).

G3   *Kant und das Problem der Metaphysik* (1990)/*Kant and the Problem of Metaphysics*, tr. Richard Taft (Bloomington: Indiana University Press, 1990).

G5   *Holzwege* (1977).

G9   *Wegmarken* (1976).

G12   *Unterwegs zur Sprache* (1985)/*On the Way to Language*, tr. Peter D. Hertz (New York: Harper & Row, 1971).

G13   *Aus der Erfahrung des Denkens* (1983).

G15   *Seminare* (1986).

G17   *Der Beginn der neuzeitlichen Philosophie* (forthcoming).

G18   *Aristoteles: Rhetorik* (forthcoming).

G19   *Platon: Sophistes* (1992).

G20   *Prolegomena zur Geschichte des Zeitbegriffs* (1979)/*History of the Concept of Time: Prolegomena*, tr. Theodore Kisiel (Bloomington: Indiana University Press, 1985). See the errata list in G61.

G21   *Logik. Die Frage Nach der Wahrheit* (1976)/*Logic: The Question of Truth*, tr. Thomas Sheehan and Reginald Lilly (Bloomington: Indiana University Press, forthcoming).

G22   *Grundbegriffe der antiken Philosophie* (1993).

G23   *Geschichte der Philosophie von Thomas v. Aquin bis Kant* (forthcoming).

G24   *Die Grundprobleme der Phänomenologie* (1975)/*The Basic Problems of Phenomenology*, tr. Albert Hofstadter (Bloomington: Indiana University Press, 1982).

G25   *Phänomenologische Interpretation von Kants Kritik der reinen Vernunft* (1987)/*Phenomenological Interpretations of Kant's Critique of Pure Reason*, tr. Parvis Emad and Kenneth Maly (Bloomington: Indiana University Press, forthcoming).

G26   *Metaphysische Anfangsgründe der Logik im Ausgang von Leibniz*

(1978)/*The Metaphysical Foundations of Logic*, tr. Michael Heim (Bloomington: Indiana University Press, 1984).

G27   *Einleitung in die Philosophie* (forthcoming).

G28   *Der Deutsche Idealismus (Fichte, Hegel, Schelling) und die philosophische Problemlage der Gegenwart* (forthcoming).

G29/30   *Die Grundbegriffe der Metaphysik. Welt-Endlichkeit-Einsamkeit* (1983)/*The Fundamental Concepts of Metaphysics*, tr. William McNeill and Nicholas Walker (Bloomington: Indiana University Press, forthcoming).

G31   *Vom Wesen der menschlichen Freiheit. Einleitung in die Philosophie* (1982).

G32   *Hegels Phänomenologie des Geistes* (1980)/*Hegel's Phenomenology of Spirit* (Bloomington: Indiana University Press, 1988).

G34   *Vom Wesen der Wahrheit. Zu Platons Höhlengleichnis und Theätet* (1988).

G36/37   *Sein und Wahrheit* (forthcoming).

G40   *Einführung in die Metaphysik* (1983)/*An Introduction to Metaphysics*, tr. Ralph Manheim (New Haven: Yale University Press, 1959).

G48   *Nietzsche: Der europäische Nihilismus* (1986).

G55   *Heraklit* (1979).

G56/57   *Zur Bestimmung der Philosophie* (1987). See the errata lists for this volume and for G61 by Theodore Kisiel in his "Edition und Übersetzung," in Dietrich Papenfuss and Otto Pöggeler (eds.), *Zur Philosophischen Aktualität Heideggers*, Vol. 3 (Frankfurt: Klostermann, 1992), pp. 106–107.

G58   *Grundprobleme der Phänomenologie* (1993).

G59   *Phänomenologie der Anschauung und des Ausdrucks. Theorie der philosophischen Begriffsbildung* (1993).

G60   *Augustinus und der Neuplatonismus* (forthcoming).

G61   *Phänomenologische Interpretationen zu Aristoteles. Einführung in die phänomenologische Forschung* (1985).

G62   *Phänomenologische Interpretation ausgewählter Abhandlungen des Aristoteles zur Ontologie und Logik* (forthcoming).

G63   *Ontologie (Hermeneutik der Faktizität)* (1988)/*Ontology (Hermeneutics of Facticity)*, tr. John van Buren (Bloomington: Indiana University Press, 1995).

G64   *Der Begriff der Zeit* (forthcoming).

G65   *Beiträge zur Philosophie (Vom Ereignis)* (1989)/*Contributions to Philosophy*, tr. Parvis Emad and Kenneth Maly (Bloomington: Indiana University Press, forthcoming).

GD   "Grundsätze des Denkens," *Jahrbuch für Psychologie und Psycho-therapie 6* (1958): 33–41.

HB   Martin Heidegger and Elisabeth Blochmann, *Briefwechsel, 1918–1969*, ed. Joachim W. Storck (Marbach am Neckar: Deutsche Schillergesellschaft, 1989).

HFH   "Hebel—Friend of the House," tr. Bruce V. Foltz and Michael Heim, in Darrel E. Christensen (ed.), *Contemporary German Philosophy*, Vol. 3 (University Park: Pennsylvania State University Press, 1983), pp. 89–101.

HJ   Martin Heidegger and Karl Jaspers, *Briefwechsel 1920–1963*, ed. Walter Biemel and Hans Saner (Frankfurt: Klostermann, 1990).

HS   Martin Heidegger and Eugen Fink, *Heraclitus Seminar 1966/67*, tr. Charles H. Seibert (Alabama: University of Alabama Press, 1979).

ID   *Identity and Difference* (English and German), tr. Joan Stambaugh (New York: Harper & Row, 1969).

LF   Letter to Manfred S. Frings, October 20, 1966 (German and English), tr. W. J. Richardson, in Manfred S. Frings (ed.), *Martin Heidegger and the Quest for Truth* (Chicago: Quadrangle Books, 1968), pp. 17–21.

LG   Letter to Martin Grabmann, January 7, 1917, in Hermann Köstler, "Heidegger schreibt an Grabmann," *Philosophisches Jahrbuch 87* (1980): 98–104.

LHC   Letter to the participants of the tenth annual meeting of the American Heidegger Conference, April 11, 1976 (German and English), in John Sallis (ed.), *Radical Phenomenology* (New Jersey: Humanities Press, 1978), pp. 1–4.

LKB   Letter to Rudolf Krämer-Badoni, April 25, 1960, in Rainer A. Bast, "Bericht: Ein Brief Martin Heideggers an Rudolf Krämer-Badoni über die Kunst," *Phänomenologische Forschung 18* (1986): 175–82.

LR   Letter to William J. Richardson, April 1962 (English and German), tr. William J. Richardson in his *Through Phenomenology to Thought* (The Hague: Martinus Nijhoff, 1963), pp. viii–xxiii.

MD   Review of Ernst Cassirer, *Philosophie der symbolischen Formen. 2. Teil: Das mythische Denken, Deutsche Literaturzeitung 21* (1928): 1000–1012.

MHG   *Martin Heidegger im Gespräch*, ed. Richard Wisser (Freiburg: Karl Alber, 1970).

N1 & N2   *Nietzsche*, 2 vols. (Pfullingen: Neske, 1961).

NI   *Nietzsche*, Vol. I: *The Will to Power as Art*, tr. David Farrell Krell (New York: Harper & Row, 1979).

NII   *Nietzsche*, Vol. II: *The Eternal Return of the Same*, tr. David Farrell Krell (New York: Harper & Row, 1984).

NIII   *Nietzsche*, Vol. III: *Will to Power as Knowledge and Metaphysics*, tr. David Farrell Krell (New York: Harper & Row, 1987).

NIV   *Nietzsche*, Vol. IV: *Nihilism*, tr. Frank A. Capuzzi (New York: Harper & Row, 1982).

NG   "Nur ein Gott kann uns retten," *Der Spiegel* May 31, 1976 (no. 23), pp. 193–219/"Only a God Can Save Us," tr. W. J. Richardson in Thomas Sheehan (ed.), *Heidegger: The Man and the Thinker* (Chicago: Precedent Publishing, 1981), pp. 45–67.

NH   Guido Schneeberger, *Nachlese zu Heidegger: Dokumente zu seinem Leben und Denken* (Bern: Suhr, 1962).

PAA   "Phänomenologie der Anschauung und des Ausdrucks (Theorie der philosophischen Begriffsbildung)," lecture course of SS 1920, transcript by Franz-Josef Brecht, the *Archiv der Dilthey-Forschungsstelle, Ruhr-Universität*, Bochum, Germany.

PC   "The Problem of the Categories," tr. Roderick Stewart, *Man and World* 12 (1979): 378–86.

PDT   "Plato's Doctrine of Truth," tr. John Barlow, in William Barrett and Henry D. Aiken (eds.), *Philosophy in the Twentieth Century: An Anthology* (New York: Random House, 1962), pp. 251–302.

PIA   "Phänomenologische Interpretationen zu Aristoteles (Anzeige der hermeneutischen Situation)," *Dilthey Jahrbuch für Philosophie und Geschichte der Geisteswissenschaften* 6 (1989): 228–74/"Phenomenological Interpretations with Respect to Aristotle: Indication of the Hermeneutical Situation," tr. Michael Baur, *Man and World* 25 (1992): 358–93.

PLT   *Poetry, Language, Thought*, tr. Albert Hofstadter (New York: Harper & Row, 1971).

PR   "The Problem of Reality in Modern Philosophy," tr. Philip J. Bossert, *Journal of the British Society for Phenomenology* 4 (1973): 64–71.

PT   *The Piety of Thinking*, ed. and tr. James G. Hart and John C. Maraldo (Bloomington: Indiana University Press, 1976).

PW   "The Pathway," tr. Thomas F. O'Meara and Thomas J. Sheehan, *Listening* 8 (1973): 32–39.

QB   *The Question of Being*, tr. Jean T. Wilde and William Kluback (New Haven: College and University Press, 1958).

QCT   *The Question Concerning Technology*, tr. William Lovitt (New York: Harper & Row, 1977).

R   "A Recollection," tr. Hans Siegfried, in Thomas Sheehan (ed.),

Heidegger: The Man and the Thinker (Chicago: Precedent Publishing, 1981), pp. 21–22.

SD   *Zur Sache des Denkens* (Tübingen: Max Niemeyer, 1976)/*Time and Being*, tr. Joan Stambaugh (New York: Harper & Row, 1972).

SDU   *Die Selbstbehauptung der deutschen Universität, Das Rektorat 1933/34: Tatsachen und Gedanken* (Frankfurt: Klostermann, 1983)/"The Self-Assertion of the German University, The Rectorate 1933/34: Facts and Thoughts," tr. Karsten Harries, *Review of Metaphysics* 38 (1985): 467–502.

SG   *Der Satz vom Grund* (Pfullingen: Neske, 1978)/*The Principle of Reason*, tr. Reginald Lilly (Bloomington: Indiana University Press, 1992).

SZ   *Gesamtausgabe*, Vol. 2: *Sein und Zeit* (1977)/*Being and Time*, tr. John Macquarrie and Edward Robinson (New York: Harper & Row, 1962).

TK   *Die Technik und die Kehre* (Pfullingen: Neske, 1962).

UZP   "Über die Zeitverständnis in der Phänomenologie und im Denken der Seinsfrage," in Helmut Gehrig (ed.), *Phänomenologie—lebendig oder töt?* (Karlsruhe: Badenia, 1969), p. 47/"The Understanding of Time in Phenomenology and in the Thinking of the Being-Question," tr. Thomas Sheehan and Frederick Elliston, *The Southwestern Journal of Philosophy* 10 (1979): 199–201.

V   "Vita," by Günther Neske with Heidegger's "imprimatur," in Günther Neske (ed.), *Erinnerung an Martin Heidegger* (Pfullingen: Neske, 1977), pp. 303–304.

VA   *Vorträge und Aufsätze* (Pfullingen: Neske, 1985).

VZB   "Versuch einer zweiten Bearbeitung," with Heidegger's accompanying letter of October 22, 1927, to Husserl, in Edmund Husserl, *Phänomenologische Psychologie* (*Husserliana* IX), ed. Walter Biemel (The Hague: Martinus Nijhoff, 1968), pp. 256–63, 600–602/"The Idea of Phenomenology," tr. Thomas Sheehan, *Listening* 12 (1977): 111–21.

WDF   "Wilhelm Diltheys Forschungsarbeit und der Kampf um eine historische Weltanschauung," ten lectures held in Kassel, April 16–21, 1925; transcript by Walter Bröcker in the *Archiv der Dilthey-Forschungsstelle, Ruhr-Universität*, Bochum, Germany; forthcoming in *Dilthey-Jahrbuch* 8 (1993), ed. Frithjof Rodi.

WHD   *Was Heisst Denken?* (Tübingen: Niemeyer, 1954)/*What Is Called Thinking?*, tr. Fred D. Wieck and J. Glenn Gray (New York: Harper & Row, 1972).

WP   *What Is Philosophy?* (English and German), tr. William Kluback and Jean T. Wilde (New Haven: College and University Press, 1956).

Other Texts

C   *St. Augustine's Confessions* (English/Latin) (London: William Heine-
            mann, 1960)/*The Confessions of St. Augustine*, tr. R. Warner
            (Toronto: New American Library, 1963).

CD   Søren Kierkegaard, *Christian Discourses*, tr. W. Lowrie (Princeton:
            Princeton University Press, 1974).

CEM   Wilhelm Dilthey, "Christentum, Erkenntnistheorie und Meta-
            physik" and "Augustinus" in his *Gesammelte Schriften*, Vol. 1: *Ein-
            leitung in die Geisteswissenschaften* (Leipzig and Berlin: Teubner,
            1922), pp. 250–67.

COA   Søren Kierkegaard, *The Concept of Anxiety*, tr. R. Thomte and A.
            B. Anderson (Princeton: Princeton University Press, 1980).

CUP   Søren Kierkegaard, *Concluding Unscientific Postscript*, tr. David F.
            Swenson and Walter Lowrie (Princeton: Princeton University Press,
            1941).

DEW   Hans-Georg Gadamer, "Der Eine Weg Martin Heideggers," *Jahres-
            gabe der Martin-Heidegger-Gesellschaft* (West Germany, 1986), pp.
            7–25.

DG   Martin Kähler, *Das Gewissen, Erste Hälfte: Altertum und neues
            Testament* (Halle: Julius Fricke, 1878).

DGE   H. G. Stoker, *Das Gewissen: Erscheinungen und Theorien* (Bonn:
            Verlag von Friedrich Cohen, 1925).

DK   Theodore Kisiel, "Das Kriegsnotsemester 1919: Heideggers Durch-
            bruch zur hermeneutischen Phänomenologie," *Philosophisches Jahr-
            buch* 99 (1992): 105–22.

DMH   Otto Pöggeler, *Der Denkweg Martin Heideggers*, 2d ed. (Pfullingen:
            Neske, 1983).

DQ   Augustine, *De Diversis quaestionibus octoginta tribus*, in *Corpus
            Christianorum*, XXXII (Turnholti: Typographi Brepols Editores
            Pontificii, 1975)/*Eighty-Three Different Questions*, tr. David L.
            Mosher, in *The Fathers of the Church*, Vol. 70 (Washington, D.C.:
            Catholic University of America Press, 1982).

DW1 &   Paul Natorp, *Deutscher Weltberuf: Geschichtsphilosophische Richt-
DW2   linien*, Vol. 1: *Die Weltalter des Geistes*, Vol. 2: *Die Seele des Deut-
            schen* (Jena: Eugen Diederichs, 1918).

EBF   Theodore Kisiel, "Das Entstehen des Begriffsfeldes 'Faktizität' im
            Frühwerk Heideggers," *Dilthey-Jahrbuch* 4 (1986–87): 91–120.

EHA   Hans-Georg Gadamer, "Erinnerungen an Heideggers Anfänge,"
            Dilthey-Jahrbuch 4 (1986–87): 13–26.

EMH   Günther Neske (ed.), *Erinnerung an Martin Heidegger* (Pfullingen: Neske, 1977).

EO   Søren Kierkegaard, *Either/Or*, Vol. 1, tr. Walter Lowrie (Princeton: Princeton University Press, 1971).

EU   Theodore Kisiel, "Edition und Übersetzung: Unterwegs von Tatsachen zu Gedanken, von Werken zu Wegen," in Dietrich Papenfuss and Otto Pöggeler (eds.), *Zur philosophischen Aktualität Heideggers*, Vol. 3: *Im Spiegel der Welt* (Frankfurt: Klostermann, 1992), pp. 89–107.

FCL   A. W. Hunzinger, "Das Furchtproblem in der katholischen Lehre von Augustin bis Luther," *Lutherstudien*, 2. Heft, 1. Abteilung (Leipzig: A. Deichert'sche Verlagsbuchhandlung, 1906).

FTR   Søren Kierkegaard, *Fear and Trembling, Repetition*, tr. H. W. Hong and E. H. Hong (Princeton: Princeton University Press, 1983).

G   Martin Kähler, "Das Gewissen," in *Realencyklopädie für protestantische Theologie und Kirche*, Vol. VI.

GBT   Theodore Kisiel, "The Genesis of *Being and Time*," *Man and World* 25 (1992): 21–37.

HA   Theodore Kisiel, "Heidegger's Apology: Biography as Philosophy and Ideology," *Graduate Faculty Philosophy Journal* 14–15 (1991): 363–404.

HAN   Victor Farias, *Heidegger and Nazism*, ed. Joseph Margolis and Tom Rockmore, tr. Paul Burrell and Bariel R. Ricci (Philadelphia: Temple University Press, 1989).

HBC   Theodore Kisiel, "Heidegger (1920–21) on Becoming a Christian: A Conceptual Picture Show" in R HS.

HCM   Michael E. Zimmerman, *Heidegger's Confrontation with Modernity: Technology, Politics, Art* (Bloomington: Indiana University Press, 1990).

HDZ   Karl Löwith, *Heidegger: Denker in dürftiger Zeit*, 2d ed. (Göttingen: Vandenhoeck & Ruprecht, 1960).

HEL   Theodore Kisiel, "Heidegger's Early Lecture Courses," in Joseph J. Kockelmans (ed.), *A Companion to Heidegger's "Being and Time"* (Washington, D.C.: University Press of America, 1986), pp. 22–39.

HL   Thomas Sheehan, "Heidegger's *Lehrjahre*," in J. C. Sallis, G. Moneta, and J. Taminiaux (eds.), *The Collegium Phaenomenologicum: The First Years* (Dordrecht: Kluwer Academic Publishers, 1988), pp. 77–137.

HMH   Hugo Ott, "Der Habilitand Martin Heidegger und das von Schaezler'sche Stipendium. Ein Beitgrag zur Wissenschaftsförderung der katholischen Kirche," *Freiburger Diözesanarchiv* 108 (1986): 141–60.

HN   Thomas Sheehan, "Heidegger and the Nazis," *New York Review of Books* June 16, 1988: 38–47.

HW   Hans-Georg Gadamer, *Heideggers Wege: Studium zum Spätwerk* (Tübingen: J. C. B. Mohr, 1983).

IPR   Thomas Sheehan, "Heidegger's 'Introduction to the Phenomenology of Religion,' 1920–21," *Personalist* 60 (1979): 312–24.

IRP1,
IRP2,
IRP3   Edmund Husserl, *Ideen zu einer reinen Phänomenologie und phänomenologishen Philosophie*, Books 1–3 (Husserliana III–V) (The Hague: Martinus Nijhoff, 1950, 1952)/*Ideas: General Introduction to Pure Phenomenology*, tr. W. R. Boyce Gibson (New York: Collier, 1962).

LA   Friedrich Nitzsch, *Luther und Aristoteles* (Kiel, 1883).

LE   Max Scheler, "Liebe und Erkenntnis," in his *Liebe und Erkenntnis* (Bern: Francke Verlag, 1970), pp. 5–28.

LH   Edmund Husserl, Letters to Martin Heidegger; May 27, 1916 to January 2, 1932 (Husserl-Archives, Louvain, Belgium).

LU1 &
LU2   Edmund Husserl, *Logische Untersuchungen, Zweiter Band*, 2 Vols. (Husserliana XIX/1 and XIX/2) (The Hague: Martinus Nijhoff, 1984)/*Logical Investigations*, 2 Vols., tr. J. N. Findlay (London: Routledge & Kegan Paul, 1970).

ME   *Meister Eckhart: A Modern Translation*, tr. Raymond B. Blakney (New York: Harper & Row, 1941).

MH   Hugo Ott, *Martin Heidegger: Unterwegs zu seiner Biographie* (Frankfurt: Campus Verlag, 1988).

MHT   Bernhard Casper, "Martin Heidegger und die Theologische Fakultät Freiburg," *Freiburger Diözesanarchiv* 100 (1980): 534–41.

ML   Theodore Kisiel, "The Missing Link in the Early Heidegger," in Joseph J. Kockelmans (ed.), *Hermeneutic Phenomenology: Lectures and Essays* (Washington, D.C.: University Press of America, 1988), pp. 1–40.

MLD   Karl Löwith, *Mein Leben in Deutschland vor und nach 1933: Ein Bericht* (Stuttgart: J. B. Metzlersche Verlagsbuchhandlung, 1986).

MV   Curd Ochwadt and Erwin Tecklenborg (eds.), *Das Mass des Verborgenen: Heinrich Ochsner (1891–1970) zum Gedächtnis* (Hannover: Charis-Verlag, 1981).

OR   Friedrich Schleiermacher, *On Religion: Speeches to Its Cultured Despisers*, tr. Richard Crouter (Cambridge: Cambridge University Press, 1988).

OWB   Theodore Kisiel, "On the Way to Being and Time: Introduction to the Translation of Heidegger's *Prolegomena zur Geschichte des Zeitbegriffs*," *Research in Phenomenology* 15 (1985): 193–226.

OWE   Thomas Sheehan, "On the Way to *Ereignis*: Heidegger's Interpretation of *Physis*," in Hugh J. Silverman, John Sallis, and Thomas M. Seebohm (eds.), *Continental Philosophy in America* (Pittsburgh: Duquesne University Press, 1983), pp. 131–64.

PA   Karl Jaspers, *Philosophische Autobiographie*, 2d ed. (Munich: R. Piper, 1977).

PDW   Karl Jaspers, *Die Psychologie der Weltanschauungen*, 5th ed. (Berlin: Springer-Verlag, 1960).

PK   Pascal, *Pensées*, tr. A. J. Krailsheimer (Harmondsworth, England: Penguin Books, 1966).

PMG   John D. Caputo, "Phenomenology, Mysticism and the '*Grammatica Speculativa*': A Study of Heidegger's *Habilitationsschrift*," *Journal of the British Society for Phenomenology* 5 (1974): 101–17.

PO   Pascal, *Pensées et Opuscules*, ed. M. Léon Brunschvicg (Paris: Librairie Hachette, 1909).

PPT   Helmar Junghans, "Die probationes zu den philosophischen Thesen der Heidelberger Disputation Luthers im Jahre 1518," *Lutherjahrbuch* 46 (1979): 10–59.

PS   Pascal, *Pensées*, tr. H. F. Stewart (New York: Modern Library, 1967).

RH   John D. Caputo, *Radical Hermeneutics: Repetition, Deconstruction, and the Hermeneutic Project* (Bloomington: Indiana University Press, 1987).

RHS   Theodore Kisiel and John van Buren (eds.), *Reading Heidegger from the Start: Essays in His Earliest Thought* (Albany: State University of New York, 1994).

TB   Thomas Sheehan, " 'Time and Being,' 1925–27," in Robert W. Shahan and J. N. Mohanty (eds.), *Thinking about Being: Aspects of Heidegger's Thought* (Norman: University of Oklahoma Press, 1984), pp. 177–219.

TC   Søren Kierkegaard, *Training in Christianity*, tr. Walter Lowrie (Princeton: Princeton University Press, 1972).

TI   Emmanuel Levinas, *Totality and Infinity*, tr. Alphonso Lingis (Pittsburgh: Duquesne University Press, 1969).

TME   John D. Caputo, *The Mystical Element in Heidegger's Thought* (New York: Fordham University Press, 1978).

UG   Albrecht Ritschl, "Über das Gewissen," in his *Gesammelte Aufsätze* (Freiburg: J. C. B. Mohr, 1896), pp. 177–203.

VVU   William J. Richardson, "Verzeichnis der Vorlesungen und Übungen von Martin Heidegger," in his *Heidegger: Through Phenomenology to Thought* (The Hague: Martinus Nijhoff, 1963), pp. 663–71.

WA   *D. Martin Luthers Werke* (Weimar: Hermann Böhlaus, 1883–)/ *Luther's Works* (Philadelphia: Fortress Press, 1955ff.). Unless otherwise indicated, the volume numbers given in Roman numerals refer to the main body of the German and English editions of Luther's works.

WFD   Theodore Kisiel, "Why the First Draft of *Being and Time* Was Never Published," *Journal of the British Society for Phenomenology* 20 (1989): 3-22.

WFH   Theodore Kisiel, "War der frühe Heidegger tatsächlich ein 'christlicher Theologe'?," in Annemarie Gethmann-Siefert (ed.), *Philosophie und Poesie: Otto Pöggeler zum 60. Geburtstag* (Fromann-Holzboog, 1988), pp. 60-75.

WSH   Theodore Kisiel, "Why Students of Heidegger Will Have to Read Emil Lask," in Deborah G. Chaffin (ed.), *Emil Lask and the Search for Concreteness* (Athens, Ohio: Ohio University Press, 1993).

WT   Edmund Schlink, "Weisheit und Torheit," *Kerygma und Dogma* 1 (1955): 1-22.

Other Abbreviations

KNS   Kriegsnotsemester
SS   Summer Semester
WS   Winter Semester

PART I

The Matter of Heidegger's Thinking

1 | Heidegger's Autobiographies

> There was hardly more than a name, but the name travelled all over Germany like
> the rumor of the hidden king.
>
> Hannah Arendt

Rumors from Freiburg

FOR YEARS WE heard rumors about an unofficial story regarding Martin
Heidegger's unpublished youthful writings prior to his 1927 *Sein und Zeit*
(henceforth abbreviated "SZ"). The rumors have included suggestions that in
these writings he had already discovered the being-question, made the turn
(*Kehre*) beyond subjectivity to being itself (such that his later turn after SZ was
a return to his youthful period), and did all this in a unique way through readings of Meister Eckhart, Luther, Kierkegaard, Aristotle's ethics, Plato's *Sophist*,
Dilthey, and Husserl.

The first wave of rumors about this *Jugendgeschichte* arrived via an anecdotal and doxographical tradition deriving from the memorabilia and reports
of Heidegger's early students. A famous example is Hannah Arendt's story
about "the rumor of the hidden king":

> the beginning in Heidegger's case is . . . the first lecture courses and seminars
> which he held as a mere *Privatdozent* (instructor) and assistant to Husserl at
> the University of Freiburg in 1919. For Heidegger's "fame" predates by
> about eight years the publication of *Sein und Zeit* in 1927. . . . there was
> nothing tangible on which his fame could have been based, nothing written,
> save for notes taken at his lectures, which circulated among students every-
> where.

Hans-Georg Gadamer has for decades praised "the revolutionary genius of the
young Martin Heidegger. Heidegger's entrance as a young teacher at the University of Freiburg in the years after the war was truly epoch-making." "To
this day," Gadamer also wrote, "hardly anything has been made public of this
event." We heard from others such as Karl Löwith, Wilhelm Szilasi, Leo
Strauss, and Helene Weiss this same story that not the years around SZ but
Heidegger's much earlier thought is the real beginning of his thoughtpath

(*Denkweg*).[1] Oskar Becker, who began attending Heidegger's courses in 1919, maintained that "*Sein und Zeit* is no longer the original Heidegger, but rather repeats his original breakthrough only in a scholastically hardened form" (DMH 351). Transcripts of Heidegger's youthful courses continued to circulate for decades in a kind of philosophical underground spanning the continents and took on the legendary status of a body of esoteric writings, similar to how Plato's lectures in the Academy were often used by Aristotle and others as the authoritative sources of his ideas.

Through his teaching, the commerce in transcripts of his courses, and the indirect dissemination of his ideas, Heidegger helped to shape a whole generation of scholars who went on to dominate the German intellectual scene for decades. Theodore Kisiel has written that "this period preceding the publication of *Being and Time* is probably the most productive and most influential period of Heidegger's career" (G20 English tr., p. xix). Thus a second wave of rumors about the hidden king arrived via an effective history of his youthful thought in the work of others. This included not only many historical studies of especially Aristotle, Christian traditions, and Husserl, but also such new movements as Gadamer's hermeneutics, Arendt's practical philosophy, Becker's mathematical theory, Rudolf Bultmann's existential theology, Habermas's critical theory, and more recently John Caputo's "radical hermeneutics" and David Krell's studies of "daimon life."[2]

Another wave of rumors has come from the philological and philosophical detective work of such scholars as Otto Pöggeler, Thomas Sheehan, and especially Theodore Kisiel, who tirelessly followed the paper trail of Heidegger's unpublished courses and essays from one archive and personal library to another, and over the years provided a series of ground-breaking studies. Heidegger's youthful writings had fallen into such oblivion by the 1960s that, when Otto Pöggeler published his research on them in his *Der Denkweg Martin Heideggers*, it was dismissed in some quarters as a "fabrication."[3]

A decisive wave of rumors has begun to arrive via the publication of Heidegger's youthful manuscripts themselves in the collected edition of his writings. The publication of these manuscripts was initiated in the early 1980s and will be completed in the 1990s. Thus it is as if we now find ourselves in a strange Kierkegaardian scenario in which an author had long ago dispatched a number of manuscripts in the mail, only for them to become lost, rumored about for years, and then eventually delivered in new circumstances after the death of the author. The history of Heidegger's youthful writings often reads also something like Umberto Eco's *The Name of the Rose*, Edgar Allan Poe's *The Purloined Letter*, or a detective novel titled "The Case of the Missing Manuscripts," which is complete with episodes about Heidegger losing and destroying manuscripts, H. L. Van Breda finding the burned remains of Heidegger's letters to Husserl on the docks of Antwerp during the Blitzkrieg,

Gadamer's copy of Heidegger's 1922 introduction to a book on Aristotle being destroyed in a bombing raid on Leipzig and then another copy of this long-lost work turning up in the papers of a minor German scholar in the 1980s (PIA 229, 273), while West Germany's leading newspaper the *Frankfurter Allgemeine Zeitung* reports Kisiel's latest archival findings and twists to the case of the young Dr. Heidegger.[4]

Errant Ways?

The rumor of the hidden king was also spurred on by Heidegger's own philosophical autobiographies. Though warning in SZ that philosophy should not involve telling a story (*mython tina diegeisthai*), he was given to sketching self-portraits (*Selbstdarstellungen*) which, when not focused on his involvement with National Socialism, usually began with his student years (1909–15), moved quickly through his early Freiburg period (1915–23) and early Marburg period (1924–28), and ended with his mature thought in the later writings.[5] "I am narrating [*erzähle*] all this to you, but not in order to give the impression that I already knew then everything that I am still asking today," he said to the Japanese interlocutor in his 1953–54 dialogue on language (G12 88/7).

But we do find Heidegger suggesting strongly that the *Sache* or topic of his thought—the question about being—was already germinally there in his youthful courses and essays. In a 1969 seminar, he told the story of his thought in terms of three central thoughtpaths into his enduring topic: namely, the "sense of being" worked out systematically in SZ and then the "truth" and "place" (*topos*) of being pursued in his later thought. Here he also spoke of the "preceding course of thinking" whereby the "question about being in *Sein und Zeit* was set on the way." Elsewhere he called the lines of thought traced in his first courses "youthful leaps," in which "I was concerned with bringing into view something completely different," was "brought onto the path of the question about being," and was not concerned merely with Husserlian phenomenology, philosophy of life, or existentialism. "The question of being, awakened by Brentano's work [*On the Manifold Meaning of Being in Aristotle*], nevertheless remained in view." He even maintained that his 1915 qualifying dissertation on Duns Scotus marked a "beginning of the way." And he was also able to include his 1919–21 essay on Karl Jaspers in the 1976 edition of his anthology *Wegmarken* (Waymarkers), which was intended to provide a record of the different approaches to his enduring topic. He suggested to Otto Pöggeler in a more restrained tone that "he found his way to the question of being and time in 1923 or 1922–23."[6]

Heidegger recounted also that these seminal thoughtpaths were not mere bridges that he burned on the way to his subsequent work, and here he quoted

Hölderlin: "As you began, so you will remain." "Provenance," Heidegger explained, "always remains that which comes toward us as future." His originary formulations of the being-question were creatively reinscribed in the palimpsests of his different ways in his subsequent thought. In SZ he noted that the "analysis of the environment and in general 'the hermeneutics of facticity' [in Division One of Part One] has been communicated repeatedly in his courses since the winter semester of 1919-20." He also acknowledged that important elements of his analysis of time in Division Two "were communicated as theses on the occasion of a public lecture in Marburg (July 1924) on the concept of time." In SS 1928, he told his students that he had already used the term "worlding" (*Welten*) in his early Freiburg period. Indeed, we now know that many other key concepts and terms of his later philosophy—for example, the end of philosophy, the other beginning, the turn, the event/enownment (*Ereignis*), there is/it gives (*Es gibt*), mystery, modern technology —were also used in his courses in 1919 and the early 1920s.[7]

But one is struck also by the discrepancies between the longstanding unofficial versions of the story of his youthful thought and the official versions offered by Heidegger and Heideggerians. For what he gave with one hand, he almost took away with the other. His evaluation of his youthful thoughtpaths is richly ambivalent. He often referred to them as mere byways (*Umwege*), errant ways (*Abwege*), blind alleys (*Irrgänge*), and a trace of the way (*Wegspur*) that showed the genuine way to his topic only indirectly or mediately (*mittelbar*). "But the way of questioning became longer than I suspected. It demanded many waystations, byways, and errant ways. What the first courses in Freiburg and then those in Marburg ventured shows the way only indirectly.[8] Heidegger looked back on his early Freiburg and Marburg courses as imperfect anticipations of *the* way, which purportedly first showed itself in SZ and then in his later writings. Despite the intelligibility of many of his criticisms, there are just as many that seem very unconvincing, and his overall downplaying and even dismissal of his youthful thought are puzzling.

To begin with, his autobiographies exhibit an impatience toward the sheer plurality and flux of the "many" ways and waystations in his youthful period. According to Heidegger's metaphor, waystations (*Aufenthalte*) are places along a thoughtpath where one tarries awhile and the topic shows itself in its *Jeweiligkeit*, temporal particularity or awhileness. His youthful thought was the "attempt to go along a path, on which I did not know where it would lead. Only its most immediate outlooks were familiar to me, because they lured me unceasingly, even though the horizon shifted and darkened from time to time." Such shifting viewpoints involved many "upsets" and "perplexities." This constantly agitated "circling around" his topic showed *the* way only mediately. But Heidegger himself insisted repeatedly that we have no access to an immediate noninterpretive understanding of his topic that would take the form of a privileged *Heilsweg*, sacred way, way of salvation. The mediation of the topic by a diversity of ways is a defining mark of postmetaphysical thinking, which is like a maze of *Feldwege* and *Holzwege*, fieldpaths and forestpaths: "Each wanders away separately, but in the same forest. Often it seems as though one were similar to the other. But it only seems so."[9] There is no royal road through the Black Forest of Heidegger's topic. On the other hand, we find him curiously privileging the beaten paths of his later thought and disparaging his youthful ways precisely because of their flux and plurality.

Heidegger also looked unfavorably on the fact that his youthful thought-paths involved "byways and errant ways through the history of western philosophy" (LR x–xi). *Umweg*, byway, means detour, roundabout way, getting off the main road. Instead of moving directly on the straight and narrow of *the* way, Heidegger had to go around (*um*) it on the backroads of certain traditions in which he was absorbed at the time: for example, the young Luther, Aristotle's ethics, Sextus Empiricus, the New Testament. But then, apart from a few very late seminars on his own thought, his later writings are themselves byways through conversations with traditions, especially Kant, Nietzsche, the pre-Socratics, and Hölderlin. Indeed, he stated in one of these later seminars that philosophy "can only be achieved on the byway [*Umweg*] of a return to the beginning." He insisted that an ahistorical and presuppositionless point of departure—"an immediate and shorter way to being"—is not possible (G15 394; G65 434). His approach to the topic was always mediated by creative reinscriptions of traditions. There was no main street to *die Sachen selbst*, only side roads through traditions. But, on the other hand, he either forgot this in his unfavorable judgment of his youthful byways, or simply preferred his later paths as *the* byways that the earlier ones had showed only indirectly, though he never explained in detail why this should be the case.

Heidegger also stressed that his youthful lines of thought were "very *unvollkommen*," imperfect, incomplete. The "something completely different" he wanted to bring into view was, "however, something at first only darkly, if not confusedly intimated," which reached its perfect or complete expression only later. His youthful thought was but a "hint" and *Wegspur*, a way-trace, a trace of the way. "I always followed only an unclear way-trace," one which often "withdrew from every attempt to say it." His insights "did not yet suffice to venture placing in discussion the being-question as the question about the sense of being." However, Heidegger elsewhere clarified that incompleteness and imperfection belong to the very style of postmetaphysical thinking, which can only pursue traces (*Spuren*) and hints (*Winke*) and is ever "on the way." Metaphysics strives for perfection, completion, in the sense of having thought in the actualization and presence of its end (*entelecheia, perfectio*), whereas the work (*ergon*) or text of postmetaphysical thinking puts itself forth as *energeia ateles*, i.e., being at work that never reaches its end and is thus imperfect. The inexhaustible being on the way of thinking from possibility to being-in-work is permeated with a *steresis*, deficiency, absence, concealment, dissemblance. Thus Heidegger's motto on the title page of the collected edition of his writings reads, "[Ongoing] ways—not [finished] works.[10] Thinking is supposed to move along unfinished streets and unbeaten paths. On the other hand, we find Heidegger oddly downplaying his youthful thoughtpaths precisely because of their incompleteness.

Finally, his autobiographies depicted his youthful ways as *Irrgänge*, blind alleys, and *Abwege*, errant ways, deviations, crooked ways, mistakes, errors. His errant ways were errors that led him away (*ab*) from the straight and narrow of *the* way. But he stressed elsewhere in the context of his later thoughtpaths that thinking consists of nothing but *Holzwege*. *Auf dem Holzweg sein* means to be on the wrong track. Thus the French translation of Heidegger's anthology titled *Holzwege* is *Chemins qui ne mènent nulle part*, paths leading nowhere. The preface reads, "In the forest are paths that, mostly overgrown, suddenly end in the untrodden. . . . Woodcutters and foresters know the paths. They know what it means to be on a forest path/wrong path." "They move in errancy [*in der Irre gehen*]. But they never lose their way [*sich verirren*]." They fall into error, but they never become aberrant, erratic, erroneous. Just as thought is ever incomplete, so it ever errs because, as *aletheia* (unconcealment), truth is permeated with concealment (*lethe*) in the form of both simple hiddenness and dissemblance. Genuine thinking is thus attentive to this dimension of concealment: "Who thinks greatly must err greatly. . . . not meant personally, but related to the errancy prevailing in the essence of truth, into which all thought . . . is thrown." All ways are errant ways, blind alleys with their blind spots. But they never lose their way, becoming erratic and erroneous, since they remain related to their topic in the play of unconcealment and concealment. Thus Heidegger could write that his "continual reference to the ontological difference from 1927 to 1936 would have to be seen as a necessary *Holzweg*." All thoughtpaths stumble errantly in the same dark forest, some more and some less than others. And Heidegger stressed that, though left behind, still these "thoughtpaths . . . wait until at some time thinkers go along them" again in critical repetition.

Why then did he, on the other hand, occasionally dismiss his youthful ways for displaying precisely this trait of errancy that defines thinking? Though he never explained any of his unfavorable judgments about his youthful thought, his main criticism regarding errancy seems to have been the one he directed against SZ, namely, that here the turn from subjectivity to the temporal giving of being itself was not adequately realized. And yet he also maintained, "It is everywhere supposed that the attempt in *Being and Time* ended in a blind alley [*Sackgasse*]. Let us put this opinion to rest. The thinking that ventured a few steps in *Being and Time* has even today not advanced beyond it." Its "path remains even today still a necessary one, if the question about being is to set our Dasein on the way."[11] Why did Heidegger not say the same about his youthful thoughtpaths?

Heidegger's unfavorable judgment of his youthful thought is summed up in the statement that "with such youthful leaps one easily becomes unjust" (*ungerecht*) to the topic (G12 121/35). *Ungerecht* also means not upright, without right, illegitimate. The same legal, moral, and religious overtones can be heard in the term *Abweg*. *Auf Abwege kommen* originally means to go astray, to stray from the straight and narrow, to fall by the wayside. *Abwegig* means way out in left field, out of it, eccentric. For example, Heidegger's own religious, moralizing essays between 1910 and 1913 in the antimodernist journal *Der Akademiker* appealed to the New Testament formula, "I am the way and the truth," and spoke of "whoever has not tread upon errant ways [*Irrwege*] and let himself be blinded by the deceitful pretence of the modern spirit, whoever ventures himself along life's journey in a truer, deeper, better-grounded relinquishment of the self in the glaring light of truth" (CA 492–93). Similarly, when one hears the later Heidegger's suggestions that the philosophical *Irrgänge* and *Abwege* in his youthful period purportedly led him away from the straight and narrow of "the way" of thinking, this language reminds one of a *Heilsweg*, a sacred way, a way of salvation, which Heidegger himself elsewhere stresses is not available.

In his autobiographies, the right hand does not appear to know what the left hand is doing. On the one hand, he indicated that his enduring topic was discovered in his youthful thoughtpaths, and that this topic is characterized by a radical openness and diversity of byways, incomplete ways, and errant ways. On the other hand, he downplayed and often even dismissed his youthful thought, placing it into a hierarchical-teleological relationship to "the way" of his subsequent writings.

Heidegger's Hands

What about this "on the other hand"? Derrida has pointed out the pervasive image of the hand in the later Heidegger, who takes thinking to be a kind of *Hand-Werk*, craft, handiwork, work of the hand.[12] This imagery first turned up in Heidegger's youthful writings. In 1922 he discussed Aristotle's statement in the *De anima* (432a) that "the soul is in a way all being," insofar as "the soul is analogous to the hand." "As the hand is the tool of tools, so the look [*eidos*] of objects comes into view only through *nous* [perceiving]" and its simple *thigein*, its intentional reaching forth and touching, which is always an *aletheuein*, being-true, an uncovering of tangible being (*Meta.* 1051b). There is not only an *oculis* but also a *manus mentis*. Similarly, Heidegger defined life's intentional having (*Haben*) and comportmental holding (*Verhalten*) onto the hold (*Umhalt*) of being as: grip (*Ergriff*), re-grip (*Rückgriff*), pre-grip (*Vorgriff*), pulling-through (*Vollzug*).

As we shall see later, this intentional hand is marked by two basic possibilities. It can have the character of Eckhartian letting-be (*Gelassenheit*) and openness toward the "mystery" of the groundless, absence-permeated, anarchically differentiated, and thus incalculable and nonmasterable *Sache* of the temporal giving of being. This is the hand that "takes the rope for the sail into hand and looks toward the wind" that carries the sails of thinking along many different routes. As metaphysics and modern technique, however, the intentional hand of thinking attempts to objectify, calculate, and master the *Sache* into the before-the-hand-ness (*Vorhandenheit*) of a present, universal, and homogeneous ground, around which it can close its conceptual fist. This is the hand with which "we make a grab [*Griff*] into the flowing stream . . . we 'still the stream,' " reducing it to "that which lies 'before the hand' in the in-itself of the 'things themselves,' " as if these were "like jewels on a platter." But all this is an illusion, since philosophy "cannot comfortably drop a knowable object into one's hands." We find the same contrast in Heidegger's later writings. "Thinking is genuine *Handeln*, action, handiwork, if *Handeln* means to lend a hand to the presencing of being" in the sense of "letting-be." It "embraces firmly and gently that which seeing brings into view; it does not grab and grasp conceptually [*be-greift*]."[13]

The ambidexterity of this noetic hand turns up also in the *mens auctoris*, the mind of the author, authorial self-interpretation, that is, in Heidegger's ambiguous gestures toward the boundaries and sense of the *Sache* of his literary corpus and especially his youthful manuscripts (*Handschriften*). As Derrida has written, in Heidegger's thinking generally there are two gestures, "two texts, two hands, two visions, two ways of listening. Together simultaneously and separately."

On the one hand, Heidegger's gentle hand of *Gelassenheit* is a generous letting-go and letting-be of the topic of thinking to generate itself in different ways in his many texts and, of course, also elsewhere. It hands thought over to the decisive criterion which is the possibility of *die Sache selbst*, the matter itself in the double sense of the being-question and the texts into which it has been woven. This authorial hand is more precisely a gesture of self-deconstruction (*Abbauen*), since from the very start it puts into question its inevitably exclusive self-interpretations that, to one extent or another, enclose the topic of the writings in its conceptual grasp and bring it to closure.

Already in WS 1924–25, Heidegger said that it is "a dubious thing to rely on what an author himself has brought to the forefront. The important thing is rather to give attention to those things he left shrouded in silence."[14] In the autobiography he later sketched out for the *Heidelberger Akademie der Wissenschaften*, he acknowledged the thoroughly interpretive character of all such autobiographies: "At each waystation the exhibited way appears in a different light and with a different emphasis for the glance backward and out of the glance forward, and awakens different interpretations." "What in the time following [my student years] succeeded and failed on the way taken eludes self-portraiture, which could name only that which does not belong to oneself. And to this belongs everything essential." Thus Heidegger also wrote, "Who lets himself get involved in being on the way to the sojourn in the oldest of the old will bow to the necessity of later being understood differently than he meant to understand himself." In the spirit of Roland Barthes's talk about "the death of the author," Heidegger maintained that "the artist remains inconsequential in comparison with the work, almost like a passageway that destroys itself in the creative process for the work to emerge." The criterion he stressed for interpretive editorial work on the manuscripts for his collected edition also applies to any reading of them. That criterion is not the retrospective self-interpretation of the *mens auctoris*, but *das dem jeweiligen Text* Gemässe, *what is fitting* to the particular text at the particular time.[15] As author, Heidegger is not the master, but only the first reader of his texts. They are out of his hands and open to other interpretations that are fitting to them.

With respect to historical accuracy, Heidegger wrote to Otto Pöggeler that, "regarding the relation of my thinking to Husserl, some gross errors have cropped up that of course can be removed only through careful philological work." Likewise, "regarding his political entanglements [in the thirties], Heidegger himself definitively said that they must be portrayed and told exactly as they happened" (DMH 343, 353). He told Hartmut Buchner that he considered the indiscriminate and historically inaccurate use of student transcripts in the original publication of Hegel's lectures to be a "deterrent example" of how not to do editorial work: "I only hope that it does not go with me someday as it did with Hegel" (EMH 51).

On the other hand, this self-deconstructive gesture, this hand that fights against itself, confirms what Heidegger himself knew to one extent or another, namely, that on an operative level he was bringing his texts and topic to closure in the self-interpretive grasp of the *mens auctoris*. We see this closure in his puzzling criticisms of his youthful writings. These criticisms are in fact aspects of his general narrative of the origins and early development of his thought, in which he often retrospectively read his later thought back into his earlier thought, such that in these instances he created a kind of *mython* in the sense of a mythic narrative, a tall tale. *Caveat lector*! Though this well-documented poetic self-stylizing and revisionism in his self-portraits seems often to have been self-conscious "irony" (DMH 351; HEL 25–26) and the playful strategy of using the earlier writings as occasions for introducing discussions of later themes, it was naively built up over the years into an official story told and retold by Heideggerians and non-Heideggerians alike.

Heidegger's autobiographies usually located the decisive beginning of his being-question in his very early study of Franz Brentano's *On the Manifold Meaning of Being in Aristotle* and of the speculative theology of Carl Braig during his student years (1909-15), then quickly leapt to how all this was worked out in his 1927 SZ and his later thought, and thus gave the impression that there was a single unbroken thoughtpath that developed from his student years, through the decade between 1916 and 1926, and to SZ and his later writings. He said little about what happened in the decade of silence between the publication of his qualifying dissertation in 1916 and SZ, downplayed its importance, and was generally reluctant to provide information about it or make his unpublished writings from this period available. Despite the legendary status attributed to these writings by his early students, and repeated requests for their publication, he published only one of them in 1973, namely, his 1919-21 essay "Anmerkungen zu Karl Jaspers 'Psychologie der Weltanschauungen.' " In his "A Dialogue on Language," he discouraged his interlocutor's interest in his SS 1920 course "Phänomenologie der Anschauung und des Ausdrucks (Theorie der philosophischen Begriffsbildung)," expressing impatience with the continual hunt after the "muddy sources" of transcripts of his youthful courses and preferring to direct the conversation to the connections between his student years and his later thought (G12 87/6).

Pöggeler reported that, though Heidegger assisted him in the writing of his *Der Denkweg Martin Heideggers* and even made available unpublished manuscripts, he only "generously tolerated my treating his early courses like Hegel's youthful writings (thus even dreaming of a future discovery of the finest thing he had worked out)." Heidegger's early encounter with Aristotle "was placed out of my reach, since the later Heidegger directed our discussion of Aristotle completely to the question of the relationship between ontology and theology" (DMH 351-52). Sheehan has written that the decisive influence of Aristotle on Heidegger's thought, which is documented in his early courses, is "among Heidegger's best-kept secrets." Though maintaining that "thinking" is really "thanking," the later Heidegger was, as has been well documented, often puzzlingly reluctant to acknowledge his profound indebtedness to those philosophical traditions that originally helped to put him on the way of the being-question in his early Freiburg period, such as the young Luther, Kierkegaard, Jaspers, Aristotle's practical writings, Husserl's Sixth Investigation, and Dilthey.[16]

Moreover, the *manus mentis* of Heidegger's self-portraits often manipulatively painted over particular historical facts about his youthful texts. In a record of his courses that he himself checked over and authorized, some were cited from his youthful period that had never been given and at least one that was held—his first postwar course of KNS 1919, in which he introduced the important terms *Ereignis* and "it worlds"—was left out. In "A Dialogue on

Language," he used his 1920 course "Phänomenologie der Anschauung und des Ausdrucks" as an occasion for exploring later themes, wrongly dating it as having taken place in 1921, and changing the title first to "Ausdruck und Erscheinung" and then to "Ausdruck und Bedeutung." He gave the impression that at that time he opposed Dilthey's concepts of "expression" and "lived experience," whereas in fact he adopted them enthusiastically in his personalist approach to the question about being, stressing in his course of SS 1920 that his "preoccupation with Dilthey [is] not to be misunderstood as a campaign against philosophy of life." Likewise, his statement that he only "found his way to the question of being and time in 1923 or 1922–23" is an underestimation, since, as we shall see, he had posed this question as early as his course of KNS 1919. He also maintained that he first used the words "hermeneutics" and "hermeneutic" in 1923 when he purportedly began the first drafts of SZ, but these terms had been used in his courses since 1919. As he had been a censor in the German postal service during the First World War, so similarly in his later years he sometimes changed a word here and there, garbled the messages, and held up the philosophical mail service between his youthful texts and potential readers.[17]

Presumably, the later Heidegger stressed the speculative theological thinking of his student years as the decisive beginning of his being-question because it, rather than his caustically antispeculative thought in the early twenties, could more easily serve as an occasion for underlining his own later speculative approach to the being-question after his "turn." But the poetic license of this retrospective interpretation became almost comical when the reader was presented with images of a seventeen-year-old student pondering the question of being on his way home from school (G12 88/7) and the *Privatdozent* of the early twenties grappling with the neo-Greek question of the truth of being (SD 87/79), whereas in fact this *Privatdozent* was rather opening his courses with Luther's virulent condemnations of pagan philosophy. Using Heidegger's own principle of "*what is fitting* to the texts," we would do well to demythologize the later Heidegger's *mython* and understand it as an interesting occasionalist literary strategy.

The autobiographies that Heidegger gave during his student years in the form of academic curricula vitae and during the early twenties in his courses and correspondence do not at all match up with his later autobiographies (cf. HL 78–80; G61 182; G63 5). From a study of these and the other relevant texts in question, we now know that during his student years he was actually pursuing traditional Neo-Kantian and Neo-Scholastic metaphysics, and that in his courses from 1919 onward he carried out a critical "destruction" of this very metaphysics, calling for the "end of philosophy" and executing the very first versions of the "turn" to a new "genuine beginning." This is the decisive beginning of his being-question, as the rumored unoffical story about Heidegger has been suggesting for years. We have also become aware that, by the time Heidegger came to write SZ, his thinking had undergone major transformations under the influence of Kant's transcendental thought, and that in the later writings it developed in still different directions under the influence of the pre-Socratics, Hölderlin, and Nietzsche, though here we also see a creative reversion to his terminology of *Ereignis*, worlding, and there is/it gives in 1919 and the early 1920s. In other words, there is a very broken line that runs from his student period to the later writings, and the major rupture occurs around 1919.

Nor is Heidegger's narrative "fitting to the texts" in sometimes suggesting a teleological plot in which his youthful texts are seen to be imperfect anticipations of, and to lead inevitably to, his later concerns and terminology. This retrospective closure is shown to be dubious in light of the different uses made of his youthful thought by Gadamer, Arendt, Habermas, Caputo, Krell, and others. The later Heidegger is only one among many readers of his youthful writings. And here he was his own check when he, on the other hand, made such statements as, "I still knew nothing of what would later trouble my thinking" (G1 55; cf. G12 88/7). The noetic hand of the *mens auctoris* encloses, monopolizes, revises, paints over, even tears out pages, but it also knows how to let go, to let the readers ponder the texts independently.

The Dangerous Supplement

This longstanding ambidexterity was finally reflected in the *coup de main* of Heidegger's handling of his collected edition, which began to be published in 1976, near the end of his life. On the one hand, he stated in the unfinished introduction that

> the collected edition should show in a manifold fashion: a being on the way in the way-field of the variable questioning of the polysemous being-question. . . . What is to be handled here [*es handelt sich um*] is the awakening of a debate on the question of the topic of thinking . . . and not communicating the mind of the author and not sketching out the author's standpoint; . . . this sort of thing . . . has no importance whatsoever. . . . The large number of volumes attests only to the enduring questionableness of the question of being and gives ample opportunities to check matters for oneself. (G1 438)

In other words, the decisive criterion for interpreting the texts is not his own retrospective self-understanding, but rather the topic itself in these texts. Thus the first prospectus of Fall 1974 and the second one of Fall 1975, which were issued by the publisher Vittorio Klostermann during Heidegger's lifetime, expressed his wish that the edition should "open up a *more exact* and deeper insight into his thinking" (emphasis added) and allow his thoughtpath to be seen "in the *sequence of its steps* more penetratingly than before" (emphasis added). "Because the collected edition is supposed to show the movement of the thoughtpath, the *chronological principle* of the genesis of the writings forms the basis of each division"[18] (emphasis added). The edition is a "collected" edition because it presumably gathers together in a chronologically exact manner the great plurality of Heidegger's textual thoughtpaths. And it is an *edition* (*Ausgabe*) in the sense of a handing out (*editio*, *Ausgeben*) of the *Handschriften*, an emancipation of the manuscripts into the open-ended movement of independent interpretation. Thus the motto of the edition that Heidegger penned shortly before his death in 1976: "ways—not works."

On the other hand, Heidegger's plans for the collected edition involved handing out the thoughtpaths in his early Marburg courses, but not those in his early Freiburg courses. The reason was both that it was unclear how many of the manuscripts from this period were extant and in publishable form, and that, as Gadamer has stated, Heidegger did not think they belonged to his authentic corpus, since he maintained that they had not yet made the real breakthrough to the being-question (DEW 9). The early Marburg courses were included in the edition because, as we read in the first prospectus of Fall 1974, Heidegger took them to "stand thematically in the compass of *Sein und Zeit*." The first prospectus stated also, "It remains reserved for a later decision whether the early Freiburg lecture courses (1916-1923) will also be published as a supplement [*Supplement*] to the second division." Regarding this "dangerous supplement" (which, in Derrida's sense of the *supplément*, *supplants* much of Heidegger's self-interpretation and lets his entire literary corpus be seen in a *different* light), note that the prospectus says "whether" and not "when," which is what it presumably should have read if the problem here was only that of waiting a few years until the surviving manuscripts could be "collected" together. This statement was repeated in the next two prospectuses of Fall 1975 and March 1978, then dropped from the fourth prospectus of April 1981, and finally replaced in the fifth, April 1984 prospectus with the announcement that the literary executor Hermann Heidegger had decided to publish the extant manuscripts from this period as a "supplement."

However, only eight of Heidegger's own manuscripts from the estimated thirteen lecture courses he held were found to be extant. The missing manuscripts are those from his three lecture courses held between WS 1915-16 and WS 1916-17, his SS 1919 "Über das Wesen der Universität und des akademischen Studiums," and his WS 1920-21 "Einleitung in die Phänomenologie der Religion," as well as the full text of his SS 1924 "Aristoteles, *Rhetorik*, II," his 1924 lecture "Der Begriff der Zeit," and 1925 Kassel lectures "Wilhelm Diltheys Forschungsarbeit und der Kampf um eine historische Weltanschauung." Many of the missing manuscripts were apparently destroyed at one time or another by Heidegger's own hand.[19] The extant lecture courses of the early Freiburg period had to be inserted almost haphazardly into the "supplement" to "Division II: Lecture Courses," squeezed uncomfortably between Heidegger's SS 1943 course on Heraclitus (vol. 55) and his 1936–38 *Beiträge zur Philosophie* (vol. 65), as if Heidegger's reading of the pre-Socratics was prior "chronologically." This priority surely reflected the later Heidegger's systematic preferences, but it and the original exclusion of the early Freiburg courses from the collected edition seem to fly in the face of "the chronological principle."

His youthful writings, these dangerous supplements, look like juvenile bricolage that one does not know what to do with and where to put. Apparently, these philosophical Gnostic Gospels did not originally receive Heidegger's "imprimatur"[20] in the summa of his thoughtpaths and thus almost have the status of apocrypha in the Heideggerian canon, or of items on an *Index Expurgatorius*. The world is profoundly indebted to Heidegger and his literary executors for holding off on plans for a critical edition and thus making his unpublished writings available so quickly in the present edition, despite its imperfections. What is perplexing, however, is that, despite the original chronological principle, he was apparently reluctant to make his early Freiburg writings available just as quickly and that, despite the associated principle that the edition should have nothing to do with "communicating the mind of the author," he seems to have verged on installing his own authorial self-interpretation of these writings into the very structure of the collected edition. The fact that the publication of his early Freiburg courses, which was begun in 1985, will be quickly completed by the mid-nineties also suggests that his reluctance to publish them was based on not only philological but also philosophical reasons.

There is a clear precedent here. In the 1980s Victor Farias discovered that Heidegger had omitted from the collected edition his eight contributions between 1910 and 1913 to the Catholic antimodernist journal *Der Akademiker* (CA 486–519; HAN 38–47; MH 62–66). They were not even mentioned either in the prospectuses, in the volume *Aus der Erfahrung des Denkens* (G13) that presented Heidegger's short publications as far back as 1910, or in *Frühe Schriften*, which claimed to have collected together "all of the early writings published by Heidegger between 1912 and 1916" (G1 438). Yet these book reviews and essays provide us with important insights into the background of his other publications at the time and into the subsequent development of his thought, including his later involvement with National Socialism. We can find another precedent not directly in Heidegger himself, but ironically in his critique of the later Husserl's retrospective downplaying, "profound revisions," and withdrawal from publication of the Sixth Investigation in his early *Logische Untersuchungen*. "The master himself no longer held his work in very high esteem" and "watched [Heidegger's early study of it] . . . in disapproval" (G12 86/5; SD 84–90/77–82).

Heidegger's Signature

One can also get a vivid sense for the ambidexterity of the Heideggerian *mens auctoris*, of his inclusion/exclusion of his youthful writings in his literary corpus, by looking at the reproduction of his signature, scrawled with his aged hand, on the title page of his collected edition: "Martin Heidegger/Collected Edition/Ways—not works." What's in a name? Who is the "Martin Heidegger" here? Who is the signatory, the signified of this signature? From whose hand does it come? Whose hand is it that hands out the collected edition to us? Were one to study all the published photographs of Heidegger that show his hands, and also all the reproductions of his signature on his photographs and in his published correspondence, which hand and signature should one single out? Heidegger himself wrote that "the name of the thinker stands as a title for *the topic* of his thinking" (N1 9/NI xv). Thus, if his topic is pluralized into a diversity of ways, we are led to believe that there is also no strict unity in the name of the thinker and that it cannot serve as a spiritual principle of identity animating a literary corpus. Derrida is arguing the same point when he maintains that the name or signature of an author is permeated with *différance*, a differing/deferring that does not allow it to serve as a principle of unity in a text or corpus.[21]

So which Martin Heidegger is the signified of his signature and the proper name on the title page of the collected edition? The "name" that "travelled all over Germany like the rumor of the hidden king"? "Heidegger I" of SZ? "Heidegger II" of the later writings? The young Heidegger of the early twenties? "Heidegger-Zero" of his earliest metaphysical writings in his student years "before Heidegger became *Heidegger*"?[22] Or a Heidegger III in the unpredictable other beginning of Western thinking that he envisioned for the very distant future? Or how about Heidegger the Nazi rector of 1933? "Just look at [Hitler's] wonderful hands!" "Heil Hitler! Martin Heidegger, Rector." "We the signatories, representatives of German science . . . firmly believe that under his leadership . . . " "Needless to say, non-Aryans shall not appear on the signature page." Is the signature on the title page of Heidegger's collected edition also supposed to signify "Martinus Heidegger," the name in the register of the Jesuit novitiate in Feldkirch, Austria that the twenty-one year old had entered to become a priest? Who are "-gg-" and "Martin Heide," pseudonyms under which the young theology student and poet published his first poetic efforts in 1911 and 1915? Who is "Martin Heidegger, Cand. math." (*Candidatus mathematicus*, mathematics candidate), the signature on his 1913 petitionary letter for the Ph.D.? Who "Dr. Heidegger Lerchenstr. 8," as we read in a June 19, 1923 letter to Karl Jaspers?[23] There never was *a* Heidegger.

Similarly, now that we are getting a chance to study his early courses and essays, we can see that his writings from 1919 onward, including SZ, make up a long chain of differing/deferring drafts of a nonbook about "Being and Time" that continues into the drafts after SZ such as his *Beiträge zur Philosophie*, similar to Derrida's image of writing as a gallery of paintings of paintings of paintings. . . . [24] Which is the real "Being and Time?" We shall see that there really never was *a* text called "Being and Time."

Following Heidegger himself, we find that his signature turns out to be a "divided seal," a "seal in bits and pieces," as Derrida said of John Searle's signature. We find a Heidegger "who is divided, multiplied, conjugated, shared. What a complicated signature!"[25] Where is the proper in Heidegger's proper name? As I show later with Heidegger's treatment of analogy in his qualifying dissertation, his name can have only an analogical unity of identity-in-difference, though this is hardly a *pros hen* analogy of attribution where the name "Heidegger" would be attributed properly to the "later Heidegger" and only derivatively to the other Heideggers. His name, signature, and topic are ruptured, decentered, disseminated into a family of different Heideggers and Heideggerian thoughtpaths. If anything, they are signs of an identity-crisis, a literary schizophrenia in the *mens auctoris*. They are only what he himself called formal indications (*formale Anzeige*), unfulfilled intentional traces that point out of their absence to analogical enactment and differentiation into a plethora of Heideggerian offspring.

But the matter at hand is even more complicated. In addition to the different Heideggers, student transcripts of his courses are being published under his own name in the collected edition, either on their own or by being woven into his own manuscript (for example, see G56/57 215–18). And there are even more hands at work in weaving the texts of the edition: those of the literary executors who have taken up the unfinished project of the collected edition and interpret the guidelines that Heidegger left behind; and those of the editors of the individual volumes who must make interpretive decisions in deciphering Heidegger's antiquated handwriting, dividing the manuscript into sections, adding punctuation, and weaving in Heidegger's marginal notes and student transcripts. In the case of volumes appearing in a foreign language, the hermeneutical hands of the translators, series editors, and copy editors are also busy. "It is also *their* edition," Kisiel has written, stressing the principle that edition is interpretation (EU 98). The hand that scrawled the signature on the title page of the collected edition turns out to be a phantom limb that lingers around after the amputation of the metaphysical myth that the author's name, the *mens auctoris*, is a spiritual principle of identity animating the literary corpus.

Though the later Heidegger *thematically* deconstructed the centrality of the mind of the author, his hermeneutical *praxis* of retrospectively stylizing and marginalizing his youthful writings, and then allowing this self-interpretation to install itself into the plan of the collected edition by excluding his youthful writings, indicates that his signature on the title page flirted with the possibility of being a master name and imprimatur for the edition. Is the collected edition a summa and system of thoughtpaths that collect the writings around his later thought as a teleological principle expressing the hidden sense and unity of his many different ways? Is his signature a forgery that covers over the differences and discontinuities of his thought? Is it, to use Derrida's terms, a logocentric signature[26] fixed on the author's intention-to-say (*vouloir-dire*), on what the author really meant to say, on the self-presence to itself of this authorial voice via its externalized interweaving into writing, which is thus like a gloved hand that wants to caress itself?

Does the sense of his texts come across as something present-before-the-hand (*vorhanden*) to be enclosed in the conceptual grip (*Begriff*) of the author's omniscient transcendental hand and then handed over to the reader? Does he fall toward an onto-theo-ego-logical reading of his own writings that anchors their sense in the metaphysical ground of the *mens auctoris*, in (as Barthes put it) "the 'message' of the Author-God,"[27] in the highhanded notion of the pluralized *Heilsweg* of his later writings? Is the analogical identity-in-difference within his thoughtpaths a *pros hen* analogy of attribution similar to how in Scholasticism the term "being" is attributed properly to God and only derivatively to other beings? Did he want his later self-interpretation to be as it were written in stone, as he literally did with his essay "Art and Space" (G13 250)? Has Martin Heidegger been caught with his hand in the jar of his collected edition? The question is ambiguous because his handling of the status of the *mens auctoris* is ambivalent. Here one will have to criticize Heidegger with Heidegger.

Edition from the Last/Ultimate Hand

This dangerous ambiguity has been aggravated by Heidegger's commentators and the literary executors of the guidelines he left behind for the unfinished project of his collected edition. Here we sometimes get the impression of a kind of hermeneutical amputation of that self-deconstructive Heideggerian hand that sweeps away the *mens auctoris* as the decisive criterion. We are sometimes left with a handicapped, monoplegic caricature that exalts the *mens auctoris* to the status of a metaphysical principle. Two years after Heidegger's death, the third, March 1978 prospectus for the edition no longer mentioned the guiding "chronological principle," but rather the principle of an *Ausgabe letzter Hand*, a last-hand edition, a handing out from the last/ultimate hand of Martin Heidegger himself. It stated that "Martin Heidegger's collected edition is in a special sense *his* edition" (EU 98). We read in the prospectus of April 1984 that "the volumes of the collected edition are edited basically in the way that the philosopher himself made his writings available: without a philological apparatus and without an index. For such an edition it remains decisive that in it *the will of the author* to gather together his life's work in *the confluent form he sketched out* is realized" (p. 4; emphasis added). The edition is thus supposed to be an "edition without interpretation," an immediate handing out of the volumes from Heidegger's hand into the hands of the reader—without the interpretive mediation of executors, editors, and translators. "The texts should rather speak immediately and for themselves." In this way, the reader's independent interpretation of the texts as *die Sache selbst* is supposed to be encouraged.[28]

But, as Kisiel has pointed out, this posthumuous last/ultimate-hand principle and the associated principle of an "edition without interpretation" actually work against the intentions of Heidegger's executors by surreptitiously giving priority to the *mens auctoris* over *die Sache selbst* in a number of subtle ways. They function as principles of hermeneutical intimidation in editorial and translation work, which, according to Heidegger himself, is inevitably interpretive, should strive for "*what is fitting* to the particular text," should be willing to take responsibility for its independent interpretive decisions, and thus presumably should, in a spirit of hermeneutical openness, inform the reader of these decisions with philological apparatuses such as notes, preface or epilogue, glossary, and index (EU 98).

But these principles also intimidate the independent interpretation of readers. For though, as Heidegger himself knew, the reader inevitably receives interpretively packaged texts at the other end of the communicative process, the idea of an "edition without interpretation" encourages the naive impression that neither Heidegger's self-interpretation nor the editors and translators have left any significant marks on the pages. Moreover, the last/ultimate-hand principle, which is centered on "the will of the author," greases the slippery slope down which neither Heidegger himself nor his executors wanted to see the reader slide, namely, the tendency to go from asking "how Heidegger himself probably would have decided" an editorial question (EU 98), to pondering how he himself would have decided a question of translation, to speculating how he himself would have decided the interpretation of his texts, as if the reader thought that he or she could walk hand in hand with the last/ultimate hand of the author, which would reach out from the collected edition to offer its master code, just as the hand of God in Michelangelo's Sistine Chapel fresco communicates the spiritual breath of life to Adam by touching his fingertip. Regarding the case at hand, there lurks the danger that the later Heidegger's operative tendencies to valorize his unfavorable self-interpretations of his youthful period, his executors' equally ambivalent elevation of the *mens auctoris* to the level of a thematic hermeneutical principle, and the tendency of many of Heidegger's commentators to fall into the metaphysical illusion of an all-knowing author will seriously bias the ongoing rediscovery and interpretation of his youthful writings.

Heidegger, Inc.

In his essay "What Is an Author?," Michel Foucault clearly saw this kind of problem in the interpretation of those authors who are historical "founders of discursivity," such as Marx and Freud. Let us add Heidegger's name. Foucault argued that the function of naming the author of a text or corpus (the "author-function") is not so much the simple attribution of the discourse to a natural individual (for example, Heidegger the man), but rather the interpretive construction of a second self, a rational being (the later Heidegger) that serves as a principle of unity for the text or corpus (Heidegger's collected edition). There is an isomorphism here between the metaphysical couplets mind/body and author/corpus. The *mens auctoris* is as it were the mind of the literary corpus, its self-identity.

The traditional interpretive rules for constructing the author have included taking the author to be a standard of quality, of conceptual coherence of doctrine, and of stylistic uniformity, in terms of which we can say that a particular text does or does not belong to the corpus of the author in question. Foucault asked, "'When undertaking the publication of Nietzsche's works, for example, where should one stop?"

> Surely everything must be published, but what is "everything"? . . . And what about the rough drafts for his works? Obviously. . . . What if, within a workbook filled with aphorisms, one finds a reference, the notation of a meeting or of an address, or a laundry list: Is it a work, or not? Why not? . . . A theory of the work does not exist, and the empirical task of those who naively undertake the editing of works often suffers in the absence of such a theory.

Foucault maintained that the author-function is usually an "ideological figure," a "system of constraint," power, and exclusion used to regulate the interpretation of the texts in question: "The author is the principle of thrift in the proliferation of meaning. . . . he is a certain functional principle by which, in our culture, one limits, excludes, and chooses; in short, by which one impedes the free circulation, the free manipulation, the free composition, decomposition, and recomposition of fiction."[29] Similarly, Barthes holds that the "Author-God" is a "religious" or ontotheological authority: "To give a text an Author is to impose a limit on that text, to furnish it with a final signified, to close the writing."[30] A direct link exists between author and authority.

So we can ask, To what extent is the name of the all-knowing author of Heidegger's corpus and of the signatory of his collected edition a literary construction erected partially (and to a great extent ironically) by Heidegger himself and then blown out of proportion by both his followers and his detractors? To what extent is this author an ideological figure constraining the interpretation of his thought within the limits of his later self-interpretations, impeding the "free circulation" of his youthful thoughtpaths as well as others, and so thriftily suppressing the rich proliferation of ways to which his topic presumably lends itself?

Foucault stressed that, in the case of "founders of discursivity," the author also produces "the possibilities and the rules for the formation of other texts," that is, for a discipline (Heidegger Studies) and tradition of discursive practices (Heideggerianism).[31] Authorial rules of quality, doctrine, and style, as well as especially the provocative "gaps and absences" in the original texts, open up possibilities of discourse and serve as reference points for debating whether a text is, e.g., a genuinely Heideggerian interpretation and belongs in the set of Heideggerian discursive practices. Foucault suggested that the creative ambiguity of the founding texts can be leveled off and the rules can become increasingly inflexible and institutionalized in the derivative discursive practices that include monographs, applications of the texts to particular issues, archival work, editing, translation, journals, conferences, university courses, and academic societies, all of which are disciplinary in a double sense of an academic field and constraint. Here the *mens auctoris*, the founder of discursivity, becomes incarnated into the institutional body of a kind of Marx, Freud, or Heidegger Corporation, a "Copyright Trust"[32] defined by literary and legal relations of ownership and rights over the founding texts and their meaning. Heidegger's linguistic "house of being" becomes Heidegger, Inc., the Institute for Heidegger Studies.

Like the idealist's transcendental self that is supposed to be instantiated in empirical egos, the literary space of the founding authorial dramatis persona, now left vacant by the death of the natural person, is colonized by Marxists, Freudians, or Heideggerians, heirs apparent who attempt to cheat finitude by immortalizing an authorial intention that now reaches out to us like a ghostly hand from beyond the grave. A new Heideggerian "scholasticism," to quote Gadamer (HW 28), becomes entrenched within the binary oppositions of the authentic over against the inauthentic, orthodox right-wing over against heretical left-wing Heideggerianism. At the extreme, this concern with a Heideggerian *Heilsweg* turns into a pseudo-religious cult of "the man," with its styles of hagiography, memorabilia, photobiography, and officialese, which is not to be confused with the philosophical chronology and biography necessary to show the historicity and variety of Heidegger's thoughtpaths.

And yet all the while this Heidegger-scholasticism remains the dupe of the rich ambiguity of the texts and of the Author-Father himself, who rarely took himself so seriously and showed his whole hand. Heidegger himself called this institutionalizing of knowledge "idle talk," "passing the word along," and "scribbling." But to what extent did his own flirtation with mythic authorial construction in his autobiographical accounts of his youthful period and in his treatment of his youthful writings in his collected edition encourage the exaggerated institutionalization of this occasionalist literary device into the Official Story about the origins of his thought that has been passed along for years? There has been much talk of a type of "damage control" exercised by orthodox Heideggerians on Farias's and Ott's documentation of Heidegger's involvement with National Socialism, but what about the possibility of damage control on the rediscovery of the dangerous "supplement" of his youthful writings that threatens to upset the Official Story? Will these writings be filed away and forgotten as errant ways, dark alleys, crooked dealings, so as to aid in averting the danger of a proliferation of unorthodox thoughtpaths and "free composition," which threatens now that an increasing number of these and other Heideggerian apocrypha are coming to light? "But where danger is grows the saving power" (VA 39/QCT 34).

An Ambiguous Apologia

This study of Heidegger's youthful writings takes up the challenge of infiltrating Heidegger, Inc., demythologizing the *mython* of the Official Story about the early development of his thought, and telling a version of the unofficial story that has been rumored for years. It ventures a deconstruction of the homogenizing, hierarchical-exclusionary gestures of a Heidegger, Inc. that is built on the very ambiguous foundation of the later Heidegger's logocentric name and signature. As a genealogy of the plurality of different thoughtpaths that Heidegger pursued in his youthful period, it attempts to expose ruptures and discontinuities, "gaps and absences," in the Heideggerian *epistemes* trembling beneath his signature, and thus disperse his proper name into a rich non-hierarchical play of thoughtpaths. In his 1986 memorial lecture before the *Martin-Heidegger-Gesellschaft*, Gadamer said of Heidegger's WS 1921–22 lecture course that "there are indeed astonishing things in this early text":

> One needs to have the courage to admit to oneself that a great man can himself still underestimate his own radiance and above all the promising richness of his beginnings. . . . He himself would not at all have counted this text among his works. . . . I can even imagine that Martin Heidegger himself would have found many new things in this, his youthful writing, had he been able to read it with the eyes of someone who was not him. (DEW 9, 14)

We can find inspiration for our project, as well as a certain fidelity and orthodoxy, in the more radical tendencies in Heidegger himself, namely, his ambivalent acknowledgment of the importance of his youthful period from 1919 onward, his principle that the *mens auctoris* is not the decisive criterion, his play-ful irony and suspicion regarding his own retrospective self-interpretations, and his theme that the topic of thinking is open to a radical plurality of ways. Accordingly, Heidegger's readings of his own thought, as well as those by Hei-deggerians, are often very un-Heideggerian! In other words, we can read and demythologize Heidegger with Heidegger as well as with Derrida, Foucault, and others.

But the ultimate aim here is not merely a historical study of Heidegger's youthful period. For one is struck by the external similarity between the case of Heidegger's autobiographies of his youthful period and what has been called *l'affaire Heidegger*, that is, the case of his autobiographies of his involvement with National Socialism. In both cases, we are faced with the official and often unreliable story of the matter, which involves revisionistic interpretation and suppression of documents. In both cases, a deconstruction of the official story that picks up the rumors of an unofficial story is called for (cf. MH 7–16; HAN ix–xxi; HN 38–47; HA 363–404).

Sheehan has written that Heidegger's autobiographical accounts of his affiliation with National Socialism are "so riddled . . . with omissions, histori-cal errors, and self-serving interpretations that these texts can be used only with the greatest caution and a constant cross-check of the facts." Consider Heidegger's alteration of his statement about "the inner truth and grandeur of National Socialism" that he made in his SS 1935 course *Einführung in die Metaphysik*, so that in the published version of 1953 it now reads, "the inner truth and grandeur of this movement (namely, the encounter between global technology and modern humanity)" (G40 208/199). To quote Sheehan, he was "thereby reading back into 1935 his much later, and in fact revised, under-standing of the historical role of Nazism. And yet, to the day he died, he con-tinued to maintain that his 1935 lecture notes read exactly that way and that he had never tampered with them." Moreover, the page of the manuscript in question is missing from the Heidegger archives in Marbach, West Germany (HN 42–43). Similarly, it is very doubtful that Heidegger made plans to in-clude in his collected edition his assorted texts on National Socialism that Farias, Ott, Schneeberger, and others have painstakingly unearthed. Will the edition include, for example, his letter of October 2, 1929 to Victor Schwoerer on the "Jewification of the German spirit," his telegrams of May 20 and No-vember 9, 1933 to Hitler, or his adresses on German radio in 1933 and 1934?[33]

Here the genitive case in Heidegger's famous phrase *die Sache des Den-kens*, the *Sache* of (the) thinking, of (Heidegger's) thinking, takes on a curious ambiguity. He liked to appeal to the original sense of *Sache* as affair, public controversy, court case. "The expression '*Sache*,' '*Sache* of (the) thinking' . . . , taken in the old sense of the word (court case, lawsuit), means a disputed case, what is disputed, that which is to be handled [*das, worum es sich handelt*]," the "case at hand" (SD 41/38, 67/61; ID 107). Heidegger's phrase is meant in the sense of "*the subject matter* of thinking," that is, the affair, court case, or controversy of being itself, which affects thinking. But it can also mean "the affair, the court case of the (i.e., Heidegger's) thinking," *l'affaire Heidegger*, the Heidegger affair, that is, how the *mens auctoris* dealt with the topic in terms of autobiographical revisionism, as well as the ideologies of fascism, ethnocentrism, genderism, anthropocentrism, authoritarianism, and other problems that Heidegger's critics, spurred on by the reinvestigation of his involvement with National Socialism, claim he himself has read into the topic of the being-question. He wanted to stay away from this rendition of the phrase *die Sache des Denkens* since, according to the first rendition, thinking takes its directives immediately from being. Thus in his book *Die Sache des Denkens*, he quoted from Hans Erich Nossack's novel *Impossible Trial*: "But the accused made a sign of dimissal. One would have to be there, he said, if one is to be summoned, but to summon oneself would be the greatest, most topsy-turvy error that one could make" (SD 58/54). I shall argue that both readings of "the *Sache* of thinking" are legitimate within limits.

Reopening the case of Heidegger's coverup of his youthful writings may not, like Farias's 1987 and Ott's 1988 studies of Heidegger's alleged coverup of his involvement with Nazism, send another shock wave through Heidegger, Inc. But a more decisive difference in the two cases is that the one opens up *a* strategy for coping with the problems of the other. For what we shall find in Heideigger's youthful explorations of the end of philosophy, the other beginning, *Ereignis*, *Es gibt*, worlding, difference, mystery, the "Dasein of personal life," poetry, and modern technology are an-archic personalist formulations of the being-question; a project of demythologizing metaphysical *mythos* and a critique of worldview-ideology; an ethical ontology which is inspired by Eckhartian *Gelassenheit*, Schleiermacher's notion of free sociality, and the kairological thinking of Aristotle, Luther, and Kierkegaard; an anarchic notion of the university; and meditations on Dasein, *Geschlecht*, woman, and animal.

When Arendt called the young Heidegger of the early twenties "the hidden king," she meant that, like the Platonic philosopher-king who shuns the *polis* and rules rather in the heavenly city of the Ideas, so "the hidden king had reigned in the kingdom [*Reich*] of thinking" prior to the *déformation professionelle* of his "flight to tyrants and Führers" and his attempt at playing "philosopher-king" in the Third Reich/Kingdom of National Socialism.[34] But, in fact, we shall see that this hidden exiled king expressed an aversion to philosopher-kings in any sense and did not want to reign even in a kingdom of thought. The negative, deconstructive, skeptical thinking of the young Heidegger is closer to Derrida's position that, "not only is there no kingdom of differance, but differance instigates the subversion of every kingdom," "the death of the king."[35] According to the young Heidegger's warnings, the very attempt to rule in the realm of thought leads disastrously to totalitarian rule in the cultural and political spheres.

We shall explore how the above-mentioned themes in Heidegger's youthful writings, including especially his project of demythologizing, can be played off against his later autobiographical myths and his ideological and impersonalist tendencies toward a metaphysical *arche*, principle/kingdom. They can help us to move beyond these particular ways in which the *mens auctoris*, the matter of *Heidegger's thinking*, formulated the *matter* of thinking, i.e., the temporal and radically differentiated giving of being. But this will be for the sake of helping to free up those ambiguous nonideological and personalist countertendencies in Heidegger's later thought itself, liberate this thought into more generous styles of thinking, and thus foster that very independent, reinscriptive thinking-further (*Weiterdenken*) of the *Sache* itself which he himself always ambiguously insisted upon. The young Heidegger—this Heidegger earlier than the early Heidegger—can be of service in finding the Heidegger or, better, the Heideggers later than the later Heidegger, as well as ways of thinking that no longer directly bear Heidegger's seal. In his 1986 lecture before the *Martin-Heidegger-Gesellschaft*, Gadamer suggested that "the worldwide reputation of Hegel was in fact not realized through his *Phenomenology* or through his *Logic*, but rather through the publication of his lecture courses. Something similar could someday perhaps happen with Heidegger" (DEW 8). Rediscovering Heidegger's *Jugendgeschichte*, this apologue of a hidden exiled king, lending our voices to the rumor and letting it speak again, playing it off against the later Heidegger, can become an ambiguous apologia for his thinking, one which only reflects the very ambiguities in this thinking itself.

The plan we will pursue is as follows. The remainder of Part One sketches out a number of family resemblances in the later Heidegger's different thoughtpaths into the topic of the being-question (1927–76), but it does not yet discuss the above-mentioned problems in his thought. This sets the stage for the body of my study as a genealogy that shows that and how these resemblances were first inscribed in unique ways in Heidegger's early Freiburg period (1919–23). Part Two, on Heidegger's student years, leads into this task by exploring how his two dissertations in his student period (1909–15) and other writings at the time did indeed anticipate his later breakthroughs to the being-question, but were still working to a great extent within traditions of western metaphysics. Part Three focuses on Heidegger's early Freiburg period, outlining his "destruction" and demythologizing of the being-question in traditional metaphysics, his concept of the end of philosophy, and his readings of primal Christianity, Husserl, Dilthey, and Aristotle. Part Four again centers on the early Freiburg period, exploring Heidegger's an-archic personalist formulations of the new postmetaphysical beginning for the being-question, his notion of ontological mystery, his method of formal indication, and its ethical significance. The final chapter critically plays off Heidegger's youthful writings against the problems in his later thought. It explores how his "turn" after 1930 was a return to the lexicon of his early Freiburg period, sketches out how SZ and the later writings effected mythic, ideological, and impersonalist reinscriptions of this earlier lexicon, and applies his youthful strategy of demythologizing to these later reinscriptions.

2 | Figuring the Matter Out

Heidegger so radically transformed the traditional being-question that he eventually stopped using the term "being" as a designation for what he was ultimately aiming at. The appellation reiterated through the many waystations or *topoi* of his thought from his student days to his latest thought was in fact the word *Sache*, which can be translated as matter, topic, issue, problem, question, point of dispute (G1 196, 211; G61 12; SZ 37/50; SD). Though Heidegger liked to appeal to the word's original sense, namely, court case or legal battle, he also maintained that the conflict and difference involved here are not initiated by the belligerence of human thought. Rather "the *Sache*, the disputed case, is in itself a dis-pute, a dis-cussion [*Aus-einander-setzung*]" (N1 9/NI xv). The sameness of the *Sache*, which contains difference in itself, is thus not to be confused with identity: "But the same [*das Selbe*] is not the identical [*das Gleiche*]. In the identical, difference disappears. In the same, difference appears" (ID 107, 111/45).

Heidegger often used subjunctive and aporetic phrases such as what is to be thought (*das zu Denkende*), what is worthy of question (*das Fragwürdige*), and what is to be said (*das zu Sagende*) as synonyms for the term *Sache*. This nameless name was not supposed to name anything actual, determinate, and singular, but rather invoked a possibility, an indeterminacy that allows itself to be reiterated and reinscribed in different and clashing ways. Heidegger's topic is not an answer, but essentially a question to be answered over and over on different thoughtpaths (N1 457/NII 192). Thus Heidegger likewise gave up the term "philosophy" in the metaphysical doublet philosophy/being and preferred to speak rather of "paths" of thinking into the topic. "What endures in thinking is only the way" (G12 94/12). The postmetaphysical name of his thinking that he reinscribed through his many thoughtpaths was precisely the word *Weg*, way or path (G1 201, 213; SZ 576/487; G61 157; SD 38/36). Though he continually placed the same topic in discussion (*erörtert*), his paths never stepped onto the identical *topos* twice.

There never was a single Heidegger, *mens auctoris*, topic, Heidegger's philosophy, since these are pluralized and differentiated into Heideggers, *topoi*, and thoughtpaths. And yet the anonymity of the term *Sache*, topic, still trembles across the expanses of his thought. How is one to get a sense for and learn how to cope with the style of this *lucus a non lucendo*, this clearing where nothing gets cleared up? How to avoid becoming completely lost in Heidegger's Black Forest of *Holzwege*? I argue that the word *Sache* is a kind of family name, an empty "formal indication," for the different Heideggers housed and trying to get along together in the family quarrel of his collected edition. I present a number of family resemblances in the different ways that he reiterated and placed his topic in discussion from his 1927 SZ, through his *Beiträge zur Philosophie (Vom Ereignis)* and *Nietzsche* in the 1930s and 1940s, and to his *Zur Sache des Denkens* and *Seminare* in the 1960s and 1970s. My philosophical family portrait sketches three traits which, as I shall show later, were first inscribed in his youthful thought: namely, the end of philosophy, a new beginning, and indeed a constant beginning or being on the way.

Using Heidegger's terminology from the early twenties to unlock the sense of his later thought, I explore how each of the above traits in his later thought is itself oriented around a multifaceted cluster of resemblances in the way that the sense of being (*Seinssinn*) is configured out into a number of intentional moments. The young Heidegger called these analogical moments the content-sense (*Gehaltssinn*), relational sense (*Bezugssinn*), fulfillment-sense (*Vollzugssinn*), and temporalizing-sense (*Zeitigungssinn*) of our intentional comportment (*Verhalten*) to being. Content-sense points to the sense of the intentional content of experience, relational sense to the sense of the manner of intending this content, fulfillment-sense to the sense of enacting, performing, actualizing, or fulfilling the horizonal prefigurement of the whole intentional relation, and the all-important temporalizing-sense to the deep radical dimension of this fulfilling as historical time. Though Heidegger toned down his use of these phenomenological terms by the time he wrote SZ, he continued to employ them right up until the unfinished introduction of his collected edition, where he dealt with "the question concerning the topic of thinking (thinking as the relation [*Bezug*] to being)" (G1 438). Configuring and laying out the matter of Heidegger's thinking into these terminological moments offers an important hermeneutical approach to figuring out the elusive sense of this matter.

Thus, the plan to be followed is: (1) how Heidegger's strategies for the end of philosophy dismantled the founded character of the traditional metaphysical configurations of the content-, relational, fulfillment-, and temporalizing-senses of being; (2) how his forays into a new beginning reconfigured these moments postmetaphysically; and (3) how his imperatives to constantly beginning anew on different thoughtpaths insisted on a constant reinscription of the postmetaphysical sense of these moments.

The Ends of Philosophy

Whether pursued along the path of the sense, truth, or place of being, Heidegger's topic arose out of the byways of deconstructing the entire western metaphysical tradition, which he viewed as a "first beginning" initiated by the Greeks and working itself out in various constellations in the Middle Ages and modernity. Deconstruction (*Abbauen*), which captures the genuine sense of Heidegger's term "destruction" (from *destruere*), means dismantling the founded "structure of the guiding question" about being in the history of metaphysics. Heidegger claimed that this enduring structure guided the development of the various traditional "fundamental metaphysical positions," in which "the questioner comes to stand within and towards beings as a whole and so co-determines the position of humanity as such in the whole of beings."[1] In other words, his deconstructions focused on the content-, relational-, fulfillment-, and temporalizing-senses of being that characterize the complex structure of the guiding question of metaphysics. Here content showed itself as causal ground, relation as *logos*, fulfillment as making-present, and temporalizing as standing presence. The history of metaphysics is a chain of reinscriptions of these characters, a series of variations on these leitmotifs. Heidegger's usual procedure was to uncover their genesis in Greek philosophy, to show how this genetic code covertly animated the Middle Ages and modernity, and then to call for the end of philosophy and a transition to another beginning. His genealogical deconstructions can rightly be called archeologies, since they endeavor to give accounts of the double *arche* (in Heidegger's sense of both beginning and reign) for western metaphysics.

Content-Sense as Ground

To describe that to which our experience of being is related, namely, world, Heidegger often used the term *Gehalt*, content (e.g., SZ §44a), or some other variation of the term *Halt*, hold, support. In his "Letter on Humanism," he wrote, "The truth of being offers the hold [*Halt*] for all comportment [*Verhalten*]" (G9 361/BW 239). This worldly hold or content is that to which we are drawn (*gezogen*), tend, and hold in the intentional relation (*Bezug, Verhältnis*) of our comportment (*Verhalten*) to it. Intentional content makes up the tenancy of our being tenants in a world. It provides us with a residence (*Aufenthalt*) and home (*ethos*) which defines our basic stance (*Haltung*) toward things. In his *Beiträge*, Heidegger wrote of the *Umhalt* for experience, i.e., the hold or content around us provided by a world's *Zeit-Spiel-Raum*, the leeway of space and time which articulates the paths of thought and action, work and play (G65 §242).

The derivative content-sense in the structure of the guiding question of metaphysics is the being (*Sein*) or beingness (*Seiendheit*) of beings in the sense of a causal ground for beings. What is interrogated (*das Befragte*) is beings, but what is sought after (*das Erfragte*) is ultimately the being of beings that can account for or explain beings as beings. "Metaphysics begins with beings, elevates itself to being, in order to turn back to beings as such and clarify them in the light of being." It "questions after being with a view to how it determines beings as beings" (G15 306–307). The *terminus a quo* and *ad quem* of the questioning is beings. Being is used to explain beings without itself having been interrogated regarding how it comes about.

The Greeks experienced being as a stable *noeton topon*, an intelligible place (*Republic* 508c), an open area of truth in the sense of unconcealment (*aletheia*), light (*phos*) or radiant appearing (*phainesthai*), and emergence (*physis*). It was seen to be the *aition* of beings (the cause of beings in the premodern generic sense of what is responsible for something), as well as the *arche*, which, as Heidegger repeatedly pointed out, has the double sense of beginning and governance (*Herrschaft*), dominion, kingdom (G9 247/BCP 228). According to Heidegger, when Heraclitus makes such statements as "time is a child playing a board game, a child's is the kingdom [*basileie*]" (fr. 52) or "war is the father and king [*basileus*] of all things" (fr. 53), he "grasps in almost poetic language the sense of the *arche* of motion" (G15 45/HS 24; SG 188). This origin/kingdom of being functions as the ruling etiological ground furnishing beings with intelligibility or sense, that is, lets them be *as* intelligible beings, unconcealed beings, phenomena, emergent beings. In Plato, for example, the being of individual beautiful beings consists in the idea of the beautiful that offers the view or look (*eidos*) through which beings can appear *as* beautiful. Metaphysics is "onto-logic" in the sense of assertoric discourse (*logos*) about being (*on*) as ground (G1 55).

Being as ground was also taken to be itself a being, the most beingly being (*to on ontos*), that is, the highest and most honored being in the hierarchical-teleological order of the cosmos. Thus the Greeks ultimately saw in being the divine (*to theion*) (ID 107–43/42–74). "That which is wise is one; it is willing and unwilling to be called by the name of Zeus" (Heraclitus, fr. 32). The same ambiguity shows itself in Aristotle's first philosophy, which begins with the question of being as being and yet ends in theology. The full topic of Greek philosophy is thus the etiotheological *topos* of the being of beings.

This structure of the content-sense of being as ground was presupposed, unquestioned, and in fact hidden in the very guiding question of metaphysics, which was therefore already half an answer. It opened up and limited the field for the outbreak of the Greek *gigantomachia peri tes ousias*, the battle of giants, of the would-be philosopher-kings, about the title to the royal *topos* of being. Thus it guided the formation of fundamental metaphysical positions that arose in Greek thought as competing answers: for example, being (Parmenides), *logos* (Heraclitus), idea (Plato), category, being-in-work (Aristotle). All these metaphysical positions were "preoccupied with finding an answer" and inattentive to the possibility of unfolding the structure of the question itself in another direction. Their strife took place against the backdrop of a deeper unanimity concealed in the very unquestioned question about being as ground.

Heidegger argued further that the etiotheological question of being makes up the "first beginning" of western thought in the sense of the double *arche* of beginning and governance for the entire tradition from the Greek to the medieval and modern epochs. He took this tradition to be a continual and varied surveying of the metaphysical topic from one end to the other into the various fundamental metaphysical positions in "the history of being." The pervasive answer to the unquestioned question about the being of beings in the medieval epoch is that this is the *actualitas* of the Kingdom of God in the sense of the *summum ens* and *summum bonum*, the highest being and good in a hierarchical-teleological order. The pervasive answer in the modern epoch is that the being of beings is the "promised land" (Husserl) of subjectivity: for example, *res cogitans* (Descartes), monad (Leibniz), sensory mind/brain (empiricism), transcendental unity of apperception (Kant), absolute spirit (Hegel), will to power (Nietzsche), transcendental ego (Husserl), and the framework or enframing (*Gestell*) of contemporary technology. "I understand by a 'kingdom,' " wrote Kant in his *Groundwork of the Metaphysics of Morals*, "a systematic union of different rational beings under common laws." If Greek philosophy was onto-theo-cosmo-logy and the medieval tradition was a hybrid Hellenic-Christian ontotheology, modernity is onto-theo-ego-logy, since the structure of being as divine ground is grafted onto some form of the human ego.

Relational Sense as Logos

Heidegger also dealt extensively with our *Bezug zum Sein*, our relation to being; the "*Bezug* of the human being to the twofold of presence and that which is present"; the "*Bezug* of human being to the truth of being." Thus "being is not absolutely for itself . . . being is not without its relation to Dasein," to human being-here (*Dasein*). He often said that all ontologies are already anthropologies and ethics, since they implicitly or explicitly sketch out the relation of our comportment in action and thinking to being. He wrote, "Every doctrine of being is ipso facto a doctrine of the essence of human being." "To think the truth of being means at the same time: to think the humanity of the *homo humanus*." In its relation to human life, being is the dwelling place, the home (*ethos*) of human being. "Language is the house of being. In its home human beings dwell." Thus, "that thinking that thinks the truth of being as the originary element of human being, which exists, is in itself originary ethics." Conversely, if there is no being without its relation to human being, "this relation to being makes up the essence of human being." It defines our "relationships of being to world, to Dasein-with, to being-in [the world] itself." Being and human being are defined by an essential intentional correlativity: "Each of the two members of the relation of the essence of human life and being already implies the relation itself."[2]

The founded relational sense in the structure of the guiding question of metaphysics is *logos* in the inclusive sense of theory, thought, and assertion about the etiotheological topic of being. Though Greek thought tended to be an objectivism that took being to be independent of thought, it was still quite aware of the relation of human life to being. "Philosophy seeks to elucidate being via reflection on the *thinking* of entities (Parmenides). Plato's disclosure of the ideas takes its bearings from the soul's conversation (*logos*) with itself. The Aristotelian categories originate in view of *reason's* assertoric knowledge" (VZB 256/111). Being is experienced as unconcealment and radiant appearance *for* human life, which is *en to noeto topo*, in the intelligible place of being. Being is the proper home of the human soul. "The home [*ethos*] of human being," sang Heraclitus, "is the divine" (fr. 119). As Arendt pointed out in her essay on Heidegger as the "hidden king," it is in the origin/kingdom (*arche*), the principle/principality (*principium*), of the intelligible place of being, the "city in *logos*," that the Platonic philosopher-king (*archon, princeps*) reigns.[3]

In this etiotheoethical topic of being, the Greek philosopher stood in an ocular relation of seeing (*idein*), contemplative gazing (*theorein*), and wondering (*thaumazein*). The thinker is a "spectator of the truth," a "lover of the spectacle of truth" (*Republic* 475e). Thus Plato took being to be an *idea*, an *eidos*, that which is seen, the outlook of being that looks back at us. The Greeks were all eyes, enchanted by the beauty, charm, and divinity of the sight of being as unconcealment and radiant appearance. This theoretical relation to being shows itself more clearly in the form of *nous*, which is usually translated as mind, intellect, reason, but means more exactly a simple mental perceiving or beholding that also animates sense perception (*aisthesis*). Far from being an idealist thesis, Parmenides's statement that "pure perceiving [*noein*] and being are the same" (fr. 3) asserts that being is the objective *noema*, that what shows itself for *nous*. This ocular-noetic relation completes itself in *logos*, discourse in the specific sense of statement. For Aristotle, the logos of philosophy is primarily *logos apophantikos*, the assertoric judgment that lets being appear through a simple pointing out (*apophainesthai*). This is what he also calls *kategorein*, the accusing or addressing of beings in terms of the schemata of the categories of being. Greek thinking thus had a strong phenomenological character, since *aisthesis*, *nous*, and *logos* are taken to be types of letting appear (*phainesthai*), making manifest (*deloun*), unconcealing (*aletheuein*) of being.

But the Greek thinkers also had another representational view of this ocular noetic-logical relation to being which was to haunt the development of philosophy. Both Plato and Aristotle metaphorically took this relation to be a container (similar to a wax tablet or aviary) which is filled with "impressions" of the world, as if being were a signet ring stamping and writing itself on the wax tablet of the soul or a flock of birds flying into its aviary (see *Theaetetus, De anima*). Connected with this view is the conception of truth (*aletheia*) not as unconcealment, but as correctness (*orthotes*) in the sense of the likeness (*ho-*

moiosis) of representations with being. But in either view, the relational sense of being is modeled on theory, knowing, assertion. *Nous* or *logos* is taken to be the ruling principle of a composite human being who is defined as *zoon logon echon*, the animal that has *logos*. The doublet of etiological ground and beings in the content-sense of being is paired in the human mind/body doublet of relational sense. As the kingly divine *nous* rules the cosmos, the king the city-state, and the father the family, so *nous* in the psychological sense rules the body. The human being thus resides authentically in the theater of being as a primal theoretician, epistemologist, logician.

The Greeks thereby initiated the ocular noetic-logical relational sense of being in the structure of the guiding question of metaphysics, which became the double first beginning (*arche*) for relational sense that was unfolded in the fundamental metaphysical positions of the entire tradition. "As the characteristic of the essence of all metaphysics, we can thus inscribe the title: *being and thinking* . . . being is grasped with the guiding thread of thinking . . . whereby 'thinking' is understood as assertoric speech" (N2 78/NIV 41). Medieval philosophy tended to inhabit the etioethical Kingdom of God, the heavenly home, in the form of *contemplatio, ratio, doctrina, scientia*. Modern thought achieves its "being at home with itself" (Hegel) in the etiotheoethical kingdom of the subject, in the "promised land" of the ego, through its reflective relation to itself in the forms of reason, experience, method, logic, science, critique of reason, dialectic, phenomenological reduction, and planning in the earthly dominion of technological enframing. The tendency in the modern period is to continue to take being in a theoretical-ocular manner to be *idea*, *eidos*, what is seen in a contemplative gazing, whether this is interpreted religiously as God, idealistically and transcendentally as the ideas or categories of reason, or as the empiricist's sensible impressions and ideas. Likewise, the representational view of perception and the definition of truth as correctness in Greek thought gained the upper hand over its phenomenological tendencies, entering into the medieval definition of truth as *correspondentia* or *adequatio intellectus et rei* and unfolding into the correspondence theory of truth and representationalism operative in modern epistemology, logic, science, and technology.

Fulfillment- and Temporalizing-Sense as Making-Present and Presence

Heidegger also dealt with the theme of *Vollzug*, the fulfilling enactment of the relational doublet of being/Dasein. "Thinking fulfils [*vollbringt*] the relation of being to the essence of humanity"; it is "the enactment [*Vollzug*] of the truth of being." At its deepest level, this *Vollzug* means a projective standing out toward (ex-istence) the lighted clearing of being: "Projection is the *Vollzug* of Dasein, that is, of the ec-static standing in the openness of being. In ex-ist-ing, Dasein discloses *sense.*" *Vollzug* is furthermore the *Vollzug der Auslegung,* the fulfilling enactment that interpretively unfolds the futural prefigurement of sense. In SZ, Heidegger maintained that it is relational sense and fullfillment- or enactment-sense that express the sense of *Personsein,* the personal *being* of the human individual: "In accord with the character of the *mineness* of this being, addressing Dasein must constantly also express the *personal* pronoun: 'I am,' 'you are.' " But he insisted that this personal enactment cannot simply be characterized negatively, as Scheler and Husserl do, by saying that Dasein is *not* a thing: "The person is no thing, no substance, no object. . . . the person exists only in the enactment of intentional acts. . . . What, however, is the on- tological sense of 'enacting,' how is the type of being of the person to be char- acterized in an ontologically positive manner?" Heidegger answered that the underlying sense of this intentional enactment is to be found in *Zeitigung,* the temporalizing of historical time. In the thirties, he stressed the distinction here between our temporalizing of the being/Dasein relation and the temporaliz- ing of this relation through the *Ereignis* of being itself. Human temporalizing stands in "*Bezug* to *Ereignis*," since it is the temporal, fulfilling enactment of this *Ereignis,* the "*Vollzug* of the projection of the truth of being" itself.[4]

The derivative temporalizing-sense in the structure of the guiding question of metaphysics is the static and homogeneous presence of the being/Dasein relation. Heidegger never tired of pointing out that *ousia,* being, substance, originally meant not only household, estate, castle, but also this in the specific sense of the property, the household goods lying present. Thus the derivative noun *parousia* means presence, present circumstances (*ta paronta*). The plural noun *ta onta,* beings, likewise means things that are present, the present in opposition to the past and the future. Philosophically, *ousia* means the secure etiotheological household and castle of presence in which thinking dwells. Since it is the identical ground of the coming to be and passing away of het- erogeneous beings, it is seen to be eternal being (*aei on*) and has the compara- tive sense of Plato's *to on ontos,* the most beingly being in the temporal sense of the most present presence, such that Plato and Aristotle also call it the most true or unconcealed (*to alethestaton*) and the most radiantly apparent (*to pha- notaton*). Being is the shining eternal kingdom standing firm above the gloomy sublunar rise and fall of heterogeneous cultures and historical periods.

On the basis of this unquestioned question about being as presence, the history of the basic metaphysical positions in Greek philosophy unfolded in an exchange of economies of presence: namely, *eon, logos, nous, eidos, energeia.* The human aspect of fulfillment- and temporalizing-sense was likewise inter- preted in terms of presence. The human being was reified and depersonalized into a present-at-hand thing, a composite substance of mind and body with the upper rational story having its true home in the eternal cosmic order. Moreover, the soul's noetic-logical relation to being was taken to be a static noninterpretive making-present or presentation before the mind, a noncreative instantiating of the eternal order.

This ousiological structure of enactment- and temporalizing-sense became archontic for the exchanges in the economies of presence that dominated the rest of the history of metaphysics. In medieval thought, the eternal soul was seen to fulfill the *nunc stans* of the eternal City of God and thereby achieve the *securitas* of salvation. In modernity, the promised land of subjectivity is seen to be inter alia the eternity of spirit, the logical atemporality of categories, or the endless reign of technological *Gestell*. The Greek mind/body doublet, which already took the soul to be a kind of knowing-machine, was transformed into the thesis of the modern Enlightenment about "man the machine," as well as into the information-processing apparatus depicted in the mechanistic psychology of empiricism, rationalism, cybernetics, and contemporary artificial intelligence research.

Heidegger's genealogical archeologies of the guiding question of the history of metaphysics attempted to unmask the derivative superstructural character of the question's structure, to deconstruct it back to its concealed ground question (*Grundfrage*), and thus to effect the end of philosophy. His rekindlings of the ancient battle of giants did not provide still more answers to the same old question. Like the stranger from Elea in Plato's *Sophist*, Heidegger arrived at the philosophical dinner party of western metaphysics as the uncanny guest who "questions the questioning" itself (N1 458/NII 193). He attempted to show that the ground/*logos*/presence configuration of the guiding metaphysical question has its birth certificate in the more basic configuration of world/praxis/time, which thus make up the focal points of the unthematic ground question of metaphysics.

Other Beginnings

Heidegger's different posings of the ground question were repetitions (*Wiederholungen*) of metaphysics that draw this question out of the depths of the guiding metaphysical question itself. His deconstructions sought not literally to destroy the first metaphysical beginning, but rather to "unfold" it into the "inner structure" of its own concealed ground question in a postmetaphysical "other beginning," "other questioning," "other thinking," and "other language." Deconstruction led to repetition as a restructuring of the structure of the question about being. The configuration of ground/*logos*/presence was refigured into that of world/praxis/time. This deconstructive repetition is a double archeology that aims at the turn (*Kehre*) of the metaphysical *arche* of the first beginning into the nonmetaphysical *arche* of the other beginning.

Relational- and Content-Sense as Praxis and World

Heidegger's deconstructive repetitions of the Greek notion of the content-sense of being stripped it of the etiotheological function of providing a divine ground for beings. "The being of beings," he wrote in SZ, " 'is' not itself a being." " 'Ground' is accessible only as sense, even if it is itself the abyss of meaninglessness" (SZ 8/26, 202/193). The content-sense of being is simply the horizon of intelligibility in the light of which things can appear and be understood *as* this or that. At various stages, Heidegger called this content-sense the "worldhood of the world," the illuminated clearing (*Lichtung*) of being, the *Zeit-Spiel-Raum*, and the "fourfold" of "earth and sky, gods and mortals." Moreover, the primary locus of sense is not a free-floating realm of ideas existing in itself, nor the noumenal universe of modern mathematical physics, but rather the concrete practical world, which includes the environing world (*Umwelt*) of our work and the interpersonal with-world (*Mitwelt*). World is the fourfold of earth and sky, gods and mortals in which these mortals concretely dwell and have their daily home. It is what Aristotle calls one's habitual dwelling place (*ethos*) and the world of the political community (*polis*). This worldly content-sense is not the naked logical meaning found in the metaphysical tradition, but rather something poetic and practical that gives itself in the form of an interpretive end for practical understanding, attunes our moodful attunement to the world, and offers itself in the shape of language for human discourse.

Similarly, Heidegger performed deconstructive repetitions of the traditional ocular noetic-logical relational sense of being, which he exposed to be "a founded mode of being-in-the-world" (SZ 80–84/86–90). The primary relation to world is not a bare theoretical one, but rather a practical and poetic dwelling with things and other persons that involves the care, mood, understanding, interpretation, and language of the whole human being. Philosophical thinking is not the static gazing of contemplation, but rather a more genuine form of dwelling and praxis that guards the house of being (G9 313/BW 193). Thus Heidegger described the philosopher as "housefriend" and thinking as "original ethics," "homecoming," "being on the way," "building" the house of being, "thanking," "remembrance," and "poetizing" (*Dichten*). Thinking shares this superlative relation of guardianship with the *poiesis* of art and the *polis*-shaping acts of politics.

Enactment- and Temporalizing-Sense as Time

Heidegger's deconstructive repetitions of the Greek notions of the enactment- and temporalizing-sense of being as presence attempted to excavate and critically develop the hidden temporal reference here to presence. The Greek question—what is being in the sense of constant presence that grounds and determines present beings *as* present beings?—already contained the unthematized and unquestioned answer that being is a specific mode of time, i.e., the present in opposition to past and future. What made this question possible as a question was the deeper concealed understanding of being as time. In such basic characterizations of being as *physis, aletheia,* and *phainomenon* (which have the temporal sense of presence), the Greeks had only a vague acquaintance with the dynamic temporal activity of emerging (*phyein*), unconcealing (*aletheuein*), and appearing (*phainesthai*) operative here (G15 331-32, 365). And Heidegger's contention was also that this dimension of time became increasingly concealed in the subsequent economies of presence that dominated the history of being.

If in the guiding question of metaphysics what is interrogated is beings, but what is ultimately sought after is the being of beings, what is interrogated in Heidegger's "other questioning" is the being of beings, the meaningful presence of beings, whereas what is sought after is not more being, but rather a third thing, namely, the radical depth dimension of the temporal happening and differentiated giving of this being of beings. If the configuration of the guiding question of metaphysics is beings/being, the postmetaphysical configuration of Heidegger's topic is beings/being/the temporal giving of being in different historical shapes. His "step back" out of metaphysics is "out beyond the conception of being as the being of beings" (G15 377-78).

Thus Heideggerians in their search for "Being" have for years been after the wrong thing. Despite Heidegger's continued use of such phrases as "the question of being," "being as being," and "being itself" right up until the unfinished introduction to his collected edition, his question was never really the question of being, but rather the more radical question of what gives or produces being as an effect. The "question of being" misleadingly suggests that being here means what it has always meant in traditional metaphysics. "The name *being* loses its naming power in the step back, because it always unwittingly says 'presence and permanence,' determinations to which the essential presencing of being can never be attached as a mere addendum." Thus Heidegger spoke of the "disappearance of being" in the step back to that which makes being possible, "When the emphasis reads: *letting* come to presence [*Anwesen lassen*], there is no more room even for the name being. The *letting* is then the pure *giving*, which itself points back to the It that gives, which is understood as *Ereignis*." The term "being" survives only in the role of "a staff borrowed from metaphysics" that helps thinking along on its path of transition to other postmetaphysical beginnings. To stress that he was not interested in the traditional notion of being, Heidegger resorted first to the distinction between beingness (*Seiendheit*) and being (*Being*), then to the archaic spelling *Seyn*, "beon," eventually to putting an X of erasure over "being," and finally to doing away with the word altogether as the name for his topic. In 1966 he flatly stated, "I do not like to use this word any more." Thomas Sheehan has suggested the obvious conclusion here: "It could be argued that we might enhance the explanation of Heidegger's subject matter by retiring the terms 'Being' and the 'question of Being' from the discussion."[5]

In his youthful thoughtpaths from 1919 through the early 1920s, Heidegger's names for the radical depth dimension of the temporal happening of being were *Ereignis*, there is/it gives, it worlds, kairological time, and movement (*kinesis*). According to his later schema of his three main thoughtpaths, the temporal dimension was named sense (temporality) in his SZ, then in his later writings truth, in the sense of the unconcealing and lighted clearing of being, and finally *topos* in the sense of the place that happens (*die ereignende Ortschaft*) (G9 331). But there were many other names in Heidegger's later writings for this radical dimension: "the possibilizing of the openness of beings" (G9 114/BW 105), the being of being (*Sein des Seins*) (G15 373), the "essential presencing [*Wesen*] of being," the "worlding" of the world, the *Ereignis* of being, the sending (*Schickung*) of being, the "there is/it gives being," the "giving" of the givenness of being, the "it lets being" (G15 363–64).

The temporalizing of being involves the having-been (*das Gewesene*) of a historical past or provenance (*Herkunft*) that is constantly circling back as a future (*Zukunft*) coming toward us in the form of possibility. In this ceaseless and varied repetition of the past in the future, the arriving (*Ankunft*) of the present is constantly opened up in new and different ways. Temporalizing is a creative "having-been-coming" of being (VA 177/PLT 184), a circular detour (*Umweg*) through the past. "History is the arrival of what has been" (GD 35/PT 48–49). But, as John Caputo has shown in taking up Derrida's critique of Heidegger, here we meet up with an ambiguity and play of countertendencies in Heidegger's thought between a residual metaphysics of the proper and a postmetaphysical thinking of difference and impropriety. Though Heidegger often suggested that this temporal process involves the creative repetition of a substantial origin, of an original presence and proper meaning (the Greek epoch of being) that comes toward us in the guise of a destiny (*Schicksal*), he just as often suggested that it is an an-archic process involving the unceasing recovery of the original absence and concealment in the questionableness and possibility of being, which is not ruled by a single metaphysical *arche* or principle, but rather gives rise to a plurality of such principles, interpretations, thoughtpaths, and epochs of being.[6]

In this sense, Heidegger's topic is the anarchic temporalizing of being out of an original concealment and impropriety. Truth in the sense of *aletheia* is always simultaneously concealment (*lethe*), *Ereignis* is always also *Enteignis*, disowning (SD 44/41). Our relation (*Bezug*) to and enactment (*Vollzug*) of the *Ereignis* of being is faced with its constant withdrawal (*Entzug*). All ways are incomplete ways, *Abwege*, errant ways, *Irrgänge*, blind alleys that end in darkness. Heidegger took this depth dimension of concealment to be "the mystery," the sheltering and giving "heart of *aletheia*," which cannot be penetrated, conquered, and controlled by human thinking. "All unconcealing [*Entbergen*] belongs in a sheltering [*Bergen*] and a concealing [*Verbergen*]. But that which frees—the mystery—is concealed and always concealing itself" (VA 29/QCT 25).

The temporal *Ereignis* of this mystery is the sending and giving of the various epochal shapes of being in the history of metaphysics. Hence he insisted that it must not be confused with any of these particular historical shapes or taken for a new one. The flux must not be confused with any of its fluctuations, the giving and sending with any of its gifts and sendings, the effecting with any of its effects. " 'Appropriation' [*Ereignis*] no longer names another manner and epoch of 'Being' " (EP xiii). "*Ereignis* is not a new stamp of being in the history of being. . . . Thinking then stands in and before that which has sent the various forms of epochal being" (SD 44/40–41). In fact, there is no substantial content, no principle/kingdom, to *Ereignis* over and above the various epochs and principles of being that it has effected, since it is an abyss of absence, concealment, possibility. As an *epoche*, a holding itself in, *Ereignis* and the concealment that sustains it remained concealed behind the various epochs of being in the history of metaphysics. And Heidegger's notion of temporalizing as repetition is ultimately directed to this effectiveness of *Ereignis* in the tradition and only secondarily to the particular epochs and interpretations of being that it has effected. He wrote: "One will not succeed in thinking *Ereignis* with the concepts of being and the history of being, and just as little with the help of what is Greek (rather precisely 'to step beyond' this)" (G15 366).

Heidegger maintained that the *Ereignis* of the different epochs of being is a groundless, mysterious, and anarchic activity of play, which is like the blooming of the rose and the playing of the child—"without why," "without ground." "The fated sending of being, it is a child, playing. . . . It plays because it plays. The 'because' sinks into play. The play is without why" (SG 188). *Ereignis* is something the same (*das Selbe*), but it is not the identical (*das Gleiche*), since it is precisely the constant play of difference (ID 111/45). In the anarchic *Ereignis* of the epochs of being, there is no transcendental criterion available for ultimately privileging and preferring one epoch over the others and subordinating them as mere means in a hierarchical-teleological relationship of progress: "Not only do we lack any criterion that would permit us to evaluate the perfection of an epoch of metaphysics as compared with any other epoch, the *right* to this kind of evaluation does not exist" (SD 62/56). There is no such thing as *the* genuine sense, truth, or topos, no master name and secret code of being, but rather only the genuinely mysterious *Ereignis* of many senses, truths, places, names, and codes of being. There is no *Heilsweg*, no sacred way or way of salvation to a heavenly kingdom of *Ereignis* in which a philosopher-king could rule. There is only the dark field of the mystery crisscrossed with a plurality of paths. The thinking of *Ereignis*, which is marked by a basic "poverty," has "abdicated the claim to a binding doctrine" (VA 177/PLT 185).

There is thus a double sense of "radical" in Heidegger's radical thinking. It points to the depth dimension (*radix*, root) of a mysterious and anarchic *Ereignis* that produces being in a plurality of different effects. But it also indicates an emancipatory gesture that deconstructs ideological claims to a proper and privileged sense of being that can be erected as a universal standard to judge and marginalize other senses of being in other historical periods, cultures, religions, and philosophical thoughtpaths. To take up residence in *Ereignis* as a dwelling place, a home (*ethos*), and perhaps even to meditate upon the possibility of an "originary ethics," does not mean to settle into a historicized version of the old metaphysical concept of a homogeneous, hierarchical, and exclusionary *ethos* (e.g., that of ancient Greek culture), though, as we shall see, there is *also* a countertendency in Heidegger's thinking toward this latter type of *ethos*.

The message that Heidegger often gave us, however, is that to dwell in the mystery of *Ereignis* is to live in the attitude of a letting-be of the play of different dwelling places and homes (*ethea*), and thus to practice a postmetaphysical ethics of ecumenism. If there is no privileged sense or epoch of being, so there is no singular *the* house of being, no kingdom of being, but rather many houses of being. Heidegger joked that searching for a universal sense of being and thus also of *ethos* over and above the plurality of ways in which these show themselves is as vain as searching at the market for an individual item called "fruit." One finds only apples, oranges, similar to how "there is being only now and then in this and that historical stamp" (ID 134/66).

The being/Dasein relation is temporalized not only out of the nonhuman depth dimension of *Ereignis*, but also out of our "relation to *Ereignis*," our "*Vollzug* of the truth of being," i.e., our temporal co-enacting and fulfilling of *Ereignis*. Though "human being does not have control over unconcealment itself," the fateful address (*Anspruch*) of *Ereignis* needs our responding (*Entsprechen*), which is at first passive but then also involves interpretively working out the epochal dispensations of being in concrete situations. "Does this unconcealing happen somewhere beyond all human action? No. But it happens also not simply *in* human being and not *through* it in the manner of measure-giving. . . . History is [not] . . . simply the *Vollzug* of human action" (VA 21, 28/QCT 18, 24). Because mortals—who live daily in the midst of death, the shrine of concealment—stand in a temporal relation to, are a site for, and play along with the anarchic play of the mysterious "heart of *aletheia*," they too share in the depth dimension of this mystery (though the later Heidegger rarely spoke of the mystery of the person): "human being truly is only when in its manner it is like the rose—without why" (SG 73). *Vollzug* means the "*Vollzug* (sheltering [*Bergen*])," letting-be, and preserving of the mystery of concealment (*Verborgenheit*) belonging to truth (G65 407).

Constant Beginnings

Heidegger's deconstruction of the first metaphysical beginning so as to effect the end of philosophy and its repetition in an other beginning—that is, his reinscription of the metaphysical configuration ground/*logos*/presence into the postmetaphysical leitmotifs of world/praxis/time—was not supposed to be a one-time thing, but something ongoing and plural. The other beginning is not an answer, but a *Sache*, a topic, a question to be answered over and over in diverse quests of thinking, an adventure in the sense of risky undertakings and endless advents (G9 363/BW 240). Always confronting us in the shape of what is *to be* thought, what is *to be* said, the other beginning is a dis-pute giving rise to different ways of pursuing it. "[Difference] appears all the more pressingly, the more decisively thinking is concerned with the same *Sache* in the same manner" (ID 111/45). Thus Heidegger's reinscriptions of metaphysics were always for him and still are for us open to deconstructive redraftings pursuing the topic in different contexts.

He insisted that his thought was not to be turned into an object: a Heideggerian philosophy, system, doctrine, object of scholarship, program, school, a Heidegger, Inc. All this is the ocular *logos* of the metaphysics of presence. Discourse must struggle constantly against it by finding ways of preserving and keeping the mysterious play of *Ereignis* in play. In SZ, Heidegger used the discourse of "the formal indications [*formale Anzeigen*] of the constitution of the being of Dasein." Formal indication, a notion that derived from Heidegger's work in the early twenties, indicates or points to what is still absent in *die Sache selbst*, what is still to be thought and is on the way to language. In fact, this pointing is at bottom the very topic of thinking itself, since, as the temporal giving of being, this topic points to its ever-repeatable fulfillment and differentiation in historical situations. Formal indication provides not fixed results, but only starting points that are to be critically repeated and followed up in independent thought toward a renewed discourse about the possibilities of the topic itself. "The answer gives a direction [*Anweisung*] . . . and it gives only this." "[Phenomenology's] essential character does not consist in being *actual* as a philosophical school. Higher than actuality stands *possibility*." Because there is a tendency to fall toward the discourse as an object for scholarly "idle talk" and "scribbling," the "difficulty of this research lies precisely in making it critical against itself in a positive sense." In other words, the formally indicative discourse of SZ is self-deconstructive in that it points into the way toward the *Sache*, toward the dispute about being. This is the note on which Heidegger's text ends: "The *dispute* regarding the interpretation of being cannot be settled, *because it has not yet been stirred up.* . . . stirring up the dispute requires preparation. Towards this alone the foregoing investigation is *on the way*" (SZ §25, 26/40, 49/61, 51/63, 577/487; cf. G9 45–67/PT 5–21).

Heidegger again took up the notion of formal indication in his WS 1929–30 course *Die Grundbegriffe der Metaphysik* and 1936–38 *Beiträge zur Philosophie* (*Vom Ereignis*), where he wrote of the "indication of the essential presencing of truth": "This thoughtful saying is a *pointing* [*Weisung*]. It indicates the free play of the concealing of the truth of being in beings as something necessary—without being a command. Such thinking never lets itself be made into a doctrine." He used this language of pointing throughout his later writings. The preface to his 1954 anthology *Vorträge und Aufsätze* stated that "an author on thoughtpaths can only point [*weisen*] without having wisdom in the sense of the *sophos*." In this volume we also read, "The following remarks lead to no given result. They point into *Ereignis*." Likewise, he gave his 1967 anthology the title *Wegmarken*, waymarkers. By following these pointers, which are like provisional maps or rough trail markers, "thinking remains fast on the wind of the topic," remains a "wanderer in the neighborhood of being."[7]

Heidegger also used the terms trace (*Spur*) and *Wink*. The temporalizing of *Ereignis* always leaves behind in language *Spuren*, traces, tracks, signs, remnants that point to the double absence of its having-been and of its coming, its no-longer and not-yet, its departure and deferral to a futural return. The word *Spur* means both a "trace" of the past and a "track" to be followed into the future, whether the matter pointed to is the gods or *Ereignis* itself. "Traces are often inconspicuous and always the legacy of a barely divined pointing. To be a poet in a needy time means: to attend, singing, to the trace of the fugitive gods" (G5 272/PLT 94).

In the world-night of the western land of evening (*Abendland*), Anaximander's fragment about *to chreon*, which Heidegger translates as *Brauch*, usage, is a trace of the way being showed itself at the dawn of thinking and a track toward what remains to be thought in a new dawn: "What properly remains to be thought in the word 'usage' has presumably left in *to chreon* a trace that quickly vanishes in the destiny of being, which unfolds in world-history as western metaphysics" (G5 369/EGT 54). *Wink*, which according to Heidegger is the basic character of language, means a sign made in departing, a gesture, wink, wave, nod, but also a signal and hint to be followed up (G12 109/24). The "*Winke* of the last god" who has departed are also hints of a possible return. Similarly, "in its making a departing sign being itself, *Ereignis* as such, becomes visible for the first time." Heidegger also called this postmetaphysical logos of pointing to the absence of his topic "sigetics," the art of wakeful keeping silent (*sigan*) that shelters the mystery of *Ereignis* and listens for its movements: "Keeping silent is the 'logic' of philosophy. . . . It seeks the truth of the essential presencing of being, and this truth is the winking-hinting conceal-ment (the mystery) of *Ereignis* (hesitant denial)" (G65 82, 70, §§37–38).

Heidegger's own writings are themselves traces and departing signs, winks and hints, which point the readers back to how the *Sache* once showed itself in his thought and point them forward into different possible ways of showing the still absent *Sache* in independent thought. It is because his thought consists of these self-deconstructive traces that Heidegger flatly denied that "there is a Heidegger's philosophy" (SD 51/48). One searches in vain for a "Heideggerian philosophy" in the sense of a set of theses that could be grasped in the concep-tual fists of either the *mens auctoris* or the reader and brought to closure. In his 1962 text on "The Problem of Non-Objectifying Thinking," he wrote, "I will attempt to give a few pointers [*Hinweise*]. . . . The impression should be avoided that what is to be handled [*es handle sich um*] is the presentation of dogmatic theses from a Heideggerian philosophy, which does not exist" (G9 69/PT 23). The phrase "Heidegger's philosophy" is a square circle. "His" thought is not a finished product but a constant beginning anew, not an answer but a questionable question, not an object but a controversial topic, not actu-ality but possibility, not presence but absence. He wrote that endlessly think-ing "must stab itself in the heart, not that thinking should die from it, but rather live transformed" (G9 417/QB 95). And regarding his question about "being and time" in SZ, which he afterward continually subjected to "imma-nent criticism" and reinscribed in new textual thoughtpaths, he underlined that "the *critical* question of what the topic for thinking should be necessarily and constantly belongs to thinking. Accordingly, the name of the task 'Being and Time' will *ändern*, alter, become other" (SD 61/55).

In his 1969 seminar in Le Thor, France, Heidegger indicated, though in an oversimplified manner, that he performed three main deconstructive repeti-tions of his own thought, namely, the three ways of the sense, the truth, and the place of being. "Three words that, by taking over from each another, at the same time mark three steps on the path of thinking: SENSE—TRUTH—PLACE (*topos*). If the question of being is to be clarified, what binds together the three successive formulations and what separates them must necessarily be disclosed" (G15 344–45, 335). What binds the three thoughtpaths is that, as "immanent criticism," each was a reinscriptive repetition of the traces in the preceeding paths toward the topic of "being and time." What separates them is that each was a dis-pute with and *deconstructive* repetition of the traces in the previous paths. Heidegger came to see later that the question about the sense of being in SZ had entangled itself in the subjectivistic metaphysical lan-guage of Kant's and Husserl's transcendental thinking (SD 47/44, G9 357/BW 235). His later thoughtpaths of the truth and the place of being took up the models of the pre-Platonic notions of *aletheia* and *physis* in the Presocratics and Greek tragedy, which were revived in the nineteenth century by Nietzsche and the poet Hölderlin. But the term "truth" became obsolete once Heidegger realized that it had meant primarily correctness of judgment also in the Presocratics (SD 78/70). The term "place" also eventually proved to be inadequate for penetrating to the ultimate there is/it gives of *Ereignis.*

Heidegger's "preparatory thinking," which aimed ultimately at the uncertain coming of a new beginning after the reign of modern technology, would doubtlessly have kept going in this chain of differing/deferring drafts of a nonbook, a nonwork, about "Being and Time," but with his death in 1976 the way of his thinking broke off in incompleteness. His memorial on the occasion of Max Scheler's death in 1928 applies equally well to himself: "Once again a path of philosophy falls back into the darkness" (G26 64/52). In fact, in the motto for his collected edition, Heidegger did say the same thing about himself: "[Incomplete] ways—not [finished] works." There is no Heidegger's Collected Works, only a lot of work still to do.

But this is where we are supposed to come in. The provisional indicative traces of Heidegger's texts are intended to point into the possibility of new and different paths for his readers to take up in independent thought toward the topic itself. Thus he wrote to William Richardson in 1962, "I hesitate with answers, for they necessarily remain only pointers. The lesson of long experience leads me to suspect that the pointers will not be taken up as a directive to get oneself underway in order to think out the indicated topic itself independently." And in the unfinished introduction to his collected edition, he also stressed that "the large number of volumes attests only to the enduring questionableness of the question of being and gives ample opportunities to check matters for oneself." In such statements, Heidegger clearly stated his wish that he be taken not as a postmetaphysical philosopher-king who has discovered *the* way to a kingdom of being, but as a guide who has pointed out ways in rough outline and thus, like Aristotle's practical philosophy, can "be of help" in the practical task of thinking. One sees this push toward independent thought also in his pedagogical praxis, where, as Gadamer put it, he was also essentially "student-less." Georg Picht reported how one day a student reading out a protocol full of Heidegger's phraseology was stopped in his tracks: Heidegger told him, "There will be no heideggerizing here! We want to get at the topic." And Walter Biemel relates that, "if someone who had read something from Heidegger tried to quote him and was especially proud of this answer, he received an almost bad-tempered answer: 'I already know what I have written, I want to know what you have to say about it.' " In his 1951–52 lecture course "What is Called Thinking?," Heidegger told the students that "we must ourselves discover the one and only way to answer the question 'what is called thinking?' . . . If we do not find out, all talk and listening are in vain. And in that case I would urge you to burn your lecture notes, however precious they may be— and the sooner the better."[8]

He also clearly expected that this independent appropriation of his indications would be critical and deconstructive, writing to Rudolf Krämer-Badoni in 1960 that "I want no 'following'—but rather fruitful dispute" and to Pöggeler in 1964 that "I think that now it is about time to stop writing *about* Heidegger. What is more important is dispute regarding the topic" (LKB 176; DMH 355). "Dispute," he wrote elsewhere, "is genuine criticism. It is the highest and only way to a true appreciation and estimation of a thinker" (N1 13/NI 4). "Those who understand genuinely are always those who come from a distance out of their own ground and soil, those who bring much with them in order to transform much" (N2 404/NII 142). The genuine sense of what has been called the thinking-further (*Weiterdenken*)[9] of Heidegger's thought is thus not simply working out its details and applying it in new contexts, but rather thinking further than Heidegger and out-thinking him when need be.

Here the *mens auctoris*, i.e., the author's reading of his writings, may be *a* provisional criterion, but it is not the decisive criterion. Heidegger's introduction to his collected edition stressed that "communicating about the author's mind" and "characterizing the author's standpoint" have "no importance" (G1 438). "The only authority is the topic itself," whose play is not to be arrested by authorial self-interpretation (G15 286). The point is to get at what the author left unsaid: "The 'doctrine' of a thinker is what is unsaid in what he says, to which human being is exposed, so that one might spend oneself on it" (G9 203/PDT 173). Heidegger seems to have wanted neither conferences on "Heidegger" nor "Heidegger scholars," but rather symposia on the topic of his thought and independent thinkers of this topic. "It would bring me the greatest satisfaction," he wrote to Manfred Frings as the organizer of a conference on his thought, "if at once—in the first moments of the symposium—the discussion succeeded in being directed purely and decisively toward the topic. There would then develop a *colloquium on the question of being* instead of a 'Heidegger-symposium' " (LF 19/17). "It would already be enough and beneficial," he wrote in 1976 to the participants of the tenth annual meeting of the Heidegger Conference in Chicago, "if every participant would devote his attention to this question in his own way" (LHC 2/4).

Similar to the repellent stance of Kierkegaard's method of indirect communication, Heidegger often expressed the desire that other thinkers who take up his waymarkers should actually think *against* him in a dis-pute that is based in the an-archic differentiation of the topic itself, such that he would have to "bow to the necessity of later being understood differently than he meant to understand himself." He resisted the heideggerization (*Verheideggerung*) (HW 95) of his questioning into a Heidegger, Inc., i.e., centering it around the *mens auctoris*, and held that we do this questioning a disservice when we become Heideggerians. Heidegger feared that, given the "almost insurmountable difficulty in communication," especially in "the age of information" (LR viii–ix; G1 438; G9 ix), his textual pointers would fall prey to the very phenomenon he criticized in his essay "The Age of the World-Picture," namely, the modern technological approach of research that he called business (*Betrieb*) (G5 83–86, 98/QCT 124–26, 139). Similar to Foucault's critique of the institutionalizing of texts into the ideology of the author, Heidegger stressed that, in modern research, thought becomes "institutionalized" and technized in universities, institutes, societies, conferences, journals, archives, collected works. This business has a twofold thrust: the construction of a world-picture and the reduction of thinking to a "standing reserve" of information. In other words, Heidegger wanted to avoid the institutionalizing of his nonobjectifying way-markers into a thriving Heidegger, Inc. that would objectify them into the framework (*Gestell*) of a Heideggerian "world-picture" complete with rules and procedures for calculatively representing the world and achieving a new metaphysical certainty. He likewise resisted the business of treating his thought as a "standing reserve" of information to be represented and ordered in the framework of the methods of historical scholarship. In the age of research, "[the learned individual] is succeeded by the researcher who is engaged in research projects. . . . He negotiates at meetings and collects information at congresses. He contracts for commissions from publishers. The latter now determine along with him which books must be written."

Thus Heidegger was always suspicious of commentaries and conferences on his thought, and originally did not want even a collected edition or an archive to which all interested scholars would have easy access. In 1973, he gave in to the wishes of others for a collected edition of his writings, but only on the condition that it not be a historical-critical edition with elaborate notes and other philological additions, which he thought would usurp the reader's independent pursuit of the pointers in the texts and encourage historical scholarship in the sense of the "collection of information."[10] Heidegger was an enemy not of historical scholarship and "careful philological work" per se, but rather of a misguided use of it as an end in itself and not as a means to questioning. "Few are experienced enough in the difference between an object of scholarship and a topic of thinking" (DMH 353; G13 77/PLT 5).

Though, as we have seen, the play of countertendencies in Heidegger's own thought has been an ambiguous handhold for the *Betrieb* of a Heideggerian world-picture in the emergence of the Heidegger-scholasticism of his commentators and in the ongoing work on the "last/ultimate-hand edition" of his writings, the kingdom of Heidegger, Inc. can only be built insecurely on the drifting sands of his self-deconstructing textual traces and topic—a philosophical *destructio* waiting to happen. Thus, let us now turn to Heidegger's *Jugendgeschichte*, this story of a hidden king, lending our voices to the rumor and letting it speak again, employing it as one important way to make Heidegger, Inc. tremble.

PART II

The Student Years

3 | Curricula Vitae

We begin with Heidegger's student years between 1909 and 1915. The young thinker was quite prolific, publishing two books, half a dozen essays, and eleven book reviews, as well as a handful of poems. In 1911 he read Husserl's statement in "Philosophie als strenge Wissenschaft" that "the impulse to research must proceed not from philosophies but from the matters [den Sachen]" themselves, and noted in the margin that "we take Husserl at his word" (HL 96). In 1915 he wrote that knowledge of being is won only "on the path of showing" (G1 213). Had Heidegger found already in his student years a thoughtpath into the postmetaphysical Sache of the end of philosophy, a new beginning, and constant beginning? No and yes. To put this schematically, no because he first pursued an ontologic with a content/relation/temporalizing configuration of logical sense/judgment/atemporality and then a speculative ontotheology with a configuration of the absolute/spirit/eternity. And yes because in developing this very ontotheology at the end of his student period he called for a breakthrough (Durchbruch) to a historical and ultimately mystical heterology of being that would involve the configuration of worldview/person/history. However, he did not succeed in freeing this gesture toward a turn to a new beginning from pervasive metaphysical elements until his courses of 1919 and those following, in which he actually deconstructed his earlier metaphysics. If the later Heidegger is a postmetaphysician flirting with residual forms of metaphysics, the student Heidegger is a metaphysician flirting with the postmetaphysical. Heidegger later saw this ambiguity in his student writings, stating that, though they were indeed a "beginning of the way," they remained caught up in metaphysical "onto-logic" and "speculative-theological thinking" (G1 55; G12 91/10, cf. 87/6).

The present chapter relies primarily on the curricula vitae that Heidegger wrote during his student years, and which are often quite different than his later retrospective autobiographies: namely, his CV of 1913 submitted along with his doctoral dissertation to the Philosophy Department of the University of Freiburg, and then revised in the 1914 publication of his dissertation; as well as his more important CV of 1915 submitted along with his qualifying dissertation.[1] Using these autobiographies of Heidegger's early development and thoughtpaths (*curricula*), as well as other writings, we shall explore how the Greek, medieval, and modern constellations of metaphysics influenced his student years in the form of Neo-Scholasticism, Aristotle, and Neo-Kantianism and phenomenology. But we shall also highlight the counteracting influences of medieval mysticism, theological hermeneutics, poetry, and the antimetaphysical thinking of Nietzsche, Kierkegaard, and Dilthey on Heidegger's notion of a breakthrough to a deeper concept of philosophy.

Neo-Neo-Scholasticism

Growing up in the small, southern, Catholic village of Messkirch, where his father was the sexton of the nearby St. Martin's Church, the young Martin Heidegger was from an early age directed toward the priesthood. He first attended a Jesuit Gymnasium in Constance (1903–1906) and then finished his studies at the Jesuit Bertholds-Gymnasium in Freiburg (1906–1909). Thereafter he entered the novitiate of the German Province of Jesuits at Feldkirch, Austria. But he did not make it through the probationary period, leaving after only a few weeks apparently due to "heart trouble" (*Herzleiden*), as he put it in his 1915 curriculum vitae. In the fall of 1909, he then registered simultaneously at the archdiocesan seminary in Freiburg and in the theology department of the Albert Ludwig University. He took theology courses on, inter alia, the Old and New Testaments, Paul's letters, John's Gospel, church history, messianic prophesy, hermeneutics, theory of revelation, moral theology, canon law, medieval mysticism, and theological cosmology, completing philosophy courses simultaneously on logic, metaphysics, and history. But, overworked and exhausted, the student had to break off his studies halfway through his third semester in February 1911, due to a renewed outbreak of his heart problem, which the seminary director and doctor described as a "nervous heart condition" of an "asthmatic nature." Heidegger followed the doctor's recommendation of spending a few weeks at home in Messkirch "to have complete rest." In April he returned to resume his studies, but his condition worsened, and he apparently spent most of the summer semester at home convalescing. His poems from this period appear to indicate depression and possibly a mild nervous breakdown, and these psychosomatic difficulties were to continue to plague him later, especially during the denazification hearings after the collapse of Nazi Germany. In the midst of his existential crisis, which included severe financial worries, the young student followed the advice of his superiors to give up the idea of becoming a priest, and withdrew from the seminary and the theology department. In the fall of 1911, Heidegger enrolled in the "Faculty of Natural Science and Mathematics" at the university, with the idea of majoring in mathematics and taking the State Examination (*Staatsexamen*) that grants the first university degree required for a teaching profession in high schools. All this was a disappointment for his parents who, having set their sights on Martin's becoming perhaps even a bishop, exclaimed, "So much for our famous son!" (MH 67ff.; HL 95; HA 383; EMH 155).

But as Heidegger's studies in mathematics, the natural sciences, and philosophy progressed between 1911 and 1913, his career plans went through a number of changes. For a while he thought of entering the philosophical profession as a philosopher of mathematics, but eventually opted for a career as a Catholic Neo-Scholastic philosopher. Though he had switched to a new faculty in 1911, he still attended Carl Braig's lectures on dogmatic theology and stayed in close contact with his old seminary. He was well prepared for his new academic project, since in his Gymnasium years and theological studies he had been immersing himself in Thomas Aquinas, Bonaventura, medieval mysticism (especially Meister Eckhart), Herman Schell, and Carl Braig of the Catholic Tübingen School (who introduced him to speculative theology inspired by Hegel and Schelling), as well as the French Catholic philosopher Maurice Blondel and the French spiritualist Ravaisson. In the philosophy department, he worked mainly under the Catholic philosophers Arthur Schneider (director of his doctoral dissertation) and Heinrich Finke (examiner for the doctoral degree). Moreover, he established close connections with the journal *Literarische Rundschau für das katholische Deutschland* and with the antimodernist Catholic journal *Der Akademiker*, where he published most of his articles.

Heidegger wanted to develop a new type of Neo-Scholasticism, a Neo-Neo-Scholasticism, which would revive the "ancient wisdom" of medieval Scholasticism and mysticism with the help of modern Christian thought, phenomenology, and Neo-Kantianism. His articles published between 1910 and 1913 in *Der Akademiker* and other Catholic journals sketched the basic outline of this Neo-Scholastic project (CA 492–93, 518–19; G1 15/PR 70). His 1913 doctoral dissertation "Die Lehre vom Urteil im Psychologismus. Ein kritisch-positiver Beitrag zur Logik" (The Doctrine of Judgment in Psychologism: A Postive-Critical Contribution to Logic) presented a fusion of Neo-Scholastic realism with modern Neo-Kantian and phenomenological logic and epistemology. Here is how his 1915 CV described his doctoral dissertation and his work leading up to it:

> My basic philosophical convictions remained those of Aristotelian-Scholastic philosophy. With time I recognized that the intellectual wealth stored up in it must allow and demands a far more fruitful evaluation and application. So in my dissertation on "The Doctrine of Judgment in Psychologism," which concerned a central problem of logic and epistemology and took its bearings simultaneously from modern logic and from the basic judgments of Aristotelian-Scholasticism, I tried to find a basis for further investigations. (HL 116–17, 80)

Heidegger's minor subjects for the doctoral degree were mathematics and medieval history. Though in 1913 he had actually wanted to choose mathematics as the topic of his subsequent qualifying dissertation (*Habilitationsschrift*) for the license to teach in the university, his interest in medieval history won out due to the encouragement of his mentors Schneider and Finke. They had handpicked him for the chair of Catholic philosophy left vacant in 1913 by Schneider's departure and therefore advised him to do a historical dissertation on Scholastic philosophy. Schneider's old chair was temporarily filled by Father Engelbert Krebs, a lecturer (*Privatdozent*) in the theology department. But he did not feel altogether confident about giving philosophy courses and sought out the help of his younger friend Heidegger in preparing his lectures. In order to take care of Heidegger's financial needs, Schneider arranged in the summer of 1913 for him to receive a yearly grant from the von Schaezler Foundation for the study of Thomistic philosophy. In his own August letter of application to the chancellery, Heidegger wrote that "the undersigned intends to dedicate himself to the study of Christian philosophy and to pursue an academic career." In his 1914 petitions for renewal, he restated his intention to dedicate himself to the "Catholic worldview" and to pursue a "career in the service of researching and teaching Christian-Scholastic philosophy" (HL 107, 114; HMH 154–56).

His doctoral dissertation thus came to serve as the basis for his 1915 qualifying dissertation "Die Kategorien- und Bedeutungslehre des Duns Scotus" (Duns Scotus's Doctrine of Categories and Meaning), which aimed at "a fundamentally new kind of treatment of medieval Scholasticism" that would appropriate and unfold the intentional content of medieval thought and mysticism with the language and concepts of phenomenology and Neo-Kantianism (G1 204). Heidegger's CV of 1915 reads,

> My increasing interest in history facilitated for me an intense engagement with the philosophy of the Middle Ages, which I recognized as necessary for a fundamental development of Scholasticism. For me this engagement consisted not primarily in a presentation of the historical relations between individual thinkers but rather in an interpretive understanding of the theoretical content of their philosophy with the aid of modern philosophy. Thus my investigation into "Duns Scotus's Doctrine of Categories and Meaning" came about. (HL 116–17, 79–80)

Heidegger's qualifying dissertation and his other student writings show us how much he was caught up in what he later called the medieval epoch of the history of metaphysics. As we shall see in more detail, the ontologic he developed appropriated the content/relation/temporalizing configuration of Scholasticism (categories/intellect/eternity) into his own Neo-Kantian and phenomenological configuration of logical sense/judgment/atemporality. Moreover, the ontotheology that he developed especially in the later conclusion to the published version of this qualifying dissertation attempted in effect to appropriate the mystical-Scholastic configuration of God/soul/eternity into his own speculative-theological configuration of the absolute/spirit/eternity, which had also been influenced heavily by Braig's speculative theology.

According to Heidegger's later self-portraits, it was through Braig's lectures and books and through conversations with him during walks that he came to be influenced by "Schelling's and Hegel's significance for speculative theology as distinct from the doctrinal system of Scholasticism" (SD 82/75). These later portraits located his decisive encounter with Christian thought in his student years, but the decisive theological influence on his breakthrough to his postmetaphysical topic actually came later, after 1915, when he absorbed himself more deeply in medieval mysticism, Paul's letters, Luther, and Kierkegaard, and in fact deconstructed his earlier Christian ontotheology.

Back in 1915, Heidegger intended his qualifying dissertation to prepare the way for an ambitious lifelong plan to continue this development of Neo-Scholasticism with a number of other works. His 1915 CV, submitted along with his dissertation, stated that "this investigation likewise generated in me the plan of a comprehensive presentation of medieval logic and psychology in the light of modern phenomenology, with equal consideration of the historical position of individual medieval thinkers." It concluded, "If I am permitted to take on the duties of scientific research and teaching, my life's work will be dedicated to the realization of these plans." Heidegger indicated elsewhere that these works would include studies of "mystical, moral-theological, and ascetic literature," the notion of truth in "Eckhartian mysticism," the "influence of Aristotle on Scholasticism," the "contrast between Thomas and Scotus," and perhaps also the "problem of a theoretical-scientific treatment of Catholic theology" (HL 117, 80; G1 204–205, 193; G1 402, 410/PC 385; LG 103).

Aristotle and the Question about Being

In 1907, Heidegger's former teacher Father Conrad Gröber presented the seventeen-year-old Gymnasium student with a copy of Franz Brentano's 1862 doctoral dissertation *Von der mannigfachen Bedeutung des Seienden nach Aristoteles* (On the Manifold Meaning of Being in Aristotle). As narrated many years later, the still teenage Heidegger thus "came across the question concerning being"—at least in its metaphysical form. The four sections of Brentano's book deal with the four senses that Aristotle ascribed to being: being in the accidental sense, being as the true, being in the sense of potentiality and actuality, and being according to the categories, of which Brentano gives the fullest treatment. The later Heidegger recounted,

> [T]he first philosophical writing through which I worked again and again from 1907 on was Franz Brentano's dissertation: *Von der mannigfachen Bedeutung des Seienden nach Aristoteles*. On the title page of his work Brentano set down the sentence from Aristotle: *to on legetai pollachos*. I trans-

late: "beings become manifest in many ways (i.e., with a view to their being)." Concealed in this sentence is the *question* that determined the way of my thought: what is the simple, unitary determination of being that permeates all its manifold meanings? . . . [W]hat then does being mean?

After working through Brentano's text, which he later called "my first guide through Greek philosophy" and the "rod and staff of my first awkward attempts to penetrate into philosophy," Heidegger's last year at the Gymnasium in 1909 saw him take the ambitious step of checking Aristotle's collected works out of the library.[2]

Heidegger also reported later that, in the last year of the Gymnasium studies, "I stumbled upon the book of Carl Braig, then professor for dogmatics at Freiburg University: *Vom Sein. Abriss der Ontologie* [On Being: Outline of Ontology] [1896]. . . . The larger sections of the work give, at the end, extensive textual passages from Aristotle, Thomas of Aquinas and Suarez, and in addition the etymology of fundamental ontological concepts." This text actually opens with a long provocative passage from Bonaventura's *Itinerarium mentis in Deum*, which takes up Aristotle's claim that being is not a genus of beings, as well as his analogy between our perception of the being of beings and the perception of bats. The passage sounds similar to claims that Heidegger will himself make in the 1920s and thereafter:

> But just as the eye intent upon the various differences of the colors does not see the light by which it sees the other things and, if it sees it, does not notice it, so the eye of the mind intent upon particular and universal beings [*entia*] does not notice *being* itself [*ipsum esse*] which is beyond all genera, though it comes first before the mind and through it all other things. Wherefore it seems very true that just as the bat's eyes behave in the light, so the eye of the mind behaves before the most manifest things of nature. . . .

The major sections of Braig's treatise deal with "Being in General," "The Essence of Beings," "The Activity of Beings," and "The Purpose of Beings." John Caputo has argued that this work and not Brentano's book on Aristotle may have been Heidegger's decisive introduction to the question concerning being, since one finds in it the central question of the unitary sense of the manifold meanings of being, as well as some of Heidegger's later terminology (e.g., *das Sein des Seienden, das Wozu, das Woher*), his use of the etymologies of basic philosophical concepts, and premonitions of his themes of a preontological understanding of being, the ontological priority of the question concerning being, and the ontological difference.[3]

Heidegger's student writings dealt with the being-question first as the question about the status of logical sense, then as the question of the categories, and finally as the question about the ultimate divine ground of categorial sense and history. The being-question was in general taken up in the context of his Neo-Scholastic project of creatively appropriating the Aristotelian-Scholastic doctrine of the categories with the help of the logical theory of phenomenology and Neo-Kantianism, especially Emil Lask's reading of Greek and medieval ontology. At the close of its analysis of judgment and the validity (*Geltung*) of logical sense, Heidegger's 1913 doctoral dissertation stated that pure logic has the ultimate task of dividing "the entire region of 'being' [*Sein*] into its various modes of reality." His first answer to the question about the unitary sense of being was that it is the atemporal validity of logical sense. His qualifying dissertation then used this pure logic for a historical exploration of the Aristotelian-Scholastic doctrine of categories specifically in Duns Scotus. "Being (*ens*)," he wrote there, "signifies the total meaning of the sphere of objects *in any sense*, the enduring moment in what is objective. It is the category of categories" (G1 186, 214).

In effect, his ontologic appropriated the content/relation/temporalizing configuration of Aristotle's metaphysics—that is, categories/*logos*/presence—into his own Neo-Kantian and phenomenological configuration of logical sense/judgment/atemporal validity. The ontotheology he developed in the later conclusion to his work on Scotus followed Aristotle's tendency to see the highest sense of "first philosophy" not in an ontological doctrine of categories, but rather in a theology of the highest divine being. Moreover, as Heidegger later maintained in the twenties and then in his lectures on Nietzsche in the forties, his early use of the term validity was part and parcel of the modern Lotzean and Neo-Kantian restatement of Platonism (G21 §§6–10; G48 302, 105–106, 25–27; N2 226/NIV 169). Influenced by Plato's position that the timeless ideal of the Good is "beyond being," Lotz and his followers held that ideas and values do not exist, but rather are located in an atemporal realm of validity.

Heidegger had at this time not really thematically discovered the being-question as the question about the connection between being and time. Though his later autobiographies often stated very ambiguously that he "came across the question concerning being" in his early study of Brentano, Braig, and Aristotle (G12 88/7), he was back then still too much caught up in "the guiding question" of the first beginning of metaphysics, which was mediated to him through Scholasticism and interpreted for him especially by Brentano, Braig, and Lask. "Philosophy," the young metaphysician wrote in 1916, "cannot for long do without its genuine optic—metaphysics" (G1 406/PC 381). The same ambiguity is found in Heidegger's later self-portraits that stressed the decisiveness of this earliest encounter with Aristotle and said relatively little about his radically different reading of Aristotle in the early twenties. Certainly his initial reception of Aristotle played an important role, but the decisive influence of Aristotle on his postmetaphysical formulation of the being-question took place rather in the early twenties. Here he in fact mercilessly deconstructed his earlier Neo-Scholastic interpretation of Aristotle with the help of Luther's critique of the Scholastic *theologia gloriae.*

Phenomenology and Neo-Kantianism

Heidegger apparently discovered phenomenology by having "learned from many philosophical periodicals that Husserl's thought was determined by Franz Brentano." He thought it might help him figure out Brentano's book on Aristotle's question of being. So in 1909, the theology student checked Husserl's two-volume *Logische Untersuchungen* (1900, 1901) out of the university library and began reading it:

> Thus both volumes of Husserl's *Logische Untersuchungen* lay on my desk in the theological seminary ever since my first semester. . . . From Husserl's *Logische Untersuchungen* I expected a decisive aid for the questioning stimulated by Brentano's dissertation. . . . I remained so fascinated by Husserl's work that I read it again and again in the following years without gaining sufficient insight into what captivated me.

Around the same time the young scholar was studying Husserl's *Die Philosophie der Arithmetik*, which "placed mathematics in a whole new light" for him. And he eagerly followed Husserl's subsequent publications. In 1911 he studied Husserl's programmatic essay "Philosophie als strenge Wissenschaft," which had appeared earlier that year in the journal *Logos*. Just as Heidegger was finishing his doctoral dissertation in 1913, the first issue of Husserl's new journal *Jahrbuch für Philosophie und phänomenologische Forschung* appeared with the editor's own work *Ideen zu einer reinen Phänomenologie und phänomenologischen Philosophie, I. Buch*. One finds Heidegger relying heavily on these works in his writings during his student years; for example, the "doctrine of meaning" that he explores in his dissertation on Duns Scotus is taken directly from the "Idea of a Pure Grammar" in Husserl's *Logische Untersuchungen* and the first volume of his *Ideen*. When he left the seminary and his theological studies in 1911, he in fact wanted to go to Göttingen to study under Husserl, but financial problems forced him to complete his studies in Freiburg.[4] Little did he know that Husserl would actually come to Freiburg in 1916 as Heinrich Rickert's successor.

In 1911 Heidegger registered instead in the "Faculty of Natural Science and Mathematics," which was originally a section of the philosophy department, but had broken away and formed a separate department one year earlier. Until 1913 he devoted himself to an intensive study of mathematics and the natural sciences, taking various courses in geometry, calculus, algebra, physics, and chemistry, while continuing to read Husserl's *Die Philosophie der Arithmetik*. Thus one finds him displaying an advanced knowledge of mathematics and physics (Galileo, Newton, Einstein, Planck) in his early publications (G1 218-51, 418-25/CT 4-7). Though he began as a mathematics candidate in the new faculty, he submitted his doctoral dissertation on the doctrine of judgment two years later to Schneider in the philosophy department, which granted him the degree. But his interest in mathematics continued. In 1913 he briefly considered doing his qualifying dissertation on the "the logical essence of the concept of number." And in 1915, he submitted "the concept of number" as the third possible topic of the trial lecture required by the philosophy department for the license to teach (HL 107, 78).

But during his doctoral studies, Heidegger was still left with plenty of time not only for Carl Braig's theology lectures, but also for a "great quantity" of philosophy courses. In his 1915 CV, he wrote,

> My philosophical interest was not lessened by the study of mathematics; on the contrary, since I no longer had to follow the compulsory courses in philosophy, I could attend a great quantity of philosophy courses and above all could take part in the seminar exercises with Herr Geheimrat Rickert. In this new school I learned first and foremost to understand philosophical problems as problems and acquired insight into the essence of logic, the philosophical discipline that still interests me most. At the same time I acquired a correct understanding of modern philosophy from Kant on, a matter that I found sparsely and inadequately treated in Scholastic literature. (HL 116–17, 79–80)

Heidegger took Schneider's courses on "Logic and Epistemology," "Spinoza's Ethics," "General History of Philosophy," and "Exercises in Epistemology," as well as Finke's course on "The Age of the Renaissance." But during this time, he came under the influence of especially Heinrich Rickert, with whom he completed courses on "Introduction to Epistemology and Metaphysics" (lecture course) and "Epistemological Exercises in the Doctrine of Judgment" (seminar), though his 1915 CV indicated that he took more than just one seminar with Rickert.

It may have been in Rickert's seminar on "the Doctrine of Judgment" that he worked out many of the ideas for his doctoral dissertation with the same title. In the preface Heidegger wrote that "to him I owe the seeing and understanding of modern logical problems." After his doctoral studies, Heidegger attended at least one more of Rickert's courses in SS 1914 and also entered into an "intense engagement with his *Die Grenzen der naturwissenschaftlichen Begriffsbildung*," as well as his *Der Gegenstand der Erkenntnis* and his essay "Das Eine, die Einheit und die Eins. Bemerkungen zur Logik des Zahlbegriffs," which was the catalyst for his first topic for the qualifying examination on "the logical essence of the concept of number." Rickert became the director of Heidegger's qualifying dissertation, which was dedicated to "Heinrich Rickert in most grateful admiration" (G1 61, 190).

In Rickert's seminars Heidegger also learned of the former's student Emil Lask, who, "mediating between [Rickert and Husserl], attempted also to listen to the Greek thinkers." "Both of Emil Lask's works—*Die Logik der Philosophie und die Kategorienlehre. Eine Studie über den Herrschaftsbereich der logischen Form* (1911) and *Die Lehre vom Urteil* (1912)—themselves showed clearly enough the influence of Husserl's *Logische Untersuchungen.*"[5] Thus one finds Heidegger's student writings relying heavily not only on Husserl but also on the above writings by Rickert and Lask, as well as on the thought of the other prominent Neo-Kantians, Wilhelm Windelband, Hermann Cohen, and Paul Natorp.

If Heidegger's later autobiographies are right, Husserl's phenomenology and also Neo-Kantianism provided him with help for the Aristotelian-Scholastic question of being he had discovered in the writings of Brentano and Braig. This can only be understood to mean that, in the early days of his student period, he applied the Husserlian and Neo-Kantian critiques of psychologism and their pure noematically oriented logic to the being-question in the form of a "logic of the categories of being," as he put it in his three-part 1912 essay on "Neuere Forschungen über Logik" (Recent Research on Logic), which sketched out the ontologic he would pursue for the next three years (G1 24). In his doctoral dissertation, this ontologic took the form of a systematic analysis of the noematic categorial sense of judgments; in his qualifying examination, it involved a historical appropriation of the Aristotelian-Scholastic doctrine of categories specifically in Duns Scotus.

Heidegger's essay on logic stressed, regarding Husserl's *Logische Untersuchungen*, that "we attach far-reaching significance to Husserl's penetrating and very appropriately named investigations. . . . in his 'Prolegomena to a Pure Logic' Husserl was the first to lay out systematically and comprehensively the essence, the relativistic consequences, and the theoretical valuelessness of psychologism." Regarding the Neo-Kantian distinction between the two worlds of spatiotemporal psychical reality and the irreducible atemporal validity of sense and value, Heidegger wrote,

> The question [of whether psychologism or transcendentalism was established in Kant's philosophy] has been decided today in favour of the transcendental-logical interpretation that since the 1870s has been represented basically by Hermann Cohen and his school, as well as by Windelband and Rickert. . . . For the problem we are dealing with, this *logical* Kant-interpretation and its development, is important insofar as the intrinsic value of the logical has been emphasized.

In the same essay, Heidegger also acknowledged the "stimulus" deriving from the mathematical and logical writings of Bernard Bolzano, Gottlob Frege, and Alexius Meinong, as well as from the *Principia Mathematica* of Alfred North

Whitehead and Bertrand Russell. He wanted to stress a metaphysical difference between being (atemporal validity of logical categorial sense) and beings (the spatiotemporal reality of the psychical and the physical), between "the hemispheres of beings and the valid" (GI 24, 19–20). He seems already to have found illuminating not only Husserl's method of phenomenological "seeing," but also and more specifically the noetic "categorial intuition" of the sense of being in Husserl's Sixth Investigation.

And it was here that Lask's writings were particularly helpful, since they not only were strongly influenced by Husserl's Sixth Investigation, but also explored the realm of the categorial more deeply than Husserl had and even went back to the doctrine of categories in Greek and medieval ontology. "Lask aspires after nothing less than a doctrine of categories that encompasses the totality of what can be thought with both its two hemispheres of beings and the valid, and his attempt can be placed among the ranks of great thinkers." Heidegger was also influenced by the account of the history of the doctrine of categories laid out in Wilhelm Windelband's *Vom System der Kategorien* (1900), Eduard von Hartmann's *Kategorienlehre* (1896), and Adolf Trendelenburg's *Geschichte der Kategorienlehre* (1846) (GI 24, 202, 197; cf SZ 289/261).

By the time Heidegger came to write his qualifying dissertation, his vocabulary had become permeated with the "terminology of phenomenology," especially with the central concept of "intentionality." Here he adopted Husserl's content/relation/temporalizing configuration of noema/noesis/enactment (*Vollzug*), just as he had taken over the symmetrical Neo-Kantian configuration of logical sense/judgment/atemporal validity. All this should indicate just to what extent he was, at this time, still caught up in the transcendental philosophy of modern metaphysics. Indeed, probably following Lask's sketch of the "categories in the history of theoretical philosophy" in his *Die Logik der Philosophie und die Kategorienlehre*, Heidegger's 1912 essay on logic and the introduction to his work on Scotus in effect laid out and aligned themselves with the three major positions (*Fragestellungen*) in "the history of the doctrine of categories," namely, Aristotle, Scholasticism, and modern Neo-Kantianism and phenomenology, whose development Heidegger took to be a progressive evolution (*Auswicklung*) (GI 310, 196, 24). But, of course, this evolution is what he later came to criticize as the three epochs of the history of metaphysics with their characteristic "fundamental metaphysical positions." In his later autobiographies, he liked to focus on his discovery of Husserl's phenomenology in his student years, saying little about his reading of Husserl after 1915, but Husserl's decisive influence should be located not in this first naive and metaphysical appropriation, important as it is, but rather in his very different postmetaphysical reading beginning around 1919, which severely criticized his earlier reception of Neo-Kantianism and phenomenology.

Poetry, Mysticism, Hermeneutics, Antimetaphysicians

Heidegger was certainly studying more than Scholasticism, Aristotle, Husserl, and Neo-Kantianism. The development of his thought during these years is a suspenseful story of tension between these traditional interests and another set of potentially volatile interests. To begin with, he had an avid interest in German and Greek literature. He later reported that "in 1905 I read Stifter's *Colored Stones* for the first time. . . . In 1908 I found my way to Hölderlin through a still preserved Reclam booklet of his poems" (G1 56/R 22). He was already studying the works of Stifter, Lessing, Goethe, Schiller, and Hölderlin in the last years of his secondary education, when he even organized a private literary circle of students that met outside of class. The report of one of his teachers after graduation stated that "at times he pursued German literature—in which he is very well read—a bit too much, to the detriment of other disciplines" (HL 88).

At the end of his high schooling he was also studying Homer, Sophocles, and Euripides, and it is reported that from this time on he spent an hour a day reading the Greek poets and historians (HL 88; OWE 133). Between 1910 and 1914 he discovered "Rilke's poetry and Trakl's poems," as well as the "translations of Dostoevsky's works" (G1 56/R 22; G12 88/7). Heidegger's authorship actually began not in philosophy, but in theology and poetry. During this time he published five poems in a Romantic genre that were titled "Dying Splendor," "Hours on the Mount of Olives," "We Will Wait," "On Still Paths," and "Consolation." These and his unpublished poems express two dominant themes. The first is his existential restlessness and depression: "Again to greet the dying splendor, again to wander between night and day. Your rustling leaves trembling with death still feel in downfall the coming need." "My life's hours on the Mount of Olives: often you have looked at me with the dark apparition of dejected apprehension." The second theme is his religious sense of the *mysterium tremendum*, which is evident in the 1916 poem "Nightfall on Reichenau" (published 1917) that clearly shows the influence of the Christian mystics he was reading at this time (G13 5–7; MH 71–72, 89). In the same vein, his 1910 literary review of a work by Johannes Jörgensen reads, "The moodful-dreaminess, the muted impressionism, seriousness, stateliness, the restrained call and admonition is entirely his style, as generally the writings of northerners—I recall Selma Lagerlöf—show something ponderous, quiet, magical. . . . With the mystics of the Middle Ages he gladly tarries" (CA 490–91).

Heidegger's interest in mysticism indicates that he was immersing himself in Christian traditions outside the strict ambit of medieval Scholasticism and modern Neo-Scholasticism. Joseph Sauer's course on "The History of Medieval Mysticism," which Heidegger took in WS 1910–11, probably sparked his lifelong preoccupation with mysticism and especially Meister Eckhart. He seems to have developed professional ties with Sauer, who was the editor of the Catholic journal *Literarische Rundschau für das katholische Deutschland*, in which Heidegger published many of his articles between 1912 and 1914. Heidegger later presented Sauer a copy of his qualifying dissertation on Scotus with a handwritten dedication. One finds allusions to mysticism throughout Heidegger's student writings, but the fullest discussion is given in his qualifying dissertation, where he explored its relation to Scholasticism and promised a future work on the notion of truth specifically in "Eckhartian mysticism."

Heidegger was also familiar with the concrete and historical concerns of theological hermeneutics. In his theological studies between 1909 and 1911, he took courses on "Introduction to the Sacred Scripture of the Old Testament," "Exegesis of Paul's Letter to the Romans," "Messianic Prophecies," "Introduction to the Sacred Scripture of the New Testament," "Theory of Revelation and of the Church," "Exegesis of the Holy Gospel According to John," and "Hermeneutics, with the History of Exegesis." His interests in history led him to enroll simultaneously in philosophy courses with Georg von Below and Heinrich Finke on the "History of the German State" and "The Age of the Renaissance (History of the Later Middle Ages)." He took another history course on "The Age of the Renaissance" from Finke in 1913, writing in the preface to his doctoral dissertation that it was Finke who "awoke a love and understanding for history in the unhistorical mathematician" (G1 61).

Finally, during these years, Heidegger was moving in the company of a number of antimetaphysicians who had attacked the foundations of western philosophy and called for a radically new orientation. He later reported that between 1910 and 1914 he started studying Nietzsche's *Wille zur Macht*, Kierkegaard's existential thought, and Dilthey's philosophy of life: "What the exciting years between 1910 and 1914 brought cannot be adequately expressed, but only hinted at through a few items given in a selective enumeration: the second, significantly enlarged edition of Nietzsche's *Will to Power*, the translation of the works of Kierkegaard . . . Dilthey's *Gesammelte Schriften*" (G1 56/R 22). As we see from the presence of Novalis and Friedrich Schlegel in the conclusion of his qualifying dissertation, Heidegger was also reading the German Romantics and absorbing their critique of modern Enlightenment rationalism.

What attracted Heidegger to the countertraditions of these antimetaphysicians, the Romantics, poetry, medieval mysticism, and theological hermeneutics was their orientation to the concrete historicity of lived experience vis-à-vis the " 'gray on gray' " of pure logic and speculative-theological thought. He maintained that the "mystical, moral-theological, and ascetic literature" of the Middles Ages was the deepest expression of "the world of lived experience

[*Erlebniswelt*] belonging to the medieval human being" (GI 203, 205; GI 409/PC 383). Regarding theological hermeneutics, he later wrote that "he was driven especially by the question of the relation between the Word of sacred scripture and speculative-theological thinking" (GI2 87/9–10). And it was not so much Kierkegaard or Dilthey who had the most visible impact on him, but rather Nietzsche's "pitiless and severe style of thinking," which focused philosophy on the "depth and fullness of life." It was these influences that, as we shall see, helped impel Heidegger toward the project of a postmetaphysical breakthrough expressed in the supplementary 1916 conclusion to his qualifying dissertation and in his 1915–16 essay on "Der Zeitbegriff in der Geschichtswissenschaft" (The Concept of Time in the Science of History). This "deeper grasp of philosophy" was to have the very different intentional configuration of worldview/person/history (GI 195–96; GI 415/CT 3). Here Heidegger was making his first gestures toward the "ground question" of metaphysics, namely, the question about "being and time," which leads to the end of philosophy.

4 | Ontologic

W HAT DOES THE later Heidegger's almost offhanded label of "onto-logic" for his earliest thought mean? In his 1912 essay "Das Realitätsproblem in der modernen Philosophie" (The Problem of Reality in Modern Philosophy), he argued that Berkley's and Hume's "*esse-percipi* formula, the identification of being and being-perceived," completely ignores the intentionality of consciousness which is always directed outward to the world. We find Heidegger focusing on the intentional relation to being throughout his student writings and dealing with it in terms of the three characteristics of noematic content, noetic relation, and finally the enactment or performance of the noesis/noema relation. In the following, I explore in turn each of these characteristics in Heidegger's early articles, his doctoral dissertation, and his qualifying dissertation.

The Kingdom of Logical Sense (Dasein, Truth, Place)

Heidegger dealt with intentionality specifically in the form of "the judgment" and defined its content-sense as pure "logical sense" (*Sinn*), that is, as the logical ground for making judgments about beings. For example, we read in his doctoral dissertation that, "as what is immanent for the occurrence of the judgment, the sense, i.e., the content [*Inhalt*], can be called the logical side of judging." And again in his qualifying dissertation, "The '*ens rationis*' means the content [*Gehalt*], the sense of psychical acts; it is being in an observing and thinking consciousness—it is the '*ens cognitum*, the thought, the judged." The thrust of Heidegger's ontologic was to maintain the status of logical sense as an "autonomous realm" (*Bereich*), a "kingdom" (*Reich*), which is distinct from the ontic spatiotemporal reality of both the psychical acts of judging and the physical world about which judgments are made (G1 2/PR 64; G1 172, 277, 166). *Das Befragte*, that which is interrogated, is psychical acts and the physical world, whereas *das Erfragte*, that which is sought after, is the logical sense at work here as the being of beings, that is, as the intelligible etiological ground that allows one to understand and explain beings as beings. With this onto-*logical* difference between logical being and spatiotemporal beings, Heidegger inserted himself squarely within the structure of the guiding question of the first metaphysical beginning of western philosophy.

Let us first examine this in his doctoral dissertation and his preceding philosophical articles. Here he presented himself as a pure logician living in the modern "age of psychology." The young champion of logic took on the task of refuting psychologism, that is, the reductionist attempt to explain the sense of judgments in terms of the spatiotemporal reality of psychical processes. The first four parts of his dissertation criticized four psychologistic theories, which respectively see judgment in terms of a "genesis" from "apperceptive mental activity" (Wilhelm Wundt), as "consisting" of "component acts" (Heinrich Maier), as a "basic class of psychic phenomena" (Franz Brentano), and as something "fulfilled" through the "action of the psychical subject that is demanded by the object" (Theodor Lipps). Heidegger's main criticism was that the very questioning in psychologism has already from the start intentionally looked away from the logical content of judgment to the psychical act of judging and is thus a theory not about the logical, but about the psychological. "Its failure to understand is not a mere *mis*understanding, *but a genuine non-understanding.*" Psychologism omits the essential "distinction between psychical act and logical content," between the noetic act of judging and the pure noematic logical sense to which the act is intentionally directed. The pure sense of the judgment "the book cover is yellow," that is, the being-yellow of the book cover, can be reduced neither to the material book nor to the psychic act of judging (G1 165, 18, 161, 22, 167ff.).

The last part of Heidegger's dissertation proceeded to outline a "pure logical doctrine of judgment." He explained that there are four distinct and irreducible kinds of reality, namely, the physical, the psychical, the metaphysical, and the logical (sense). Since sense is not to be confused with the other realms, one must say not that it "exists" or that "it is," but rather that *es gilt*, it validates, it has validity. The being of sense is *Gelten*, validating, validity. As such, it is indeed "a something" that "lies before us" and "is here [*da*]" for judgment. Thus, in a surprising anticipation of his later terminology, Heidegger here called logical sense "a manner of Dasein," being-here—the very term that in the twenties will equivocally come to mean rather the founding prelogical sense of historical being-in-the-world. But in 1913 his position was that the being-here of logical sense has an irreducible givenness that cannot be "explained" through anything else. "What is the sense of sense? Does it make any sense to question after this? . . . Perhaps we stand here at something ultimate and unreducible, for which a further clarification is ruled out. . . . one will never get beyond description." Appealing to Husserl's Sixth Investigation and to his "Principle of Principles" in the *Ideen*, Heidegger argued that one can only show (*aufweisen*) and describe sense through evidential acts of nonsensuous categorial intuition. The Dasein of valid categorial sense can become a phenomenon for phenomenological seeing within a kind of transcendental empiricism. Following Kant's denial of intellectual intuition, the empiricist's restriction of intuition to the sensible is "a dogmatic claim that ill suits him as an empiricist" (G1 165–71; G1 9–10/PR 68).

Heidegger's dissertation concluded with the claim that his investigation into judgment provides the "preparatory work" and "basis" for the wider project of erecting a "pure logic" which would include ontology in the form of a doctrine of the categories that articulate being into its manifold senses. "And only when a pure logic is erected and elaborated on such a basis," he writes, "will one be able more securely to deal with epistemological problems and divide the entire realm of 'being' [*Sein*] into its various modes of reality, bring into relief their peculiarity accurately and determine the kind and scope of knowledge belonging to them with certainty" (G1 186). Heidegger had already explained, in his 1912 essay on "Recent Research on Logic," that the highest part of logic is the doctrine of categories.

The first level of this doctrine is concerned with the a priori "categories of being" that provide the transcendental "conditions of knowing" any "sensible beings" whatsoever. These categories of the being of beings were first worked out in a realist context by Aristotle and then reshaped by Kant's "transcendental logic" into the objectness of the objects of experience. "Kant worked out the logic of the categories of being. . . . [B]eing has lost its translogical independence, being has been reworked into a concept of transcendental logic. This does not mean that objects are stamped into nothing but logical content; rather, only objectness, thingness over and above the thingly, being over and above beings is logical value, formal content." The division of being into its various modes of reality also involves concretizing the doctrine of categories within the regional ontologies that investigate the categorical structures of the various sciences. "Besides fundamental concepts (categories) . . . logic studies the logical structure of the individual sciences . . . fences them off against each other as special provinces and finally strives back to unity in a system of the sciences" (G1 23–25).

The second level of the doctrine of categories, which was opened up by the Neo-Kantian Lask, is concerned with the "philosophical categories" that provide the transcendental conditions of knowing the categories of being themselves and are therefore categories of categories, forms of forms. Philosophical categories are such "reflexive categories" as "identity" and "something in any sense," but the highest is "validity," which is the constitutive form of all other categories. "Just as being is the 'regional category' for sensibly intuited material, so validity is the constitutive category for non-sensible material." Though Aristotle and Kant overcame the Platonic "hypostatizing of the logical into a metaphysical being," they mistakenly "restricted the problem of the categories to sensible beings" and failed to see that categories are themselves another "area of application" for still higher categorial determinations. This higher level of the doctrine of categories presumably also has to do with the division of being into its various modes of reality, since the different senses of being are precisely each an "in-one-another of the valid and validity," of the form "validity" and the matter "being" (G1 25). The ultimate "sense of sense," of the being of beings, is validity. It was in this manner that Heidegger answered the question that he later claimed he was vaguely pursuing in his student years, namely, "what is the simple, unitary determination of being that permeates all its manifold meanings?" His project of a pure logic amounted to a phenomenological and transcendental ontologic of the Dasein of the valid categorial sense of the being of beings.

Validity means basically three things in Heidegger's student writings. In outlining these, we can follow his own self-critique in 1919 and the 1920s (see G56/57 §§13–20; G61 85–99; G63 §§8, 12; G21 81; SZ §33). First, validity means the form of *ideality* possessed by the sense of a judgment, which does not "exist" in the brute reality of space and time. Just as Plato's idea of the good is the form of forms, of the being of beings, but is itself "beyond being," so validity is the higher form of all logical sense of beings. For the manner of Dasein belonging to sense, "Lotze has found the decisive term in the German language: next to an 'it is' there is an *es gilt*, it validates, it has validity. The form of reality of the identical factor uncovered in the process of judgment can only be validating, validity. The being-yellow of the bookcover always validates, but never exists" (G1 113, 170).

Validity also means the validity of the predicative sense of a judgment *for* the logical subject of the judgment. "The book cover is yellow" means that "being-yellow has validity for, holds for the book cover" (*vom Einband gilt das Gelbsein*). The copula "is" means nothing more than that the predicative meaning-content (being-yellow) has validity for the meaning-content in the subject position (book cover). In another surprising anticipation of his later terminology, Heidegger stated that here we have answered the "question concerning the 'sense of being' "—a question he will pose later in a much different and historical manner, though still maintaining a moment of ipseity in content-sense vis-à-vis relational sense. But in his doctoral dissertation he first reduced being to the copula and then interpreted the latter as validity. "The validity of this for that signifies the logical concept of the copula. The question of the 'sense of being' in the judgment is thereby simultaneously settled. This being means not real existing or some relation in this, but validity. . . . the copula signifies 'has validity for.' " The *is*-yellow or *being*-yellow of the book cover means that "yellow" *has validity for* the book cover. The "is," being, really has no active verbal sense, but rather means only the static relational "sense-structure" of the "validity of one meaning-content for another." "The copula has no necessary relation to the verbal form 'is,' but rather represents something eminently logical, insofar as its form of reality is precisely validity" (G1 175, 178).

However, the sense of being, of the copula "is" in the judgment, not only means the validity of one meaning-content for another, but also entails the validity of these meaning-contents for the sensible being about which the judgment is made. Valid categorial sense is precisely the objectness of objects, the thingness of things, the being of beings. It makes up the transcendental "conditions of knowing" beings. "I know and can only know about reality in and through what has validity." These conditions are in the first place the higher categories of substance, quality, relation, causality, etc. that apply to any being whatsoever and are studied in the doctrine of categories. "The fundamental question of logic directs itself towards the conditions of knowing in general. Logic is theory of theory, the doctrine of science." But the conditions of knowing beings also include the material-categorial concepts used in judgments: for example, "book cover" (substance) and "being-yellow" (quality). In the judgment "the book cover is yellow," the sense of the being-yellow of the book, of the book-as-yellow, allows one to know the sensible object *as* a book and *as* yellow, and thus has validity for the sensuously existing yellow book. This validity-for is precisely a positing (*Setzung*) of something as existent (its that) and a determining (*Bestimmen*) of it *as* something (its what). "We can say that all knowledge is a seizing of the object, a determining of the object. . . . What has validity for the object determines it at the same time." "Knowing means embracing the material with the form. Accordingly, in the judgment, the categorial form (predicate) is expressed of the alogical material as subject" (G1 166, 23, 175, 33; G1 5/PR 66).

The validity of the sense of judgments *for* beings derives not just from its constitutive role, but also from its truth or correspondence with these beings themselves. Following Husserl's *Logische Untersuchungen*, Heidegger maintained that the primary locus of truth is the noematic sense of the judgment. The psychical activity of judging is true only in a "derivative sense." "What is true is rather the content of the representation, that which we mean, the sense." Since judging is an intentional determination of a being (the book) as something (yellow), truth as correspondence means that the noematic content (book-as-yellow) corresponds with and is "fulfilled" by the sensible book itself. Falsity or not being valid-for means "not-being-fulfilled." "Insofar as a meaning-content has validity for the object of judgment by determining it, the judgment is true or false. The old concept of truth *adaequatio rei et intellectus* can be elevated to the purely logical, if *res* is conceived as object and *intellectus* as determining meaning-content" (G1 31, 34, 176). The validity-for or truth of the logical sense of judgments actually means that this sense both makes possible knowledge of beings (Kant's transcendental truth) and is fulfilled by these beings themselves (correspondence).

Finally, validity means the universal and normative bindingness of the ideal sense of judgments on all judging agents. "Valid sense functions as a norm for psychical acts of thought." Heidegger's project of a pure logic meant more precisely, therefore, a phenomenological ontologic of the Dasein of the categorial sense of the being of beings which is valid in the triple sense of ideality, validity-for (truth), and bindingness. Being is an ideal etiological ground that is universally valid for beings and universally binding on human judgments. His is hardly a logic in the narrow sense, but rather a transcendental ontologic of the conditions of the possibility of knowing any beings whatsoever. Thus the last line of his dissertation states that this work "strives to be a philosophical work in that it was undertaken in the service of the ultimate whole" (G1 176, 187).

Heidegger's qualifying dissertation on Duns Scotus extended precisely this ontologic. It did so by means of a critical "repeating" and "unfolding" of the "objective meaning-content" of the medieval Aristotelian-Scholastic doctrine of categories with the help of modern Neo-Kantianism and phenomenology. One of the key texts he examined here, the *Grammatica speculativa sive de modis significandi*, was later discovered to have been written not by Scotus, but rather by the Scotist Thomas of Erfurt. Little would Heidegger have cared, since he wanted to pursue a *"problem-*historical" treatment of the *Sache* of the text, as opposed to a "literary-historical" analysis focused on the *mens auctoris.* As the medievalist Martin Grabmann wrote, "he has in principle renounced the genetic-historical manner of treatment and rendered the texts and the trains of thought into the language and terminology of Lotze, Husserl, Rickert, Lask, and Windelband." In fact, Heidegger claimed that Scholasticism and its doctrine of intentionality were already a "noematically oriented" phenomenology without an explicit "phenomenological reduction" back to the psychical acts of the human subject (G1 211, 193–205; LG 107).

Part one of Heidegger's study dealt with Scotus's doctrine of categories and began with its *metaphysica generalis* of the transcendentals, that is, of the highest categories that transcend any particular genus of beings: namely, being (*ens*), one (*unum*), true (*verum*), good (*bonum*). Being means "something in any sense," "the experienceable in any sense." Using the language of modern transcendental philosophy, Heidegger interpreted *ens* to mean the very objectness of objects of experience: *"Primum objectum est ens ut commune omnibus.* This *ens* is given in every object of experience, insofar as it is simply an object. . . . *Ens* signifies nothing else than the condition of the possibility of knowledge of any object whatsoever." It meant for Heidegger literally *Gegenständlichkeit,* a standing-over-against consciousness; ob-jectness, thrown-against-ness. In light of this category, we determine and illuminate any particular being simply *as* a being, as an ob-ject present to us, illuminated for us. "The 'over against' itself is already a determinate view toward [*Hinsicht*]. . . .

By the fact that a something (*ens*) is in any sense consciously given to me, that I make something into an object of my consciousness, the concept of determination has already started to function." Without this "first moment of clarity," I would "live blindly in absolute darkness." Heidegger maintained that Scotus should not have dealt with the mode of being (*modus essendi*) merely as an "absolutely objective reality." Rather, he should have differentiated between a noematic *modus essendi passivus* (the passive mode of being), that is, the way a being undergoes determination as an illuminated ob-ject, and a noetic *modus essendi activus* (an active mode of being), that is, the way our intentional act determines and illuminates the being as an ob-ject (G1 214–17, 318, 223–24, 320). The other transcendentals, which likewise function as universal conditions of the possibility of experience of objects, are convertible properties of being. Every being is *an* object (*unum*), a true object in the sense of being related to knowledge (*verum*), and an object of desire and will (*bonum*).

Being is "the category of categories," the "primal element," the "primal category," "an ultimate, a highest, behind which one cannot question further back" (G1 215, 219). All other categories, whether the other transcendentals or the categories of specific regions of being, are located within its luminous horizon. In Scholasticism it was *metaphysica specialis* that dealt with the narrower categories of specific regions of being, which were roughly identified as the divine (theology), the world (cosmology), and the soul (psychology). According to Heidegger, Scotus demarcated being more specifically into the regions of the physical, the psychical, the supersensible or metaphysical, the mathematical, and the logical. In the remainder of the first part of his work, Heidegger discussed primarily the categories of the mathematical and the logical realms, dealing at length with the two transcendentals relevant here, namely, *unum* and *verum*. He left *bonum* out of consideration altogether since his concerns were primarily logic and mathematics.

He found in Scotus a sharp distinction between real being (*ens reale*) and the logical being (*ens logicum*) of valid categorial sense, which is subject to its own peculiar categories. He pointed to a primary onto-logical difference between *ens logicum* and all other regions of being, insofar as the world of logical sense cuts across all of them and allows them to be known. "Insofar as knowledge is sought and gained of them, all regions of reality are able to be encountered through nonsensuous valid forms of sense." If they are to be known, they must "enter into the world of sense." The *ens logicum* is for Scotus an *ens in anima* precisely because it is the "noematic sense" that makes up the "intentionality of the correlate of consciousness." One must here distinguish between the noematic *modus intelligendi passivus* (passive mode of knowing), that is, the way sense undergoes being known, and the noetic *modus intelligendi activus* (active mode of knowing), that is, the way that the intellect intends this sense. Our "natural attitude" is caught up primarily in *prima in-*

tentio, first intention that is directed toward objects and not toward the noematic sense that makes the knowledge of these objects possible. This sense can, however, be thematized through a *secunda intentio*, a second intention that is a kind of step back and "turning of the gaze" from *ens reale* to *ens logicum*. "Everything existing in the metaphysical, the physical, and the psychical worlds of objects, as well as mathematical and even logical objects, are grasped in the realm of the '*secunda intentio.*' In it alone is there knowing of objects. The most cardinal distinction in the modes of reality is that between consciousness and reality," where consciousness is taken here specifically with regard to its noematic correlate of categorial sense (G1 277–87).

The primary category of *ens logicum* is not any of those categories applicable to the other realms, but rather validity, validating. Here Heidegger reiterated the three primary characteristics of the validity of categorial sense in judgments that he had outlined in his doctoral dissertation: unchanging ideality, validity-for objects, and universal bindingness for knowing subjects. Regarding the second characteristic, he maintained that logical sense makes up the transcendental category of "true" that is convertible with being; it is *on hos alethes*, *ens tanquam verum*, being as truth. On the one hand, it is transcendental truth (*verum transcendens*) in the Neo-Kantian sense of the condition of the possibility of knowing objects, whereby they are intentionally determined and thus "assimilated." The sense of judgments has the function of the "epistemological constitution of real objects." On the other hand, this sense is truth in the manner of "conformity with the objects" (correspondence), insofar as what is expressed in the sense of a judgment is virtually (*virtualiter*) contained in the object, which can thus fulfill the judgment precisely through being determined by it (G1 267–78).

The second part of Heidegger's qualifying dissertation turned specifically to the Scotist text *Grammatica speculativa sive de modis significandi* (Speculative Grammar Or On the Mode of Signifying), which he took to be a precursor of Husserl's "doctrine of meaning," that is, a science of the categories of meaning (*Bedeutung*). Meaning is a specific domain within the realm of *ens logicum*. Meanings are the individual elements out of which the complex sense of a judgment is built up. The judgment "the book cover is yellow," that is, the sense of the being-yellow of the book cover, contains the meanings "book cover," "is," and "yellow." In turn, both "sense and meaning are expressible through linguistic forms," the latter through individual words and the former through whole sentences. "As affixed to meaning and sense, these linguistic forms are expressions." The intrinsically alogical material sounds and marks in spoken and written words function together in a meaningful expression due to "meaning-bestowing acts" of the intellect that animate the material signifiers with meanings. In meaningful expressions there is thus an intentional stratification of signs in the "noematic nucleus" that runs from the expression (*modus significandi*) through the meaning and sense understood (*modus intelligendi*) to the being that is immediately intuited (*modus essendi*). "The linguistic form is a sign of the meaning, the sense, which in turn is a 'sign' of the object. . . . Things stand in thoughts, and these are affixed to words and sentences." The doctrine of meaning that Heidegger found in the Scotist text means a pure a priori grammar of the categorial forms of meaning and the rules of combination that are operative in all empirical-material languages. The focus of Heidegger's study of the Scotist text was the eight categories of meaning that make up the main parts of speech: noun, pronoun, verb, adverb, participle, conjunction, preposition, and interjection (G1 290–99, 317).

Meaning possesses the same kind of validity as sense. "For those who live in here-and-now speech, the spheres of existing grammar and that which is validly logical are fused into one," but the categorial structures of meaning also have an ideal subsistence apart from the spatiotemporal reality of empirical languages, for which meaning is universally binding. "Logical forms have their own reality, even when they are not linguistically expressed," in the same way that a real being can still exist without being known through the meaning and sense of judgments (G1 295, 291). Likewise, meaning has validity for objects in that it is based on the categories of being and enters into the sense of judgments. For example, the general function of the noun is to express being, the object as object. The *modus significandi* is intentionally directed through the *modus intelligendi* to the *modus essendi*.

In Heidegger's ontologic, the ideal realm of categorial sense that is valid for objects in the double sense of condition of possibility and correspondence is the being of beings, the etiological ground of beings. This was his bold reinscription of the content-sense of the guiding question of metaphysics, his translation of Plato's intelligible *topos* into the Lotzean and Neo-Kantian transcendental lexicon of validity and logical sense. "It is indeed more than a popular expression of the logicians," he wrote, "to speak of the logical place [*Ort*] of a phenomenon. . . . 'Place' in the logical sense is based on order. What has its logical place fits itself obediently into a determinate totality of relations." Categorial sense is a kind of logical *agora* that is fenced off by the transcendental categories and subdivided into the more specific categories of the various regions of being. As *Erörterung des Geltens*, a placing validity in discussion, knowledge can thus take the form of a "system" of "the totality of what is knowable," in whose framework (*Fachwerk*) any philosophical discipline, science, or piece of knowledge can be assigned its logical place. Philosophy turns out to be an *instrumentarium logicum*, a logical instrument for surveying the landscape of sense, taking the categories of being into our conceptual grip, and grounding our knowledge of beings (G1 207–12, 23, 223; for the term "*Ort*," cf. 174, 181, 183, 223).

We have found Heidegger naming the being of beings not only "place," but also "truth" and "Dasein"—the very names of three of his later thought-paths. But a postmetaphysical characterization of the content-, relational, and temporalizing-senses of the place, truth, and Dasein of sense, including the aspect of historical difference, is clearly missing here. In fact, Heidegger confronted philosophy with an ontological option between, on the one hand, a fluctuating historical realm of spatiotemporal existence and, on the other, a transcendental atemporal realm of unchanging logical validity. On the one hand, pure logic and *Wissenschaft*. On the other, "psychologism," "relativism," "anthropologism," historicism. Regarding content-sense, this option meant more specifically the doublets: logical sense and worldview; validity and spatiotemporal existence; ideal and real; form and matter; identity and difference. Heidegger acknowledged that, for those who live here and now in the *prima intentio* of the natural attitude, logical sense and meaning are indeed fused into one with the immediate environing world (*Umwelt*), with *Existenz*. For they are the form that informs the matter of known objects and the soul that ensouls the material signs of language. Sense and meaning are like a transcendental mind animating the flesh of the world.

But Heidegger insisted that there are two different ontological orders here, a dualism of two "worlds," the two "hemispheres of beings and the valid," which philosophy must distinguish. In "the critique of psychologism there comes to light the heterogeneity of any psychical and therewith spatiotemporal reality whatsoever and the logical." The "world of sense," which is disclosed in *secunda intentio*, is a "kingdom [*Reich*] of validity . . . over and against sensible being." "The '*ens logicum*,' i.e., sense . . . has shown itself to be a unique world over and against real being." "Duns Scotus teaches the freedom of the region of meaning from *Existenz*." Philosophy "lives in a tension" between these two worlds and is thus placed before an ontological option in its basic orientation. Heidegger's "decision" was not to opt for spatiotemporal existence to be the "foundation" and "anchor" of logical sense, as psychologism and historicism do, but rather to uphold the "absolute rule [*Herrschaft*] of logical sense over all worlds of knowable and known objects" (G1 110–14, 213, 23–24, 279–80, 290, 301, 92, 195).

Prior to becoming the hidden exiled king of 1919 and the early 1920s, when he would renounce his earlier metaphysics, Heidegger's "battle [*Kampf*] against psychologism" reigned in the "entire realm [*Gesamtbereich*] of 'being'," in the "kingdom" of a Kantianized Platonic intelligible *topos*, Dasein, and truth of being. The young logician handed down a severe judgment on all subjectively and historically oriented epistemologies: "Precisely through the absolute primacy of valid sense, the rod is condemningly broken over [*der Stab gebrochen über*] all physiological, psychological, and economic-practical epistemologies, and the absolute validity of truth, genuine objectivity, is irrevocably founded." (It was no accident that he left out *bonum* in his study of the medieval transcendentals.) The introduction to his qualifying dissertation asserted that "the religious, political, and cultural moments" in the very different worldviews of the Greeks (naturalism), the Middle Ages (theocentrism), and modernity (self-consciousness) are indeed "indispensable for understanding the genesis" of Aristotle's doctrine of categories of the natural world, the medieval analogical doctrine of categories, and the modern transcendental doctrine of categories. But, taking up Husserl's notion of *epoche*, he kept a firm grip on the principle that "these moments can, however, be disregarded in the pure philosophical interest that as such moves precisely only around the problems in themselves." Logic must suspend (*ausschalten*) these concrete worldviews so as to extract the pure noematic sense of the logical problems in themselves (GI 186, 273–75, 196). The kingdom of valid categorial sense that was disclosed in Scholasticism was actually the condition of the possibility of the medieval world, which thus must be subjected to a phenomenological reduction (*secunda intentio*) back to its logical foundation. That which was first in the *ordo cognoscendi* (order of knowing), namely, the *prima intentio* of the medieval world, was actually second in the *ordo essendi* (hierarchical order of being).

The Judgment

What is the relational sense in the structure of Heidegger's guiding ontological question concerning being? What did he mean when he wrote of "the various ways of intentional relation [*Beziehung*]," "the various ways in which consciousness is intentionally related [*bezogen*] to the objective"? We find him characterizing this relation generally and foundationally with such terms as "consciousness," "noesis," "thinking," "intellect," "reason." He held that the categorial sense given to psychical acts is a "being in an observing and thinking consciousness," a known-being (*ens cognitum*), a being in reason (*ens rationis*). To the etio-logical ground of valid categorial sense that makes up the content-sense of being corresponds an ocular noetic-logical relational sense. Its full sense is judgment. Heidegger's 1913 statement that "all knowledge is always judgment" was reiterated two years later in his qualifying dissertation: "All knowledge is judgment." "I understand real objects only precisely through knowledge, judgment" (GI 319, 277, 174, 268, 273).

The noetic act of judging is marked by the three moments of showing, predication, and communication (cf. G21 §11; SZ §33). As Heidegger put this in his dissertation on Scotus, the stratification of the objective noematic nucleus (for example, the book) into the passive *modi essendi, intelligendi,* and *significandi* (the shown-known-said book) is lined up with the three corresponding active modes, namely, the "act-qualities" and "act-strata" of showing, knowing, and expressing that "mesh into one another" and are "dependent on each other." The intuited object comes to be known through judgment and put into words. Every judgment presupposes the intuitive *modus essendi activus* that makes up "those acts in which immediate givenness comes to consciousness here and now." This mode is a "bringing-something-to-givenness-for-oneself," showing (*Aufzeigen*), revealing (*manifestari*), uncovering (*Aufdecken*). Thus Aristotle called the assertion or judgment "*apophansis, logos apophantikos,*" since it is a statement (*logos*) that contains the moment of an explicit bringing to light and showing (*apophainesthai*). "What is the sense of this showing? What is shown stands before us in its self and can be immediately grasped [*erfasst*]." This revelatory determination by the *modus essendi activus* of a being *as* a being, as an ob-ject, is an act of unconcealing from the "darkness" of nongivenness to the "clarity" of givenness. Following Scotus and Aristotle, Heidegger stressed that this unconcealing of beings is "always true," since here truth means simply bringing to givenness and clarity, being-true in the literal sense of the Greek *a-letheuein*, unconcealing (though he had not yet made this etymological connection). "Truth fulfills itself in givenness and does not reach beyond it." Thus "the truth of '*simplex apprehensio*', of the simple having of a being has for its opposite not falsity, but rather non-consciousness, non-knowing," that is, a simple nonshowing and nonhaving of the being in question. The false representation that "grasps the object in a determination that does not fit it" is still true in the sense of the revelatory determination by the *modus essendi activus* of something as a given ob-ject. "The given as something given becomes each and every time an object" (G1 317–20, 268, 169–70, 165, 213, 216, 278, 224).

Without this immediate showing of the object, the other two moments of judgment—the predicative act of the *modus intelligendi* and the assertoric act of the *modus significandi*—would have nothing to build on, since they are just more explicit and determinate ways of intentionally showing the object. *Praedicari est intentio.* Through predication, which makes up the judgment proper, "reality is somehow interpretively grasped [*aufgefasst*], something is broken out of it and thereby differentiated, delimited, and ordered." Unlike the simple showing of the active *modus essendi*, predication is a complex act that explicitly differentiates (*diairesis*) the object into subject ("the book cover") and predicate ("yellow"), and through the copula synthetically judges the latter to hold or have validity for the former ("the book cover *is* yellow," "being-yellow holds for the bookcover"). The predicate is literally ex-pressed (*aus-gesagt*) of the subject, which is thus interpretively determined and grasped *as* something (book cover-as-yellow). As interpretive determination, predication has the possibility of being false: "The knowledge whose truth has falsity for its opposite is judgment. The judgment is that which may be called true in the authentic sense." Finally, the determinative showing of the object in judgment completes itself by being linguistically expressed or asserted (*ausgesagt*, said out) and shown *to* others in the form of communication (*modus significandi*). "In the enactment [*Vollzug*] of the judgment 'the bookcover is yellow' my psychical activity usually reveals and announces itself in a spoken or written sentence. . . . [T]he being-yellow of the bookcover, i.e., the static moment, is what is communicated, the content or the sense of the sentence" (G1 280–81, 268, 170, cf. 305).

Seen from its three basic act-strata, then, judging is a communicative showing that determines something as something. Here Heidegger modeled intentionality on the ocular or theoretical attitude, which arises from a deficiency in practical dealings that simply tarries alongside the world, observes and discusses it, and gets radicalized into an autonomous activity in philosophy and science. This is vividly portrayed in his own comparison of the reflective attitudes of the businessman and the logician:

> A businessman plans, for example, a big undertaking. After long reflection and discussion with friends he comes to the conclusion that the plan is senseless, i.e., cannot be carried out. . . . There can be talk of sense always only where reflection, weighing, construing, determining is present. Sense stands in closest connection with that which we describe very generally with thinking.

For logical judgment, the world is no longer something ready-to-hand (*zuhanden*) for practical dealings; rather, the transcendental category of being means precisely *Vorhandensein*, being-before-the-hand and *Gegen-ständlichkeit*, objectivity, standing-over-againstness. The Dasein of sense means that "with this identical factor, a something lies before us, is here." Being is a present-before-the-hand Dasein, truth, or place of sense in which an observing, predicating, and assertoric consciousness dwells—a kind of logical neighborhood and *ethos*:

> Here there can of course be no thought of a *spatial* distance and neighborhood [my italics]. . . . Consciousness is a unique kind of relation. As everything standing over against me in natural reality is something different as soon as I myself am differently localized, and as nonetheless precisely in the "over against" the identical moment of the pure over-against maintains itself, so it is with experience, consciousness. (G1 169–72, 223)

Here, in his early etio-etho-logical topic of being, we encounter Heidegger's hands again. Heidegger quoted Kant's statement that "we can reduce all *Handlungen*, actions/handlings, of the understanding to judgments." The showing of the *modus essendi activus* is precisely an act of "ob-jectification" and *Vor-stellen*, a throwing/placing with and before the *manus mentis*. Being is *"handfeste" Wirklichkeit*, "handfast" reality. As predication, this showing of the object becomes further an explicit *Bemächtigung*, an overpowering interpretive seizure of the object as something. "All knowledge is object-*Bemächtig-*

ung, determining the object. . . . Something [subject] is seized, determined through something," namely, through the predicate, the *kategoria* in the literal sense of "charge," "accusation." In the *agora* of categorial sense, being is arraigned in many ways. "Categories 'clasp' material encountered in its givenness, get it into their power [*in ihre Gewalt*], as it were" (G1 30, 268, 317–18, 175, 281). Knowledge is a kind of power, a judgment is a conceptual fistful of beings, which techno-logically enframes beings in terms of the "framework" of the *Reich* of logical categories. The later Heidegger knew from firsthand experience what he was talking about when he criticized modern metaphysics as technological enframing (*Gestell*) that uses a framework of concepts and methods for representing and mastering being.

The founding/founded doublet of valid logical sense and spatiotemporal existence in the content-sense of Heidegger's ontologic is mirrored in the relational sense with its stratified doublet of judgment versus nonjudgmental acts. The "emotional-practical side of mental life . . . the world of ends, norms, values, and goods . . . in aesthetic contemplation, in religious belief, in custom, law, and morality" is founded on judgment and its noematic logical sense. Just as the material sounds and marks of words are intrinsically alogical and need to be affixed to and animated by the "meaning-bestowing acts" of the *modus significandi activus* if they are to signify something intentionally, so moods, desires, actions, and all psychical aspects of the "activity of judging" are in themselves nothing more than a stream of spatiotemporal processes (*Vorgänge*) that need to be affixed to, ensouled by, and meshed with intentional acts of *noesis*, of the *modus intelligendi activus*, if they are to have an intentional referent. Following Aristotle, Heidegger thus maintained that judgment is the locus of truth; it alone can be true or false since, as *logos apophantikos*, it alone shows or points out beings. "A psychical activity of judging can never be true or false; it exists or does not exist like the 'flowing' of an electric current that stands outside the either/or of 'true and false.' " By itself, mood would not be a *modus essendi activus*, a mode of actively disclosing being, but rather a mere *Gemütsbewegung*, psycho-physical e-motion. It did not yet occur to Heidegger that the senses, desire, mood, action, practical understanding, and everyday speech have their own and more originary form of intentionality and sense. The enthusiastic businessperson can see the *sense* of the big undertaking, the enraptured viewer can encounter a *"meaningful* art work, e.g., Rodin's 'Balzac'," and the newspaper article can recount favorably that "a *sensible* gift was presented to the anniversary couple" precisely because in all these cases (which include *techne* and *phronesis*), "reflection, weighing, construing, determining is present," that is, the intentionality of thinking and judging. "Sense stands in closest possible connection with what we very generally call thinking." Do we usually walk around making judgments like this? In 1913 Heidegger thought so. When the doctoral student "takes his usual walk" on

the fieldpath (*Feldweg*) near his hometown of Messkirch and, lost in meditation, suddenly sees a yellow pen on the ground that reminds him of the book
with the yellow cover he has been reading, this is possible because "I once
again make the judgment: 'The book cover is yellow.' " All this is ironic in
light of how Heidegger again used his books in SS 1923 and then the
Messkirch fieldpath in his later writings as illustrations of the temporality of
being (G1 91, 268, 47, 397, 167–75; G13 87–90/PW 32–39).

There is a complicated stratification and founding of act-qualities that
runs as follows: the active *modi essendi, intelligendi, significandi*, and then affixed to these the desiderative, emotional, and volitional acts of practical life.
The relational sense of moral life, art, and religious life, which take a practical
interest in things, is founded on the theoretically oriented relational sense of
judgment. For example, everyday nonassertoric discourse is seen to be affixed
to and animated by the meaning-intention of assertion as the founding mode
of the *modus significandi*. "Apart from the act of assertion," Heidegger wrote,
"still other types of the subject's taking up a position to the state of affairs
[*Sachverhalt*] are possible; it can be a wished, questioned, commanded,
doubted state of affairs"—for example, "the book cover should be yellow"
(the wished-commanded-yellow-book-cover). But "that Duns Scotus assigns
them to the accidental modes and thus to the founded functions of signification indicates that even he understands them not as mere simple acts, but
rather as acts affixed with varied complications." The "above-mentioned
modes can all be reduced to [the assertoric infinitive form of the verb that
merely *vor-stellt*, puts forth], since they all contain the state of affairs that is
somehow colored by the act-quality." What is initially given noematically
through the judgment or assertion as *Vor-stellen* is something present-before-
the-hand in its naked truth, which is then clothed, painted, and rounded out
by the desiderative, emotional, and volitional acts of the *manus mentis* into a
full-blown thing with value-predicates. To take Heidegger's own example,
there is a noematic stratification of the shown-known-said-desired-felt-used-
poetized book on the fieldpath. But strictly speaking, there is no noematic correlate of these types of nonjudgmental acts; rather, they express our attitudes
toward the present-to-hand objects known through judgments. They are only
Begleiterscheinungen, accompanying phenomena. For instance, the interjection
"Oh!" or the grunt "too heavy!" at a hammer "does not determine the meaning-content of the verb as such, i.e., the state of affairs meant in it; its determinative function is directed to the relation of the verbal act of meaning to consciousness. Concrete forms of interjection arise in accord with various
emotions such as pain, sadness, joy, admiration, fear, and horror" (G1 387,
111, 398).

Heidegger's onto-logical difference between valid sense and spatiotemporal beings is paired with a basic psycho-logical difference, namely, his Neo-

Kantian version of the traditional distinction between mind (*nous*) and body. In the same way that spatiotemporal objects are bearers of the autonomous kingdom of sense, and the material sounds and marks of language "bearers of meanings," Heidegger suggests that the individual psycho-physical subject is the bearer or vehicle (*Träger*) of a logical "consciousness in general," a "transcendental-logical" understanding that is actualized and "imbedded" in it. "Geyser's critique of the 'trans-individual I,' " he writes,

> does not seem to me to be completely accurate. The formation of this concept grew precisely out of an attempt to make truth and its validity independent of the individual subject. It is to be understood purely logically as the system of valid forms of knowledge, which as needs be are deposited [*eingelagert*] in an individual subject in its here-and-now [*aktuell*] knowing, just as Geyser must require a "bearer" for pure intentional thoughts. (G1 295, 153, 19, 30, 34–35)

Heidegger's dualism places us before an ontological option in the relational sense of being between the doublets form and matter, mind and body, the transcendental and the psychological, knowing/judging/asserting and mood/desire/action/practical discourse. "Philosophy lives in a tension with living personality"—and has to decide. Heidegger here condemns Heinrich Maier's position that "thinking the ideals of thought is not absolutely necessary, but rather striving after them. The 'anchoring ground of this striving and therewith logic itself is . . . ethical willing, the willing of an ethical ideal'. . . . the ultimate basis of logic is an emotional act, a representation of covetous desire." Oddly enough, Maier's position will later be approximated by Heidegger himself in his analysis of technological "will to power" as the underlying characteristic of modern knowledge. But in these early years he likewise rejects the position of Karl Vossler, a follower of Wilhelm von Humboldt, that "linguistic thought is a matter for itself, something autonomous and especially something essentially other than logical thought," that "in and of itself all speaking is alogical," and that "logic first begins after language or in the middle of language, but not before it or without it" (G1 195, 108, 338; PMG 113). Heidegger will later make a sharp about-face by taking up this very position himself in the twenties (cf. SZ §34).

In his student writings, however, he rejected these attempts at psychologistic and historicist relativism that invert the *ordo essendi*. One must not take the dangerous route of "physiological, psychological, and economic-practical epistemologies," but rather the path of pure logic. Just as Heidegger suspended the various historical worldviews that have been fused with the noematic content-sense of the traditional doctrine of categories and considered only the pure logical sense that founds these worldviews, so he suspended the nonjudgmental acts of relational sense that are meshed with judgment and performed

a reduction back to purified acts of judgment. Though he felt that a phenomenology of emotional and volitional acts in connection with Brentano's *Psychologie vom empirischen Standpunkt,* Scholastic psychology, and the "mystical, moral-theological, and ascetic literature" of the Middle Ages is an
"urgent" task, he still maintained in both of his dissertations that "these phenomena do not have logical priority over the problem of the judgment, so that
they can be left out of consideration." In his doctoral dissertation, he wrote
that " 'pure logic' has nothing to do with [these phenomena]. . . . a 'logical
feeling' exists as much and as little as wooden iron." "The results of researching the connection between logical experiences and the other events of
consciousness are completely worthless" (G1 48, 287, 205, 112–13, 155). His
qualifying dissertation did lighten this judgment, but still argued that, though
fused together in the naive natural attitude of concrete life, the two types of
acts belong to ontologically different realms.

The Battle of the Giants about Being

How did Heidegger's ontologic characterize the enactment- and temporalizing-senses of the intentional judgment/sense relation? In both dissertations,
he emphasized a sharp quasi-Platonic and Lotzean ontological difference between the two heterogeneous worlds of the *atemporal* validity of sense (ideality) and the sensible spatio*temporal* existence of psycho-physical being. Following Bergson and others, Heidegger described the here-and-now enactment
(*aktueller Vollzug*) of the judgment as a flowing stream of consciousness—"an
enacting and happening [*Geschehen*] that runs its course in time," "a flowing
and inconstant reality," "a constantly flowing psychical stream." It is a process
(*Vorgang*) that consists of *Ereignisse,* events; and whether these *Ereignisse* are
judgmental or nonjudgmental acts, they are always marked by difference (*Ver-
schiedenheit*), alteration (*Änderung*), change (*Wechsel*), wandering (*Wandeln*),
since they take place from moment to moment (*Augenblick*), from situation to
situation (*Situation*), often surfacing and disappearing of a sudden (*plötzlich*)
and in the blink of an eye. They are *jeweilig,* for a while at a particular time.
"The same psychic situation of consciousness can never repeat itself" (G1 23–
24, 155–70, 276–78, 365, 354, 284–87, 317–19, 205).

But the temporal enactment of intentionality belongs to a different realm
of reality than the noematic Dasein of the atemporal sense that is present in
the judgment. Sense is "ideal trans-temporal identical sense," "something enduring and identical," "sameness." It is characterized by *Veränderungsfremd-
heit,* foreignness to alteration. "The judgment of logic is sense, a 'static' phenomenon that stands beyond all development and alteration and therefore does
not become, arise, but rather has validity, validates." The meaning of the terms
in a judgment and the sense of the whole judgment "are subject to no altera-

tion. They are timelessly and identically the same." "Logical and mathematical states of affairs are not temporally conditioned." Sense is likewise not affected by the time of its physical referent: "Whether the meant object exists, alters itself, or disappears, the meaning remains untouched by this change" (G1 22, 168, 179, 293, 390, 301).

Heidegger exemplified this nonsituational character of sense with the judgment "the book cover is yellow." In the first moment of enacting this judgment, the situation was that he was sitting in his study and the judgment "suddenly surfaced in me"; in the second situation, he arrived at the judgment through comparing his books in a moment of absentmindedness; the next time, he was out walking on the fieldpath, saw a yellow pencil on the ground, and came to the judgment by way of memory and association; and in the final situation, the judgment was made in the form of an answer to a friend's question about how the book is bound. But "in all these 'modifications of consciousness' in the moment [*Augenblick*] of making the judgment, in all the difference of times here, I meet up with a constant factor in each act of judgment—each and every time I intend to say: 'the bookcover is yellow.' . . . Therefore there remains only the possiblility of locating it outside the constantly flowing psychical stream." One finds the same view in Heidegger's qualifying dissertation, which asks whether the logical *ens rationis* is to be "understood in the sense that it belongs to the soul like a memory that surfaces suddenly in the life of the soul, or like the feelings of sorrow and joy that shake us inwardly often only for a moment [*Augenblick*] and then disappear," in order "to sink away and make room for other psychic *Ereignisse*?" "But then the judgment would be true only for as long as the enactment of the activity of judgment endured" (G1 167–68, 276).

The "manner of Dasein belonging to the static moment in the dynamic activity of the process of judgment" is precisely the constant standing-present-over-against-ness (*Gegenständlichkeit*) and being-present-before-the-hand (*Vorhandensein*) of valid sense. Walking along the fieldpath may be a temporal event, but not its sense. "Maier says that, when I perform it under a dull heavily clouded sky, the judgment 'it is not raining' has a different sense than when I enact it in the face of a smiling cloudless sky. I mean that the sense remains the same since in both judgments there is indeed stated: rain is not *vorhanden*, present-before-the-hand." The constant being-here of valid sense is the superlative expression of the transcendental "being" (ob-jectivity) since it is enduring ob-jectivity, the most objective objectivity, and thus (in Plato's sense) the most beingly being, the most present presence. "Everything standing over against me in natural reality is something different as soon as I myself am differently localized" and yet "nonetheless precisely in the 'over against' the identical moment of the pure over-against maintains itself" (G1 112, 223).

The judgmental showing, predication, and communication of sense have the temporal meaning of *Gegenwärtigen*, making-present-over-against oneself and *Gegenwärtighaben*, having-present-over-against oneself. *Vergegenständlichung* (objectification) and *Vorstellen* (representing) thus amount to a throwing/placing into presence before the *manus mentis*. The *modus essendi activus* acts upon being and makes it present in the *modus essendi passivus*. More literally, *Gegenwärtigen* means waiting-against, tarrying, dwelling in the logical neighborhood of presence (*ousia*). Heidegger wrote, "Through the meaning-giving act it becomes possible for me to live in the meaning of a word, to *make-present* [*vergegenwärtigen*] its meaning to myself here and now." "I must precisely have ['A'] *present* in order to reject it, i.e., to posit it as not being." In enacting the judgment "the book cover is yellow" in the different situations, in each case I "let the book become *present* [*präsent*] in its format and size," whether expressly or not (G1 302, 117–23, 167; G1 8/PR 67; emphasis added).

The making-present of judgment involves the here-and-now instantiation of sense into the situational spatiotemporal objects that are interpretively predicated as-something and whose content provides this predicative sense with its *jeweilige Erfüllung*, its fulfillment at a particular time. Sense is categorial form that through the judgment "embraces" and "forms" the material content of things, making it knowable. Homogeneous, univocal concepts thereby get instantiated into the heterogeneity and analogicity of individual beings that, as Duns Scotus saw, are defined by haecceity, such-now-here-ness. Individual things are occasions for judgment. In "all the different instances" in which Heidegger makes the judgment "the book cover is yellow," the "circumstances that are able to occasion [*veranlassen*] me to to make the judgment vary," but whether "stimulated by the color of the pencil" on the fieldpath or stimulated by comparing his books, his judging instantiates the same noematic sense. "The real gives as it were only the *stimulus* (*occasio*) and provides the *point of departure* for the creation of ordering relations that have no adequate correspondence in the real." But this making-present is also an instantiation of sense into the knowing subject. "Through individual psychical acts of judgments ... the sense of the judgment becomes at a particular time [*jeweils*] consciously and in a certain respect 'really' given for the knowing subject and is taken up into the mental life of the actual individual." "The logical is imbedded in the psychical," "deposited in an individual subject in its here-and-now knowing." *Ens logicum* is *ens in anima*, noematic being instantiated in the soul (G1 354, 365, 195, 167, 281, 278, 30, 275). On a larger scale, logical categorial sense is instantiated in and meshed with the "life-attitude" and the "religious, political, and cultural moments" of the valuative worldviews of Greek thought (naturalism), medieval Scholasticism (theocentrism), and modern thought (self-consciousness).

Heidegger's ontological difference between time and atemporal validity placed philosophy before still another primal alternative in its basic orientation. In his 1913 review of the book *Zeitlichkeit und Zeitlosigkeit* (Temporality and Atemporality), he gave a Neo-Kantian reformulation of the Greek *gigantomachia peri tes ousias* that was waged between Parmenideans and Heracliteans as to whether being is unchanging reality or the flux of becoming. "Parmenides and Heraclitus cannot die. . . . the problem—how is the abyss between the atemporal reality of abstract thought and the temporal reality of sensory perception to be bridged?—still holds thinking fast in a situation of conflict." "The major phases of the historical development of the problem" of whether to ground the supposedly atemporal in the temporal or to ground the temporal in the atemporal include also the disputes between Plato and Aristotle, between modern rationalism and English empiricism, and presently between Neo-Kantian logic and the "absolutizing of psychological-historical thinking" in psychologism and historicism, which includes the "Heraclitism of Bergson" that affirms that we are caught up in a "constantly flowing psychical stream" (G1 46, 305, 168).

Heidegger's ontological resolution of this conflict was to opt for the priority of atemporal validity as the foundation of the sense present in the realm of historical experience. Though sense is imbedded in temporal experience and indeed in cultural worldviews, there are two ontologically heterogeneous realms here. The temporal aspects are to be suspended and subjected to an eidetic reduction that extracts atemporal sense (essences) from historical facts. In the words of Heidegger's doctoral dissertation, temporal experience is only the "first basis of operation" for the "will to the logical" "to go through" so as to detach the logical sense that founds it. "But the stream and its accompanying phenomena in the judging subject cannot in any sense interest logic as logic." "That which ever has the character of running its course in time, of being active, remains necessarily foreign to the region of pure logical theory." In the preface to the doctoral dissertation, Heidegger fittingly described himself as an "unhistorical mathematician" (G1 29, 169, 111, 164, 61).

Though his qualifying dissertation makes a significant advance on his earlier dissertation in that it acknowledges the imbedding of sense in historical worldviews, it does not present a decisive break, but rather is at bottom only a more sophisticated and enlightened form of idealism. Its *"problem*-historical method" indeed insists that the different historical "posings of the question" about the categories of being in Greek thought, Scholasticism, and modern thought must be made a part of the systematic logical problem of the categories, but this is not for the sake of understanding their situatedness in and genesis out of the historical worldviews of Greek naturalism, medieval theocentrism, and modern self-consciousness. Rather, history is to be suspended and used as the wider operational basis for performing the eidetic reduction back to "the problems in themselves," that is, back to the pure atemporal noematic sense of the different posings of the problem. Heidegger's method is *problem-historical*, not problem-*historical*.

> Even if the religious, political, and (in a narrower sense) cultural moments of a time are indispensable for understanding the *genesis* and the historical conditionedness of a philosophy, these moments can, however, be disregarded in the pure philosophical interest that as such moves precisely only around the problems *in themselves*. Understood here as a *historical* category, *time is as it were suspended*. . . . Therefore the history of philosophy has an essential relation to philosophy so long and *only* so long as it is not "pure history," a science of facts, but rather has projected itself into the pure philosophical system.

This notion of the recurrence of essential questions in history not only shows the influence of the Neo-Kantian Windelband, but also has a definite Hegelian heritage. Even though categorial sense arises initially in the for-itself of historical worldviews, it must be "cancelled, lifted up [*erhoben*] into the concept," subjected to "a cancellation, a lifting up [*Aufhebung*] into the systematic," into the " 'gray on gray' of philosophy" that deals with the logical kingdom of the in-itself. "The entire *seemingly purely* historical investigation is lifted up [*gehoben*] to the level of a systematic-philosophical treatment." The motto of Heidegger's qualifying dissertation is even from Hegel: "With a view [*Rücksicht*] to the inner essence of philosophy there are neither predecessors nor successors" (G1 196, 207, 399, 203, 17, 204, 193).

Thus Heidegger's study of medieval thought stressed that the "enriching and in general the possibility of a systematic-philosophical understanding of the doctrine of meaning [in Scotus] is *not* to be gained" through "research into the *historical* conditions and the genetic formation of the region of knowing concerned." "We are not concerned with *happening, coming to be* and *passing away*, with processes, events." Likewise, the study of the intentional acts of the *modi essendi, intelligendi,* and *significandi* belongs not to psychology (which views them as a stream of temporal psycho-physical acts here and now), but rather to phenomenological logic, which treats them with a view to their noematic achievements (*Leistungen*), their "sense-giving function." And though in them "the different modes of the intentional relation receive their here-and-now enactment," they are ultimately to be studied as essential "act-qualities" or "act-characters" that have been lifted out of the stream of experience (G1 276, 207, 320, 284–87, 317–20).

Heidegger's ontological difference between the temporal and the atemporal in the doublets of logical sense and worldview, meaning and sign, judgment and nonjudgmental act, mind and body, ideal and real, form and matter, still left him with the old Platonic problem of *methexis*, participation, that is, how the abyss between atemporal kingdom of sense and time is to be bridged. In using historical factuality as our operational basis, "we have to do precisely with the strange fact (concealing in itself problems perhaps never able to be completely illuminated) that the logical is imbedded in the psychical." There is a "strange and intimate" "intertwining" of the two. The "relation is a fact," but "the problem is how does *validating* sense [come to] function as a norm for *psychical* acts of thought" that "affirm" it? Heidegger did not deal explicitly with this problem of *methexis* until the 1916 supplementary conclusion to his study of Scotus. But the earlier answer that he assumed was that the ontological abyss between the above and the below is bridged through informing, animation, ensouling, fusing, depositing, that is, through the overpowering embrace and imbedding of form and matter that is carried out in the temporal enactment of judgment as instantiation. Denying Plato's metaphysical " 'hypostatizing' of the logical into a metaphysical being" that is completely separate, he took up the more Aristotelian position in its modern epistemological Neo-Kantian expression that form always functions with matter in the composite reality (*to synholon*) of the known and judged object (G1 30, 292, 176, 24).

5 | Heterology

IN REKINDLING THE ancient "battle of gods and giants," of Eleaticism and Heraclitism, Heidegger's two dissertations reinscribed the content/relation/temporalizing configuration of the first guiding metaphysical question about being (ground/*logos*/presence) into the logical sense/judgment/atemporality configuration of his own modern ontologic. He gave one more answer to the same old guiding question without questioning this question itself. Heidegger's battle would soon, around 1919, actually join forces with his early opponents of historicism, psychologism, and skepticism, reverse its previous decision concerning the relation of founding between logical sense and historical lifeworld, and thereby displace the concepts of sense, Dasein, truth, and place from the former into the latter. Logical sense will no longer be interpreted as "something ultimate and unreducible, of which a further clarification is ruled out," but rather deconstructed. Not indeed back to some naked blind physical or psychical reality, but rather back to the facticity of sense in historical lifeworlds. The first and most decisive "turn" in Heidegger's thought, from being to the differentiated temporal giving of being, is to be found in the silent decade between his 1916 Scotus book and SZ. But there are portentous signs of this turn already in two texts from 1915–16 that I have not yet discussed.

Heidegger finished his qualifying dissertation on Scotus in the spring of 1915, presented it to the philosophy department in July, received his official *Privatdozent* status early in August, and was already teaching his first course in November, while simultaneously doing military service since August. Sometime between spring 1915 and fall 1916 when his study of Scotus went to press, he wrote a short supplementary conclusion for the book version that was titled "Das Kategorienproblem" (The Problem of the Categories). The other text in which we catch glimpses of Heidegger's turn is his 1916 journal article "Der Zeitbegriff in der Gesichtswissenschaft" (The Concept of Time in the Science of History), which was based on the July 1915 trial lecture he delivered as one of the requirements for the license to teach (HL 77–82; GI 191). In these two texts, Heidegger called for a "breakthrough" to a deeper historical notion of philosophy, which took the shape of a heterology of being. He also called for an even deeper breakthrough to an ultimately *mystical* heterology.

He made these gestures by taking up and radicalizing the themes of mysticism, worldview, value, personality, history, difference, haecceity, and analogy that had already surfaced in his qualifying dissertation, though they had been subjected to a phenomenological suspension there. His supplementary conclusion was a *supplément* that both added to and supplanted the body of his dissertation, allowing the themes therein to be reiterated in a different light.

Because of this tension between the body and the supplementary conclusion of Heidegger's work on Scotus (cf. PMG 112), we have waited until now to treat the more historical concerns of Heidegger's student writings. The present chapter examines his historical heterology, whereas the following chapter explores the ultimately mystical sense of this heterology. More specifically, the present chapter pursues the following plan: (1) Heidegger's growing dissatisfaction with pure logic and his yearning for a breakthrough to a more concrete, historical doctrine of the categories of being; (2) his account of the history of the doctrine of the categories; and his reinscriptions of (3) content-sense as worldview, (4) of relational sense as personality, and (5) of enactment- and temporalizing-sense as historical differentiation.

Restlessness and Breakthrough

After completing his two dissertations, all the poetry, mysticism, hermeneutics, Dilthey, Kierkegaard, Nietzsche, and who knows what else that the young logician and Neo-Scholastic had been reading started to catch up with him. The philosophical tension between timelessly valid sense and spatiotemporal reality was at this time also a tension within Heidegger's own philosophical personality—and it would soon snap. His phenomenological suspension (*Ausschalten*) of the flux of spatiotemporal reality was also a suppression of his own philosophical impulses. *Ausschalten* ordinarily means "turning off" something—the water or the electricity, for example. Between 1915 and 1919, the damming up of Heidegger's philosophical and religious impulses finally burst, and we have been trying to cope with this explosion ever since.

A religious and philosophical personality such as Heidegger could not long remain satisfied with pure logic. "It is now the appropriate place," he wrote at the opening of his supplementary conclusion, "to allow the hitherto suppressed spiritual *restlessness* a chance to speak." His essay on time likewise opened with a Nietzschean call for the liberation of the personal " 'drive that philosophizes' ": "In the last few years a certain 'metaphysical urge' has awoken in scientific philosophy. Staying put in mere epistemological theory no longer suffices. . . . One has to read this as a deeper grasp of philosophy and its problems and see in it the will of philosophy to power." Given the pervasive Neo-Kantian atmosphere of the discipline of philosophy in the days of Heidegger's apprenticeship, his suspension of concrete historical life was an *ascesis* for the theology-student-turned-philosophy-student in the double sense of denial and institutional disciplining. The preface added to his 1916 Scotus book announced that the earlier dedication to Heidegger's Neo-Kantian teacher Rickert was now also intended to express the fact that, "in completely free adherence to my own own 'standpoint'," philosophy of value and worldview is "called to a decisive movement forward and deepening of its work on philosophical problems. Its orientation to the history of the spirit provides a fruitful basis for creatively shaping philosophical problems from out of strong personal lived experience" (G1 399/PC 378; G1 196, 191; G1 415/CT 3). After giving up his theological studies, Heidegger had tried his best to become a Neo-Scholastic, a mathematician, a phenomenological Neo-Kantian, a pure logician, but it was not in him. Instead, after 1915 he turned into Heidegger the young romantic and passionate rebel who advocated a fundamental critique of his own metaphysical heritage and a revolution to a new postmetaphysical beginning.

His position was now that the question of the categories of being cannot remain on the theoretical level of epistemology and logic. "An ultimate clarification of this question," he wrote, "will not be gained by staying put within the logical sphere of sense and its structure. Logic and its problems are not at all able to be seen in a true light if the context *out of* which they are interpretively read does not become a translogical one." Philosophy has to make a deconstructive breakthrough to its prelogical "authentic depth dimension," which is located in the "world of lived experience" and is ultimately the theme of a mystical metaphysics. "Philosophy cannot for long do without its authentic optic—metaphysics. . . . it must be called a principial and disastrous error of philosophy as 'worldview' . . . if it does not—and this is its most authentic vocation—aim at a *breakthrough* into true reality and real truth." Heidegger no longer spoke of pure logic as the highest type of philosophy, but of "the deeper, worldview essence of philosophy" (G1 405-10/PC 381-384). Thus he made a gesture toward reversing his earlier stand on the relation of founding between purportedly atemporal logical sense and the concrete historical sense of worldviews, and thereby redeciding the ontological option that he had set up between these two spheres. His thought entered a *krisis* (the first of many to come) in the double sense of danger and decision, which would lead eventually in 1919 and thereafter to a clear abdication of his earlier claim to a homogeneous, unchanging kingdom of the sense of being.

Heidegger had already explained, in the introduction to his qualifying dissertation, that the history of philosophy is not so much a linear "devolving" from questions to solutions and then to new questions as rather an "evolving" and "drawing-out" of the same past questions that are continually repeated (*wiederholt*) down through the ages in new formulations. Progress "lies mostly in the deepening and the new beginning of the placings of the question." Thus "when history ceases being merely the past, it drives the most effective thorn

into the spirit" (Trendelenburg). This reiteration of past questions in new beginnings is "ever beginning anew" and "never complete, but always on the
way in finding the truth." The "history of philosophy has an essential relation
to philosophy" in that philosophy is understood historically and history philosophically. This is what Heidegger meant by his hybrid "problem-historical"
approach to the problem of the categories of being, which was repeated,
placed, and "stamped" in different ways in the Greek, medieval, and modern
"epochs of spiritual history"—and now again in the new beginning in his supplementary conclusion. However, the introduction had indeed aimed at an
eidetic reduction of history into a "pure philosophical system" of atemporal
logical sense. But if the problem-historical method is rethought in light of the
advances Heidegger made in his conclusion, then his notion of the "history of
the doctrine of categories" starts looking like his first appellation of his later
notion of *Seinsgeschichte*, the history of the three epochs of being. Method in
the literal sense of way-toward the *Sache* of the categorial sense of being starts
looking like a problem-*historical* approach, which also prefigures his later
themes of the end of philosophy (deconstruction of the epochal topology of
being back to its historical depth-dimension); a new beginning (repetition that
turns from being toward its temporal giving); and constant beginning of this
new beginning. Heidegger's conclusion in effect gestured toward the end of
philosophy by attempting to break-*through* the traditional guiding question
about the categories of being, as well as through his own modern onto-logical
configuration of this question (logical sense/judgment/atemporality), so as to
get back to the depth dimension of historical lifeworlds. From this ground
question, his breakthrough to a new beginning of worldview-oriented philosophy attempted to reinscribe the problem of the categories in the configuration
of worldview/person/history (G1 196–202; G1 416, 429/CT 3, 9; G1 408/PC
383).

The History of the Doctrine of Categories

Heidegger's conclusion lifted his previous suspension of "the genesis and
the historical conditionedness" of philosophy in "religious, political, and cultural" values and gave free play to the historical genealogy of the Greek, medieval, and modern formulations of the doctrine of categories that he had
hinted at in the introduction. The latter had tentatively suggested that the epochal formulations are at bottom conceptual expressions of the historical
worldviews belonging to the philosophizing personalities in question. Each
formulation was a historical and "personal position-taking." The history of
philosophy is thus able to appear in terms of the "underlying value-judgments
of the philosophers." Here Heidegger appealed to Nietzsche's concept of the
will to power, of the personal drive that philosophizes, and to Nietzsche's idea

that "what is most [philosophy's] own is to claim validity and function as a value for life." Heidegger's conclusion took up these suggestions into his principle of the "immanence" of sense in translogical worldviews, stating unequivocally that this principle was operative in the three epochal formulations of the categories and that a genealogy needed to be carried out for each of them (G1 407–408/PC 382–83; G1 195–96).

The principle of analogicity permeating the Scholastic doctrine of categories seems to be a mere "schoolroom concept." But not so. It is the view that "being" is neither a univocal nor an equivocal term, but rather is differentiated analogically into levels stretching from the highest supersensible reality (namely, God to whom "being" is properly attributed) to the lowest sensible reality (to which "being" is attributed by virtue of God's emanation into it and thus its participation in divine reality). Heidegger claimed that this doctrine of the analogy of attribution is the philosophical articulation of the prephilosophical theocentric worldview of the Middle Ages ("spiritualism"), which lives within a tension in the God/believer relation between, on the one hand, the community of all things in God who is being and, on the other, the difference between creator and creation as well as the sheer multiplicity of the created world. In its personal, loving, and faith-grounded relation to God, medieval Dasein lives the categorial sense of being as identity-in-difference and difference-in-identity. Aristotle's notion of the analogical unity of "being" that is "said [attributed] in many ways" was cut to measure for giving philosophical expression to this tension in medieval life. The analogical doctrine of categories "contains the conceptual expression of the qualitatively fulfilled, value-laden, and transcendently related world of lived experience belonging to medieval humanity; it is the conceptual expression of the specific form of inward Dasein anchored in the transcendent and primal relation of the soul to God." The "natural environing world [*Umwelt*] (and for medieval humanity simultaneously also the supersensible world of which it is just as constantly and penetratingly conscious) is already categorially determined"—and then subsequently ex-pressed in the analogical doctrine of categories in Scholastic philosophy (G1 408–409/PC 383; G1 255).

Since the experiential world of medieval Dasein reaches its highest pitch in mysticism, Heidegger stated that, if one wants "to penetrate into the living life of medieval Scholasticism," then a "thorough philosophical—more precisely a phenomenological—elaboration of the mystical, moral-theological, and ascetic literature of medieval Scholasticism" is "especially urgent." The Scholastic doctrine of categories is not an abstract, lifeless, and powerless rationalism, but rather the conceptual expression of the "life-will" of medieval mysticism, which for its part is not "irrational lived-experience" but rather experience laden with sense and value. "Scholasticism and mysticism belong essentially together for the medieval worldview. The pairs of contrasts—rationalism/irrationalism and Scholasticism/mysticism—do not coincide. And where such an equation is attempted, it rests on an extreme rationalization of philosophy. As a rationalistic construction detached from life, philosophy is powerless." Scholasticism without mysticism is empty; mysticism without Scholasticism is blind. But given its connection with lived experience, Scholasticism "decisively enlivened and intensified a cultural age," becoming a "driving force and enduring power . . . for the whole attitude of life belonging to medieval humanity." In Heidegger's Nietzschean language, Scholasticism was philosophical will to power that was empowered by and in turn empowered the "eternal yea-saying" to *unio mystica* (G1 205–206, 193; G1 410, 406/PC 382–83).

Heidegger claimed further that Aristotle's doctrine of categories was the philosophical expression of the "naturalism" of the Greek worldview, which was absorbed in the sensible environing world of natural reality. These categories "appear as a specific class of a specific region and not as *the* categories *as such*," which also include those of supersensible being, psychic life, and logical being. The stereotypical opinion about Scholasticism's " 'slavish' relation to Aristotle" is unfounded, since Aristotle's categories of natural being "were uniquely fitted into the whole of the metaphysical world-picture" of medieval philosophy. "For the medieval human being, reality as reality, as the real environing world . . . appears as dependent on and evaluated according to transcendent principles"; that is, it is fitted into the analogical ordering of the relationship between God and the created world. Medieval spiritualism was theocentric and Greek naturalism cosmocentric (G1 263, 211, 287, 194, 199).

Modernity, on the other hand, is anthropocentric. For medieval and Greek humanity, "the stream of one's own life . . . lies for the most part submerged, it is not recognized as such." Medieval thought is characterized by an "absolute devotion and temperamental immersion in the traditional material of knowing. . . . the value of the *Sache* (object) dominates over the value of the I (subject). . . . the individuality of the individual thinker goes under as it were into the fullness of the material" and ultimately into the mystical depths of the *Deus absconditus*. Given that its spiritual life is so "noematically oriented," so "tied down to transcendence" in the "onesided direction of its gaze," the medieval worldview "renders impossible the 'phenomenological reduction' " of noematic sense back to the intentional noetic life of the subject, to its "dynamic-flowing reality." But modernity is oriented precisely to subjectivity; it is the worldview of self-consciousness and self-assertiveness. Apparently following Hegel's reading of the modern subjective turn in the Cartesian philosophy of the *cogito*, in the Lutheran religiosity of "the heart," in Romantic aesthetics of feeling, and in the rationalist ethical-political thought of the Enlightenment and the French Revolution, Heidegger maintained that modernity attempts to absolve itself from its former dependence on the environing world and from its "anchor" in the mystical depth dimension of God. Using Hegel's language, Heidegger wrote that modernity is *bei sich selbst*, at home with itself. The God-consciousness of the Middles Ages lacks the essential character of modernity, namely, "liberation of the subject from being tied down to its surroundings, securing oneself in one's own life. . . . it sees itself placed into a metaphysical tension; transcendence holds it back from a purely human attitude over and against the whole of reality." In its self-conciousness, the will to power of modernity attempts to relate itself to itself as its own ground, certainty, and security, which is to be unfolded through its self-development. And the "consciousness of methods" that makes up the "basic character of modern science is only a reflection of modern culture in general, which has asserted itself through the self-consciousness of its self-development as something new" (GI 198–205; GI 409/PC 384).

Method is the modern form of the will to power of philosophy. It is a "strongly developed drive of questioning and courage of questioning, the constant control of all steps of thinking." What Heidegger had in mind here is also Kant's account of the Copernican revolution and transcendental tribunal of reason beginning with Galileo and Descartes, in which knowing no longer begins with being, but rather performs a "certain intellectual shift back" onto itself in order "to master" the initial formulation of problems in terms of concepts, hypotheses, and methods that are subsequently applied to the search for solutions in the actual investigation of reality. In "reflecting on the way to be taken," it is "constantly sharpening the knife," often even to the point of finally having "nothing to cut." Modern thought is neither cosmological nor theological, but epistemo-logical, an account of the categories and methods of knowing itself that make possible any knowing of objects. In philosophy, methodical consciousness culminates in transcendental philosophy, where the old notion of independent "being is reworked into a concept of transcendental logic." In natural science, it takes the form of "the will of philosophy to power in the sense of the intellectual forces of the so-called 'natural-scientific worldview.'" The "basic tendency of physics" is no longer to begin with "observation" of "appearances surfacing in immediate reality," as ancient and medieval philosophy of nature did in order to arrive at essences by way of induction and further to speculate about their "hidden causes." Rather, modern physics's hypothetical mathematization of the world, in which only the quantifiable "primary" qualities of objects are considered, leaves behind the spirit of traditional physics as *sozein ta phainomena*, saving the phenomena. "The intuitive-sensible qualities of the defined phenomenon are extinguished and completely elevated into the mathematical." Modern physics begins with the projection of mathematically formulated hypotheses, in terms of which "laws are arrived at in purely deductive manner and then subsequently confirmed experimentally."

Thus "Galileo's science signifies something basically new in terms of method. It seeks to become master over the multiplicity of appearances through laws; and *how* it arrives at laws—this is its peculiarly new achievement." The will to power of modern mathematical physics seeks to make us "masters and possessors of nature" (Descartes) (G1 415–23/CT 3–6; G1 198–200).

The will to power of method in the philosophical and scientific categories of being is empowered by and empowers the self-assertiveness of the modern worldview. Does Heidegger here anticipate his later theme of the modern epoch of being as that of technology and will to power? One thing that is certain is that he has come a long way from the purely logical concerns of his doctoral dissertation by displacing categorial sense into the depth dimension of the factical worlds of historical epochs. The "sense of being" has been displaced from the copula of the judgment and its content into the factuality (*Tatsächlichkeit*) of value and significance (*Bedeutsamkeit*). The Dasein of logical sense has become the Dasein of the "world of lived experience." The logical *verum transcendens* has become a "breakthrough into true reality and real truth." The "logical place" of sense has become historical "context," a historical "cosmos of categories," the "placing of the question" of being in worldviews, the "here" of sense for historical Dasein (G1 213; G1 408, 401/PC 383, 379).

Heidegger's principle of the immanence of categorial sense also anticipates his notion of philosophy as a hermeneutics of facticity with its double genitive. The objective genitive, in which "of" signifies "taking as its object," means that the Greek, Scholastic, and modern philosophy draw their categories out of the factuality of the worldview of the times. The "context *out of* which" the categories "are interpreteted," read off (*abgelesen*), and lifted out (*aufgehoben*) is a translogical one. "Out of the depths and fullness of personality, philosophy draws its content." It is and should be a "listening in on," a "living into," an "empathetic understanding" of "the immediate life of subjectivity and its immanent contexts of sense." A hermeneutics of facticity in which the "of" signifies "belongs to" (subjective genitive) means that each of the doctrines of categories was at bottom also an "intensifying" and "enlivening" of the interpretative expression of the living spirit of the times itself. Heidegger's use of such terms as objectification, empathy, understanding, "forms of life," and *Aufheben* suggests that the first source of his hermeneutics of facticity is the theory of concept-formation in Hegel and Dilthey. A doctrine of categories is the times expressed in thoughts, a "form of life" lifted up into the " 'gray on gray' " of the "abstract world" of concepts. The owl of hermeneutics spreads its wings in the falling dusk of factical life. The *Ur-sprung*, the original place from which philosophy leaps into work, is worldview. *Hic mundus, hic saltus*. Here is worldview, dance here. Immanent categorial sense is the rose in the cross of factical life that "drives the most effect thorn into the spirit" of philosophy (G1 195, 203; G1 401–11/PC 379–84; G1 426/CT 8).

Worldview

Heidegger's repetition of the problem of the categories focuses on three "potencies" and "requirements" that need to be satisfied if this problem is to shake off its traditional "impoverished" and "deathlike emptiness," its "gray on gray," and to enrich itself with the fullness of "life's golden tree." Though these possibilities "condition each other," the first involves a reinscription primarily of the content-sense (categorial sense) of the problem of the categories, so that it contains right within itself a principial reference to worldviews. In the first place, this means "the descriptive demarcating of the different regions of objects into realms that are categorially irreducible to each other," as well as gathering these categorial realms together within the ultimate sphere of the transcendental categories. This possibility was already seized upon in the body of Heidegger's work, where he applied the transcendentals to the different realms of reality (the physical, the psychical, the divine, the logical), but "here a strictly *conceptual* and in a certain sense onesided presentation was demanded with conscious suspension of the more deeply penetrating metaphysical connections of the problem." The body of the work had not sufficiently stressed that the transcendentals and the different regional categories are to be located in and read off from the ways in which they are immanently given in worldviews to prephilosophical life (G1 399–401, 408/PC 378–79, 383; G1 203).

But these metaphysical aspects of the problem are clarified "only when a second basic task of each and every doctrine of categories is recognized," namely, "the insertion of the problem of the categories into the problem of the judgment and of the subject." Heidegger noted here that the medieval grammar he had dealt with in the body of his work exhibits a "refined disposition for listening in on the immediate life of subjectivity and its immanent contexts of sense," since it relates the *modus intelligendi* to the *modi significandi* and *essendi* of "everyday prescientific speech" and " 'prescientific' knowing." Acknowledging the relationship of (1) noematic categorial sense to noetic acts, (2) the act-level of knowing to that of living discourse in pretheoretical life, and (3) these act-levels to the act-level of showing material being "leads to the principle of the material determinateness of all forms." Heidegger had already introduced this principle in the body of his work, but now took it more seriously and expanded upon it. By "material" Heidegger meant the *modus essendi*, which is "immediately given empirical reality," "that-which-stands-over-against consciousness in an absolute sense, 'handfast' reality that forces itself unresisted upon consciousness and can never be pushed aside." The principle of material determinateness means, in the first place, that forms (categories) are *always already* meshed with the matter of being, that is, fulfilled and made determinate by it in pretheoretical acts of showing, knowing, and speaking/writing. Form is not first given by itself in theoretical knowing and then subsequently applied to an "irrational" and "blind factuality" of being. Concrete being has already had form applied to it and been made determinate through categories. Factuality is already meaningful, meaning is already factual. Matter determines (interpretively fulfills) form, form determines (interpretively intends) matter. There is a reciprocity of determination at work here that cannot be broken asunder into two elements that are accidentally pieced together. It is precisely this material determinateness of categorial form that Heidegger found operative in the naturalistic, mystical-theocentric, and self-assertive worldviews of the Greeks, the Middle Ages, and modernity. For medieval humanity, for example, "the natural environing world and the supersensible world . . . are *already* categorially determined" (emphasis added) (G1 401–402, 406/PC 379–80, 382; G1 306, 318, 255).

The principle of the reciprocal determination of matter and form is also called the "transcendental-ontic composition of the concept of the object." The transcendental "being" (objectness) and all other categorial conditions of the possiblity of objects are always already ontically fulfilled, interpreted, determinate. As Heidegger would later say, being is always the being of beings; the ontological is to be found nowhere else than in the ontic, and the ontic is already ontological. In reference to his earlier problem of the *methexis* of ideal sense and spatiotemporal reality and, more particularly, of how valid sense can function as a binding norm for judgments, Heidegger wrote that, once the transcendental-ontic nature of the object is taken into account, "then the problem of 'application' of the categories loses its meaning." His new solution was not to try to explain genetically how ideal sense comes to be intertwined and imbedded in real being, but rather to step beyond the presuppositions of this pseudo-problem by simply acknowledging "the strange fact," never to be "completely illuminated," that the ideal is *always already* in the real, a predicament that SZ will call the "enigma" of "facticity" and "thrownness." The transcendental-ontic nature of the object can also be called "the principle of immanence," that is, categorial form is immanently determinate in the ontic matter of the worldviews of living spirit. The "immediate life of subjectivity" lives in "contexts of sense that are immanent to it" and whose validity it has always already affirmed pretheoretically. "Only in the orientation to the concept of living spirit and its 'eternal affirmations' (Fr. Schlegel)," Heidegger wrote, "will epistemological logic remain protected from an exclusive limitation to the study of structures and make logical sense into a problem also in accord with its ontic significance" (G1 406–407, 401/PC 382, 379; G1 30).

Before categorial sense is expressed in a philosophical doctrine of categories, it already functions teleologically as ethical, aesthetic, and religious *value* that is affirmed and actualized in historical worldviews. "The valuative already lives in a primally authentic manner in" the teleological consciousness of living spirit. Here Heidegger reintroduced being under the convertible aspect of the transcendental *bonum* that had been left out of consideration in the body of his work. As Nietzsche had said about philosophy, "what is most its own is to claim a validity and function as a value for life." The validity of sense that philosophy deals with is originally affirmed not logically, but rather in terms of this value for life. Here validity means the concrete ideality of valuative sense *in* a historical worldview, validity or truth *for* the things of this world, and valuative bindingness *on* the living spirit inhabiting it. "Whether validity means a unique form of 'being' or an 'ought'," Heidegger wrote, "or neither of these, but rather is to be grasped only through deeper lying groups of problems contained in the concept of living spirit and doubtlessly closely connected with the problem of value can not be decided here." Before we know the validity of the truth of categorial sense, we live it as value. Here Heidegger promised a future "investigation of being, value, and negation," but did not get around to it until his 1919 courses where he traced the Neo-Kantian impersonal *es gilt*, it validates, back to the more original *es wertet*, it values, and ultimately to *es weltet*, it worlds (G1 405–407/PC 381–82).

Heidegger's 1916 essay on the concept of time in historical science already makes the move from logical sense to practical "ontic significance" (*Bedeutung*). Past and present things and events (*Ereignisse*) have "qualitative" significance for the "interest" of the historian and are singled out because of their "relation to values," of which they are unique "actualizations" and "objectifications." The quantitative numerical determinations that historical chronology works with, such as dates, spans of time, numbers of people, are only "convenient numerical markers" for the qualitatively significant *Ereignisse* of history. "Considered in themselves they have no sense." To make this same point later in SZ, Heidegger actually referred back to his essay on historical time (SZ 553/471). Regarding "the famine in Fulda in the year 750," the "number 750 and every other historical date has sense and value only with reference to the historical significance of the content." The other example Heidegger used is partly motivated by the fact that he was writing during World War I. He noted that "later military history will certainly be interested in *how long* the Mackensen army took to carry the offensive forward from the Carpathian mountains to the Russian-Polish fortress." But "the *quantitative* determination—approximately 12 weeks—has value and significance for the historian not *in itself*, but rather only insofar as from this the tremendous combat strength of our allied troops and the success of the whole operation can be understood." Likewise, the beginning of numerical calendars shows that "they always start at a historically significant *Ereignis* (founding of the city of Rome, birth of Christ, Hedschra)." Regarding more particularly the beginning of the calendrical year, Heidegger pointed out that Christians were originally displeased that it was set on the first of January, " 'since it had no relation what-soever to the Christian religion.' Thus the Church moved the celebration of the Circumcision to this day in order to give it a religious *significance.* It was always significant celebrations—Easter, Christmas—at which the beginning of the year was set" (G1 406/PC 382; G1 426-33/CT 7-10).

The principle of material determinateness is what Heidegger meant by the breakthrough into *die wahre Wirklichkeit und wirkliche Wahrheit,* which needs to be translated here as "the true actuality and the actual truth." Here the double sense of truth as validity-for, namely, transcendental truth and truth as agreement, means first that true categorial form has always already actualized itself interpretively in matter by determining it as-something and thus rendering it into a true actuality; and second that matter has always already interpretively actualized and determined true categorial form, thus making it actual truth. The concepts of truth and of material determinateness also express "the essential interconnection of the object of knowledge and the knowledge of the object," since knowledge is always knowledge of the object (matter) through forms. Without the material determinateness of categorial forms in pretheoretical life, their truth and our knowledge of them would take on an unreal character. Only through the principle of material determinateness "will a satisfying answer be possible as to how *'unwirklich'* ['unreal'/'nonactual'] 'transcendent' sense guarantees true *Wirklichkeit* [reality/actuality] and objectivity" (G1 402, 406/PC 380, 382).

As Husserl explained in his Sixth Investigation, truth is an experienced noematic identification or "harmonizing" between the object given in an unfulfilled meaning-intention and the object as it gives itself in an immediately fulfilling intuition. But life is textured with a whole domain of already enacted and experienced identifications, that is, with truth, in which we habitually move without thematically apprehending this truth itself. This seems to be what Heidegger meant by the "real truth" that living spirit experiences in its immanent translogical contexts of sense, which include the categorial realms of the physical environing world (*Umwelt*) in which "we move about daily"; "personality"; and the divine. Likewise, the transcendental categories of being, one, true, and good are already operative in " 'prescientific' knowing" and make up what Heidegger will later call our preontological understanding of being. As Scotus put it, *primum objectum intellectus est ens.* For without this immanent categorial understanding, "I would live blindly in absolute darkness" (G1 38, 213-14, 224; for *Umwelt,* see 199, 213, 255).

We live in the truth before we know it. "Validity," Heidegger wrote, "is the sphere in which I, as a subject here and now, must live in order to know both the what and the that of something." Here he made the breakthrough from reflective logical sense and category to inconspicuous "context" and "world" in which we are thrown and prereflectively absorbed. He indicated that he was led to this breakthrough via the work of Lask, which was influenced by Husserl's Sixth Investigation and later, around 1913–15, apparently by American pragmatism. Heidegger wrote that Lask's "philosophical creativity" is "unusually rich in fertile perspectives." Reminiscing in 1919, he confessed that to Lask "I personally owe very much. . . . He was one of the strongest philosophical personalities of the times, a profound man." "In the ought and in value Lask discovered as ultimate lived experience *the* world that is just as much not-material [*nicht-sachlich*] and non-sensuously metaphysical as not immaterial and extravagantly speculative, but rather factual. . . . categories [appear] as value and form in Lask." Kisiel writes that for Lask the original realm of sense "contains a precognitive lived element, such that it is simply 'lived through' and not itself known. I live in the category as in a context such that I simply experience its illumination; I thus 'live in its truth.' " In his study on "Living and Knowing," Lask proceeded "in a decidedly 'mystical' vein with his descriptions and examples. . . . our first experience of the categories is such that we are 'lost' in them in 'pure absorption,' for example in aesthetic, ethical or religious 'dedication' (*Hingabe*) in which we find ourselves simply 'given over' to the given form, meaning, value" (G1 166, 191; G1 407/ PC 382; G56/57 180, 122; WSH).

Heidegger picked up on this analogy between experience in general and the way that medieval life and especially mysticism are characterized by an "absolute devotion [*Hingabe*] and temperamental immersion" in the noematic material of knowing and ultimately in the mysterious depths of the *Deus absconditus*. And Heidegger did so because, following Eckhart and others, he was attempting to ground the ontological question of the categories of being in the "genuine optic" of "metaphysics," which here means mystical theology. It is important to get a sense for the term *Hingabe* since it will turn up again in Heidegger's 1919 courses. It means not only "devotion," but more particularly "abandonment," "surrender," "giving [oneself] away to" something. *Sich Gott hingeben* means "to surrender oneself to God"; *er gab sich ihr hin* means "he surrendered himself to her"; *mit Hingabe singen* means "to sing with abandon." Thus Heidegger wrote that, in the "primal relation of the soul to God," the self "goes under" and is "submerged" in its world. "This moodful self-surrendering [*Sichausliefern*] to the material holds the subject spellbound as it were." This *Hingabe* carries the mystical overtones of Meister Eckhart's *Gelassenheit*, abandonment, releasement, letting-be. The "in" of Eckhart's notion of living "in God," "in the light of God" ("in him we live and move and have our being") has a sense of precognitive immersion similar to Heidegger's notion of "the sphere of validity *in* which I must live" and to his later concept of "being-in" the world (emphasis added). Hence he insisted that reading the categories off of worldviews has to take the form of an immersive "living-into," "listening-in," and "openness of empathetic understanding" (the German *Aufgeschlossenheit* has the ring of Eckhart's *Gelassenheit*). His use of such terms as "temperamental," "moodful," "active love," "inward Dasein," "worshipful God-intimacy" suggests a strong emotional element in this precognitive absorption in the world. If we also factor in here the *modus signifi-candi* of "living discourse" as found, for example, in "mystical, moral-theological, and ascetic literature," then we already have an early version of Heidegger's later account of the three basic existentials of being-in-the-world, namely, mood, understanding, and discourse (G1 198–200, 406; ME 209, 304; G1 408–10/PC 383–84).

Heidegger stated that "I hope to be able to show on another occasion how Eckhartian mysticism first receives a thorough philosophical clarification and appraisal from out of [the principle of the material determinateness of form and its inclusion of the subject-object correlation] in connection with the metaphysics of the problem of truth." What Heidegger seems to have had in mind here is Eckhart's novel presentation of the medieval theory of the transcendental truth of being, that is, of the convertability of being with truth in the sense that all beings (matter) are true, intelligible, illuminated since they conform to and participate in the luminous ideas (form) in the mind of God. On this cosmic level, the principle of the material determinateness of form means that, while the ideas of the divine intellect determine the world and make it intelligible, the temporal world of creation for its part differentiates the unity of these ideas into a multiplicity of analogical manifestations. "Creatures are created after the idea and likeness of something in God," writes Eckhart. "Every being and every single thing has all its being, and all its unity, truth and goodness immediately from God." As if in a mirror, created things are lit up, are in the light ("in God," as Eckhart says) since they are made intelligible by participating in the light of the divine intellect. Thus, according to Eckhart, we must learn to find God "in" all things, even in the midst of the most commonplace situations. "What is an object stands in clarity. . . . [I]t [is] graspable, knowable, understandable," echoed Heidegger in the context of modern displacement of form from the divine into the human-transcendental intellect (G1 402/PC 380; ME 283, 278; G1 224).

Heidegger's claim that the principle of the material determinateness of form (transcendental truth) also includes the truth of the subject-object relation can also be found in the theory of truth in Eckhartian mysticism. As Caputo has argued, Heidegger's study of Eckhart probably also planned to show this. Spoken in the language of Neo-Kantianism, the point is that, since knowledge is always knowledge of matter through forms, the material determinateness of form also means the material determinateness of knowledge. Knowledge is the site and vehicle of the form-matter relation. In Eckhartian mysticism, this point is expressed by saying that God the Father constantly emanates and gives birth to the Son (the Logos, the Word) in the human soul. "Man is created after the image and likeness of the entire substance of God." "God falls into the intellect as truth, into the will as goodness." "The soul is intellectual after the image and species of God." That is, the human soul is a microcosmic *imago* and agent of the transcendental truth of the macrocosmic form-matter relation in God's reality. "The soul is composite of everything," writes Eckhart, paraphrasing Aristotle's statement in the *De anima* that "the soul is in a way all beings." Here Eckhart, and indirectly Heidegger, seems to be drawing on the medieval Neo-Platonic rendition of Aristotle's active or agent intellect (*nous poietikos*), which is seen as an inborn *lumen naturale* capable of illuminating objects and making them knowable because it is constantly illuminated by the light of the divine intellect, the Logos (PMG 115–17; ME 283–85, 140, 303–304; cf. TME Chaps. 3, 5).

Personality

Heidegger's second requirement for revitalizing the doctrine of categories is "the insertion of the problem of the categories into the problem of judgment and of the subject," which in effect calls for rethinking the relational sense of the subject that intends categorial sense. The requirement means first that the categories are inseparable from the human subject: "Category means the most general form of the determination of the object. Object and objectivity have sense as such only *for* a subject." In the second place, Heidegger here called for a breakthrough to the translogical depth-dimension of the subject as "living spirit" that lives "in" historical worldviews. "Within the richness of the directions of the formation of living spirit," he wrote, "the theoretical attitude is only *one* such direction." "The epistemological subject does not clarify the metaphysically most significant sense of spirit. . . . only by being placed into this sense of spirit will the problem of the categories receive its authentic depth-dimension and enrichment." Living spirit is "real life," "the immediate life of the subject," the "depth and fullness of life," "living life," "living knowing and speaking," "prescientific knowing," "everyday prescientific speech." Drawing on the *Lebensphilosophie* of especially Dilthey and Nietzsche, Heidegger also described living spirit as "historical personality," "living personality," "the personal life of the individual," "the stream of one's own life," "personal lived experience," "inward Dasein," which, as we shall see, is essentially defined by the "individual-being" of haecceity. But living spirit is also the communal being of "associations and organizations (state)" (G1 401–409/PC 379–383; G1 264, 191–99; G1 426/CT 8).

Heidegger's second requirement has more specifically to do with "the individual act-strata (*modus significandi, intelligendi, essendi*) . . . and their relation with each other." Here again he took as his model "the listening-in on the immediate life of subjectivity" that is found in medieval Scholasticism; in "mystical, moral-theological, and ascetic literature"; and specifically in Eckhart's mysticism. As we saw above, the first model for Heidegger's notion of a prereflective "being-in" the world with its existentials of mood, understanding, and discourse was the noematically oriented intentionality of "absolute devotion and temperamental immersion" in God. The doctrine of meaning found in medieval grammar, as well as religious literature, shows how understanding (*modus intelligendi*) is related to the emotionally absorbed, prescientific encounter with "immediately given empirical reality" (*modus essendi*) in living discourse (*modus significandi*). Here understanding takes the form not of a theoretical judging, but of a practical teleological understanding that is oriented to categorial sense in the form of value and whose ultimate end is God. Thus Heidegger called for a "teleological interpretation of consciousness." In Aristotelian terms, this means that practical understanding is desiderative understanding and understanding desire. As Heidegger would later put this, understanding is a mode of "care," of practical interest; but back in 1915–16 he made this point by saying, in a curious fusion of Eckhart and Nietzsche, that understanding is not pure observation and judgment, but rather is permeated by "devotion," "love," "life-will," "drive," and "will to power" that are immersed in categorial sense in the form of teleological values (G1 401–10, 406/PC 379–84).

The Difference that History Makes

Heidegger's third requirement for the problem of the categories involves rethinking the temporalizing sense of the spirit/worldview relation by displacing it from the realm of atemporal validity into the translogical depth-dimension of history. "History and its cultural-philosophical and teleological interpretation must become a meaning-determining element for the problem of the categories, if one wants to consider working out the *cosmos* of categories so as to get beyond an impoverished, schematic table of categories." Categorial sense has to be seen as historical *telos*, value, cosmos, worldview. The material determinateness of form, the transcendental-ontic concept of the object, the principle of immanence, the notion of true actuality and actual truth all mean that categorial sense (form) contains right within itself a reference to its historical fulfillment in the matter of the *modus essendi*. As Heidegger had already written in the body of his work, "form is a correlative concept; form is the form of a material, all material stands in form. Moreover, the material stands always *in einer ihm angemessenen Form*, in a form befitting it, measured to it; put differently, form receives its meaning [*Bedeutung*] from the material." As validity-for (*Hingeltung auf*), a view-toward (*Hinsicht*), categorial form is the noematic expression of intentionality, that is, the directedness of an unfulfilled intention toward its fulfillment in matter. "Forms are nothing other than the *objective* expression of the different ways in which conscious-ness is *intentionally* related to the objective." "The homogeneity of the logical realm of validity lies in intentionality, the character of validity-for. . . . Inten-tionality is the 'regional category' of the logical realm" (G1 408/PC 383; G1 251, 223, 319, 283).

Correlatively, "living spirit is as such essentially historical spirit in the wid-est sense of the word." It is more specifically a historically teleological con-sciousness: "For the theory of truth, [the metaphysical optic of philosophy] signifies the task of an ultimate metaphysical-teleological interpretation of con-sciousness. In it, the valuative already lives in a primordially genuine manner, insofar as it is meaningful living action that actualizes [*verwirklicht*] sense." This historical actualizing of the intentional spirit/worldview relation is what Heidegger also called its here-and-now enactment (*aktueller Vollzug*), fulfill-ment, and performance (*Leistung*) especially through the *modi significandi* and *essendi*. Thus he wrote that history is "the objectification of spirit [i.e., of value] enacting itself in the course of time" and that "spirit is to be grasped only when the whole abundance of its performances, i.e., its history, is lifted up into it" (G1 406–408/PC 381–82; G1 319; G1 426/CT 7). The "problem of truth" requires a teleological interpretation of consciousness and categorial sense because, as we have seen, truth is precisely "actual truth" (historical ful-fillment of form) and "true actuality" (historical determination of matter through form).

The enactment of the intentional relation is precisely the ongoing historical enactment of this truth. Taking up Dilthey's terminology, Heidegger main-tained that truth has always already somehow been achieved, the *telos* of cate-gorial sense already actualized in the historical *Wirkungs- und Entwicklungs-zusammenhang*, the effective and developing context, in which spirit lives at any time. The latter is always caught up in a web of already achieved fulfill-ments, enactments, or objectifications. But all this is developmental. The norms or values that *have been* actualized are still in need of further fulfillment, are *not yet* exhaustively realized, and thus have to be repeated and actualized again in here-and-now fulfillment. This is seen, for example, in the fact that the his-torian's "selection of the historical out of the abundance of what is given is based on a relation to value," on a valuative "interest" that the futurally ori-ented present has in the past. "The past has sense always only when seen from the present." And a past event is seen more particularly as only one realization of the value or values involved. The historical time of human spirit—including individuals, groups, institutions, and other cultural realities—is thus a circular flow through past, future, and present, a position that Heidegger had already anticipated in the introduction to his qualifying dissertation when he said that the history of philosophy is really a continual evolution, drawing-out, and re-inscription of past philosophical beginnings. "In its abundance and variety of forms," we read in Heidegger's essay on history, "this creation of culture runs its course temporally, undergoes development, is subject to the most diverse transformations and reformations, takes up the past in order to work it over further or to combat it. This creation of culture . . . is at bottom the objectification of human spirit" (G1 426-27/CT 7-8).

The enactment-sense of this historical teleology is quite different from that of judgment, which, as we have seen, consists in a making-present and instantiation of sense that remains essentially unaffected by the concrete historical situation in which the act of judgment runs its course. But Heidegger's more insistent reaffirmation of the principle of the material determinateness of form in the conclusion to his work on Scotus suggests that forms are actually *interpretively* determined by the matter of the *modus essendi*. In being applied to material particularity, form has always already fit itself interpretively to matter. Heidegger suggested that, in the hermeneutical "as" of intentionality (truth), there is an essential reciprocity of interpretation between form and matter, sense and being, universal and particular, meaning-intention and intuition, persistence and situation. He attempted to step outside of his previous Neo-Kantian staging of the ancient battle of the giants, that is, outside of his compartmentalized doublets of valid logical sense and naked spatial realities, reason and dumb psychic processes, atemporality and time, as well as the corresponding doublet of pure logic and historicism.

Meaning is historical, history is meaningful. The so-called "facts" of history are nothing but abstractions from the values of which they are fulfillments, and these values are themselves found only in such facts. Likewise, "one has not in the least understood [the historical activity of spirit] if it is neutralized into the concept of a biologically blind factuality." "Historical science has human being for a theme not as a biological object, but rather insofar as the idea of culture is actualized through its spiritual-bodily achievements" (G1 402, 406/PC 379, 382; G1 426/CT 7). Hence medieval mysticism is already "Scholastic" (not irrational experience), and Scholasticism already mystical (not rationalism). The point is to explode the very presuppositions of the question of *methexis*, of "application," of "bridging" heterogeneous realms because the historically teleological form-matter relation of intentionality is itself already the hermeneutical bridge and *methexis*, which then gets broken asunder by idealists and realists, psycho-biologists and logicians, Heracliteans and Parmenideans.

The most radical expression of this interpretive interplay of form and matter is Heidegger's specification of the principle of material determinateness of form as that of the "form-differentiating" or "meaning-differentiating function of material," which his supplementary conclusion takes up from the body of his work and radicalizes into "value-differentiating" and history as "the meaning-determining element for the problem of the categories" (G1 314; G1

405, 408–409/PC 381, 383). The matter of the *modus essendi* has always already effected and continues to effect an interpretive, analogical, and historical differentiation (*Differenzierung*) of form. And it can do this because it is *Differenz*, alterity, heterogeneity in the twofold sense of the "heterothesis" of being in general and the haecceity of *ens reale*. Let us examine these two senses of difference, beginning with heterothesis.

On its own, being—the "something in any sense"—is indifference, the undifferentiated, the indeterminate determinate, continuum. "*Aliquid indifferens concipimus*: we latch onto something lying in advance of every determinate categorial forming." This primal element (*Urelement*) is "the first moment of clarity," the pure "over-against," "before us," there is/it is given (*es gibt*). The something is an obscure "twilight" element spread out over the "blindness" of "absolute darkness," over the "nothing," and intimated in those indeterminate experiences of not knowing in the least what is "before us," as Heidegger suggests, but also perhaps in falling asleep, moods, the moment of death, or the mystic's breakthrough to the divine abyss where all "names" fail. Being is the "persevering moment" that "remains preserved in every *object*, however it may be differentiated in its fullness of content" (G1 214–15, 223–24).

But by itself the *ens* is not enough to give one an experience of an object; it gives only a pure light in which all cows are white. One also needs the other "constitutive elements for an object in any sense," namely, the convertible transcendental properties of *unum, verum, bonum*. "Every *ens* is an *unum*." Here Heidegger made a very interesting point, namely, that *unum* is "convertible" and "equiprimoridal" with *alter, das Andere*, the other; the *idem* (same) with the *diversum* (different). In the sentence "something is a something," the something is related to itself as this same something precisely through its relation to the other that it is not. " 'Something is what it is only in its limit,' says Hegel." The above sentence thus says at bottom that "something is *a* something—not its other," for which it itself is in turn the other. "It is a something and, in being-something, it is *Nicht-das-Andere-Sein*, being-not-the-other. . . . The one and the other are given in an equally immediate way with the object in any sense . . . the one *and* the other, 'heterothesis,' is the true origin of thinking as seizing hold of the object." *Definitio fit per genus proximum et differentiam specificam.*

Being-an-object is a primal *Sachverhalt*, a relational comportment, namely, the *Bewandtnis* (involvement) "that it is identical with itself and different from an other"—a *Be-wandtnis* that bears the same and the different apart and toward each other face to face. Being always looks the other way, diverted, deviant, otherwise, improper, alien. The hetero-thesis right within being itself is the simultaneous giving of the *hen* (one) and the *heteron* (other), a primal splitting that is the first tear in the sock of being, the first wound in the innocent heart of the something, the first wrinkle in the primal element of the *es gibt*.

This giving "adds no positive content to the concept of the object," but rather is a pure "negation." The *unum* "means in itself a *privation* insofar as an object is precisely *not* the *other*."

The full determinateness of the *modus essendi* (*es gibt*) is thus I-intentionally-give (active mode) and there-is-given (passive mode) being "as" a different being—and also "as" a true (interpreted) and good (desirable) being. This is the minimal determination needed for even the most naked and indefinite object to be given, whatever it happens to turn out to be—a thing, a mood, a concept, a god. " 'There is given [*es gibt*] no object if there is not given [*es gibt nicht*] the one and the other' [Rickert]." Thus Heidegger surprisingly maintained that alterity, difference, is a transcendental that is convertible with being. "The one and the other are transcendentals, primal determinations of the object and as such convertible with the object" (G1 217-24, 229-31, 381). Being is said in many different ways. This is Heidegger's transcendental heterology of being that cuts across the categorial realms of the *ens logicum* and the *ens reale*.

However, in the realm of "real existence" with its three categorial domains of personality, environing world, and God, heterothesis takes the form of *haecceitas*, haecceity. Scotus's term is formed from the pure indexical *hic*, which can mean all of "this," "now," "here." Heidegger thus translated it as "such-now-here-ness," but also as "individual-being." Every existent being is an individual, a such-now-here. Haecceity points to the realm of factuality and thus to "alogical material" that cannot be grasped through a species-concept. "As individual it always contains a more, and regarding this the species-concept expresses nothing. Thus it is to be said that the individual as individual cannot be completely grasped. There is always an inexpressible residue left remaining." The individual is "an irreducible ultimate." *Individuum est ineffabile.* An eidetic phenomenological reduction of the individual qua individual is impossible. Real being is "an unsurveyable multiplicity of individual objects," a "heterogeneous continuum" that cannot be overpowered, gathered up, and calculated in the grip of universal concepts. The "uniqueness and once-ness [*Einmaligkeit*]" of the individual is bound up with both its spatiality ("here") and its historicity ("now," at this time). The individual maintains itself in "its never before having-been-here and never repeatable individuality." Each this-now-here is *jeweilig*, at a particular time, for a while (G1 276, 252-55, 33, 351-52, 365; G1 427/CT 8).

Heidegger wrote that "*individuum* means: determinateness as this unique determinateness that could never be met up with at another time and somewhere else and essentially resists being analyzed still further into independent qualitative moments" and that "the form of individuality (*haecceitas*) is capable of providing a primal determinateness for real actuality." In other words, the individual is not a pure irrational, a surd, a *factum brutum*. It is understood *as* an individual precisely through the category of such-now-here-ness, through "individuality as *essence*," a *Bewandtnis*, "viewpoint," "form." The beauty of Scotus's concept of haecceity is that here the *principium individuationis* is not only—as Aristotle and Aquinas seemed to maintain—the materiality of the individual that individualizes a universal form, but rather is also something right within form, categorial sense, being itself, namely, the form of haecceity that allows material particularity to appear. Rationalists and idealists take the way of universal essence, nominalists and empiricists the way of material particularity, but Scotus takes the *via media* of haecceity that links these two realms. The "once and only once" (Rilke) of an individual person— for instance, this Socrates here and now—is due not only to the body and its interweaving in the material world (otherwise it would simply instantiate the universal "human being" or Aristotle's eternal "active intellect"). It is due also to the very being or sense of the person (the soul), whose essence thus must lie in, for example, a kind of this-Socrates-ness. "For Duns Scotus the soul is, 'as an individual, something primary that in itself, i.e., apart from the fact of its unification with the body, already consititutes a substance for itself and thus is not first individuated through embodiment' " (G1 253, 352, 318, 264, 277). The haecceity of the being of the person is what the Heidegger of the 1920s will call the "mine-ness" of Dasein.

For all domains of real being, the "such" of such-now-here-ness is not just the element of materiality, but rather also the "such" of categorial sense (being) that Heidegger calls concrete historical "significance." The such-now-here means sense-now-here. Thus heterothesis in the realm of real being takes the more determinate form of I-give and there-is-given being as a different being that is uniquely such-now-here. The transcendentals of identity and difference are specified as the "primal determinateness" of haecceity, as existential-historical individuality and alterity. "Each is an other. . . . Empirical actuality is everywhere other." As Heidegger himself suggested to Löwith, 1927, this haecceity right within the sense of being itself is what he came to call the facticity and temporal particularity or awhileness (*Jeweiligkeit*) of being (G1 254; BL 37).

Haecceity is found not only in the psychical realm of persons, but also in the natural environing world; for example, "two apples on the same tree do not have the same 'view' to the heavens, each is . . . different from the other." Haecceity even belongs to divine being, namely, to the "actuality of the absolute being of God," the persons of the trinity, and the angelic realm, though the historical aspect of individual-being applies here only to the sphere of divine emanation. In his essay on time, Heidegger extended the analysis of haecceity to the "qualitative otherness" and "uniqueness" of the objects of historical science, namely, "associations and organizations (the state)," *Ereignisse* such as "the famine in Fulda in the year 750" or "the birth of Christ," and entire "epochs," whose unique contexts make possible the authentication of historical "sources" (e.g., documents such as papal letters), as well as the interpretation of the significance of the individual "facts" made available in such sources. The naturalistic, mystical-theocentric, and self-reflective worldviews of the Greeks, the Middle Ages, and modernity are marked by "originality," such that, for example, the "intellectual milieu" out of which modern logic emerged is "a totally other than that of Scholasticism" (G1 252–53, 264; G1 426–32/CT 8–10).

Heidegger highlighted the alterity of "qualitative" historical time by contrasting it with the "quantitative" concept of time in physics, which "is not in a position to grasp empirical actuality and further the *historical* in its *individuality*." For it, time consists of a series of *homogeneous* time-points that differ only with regard to their position in a series, but historical time is defined by the *heterogeneity* in the qualitative "significance" of the different times, by the "otherness of objectifications of human life." "What is past *is* not only no longer . . . it *was* also an *other* than we and our context of life today in the present are. . . . Only where this qualitative otherness of past times comes into the consciousness of the present has the historical sense awakened." Moreover, whereas physics attempts to get at precisely "the lawfulness of the movement" of the series insofar as it can be expressed in mathematical equations, "there is no law that determines how the *times* follow one another" (G1 262; G1 427, 431/CT 8–10).

We are now in a position to understand Heidegger's principle of the meaning-differentiating function of the matter of the *modus essendi* in the supplementary conclusion of his work on Scotus. Transcendental heterothesis makes it possible that the realm of categorial sense has in the first place been differentiated into different concepts or categories; the haecceity of existence makes it possible that the latter have been differentiated into different individual and historical senses. There is thus a two-tiered movement from indifference to difference, from homogeneity to heterogeneity. All this means that, if real being is not characterized by homogeneity, identity, univocity, neither is it pure heterogeneity, difference, equivocity. Rather the full "categorial structure of the real world" is "completely ruled by analogy." The "*analogata* are found in a determinate relation of belonging-together. What stands in analogy is neither totally different, nor totally same." Real being is unity-in-multiplicity and multiplicity-in-unity. This analogical order stands somewhere between and beyond the extremes of multiplicity and unity, since it has always interwoven them. There is always "a multiplicity *in* the unity" of meaning (e.g., the different here-and-now unique senses of "apple"), and in turn there is always "a unity *in* the multiplicity" (e.g., the multiple senses are *of* "apple") (emphasis added). Heidegger wrote, "Insofar as the '*commune*' is found *differently* in the different areas, *multiplicity* also remains preserved in analogy. . . . homogeneity and heterogeneity are *interwoven* in a peculiar manner. . . . There results a peculiar unity in the multiplicity and a multiplicity in the unity" (G1 255–57). The "actual truth" to which his conclusion wants to make a breakthrough is just this unity-in-multiplicity of the analogical categorial structure of real being. Truth (unity of transcendental truth) is already actual (differentiated) truth, actuality (multiplicity) is always true (unitary) actuality.

As futural *telos* and unfulfilled intentional directedness to objects, form is repeatedly fulfilled and analogically differentiated in the haecceity of the present. Differentiating takes place through the "individualizing function" of meaning (*modus appropriati*). Whereas the "generalizing function" (*modus communis*) reads off from individual objects a universal and lets it be seen "in view of its function, of the possibility based in it of being-said of many individual objects," individualizing acts fulfill and differentiate the noematic sense with individual beings. "The singular individual object or the meaning that expresses it in the mode of singularity is *no longer* able to be intentionally related to *several* objects." This happens in a superlative manner in the *modus appropriati* of proper names, which are geared to the haecceity of persons, since "at each time they mean an individuality, and indeed this one per se. . . . [the meaning-content] belongs to this and *only* this intended individual." In addition to first and family names, which clearly "bear in themselves a *historical* moment," Heidegger also mentioned "the epithet, whose form of meaning is determined *a proprietate eventus*, i.e., by a unique and especially significant *Ereignis*, to which the one who is named at any particular time [*jeweils*] stands in a specific relationship." "It is no accident that Duns Scotus gives the example of Scipio Africanus, a *historical* personality" (G1 350–54, 364–65).

Heidegger suggested that even proper names such as the family name are analogical—a point that, as I have already suggested, can be applied to his own name. A family name ("Heidegger") is analogically differentiated into the individual members, whose first names or epithets ("young," "early," "later") indicate that through them "individuals bearing the same names are different. . . . [T]he named individuality appears to us *as* a different individuality." An epithet such as "thinker of the *Ereignis* of being" can be analogically differentiated according to how the ones who are so named (the young/early/later thinker) "stand in a specific relationship" to the historical *Ereignis* from which the epithet derives (the *Ereignis* of being) (G1 365). Presumably, a proper name such as "Heidegger" would also have to be seen as in some way analogically differentiated in all the signatures that fulfill it. The *modus appropriati* looks like it is defined just as much by a mode of impropriety. The family name "Heidegger," "Heidegger's *Sache*," has only the analogical unity of identity-in-difference, because it is defined by a fundamental heterothesis and haecceity. It is an uncontrollable plethora of differentiating thoughtpaths that flow out of, in, and back to a single *Sache*.

But all categorial sense is subject to individualizing acts of meaning that analogically differentiate. "In analogy," Heidegger wrote, "the direction of fulfillment differentiates itself insofar as it is aimed at different spheres of actuality and from here differentiates the general meaning-content." The "creation of culture" within the circular teleological movement of history is just this analogical fulfillment, which Heidegger referred to as the "objectification" and "differentiation of value" within the haecceity of individual personal life, social institutions, world-historical *Ereignisse*, and whole epochs. "The times of history differentiate themselves qualitatively. . . . [E]ach is in the structure of its content an other. The qualitative in the historical concept of time signifies nothing other than the condensation—crystallization—of an objectification of life that is given in history." The historian studies the rich abundance of individual forms and shapes of historical life as a great treasury of crystallized differentiations of value. "The goal of historical science is accordingly to present the effective and developmental context of the objectifications of human life in their uniqueness and singularity, where such uniqueness and singularity are understandable through their relation to cultural values." Living within the haecceity of our own time, we can still "understand the past since it cannot be an *incomparable* other." Rather, present and past times stand within an analogical identity-in-difference (G1 334; G1 409/PC 383; G1 431, 427/CT 8–10).

The Analogical Doctrine of Categories

Heidegger's warnings in his supplementary conclusion against a "*merely* objective-logical manner of treating the problem of categories," against "an impoverished schematic table of categories," gesture emphatically toward the impossibility of access to a univocal *Reich*/Kingdom of pure, identical, and ahistorical categorial sense in itself that has not always already been historically differentiated and woven into cultural contexts. The categories of being are neither univocal nor equivocal, but rather have a disseminated analogical unity—an identity-in-difference that is also a difference-in-identity. Heidegger offered a very apt metaphor for this. If univocity is like a single line, and equivocity like a criss-crossing of divergent lines, analogy is like the single point of light out of which many rays splinter and flow forth: "There prevails no pervasive identity, but also no complete difference—rather a peculiar interweaving of both: identity in the difference and difference in the identity. . . . with analogical expressions, the identity in the difference [is like] a bundle of rays flowing together in a single point" (G1 334–35; G1 407/PC 382). The very categories of real being are such intentional bundles. The doctrine of categories thus steps beyond the doublets of absolutism/relativism, monism/dualism, universality/particularity, and logic/historicism by taking the *via media* of analogy. The battle of giants about being is a lovers' quarrel since Parmenides (the one) is already Heraclitus (the many), and Heraclitus already Parmenides.

The categories of real being contain within themselves the transcendental category of difference (heterothesis) in the form of the pure indexicality of haecceity ("such-now-here!"). The "transcendental-ontic" nature of the object (*ens*) means that categorial form is precisely an intentionally unfulfilled noematic pointing toward the ontic matter that fulfills and analogically differentiates it. Already in the introduction to his work on Scotus, Heidegger had suggested that, with the term "method," "not only the knowing of principles is meant, but rather actually the knowledge of the connection between them and that for which they are principles. Not only the that and the what, but rather the *how* of the principial connection is the important matter." We now know that this how means pointing into the way of analogical differentiation. In metaphysics as a science of "first principles" (*archai*), these *archai* are not a univocal kingdom, but literally "starting points" (*Ansätze*) for method, which likewise can be taken in the literal sense of "way toward," a "way of discovery" that is always "on the way." In his exposition of the theory of signs in Scotus and Husserl, Heidegger had also said that "meaning [is] a 'sign' of the object," since what the material signifier is to it, it is to objects, namely, a relational pointing toward (*Hinzeigen, Hinweisen*) or indicating (*Anzeigen*). *Bedeutung*, meaning, significance is literally a *be-deuten*, pointing to, sign-ifying. Now given Heidegger's inextricable insertion of the problem of the categories into this living historical domain of the *modus significandi*, these categories themselves—which "meaning" fulfills and differentiates—look like they have an *essentially* indicative function. Thus Heidegger also intimated to Löwith in 1927 that in the twenties he came to use the term "formal indication" for his earlier concept of categorial form which points to its analogical differentiation in the historical haecceity of matter (G1 197–201; G1 416/CT 3; G1 295–98; BL 37).

Heidegger was particularly influenced by a fundamental distinction in the theory of "concept-formation" developed by Dilthey, Simmel, and especially Rickert, namely, the distinction between "generalizing science" and "individualizing science," which Heidegger saw as corresponding to the "generalizing" and "individualizing" functions of meaning in Scotus. Generalizing science, which is characteristic primarily of the natural sciences, sees particularities simply as instantiations of the universal that it reads off from them and likewise sees the universal in its function of being able to be instantiated in particularities. This type of science does not at all work with the category of haecceity either as it is found in the unique particularities themselves or as it might function right within genus-species hierarchies and systems of laws. Through the abstractive method used here, haecceity "comes to be lost" both in the concrete matter and the categorial form. But the individualizing science that is characteristic of the historical sciences does work with haecceity on both these levels; it studies historical particularities as "unique" objectifications and differentiations of value, which it in turn sees in its function of *pointing* into actual and possible differentiation. Thus individualizing science cannot work simply with species-concepts. "The ordering in the realm of the real is *not* that of pure generalizing in terms of genus, whereby the meaning of the genus is given to each of the 'subsumed cases' *in the same sense*, as this is the case in, for example, a system of zoology and botany." Since the individual "cannot be known through the lowest species-concept that comes closest to it," is "ineffable" for it, "new moments of meaning have to be added," namely, the category of haecceity and the very act of intentional individuation. As Heidegger will say repeatedly in the early twenties, being is not a genus (G1 350–54, 253, 365, 261; G1 433/CT 10).

The doctrine of the categories of being must then also have the character of an individualizing science that, in incorporating history as a meaning-differentiating element, views the categories as analogically differentiable and historical realities as unique differentiations. Heidegger stressed that the categories can thus provide "the conceptual means and ends for comprehending the individual epochs of spiritual and intellectual history in a living way," for "the living understanding of a 'time' " in Dilthey's sense of "empathetic understanding" (G1 408, 401–402/PC 383, 379). There is something like a generalizing moment in the doctrine of categories, but one should call it rather formalization, as Heidegger later does in the early twenties. Formalization occurs by relaxing the intentional pointing of form into its differentiation in matter, holding it in abeyance, and lifting it out as an unfulfilled intention. The indexicality of categorial haecceity, of the "such-now-here!," is thereby neither extinguished in a univocal doctrine of categories, nor brought to closure in existing historical objectifications (worldview), but rather held open for new and different fulfillments.

6 | Mysticism, Ontotheology, Antimodernism

HEIDEGGER'S HISTORICAL HETEROLOGY of being is ultimately based on a Neo-Eckhartian "breakthrough" to the deepest depth-dimension of a *mystical* heterology. *Durchbruch* is a fundamental idea in Eckhart's mysticism and means the breakthrough to the realization of the *unio mystica* vis-à-vis the birth of the Logos (Son) in the soul, whereby—to put this in Heidegger's language—divine truth is made actual (actual truth) and analogically differentiated in the matter of the individual soul, which in turn lives in the truth (true actuality). "In breaking-through I discover that God and I are one," says Eckhart. Heidegger's academic interests in medieval mysticism extended back to the course he took on this topic in 1910 and were expressed already in his *Der Akademiker* articles between 1910 and 1913. In 1911 he wrote of "the mystical element that from time to time intensely *breaks forth* [*hervorbrechend*]" (emphasis added). In a passage from the same year that sounds autobiographical in light of his despondent "dark night of the soul" poems around the same time, he insisted that

> alongside the connoisseurship in philosphical questioning that has gradually become a sport [in modernism], there *breaks forth* unawares—right in the midst of all self-awareness and self-satisfaction—a longing for self-contained, conclusive answers to the ultimate questions of being [*Sein*], which from time to time flash up suddenly like this and then lie unresolved for days like leaden weights on a tortured soul that is poor in both end and way. (emphasis added)

In a 1912 article, he also critically discussed the treatment of mystical experience in William James's psychology of religion (ME 232; CA 494–97, 502–503).

By the time Heidegger composed the supplementary conclusion of his work on Scotus, this Eckhartian notion of the breaking-forth of the mystical had become his idea of the highest vocation of philosophy as "a *breakthrough* to the true actuality and the actual truth." Likewise, his essay on the concept of time opened with the statement that "confinement in epistemological problems does not allow the questions about the ultimate end of philosophy to arrive at their immanent meaning. Hence the tendency to metaphysics that one moment is covered up and the next is openly *breaking [tretend]* into the light of day." The "true worldview" of "the deeper, worldview essence of philosophy" was ultimately to be a "philosophy of living spirit, of active love, of worshipful God-intimacy [*Gottinnigkeit*]," a term that—along with "inward [*inner*] Dasein"—has the ring of Eckhart's central notion of *inne sein*, being inward-at-home and finding God in the depths of the soul (GI 415/CT 3; GI 407-10/PC 382-84).

In the following, we shall examine: (1) the influence of Eckhart's notion of the analogical birth of the Logos on Heidegger; (2) Heidegger's own mystical heterology that was also influenced by Hegel and German Romanticism; and finally (3) the residual metaphysical traces of ontotheology and worldview in his heterology of being and time.

The Analogical Birth of Logos in Eckhart

We should recall that Heidegger saw the Scholastic doctrine of analogy as the conceptual expression of the spiritual worldview of medieval Dasein (sacramentalism) that reached its highest pitch in mysticism. Here the content-sense of God is experienced not as logical sense, but as teleogical value, the *summum bonum*, the measure of perfection (*mensura perfectionis*), the ultimate "optic." "As absolute actuality that centers in itself, the '*unum infinitum*' is the highest value [*das Höchstwertige*], the absolute measure for all actuality." In its "transcendent and primal relation to God," its "eternal yea-sayings," the relational sense of medieval "inward Dasein" is stretched ecstatically, moodfully, and devotionally toward and into the mysterious depths of the divine *telos*. Medieval life is precisely this "metaphysical tension," this "stretching itself along into the transcendent," which reaches its tautest expression in mystical love poetry (Heidegger would later call this stretching-along "care" and "ecstatic" "temporality") (GI 260-62, 199; GI 409/PC 384). The deep temporalizing-sense of this intentional God/Dasein relation is the analogical differentiation of homogeneous divine form within the heterogeneous matter of creation, that is, the enactment of truth as the principle of the material determination and differentiation of form.

God is the one (*monas*), the infinite one (*unum infinitum*); one must speak of the *unitas Dei*, the unity of God. *Esse divinum*, divine being, is ultimately the undifferentiated "primal element" of the transcendental "being," of the there is/it gives. Here in his creative exposition of Scotus, Heidegger used Eckhart's phrase that God *west*, essences/presences. "In the strictest, absolute sense *only* God is. He is the Absolute, which is existence that exists in essence and 'essences' in existence. The actuality of nature, that which is sensibly real, exists only as created reality; it *is* not existence like the absolute, but rather *has* existence through '*communicabilitas*,' " impartability (GI 258-61). Heidegger was apparently appealing to Eckhart's novel notion that being is God (*esse est deus*) and that, in themselves, creatures would be a "pure nothing." God is like the sun that emanates the homogeneous medium of light in which things can participate and thus appear, or like the formal element of whiteness in which white things can appear as white. Beings are "in God," in being, "in the light." As the Neo-Platonic "Godhead" that precedes the differentiation of the trinity and creation, "God is one," simplicity, the "negation of negation," the dark hidden "ground" that is an abyss (*Abgrund*), the divine "wasteland" that transcends all "names."

But this *Deus absconditus* is also a dynamic efflux, emanation, and differentiation into the persons of the trinity and into the multiplicity of the created temporal world. For Eckhart, writes Caputo, "creation is the overflow, the spilling over of this inner life-process into time and number and multiplicity." In the relation to God and to each other, creatures "are" analogically, since, as Eckhart explains, being is attributed properly only to God from whom, "immediately, all being is," just as "all things are white from whiteness itself." "The good and likewise being have an analogical relation in God and in creatures. For goodness itself, which is in God and which is God, is the quality by which all men are good" (TME 109; ME 302, 278, 276). According to the mystical Neo-Platonic light-theory of transcendental truth to which Eckhart is appealing, the divine mind—the "father of lights"—is the very lighting process of creation; it is an illuminated clearing (*Lichtung*) in which all things appear as mysterious analogical emanations, gifts, sacraments, lights, images, signs, signatures, symbols, traces and tracks (Bonaventura's *vestigia*) of the *mysterium tremendum*, which is reached on the path of the *via negativa*. For medieval mysticism, the world is like a book of magical words inscribed by the absent finger of God, like a mirror in which an absent face peers and is reflected in myriad images. The centripetal theocentrism of the mystical *via negativa* is also a centrifugal and heterological theophany.

One of Eckhart's most unique contributions to the mystical tradition is his idea of the personal and analogical birth of the Son, the Logos, in the haecceity of individual souls. The soul is not only the microcosmic site of the transcendental truth of the macrocosmic form/matter relation in God's reality; it is also itself matter that performs a form-differentiating function. "The Logos became flesh and dwelt *en hemin*, in us." For Eckhart, the matter of the soul is formed over (*überbildet*) into the Logos, of which it is thus an image (*Bild*), an appearance. In the deep "ground" of the soul, Eckhart explains, there is a divine agent or faculty (*Kraft, virtus*) that is the manger-like site ("the little castle in the soul," the "cabin" [*Hut*], "the little spark" [*Fünklein*]) into which the intelligible light of the Word has been incarnated. "She [the soul] is illuminated and radiates [the Word] as the one and only pure, clear light of the Father. . . . In this faculty, God is perpetually verdant and flowering." Eckhart is not saying that human individuals are the Logos per se; rather, they are the Logos analogically, that is, actualizations that differentiate it via the matter of their unique lives. The one Word, Light, and Kingdom in which the Father has been manifested, namely, the eternal Son, in turn differentiates itself into many little words, sparks, castles, sons, and daughters. "We receive *in time* when we *are*, and are sons." Selves, Eckhart says, are like different loaves of sacramental bread into which the divine form has dispersed itself, like mirror images into which a single face has been refracted. In relation to creation, the Logos is just this whole analogical nexus of identity-in-difference. In defending before the Church authorities his statement that "between the only begotten Son and the soul there is no distinction," Eckhart explains that "matter and form are one in being; living and working. Yet matter is not, on this account, form, or conversely . . . just as God is one in all things by essence, so the Son is one God in all sons-by-adoption, and they through him, and in him, are *sons-by-analogy*" (emphasis added). "An example is found," he continues, "in the images produced in many mirrors by the face of one person looking therein. . . . God, undivided and One by essence, is inmost and closest to each one of us." For Eckhart there is a mystical analogical community of persons that are all *differently* in the *same* body of the Logos. "A holy soul is one with God, according to John 17:21, That they may all be one in us, even as we are one" (ME 209–11, 292, 302–304).

Is there in Eckhart's notion of the birth of the Logos a human enactment-sense corresponding to the deep temporalizing-sense of God's efflux and influx? Eckhart's quaint Germanic imagery is bound up with a profound personalism that antipates many of the insights of Lutheran Protestantism. "It would mean little to me that the 'Word was made flesh' for humanity in Christ, granting that the latter is distinct from me, unless He also was made flesh in me personally." According to Eckhart, the soul "co-bears" the divine birth of the Logos and co-works or co-acts (*mitwirkt*) with the actualization of God. Following the Aristotelian tradition, Eckhart sees "life" as *kinesis* from potentiality to being-in-work that has its own principle in itself and is therefore "without why," that is, without a ground outside of itself. "Life lives out of its own ground and wells forth out of what is its own, thus it lives without why." The Divine Life is just this movement of overflow from the abyss of the Godhead into the analogical differentiation of actuality, and the soul is the co-worker or co-actualizer of this differentiation within the matter of itself and its world. "What is my life? That which is moved from within out of itself. . . . If we live with Him, then we must also co-work with Him from within" (TME 115, 102ff., 122–23, 108–109; WFH 73).

In the first place, this personal enactment-sense is contemplative detachment (*Abgeschiedenheit*), being-inward-at-home, and *Gelassenheit* in the triple sense of releasement from willfulness, surrendering-to, and letting-be of the birth of the Logos within the rythmn of the Word and silence, Parousia and Kairos, gift and gratitude. But this contemplative activity completes itself in the realm of "works," of plough and pen, market and office, marriage and monastery. "Not that one should give up, neglect or forget his inner life for a moment," writes Eckhart, "but he must learn to work in it, with it, and out of it, so that the unity of his soul may break out into his activities and his activities may bring him back to that unity." Meditation and work, inner and outer, mystery and commonplace, abyss and surface, form and matter, simplicity and multiplicity, eternity and the tower-clock are intimately bound together in a daily circular rhythm of opening and closing, efflux and influx, dissemination and gathering. The analogical unity of the soul with God extends all the way down from the abyss of the Godhead to the emanation of the Logos and its realization in the everyday world. In Eckhart's thought, one finds not only the great mystery of God, but also the mystery of the human person, since the ground of the soul is actually a groundless abyss and absence that provides the deepest point of unity between soul and Godhead. "It is neither this nor that. . . . it is free of all names and naked, apart from all forms." Who is looking out of the absence and darkness behind the human face in the shimmering mirror of creation? "The eye with which I see God is the same eye with which God sees me. My eye and God's eye are one eye," answers Eckhart (TME 118–27; ME 37, 301, 288).

Mystical Heterology

Heidegger took up this Eckhartian "metaphysics of the problem of the truth" (i.e., the material differentiation of form) in his interpretation of the medieval doctrine of analogy vis-à-vis Scotus and in his own Hegelian and Diltheyan reformulation of medieval mysticism. He explained that for Scotus God, the absolute, is being and, as an "active creative principle," God "imparts" or "communicates" being to created things. God is the *monas* that functions as the primal wellspring (*Quelle, Ursprung*) of "the multiplicity of objects according to their essential being." "Unity is the *measure* of the multiplicity that springs forth from it. . . . The '*number*' of created realities arises '*per sui communicabilitatem.*' " Thus there arises an analogical and hierarchical ordering for two reasons. First, "being" and the other transcendentals are attributed properly to God and only derivatively to created things. "Although both are real, creator and creation are, however, real in a *different* manner. Here we meet up with the moment of heterogeneity in analogy." Moreover, created things "have," "participate in," or actualize the valuative measure of God's being in *different* degrees. "Every individual object of natural actuality has a determinate valuableness, a grade of being-actual. This increases itself all the more, the more intensively the object participates in the absolute actuality" (GI 258–63; GI 410/PC 384).

This analogical differentiation finds its richest expression within the haecceity of "the *historical* in its *individuality*," which means especially the world of "the spiritual individual," "historical personality," even though all this remained for the most part unthematic in medieval philosophy. Heidegger took up this theme suggested in the body of his work on Scotus and radicalized it in the supplementary conclusion, as well as in his essay on the concept of time. In his exposition of the medieval "form of inward Dasein anchored in the transcendent primal relation of soul to God," we also meet up with something like Eckhart's notion of the analogical birth of the Logos in persons and with the personal enactment-sense corresponding to the deeper "creative principle" of God. Though the primal relation that defines especially mysticism seems to be only a one-way stream flowing into the mysterious source of the *Deus absconditus* in which the self is completely immersed, it is simultaneously the reverse direction of the emanation and pouring forth of God into the life and the world of the individual person. "Transcendence," Heidegger wrote, "does not signify a radical, self-relinquishing distancing from the subject—there persists precisely a life-relation built on correlativity." It "is to be compared to the back-and-forth flowing stream of experience in mutually attracted spiritual individuals. . . . The placing of value does not gravitate exclusively to the transcendent, but rather is as it were reflected back from its fullness and absoluteness and comes to rest in the individual." This pouring forth (*communicatio*) of God into the heterogeneity and haecceity of persons is precisely the process of analogical differentiation with its hierarchical grades of being. "In virtue of distancing or approaching . . . the multiplicity of the life-relations between God and soul are altered. . . . The metaphysical interlocking through transcendence is simultaneously the source of manifold oppositions and thus of the richest living of the immanent personal life of the individual" (GI 263; GI 409/PC 383).

This personal life is a teleological consciousness that co-enacts and fulfills the divine *telos* in the religious, moral, political, and artistic realms of its historical world. "In the whole medieval worldview, because it is already radically and consciously *teleological*, there lies a whole world of manifold differentiations of value." It is this personal enactment-sense that Heidegger seems to have wanted to get at in his planned study of "scholastic psychology" through a "phenomenological elaboration of mystical, moral-theological, and ascetic literature." Since the "concepts" that Scholasticism used in its "anthropology" were "very insufficient" for getting at "the complex involvements of historical personality, its own being, its conditionedness and manifold working-out, its wovenness into the surroundings," Heidegger's plan seems to have involved using the personalist terminology of Nietzsche, Dilthey, and others to study nonphilosophical medieval literary sources in which he could find a rich, even if unthematic experience of enactment-sense. Here he wanted to fathom how the teleological relation to God is actualized and differentiated in "the stream of one's own life in its manifold entanglements, turns, and conversions, in its multi-shaped and widely branching-out conditionedness." It was this concern that to some degree originally led Heidegger to the Duns Scotus who is both the airy *doctor subtilis* and the thinker of the haecceity of being. "He has a greater and more acute closeness to real life (*haecceitas*) than the Scholastic philosophers before him, and to a greater extent has discovered the multiplicity and possibility of tension in real life." "He is equally familiar with 'shapes of life' and with the 'gray on gray' of philosophy" (G1 409/PC 383; G1 200–205).

Heidegger took up this medieval mystical configuration into his own systematic position that was also expressed and modernized with the help of Hegel, German Romanticism, and Dilthey. What attracted him here were critiques of the rationalism of the modern Enlightenment and restatements of the medieval Neo-Platonic theory of divine emanation within the concrete particularity of history, communities, religion, myth, morality, art, and personal life. As he would suggest in the twenties, German idealism, Romanticism, and hermeneutics are inseparable from the theological influences of Rhineland mysticism and Lutheranism. He later recounted that, between 1910 and 1914, he developed a "growing interest in Hegel and Schelling" through his teacher Carl Braig, a leading figure in the speculative Catholic Tübingen School. From Braig Heidegger "heard for the first time of Schelling's and Hegel's significance for speculative theology in distinction to the doctrinal system of Scholasticism. Thus the tension between ontology and speculative theology as the structure of metaphysics entered the horizon of my searching." The closing paragraph of Heidegger's conclusion stated that his rough sketch of a new doctrine of categories and a philosophy of "worshipful God-intimacy" stood before "the great task of a principial confrontation with the system of historical worldview that is the most powerful in fullness as in depth, wealth of lived experience, and concept-formation . . . that is, with Hegel." In Heidegger's appropriation of medieval mysticism in Hegel's modern language, the content-sense of God was inscribed as "the Absolute," "the absolute spirit of God"; relational sense was stamped as "historical spirit"; and the deep temporalizing-sense took the shape of the "heterothesis" that was inspired not only by Scotus and Rickert, but also by Hegel. For Hegel, absolute spirit is in-and-for-itself, a dialectical identity-in-difference, insofar as it is both a "kenosis" of the in-itself of the Logos into the rich historical multiplicity of the for-itself and a synthetic elevation (*Aufhebung*) of this multiplicity back up to the in-itself. Like Eckhart's metaphor of the Logos differentiating itself in many different sacramental loaves of bread, Hegel conceives of absolute spirit as eternally pouring itself forth into the chalice of history, such that the "kingdom [*Reich*] of spirits" in turn hands this chalice filled with myriad shapes of life back up to the "throne" of the king. "Only from the chalice of this kingdom of spirits," Hegel writes at the end of his *Phenomenology of Spirit*, "foams forth for him his infinity." Heidegger's appropriation of Hegel's position reads, "Spirit is to be grasped [*zu begreifen*] only when the entire abundance of its accomplishments, i.e., *its history*, is lifted up [*aufgehoben*] into it; with this constantly growing abundance in its philosophical conceptualization is given an ongoing and increasing means for a living grasp of the absolute spirit of God" (G1 56/R 22; SD 82/75; G1 408-11/PC 382-84; G1 260).

Heidegger's essay on time also incorporated this Hegelianized mystical configuration, but now with a strong Eckhartian and Diltheyan twist. It should not be forgotten that Heidegger saw this essay as the extension of his earlier treatment of the medieval notions of haecceity and analogy into the realm of history and personality. Thus it dramatically opens with a motto from Eckhart's sermons, expressing the notion of the analogical emanation and differentiation of God within time: "Time is that which changes and multiplies itself [*mannifaltigt sich*], eternity holds itself in simply [*einfach*]" (G1 253, 264; G1 415/CT 3; MH 87). For Heidegger, history is the principle of the material differentiation of form and value that ultimately reach back into the mysterious depths of God. As such, history is ultimately the creative divine efflux of objectification and differentiation into a rich panorama and sacramental treasury of heterogeneous effects (*Wirkungen*), crystallizations, shapes (*Gestalten*), epochs, *Ereignisse*, cultural worlds, institutions, and personal worlds—a process that in 1919 Heidegger would explicity call *Ereignis* and "it worlds." Influenced by the preceding historical contexts from which they emerge, epochs and worlds nonetheless to a great extent erupt vertically and an-archically into being without a necessary "law that determines how the times follow one another." Heidegger's mention of the "founding of the city of Rome, birth of Christ, Hedschra" as examples of unique world-originating *Ereignisse* suggests that he may be working here with some notion of *Heilsgeschichte*, sacred history.

The conclusion to his book on Scotus also shows the influence of the mystical strands of German Romanticism. Its motto reads, "Everywhere we seek *das Unbedingte*, the unconditioned and always find only *Dinge*, things," that is, historically conditioned objectifications and differentiations. This passage is from the fragments of the poet Novalis, a passionate proponent of antimodern medievalism who was influenced by the mystic Jakob Böhme, Friedrich Schlegel, Schelling, and Fichte. His *Hymnen an die Nacht* (Hymns to the Night), one of his best-known works, express a longing to escape the harsh light of the finite world of multiplicity and opposition into union with the divine undifferentiated ground of "night." "Back I turn to the holy, ineffable, mysterious night. . . . Now I awake, for I am thine." In speaking of "living spirit and its 'eternal yea-sayings,' " Heidegger's conclusion also quotes the other seminal Romantic figure, namely, Friedrich Schlegel, who, similar to his friend Novalis, brought together strands from Spinoza, Schelling, and Schleiermacher into the view of history and especially the art of the genius as symbolic expressions of the Godhead. Heidegger's 1916 poem *Abendgang auf der Reichenau* (Nightfall on Reichenau) sounds remarkably similar to Novalis's hymns, to the motto from Eckhart at the start of his essay on time, and to Eckhart's metaphor of the Godhead as a "wasteland" from which, however, a diverse abundance of life emerges: "Over the waters flows a silvern glimmer to dark and distant shores; and in summer-weary, dew-damp gardens falls, like a lover's word withheld, the night. . . . and what the shining summer day has created for me rests fruit-heavy—from eternities a cargo beyond sense—in the gray desert of a great simplicity [*Einfalt*]." Heinrich Ochsner recounted that, at the time of the composition of this poem on the island Reichenau on Lake Constance, his friend Heidegger sent him a postcard with allusions to mysticism. Two very provocative oral remarks about the relation of form (sense) and matter (being) that Heidegger made to Ochsner in 1916 also resonate with Romantic mysticism and hearken back to his motto from Novalis: "The immanent structure of philosophy is a back-and-forth between sense and being. In this duality lies the tragedy of the philosopher." "Searching for oneself and not being able to find oneself is the innermost rhythm of philosophy" (G1 399/PC 378; G1 406/PC 382; G13 7; MV 264, 269).

These statements indicate that Heidegger sees human life, as well as philosophy, to be haunted by a *mysterium tremendum*, a concealment and absence that cannot be fully penetrated and mastered. The word *verhalten* (withheld) in his 1916 poem seems already to have some of the sense of his later term *Entzug*, the withdrawal of being into *lethe*, concealment, which permeates the experience of "tragedy." His stress on the "conditioned" character of knowing suggests that we are always far too woven into and entangled within the *textum* of the analogical differentiation of history to be able to lift ourselves out of time and make a clean breakthrough to the univocal kingdom of an infinite mystical depth-dimension, the Kingdom of God. We only glimpse it from within an analogical and historical text of identity-in-difference that is like "a bundle of rays flowing together in a single point."

Heidegger stressed that the personal enactment-sense whereby this text is co-actualized is thus not to be dissolved into a divine absolute, just as it was not in the medieval view of the analogical book of the created world. "In the end," he wrote, "the notion of transcendence must become all-governing [*allbeherrschend*] in a philosophy. But that can happen only when the realm of the governance [*Herrschaftsbereich*] of transcendence is fixed in its limits and taken up on all sides into one's own life" (G1 200). Here he follows the stress on unique individual personality in Romanticism, as well as Kierkegaard's and Nietzsche's critiques of idealism, which he has been reading in selections since around 1910.

In his ground-breaking work *The Mystical Element in Heidegger's Thought* in 1978, John Caputo showed how there was an "analogy" between Heidegger's thought and Eckhart's mysticism, but now we know that in 1915–16 Heidegger's thought ultimately *was* philosophical mysticism. His project was not only a new type of modernized Neo-Scholasticism, but also a highly creative repetition of medieval mysticism within the modern thought of phenomenology, Hegel, the German Romantics, Dilthey, and Nietzsche. One could call this the beginning of Heidegger's early mystical-personalist thought-path that extends into the early twenties. This mystical-personalist heterology of being has the intentional configuration of worldview/person/mystery (differentiating). The separation and analogy between Heidegger's being-question and mysticism would come later around 1919 when he leaves the Catholic Church and, while struggling to sort out his religious orientation, declares that philosphy must not be a religious "worldview," but "primal science"—all the while using his rich knowledge of mysticism, alongside of Kierkegaard and Luther, as a comparative model for his analyses of being in general.

Ontotheology and Antimodernism

In 1915–16 Heidegger had still not made the decisive breakthrough to the question of being and time. His first answer to the question about being, in his doctoral dissertation and in the body of his work on Scotus, was that being is the atemporal validity of univocal logical sense that is *separate* from the realm of history, which must therefore be suspended in ontology. His answer in the supplementary conclusion is that being is an analogical identity-in-difference that is *inseparable* from history, which must therefore not be suspended. The former answer offers a straight line, the latter a bundle of heterogeneous rays flowing together in a single point. Categorial sense and history seem to be always already so interwoven in the *textum* of analogicity that philosophy is in the tragic predicament of looking for pure unconditioned sense but finding only meaningful "things," and looking for pure things but finding only interpreted sense.

And yet Heidegger clung to the metaphysical *ideal* that philosophical speculation could still somehow transcend this contextual analogicity and view it under the aspect of the eternity of God as consisting of the *ontologically* separate realms of sense and existence, universality and particularity, time and eternity. He wrote at the close of his supplementary conclusion that "in the concept of living spirit and its relation to the metaphysical 'origin' [*Ursprung*], there opens up an insight into its metaphysical ground-structure in which the uniqueness and individuality of *acts* is merged into a living unity with universal validity and the subsistence-in-itself of *sense*." And this seems to allow the old problem of *methexis* to arise again in a new form: "Objectively put, there lies before us the problem of the relationship of time and eternity, alteration and absolute validity, world and God, which is reflected theoretically and scientifically in *history* (value-formation) and *philosophy* (validity of value)" (G1 410/PC 384).

What these passages suggest is that, for Heidegger's "speculative-theological thinking," history has been "lifted up" in Hegelian fashion into the *Reich* and "throne" of "the absolute spirit of God," who is truth in-and-for-itself. Though the Echartian notions of the divine abyss and its efflux in the background of Heidegger's thinking do not seem to be caught up in an ontotheological concept of God (TME 130), his concepts of "the transcendent," "depth-dimension," "metaphysical 'origin,'" "transcendent principles," the "realm of the governance of transcendence," do have the sense of a statically present causal ground, a *summum ens* and *summum bonum*, which sends the analogically differentiated historical worldviews and epochs, but itself remains untouched by the historical. Heidegger reduces being to a static divine entity since he is ultimately working with precisely a hierarchical *pros hen* analogy of attribution in which being is properly attributed to the divine entity called God. Though expressed in the context of a historically self-conscious, sophisticated idealism, we are still left with a version of the Greek concept of the divine *arche*, origin/kingdom, the Kingdom of the ontotheological God, where the philosopher reigns in the manner of "grasping [*Begreifung*] the absolute spirit of God" (G1 408–409/PC 382-83; G1 199, 201). The intentional configuration of this speculative ontotheological thinking is the absolute/spirit/eternity. In 1915–16 Heidegger made metaphysics tremble, but in the end left its guiding question in place.

Heidegger's mystical and Neo-Scholastic project was entangled in the metaphysics of presence also because it attempted to offer "the true worldview," namely, the historical *arche* of the Christian medieval epoch as it can be reformulated in the modern "Catholic worldview" (G1 408/PC 382). It thereby confused the historical differentiated giving of being with one of its effects and brings this giving to closure. In Heidegger's student writings, from his early *Der Akademiker* articles to the conclusion of his book on Scotus, we find the project of a struggle (*Kampf*) against the alleged fallenness and unruliness of modern individualistic liberalism, and a proposed revolutionary return to the deep theistic worldview of the past, which he thought could provide a ground and anchor for modern subjectivism. Let us examine the outlines of this project, since we will later be comparing it to Heidegger's cultural critiques in the early twenties and then in his later writings.

This project was originally influenced by the antimodernist crusade of

Pope Pius X, which began with his "Modernism Encyclical" in 1907 and was supported by, among other academics, Heidegger's teacher Carl Braig, who is actually thought to have coined the term "modernism." The ultraconservative Catholicism of Heidegger's early *Der Akademiker* articles speaks passionately against the "boundless autonomism," the "spiritual and moral sovereignty of the ego," "currents of free-thinking," and "individualistic ethics" in modernism. "The Church will, if it is to remain true to its eternal treasure of truth," he wrote, "justifiably combat the destructive influence of modernism, which is not conscious of the sharpest contradictions in which its modern views of life stand to the ancient wisdom of the Christian tradition." Crudely employing the New Testament themes of the fall, the lusts of the flesh, and worldliness, Heidegger painted modernism as a cultural sickness in the sense of a de-cadence, a falling away from the traditional depth dimension and *telos* of God into the multiplicity of the world, into the distractions of the present. The language of the young theology student's 1910 essay on the seventeenth century Viennese preacher Abraham a Sancta Clara sounds very much like that of the analysis of falling in SZ and the critique of modernity in his later writings:

> The frenzied innovation that upsets foundations, the crazed leaping away over the deep spiritual content of life and art, the modern sense of life guided by the continually shifting stimulus of the moment, the occasionally suffocating sultriness in which every kind of contemporary art moves, these are moments that point to decadence [*Dekadenz*], to a sorry falling away [*Abfall*] from health and the otherworldly value of life.

Likewise, his 1910 review of *Lies of Life and Truth of Life*, by the Catholic convert Johannes Jörgensen, speaks against the fact that "in our day one talks much about 'personality'. . . . The person of the artist moves into the fore-ground. Thus one hears much about interesting people. Oscar Wilde the dandy, Paul Verlaine the 'brilliant drunkard,' Maxim Gorky the great vaga-bond; the superman Nietzsche—all interesting people." But this individualism leads to *Verwesung*, decay, the loss of essence, "despair," "horror and sin," "death," a "wretched Dasein," "errant paths" that exile one from the *Reich* of "the light of truth." "Their life was an intoxication," Heidegger preached. "And further and further they drifted downwards to the point where they loved death and despair and 'called decay holy.' " "See that line of witnesses, how they went astray and held a revolver to their foreheads. So none of them had the truth" (MH 62–66; CA 484, 486–93; G13 3).

In the midst of this fall, need, and danger comes a call to conversion, to a *Kehre*. Here Heidegger made his treatment of the convert and "modern Au-gustine" Jörgensen a model for the whole of modernism. "And now and then when the mad frenzy faded, the call came from afar out of the deepest depths of his tortured inwardness: 'Oh, tired soul, come here!' . . . The Darwinist roused himself." More philosophically, he writes in another essay that Neo-Scholasticism "is called to progress." To what is the call calling? To *Bekehrung*, to a Jörgensen-like conversion, a turning back to and preservation of the *telos* of the divine depth dimension that is housed in "the ancient wisdom of the Christian tradition," in "the great indestructible connections with the past," which include the traditional German Catholicism living on in the hearts of *das Volk*, the people. This model of fall, call, and return is the sense of Heidegger's Neo-Eckhartian language in his *Der Akademiker* articles and other writings about "a longing [that] *breaks forth* unawares—right in the midst of all self-awareness and self-satisfaction" in the modern epoch of subjectivism (CA 489–97, 518–19).

This calling back is no mere reactionary flight into the past, but rather a revolutionary conservatism that wants to "look forward by looking back" (*vorwärtsschaut rückwartsblickend*). The deconstructive breakthrough to the traditional depth-dimension is the outbreak (*Aufbruch*) of retrieval and renewal. In his essay on Abraham, Heidegger waxed on about how "the health of the people in soul and body, this is what this truly apostolic orator strove for. Thus his fearless weighing up of every earthly, overrated opinion of life in this world." Stressing the roots of Abraham's work in "the Bible, the Church Fathers, the Scholastics, the mystics," Heidegger expressed his lament over modernity and his pitch for revolutionary change:

> That the external culture of our times and its fast living would indeed look forward by looking back more! . . . Models such as Abraham a Sancta Clara must remain preserved for us, silently continuing to have an effect in the soul of the people. May . . . his spirit [*Geist*] became a powerful ferment for the preservation of health and, where need cries out, for the renewed healing of the soul of the people.

Already by at least 1912 Heidegger began separating himself from the reactionary flight of the Church and advocated his own Neo-Scholastic project of a repetition of the Christian past within the conceptuality of modern thought. In a 1912 *Der Akademiker* article, for example, he quoted the Scholastic historian M. de Wulf: "Neo-Scholasticism is mobile like everything that lives; stopping its evolution would be the sign of a new decadence" (G13 3, CA 518–19; MH 83; HL 113).

The enactment-sense of this revolutionary project, which looks forward by looking back and looks back by looking forward, takes the form of the heroic *Kampf* of the cross-carrying Christian soldier on the *Heilsweg* to the Kingdom of God, a soldier who is reinterpreted along the lines of a spiritualized Nietzschean biologism of the will to power and ascending life. Struggle means first struggle *against* in the sense of ascetic denial, critique, and death of the fallen self, the old Adam of modernism. Heidegger here appealed to "whoever has not tread upon errant ways and let himself be blinded by the deceitful pretence of the modern spirit, whoever ventures himself along life's journey in a truer, deeper, better-grounded denial of self [*Entselbstung*] in the glaring light of the truth." The essay on Jörgensen reads, "And so individualism is the false standard of life. Therefore banish the will of the flesh, the doctrine of the world, of paganism. And again a biological prerequisite. Higher life is conditioned by the destruction [*Untergang*] of the lower forms." So "die, kill what is lower in yourself, work with supernatural grace and you will be resurrected. And thus the strong-willed, hopeful poet-philosopher now rests in the shadow of the cross." Heidegger was advocating the eclipse not of personality per se, but of "individualistic ethics"—the attempt to ground personality through nothing other than itself. He wanted rather to ground personalist ethics in the traditional depth-dimension of God: "The much-ballyhooed cult of the personality can thus only flourish when it remains in the most inward contact with the richest and deepest source of religious-ethical authority." Modern individualism was to be grafted onto medieval participation. Thus we find Heidegger stating that "self-development must not take a back seat" and that "one only possesses truth in a genuine sense when one has made it one's own" (CA 490–493, 496–99).

Kampf also means struggle *for* in the sense of the severity of willing and actualizing the divine *telos* that has been recaptured. This involves "difficulty," a "powerful struggle" (*Ringen*), "tireless searching," "the long arduous path," "the ultimate step to the peak of truth." "It was not the urge for sensation that drove [Jörgensen] to conversion," Heidegger told his readers, "no, rather deeper, more bitter seriousness." His poetic description of Jörgensen, the model Christian soldier, continued: "And again the night sank in, leaden, without stars, the night of death. . . . A strong hand struck him. He saw. . . . With iron consistency, he marched onward, upward" past the "wretched Dasein" of the aesthetes and dandies who lay fallen by the wayside, "weak," "sick," and utterly ruined with "revolvers to their foreheads." According to Heidegger's Nietzschean vocabulary, "religion [is] the most fundamental power of life"; to all "scientific work there belongs a certain base of ethical power." "Philosophy means an unflinching struggle [*Ringen*] for truth." One must be strong and hard (CA 486–89, 496–97, 504–505, 516–17).

This antimodernist project turned up again in a less severe form in Heidegger's other student writings. His more philosophical articles and reviews between 1912 and 1914, as well as his 1913 doctoral dissertation, had already carried forward his Neo-Scholastic project by taking up the concerns of medieval thought within the modern movements of phenomenology and Neo-Kantianism. His account of the history of the doctrine of categories, in his book on Scotus, contrasts "modern culture in general" to the cosmological and theistic-mystical worldviews of Greece and the Middle Ages. Modernism is the worldview of self-consciousness, method, subjectivism, self-assertiveness, and mastery, which has absolved itself from its traditional grounding in the depth dimension of God, is now "at home with itself," and attempts to find its ground in itself. In his supplementary conclusion, Heidegger expanded his critique of modernism against the backdrop of his praise for the medieval theory of the analogicity of being. Because it was "anchored in the primal transcendent relation to God," the spiritualism of medieval culture lived in an analogical identity-in-difference, in a rich back-and-forth tension between God and world, eternity and time, universal and particular, individual and *ens commune*. It was neither a "monism" nor a "dualism," but a mystical analogism. If Greek thought often tended toward cosmic tautology, a monistic identity without difference, modern culture tends to lose itself in heterological difference without identity, multiplicity without unity, haecceity without homogeneity. It has lost its "anchor" in the unifying transcendent *telos* of the mystical depth-dimension of God, forfeited its vertical gravity, and is adrift in the superficiality of the horizontal flux of history. The "wealth of experience" in modernity, Heidegger wrote, is "conditioned by a *flighty breadth of content*. In this shallow-running attitude of life, the possibilities of a growing insecurity and complete disorientation are far greater and almost limitless." Medieval life highlights the problem with modernity: "In contrast, the basic shape of the form of medieval humanity's life does not at all lose itself in the breadth of content in sensible reality and does not anchor itself there. Rather, it subordinates this—as *in need of an anchor*—to the necessity of a transcendent end." Willing to be "at home with itself," modern life suffers from a metaphysical homelessness, just as Jörgensen experienced a "longing for home." It lacks the ethos of the "primal hold [*Urverhältnis*] of the soul toward God." Theological metaphysics is primal ethics of the transcendent Kingdom of God (G1 198, 263; G1 409/PC 384; CA 494–95).

And again in the midst of this crisis and danger, we hear the voice of a call to *Kehre*. Philosophy's "most authentic calling" is to "aim at a *breakthrough* into the true reality and real truth"; it "is called to a decisive movement forward and deepening." Heidegger cited as a model here the "dominance of the notion of authority and the high esteem for all tradition" in the medieval world, its "devotion" to "the material of knowledge that has been handed down" (G1 406/PC 382; G1 191, 198). What he himself was aiming at was again a radical retrieval of the mystical "anchor" and "transcendent end" preserved in the medieval tradition, so that modern personalism and individualism could be grounded in this depth-dimension. He wanted to personalize mysticism and mysticize personalism.

We also find again the enactment-sense of the critical struggle *against* the subjectivistic hubris of modernism, but now in the more academic form of the "battle [*Kampf*] against psychologism," the "turning away [*Abkehr*] from psychologism," the "overcoming of psychologism." Heidegger's battle against psychologism picked up where his earlier battle against modernism in the *Der Akademiker* articles left off. The opening of his doctoral dissertation makes it clear that psychologistic logic is only one manifestation of the modern "age of psychology," which also includes "ethical and aesthetic investigations, pedagogy and the practice of law," "modern literature and art." One of his 1911 *Der Akademiker* articles already began the critique of psychologism, opening with the statement that "philosophy, in truth a mirror of eternity, today only reflects subjective opinions, personal moods, and wishes. . . . A strict ice-cold logic is inimical to the refined *feelings* of the modern soul. 'Thinking' can no longer let itself be constrained in the unshakeable eternal limits of fundamental logical principles" (G1 275, 18, 43, 63, 198–205; CA 496–97).

His 1912 article in the same journal carried the critique into the field of the study of religion. Taking up Braig's critique of modern psychology of religion, Heidegger conceded that "one will still have to attribute a not-unimportant significance" to William James's pragmatic analyses and to the stress on "subjective religious experience" in "modern Protestant theology that is oriented toward Kant, Schleiermacher, and Ritschl," since "religion determines psychic life in a unique way." But one must ensure that "empirical-psychological explanation" is not allowed to reduce "the supernatural side (grace)"— that is, the "content" of intentional religious experience in conversion, prayer, love, faith, and mysticism—to the intentional acts, especially to those of a "subconscious." The deepest inspiration for Heidegger's critique of psychologism in his two dissertations is not so much the pure logic of Neo-Kantianism and phenomenology as rather "Aristotelian-Scholastic philosophy that has always thought realistically" and its religious "devotional" attitude. One also has to factor in here Heidegger's alliance of antimodern Neo-Scholasticism with the Romantics' critique of modern rationalism and their return to medievalism (CA 504–505, 512–13; G1 15/PR 70).

On December 13, 1915, after the completion of his qualifying dissertation, the *Privatdozent* Heidegger—at the time doing military service first as a rifleman and then in the Freiburg Office of the Postal Censor—filed a request for another von Schaezler stipendium, writing to the chancellery that "he is orienting his life's scientific work toward the realization of the intellectual goods laid down in Scholasticism for the sake of the spiritual *Kampf* of the future for the Christian-Catholic ideal of life." This *Kampf*-mentality expressed itself in still another way in Heidegger's depictions of the heroicism of the lonely early death of Lask in the First World War, who was "torn from us all too early by a bitter destiny." In the same spirit, Heidegger wrote in the preface to his book on Scotus: "The philosophical creativity of Emil Lask, to whom in his distant soldier's grave a word of grateful and respectful memory should be said here, is evidence" for how Neo-Kantianism can lead to "the shaping of problems out of strong personal experience." As with his example of "the tremendous combat strength of our allied troops" in his essay on history, military life and philosopical life are strangely interwoven here. On a more philosophical note, his essay on history had opened with the affirmation of the "will of philosophy to power" in the awakening "metaphysical urge" in the very midst of the modern "intellectual forces of the so-called 'natural-scientific worldview' " (HMH 159; HL 77, 81–82; G1 407/PC 382; G1 191; G1 415/CT 3). The battle-bright young scholar was making ambitious lifelong plans for futher campaigns in Neo-Scholastic philosophy, but he was soon to lay down his kingly armor.

PART III

The End of Philosophy

7 | Demythologizing Metaphysics

Abdication

HEIDEGGER DID NOT get the chair of Catholic philosophy at Freiburg University to which he had been aspiring since 1913 with the help of his mentors Finke and Schneider. Upon receiving his license to teach in 1915, the eager lecturer had to be satisfied with assisting the temporary replacement Father Krebs with providing philosophy courses for theology students. He delivered lectures on "Die Grundlinien der antiken und scholastischen Philosophie" (The Basic Outlines of Ancient and Scholastic Philosophy) in WS 1915–16 and on "Der deutsche Idealismus" (German Idealism) in SS 1916. In WS 1916–1917, he took over the temporary position from Krebs and lectured on "Grundfragen der Logik" (Basic Questions of Logic). But Heidegger's hopes for the chair had already been bitterly disappointed by the middle of 1916 when the philosophical faculty instead nominated Josef Geyser, who arrived in Freiburg in SS 1917. Heidegger felt betrayed by his own mentors in the intrigues of university politics. Small consolation that in October 1917 Paul Natorp considered him as a candidate for a position in the history of medieval philosophy at Marburg, since he was placed only third on the nomination list (HL 82; MHT 539; MH 87).

His growing estrangement from Neo-Scholasticism was not only institutional, but involved a profound confessional, theological, and philosophical conversion in the wartime years after 1916. Among the students in his very first course of WS 1915–16 was Elfride Petri; they became engaged one year later and were married on March 21, 1917 by Father Krebs in a quiet wartime wedding in the university chapel. Shortly before, Heidegger's fiancée had visited Krebs to discuss her wish to convert from Protestantism to Catholicism, but was advised that she should wait until after the wedding to make such a difficult decision. She visited him again during Christmas of 1918 with some weighty news that he recorded in his journal: "My husband no longer has his faith in the Church, and I did not find it. His faith was already undermined by doubt at our wedding." It was she who had "pushed for the Catholic wedding and hoped to find faith with [her husband's] help." Together they "read much,

133

discussed, thought, and prayed a lot," but the result was that "both of us now think in a Protestant manner (i.e., without a fixed dogmatic tie), believe in the personal God, pray to him in the spirit of Christ, but without Protestant or Catholic orthodoxy" (HL 82; MH 99–101, 108).

On January 9, 1919, Heidegger himself wrote to Krebs, reminding him of his wife's visit and explaining that "over the last two years I struggled for a basic clarification of my philosophical position. . . . [However] epistemological insights extending to the theory of historical knowledge have made the *system* of Catholicism problematic and unacceptable to me, but not Christianity and metaphysics—these, though, in a new sense." He assured Krebs that he had lost neither his Christian faith, nor his "deep respect for the Catholic life-world," nor his philosophical interests in "the Middle Ages." He concluded with a statement that has the ring of Luther's "Here I stand." "I believe that I have an inner calling to philosophy, and, through fulfilling it in research and teaching, a call to achieve what stands in my power for—*and only for*—the eternal vocation of the inner person and thus to justify my very Dasein and activity before God" (MH 105–106). With this remarkable letter of declaration, Heidegger's *Kampf* for the historical *arche* of the "Catholic worldview," for his "career in the service of researching and teaching Christian-Scholastic philosophy," and for the Aristotelian-Scholastic metaphysics at work here officially ended. The ultraconservative Catholic had become a liberal Protestant and, given his continued interests in medieval mysticism, the exponent of a kind of free Lutheran mysticism.

On the philosophical level, the former Neo-Scholastic and Neo-Kantian now became an antiphilosopher for whom metaphysics was no longer "acceptable" in light of "the theory of historical knowledge." His "restlessness" about the "requirement" to incorportate history into the categories of being had been intensifying ever since 1915, and he now gave up his idea of fulfilling this requirement in the context of traditional philosophy. He began to speak of the end of philosophy and a new beginning for both ontology and theology. In his first postwar course of KNS 1919, Heidegger announced that "phenomenological critique" leads to "the catastrophe of all (previous) philosophy" and "a completely new concept of philosophy." On August 19, 1921, he wrote to his student Karl Löwith that "I am no philosopher. I do not presume even to do something comparable; it is not at all my intention." In WS 1921–22, drawing on the young Luther and Kierkegaard, he told his students that post-metaphysical thinking is a kind of skepticism, and that "skepticism is a beginning, and as the genuine beginning it is also the end of philosophy." Again on May 9, 1923, he told them "that, as far as he was concerned, philosophy was over."[1]

Heidegger now clearly resolved the ontological alternative posed in his student writings by affirming that categorial sense and God are not merely externally interwoven into history, but rather are themselves historical. In subjecting his earlier pure logic and speculative theological metaphysics to a radical destruction, he now became a kind of exiled hidden king who decisively abdicated the *Reich* of the place, Dasein, and truth of pure logical sense, as well as the speculative ontotheological Kingdom of God. We read in KNS 1919 that his "completely new concept of philosophy" means that "philosophy would then lose its most ancestral privileges, its superior kingly [*königlich*] vocation." Heidegger was here discussing inter alia Kant's *Kritik der reinen Vernunft*, and his own "phenomenological critique" reminds one of the "tribunal" of Kant's "critique of pure reason" in his Preface to the First Edition: "Time was when [metaphysics] was titled the Queen [*Königin*] of all sciences. . . . Now the changed fashion of the age brings her only scorn, and the matron, exiled and abandoned, mourns like Hecuba: *Modo maxima rerum . . . nunc trahor exul, inops,*" once the greatest in the kingdom . . . now dragged off in exile, in poverty (Ovid, *Metamorphoses* xiii, 508–10). Heidegger's "radical separation" and attempted reconciliation between critical "science" and the speculative "metaphysics" of worldview-philosophy, which aims to solve "the ultimate questions," also reminds one of Kant's juxtaposition between "the skeptics, a species of nomads, who despise all durable cultivation of the land," and the speculative "dogmatists" ("her dominion, under the administration of the dogmatists, was at first despotic"). Concerning his new "genuine beginning" in WS 1921–22, Heidegger's lecture notes stressed, "No fantastic representation of new categories that comfortably lead us into a new kingdom [*Reich*]," which would be "before the hand" and in which one could reign as philosopher-king, "prophet," "Führer." This new beginning is not "salvation," a "saving coast," "something established which is there fixedly in terms of time and place, and . . . to which one travels as if to a castle in the mountains [*Feldbergturm*]." And again, "It is of course the most comfortable thing to place onself immediately outside of the world and life into the kingdom [*Land*] of the blessed and the absolute." In SS 1923, Heidegger likewise criticized the Neo-Kantian "kingdom [*Reich*] of sense," the Platonic "place" of "validity, value, subsistence (over against 'sensible reality')," which "as that which dominates and reigns everywhere . . . makes up authentic being."[2]

Heidegger's letter of January 9, 1919 to Krebs spoke of *Verzicht*, a term which means the renunciation or abdication of a claim, right, authority, office, throne. A few months later, he wrote to Elisabeth Blochmann that "the new life we want . . . has *verzichtet*, renounced/abdicated, being universal." In WS 1919–20, he stated that "[philosophy] renounces/abdicates the 'system,' the ultimate partitioning of the All into realms," "metaphysics—the crown of the philosophical disciplines." We read from WS 1921–22 that "philosophy may not . . . presume to possess and define God" or to preach a "religious ideology"; rather, practicing "factical 'asceticism,' " the philosopher with his or her particular worldview "must withdraw and *verzichten,* go without, renounce, abdicate." This concept turned up also in other terms such as refusal (*Ablehnung*) and giving up (*Aufgeben*). For example, "The ideality of values and the like, which have been dressed up as transtemporal and posited as eternally valid on a noble throne [*in thronende Vornehmheit*], flutter about like phantoms. . . . Philosophy must think about giving up . . . the swindle of its aestheticizing intoxication of itself and its contemporaries." One "does not have the right [*Recht*] to set up in principle and in general absolute knowledge of truth as the rule of measurement for philosophy." A "claim [*Anspruch*] should not be made to absolute knowledge as the norm" (MH 107; HB 15; G58 239, 21; G61 198, 14, 111, 163–64).

In Heidegger's courses and unpublished essays of 1919 and the early 1920s, we already find clear and novel inscriptions of the three family resemblances in his later paths into the *Sache* of his thought, namely, the end of philosophy, a new beginning, and constant beginning anew. Part Three of this study explores how, in the decade of silence between his qualifying dissertation and the publication of SZ, the young Heidegger envisaged the end of philosophy, whereas Part Four examines the new beginning of his anarchic-personalist thoughtpaths and the constant beginning of his method of "formal indication." We will examine the young Heidegger's writings both in his early Freiburg period (KNS 1919 to SS 1923) and in the first part of his Marburg period up to WS 1925–26, though the focus will be on the former period.

By right, each of his courses and essays leading up to SZ deserves a separate and detailed chronological treatment, but this task exceeds the scope and limits of my study. Instead, I offer still another portrait of family resemblances in these writings, though I do outline the different stages that Heidegger's thought went through after 1919. I focus more on the early Freiburg period, as made accessible through the "*supplement*" to Heidegger's collected edition, because it expresses more clearly the type of daring, antiphilosophical, and experimental type of thinking that Heidegger was doing before SZ. It reminds one far less of Kant than of the ancient skeptics, the mystics, the young Luther, Kierkegaard, and even Derrida. Heidegger was at this time a great skeptic, destroyer, and demythologizer of western metaphysics, and this flury of criticism and innovation remains perhaps unmatched in his entire corpus. Even though his plan for the end of philosophy and a new beginning were still operative in his courses of SS 1925 and WS 1925–26 and in his 1927 book SZ, it had already been modified and tamed under the influence of the transcendental thought of Husserl and Kant. The early Freiburg period gives one a better sense of how the text about "being and time" that later became the plodding scientific treatise called *Sein und Zeit,* an aberration in Heidegger's own eyes, was originally supposed to read. And, just as important, this period allows one to understand how it could be that his *Kehre* after 1930 was actually made possible by a return to and creative reinscription of his youthful thought.

The present chapter sketches the young Heidegger's project of carrying out a destruction of the history of metaphysics and repeating the question about being with the aid of certain antimetaphysical traditions that could be uncovered through this destruction (primarily "primal Christianity," Aristotle's practical writings, Husserl's Sixth Investigation). Here in his notion of the end of philosophy, we find Heidegger in effect dismantling the guiding question of the Greek, medieval, and modern epochs of the first metaphysical beginning. More specifically, I examine: (1) Heidegger's understanding of metaphysics as a kind of myth-making that needs to be unmasked and demythologized; (2) the intimate connection between his project of destruction and his plans for a phenomenology of religion; and (3) how this connection is displayed in the list of his courses and publication plans between KNS 1919 and SS 1921.

Metaphysics as Myth

The young Heidegger now took metaphysics to be a kind of phantasy, myth, dreamland. He referred to it as "mythical and theosophical metaphysics," a "phantasy of life and thinking," "this fantastic path to the transhistorical," "religious ideology and phantasy," "a dream of ideal possibilities of absolute knowledge," "a soporific opiate," a "dream-condition." In WS 1919–20, he insisted that "the primal region of philosophy is . . . nothing mythical." In WS 1921–22, he quoted Kierkegaard's statement that "philosophy has aroused the illusion that human beings could, as one prosaically says, speculate themselves out of their own good skin and into pure light." In SS 1925, he contrasted "the matter itself" of intentionality with Rickert's "mythical concept of representing" and with "the old mythology of an intellect which glues and rigs together the world's matter with its own forms." In KNS 1919, he read to his students Plato's criticism of the mythopoetic thinking in the pre-Socratic battle of the giants about being (*Sophist* 242c): "It seems to me," his translation ran, "that each of them (the old philosophers of being) tells a *mython*, a myth, a story, as though we were children." In WS 1924–25, he extensively discussed this passage and its critique of "wild speculation" ("they 'tell stories' without authentic *logos*"), highlighting it again in SZ: "If we are to understand the problem of being, our first philosophical step consists in not *mython tina diegeisthai*, in not 'telling a myth, a story.'" His new nonspeculative and hyper-empirical sense of philosophy, which he called "skepticism," wanted to focus on the historical and personal temporalizing-sense of being, which he called *Ereignis* (1919), kairological time (1920–21), and *kinesis* (1921–23). For the young Heidegger, being is marked by an irreducible kinetic-personal physiognomy; it has no unchanging universal content. By the phantasy and myth of metaphysics, he thus meant that, with its pretensions to "absolute knowledge," it "childishly closes its eyes" to the "difficult" *kinesis* of life, and falls asleep in the tranquil dream of a "pure present" and kingdom of impersonal universality.[3]

Heidegger maintained that metaphysics is an extension of the tendency to falling in prephilosphical life. To use the terminology of WS 1921–22 and SS 1923, life is the ongoing attempt to mask (*maskieren*) the kinetic-personal physiognomy of being with the static and impersonal dominion of *das Man*, the anonymous public "They" (what "they" know, say, do, own, etc.). This masquerade (*Maskierung*) is also the hyperbolic or excessive (*das Hyperbolische*), insofar as it involves falling away from one's unique historical situatedness into the abstract Beyond (*hyper*) of the They. Heidegger called this masking "larvance" or "ghostliness" (*Larvanz*), a term coined from the Latin word *larva*, which means both ghost or phantom and mask. Life becomes ghostly and phantom in the public abstractions of the They; one's life is in a state of "ambiguity"; it looks like it is concretely there and is being lived fully, but really it is not. This hyperbolic phantom life is in a state of *Entfremdung*, alienation (G61 140; G63 15). Here Heidegger laid out a whole set of categories belonging to the masquerade of this phantom life (see G61 100–155).

Inclination (*Neigung*) means a certain intentional directness in which life abandons itself to the pull and drag of its world. It includes the categories of disposition (*Geneigtheit*), being-carried-along (*Mitgenommenwerden*) by the world, dispersion (*Zerstreuung*) into the world, and worldly self-satisfaction (*Selbstgenügsamkeit*). Glutting and satiating itself with the world, "life 'has itself' and experiences itself always only in the shape of its 'world' " (G61 101). The effacing of distance (*Abstandstilgung*) means that, within inclination, the distance between self and world is erased. It too contains a multiplicity of categories. In distantiality (*Abständigkeit*), distance turns up as the concern for the distance between my worldly status and the anonymous They (what they know, say, do, own). The They provides an "interpretedness" of life that is characterized by "averageness" and "publicness," and as such it functions as the measure with which one pursues and comparatively calculates "rank, success, position in life (world)," "importance," "preeminence, the first, the closest, highest, and most" (G63 31; G61 103, 106–107). Lost in the Beyond of the high and mighty They, life lives in the category of the hyperbolic and thus also in the categories of overlooking oneself and going wrong (*Versehen*), mismeasuring (*Vermessen*) one's unique historical situation, and thus missing the mark. "Life mismeasures itself; it misapprehends itself regarding the measure fitting to it (measure not quantitative)" (G61 103). For Heidegger, *Vermessen* also carries the sense of presumption, pride, hubris.

Finally, the category of obstruction or blocking-off (*Abriegelung*) means that life is concealed, alienated, blocked off from itself. It has disguised itself from itself with the "mask of public interpretedness" and leads a larvant phantom life of ambiguity, illusion, pulling the wool over one's eyes (*Sich-etwas-Vormachen*). "This 'They' is *the* 'no one' that circulates like a phantom in factical Dasein, a how of the specific disaster of facticity." Life is characterized by *Diesigkeit*, a certain fogginess coming from the smoke screen of the They that can never be completely dissipated. "Hyperbolic Dasein" constantly cultivates possiblities of missing (*Verfehlen*) the shifting mark of its situational life, and as such cultivates the elliptic (*das Elliptische*) in the sense of "leaving itself behind," "omitting itself, and "falling short" of itself. Still other categories belonging to obstruction are waylaying itself (*Sich-aus-dem-Weg-gehen*) and blinding itself (*Blendung*). "Life blinds itself, sticks out its own eyes," Heidegger said bluntly. This hyperbolic masquerade is at bottom a "flight" in the face of the "difficult," namely, passionately living and choosing in the midst of the flux of things. Instead of this, inauthentic life seeks taking-it-easy (*Erleichterung*), "carefreeness," "security," and comfort (*Bequemlichkeit*) in the static and impersonal conventions of the They. "Dasein speaks of itself, it sees itself as such and such, and yet it is only a mask that it holds before itself, in order not to be frightened by itself. Defense against 'the' anxiety" (G61 108; G63 32).

The above-discussed categories belong primarily to the relational and enactment-senses of factical life. Heidegger also showed their deeper kinetic temporalizing-sense in the categories of relucency (*Reluzenz*), prestruction (*Prestruktion*), ruination (*Ruinanz*), not-having-time, and the effacing of time (*Zeittilgung*). Inclination is temporally relucent in that it lets the world shine back on itself as a future, and it is prestructive in the sense of developing (*Ausbildung*) in advance secure possibilities into which it falls away from itself. These fixed relucent possibilities are built up and temporalized as "structure," as images, pictures, or paradigms (*Bilder*) of life, which make up the goods of worldview, culture, and education (*Bildung*), in which life is disposed, carried along, dispersed, and self-satisfied.

Similarly, distantiality is relucently prestructive insofar as it futurally develops and lets shine back on itself the hyperbolic possibilities and standards of the They, with which it can proudly but mistakenly take measure of itself. Finally, obstruction is relucently prestructive in that it allows itself to come futurally toward itself wearing the phantom mask of the They, dressed up in its structures and pictures, thereby "scaring itself away, as it were," and not allowing itself to come toward itself genuinely. It "makes it its business that . . . it should never come into the embarrassment . . . of having to look . . . life in the face [*ins Gesicht*]" (G61 123–24).

The category of ruination expresses the fact that the *kinesis* of inauthentic life is not only a "toward itself," but simultaneously the "against itself," "away from itself," and "out of itself" of falling-away, which Heidegger now called the plunge or crash (*das Sturz*) out of authentic time and into the dominion of the They.[4] Ruination (coined from the Latin word *ruina*, falling down, collapse) also involves the temporal categories of "1. the tempting (the tentative), 2. the comforting (the quietive), 3. the alienating (the alienative), 4. the annihilating (the negative; active, transitive)." Ruinant life tempts, comforts, alienates, and annihilates itself temporally in that the terminus of its crash (namely, the impersonal and static realities of the They) entails the vacancy (*die Leere*) and nothing (*Nichts*) of "there is nothing [and no one] here" and "there is nothing going on." "What happens? Nothing." "The nothing of factical life is that of its own not-coming-forth" (G61 123, 140, 147–48; G63 32).

More precisely, the terminus of the fall is the *presence* (*Präsenz*) of the present (*das Gegenwart*). Here the present is "the public interpretedness of the today." Heidegger's notes read, "Dasein as historical present, its own. Being in the world, being lived by the world; present-everyday. . . . The today ontologically: the *present of the most immediate*, the They, being-with-one-another; 'our times.' " Tarrying in this today, Dasein "makes itself present [*präsent*] for itself and holds itself in this presence [*Präsenz*]." It is in the nothing-happening and the no-one of this presence that Dasein attempts to mask, to alienate, to comfort, and to annihilate itself. Faced with the difficulty of being, personal historical life falls prey to a death-wish of effacement: it is that which "should be finished, annihilated." Heidegger coined the term "the quietive" from the Latin word *quies*, which means rest, repose, sleep, the sleep of death (cf. the English "quietism"). "Care lays down more and more on life and finally remains lying down on it" (G63 79, 29–30; G61 107, 140). Life wants to fall asleep, to die, to rest in peace in a comforting dreamland of presence. It lives as a phantom, a ghost of itself.

This collapse into the presence of the today is what Heidegger also called the "effacing of time," that is, of the kinetic-personal physiognomy of the temporalizing of historical situations. Distracted in the today of *das Man* and thus having "no time" for its own time, life literally "has no time" in the sense of having effaced it. "Factical ruinant life 'has no time' because its basic movement, ruinance itself, takes away 'time'. . . . Ruinance takes away time, i.e., it seeks to efface the historical from facticity. The ruinance of factical life has this enactment-sense of the *effacing of time*." Rather than having time for its "kairological" (situational) time by "sitting still, waiting . . . 'giving it time' " in a stance of "wakefulness," life reduces the future to an extension of the present of the today, of the They, and proceeds "to calculate in advance" what will and will not happen, to whom it will happen, when it will happen, and in what measure. The future is taken as an available, calculable present that has not yet arrived. Hyperbolically obstructed and blinded in this way, life temporalizes itself elliptically, that is, by contantly going wrong and missing "the fitting measure" in the *kairos*, the moment (*Augenblick*). "Obstruction has the specific enactment- and temporalizing-character of the elliptical" (G61 140, 108; G63 19; BZ 20).

Since Heidegger understood philosophy to be life interpreting itself, he applied the above categories to philosophy itself, namely, masking, ghostliness, the They, the hyperbolic and the elliptical, presumptuous mismeasuring, ruination, alienation, comfort, security, effacing time. Metaphysics is likewise afraid of the difficulty of life and suffers from the same lack of nerve. It too effaces the original kinetic-personal physiognomy of being with its masquerades, phantoms, and myths about a dreamland of presence. It is just a more refined type of hyperbolic phantom life. Heidegger's notes read, "Organized distantiality and ruination, as Platonism in philosophy. The 'before' of the theoretical attitude returns relucently here as the high value of objectivity" (G61 122). As we will explore in detail in Part Four, Heidegger's new beginning viewed the temporal happening of being as ultimately groundless, absence-permeated, anarchically differentiated into personal life, and hence incalculable and nonmasterable. Thus we find him speaking of "the mystery . . . of all life" (HB 14). What both cultural life and traditional philosophical life share is the masquerade of being as a fixed presence that is homogeneous, universal, before-the-hand, and thus able to be calculated and mastered. Both manifest a will to totalization, closure, and what Heidegger already understood as the "technization" of being.

In cultural life, this illusion takes the form of the dominion of the public conventions of the They; in philosophy, it shows up as the ideal of a *Reich* of unchanging, universal, and impersonal truth, and as the myths and worldview-ideologies that get constructed in the pursuit of this ideal. These make up the great Beyond of hyperbolic philosophy, the Meta of metaphysics. Here Heidegger quoted Spranger: "We all—Rickert, the phenomenologists, the movement connected with Dilthey—meet one another in the great struggle for the *timeless in the historical* or *beyond* the *historical*, for the *kingdom* [*Reich*] *of sense* . . . which leads beyond the merely subjective toward the objective and the valid." In fact, Heidegger took metaphysics to be a kind of public philosophical They. "Even philosophy is in publicness; it *is* here in the manner of everything public, i.e., it presents [*präsentiert*] itself in this." "Objective philosophy" offers "objective agreement, 'We all . . . ,' i.e., it presents [*präsentiert*] to Dasein itself the prospect of the peaceful security of the universal unanimous 'yes.'" The phantom mask that philosophy uses to flee the difficult is "the Holy Ghost of Knowledge," the "pure ghost" of "absolute truth." "The illusion of purely objective absolute philosophy" is "the masked cries of *anxiety* in the face of philosophy." "The 'we all' in Spranger is only the mask of insecurity: no one has seen it, no one believes it, each is too cowardly to admit it."

The tendency in everyday life toward "the quietive" and "taking-it-easy" is taken up into the more sophisticated aesthetic quietism of philosophy, which wants to take a permanent holiday from the unrest of factical life, sleep, and die in the "metaphysical comforts," "soporific opiate," and "dream of ideal possibilities of absolute knowledge." The metaphysician does not want to be "disturbed on his walks through world, soul, and God." "The whole of modern philosophy is . . . based on easygoingness" (Kierkegaard).[5] Metaphysics, too, is life's secret death-wish.

Philosophy is just a more rarified expression of the falling away into illusions of *presence* which is found in the effacing of kairological time in prephilosophical life. It is a type of "interpretedness of the today." Here Heidegger showed that contemporary philosophy of history reduces the past, present, and future to "an objective-historical phenomenon (my life seen as being played out in the present)." Specifically regarding Oswald Spengler and Neo-Kantianism, he asked, "Which being [*Sein*] stands here in prehaving? Before-the-hand being, present-being [*Gegenwärtigsein*], change in the present, transformation of culture." Historical time is here fully present for theoretical "curiosity" in order to be surveyed, classified, and then "calculated in advance" regarding its futural aspect (e.g., Spengler's eschatology of "the decline of the West"). Heidegger's notes read, "The not-yet, in itself as the present in *calculation*; comparative reading-off." Against this speculation, he also wrote, "The today and the 'generation.' Against fantastic world-history. Instead of this on the ground, and let it be that of radical concrete questionableness." Similarly, in their orientation to the atemporal validity of logical sense and values, Neo-Kantian transcendental logic and value-philosophy reduce all historical experience back to the "kingdom" of "the *transtemporal in-itself*, being, validity, value, subsistence (over against 'sensible reality')." "Temporality is ordered and filed away into the eternal." Both historical science and philosophy are more sophisticated theoretical ways in which "Dasein . . . makes itself present for itself and holds itself in this presence." Whereas "historical consciousness lets Dasein be encountered in the full wealth of its objective *having-been-being* [*Gewesensein*], philosophy lets it be encountered in the unchangingness of *always-so-being*. Both bring Dasein itself before its highest possible and pure *present* [*Gegenwart*]." Both are modes in which Dasein is intent upon the myth of "*having itself there objectively*," as a present, calculable, secure object (G63 33, 43, 54–65, 106, 41, 79; G9 32; BZ 23–25).

In KNS 1919, Heidegger introduced a set of terms that can be conveniently used to get at how, throughout his early Freiburg period, he saw the history of philosophy to be a mythologizing of the entire intentional configuration of being-sense (G56/57 63–94). It not only dehistoricizes (*entgeschichtlicht*) the temporalizing-sense of the *Ereignis* of the person/world relation into the phantasy of a pure presence, but also designifies (*entdeutet*) or, to use

Heidegger's term from SS 1925, deworlds (*entweltlicht*) content-sense by reducing the immediate significance of the "it worlds" of the environing world to an objective reality, to a thing (realism) or an idea (idealism) (G20 266/196). Likewise, it delives (*entlebt*) relational sense by reducing personal Dasein to some form of reason, spirit, or epistemological consciousness.

What was at work in the young Heidegger's concept of "the end of philosophy" was a critique of these philosophical ideologies, an unmasking of these masquerades, a demythologizing of these myths, a deconstructing of these kingdoms. He himself did not use the term "demythologizing." It was the theologian Rudolf Bultmann who, during their collaboration in Marburg beginning in 1923, learned this type of "questioning kairological-critically 'in one's time'" from Heidegger, applied it to the specific domain of Christian experience, and gave it the label of "demythologizing."[6] Myth in Bultmann's sense means any outdated imaginative representation of the believer/God relation that abstracts from and is alien to the experiential "now" character of this relation in the historical *kairos*; for example, the content-sense of eternal life with God, or the lordship of the risen Christ in the Ascension, are mythologized, deworlded, delived, and dehistoricized in terms of the ancient mythopoetic cosmology of a heavenly Kingdom in the distant upper reaches of the universe. But the concept and the project of demythologizing were already there in Heidegger. He wrote, for example, "absolute knowledge: . . . at bottom a dream. . . . one should be on guard against the use of the idea of absolute truth as a soporific opiate" (G61 164). However, neither in Bultmann's theological sense nor in Heidegger's ontological sense does demythologizing mean the disenchantment of the world, i.e., banishing mystery, the poetic, and the religious. Rather, it means bringing their worldly, personal, and historical dimensions into play.

For Heidegger, destruction (*Destruktion*) meant more specifically *Abbau*, a dismantling or deconstructing of the constructions and obstructions of the history of philosophy. "*Abbau*, this means here: regress to Greek philosophy, to Aristotle, in order to see how something original came into a falling away and covering over, and to see that we stand in this *falling away*." Destruction is a "counter-ruinant movement" that drags metaphysics back from its comfortable masquerades and brings it face to face with the original kinetic-personal physiognomy of being in all its "questionableness" and difficulty. As a critique of metaphysical ideology, it awakens philosophy from its sleep and alienation in a Beyond: "Hermeneutics has the job of . . . going after the alienation of self with which Dasein is strapped. . . . terminologically, [this understanding] is fixed in advance as *the being-awake* of Dasein for itself." Thus destruction works in the service of *Wiederholung*, repetition, which is taken in its literal sense of "fetching back" the original questionableness of life: "Philosophy is a basic how of life itself, such that in each case it repeats and fetches it back [*wieder-holt*] authentically, brings it back from its falling away." Heidegger claimed that this deconstructive repetition only radicalizes "the tendency of factical life to 'be' in the mode of bringing-itself-to-having." The latter is "the conscience," which simultaneously discloses the "guilt" of having fallen and constantly falling (G63 76, 15; G61 153, 80, 171, 62, 88, 109; G9 33).

Heidegger's demythologizing of metaphysics sought to erase the traditional mythic inscriptions of the intentional configuration of being-sense, and attempted to retrace its original kinetic-personal physiognomy in his own new beginnings. Taking up his earlier schema of the three major epochs and worldviews in the history of philosophy, he aimed his genealogical destruction at "the very first beginning" in the Greek world and at its "transformations" and "restructurings" in the "Middle Ages" and "modernity" (G61 170, 2-3). In examining his destruction of medieval Scholastic metaphysics, Greek metaphysics in the figure of Aristotle, and modern metaphysics in the figures of Husserl and the Neo-Kantians, we will also see that he uncovers certain antimetaphysical traditions, namely, primal Christianity, Aristotle's practical writings, and Dilthey and Husserl's Sixth Investigation, which serve as models for his own thought, since he held that they had already addressed the ground-question of metaphysics, the question about "being and time." Heidegger retrieved, reinscribed, and weaved together these influences into the bricolage of his various textual drafts of his new postmetaphysical beginning. In fact, our major focus in Part Three will be these historical influences on his thought. To begin with, however, it is important to look briefly at how his phenomenological ontology was intimately bound up with his project of a phenomenology of religion.

Ontology and Phenomenology of Religion

The details of Heidegger's theological and philosophical conversion in the wartime years of 1917-18 are becoming more known to us today, but they are to a great extent still shrouded in darkness. Neither his own manuscripts nor student transcripts for his courses from WS 1915-16 to WS 1916-17 appear to be extant. The university catalogues announced that he was giving courses on "Hegel" for SS 1917, on "Plato" for WS 1917-18, and on "Lotze and the Development of Modern Logic" for SS 1918, but he did not deliver them since he was actually away most of the time doing military service, which included a two-month sojourn at a meteorological station on the western front (HEL 23; MH 104-105). But we do know that during these interim years he made a new turn to Husserl's phenomenology and to its application in a phenomenology of religion.

When Husserl arrived in Freiburg in 1916 as Rickert's successor, Heidegger began soliciting Husserl's personal support of his studies and career, making visits, sending letters, and presenting Husserl with copies of his essay on time and his qualifying dissertation, which Husserl helped to get published. But during 1916 and early 1917, Husserl kept the young lecturer at arm's length, apologizing in a few postcards that his busy schedule did not allow him to do more. In the winter of 1917–18, Husserl became more enthusiastic and actively took on the role of fatherly supporter, writing on March 28, 1918 to the "Home Guard Soldier Martin Heidegger" about Heidegger's immanent return from "the field" to university life, and about how "I will sincerely and gladly do my part to put you back *in medias res* and familiarize you with this *res* in *symphilosophein*," co-philosophizing. Then came a long intimate letter on September 10, 1918, in which Husserl discussed in detail his own recent work and plans for Heidegger's work (LH). When Heidegger was eventually discharged from military service on November 16, 1918 and returned to Freiburg, he finally "met Husserl in his workshop," writing to Blochmann on January 14, 1919 about his "intensive work with Husserl" and again on May 1 about his "continual learning in community with Husserl." The two were working together so well that Husserl had submitted a request on January 7 to the ministry of education for Heidegger's promotion to the unprecedented position of assistant to his chair. Due to Husserl's persistence, the request was granted in the following year, but with the stipulation that the assistantship be restricted to the person of Heidegger. He was now officially Husserl's assistant and remained such until his departure to Marburg in 1923. The Neo-Scholastic had become a card-carrying phenomenologist. Husserl would often say to his "favorite student" and "phenomenological child" that "you and I are phenomenology." Heidegger returned this compliment in 1923, with his autobiographical statement that "Husserl gave me my eyes."[7]

But Heidegger's phenomenological turn was bound up with a reformulation of the phenomenology of religion that he had already announced in his work on Scotus and that was supposed to entail "a phenomenological elaboration of mystical, moral-theological, and ascetic literature," including especially "Eckhartian mysticism." These plans were still alive when Heidegger wrote to the medievalist Martin Grabmann on January 7, 1917 about a possible review of his book on Scotus and stressed that "your friendly postcard and a letter from Bäumker are for me the most valuable incentives for further works in the area of medieval Scholasticism and mysticism." In his letter of September 10, 1918 to Heidegger on the front, Husserl wrote, "Thus each to his own as if the salvation of the world depended upon it alone and so I in philosophy and you as weatherman and in the side job of phenomenologist of religion" (LH). During the preceeding summer, Heidegger and his friend Ochsner had brought Rudolf Otto's *Das Heilige* (The Holy) to the attention of Husserl, whose letter of September 10 suggests that Heidegger may have been thinking of doing a review of this work. "I am reading with great interest Otto's book on *Das Heilige*, an attempt in fact at a phenomenology of the consciousness of God. . . . Too bad that you do not have time to write a (deeply penetrating) critical review." Then in his letter of January 9, 1919 to Krebs, Heidegger himself mentioned "my phenomenological investigations of religion that will draw heavily on the M.A. [Middle Ages]," and in May of 1919 he wrote to Blochmann about his "phenomenology of religious consciousness."[8]

His initial phenomenology of religion around 1915–16 was moving in the direction of a historical mystical-personalist heterology. But it was still permeated with metaphysical and ontotheological elements from the Aristotelian-Scholastic worldview of Catholicism, from the speculative theological thinking of German idealism, and from the ontologic of Neo-Kantianism and Husserl's phenomenology. In his courses from KNS 1919 onward, he now repeatedly expressed the view that the Aristotelian and Neo-Platonic conceptuality of both Catholic and mainstream Protestant theology amounted to a foreign infiltration and distortion of the concrete historicity of the primal Christianity (*Urchristentum*) of the New Testament, which had nonetheless violently reasserted itself at key historical points, namely, in Augustine, the medieval mystics, Pascal, Schleiermacher, Kierkegaard, and especially the young Luther's attack on Aristotelian-Scholasticism. Heidegger wrote in WS 1919–20,

> The ancient Christian achievement was distorted and buried through the infiltration of classical science into Christiantity. From time to time it reasserted itself in violent eruptions (as in Augustine, in Luther, in Kierkegaard). Only from here is medieval mysticism to be understood. . . . [After Augustine] the struggle between Aristotle and the new "feeling for life" continued in medieval mysticism and eventually in Luther.

And in the same course we read again, concerning the Greek philosophical infiltration,

> A tangled process that was continually interrupted [*unterbrochen*] by the claims of the basic, genuinely primal Christian attitude, at one moment with sweeping elemental force as one finds in an Augustine, and then *isolated* in quiet seclusion and practical lifestyle (medieval mysticism: Bernard of Clairvaux, Bonaventura, Eckhart, Tauler, Luther).

Heidegger drew his reading of the historical interconnection between Christianity and philosophy from such sources as Dilthey's studies, "Christianity, Theory of Knowledge, and Metaphysics" and "Augustinus" (1883); Max Scheler's 1916 essay "Liebe und Erkenntnis"; and Paul Natorp's two-volume wartime book *Deutscher Weltberuf: Geschichtsphilosophische Richtlinien*, which Husserl had recommended to Heidegger in his letter of September 10, 1918. In his account of the history of Christianity in WS 1921–22, Heidegger said that "Dilthey had a sure instinct here, just as he did everywhere in his research of our cultural history."[9]

"The historical," Heidegger wrote in KNS 1919, "is somehow co-given in the essence of Christianity itself. . . . [A]part from a few imperfect attempts in the new Protestant theology, there is not even the slightest consciousness that a problem with the greatest consequences lies here." This is the realization that he had come to in the interim war years of 1917–18, judging from his letter of 1919 to Krebs and from his counsel to Blochmann on November 7, 1918 that "what you search for you find in yourself, there is a path from primal religious experience to theology, but it *need not* lead from theology to religious consciousness and its vivacity." Following in the footsteps of such protest-ant figures as Luther and Kierkegaard, Heidegger's newly conceived phenomenology of religion became the project of a destruction of the Greek conceptuality underlying traditional theological thought, one which would penetrate to the historicity of "the religious lifeworld" of primal Christianity and find a more adequate conceptuality for it with the help of Husserl's phenomenology and Dilthey's philosophy of life. We read in WS 1919–20,

> The great revolution [of Christianity] against ancient science, against Aristotle above all, who, however, actually prevailed once again in the coming millennium, indeed should have become the Philosopher of official Christianity—in such a manner that the inner experiences and the new attitude of life [of Christianity] were pressed into the forms of expression in ancient science. To free oneself and radically free onself from this process, which still has a deep and confusing after-effect today, is *one* of the innermost tendencies of phenomenology.

In the following semester, Heidegger called for the "destruction of Christian philosophy and theology" (G59 12). His idea of the end of philosophy also meant the end of theology and a new beginning for it. The intentional configuration of *summum ens*/contemplation/presence in medieval Scholasticism and Heidegger's own earlier speculative configuration of the absolute/spirit/atemporality had to be dismantled back to the more originary configuration of *Deus absconditus*/faith/kairological time in primal Christianity. "Neither in Catholic nor in Protestant theology to this day has a methodologically clear concept of this science [of theology] arrived at its *Durchbruch*, its breakthrough," wrote Heidegger in 1919, with his old Eckhartian language in mind (G56/57 26, 18, 134; HB 10; G58 61).

During 1917–19 he seems to have been very attracted to the Protestant theologian and Romantic philosopher Friedrich Schleiermacher, giving a talk on August 2, 1917 before a private circle on "the problem of the religious" in Schleiermacher that focused on "the second discourse of [his] *Discourses on Religion*." "The impression it made on me still lingers through the whole week," wrote Ochsner, from whom this information about Heidegger comes.

Heidegger's enthusiasm must have been great because that Easter he had actually been giving away copies of Hermann Süskind's 1911 study *Christentum und Geschichte bei Schleiermacher* (Christianity and History in Schleiermacher), which, "coming from [Ernst] Troeltsch, rendered the absoluteness of Christianity that was still claimed by Schleiermacher into the highest form of truth given to us in a 'free Christianity' and thus inserted it into history." Even when Heidegger was away doing military service, he was still studying; for example, he wrote from the western front to Blochmann on October 2, 1918 that "in my last free days [training in Berlin-Charlottenburg] I still worked splendidly in the royal library. . . . Now and then I even get down to work [here on the front]." Blochmann was planning to do a dissertation on Schleiermacher, and we find Heidegger's letter of November 7, 1918 providing her with a detailed plan for her work that stressed Schleiermacher's letters and "youthful writings" (*Monologen*, 1800; *Weihnachtsfeier*, 1806; *Reden über die Religion*, 1799), and highlighted the most important secondary sources (Dilthey's *Leben Schleiermachers* and recent dissertations on "Schleiermacher's philosophy of history," especially Hermann Süskind's study). On January 14, 1919, Heidegger—now back in Freiburg and "rummaging" in the university library—offered more bibliographic entries on Schleiermacher for Blochmann's dissertation, mentioning Dilthey again. On January 24, he invited Blochmann to come to Freiburg at least for KNS 1919 and perhaps even to do her dissertation there under his guidance (MV 92; DMH 326; HB 9–13).

The next day Heidegger began his first postwar course in which early on he presented a reading of the development of Christianity in its relation to Greek philosophy, and in the summer semester he said of Schleiermacher that "he discovered primal Christianity." In the second discourse on religion, which according to Ochsner "contains the essential content of Heidegger's talk" in August of 1917, Schleiermacher distinguishes religion sharply from metaphysics and morals, as well as from theological doctrine; he argues that religion is based autonomously in the immediate intuition of the historical manifestation of the infinite in the unique particularities of the world and, more specifically, in the personal self-consciousness of the "*feeling* of dependence" on the infinite. "Religion's essence is neither thinking nor acting, but intuition and feeling." Schleiermacher's regress to primal religious experience, Heidegger noted in 1919, "influenced in a decisive way Hegel's youthful works on the history of religion and indirectly Hegel's whole specifically philosophical system, in which the decisive ideas of the German [intellectual] movement in general condensed into their high point" (G56/57 18, 134; MV 92; OR 102).

Heidegger was also reading the mystics for his phenomenology of religion. Around the summer of 1918 he was examining Adolf Deissmann's studies on Pauline mysticism (*Paulus*, 1911; *Die neutestamentliche Formel "in Christo*

Jesu", 1892), and in the fall he read Bernard of Clairvaux and Theresa of Avila while on the front. For WS 1919–20, he scheduled a lecture course titled "Die philosopischen Grundlagen der mittelalterlichen Mystik" (Philosophical Foundations of Medieval Mysticism), but he canceled it apparently due to lack of time to prepare for both this and the other lecture course he was teaching. But, according to Kisiel, his notes for this course and other documents show that he had been reading and was planning to deal with not only "Eckhart's hortatory tracts and popular sermons, but also Bernard's *Sermons on the Song of Songs*, Theresa's *Interior Castle*, Francis of Assisi's *Fioretti*, and Thomas à Kempis's *Imitation of Christ*" (Heidegger gave a copy of the latter to Löwith at Christmas, 1920), as well as perhaps Angelus Silesius, Augustine, Rudolf Otto's *Das Heilige*, and Natorp's treatment of Eckhart in his *Deutscher Weltberuf*. Like his work on Scotus, Heidegger's first course of 1919 interpreted medieval mysticism as a fusion of the "religious lifeworld" of early Christianity and the "researching lifeworld" of Scholasticism. "The original motives and tendencies of both lifeworlds enter into and flow together in mysticism. It thereby gains the characteristic of a free flowing movement of the life of consciousness." Heidegger's WS 1921–22 lecture course likewise pointed out the rediscovery of primal Christianity in the Rhineland mysticism of Eckhart and his follower Tauler.[10]

In KNS 1919, Heidegger wrote that, after the flourishing of high-medieval mysticism, "religious consciousness wins its new position with Luther." All indications are that, sometime shortly after the war, Heidegger entered into an intensive study of Luther's writings, perhaps partly on the prompting of Natorp's focus on Luther in his *Deutscher Weltberuf*. Jaspers recalled that, during his visit with Heidegger in April 1920, "he sat alone with him in his den, watched him at his Luther studies, and saw the intensity of his work." Julius Ebbinghaus recounted that after the war his friend Heidegger "had received the Erlangen edition of Luther's works as a prize or gift—and so we read Luther's reformatory writings for a while in the evenings we spent together [one per week]. Out of this grew my essay 'Luther and Kant.' " The time of Heidegger's library acquisition may have been 1921 since in September of that year Husserl reported back to his Canadian benefactor, Winthrop Bell, that "I gave the first 1000 marks to our outstanding Heidegger . . . he can now buy several source-books important for his philosophy of religion." Heidegger and Ebbinghaus even gave a seminar together in 1923 on "Die theologische Grundlagen von Kant, *Religion innerhalb der Grenzen der blossen Vernunft*" (The Theological Foundations of Kant's *Religion within the Limits of Mere Reason*), which explored the influence of Luther on Kant and German Idealism. In 1922 Heidegger planned to publish a journal essay on "The Ontological Foundations of Late Medieval Anthropology and the Theology of the Young Luther," but like so many of his publication plans it never appeared.[11]

Heidegger's preoccupation with Luther continued after his move to the University of Marburg in 1923. Upon arriving, for example, he immediately joined Rudolf Bultmann's seminar on the ethics of Saint Paul, introducing into the discussion Luther's interpretations of *Genesis* and *Exodus*. According to Löwith, "Heidegger held a seminar with [Bultmann] on the young Luther" (MLD 29). In fact, Heidegger and Bultmann collaborated intensely in a number of joint seminars and study groups that included reading the Gospel of John in regular Saturday sessions.[12] In the same period, Heidegger is reported to have delivered a lecture on Luther's commentary on Paul's letter to the Galatians in one of Bultmann's seminars, and even took over the Protestant theological seminar of a colleague who had fallen ill. "At Marburg," wrote the visiting British scholar W. R. Boyce Gibson, "it is not [Rudolf] *Otto* that the theologians came to hear but *Heidegger*." Bultmann maintained that "Heidegger himself never made a secret of the fact that he was influenced . . . most notably by Luther." Gadamer's recollection is also that Heidegger's "inspiration came from the young Luther." The Luther scholar Edmund Schlink went so far as to maintain that "Heidegger's existential analytic of human Dasein is a radical secularization of Luther's anthropology." Heidegger's teaching and publications in the twenties had a tremendous impact on the course of German Protestant theology in such figures as Bultmann, Paul Tillich, and Heinrich Ott. He was always known in Germany *also* as something of a theologian and Luther expert, such that we find him, for example, having assisted the Luther scholar Gerhard Ebeling in his 1961 work on Luther's *Disputatio de Homine*. Heidegger even had a line from Luther's translation of the Old Testament engraved above the door of his house in Zähringen: *Behüte dein Herz mit allem Fleiss; denn daraus geht das Leben* (Shelter your heart; for from it life flows forth) (Prov. 4:23).[13]

Heidegger found the same rediscovery of primal Christianity in Pascal and especially Kierkegaard. "We also shared a passion for Kierkegaard," wrote Jaspers about his visits with Heidegger from 1920 onward. Heidegger had first begun reading Kierkegaard around 1911 in the translations that appeared in Ludwig von Ficker's journal *Der Brenner* (HA 389). Then in spring 1919 Jaspers's *Psychologie der Weltanschauungen* appeared and presented an extensive treatment of Kierkegaard's notions of "human existence," "death," "guilt," "the moment of vision," "repetition," "indirect communication." In 1919–21 Heidegger worked on an unpublished review of this work that led to both his friendship with Jaspers and his first intensive reading of Kierkegaard's works.

In dealing with these religious sources, Heidegger's concern was both a general phenomenological ontology of being and a regional phenomenological theology of primal Christianity, both a new ontological language and a new theological language. The phenomenologist of religion was also an ontologist, the ontologist also a theologian. In his philosophy courses he talked about theology, and in his religion courses he talked about philosophy. There was a peculiar back-and-forth, cross-fertilizing movement in his youthful thought between religion and ontology, such that each was supposed to make the other possible. To begin with, the destruction of the Greek philosophical conceptuality of theology back to primal Christian sources, which Heidegger found carried out in key religious thinkers, became a model not only for his own *theological* deconstruction, but also for his wider project of the end of *philosophy* itself, that is, for his destruction of Greek, medieval, and modern metaphysics back to its ground-question of the historicity of being.

This is the philosophical way that he used Paul's attacks on the vanity of Greek philosophy, the mystics' *via negativa* to the efflux of the Divine Life, Luther's scathing critiques of the *theologia gloriae* of Aristotelian Scholasticism, Schleiermacher's antimetaphysical regress to the feeling of absolute dependence, and Kierkegaard's parodies of modern speculative thought in the name of the earnestness of ethico-religious *Existenz*. Heidegger had become a philosophical rebel, and his first allies in this reawakened battle of Greek giants about being were neither Heraclitus nor Aristotle, but a group of anti-Greek and antiphilosophical Christian thinkers. Expressed schematically, the redecision of his earlier ontological option meant that the intentional configuration of traditional ontology (ground/*logos*/presence) and of his own earlier phenomenological ontologic in particular (logical sense/judgment/atemporal validity) were to be dismantled back to and repeated from out of the configuration of their postmetaphysical ground-question (world/person/time). Armed with the analogical model of the Biblical exhortation, "Return you sons of men!" from the idolatry of the present world (see his note on the "history of salvation" in SS 1923, "Christ the turn [*die Wende*]"), Heidegger was making his first decisive turn (*Kehre*) and step-back from being to the "genuine beginning" of his lifelong topic of the mysterious depth-dimension of the differentiated temporal giving of being, which he inscribed in a number ways as *Es gibt*, *Welten*, and *Ereignis* (1919), as kairological time (1920–21), and as *kinesis* (1921–22) (G63 111).

Heidegger the ontologist was interested not only in the negative critical force of his favorite religious thinkers, but also in their rich positive analyses of the historical nature of primal Christian experience. He took the Christian experience of such realities as mystery, Parousia, Kairos, wakefulness, and falling to be a specific "ontic" model from which to read off and formalize general and ontically noncommittal "ontological" categories that would make up his new beginning for phenomenological ontology. As Kisiel has pointed out, there is an analogy in the young Heidegger between mystical experience and experience in general (GBT 30). But Heidegger also exploited the analogy between the *Deus absconditus* of Pauline kairology and the nonobjectifiable dimension of concealment that belongs to the historicity of being in general. Around

1921 he also started using Aristotle's investigations of moral life as an ontic model, and in the 1930s he turned to the model of mythopoetic experience in premodern cultures. Referring to the fact that many of the major German philosophers had actually begun in Protestant theology, Heidegger told his students bluntly in 1921 that "Fichte, Schelling, and Hegel were [Lutheran] theologians, and Kant is to be understood theologically, so long as one is not inclined to turn him into the rattling skeleton of a so-called epistemologist." Like Dilthey, "Fichte, Schelling, and Hegel came out of *theology* and take from it the basic impulses of their speculation." Heidegger, too, was a Lutheran theologian, confessing to Löwith in 1921 that "I am a 'Christian theo*logian*.' " In extracting from Christian experience the universal ontological sense of historicity, Heidegger knew that he was taking up the strategies of Kant, the German Idealists, Dilthey, Kierkegaard, Jaspers's *Psychologie der Weltanschauungen*, and Scheler, who all carried out a "formalizing detheologization" of Christian experience. For example, in the correspondence between Dilthey and Count Yorck that Heidegger read with great interest in 1923, Count Yorck writes that "dogmatics was the attempt to formulate an ontology of the higher, the historical life." And Dilthey echoes him in maintaining that Christianity must be lifted up into something like a "transcendental theology." That is, "all dogmas must be brought to their universal value for all human life. . . . they are the consciousness of the trans-sensuous and trans-rational nature of historicity pure and simple." "If the dogmas . . . are untenable in their restriction to the facts of Christian history, then in their universal sense they express the highest living content of all history."[14]

Rudolf Bultmann went too far in stressing Heidegger's indebtedness to Christian sources when he said that his work in the twenties was "no more than a secularized, philosophical version of the New Testament view of human life." In the first place, in 1919 Heidegger gave up his previous equation of philosophy with the "true worldview," namely, the "Catholic worldview" of Neo-Scholasticism. He now maintained a sharp separation of worldview and ontology, which as "primal science" can provide only a formal content that is religiously noncommittal and therefore is not restricted in its ontic application to the particular positive domain of Christian experience. Around 1921–22, he expressed the same point by insisting that philosphy must be "atheistic in principle," not because it holds that God does not exist, but because, first, access to God is based on faith and, second, the formal indications of ontology must be capable of being applied to nonreligious experience also. The "questionableness [of being] is not religious, but rather is able to lead one in the first place at all into the situation of a religious decision. . . . In its radical self-supporting questionableness, philosophy must in principle be *a-theistic*."[15] Bultmann's claim is reductionistic also because Heidegger's ontology was decisively influenced not only by religious sources but also by Aristotle, Husserl, Scheler,

Jaspers, Lask, Natorp, and Bergson, as well as by such sources as Plato's dialogues (G61 48; G19), the ancient skeptics (G21 4, 19–25; VVU 664), Seneca (G20 420/303), Tolstoy (SZ 337/298), Dostoevsky (G1 56/R 22; HW 12, 21), Van Gogh's letters (G63 32; HJ 26; MLD 28), William James,[16] and perhaps also Ortega y Gasset[17] and Georg Lukács.[18]

Heidegger thought that he could simultaneously be both an ontological and a theological thinker. "He saw himself—at that time—as a Christian theologian," writes Gadamer. "All his efforts to sort things out with himself and with his own questions were provoked by the task of freeing himself from the prevailing theology in which he had been educated, in order that he could become a Christian." Heidegger wanted to apply his new phenomenological ontology to the regional task of developing a new theological conceptuality. Since the conceptual basis of theology had after all been provided originally by Platonic and Aristotelian philosophy, theo*logical* reform presupposed philosophical reform. Only a new ontological language able to do justice to the historicity of being in general would be able to displace the static objectifying language of Aristotlelian Scholasticism that underlay Christian theology. In KNS 1919, Heidegger explained that, after the synthesis effected in the age of mysticism at the end of the Middle Ages, Luther's reformation had the result that the *religious* lifeworld of New Testament Christianity and the *philosophical* lifeworld of Aristotelian Scholasticism "split apart." As Heidegger indicated later in 1921, neither Luther nor his followers succeeded in finding a new conceptuality for Luther's own Scriptural rediscovery of primal religous consciousness. Rather, everything fell back into a new "Protestant Scholasticism which, through Melanchthon, was immediately supplied with specifically interpreted Aristotelian motives. This dogmatic with its essential Aristotelian directions is the soil and root of German idealism." Reformation theology and the German philosophy built on it led to a "derailing of the new motifs of Lutheran theology" and "succeeded to only a very small extent in giving a genuine explication of Luther's new basic religious position and its immanent possibilities." Heidegger likewise thought that, due to Kierkegaard's entanglement in Hegelian dialectics and Dilthey's external "ocular" approach to history, these two figures likewise failed to develop a conceptuality fully adequate to Lutheran historical insights.[19]

Such a conceptuality became the very task of Heidegger's application of his new historically oriented phenomenological ontology to a phenomenology of religion. In his letter of 1917 to Grabmann about his "further works in the area of Scholasticism and mysticism," Heidegger added the proviso, "But beforehand I want to acquire sufficient assurance about systematic problems, something that aims at an investigation of philosophy of value and phenomenology *from the inside out.*" On May 1, 1919, he wrote to Blochmann that "my own work is very concentrated, principial and concrete: basic problems of phenomenological methodology . . . constantly penetrating anew into the genuine origins, preliminary work for a phenomenology of religious consciousness." His statement in his 1921 letter to Löwith that "I am no philosopher" was followed by the explanation that in fact "I am a 'Christian theologian.' " This meant both that his own way of doing philosophy (in contrast to Löwith's and Becker's) was to start from the historical *logos* of Christianity, and that he was also searching for a fitting conceptual *logos* with which to speak about religious experience. In a theological discussion in which he participated in 1923, he threw out the challenge that "it is the true task of theology, which must be discovered again, to find the word that is able to call one to faith and preserve one in faith." He repeated this challenge in his discussion of the relation between ontology and theology in his lecture course of SS 1925 and in SZ: "Theology is seeking a more original interpretation of the being of the human being toward God, prescribed from the meaning of faith and remaining within it." After centuries, theology is only now "slowly beginning to understand once more Luther's insight that its dogmatic system rests on a 'foundation' that has not arisen from a questioning in which faith is primary, and whose conceptuality is not only not adequate for the problematic of theology, but rather conceals and distorts it" (LG 104; HB 16; BL 28–29; HW 29; G20 6/4; SZ 13/30).

Heidegger's Courses from KNS 1919 to SS 1921

This peculiar back-and-forth movement between religion and ontology shows up in the series of courses, talks, and publication plans that Heidegger began in 1919.[20] His three lecture courses of 1919 are titled "Die Idee der Philosophie und das Weltanschauungsproblem" (The Idea of Philosophy and the Problem of Worldview), "Phänomenologie und transzendentale Wertphilosophie" (Phenomenology and Transcendental Philosophy of Value), and "Über das Wesen der Universität und des akademischen Studiums" (On the Essence of the University and Academic Studies) (G56/57). On November 7, 1918, he wrote to Blochmann that he had also scheduled a "seminar on: the problem of the categories," which was of course the very title of the *supplementary* conclusion to his work on Scotus (HB 12). In these courses he took as his main theme phenomenological and Neo-Kantian ontology and referred explicitly back to his earlier doctrine of categories and his essay on the concept of time in 1915–16 (cf. G56/57 169, 180). Here he was moving from religion and, more specifically, mysticism to ontology in order to rethink the latter historically with the aid of the former; he thereby for the first time unequivocally reinscribed his earlier phenomenological and Neo-Kantian configuration of logical sense/judgment/atemporality into the new postmetaphysical configuration of world/person/time.

In WS 1919–20, he then planned to hold the course titled "The Philosophical Foundations of Medieval Mysticism," in which he was to move in the opposite direction of applying his new ontology to a phenomenology of mysticism. This course was to have been taught alongside the other course he announced on "Grundprobleme der Phänomenologie" (Basic Problems of Phenomenology) and along with the seminar titled "Übungen im Anschluss an Natorp, *Allgemeine Psychologie*" (Seminar in Connection with Natorp's *General Psychology*). But Heidegger replaced the course on mysticism with an expansion of the course on phenomenology, from a one- to a two-hour course (G58). Heidegger may very well have replaced the course on mysticism not only because of the official reason given, namely, lack of time, but also and primarily because he felt that he had still not adequately worked out the philosophical conceptuality and methodology needed for executing the concrete analyses of his phenomenology of religion (HL 94–95; HBC). In SS 1920, he continued with a lecture course on "Phänomenologie der Anschauung und des Ausdrucks (Theorie der philosophischen Begriffsbildung)" (Phenomenology of Intuition and Expression [Theory of Philosophical Concept-Formation]) (G59), which was accompanied by a "Colloquium in Connection with the Lecture Course." In 1919–21, Heidegger was also working on his review essay titled "Anmerkungen zu Karl Jaspers 'Psychologie der Weltanschauungen' " (Comments on Karl Jaspers's *Psychology of Worldviews*), which he used as an occasion to reflect systematically on rethinking ontology via Jaspers's reading of Kierkegaard.

It was not until WS 1920–21 that Heidegger ventured in the opposite direction of concretizing the formal indications of his ontology in a phenomenology of religion. In this semester, he held the course "Einleitung in die Phänomenologie der Religion" (Introduction in the Phenomenology of Religion) (EPR), the first part of which dealt with general methodological and conceptual considerations in connection with especially Ernst Troeltsch's philosophy of religion. Once the students had gone to the dean to complain about the lack of religious content in the course, Heidegger now finally had no choice but to enter into interpretations of concrete religious phenomena, and so in the second part of the course he gave a powerful phenomenological analysis of kairological time and the nonobjectifiability of God found in Paul's letters on the Second Coming (HBC). Simultaneously Heidegger held the seminar for "Beginners: In Connection with Descartes's *Meditations*." Then in SS 1921, he gave a lecture course on "Augustinus und der Neuplatonismus" (Augustine and Neo-Platonism) (G60), in which he investigated how Augustine's understanding of the historicity of New Testament Christianity was obscured through his adoption of Neo-Platonic conceptuality. In both courses on religion, Heidegger suggested that the young Luther's "theology of the cross" was one of his major catalysts for going back to the historical consciousness of primal Christianity.

In WS 1921–22 he opened a series of courses on Aristotle that began to a great extent from the interpretations of Aristotle found in Luther and Kierke-gaard. In 1922 Heidegger pondered publishing his essay on "The Ontological Foundations of Late Medieval Anthropology and the Theology of the Young Luther," and in SS 1923 he held his seminar with Ebbinghaus on the influence of Luther on Kant and the German Idealists. When he left for Marburg in WS 1923, he continued his religious investigations in seminars and study groups with Bultmann, as well as in the theological talks he gave in the theology department. He also planned another course on Augustine for SS 1924, but did not hold it (ML 17).

Heidegger delivered the final fruits of his phenomenology of religion in his lecture "Phänomenologie und Theologie" (Phenomenology and Theology), which was delivered in 1927 before the Protestant theological faculty in Tübingen. Here he showed the theologians how such formally indicative ontological concepts as history, guilt, falling, and conscience in SZ could indirectly make possible a new theological language that would finally be able to do justice to Luther's statement that "faith means surrendering oneself to matters [*Sachen*] that we do not see." By this time, however, Heidegger's interests in Christian theology and his own Christian faith were already on the wane, and his Tübingen lecture remained unpublished until 1970. But he seems to have begun to distance himself from his project of a phenomenology of religion already in WS 1921–22, and did so partly under the influence of the Christian skeptic Franz Overbeck, who insisted on the impossibility of treating Christianity in a science. Though he collaborated intensely with Bultmann and other theologians in Marburg from 1923 to 1928, his attitude toward theology was always ambiguous and even suspicious. Writing to Blochmann on August 8, 1928 about his Tübingen lecture, he confided that "I am personally convinced that theology is *no* science. . . . And so my work in Marburg was always consciously doublesided—helping and yet quite disconcerting—and I freed more than one from theology." If the early development of his religious interests can be broken down into three phases, namely, the antimodernist Neo-Scholastic phase (1909–12), the mystical Neo-Neo-Scholastic phase (1913–16), and the free Protestant mystical phase from 1917 into the early 1920s, then treatment of a fourth phase would have to show that sometime in the later 1920s he began to identify with the experience of the death of God in Nietzsche and Hölderlin, as well as with their aspirations for the birth of a new and more Greek God.[21]

8 | Primal Christianity

T HOUGH HEIDEGGER HAD announced to Krebs early in 1919 that, despite his "deep respect for the Catholic lifeworld," the Scholastic "system of Catholicism" was now "unacceptable" to him, it was not until his lecture courses of WS 1920–21 ("Introduction in the Phenomenology of Religion") and SS 1921 ("Augustine and Neo-Platonism") that he carried out a sustained destruction of the Greek philosophical conceptuality of Scholasticism back to the primal Christianity of the New Testament. His model here was not only, as it had primarily been in 1919, medieval mysticism's negative breakthrough to the mysterious nonobjectifiable efflux of the Divine Life; rather, he now emulated the more direct return to the eschatology and kairology of Pauline *theologia crucis* that he found in Luther's virulent attack on the *theologia gloriae* of Aristotelian Scholasticism and in Kierkegaard's critique of modern speculative thought. I begin with the latter because it allows us to understand Heidegger's claim that medieval mysticism can only be understood as a reassertion of primal New Testament Christianity against its philosophical Hellenization (G58 62, 205). His appropriation of the mystical tradition, especially in 1919, will be dealt with in Part Four. Expressed schematically, the present chapter shows how Heidegger dismantled and demythologized the intentional configuration of medieval Scholasticism (*summum ens*/contemplation/presence) back to that of primal Christianity (*Deus absconditus*/faith/kairological time), and how he creatively reinscribed the latter in his own new beginning for ontology (world/person/time).

Ontologia Crucis

The second part of Heidegger's "Introduction in the Phenomenology of Religion" focused on Paul's letter to the Galatians, second letter to the Corinthians, and two letters to the Thessalonians in order to get at the factical experience of life in primal Christianity (DMH 36–37; IPR 319). Here he showed that the ultimate content-sense of Christian faith, namely, God, is experienced not in terms of the abstract notion of substance, the objectified Kingdom (*ousia*) of God, but rather as the hidden God who has been historically revealed in the Incarnation and Crucifixion, and will again be revealed in the Parousia, the Second Coming, the incalculable coming Kingdom.

In two texts from the late twenties that draw on his earlier phenomenology of religion, we also read that in the New Testament the term *kosmos*, world, does not mean what it does in Greek philosophy, namely, either a cosmic framework of intelligible structures or a collection of things, each of which is a "what" composed of form and matter. Rather, *kosmos* expresses (1) the "how" or sense in which beings are encountered in factical life, and simultaneously (2) this how as a way of existing and being-in-the-world. "In Paul (cf. 1 Cor. and Gal.) *kosmos houtos*, this world, means . . . the condition and the situation of human being. . . . *Kosmos* is the being of human being in the how of an attitude that has *turned away* from God (*he sophia tou kosmou*, the wisdom of the world)." And in its temporal meaning, "this *kosmos*, this how, is defined by its relation to the already dawning *kosmos*, to the coming futural age (*aion ho mellon*). The condition of all beings is regarded in relation to the *eschaton*, the final situation" (G9 143/ER 51; G26 222/173).

In WS 1921–22 Heidegger maintained that "even the primal Christian contexts of life" in Apostolic and Pauline literature were themselves "already permeated with a process of 'Hellenization'." They were "co-defined by the specifically Greek interpretation of Dasein and conceptuality for Dasein (*Termini*). Through Paul and in the apostolic period and especially in the 'patristic' period, a molding into the Greek lifeworld came about," and eventually the embodiment of the spirit of the New Testament into a philosophical Christianity, Inc. In his course of SS 1921, "Augustine and Neo-Platonism," Heidegger showed that the development of Christian theo*logy* and philosophy in the patristic period and in medieval Scholasticism fell further away from the factical historical understanding of primal Christianity. They understood Greek thinking to be providing "conjectures" (Augustine) about the truth of the Christian message, and saw the adoption of Greek conceptuality to be further legitimated by Paul's statement that the "invisible things of God, his eternal power and divinity, have clearly been seen, being understood from what has been made" (Rom. 1:20), i.e., from his works. Heidegger focused on how Augustine obscured his own understanding of primal Christianity by adopting the Neo-Platonic concept of *fruitio Dei*, the enjoyment of God. Augustine here takes over the notion of God as the highest being (*summum ens*) and highest good (*summum bonum*) in a hierarchical scale of beings which are present-before-the-hand, before the *manus mentis* for either "use" or "enjoyment." "Perversion" is supposed to consist in enjoying worldly things intended for use as means to union with God, and in using what is to be enjoyed, namely, God, as a means to worldly ends. Augustine writes in his *De doctrina christiana*, "We should use this world and not enjoy it, so that the 'invisible things' of God 'being understood by the things that are made' [Rom. 1:20] may be seen. . . . The things that are to be enjoyed are the Father, the Son, and the Holy Spirit."[1] Heidegger showed how in this way the very beginnings of Christian theology fell prey to that Greek "ontotheological" thinking which proceeds from beings (*das Befragte*) back to a divine etiological ground (*das Erfragte*), which was now interpreted as an intelligible *basileia tou theou*. The personal, historically experienced God of the Old and New Testaments was objectified in speculative thought as the first cause of beings.

The way was thus paved for the use of Aristotle and Neo-Platonism in the Aristotelian-Scholastic "doctrines of God, the trinity, innocence, sin, and grace." As Heidegger explained in his 1922 essay on Aristotle, "this means that the idea of human being and the Dasein of life that is initiated in advance in all of these spheres of theological problems is based on Aristotelian 'physics,' 'psychology,' 'ethics,' and 'ontology'. . . . Simultaneously, Augustine is also decisively at work here and, through Augustine, Neo-Platonism." Here the believer/God relation is forced into the foreign Aristotelian notion of "*theion*," the divine, as first cause and "*noesis noeseos*, thought of thought," the divine *manus mentis* that caresses itself (*thigein*). This pure emotionless thought, which also characterizes the contemplative-theoretical relation to the divine (*theoria*), is seen to be a constant being-in-act (*energeia*) and thus a pure presence-before-the-hand. This Aristotelian framework is the motivational source of "the basic ontological structures that later decisively determine divine being in the specifically Christian sense (*actus purus*), the inner Divine Life (the Trinity), and therewith simultaneously the being of the relationship of God to human being and therewith the very sense of the being of human being itself." Thus "Christian theology, the philosophical 'speculation' standing under its influence, and the anthropology that always also develops in such contexts all *speak in borrowed categories that are foreign to their own field of being*." Aristotle's notion of divine *nous* "does not have the slightest thing to do with the God of Thomas." To use Heidegger's terminology in his 1919 courses, the Greek conceptuality of the patristic and Scholastic periods brought about a "theorizing" of primal Christianity and more particularly a designifying, deworlding, and mythologizing of its concrete historical content-sense. Heidegger wrote, "The historian of religion is concerned with Jesus just as he is experienced by someone religious. . . . Thus we have here a minimum of theorizing" (PIA 250, 263; G21 123; G56/57 207; G20 233/173).

Now enter the young Augustinian Martin Luther, who attempts to return to the primal *theologia crucis* in Paul and also in Augustine himself. "Luther's counterattack," wrote Heidegger in WS 1921–22, "was now enacted religiously and theologically against the Scholasticism that had been consolidated through the reception of Aristotle. . . . What is at stake here is something decisive" (G61 7). In his WS 1920–21 course, Heidegger had said that Luther understood the experience of time in Paul's letters and that this was the reason why Luther opposed Aristotelian Scholasticism so passionately (IPR 322). In his SS 1921 course, Heidegger introduced Luther's early 1518 *Heidelberg Disputation* and focused on the contrast in the nineteenth and twentieth theses between the *theologia gloriae* of Aristotelian Scholasticism and Paul's *theologia crucis* (DMH 40). Thesis 19 attacked the Scriptural basis in the letter to the Romans that had been used to justify the adoption of Greek philosophical methods and concepts: "That person is not rightly called a theologian who looks upon the invisible things of God as though they were perceptible through things that have been made [Rom. 1:20]." Thesis 20 states, "He deserves to be called a theologian, however, who understands the visible and manifest things of God seen through suffering and the cross. The manifest things of God, namely, his human nature, weakness, and foolishness, are placed in opposition to the invisible. . . . Isaiah says, 'Truly, you are a hidden [*absconditus*] God.' "

Since God is a mystery "hidden in suffering," in the cross, there is here nothing present before-the-hand that can be conceptually objectified, built up into the speculative dominion of a Christianity, Inc., and calculated in *theoria*, contemplation. There is no starting point in "the humility and shame of the cross" for ontotheological speculation to move from the visible to knowledge of the invisible, because what is given here is not the eternal, power, glory, the kingdom, but the very opposite: time, weakness, suffering, exile, the death of the King on the cross. *Outos estin Jesous ho basileus*, this is Jesus the King (Matt. 27:37). The cross is "a scandal to the Jews and *moria*, foolishness, stupidity, absurdity to the Greeks" (1 Cor. 1:23). What confronts human reason is "the paradox" (Kierkegaard) (WA I 361–62/XXXI 52–53). The only theological access to this *Deus absconditus* and the "glory" here is through an anxious and wakeful *theologia crucis* that *believes* in "matters that we do not see." As Heidegger stated in his lecture "Phenomenology and Theology," "theology is not speculative knowledge of God" (G9 59/PT 15).

According to Luther, the *theologia gloriae* taken over from Greek metaphysics wants precisely to see "God in his glory and majesty," to have God present as the first cause and highest good manifested through created works. A "theologian of glory (that is, someone who does not know along with the Apostle the hidden and crucified God, but sees and speaks of God's glorious manifestation among the pagans . . .) learns from Aristotle that the object of the will is good. . . . He learns that God is the highest good [*summum bonum*]" (WA I 614/XXXI 227). As Heidegger later pointed out, *gloria, doxa*, is the name for how the Greco-Roman thinkers experienced being in its look, its appearance (*eidos*). "If the appearance and look, in accordance with what emerges in it, is a distinguished one, *doxa* means splendour and glory. In Hellenistic theology and in the New Testament, *doxa theou, gloria Dei*, is the glory of God" (G40 110/102).

The word "glory" in the young Luther's *Heidelberg Disputation* is nothing less than his appellation for how, in Greek metaphysics and in Christian theology, the being of the divine appears as the speculative kingdom of an exalted radiant presence that is "enjoyed" by quietistic, ocular-aesthetic contemplation. For Luther, "glory" names the Greek onto-etio-theo-logical experience of the being of beings as presence; radiant light, splendor, beauty; the wondrous and extraordinary, the elevated and exalted; and power, majesty, dominion. We read in Aristotle's *Nicomachean Ethics*, for example, that metaphysics is "intuition of the things that are by nature most exalted and honored [*ton timiotaton*]. . . . [T]hose like Anaxagoras and Thales . . . know things that are strange and out of the ordinary, marvelous, difficult and divine, but useless" (1141b). Similarly, Plato understands the concrete temporal world of particularity as *me on*, which means not absolute nonbeing (*ouk on*), but rather a relative and valuative not-being something or other. For Plato this not-being means deficiency, lack, absence, darkness, pollution, ugliness, falsity, and evil in relation to the heavenly *topos* of the exemplary true being (*ontos on*) of the universal "idea" in its purity, stable presence, divinity, light, beauty, and goodness. Plato's imagery represents the idea as being exiled, polluted, wounded, crippled with absence and imperfection through its worldly temporal instantiation (*eidolon*).

For Luther, this *theologia gloriae* suffers from presumption (*praesumptio*) and *superbia*, the pride that willfully and hyperbolically oversteps its limits, elevates itself into the Beyond (*super*) of its speculative visions, and thereby seeks to satisfy its desire for dominion (*dominium*), power (*potestas*), empire (*imperium*). In Theses 23 and 24, Luther translates Paul's term *kauchesis*, boasting, as *gloriatio*, glorying in philosophical speculation or the Rule of Law. Since philosophical theology is intoxicated, "puffed up," "blinded," "hardened," and "built up" (*aedificatur*) into a speculative construction, Luther takes up not only Paul's advice in Colossians 2:8 to "see to it that no one steals you away through philosophy and empty fraud" (WA LVI 372/XXV 362), but more specifically the concept of "destruction" in 1 Corinthians. Here one reads that, through the cross which is foolishness to the wisdom-seeking Greeks, " 'I [God] will destroy [*apolo*] the wisdom of the wise' " (1:19). Paul continues in this remarkable passage to show in effect how, through the Kenosis, Incarnation, and Crucifixion, there takes place a dismantling of what the Greeks understood by "being" into the very "not-being" from which they sought to escape. He invites his readers to "think of what sort of people you are whom god has called. Few of you are wise . . . few of you are powerful; few of you are of high and noble birth [*eugeneis*]." However:

> God chose what is foolish in the world to shame the wise, what is weak in the world to shame what is strong, and he chose what is without genus, race, origin [*ta agene*] in the world, and what is lowly and null, and that which is not [gloriously present] [*ta me onta*] in order to bring to nothing that which is [gloriously present] [*ta onta*], so that no one may boast and glory before the face of God.

Heidegger in fact quoted this passage in his lecture course of SS 1928, translating *ta agene* as *das Abkunftslose*, the originless, and *ta onta* as "that which is, what rules [*das Herrschende*]" (G26 222/173).

Similarly, Luther's *Heidelberg Disputation* insists that the *theologia gloriae* has to be "emptied," "crucified," "annihilated." What is needed is not to progress forward (*procedere*) to ever-higher speculative heights, but rather a kind of theologial reduction in which one goes backward (*retrocedere*) into the "foolishness" of the cross. And, fatefully for the young Heidegger, Luther's Theses 19 and 20 translate the term "destroy" in 1 Corinthians into the Latin word *destruere*, to pull down, to dismantle, to de-stroy, to deconstruct. Like all other types of *superbia* that glory in "works," the hyperbolic works of speculative theologians that have been built up and hardened must be "destroyed [*destructus*], reduced [*redactus*] to nothing through the cross and suffering":

> [I]t does him no good to know God in his glory and majesty unless he recognizes him in the humility and shame of the cross. Thus God 'destroys [*perdit*] the wisdom of the wise'. . . . So also, in John 14:8, where Philip spoke according to the theology of glory: "Show us the Father." Christ immediately dragged back [*retraxit*] his flighty thought and led him back [*reduxit*] to himself. . . . through the cross works are destroyed [*destruuntur*]. . . . (WA I 362–63/XXXI 52–55)

Following Paul's dismantling of the Greek concept of being into not-being, Luther's deconstruction of the *theologia gloriae* and reduction to the facticity of "the cross" reverses the Platonic valorization of the *ontos on* of the universal *eidos*, the radiant form and look of being, over against the *me on* of the concrete temporal world of particularity with all its privations. Remembering that Luther's terms *species* and *forma* are common Latin translations of *eidos*, we read: "God's works always appear deformed [*deformia*] and evil. . . . [This] is clear from Isaiah 53:2: 'He has neither radiant form [*species*] nor beauty'. . . . we appear as nothing, foolish, and wicked. . . . there is neither radiant form nor beauty in us, but our life is hidden in God" (WA I 356–57/XXXI 43–44). Luther also writes that "the love of God which lives in human being loves what is sinful, evil, foolish, and weak. . . . the love of the cross . . . turns to where it does not find good it may *enjoy* [*fruatur*]." But "by nature the intellect cannot comprehend an object which is *nothing* [*nihil*], i.e., the poor and needy, but only *being* [*entis*], i.e., the good, the true. Thus it judges according to the *visible outward form* [*faciem*], grasps the outer human mask" (WA I 365/XXXI 57; emphasis added).

The same contrast is made in 1 Corinthians with the Greek term *genos* (race, genus, origin), which can function as a synonym of *eidos* (idea, form, species). Paul sets off against each other *eugeneia*, high and noble race/genus/origin, and *ageneia*, race-, genus-, origin-lessness. (Compare Aristotle's statement in the *Nicomachean Ethics* that one needs *eugeneia* for happiness in contrast to "the human who is very ugly in form and appearance [*idea*] or lacking in race/genus/origin [*dusgenes*]" [1099b].) For Paul and Luther, neither God nor human beings are encountered in terms of the glory of the Platonic *eidos* or in terms of any abstract universality at all. Rather, the event and the symbol of "the cross" mean that God and human beings appear in "the flesh" of historical particularity with all its privation, absence, and de-formity. For Luther, God is encountered factically as the crucified God, "God who is dead, the anguish of God, the blood of God, the death of God" (WA L 590).

Whereas the *theologia gloriae* of Greek and Scholastic metaphysics turns "everything upside-down" by seeing concrete historicity to be derivative of the ontotheological ground that it contructs speculatively, the destruction performed in Luther's *theologia crucis* sees such constructions to be derived from a falling away from the historicity of "the cross." "God can be found only in suffering and the cross" (WA I 613/XXXI 225; I 362/XXXI 53). Long before Nietzsche, Luther had already killed the ontotheological God of western metaphysics. As Scheler writes in his 1916 essay "Liebe und Erkenntnis," which makes much of the philosophical significance of the Pauline reversal of *ontos on* and *me on*, and anticipates Heidegger's whole philosophical project of using primal Christianity, "a radical *reversal* of love and knowledge and of value and being is enacted in Christian experience." In "original Christianity," "there is in no sense whatsoever an 'idea,' a 'law,' a 'substantial value' or a 'reason' over and above the *personal figure* [of Christ]" (LE 8–11, 18–19).

Convinced that Aristotle had replaced the New Testament in the Christianity, Inc. of the medieval universities, the young Luther also aimed his destruction directly at the *ontologia gloriae* of the "blind pagan Master Aristotle" himself. He wanted to "unmask" the fantastic dreams (*somnia*) of this "showman" and "swindler," whose "*Physics, Metaphysics, De anima,* and *Ethics* . . . glory in natural things." Reading them, he scoffed, is "as if someone were exercising his talents and skills by studying and playing with dung." In addition to its twenty-eight "theological theses" against Scholasticism, Luther's

Heidelberg Disputation contains twelve "philosophical theses" that primarily
criticize Aristotle, but also discuss Plato, Anaxagoras, Pythagoras, and Parmenides. In the "proofs" to these "philosophical theses," one finds Luther
moving freely in quoted passages from one end of Aristotle's corpus to the
other. He was not simply a dilettante who was good at swearing at "that
damned, arrogant, mischievous pagan." He had studied Aristotle's writings in
detail, delivered lectures on the *Nicomachean Ethics* in 1508-1509 and on the
Physics in 1519, and claimed that "I know this book [*Physics*] inside out" and
"read . . . Aristotle with even more understanding than Saint Thomas or Duns
Scotus." In 1517 he was working on "a small commentary on Book One of
the *Physics*," in which he planned "to disclose to many the true face of that
actor who has fooled the Church so tremendously with the Greek mask." But
his study was never completed in this form; instead, it was taken up into his
1517 *Disputation against Scholastic Theology* and his 1518 *Heidelberg Disputation*.[2]

The former work presented such theses as the following: "44. Indeed, no
one can become a theologian unless he becomes one without Aristotle. . . . 50.
Briefly, the whole of Aristotle is to theology as darkness is to light. This in
opposition to the Scholastics." The ultimate purpose of Luther's disputation of
1518 was to show that "one gains no aid whatsoever from [Aristotle], either
for theology and sacred letters or even for natural philosophy." Its philosophical theses thus open with the proposition that "he who wishes to philosophize
in Aristotle without danger must first become completely a fool in Christ. . . .
science inflates. . . . [But] all trust, life, glory, virtue, and wisdom of human
being is in Christ alone. But Christ is hidden [*absconditus*] in God. Thus what
is inwardly and outwardly visible to the eyes is nothing with which a human
being can be presumptuous" (WA I 226/XXXI 12; IX 170/XXXI 70). Taking
up Aristotle's *Physics* and *Metaphysics*, the third philosophical thesis critically
discusses his notion of the eternity of the world and of "the eternal being" as
"what moves in infinite time." About Aristotle's vision of the divine as *noesis
noeseos*, Luther writes elsewhere that this "supreme being sits above the sky
and sees nothing of what happens, but rather, as in the painting of blind for-
tune, he eternally rattles the heavens around each and every day." Aristotle
"treats the religious in such an icy manner," for here the divine is not encountered as the loving personal God manifested in the historical facticity of the
Incarnation and Crucifixion (PPT 35-37; LA 6, 32).

The *Heidelberg Disputation* also asserts that Aristotle's view of the world
provides little for "natural philosophy. For what could be gained with respect
to the understanding of things if you could quibble and trifle about matter,
form, motion, measure, and time—words taken and copied from Aristotle?"
(WA IX 170/XXXI 70). In Luther's 1515-16 *Lectures on Romans*, which, according to Edmund Schlink, "strongly influenced" the young Heidegger (WT

6; G58 204), the Aristotelian understanding of the world in terms of the static, present-at-hand *eidos* and "the categories" of being is contrasted with the Pauline understanding of *kosmos*. Here Luther gets at the sense of world in Paul that Heidegger himself stressed, namely, the historical how or sense of beings that is concretely lived in being-in-the-world. "Alas, how deeply and disastrously we are ensnared in discussions about categories and essential determinations; in how many stupid metaphysical questions are we involved." But "the Apostle philosophizes and thinks about the world in an other way than the philosophers and the metaphysicians. . . . [Y]ou will be the best philosophers and the best investigators of the world if you learn with the Apostle to consider creation as it waits, sighs, and travails" in "anxious expectation" of the coming age (WA LVI 371–72/XXV 360–62). Or, alternatively, "the world" means for Luther a way of existence, namely, "glory," which has turned away from God, from "the wisdom that is foolishness to the world" (WA I 363/XXXI 54). It is because Luther wants to understand the world not from the Greek theoretical standpoint, but from the practical perspective of the Christian religion that he can say that "a potter has more knowledge of natural things than is written in those books" of Aristotle's (WA VI 458/XLIV 200). To use Heidegger's terminology, Luther thought that the concepts of "form" and "matter" in Aristotelian Scholasticism led to the deworlding of the factical world of primal Christianity (G20 235/174).

Luther performs a destruction of Greek and medieval metaphysics with the help of not only the philosophizing of Paul, but also the practical philosophy of Socrates and Seneca (cf. WA LVI 371/XXV 361), and even certain unexploited aspects of Aristotle himself, most notably the notions of *kinesis* and *phronesis* in his practical thought. But he also seems to carry out a repetition of the sense of philosophy. The "best philosophers" philosophize "in a different way than the philosophers and the metaphysicians." And in the *Heidelberg Disputation* we read that "no one philosophizes well unless he is a fool" (WA I 355/XXXI 41).

Do these "philosophical theses" suggest an end and new beginning not only for theology, but also for philosophy, as some (including Jaspers) have suggested (WT 16–22; DMH 41)? Heidegger seems to have thought so. He maintained that the young Luther's destruction of Aristotelian Scholasticism and his return to the historical consciousness of primal Christianity simultaneously provided the basis for and was covered over by both Melanchthon's "Protestant Scholasticism" and German Idealism. These movements "succeeded to only a very small extent in giving a genuine explication of Luther's new basic religious position and its immanent possibilities," because they fell back under the spell of Greek conceptuality. Heidegger wanted to use these possibilities to rethink not only theology, but also ontology. Neither Luther nor the theological and philosophical movements he inspired finished the deconstructive commentary on Aristotle and Aristotelian Scholasticism that the young Luther had started. My conjecture is that it was Heidegger who, as it were, finished it. In an autobiographical sketch from SS 1923, which is quite different from his later self-portraits of his development, Heidegger stated, "Companions in my searching were the young Luther and the paragon Aristotle, whom Luther hated. Kierkegaard gave impulses" (GA63 5). In the 1922 introduction to his planned book on Aristotle, he wrote that "for the sake of carrying out the task of the phenomenological destruction [of the history of ontology], these researches set their sights on late-Scholasticism and Luther's early theological period" (PIA 252).

In a 1922 letter to Paul Natorp, Husserl wrote that, in its oral form, Heidegger "opened his Aristotle course on November 2, 1921 by citing Luther's condemnation of the *Metaphysics, De Anima,* and *Ethics* of the 'pagan Master Aristotle'!"[3] The reference is to Luther's *To the Christian Nobility of the German Nation:*

> What else are the universities . . . than what the Book of Maccabees calls *gymnasia epheborum et graecae gloriae?. . . .* the blind pagan Master Aristotle rules far more than Christ. . . . Aristotle's *Physics, Metaphysics, De anima,* and *Ethics* . . . should be completely discarded along with the rest of his books that glory in natural things. . . . (WA VI 457–58/XLIV 200–201)

Indeed, we do find in the published text of this course a loose page titled "Motto and Grateful Indication of Sources," in which there are two quotations from Luther (GA61 182). One consists of the last two lines of the following passage in Luther's *Preface to St. Paul's Letter to the Romans:*

> And here we must set a limit for those arrogant and high-climbing spirits, who first bring their own thinking to this matter and lift themselves on high to search the abyss of divine predestination. . . . without suffering, the cross, and the distress of death, one cannot deal with predestination. . . . The old Adam must die before he can suffer and endure this thing and drink the strong wine of it. Therefore, see to it that you do not drink wine while you are still an infant. Every doctrine has its measure, time, and age.[4]

The other motto was taken from Luther's *Commentary on Genesis:* "Right from our mother's womb we begin to die" (WA XLII 146/I 196). Heidegger also provided two mottos from Kierkegaard, who—as the great destroyer of modern speculative thought—is the counterpart to Luther's destruction of medieval Scholasticism. The first is from Kierkegaard's *Training in Christianity:*

> From both a Christian and an ethical point of view, the whole of modern philosophy is based on thoughtlessness and easygoingness. . . . as abstract, philosophy floats in the indefiniteness of the metaphysical. Instead of admitting this and so directing human beings (individual human beings) to the ethical, the religious, the existential, philosophy has aroused the illusion that

human beings could, as one prosaically says, speculate themselves out of their own good skin and into pure light. (TC 83)

And immediately beneath this motto we read another: " 'But what philosophy and the philosopher find difficult is stopping.' Kierkegaard, *Either/Or*, Vol. I. (Stopping at the genuine beginning!)" (EO 38).

What these passages suggest is that Heidegger's very term *Destruktion* and its sense came not only from Kant's notion of "critique," but more so from Luther's 1518 *Heidelberg Disputation*. Recall that Jaspers saw Heidegger hard at work on his Luther studies as early as the spring of 1920, and Heidegger seems to have first used the term *Destruktion* in his WS 1919-20 lecture course, which actually referred to Luther's *destructio* of Aristotle (G58 139ff., 61-62, 205). The following semester he called for the "destruction of Christian philosophy and theology" (G59 12). It was presumably Luther who was the main inspiration for his deconstructive regress to primal Christianity in his religion courses of WS 1920-21 and SS 1921. Finally, these passages also tell us that, as Gadamer and Pöggeler have suggested, Heidegger's very project of "the end of philosophy" (that is, the destruction of the Aristotelian being-question back to historicity) and a new "genuine beginning" in WS 1921-22 derived primarily from his readings of Luther, Kierkegaard, and other anti-Greek Christian sources (cf. HW 145).

The young Heidegger saw himself at this time as a kind of philosophical Luther of western metaphysics. He surely knew that the Lutheran "theologian" Hegel had already taken up the contrast between *theologia gloriae* and *theologia crucis* into his own alternative between the contemplative "kingly [königlich] road" to "the empyrean" that is traveled in "the robes of a high priest" (that is, immediate ahistorical intuition of the Absolute) and the "stations" of "the way of the soul" (cf. "stations of the cross"), that is, the Greek *eidos* and *nous* now seen as developing within the "suffering," "anxiety," and "death" of history, which ends in the "Calvary of Absolute Spirit." Heidegger's *ontologia crucis*, that is, the attempt to think being through "the cross" of historicity and factical life, wanted to effect an even more radical philosophical Calvary and Good Friday for metaphysics and its speculative claims about "salvation." One senses an echo of Luther even in the later Heidegger's contrast between metaphysics as "the way of salvation" and postmetaphysical thinking as "a fieldpath, a way across the field."[5] The young Heidegger's destruction of the hyperbolic, mythic sense of being in *ontologia gloriae* wanted to see it crucified, as it were, on the cross of facticity, and resurrected through the *skandalon* and "foolishness" of historicity. One of Heidegger's great contributions in the early twenties was his providing an ontological language and an opening within academic philosophy for such marginal traditions in which the end of philosophy and new postmetaphysical beginnings had already implicitly occurred. He would do the same for Nietzsche, Hölderlin, and the early Greek thinkers in his later writings.

The Thorn in the Self

Heidegger's "Introduction in the Phenomenology of Religion" pursued a number of themes in the factical relational sense of primal Christian experience, which is not contemplation or objective knowledge, but rather anxious, uncertain, and wakeful faith in the Parousia of the hidden God. He introduced Paul's theme of mystical charisma and the thorn in the flesh in 2 Corinthians 12:1–10, where we encounter Heidegger's term "the hyperbolic" in relation to aesthetic visions of the heavenly Kingdom, of *paradeison*, the pleasure-garden, paradise. Paul says, "I will not boast and glory on my own behalf. . . . To keep from exalting [*hyperairomai*] in the excess [*hyperbole*] of revelations, there was given me a thorn in my flesh. . . . That is why I approve of weaknesses, insults, hardships, difficulties." Heidegger emphasized here "how the turning to facticity is based precisely in the renunciation of visions and revelations [about the Parousia] . . . , in the refusal to boast and glory in a special gift, and in taking upon oneself one's weakness" (DMH 37).

Following Dilthey, Heidegger's lecture course of WS 1919–20 had already maintained that Christianity was a "great revolution against ancient science, against Aristotle above all," in that, in contrast to Greek "objective metaphysics" of the *kosmos*, it effected a unique "concentration of life on its selfworld":

> The most profound historical paradigm for this noteworthy process of shifting the centre of gravity of factical life and the lifeworld into the selfworld and the world of inward experience is given to us in the emergence of Christianity. What lies forth in the life of the primal Christian communities signifies a radical reversal of the directional tendency of life, and is here mostly thought of as denial of the world and asceticism (*The Idea of the Kingdom of God, Paul* [cf. Ritschl regarding everything here]). Here lie the motives for the development of completely new contexts of expression which life fashions—even up to that which we today call *history*.

This tendency was then reasserted against objective Greek metaphysics in Augustine's *Confessions*, in the medieval mystics such as Bonaventura and Eckhart, in Luther, in Kierkegaard, and also generally in the Christian tradition of "autobiography":

> Only from these newly breaking forth basic motives for a new positioning of the selfworld can it be understood why we are confronted in Augustine with something like his *Confessiones* and *De civitate Dei*. *Crede, ut intelligas* [believe in order to understand]: live your self in a living manner—and only on the basis of this experience, your ultimate and fullest self-experience, does knowing get built up. In the phrase '*inquietum cor nostrum*' [our heart (is)

restless], Augustine saw the great unceasing restlessness of life. (G58 56–62, 205; CEM 250–67; EBF 104–105)

Speaking of the sources of his notion of "factical life" later in 1922, Heidegger wrote that "the term *zoe, vita,* signifies a basic phenomenon in which the Greek, the Old Testament, the New Testament–Christian, and the Greek-Christian interpretations of human Dasein are centered" (PIA 240).

He also emphasized that Kierkegaard "explicitly seized upon the problem of existence as an existentiell problem, and thought it through in a penetrating fashion" (SZ 313/278, 331/293, 447/388). In SS 1923, Heidegger had quoted Kierkegaard's critique of the view of the individual as a mere instantiation of the universal "rational animal": "To be a human being means: to belong as an example to a race endowed with reason, so that the race, the species, is higher than the individual, or that there are only examples and no individuals." In this course, Heidegger prefaced his analyses of "one's own Dasein" and factical being-in-the-world with the acknowledgment that "strong influences on the explication presented here come from Kierkegaard's work" (G63 108, 29–30). One of the mottos that he took from Kierkegaard for his WS 1921–22 lecture course highlighted precisely Kierkegaard's key theme of "the individual human being." He also appealed to Kierkegaard's concept of the "passion" of the existing individual and his contrast between "subjective truth" and "objective truth," in order to work out a definition of the *Sache* of ontology as not only "being" (content-sense), but also the individual philosopher's passionate historical comportment to being (relational and enactment-sense). "Existentielly-philosophically, the genuine principle is only to be won in the fundamental experience of passion. . . . 'In principle' one can be and have everything (Kierkegaard)." Heidegger also appealed to Socrates's understanding of the philosophical quest after being as a "way of life," and here, too, he was undoubtedly following Kierkegaard's reading of Socrates as the preeminent thinker of "subjective truth" (G61 182, 24, 37, 60, 42–52).

In the words of Jaspers's *Psychologie der Weltanschauungen,* Kierkegaard stressed "factical individual existence" over against the universal "man in general," the Idealists' concept of the self as a "fantastic being" of pure thought, and "objective truth" that is "indifferent to the existing person." Jaspers quotes many passages from Kierkegaard that stress the personal relational and enactment-sense of passionate "subjective truth." For example, "Such an abstract thinker, one who neglects to take into account the *relation* between his abstract thought and his own existence as an individual . . . makes a comical impression upon the mind even if he is ever so distinguished, because he is in the process of ceasing to be a human being." Like the foolishness and paradox of the Incarnation, "the self signifies precisely the contradiction that the universal is posited as the individual." "That the truth becomes a paradox is based precisely on its *relation* to an existing subject" (PDW 106-107, 245-46, 384-86, 418-19; emphasis added).

Heidegger's initial reception of Kierkegaard came through his 1919-21 review-essay on Jaspers's book, in which he worked out one of the first versions of his new beginning, and in the following years he continued to rely heavily on Jaspers's detailed expositions here of such Kierkegaardian concepts as *Existenz* (PIA 245), "the individual," "subjective truth," "passion," "anxiety," "death," "dispersion," "curiosity," "being closed off," "conscience," "guilt," "becoming manifest," "indirect communication," "time," and the moment (*Augenblick*). Jaspers's doctrine of the "limit-situations" of death, guilt, accident, situationality, suffering, and struggle, to which Heidegger acknowledges his early indebtedness in SZ, was heavily influenced by Kierkegaard, as well as by Nietzsche (SZ 399/348).

Care

In various texts, Heidegger laid out the basic characteristics of factical life found in primal Christianity, including care, understanding, mood, anxiety, death, language, falling, and conscience. In 1919, he had continued to model his concept of intentionality on the mystical experience of self-surrendering devotion (*Hingabe*) to and immersion in the *mysterium tremendum*. In the early twenties, he went on to explore how the basic relational sense of life in the New Testament is care (*merimna, phrontis; sollicitudo* in the Vulgate). Here care means preeminently care for the self/God relation, that is, "care for the things of the lord" in contrast to "care for the affairs of the world."[6] Thus Heidegger used as the motto of his SS 1920 course Thomas à Kempis's *Imitation of Christ*: "The inward man puts the care [*curam*] of his self before all other cares (Matt. 16:26)" (G59 1). Heidegger also focused on how for Augustine *quaestio mihi factus sum*, I have become a question to myself, such that "our heart rests not until it rests in thee," in God. "What is closer to me than myself?" Augustine asks, and yet "I labour here and I labour within myself, and I have become to myself a land of difficulties [*difficultatis*] and much stress." "I am a burden to myself" (G21 211; SZ 59/69; C 118, 146/226, 236). Indeed, Heidegger's SS 1921 course on Augustine was centered on the latter's notion of care (*cura*) in its two basic directions of using (*uti*) and enjoying (*frui*) (G60; HBC). Heidegger noted that it was Scheler who, in his essay "Liebe und Erkenntnis," introduced into phenomenology the implications of Augustine's and Pascal's insight that intentional acts of knowing are grounded in acts of "love" that "take an interest" in the object. "Scheler, accepting the challenges of Augustine and Pascal, has guided the problematic to a consideration of the relationship of founding between acts which 'represent' and acts which 'take an interest.' "[7]

In such " 'edifying' writings" as "The Anxieties of the Heathen" and

"The Lilies of the Field and the Birds of the Air," which Heidegger read in translation at least as early as 1924 (EMH 111), Kierkegaard pursues meditations on the New Testament concept of care (*Sorge* in the German translations that Heidegger read), and in his philosophical texts Kierkegaard accordingly defines the relation of the self to itself and its world as "interest" (SZ 313/278; CUP 268; CD 311–56, 7–93). In his *Heidelberg Disputation*, Luther writes that "one urges [the ill] to seek medical care [*cura*]. . . . [W]e make [people similarly] anxiously caring [*sollicitos*] about grace" (WA I 361/XXXI 51). In Luther's commentary on Chapter Three of Genesis, which deals with the fall, anxiety, death, flight, and conscience, and to which Heidegger often referred (cf. G61 182; G20 404/292; SZ 253/235), Luther discusses various senses of care (*cura*) in connection with the statement that "by the sweat of your brow you will earn your bread" (3:19) (WA XLII 157–60/I 210–15). In WS 1921–22, Heidegger wrote that "the factical movement of life is caring (*curare*)" and that, "in its most widely conceived relational sense, life is: anxiously caring for one's 'daily bread' " (G61 90; PIA 240). In SZ we read that "the way in which 'care' is viewed in the foregoing existential analytic of Dasein is one which has grown upon the author in connection with his attempts to interpret the Augustinian (i.e., Helleno-Christian) anthropology with regard to the principal foundations arrived at in the ontology of Aristotle" (SZ 264/243).

Heidegger acknowledged in 1925 that it was "seven years ago" that "I first came across the phenomenon of care" while investigating "the ontological foundations of Augustinian anthropology" (G20 418/302). It was not Konrad Burdach's 1923 article on "Faust und die Sorge" that first led Heidegger to the concept of care, but his earlier studies of such works as Scheler's 1916 essay "Liebe und Erkenntnis" on Augustine. In 1928 Heidegger wrote that, in contrast to Husserl's description of the basic structure of intentionality as a cognitive *noesis*, "Scheler first made it clear, especially in the essay 'Liebe und Erkenntnis,' . . . that even, for example, love and hate ground knowing. Here Scheler picks up a theme of Pascal and Augustine" (G26 169/134).

Understanding and Mood

Through an analysis of especially the first twelve verses of 1. Thess., Heidegger's WS 1920–21 lecture course exhibited how understanding, mood, and language show up in primal Christianity (IPR 320–21). He pointed out that one finds here a repetition of the word "to know" (*eidenai*): "You know what kind of men we proved to be. . . . " "But concerning the time and the moment [*kairos*] [of the Parousia] I do not need to write to you, for you already know well . . . " (5:1). This kind of knowing means not theoretical knowledge, science, contemplation, but "experiential knowledge" and "comprehension of the situation" of the Parousia. Elsewhere in the New Testament, one finds this situational knowing being called *phronesis*, practical understanding or wisdom. For example, "He has made known to us in all wisdom and practical insight [*phronesei*] the mystery of his purpose according to . . . the fullness of the fitting moment [*ton kairon*]" (Eph. 1:9–10). "The Kingdom of heaven shall be compared to ten maidens who took their lamps and went to meet the bridegroom. Five were foolish, five were practically wise [*phronimoi*]" (Matt. 25:2–3; cf. Luke 12:42; 1 Cor. 10:15).

Heidegger also showed that, in the first twelve verses of 1. Thess., there is an emphasis on moods that function together with situational knowing. For example, "your labor prompted by love, and your endurance inspired by hope"; "in spite of much anxiety, you welcomed the message with joy"; "we had previously suffered." In the New Testament, mood is often designated by the term "the heart" (*kardia*): "God, who commanded the light to shine out of darkness, has shined in our hearts" (2 Cor. 4:6); "great sorrow and unceasing anguish in my heart" (Rom. 9:2); "their foolish hearts were darkened" (Rom. 1:21).

As Scheler and, following him, Heidegger pointed out, Augustine and Pascal stressed the moods of love and hate. In SZ and in his 1924 lecture "Der Begriff der Zeit," Heidegger quoted Augustine's statements that "the only way to truth is through love," and that "passing things that are encountered bring you [my soul] into a moodful state of mind [*affectio, Befindlichkeit*]."[8] "The heart," writes Pascal in a similar vein, "has reasons that reason does not know." In SZ Heidegger quoted Pascal's statement that, "while, in human matters, we are accustomed to inculcate that 'we must *know* before we can love,' an expression which has became proverbial (*ignoti nulla cupido*), divine wisdom teaches that, in regard to spiritual things, we must '*love* in order to know them.' "[9] In SS 1925, Heidegger wrote that "what we have set forth here as the being-in of Dasein and characterized in detail is the ontological fundament for what Augustine and above all Pascal already noted. They called that which actually knows not knowing but *love* and *hate*" (G20 222/165). As has often been pointed out, Heidegger also drew from the rich analyses of moods in Kierkegaard. We even find him calling upon St. Francis in 1919 (G56/57 211).

Anxiety

According to Heidegger, a basic mood permeating primal Christianity is "anxiety" over the believer/God relation. 1 Thess. 1 mentions not only the "joy" of hope, but also *thlipsis*, affliction or anxiety in the face of the uncertainty of the time and shape of the Parousia. In WS 1920–21, Heidegger made the point that "the Christian state of wakefulness in factical experience means a constant, essential and necessary insecurity" (IPR 322). In the New Testament, anxiety is also expressed as that "fear and trembling" experienced in "fear of God" (cf. 1 Cor 2:3; Phil. 2:12). In SZ we read that the phenomena of "anxiety and fear . . . have come within the purview of Christian theology ontically and even ontologically. . . . This has happened whenever the anthropological problem of the being of human being toward God has won priority and when questions have been formulated under the guidance of phenomena like faith, sin, love, and repentance" (SZ 252-53/235). And regarding his own analyses of anxiety and fear, Heidegger said that "here I am only trying to provide the [ontological] concepts for things which are usually treated in a nebulous way . . . in theology" (G20 404-405/292).

Drawing on A. W. Hunzinger's study of "the problem of fear . . . from Augustine to Luther" (G20 394/285; FCL 5-42), Heidegger pointed out that, on a Scriptural basis, Augustine developed the notion of pure or chaste fear (*timor castus*) of God, which is motivated by a pure love of God and hope of the self's future community with God. This was the theme with which Heidegger's analysis of Augustine's notion of *cura* in SS 1921 concluded (G60). That concerning which the self anxiously fears is not anything in the created world, but rather the *bonum futurum* of its very community with God or, alternatively, the *malum futurum* of loss of community that threatens in the form of "the sting of death." According to Augustine, this pure fear is eternal, because love of God is eternal. God is thus experienced as an everlasting "*mysterium* tremendum *et fascinans*," a *great* and awesome mystery (HBC). In servile fear (*timor servilis*) of God, on the other hand, the primary object of one's love or care is not the self/God relation, but the world. Thus that concerning which one fears is not the self/God relation, but those worldly possessions and attachments which are threatened by the possible punishment of God. This fear is servile, the fear of the slave, because it comports itself to God externally out of fear of the master's punishment and the loss of its worldly attachments. In contrast, pure fear acts inwardly and freely toward God out of love and anxiety over the self's union with God. Heidegger maintained that, like Thomas, Augustine also "caught a glimpse of [anxiety in a general anthropological context] in a short study *De metu* within a collection of questions, 'On Various Questions of the Eighty Tribes' " (G20 394/285, 404/292). Here Augustine uses the term *metus* to cover a whole range of moods from simple fear to anxiety (*anxietas*) and terror (DQ 47-53/62-67; cf. Thomas Aquinas, *Summa Theologiae*, II^1, qu. 41-44 and II^2, qu. 19).

Heidegger also acknowledged the "impressive" manner in which "Luther dealt with the phenomenon of anxiety in the traditional context of an interpretation of 'contrition' and 'penitence' in his commentary on [Chapter 3 of] Genesis." Here Luther describes the *anxietas* that comes with original sin and separation from God: "Adam and Eve . . . are so filled with fear and trembling that when they hear a breath or a wind, they immediately think that God is approaching to punish them. . . . what a grave downfall, to plunge from the utmost security and lack of care [*securitas*] . . . into such horrible trembling." Luther also describes the resultant and pervasive anxiety of all human life, including his own inner distress over the question of salvation that eventually drove him to break with the Church: "We see it to be just so in the case of frightened people: when they hear the creaking of a beam, they are afraid that the entire house will collapse; when they hear a mouse, they are afraid that Satan is there and wants to kill them. By nature we have became so thoroughly terrified that we fear even the things that are safe."[10]

In WS 1921-22, Heidegger wrote: "Concerning life and restlessness [*Un-ruhe*], cf. Pascal, *Pensées* I-VII; the description [is] valuable" (G61 93). *Un-ruhe* is Heidegger's translation of Pascal's term *inquiétude*, inquietude, that restlessness and homelessness which propels human life into constant motion and distraction. "Man's condition: inconstancy, boredom, anxiety." For Pascal, the individual is thrown contingently into the world, "without knowing who put him there, what he has come to do, what will become of him when he dies." "I am afraid and am amazed to see myself here rather than there, now rather than then." "I am moved to terror like someone transported in sleep to some terrifying desert island, who wakes up quite lost and with no means of escape" (PO 387, 325, 646/PK 36, 48, 88). Heidegger claimed that "the one who has gone the farthest in analyzing the phenomenon of anxiety— and again in the theological context of a 'psychological' exposition of the problem of original sin—is Søren Kierkegaard" in his work *The Concept of Anxiety* (SZ 253/235, 313/278; G20 404/292). Kierkegaard argues theologi-cally that the awareness of freedom in anxiety makes possible the choice of evil in the original sin, which then further aggravates this anxiety. But he also pre-sents a general psychological account of anxiety as the disclosure of the "noth-ing" and "dizziness" of futural possibility: "The possible corresponds pre-cisely with the future. For freedom, the possible is the future, and the future is for time the possible. To both of these corresponds anxiety in the individ-ual." Just as Augustine distinguishes between *timor castus* and *timor servilis*, so Kierkegaard (and Heidegger followed him here) distinguishes between "fear" directed toward "something definite" in the world and "anxiety" di-rected toward the "nothing" of "the possibility of possibility," that is, toward the self's freedom and possibility as such (COA 42-44, 61, 91, 96; cf. PDW 419-32).

Death

In primal Christianity, anxiety is concentrated on *Todesangst*, anxiety over the "sting" of death (1 Cor. 15:56). In SZ, Heidegger wrote that "the anthropology worked out in Christian theology—from Paul to Calvin's *medi-tatio futurae vitae*—has always also kept death in view in its interpretation of 'life' " (SZ 331/293). And in his 1925 Kassel lectures, he even said that "through Christian theology the problem of death entered for the first time into connection with the question of the sense of life" (WDF 20). For Paul, death is not something at the end of life, but rather we are constantly dying: "daily I die"; "dying, and yet we live"; "we are in anxiety in all ways. . . . we who are living are always being given over to death" (1 Cor. 15:31; 2 Cor. 6:9, 4:8–11). Heidegger's notes for his SS 1923 lecture course read, "Cf. above all Paul: glory of *christos* as the redeemer; abandonment of humanity into distress and death" (G63 111). In SS 1925, he accordingly converted the Cartesian *cogito sum* into the New Testament "*cogito moribunbus,* I am dying. . . . [The indefiniteness of the time of death] in no way weakens the certainty of its coming, but rather gives it its sting" (G20 437/317).

The motto from Luther's commentary on Genesis 3:15 that Heidegger used in his WS 1921–22 lecture course ("Right from our mother's womb we begin to die") leads us straight to Luther's description here of life as a *cursus ad mortem*. We find an exact translation of this Latin text in Heidegger's phrase *Vorlaufen zum Tode,* running ahead toward death. In connection also with Genesis 2:17 ("surely we will die"), Luther writes, "Paul says: 'Daily we die'. . . . [Life] is nothing else than a perpetual running ahead toward death. . . . Right from our mother's womb we begin to die. . . . In life we are in the midst of death. . . . our life can be called death." And in the *Heidelberg Disputation* we read, "What person is not in horror and despair in the face of death?" (WA XLII 84, 146/I 110, 196; I 374/XXXI 69). Likewise, according to Pascal in his *Pensées,* the inquietude of the human "reed" is caused especially by the all-pervasive imminence of death: "Imagine a number of men in fetters, all condemned to death, and some killed daily in the sight of the rest, and those who are left, reading their own fate in that of their fellows, waiting their turn, looking at each other in gloom and despair. That is a picture of the human condition" (PO 426/PS 81).

Heidegger's notes for his SS 1923 lecture course read, "The experience of death in general; death—life—Dasein (Kierkegaard)" (G63 111). In SZ, he indirectly referred the reader to Jaspers's review of the limit-situation of death in Kierkegaard (SZ 331/293). Here we learn that, for Kierkegaard, "my death is for me not at all something in general" and "objective" (either as a biological occurrence or as a universal truth), but rather the "subjective relation to [my] death." We do not have the benefit of "the late Herr Soldin" who " 'when he was about to get up in the morning . . . was not aware that he was dead.' " According to Kierkegaard (and here Heidegger followed him point for point), death is a constant spur of care and anxiety about the self; absolutely individual and individuating; and uncertain as to its time and thus to be anticipated at every moment. Jaspers quotes Kierkegaard, "To the degree that I become subjective, the uncertainty of death increasingly permeates my subjectivity dialectically. It thus becomes ever more important for me to think it in connection with every factor and phase of my life; for since the uncertainty is there at every moment, it can be overcome only by overcoming it at every moment" (PDW 269-70; CUP 148-49).

Language and Interpretation

There is also a strong emphasis on language in primal Christianity. In his WS 1920-21 lecture course, Heidegger noted that "the situation of [1 Thess.] is designated as 'preaching' " (IPR 320). In the first twelve verses and following, one finds also a repetition of terms expressing the content of Christian experience as message (*euangelion*) and word (*logos*), as well as the interpretive proclaiming (*euangelizesthai*) of this message. For example, "you received the word"; "from you the word of the lord has sounded forth." Whereas Greek thought has a primarily ocular orientation to seeing with the *oculus mentis*, "the ears alone," as Luther put it, "are the organs of a Christian person" (WA LVII³ 222/XXIX 224). This emphasis on language and interpretation was taken up into the tradition of theological hermeneutics, where *hermeneuein* means both "to say" and, more specifically, "to interpret" sacred writings in light of not only past but also present circumstances. As Kierkegaard emphasized with his notion of "contemporaneity," the Word is supposed to remain a "living word" that is always interpretively *in nobis* and *pro nobis*, in and for us. Similarly, the inflexible *superbia* and glory of the Law are overcome by the interpretive, situational orientation of the Spirit as love, which is exemplified in the Parable of the Good Samaritan (HW 29-40).

The precedent for theological hermeneutics lies in the New Testament itself, when Jesus interprets the meaning of the Old Testament writings (covenant, law, prophecies, messianism) with regard to the new situation that he presents. "And beginning with Moses and all the prophets, he interpreted [*diermeneusen*] to them in all the writings the things concerning himself" (Luke 24:27). In his SS 1923 lecture course on "the hermeneutics of facticity," Heidegger referred to this passage through a quotation from Kierkegaard in order to point out the factical, nonarbitrary basis of interpretation: "Life first lets itself be clarified when it is lived through, just as even Christ first began to explain the scriptures and to show how they taught about him—after he was resurrected." To make the same point, Heidegger's KNS 1919 course had already quoted Jesus' statement in Matthew 19:12, "Who can grasp [this word], let him grasp it" (G56/57 5).

In SS 1923, Heidegger also provided a detailed account of the history of theological hermeneutics from the Byzantians Philo and Aristeas, through Augustine, and finally to the "Hermeneutica sacra" of Protestant thought from the fifteenth century onward (M. Flacius Illyricus, S. Pagnino, W. Frantze, S. Glass, Johannes Jakob Rambach). Schleiermacher's "general hermeneutics" expanded the discipline to include the "theory and doctrine of the art of understanding of foreign discourse in general." Eventually Dilthey rendered hermeneutics into the "methodology of the hermeneutical human sciences." Heidegger followed these generalizing tendencies in Schleiermacher and Dilthey, but criticized their technical notion of hermeneutics as the "giving of rules for understanding" and attempted to locate interpretation originally in life itself. This move was already intimated in Dilthey's analysis of interpretation as the structure of "understanding as such" and exemplified even earlier in the hermeneutics of Philo, Augustine, and Luther (for example, Philo's notion of the interpreter as the *hermeneus theou*, the interpretive herald and messenger of God). For Heidegger, hermeneutics had to be extended ultimately to ontology, which now became in SS 1923 a "hermeneutics of facticity," that is, a self-explication of the interpretive understanding of being in factical life. "Hermeneutics," he wrote, "is the *Kundgabe*, proclaiming, making-known of the being of a being in its being to-(me)" (G63 10-16, 3).

Falling, Authenticity, Inauthenticity

In WS 1920-21, Heidegger explained that Paul differentiates between two basic ways of existing and makes a division into "two groups of people." Some have fallen away from the anxious care and situational temporality of the believer/Parousia relation into the world (cf. Paul's statement that "you have fallen away from grace" [Gal. 5:4]). "The first are those who urge peace and security. They are, says Heidegger, absorbed and totally dependent on the world in which they live. . . . They cannot be saved because they do not possess themselves, they have forgotten the authentic self. They live, says St. Paul, in darkness." However, "the second group lives not in darkness but in the light of day. The word 'day' . . . has two meanings: first of all, the light of self-comprehension, and secondly, the Day of the Lord itself" (IPR 322).

In SS 1923, Heidegger prefaced his account of falling, inauthenticity, and authenticity in life in general with a discussion of the particular domain of Christian experience. "For faith, human being is just as it now meets one and is, 'fallen' or redeemed through Christ." And in his notes, which indicate also the theological model of his ontological concept of *Kehre*, he dealt with the Christian analogues of his authentic/inauthentic distinction. "The fall is absolute. . . . Cf. above all Paul. . . . Flesh—*Spirit*. . . . Explication of facticity: of being-unredeemed and being-redeemed: *huioi theou* [children of God], Rom. 8:14. Death—life; sin—justification; slavery—sonship . . . Christ the turn" (G63 28, 111). In WS 1925-26, he emphasized more clearly that "this peculiar connection, that between the authenticity of the being of Dasein and concern that falls [toward worldly living and possessions], experienced a specific apprehension in Christianity and in the Christian interpretation of Dasein" (G21 232).

Corresponding to Heidegger's distinction between care lost in the world

178 | *The End of Philosophy*

and care anxiously directed toward the self, the New Testament contrasts "care for the things of the lord" with "care for the affairs of the world," as in the Martha/Mary contrast or in the parable of the lilies of the field. " 'Martha, Martha,' the lord answered, 'you are anxiously concerned [*merimnas*] and upset about many things' " (Luke 10:41). "No one can serve two masters. . . . Do not be anxiously concerned [*merimnate*] about your life, what you shall eat or drink. . . . Care [*merimnesei*] not for the morrow" (Matt. 6:24-34). In WS 1921-22, Heidegger wrote that, "as a character of movement, the *tentative* [the tempting] [was] first made visible by Christianity. . . . [But] it is one way or another present in contemporary 'non-Christian' life" (G61 154).

Worldly care is "tempted" by and falls away not only toward the environment of material needs and possessions, but also and primarily toward the public world, which Heidegger called the They. As he wrote in SS 1928, the Pauline concept of "this world," "the wisdom of the world," which has "turned away from God," means "the human community" in its set "comportments, evaluations, ways of behaving and approaching things" (G26 222-23/173-74). The "god of this world," "the care of the age," covers everything from worldly position, security, reputation, prestige, fame, and power to religious idolatry, the Law, and the wisdom of Greek philosophy (2 Cor. 4:4; Matt. 13:22). For Paul, as for the young Heidegger, philosophy is an expression of fallen life: "See to it that no one steals you away through philosophy and empty deceit, which depend on human tradition and the basic principles of the world" (Col. 2:8). Terms like "flesh," in the negative sense of the "lust of the flesh," and the "eyes" have the same wide range of expression. Like Bultmann, Heidegger took these and other terms ("body," "spirit," "heart") to be existential categories expressing "the how" of a way of existing. His notes in SS 1923 read: "Flesh—*Spirit* . . . : to be in them, a *how*" (G63 111).

In language that Luther would later pick up on, Paul describes the fall into the world as an illusory sense of contentment, self-satisfaction, security, "pride," being "puffed up," and "boasting," "glorying." Further, this falling is *hamartia* in the sense of not only "evil," but more specifically "error," "missing the mark," "going wrong." As Heidegger put this in WS 1920-21, "they do not possess themselves" in the concrete situation because they are lost and alienated in "the world" of public norms, the Law, eschatological prophecy, philosophy. According to Paul, they live in darkness, blindness, drunkenness, and sleep. Thus they overlook and miss the mark of the situational demands of neighborly love and the Parousia. They lack "the light of self-comprehension," wakefulness, readiness, practical wisdom (*phronesis*). "Be attentive, or your hearts will be weighed down with dissipation, drunkenness, and the cares of life, and that day will come upon you suddenly like a trap. . . . Be wakeful at all moments [*en panti kairo*]" (Luke 21:34-36).

In WS 1920-21, Heidegger discussed Book Ten of Augustine's *Confes-*

sions, where we read that "they fall [*cadunt*] into that which is in their reach and are content" (DMH 38; C 136/232). In SS 1928, he showed how Augustine's understanding of *mundus* (as in his statement that "the just are not spoken of as the world") derives not from the Greek, but from the New Testament concept of *kosmos* (G26 223/174). In SS 1925, his treatment of the category of falling (including idle talk, curiosity, dispersion, temptation, entanglement) discussed the concept of "the lust of the eyes" in Book Ten of the *Confessions* (G20 379/274; SZ 227/215). But here we in fact find all of the above Heideggerian terms in Augustine's discussion of "falling," which he describes as "temptation," "dispersion," and "entanglement." He explains three forms of this falling, namely, the "lust of the flesh," the "glory" and "ambition of the world," and the "lust of the eyes."

The last is also called *curiositas* (from *cura*, care) in the sense of "the idle care" that simply wants to "see" and know things in order to be distracted by them. In everyday life, it can even take the form of idle talk: "There are very many occasions . . . in which this curiosity of ours is tempted everyday, and it is impossible to count the times when we fall. We often at first listen tolerantly to someone's idle talk, so as not to give offense to the weak; but then we gradually become attracted [*advertimus*]." The smallest thing "may divert [*avertit*] me from some serious thought." This curiosity or lust of the eyes also manifests itself in religion, science, and philosophy, where one finds a sophisticated seeing and knowing for its own sake: "This empty curiosity is dignified and masked by the names of learning and science. . . . it is called in the divine language the lust of the eyes. . . . Hence also men proceed to investigate the concealed working of nature beyond our ken, which it does no good to know and which men want to know only for the sake of knowing" (C 174-80/245-47). In his analysis of curiosity in 1922, Heidegger used the German term *Neugier*, curiosity, to translate Augustine's Latin, "*Neugier* (*cura, curiositas*)" (PIA 241).

He also employed Augustine's analysis to thematize how Greek *theoria*, gazing, falls into the world, which is now encountered as the presence-at-hand of the *eidos*, the seen. This critique of "seeing" is of course already found in Paul, since eschatological consciousness is precisely "hope for what we do not see," namely, the futural Parousia of the *Deus absconditus*. "We live by faith, not by what is seen [*dia eidous*]," that is, the present world. "We consider not the seen, but the unseen" (Rom. 8:25; 2 Cor. 5:7, 4:18). Heidegger also followed Augustine's understanding of falling as the self's attempt to flee from itself, forget itself, and find a state of "contentment": "They love the light of the truth, but hate it when it shows them up as wrong. . . . they love truth when it reveals itself, but hate it when it reveals them. . . . this human soul of ours—blind and lazy, foul and unsightly—wants to be concealed, unknown, forgotten [*latere*]" (C 140/233-34).

In dealing with falling as constant restlessness and *kinesis* into the world, Heidegger's lecture course of WS 1921–22 referred to Pascal's detailed discussions in the *Pensées* of *divertissement*, diversion (literally, *turning away*) as the perpetual "agitation," "unrest," and "motion" of flight from anxiety and boredom. "Our nature lies in motion; absolute rest is death." "Nothing is so unbearable to a human being as to be at rest, without passion, business, amusement, occupation. It is then that one feels one's nothingness, foolishness, insufficiency, dependence, emptiness. Immediately there will issue from the depth of one's soul boredom, blackness, gloom, chagrin, vexation, despair." Pascal goes to great lengths to show that this diversion belongs to the very being of human life and can thus be found in everything from occupations, leisure, sport, and conversation to public life and the pursuit of knowledge in philosophy and the sciences. In his discussion of the *natura hominis* in SS 1923, Heidegger quoted Pascal's statement that "when everything is equally moving about, nothing apparently seems to be moving, as on a ship. When everyone goes overboard and to excesses, no one seems to. He who, like a fixed point of reference, *halts* makes us notice how the others are carried away (PO 387–88, 503/PS 57; G63 109).

In SS 1923, Heidegger also described Luther's view of fallen humanity: "Cf. Luther: *Porro caro significat totum hominem, cum ratione et omnibus naturalibus donis.* This in the *status corruptionis . . .* to it belong *ignorantia Dei, securitas, incredulitas, odium erga Deum. . . . This* as such *constitutive!*" (G63 27). In his *Heidelberg Disputation*, Luther's treatment of falling (*cadere*) and "the world" focuses on the flight from anxious care for the self/God relation (*timor Dei*) into the *securitas*, "power, glory, pleasure, satisfaction," and enjoyment (*fruitio*) derived from the shining form and outward spectacle (*eidos, species*) of the rule of the Law and works. "Human works," he writes, "always appear outwardly beautiful in form [*speciosa*], but inwardly they are filthy. . . . God does not judge according to appearances, but searches 'the minds and the hearts' [Ps. 7:9]" (WA I 226, 356–60, 365–66/XXXI 11, 43–50, 57–59). In his commentary on Chapter Three of Genesis, Luther explains that "not only Paradise but the whole world is 'too narrow' to conceal [*latere*] [Adam] safely. And now, in this anxiety [*anxietas*] of the soul, he reveals his stupidity by seeking a remedy from sin through flight from God. . . . He has stupidly hoped to be able to conceal himself. . . . 'I was in fear . . . and I concealed myself' " (XLII 129–30/I 172–74).

This *superbia* and "presumption" mean that, "completely puffed up, blinded, and hardened," "under the power of darkness," the self is alienated from itself into a Beyond. For "Luther . . . humanity is 'drunk with sin,' " wrote Heidegger in his analysis of falling in SS 1925 and in SZ (G20 391/283; SZ 238/224). In his *Lectures on Romans*, Luther states that "thus they are their own obstruction [*obex*] against the divine light. . . . [They] put up an obstruction against themselves [*obicem sibi*] and an alienating obstacle against the light of understanding." He points out that this happens through falling away (*declinatio*) from the situational understanding of God into either "excess" (inflexible presumption about one's knowledge of God and the good) or "deficiency" (dispersion into worldly pursuits).

Here he explains the Christian search for God with the aid of Aristotle's notion that the good is always disclosed to *phronesis* in a situation as the fitting mean between deficiency and the hyperbolic, excess. "The condition of this life is not that of having God, but of questioning after and seeking God" in historical situations. There are "those who have fallen away to the left and those who have fallen away to the right." "The former do not understand and question after God because of deficiency and omission; the latter are in the same situation, but because of excess and overdoing. For these men are excessively righteous, excessively intelligent, excessively seeking, so that in their own minds they are incorrigible." This "self-satisfied" approach thus always fails to hear the Word in situations and goes wrong: "[They] picture him to themselves in the way they want him to be. . . . Thus they stray away and go wrong. . . . For here God speaks, but he speaks in such a way that neither the person nor the place nor the time nor the word appears such to pride that God is speaking through that person and in such circumstances." In both types of falling, life "ruins" itself: "Together they have gone wrong and become useless. . . . [Paul] depicts their fate. First is ruin, i.e., they are worn down, diminished, and humiliated in body and soul . . . [they are] 'like chaff which the wind drives away' [Ps. 1:4]. . . . they prosper in nothing they undertake . . . they are oppressed and crushed in many ways" (LVI 238–46/XXV 223–32).

In this remarkable section of the *Lectures on Romans* and in the *Heidelberg Disputation*, we surprisingly find many of the major terms of Heidegger's own description of falling in WS 1921–22, namely, falling away, *securitas*, self-satisfaction, presuming and mismeasuring (*Vermessen*), the hyperbolic (excess; cf. *superbia* in Luther and *hyperbole* in 2 Cor. 12), the elliptic (deficiency), going wrong, ruination. Most telling is the similarity between two terms that I have translated as "obstruction," namely, Luther's term *obex* (bolt, bar, barricade) and Heidegger's very prosaic term *Abriegelung* (bolting, barring, barricading). We also find that much of the terminology of this lecture course on Aristotle actually consists of Germanizations of Latin terms gleaned from the texts of Augustine, Thomas, Luther, and others: for example, *das Quietive* (the quietive), *das Alienative* (the alienative), *das Tentative* (the tentative), *Ruinanz* (ruinance), *Larvance* (larvance), *Horrescenz* (horrescence). The Latin term *horror*, dread, is found often in Luther's commentary on Genesis 3 (cf. WA XLII 127–34/I 171–80; G61 138).

In Jaspers's exposition of Kierkegaard's thought in *Psychologie der Weltanschauungen*, we again find the primal Christian account of falling as flight from anxiety over the self/God relation. In fact, Kierkegaard extends this ontic account into an ontological analysis of a fundamental "either/or" that characterizes all life. As opposed to the "ethical" stage of life, that is, passionate *Existenz*, the "aesthetic" stage is defined by immediate enjoyment of the world without any reflection back on the self, which is thus "forgotten." This stage can be found in the hedonist practicing the "rotation method" of generating novel distractions, in the conformist surrendering to the "monstrous abstraction" of the public, and in the "objective" philosopher lost in fantastic speculations and oblivious to "subjective truth."

In Jaspers's study and in Kierkegaard's own texts, we read that the flight from self is characterized by idle talk (*Gerede*), curiosity (*Neugier*), temptation (*Versuchung*), dispersion (*Zerstreutheit*), and comfort (*Beruhigung*). "The ways of diversion and obscuring [the self]," writes Jaspers (quoting Kierkegaard), "are numerous . . . '*comfort* that wants to think about it at another time,' '*curiosity* that never gets beyond curiosity' . . . the 'weakness that *comforts* itself with the company of others' . . . 'mindless hustle and bustle.' " He quotes Kierkegaard still again: "Or through diversions or in other ways, e.g., through work and hustle and bustle as a means of *dispersion*, he attempts to preserve for himself darkness and obscurity concerning his condition." Thus "this *being closed off* [*Verschlossenheit*] that . . . hides from itself, obscures, and evades is the force running counter to the process of *becoming manifest* [*Offenbarwereden*]. Kierkegaard calls this becoming manifest freedom, and this *locking oneself up* non-freedom, bondage." And in another quotation from Kierkegaard, we read, "And here lies the profundity of *Dasein*, namely, that non-freedom takes captive precisely itself." One's life becomes permeated by nontransparency (*Undurchsichtigkeit*) and ambiguity (*Zweideutigkeit*).

Regarding the "either/or" of life, Jaspers writes that "the human being can either want to 'become manifest,' transparent, and lucid; or one can struggle against becoming manifest, overlook oneself, conceal oneself, and forget oneself. Both forces, which are present in every human being, are in battle with one another" (CD 324, 344, 353; PDW 421–24, 431). In Jaspers's study and in the German translations of Kierkegaard that Heidegger was reading, we meet up with many of the key terms of Heidegger's own descriptions of falling and the inauthenticity/authenticity distinction from his lecture course of WS 1921–22 (with its motto from Kierkegaard's *Either/Or*) to SZ: namely, *Existenz*, temptation (*Versuchung*), curiosity (*Neugier*), idle talk (*Gerede*), ambiguity (*Zweideutigkeit*), dispersion (*Zerstreuung*), comfort (*Beruhigung*), and closing off (*Verschliessen*).

Conscience

In primal Christianity, the conscience is seen to be the agency that calls the individual back from fallenness to the self/God relation and thus effects a

Kehre, a turn. (For the following, see DG 216–93; G; UG 177–80; DGE 25–30.) In using studies of the conscience in Christian, Greco-Roman, and modern traditions by Martin Kähler (1878), Albrecht Ritschl (1896), and H. G. Stoker (1925), Heidegger sought to recuperate also a religiously and morally neutral, ontological concept of conscience (SZ 361/317). We learn in these studies that the Latin term *conscientia* and the Greek term *syneidesis* originally meant simply "consciousness" or "self-consciousness." *Synteresis*, the synonym often used in Patristic and Scholastic literature for *conscientia*, meant originally "vigilance," "guarding," "taking care of," "preservation." In ethical literature (Stoicism, for example), the term *syneidesis* took on the specific meaning of a *moral* self-consciousness that, on the basis of rules and principles, reprimands regarding past actions and exhorts regarding present or future actions.

It was primarily Paul who introduced this Greco-Roman moral concept into the new context of Christianity. In the New Testament conscience (*syneidesis*) (1) is private and personal (1 Cor. 10:29); (2) is associated with memory (2 Tim. 1:3–9); (3) leads to the "manifestation" of what was "hidden" (2 Cor. 4:2–6, 5:11) and thus performs the function of bearing witness or attesting (*martyrein*) (Rom. 9:1); (4) is the conscience of errancy (*syneidesis hamartion*) and guilt (Heb. 10:2; Rom. 13:5–8); (5) awakens the anxiety of fear of God (Heb. 10:22–31); and (6) has the character of a call issuing ultimately from the divine Word and is thus conscience of God (*syneidesis theou*) (1 Pet. 2:19). Similarly for Augustine, *conscientia* is the guilt- and anxiety-ridden recollection of the self's relation to God, that is, the awakening of *timor castus*. It is the experience of being called back from fallenness and self-concealment: "You were within me and I was outside of myself. . . . You called, you cried out, you shattered my deafness: you flashed, you shone, you scattered my blindness" (FCL 36–37; C 146/235).

The Patristic and Scholastic term *synteresis*, vigilance, which is found for example in Jerome, Albertus Magnus, and Thomas, signified originally an inextinguishable spark (*scintilla*) of reason, an inborn power tending naturally to the good that is preserved in spite of the individual's fallen condition (G; DGE 25–29). Though *synteresis* was often used interchangeably with *conscientia*, its narrower sense was equated (especially by Thomas in an intellectualized form) with Aristotle's concept of practical reason (*nous*) and meant the *potentia* or *habitus* of practical principles and ends. The other aspect of conscience, namely, *conscientia*, was thought to be the application and the *actus* of these ends in particular situations. The *lumen naturale* of *synteresis* is "what cannot be lost" and cannot err, since it is the inborn knowledge of principles, whereas *conscientia* can err since it deals with the variability of situations. Latin mystical writings employed the Scholastic concept of *synteresis* in a novel way so that it meant the tendency and receptivity for immediate contact with God (cf., Eckhart's "little spark"), and here the mystics were actually going back to Jerome's understanding of *synteresis* as a faculty beyond reason, will, and desire. But both the mystical and the moral interpretations of *synteresis* saw it as the power of disclosure and illumination that counteracts the tendency to falling and self-concealment. It was perhaps the Scholastic association of *synteresis* with Aristotle's practical reason that Heidegger had in mind when, in his SS 1923 seminar on the *Nicomachean Ethics*, he dealt with the statement in Book Six that, unlike technical skill, *phronesis*, which has the self as its *telos*, cannot be forgotten (1140b). "Gentlemen, what is this?," he asked the students dramatically and ended the seminar by declaring: "This is the conscience!" (HW 31–32; EHA 23; G19 56).

Heidegger noted that Luther's commentary on Genesis 3 deals with not only the primal "anxiety" of Adam, but also the conscience as the awakening of the anxiety of "contrition" and "penitence" in Adam, who has attempted to flee and hide himself (SZ 253/235). "After their conscience had been convicted by the Law, Adam and Eve were terrified by the rustling of a leaf. . . . The words 'where are you?' [that God called to Adam] are words of the Law, which through God are directed to the conscience. . . . He wants to show Adam that though he had hidden, he was not hidden from God" (WA XLII 127–31/I 170–76). For Luther, the conscience is a faculty through which the divine Word calls directly to the individual without the mediation of the Church (the so-called "freedom of conscience"). Its function for Luther is so important that it seems to be co-primordial with faith. He was largely responsible for introducing into the development of Protestant theology the original meaning of *conscientia* as "consciousness," where the latter now means specifically consciousness of the self/God relation. This Lutheran concept of the autonomy of the conscience then influenced Kant's ethical thought and the notion of the "certainty" of "self-consciousness" in the German Idealists, who, as Heidegger noted, were former Lutheran theologians (G; DGE 32–35).

Heidegger studied closely the treatment of the limit-situation of "guilt" in Jaspers's *Psychologie der Weltanschauungen*. Heidegger's SS 1925 lecture course and SZ even borrow their quotation of Goethe's saying that "the human actor is always without conscience" from Jaspers's study (SZ 382/334, 399/348; G20 441/319). The second half of Jaspers's discussion of guilt is in fact a review of Kierkegaard's treatment of the same topic. For Kierkegaard, it is the conscience that leads the individual from "being closed off" to "becoming manifest," from "dispersion" to self-recuperation, from objective to subjective truth, from the anonymous publicness to the secret of "hidden inwardness." "This is the secret of the conscience; this secret that an individual life has with itself: that it is simultaneously individual and universal." Kierkegaard distinguishes the individual's conscience sharply from the "external" and "comparative" view of the conscience oriented to standards in public norms, legal systems, or the institutional Church. The proper mode of attunement to conscience is thus not public "idle talk," but keeping silent (*Schweigen*) and listening (*Gehorsam*) in the hidden inwardness of one's own existence. Conscience discloses radically individual guilt and thus individualizes: "The concept of sin and guilt posit precisely the single individual as the single individual." But, at its deepest level, this guilt does not have to do with isolated particular actions at isolated times, nor is it imposed on the individual from external standards; rather, it is the condition of being "essentially guilty." Guilt belongs to the finitude of one's very being (a limit-situation). More particularly, Kierkegaard sees guilt as a "disrelationship" or estrangement of the self from its possibilities and primarily from its possibility of "eternal happiness" in God. When this guilt is chosen and taken up into one's futural possibility, it becomes the "eternal recollection" and "absolute consciousness of guilt" that incite constant anxiety and passion to strive for an eternal happiness from which one is essentially removed. "Another figure comes into being with the in-itself of freedom, namely, guilt. . . . it is the greatness of freedom that it always has to do only with itself, that in its possibility it projects guilt and accordingly posits it by itself. . . . The relation of freedom to guilt is anxiety." According to Kierkegaard, "it is this totality of guilt that makes it possible that in the particular instance one can be guilty or not guilty" (PDW 274, 277–80, 333; CUP 468–93; CD 322–46; COA 98, 108–109).

Like the German Idealists and the ontological tendencies in Kierkegaard's account of conscience, Heidegger sought to extract from the Christian experience of conscience the "ontological condition" for all ontic, moral-religious concepts of conscience, as well as an ontological concept of *Kehre* (SZ 406/354). In the early twenties, his concept of conscience and guilt were still quite simple and undeveloped, but by the time he got to SZ these concepts had become highly articulated phenomena in which we recognize an ontological reinscription of many of the above-discussed features in the Christian tradition and especially in Kierkegaard (SZ §§54–60). For Heidegger, as for Kierkegaard, the conscience is not the "public conscience" of the They, but is "in each case mine" and "individualizes." It has the character of a "call" that issues from the "authentic self" and is addressed to the "inauthentic self" that has fallen away into the world. It is the call and "renewal" of anxious care. It is heard and responded to not in the idle talk of the They, but rather in "keeping silent" (Heidegger was especially interested in this Kierkegaardian concept of *Schweigen* when he read "The Lilies of the Field . . . " in 1924) (EMH 111).

By calling the self that has been "closed off" back to itself from "dispersion" in the world, and thus by "disclosing" the self, the conscience attests or bears witness to (*bezeugt*) the possibility of the authentic self, similar to how Paul sees the conscience to be a "witnessing." The conscience "summons" the self to "project" itself resolutely and passionately upon an essential "guilt," which is a double lack or "not" belonging to Dasein's very being: namely, (1) it is "thrown" into existence (which includes falling) and thus unable to master its basis; and (2) it is unable to realize all of its possibilities. This last point is very similar to Kierkegaard's idea of "essential guilt" and the "eternal recollection" that "projects guilt." Moreover, there is an analogy here between Heidegger's concept of "authenticity" and the religious concept of "rebirth," "redemption," and "justification." For Heidegger, Dasein's authenticity means not that it idealistically escapes the guilt of falling altogether, but rather that it takes this guilt upon itself and achieves a new, freer relation to it, similar to how (as Heidegger said in 1927) "in the Christian happening of rebirth the pre-faithful, i.e., unbelieving, existence of Dasein [i.e, the fallen condition of sin] is lifted up [*aufgehoben*] therein. *Aufgehoben* does not mean done away with, but taken up into the new creation" (G9 63–64/PT 18–19; cf., G63 28, 111).

In his SS 1921 lecture course "Augustine and Neo-Platonism," Heidegger showed how Augustine compromised his own understanding of the relational sense of primal Christianity by adopting the Greek notion of the *theoria (contemplatio)* and "enjoyment of God." In the treatment of anxiety in his "On Various Questions of the Eighty Tribes," Augustine writes that "the perfectly blessed person possesses that quality [of absence of fear] by the tranquillity of the soul." And the *beatitudo hominis*, the happiness and blessedness of human being, lies precisely in contemplative enjoyment of the eternal: "Who can know to what extent something is good when he does not enjoy it? . . . what else is it to live happily and blessedly but to possess an eternal object through knowing it? . . . If desire is in accord with the mind and reason, it will be possible for the mind to contemplate the eternal in great peace and tranquillity." Here in Augustine's speculative anticipations of the afterlife, the anxious, uncertain, situationally oriented, and wakeful faith in the Parousia of the hidden unseen God (the Word that is listened for) is Hellenized, ocularized, theorized, and delived down to the remnant of a quietistic, ocular-aesthetic contemplation and enjoyment of the Paradise of God as *summum bonum*. The restless motion of life ("our heart rests not [*est inquietum*]") is depicted as coming to a standstill in the *tranquillitas* of the *visio beatifica*, the happy and blessed vision of the Kingdom of God, who is a *prae oculis esse*, a constant being before the eyes ("it rests [*requiescat*] in thee"). But for Heidegger the *concupiscentia oculorum* of this contemplative quietism amounts rather to the factical self falling away from the historical believer/God relation into those speculative, objectified visions of God (dead idols) and the resultant intoxication, sleep, and blindness against which Paul had counseled in his suspicions of mystical charisma and Greek philosophy. Augustine here loses the original Christian "intensification of life in its selfworld" and falls back into the Greek "objective metaphysics" of the intelligible place of the *kosmos* (DMH 39–42; DQ 49–52/63–66).

Thus he helps prepare the way for the development of Scholasticism, where the relational sense of Christianity is solidified into an emphasis on contemplation, doctrine, method, and the summa, which are used as the means to achieving the certainty and security of salvation. In WS 1925–26, Heidegger argued that Aristotle's notion of happiness (*eudaimonia*) as contemplation of the pure presence of the divine (which unlike the "not yet" and "unfulfilled" character of practical willing "no longer points out beyond itself and is fulfilled in itself") entered into the *beatitudo* of Augustine's "enjoyment of God" and then into Thomas's beatific "vision of God," which were reflected in turn in Descartes's "clear and distinct perception," Kant's "intuition," Hegel's "thought thinking thought," and Husserl's "essential intuition" as articulated in his "principle of principles" (G21 114–23). Heidegger later took up this historical connection and showed more explicitly how in modernity the medieval attitude of *fruitio* was transformed into a methodical, technical will to certainty that constructs and enjoys its "world-pictures." In his analysis of twentieth century technology, he showed how *fruitio* reappears here as the will to power of the technological city of Enframing, which enjoys the world as the presence-before-the-hand of a "standing reserve" of "consumer goods." Accordingly, God as *summum bonum* now becomes the "highest value" of philosophy and the salvation-"industry" of corporate religion, of Christianty, Inc.

It is precisely the quietistic, ocular-aesthetic relational sense of Greek and medieval metaphysics that Luther characterizes as *gloriatio*, glorying. Whereas the ocularism of Greek metaphysics can be seen in its emphasis on *theoria* (a metaphorical term that signifies the spectator [*theoros*] at the festival of the being of beings, as it were), its "aesthetic" aspect in Kierkegaard's sense can be seen in the experience of this seeing as noetic desire (*orexis*) that is completely filled by the radiant presence-before-the-hand of being and is thus the highest stage of pleasure (*hedone*). This desire is in fact described by Plato as "eating" at the "feast of *logos*," such that the being of beings appears here as a kind of cosmic banquet table of Ideas at which the reverent philosophical guest sits (*Republic* 585–86; *Timaeus* 20c). The mind is for the Greeks a second spiritual stomach. It is thus no accident that Luther used such epithets as "theological pigs" to curse at the "theologians of glory," or referred to "reason" as a "beast" and "whore" (recall Plato's analogy of the act of knowing with the sexual act) (WA LVI 274/XXV 261). "Philosophy," Luther writes in the *Heidelberg Disputation*, "is a perverted love of knowing" similar to "fornicating outside of marriage, for human beings never use but rather enjoy [*fruitur*] creation" (PPT 34–35). The quietism (from *quies*, rest) of Greek metaphysics can be seen in its description of theory as that state in which the motion of desire comes to rest and its lack is fulfilled with the complete possession of eternally present being, which state constitutes happiness (*eudaimonia*) and bliss (*makaria*). This perfect being-in-end (*entelecheia*) is depicted as a type of leisure (*schole*, from which derives "Scholastic"), comfort (*hrastone*), recreation (*diagoge*), and freedom from the restless *energeia ateles* of practical life, whose ends are historically variable and on the move (SZ 184/177). The intelligible *topos* of the divine being of beings appears as the ideal of a kind of cosmic paradise where the philosopher-king goes on vacation from factical life.

Thus, Luther's *Lectures on Romans* argues that, in its Hellenically inspired study of the categories of being, the *theologia gloriae* of Scholasticism replaced Pauline "anxious expectation" of the Parousia with the contemplative enjoyment of the present world. The metaphysicians of glory "esteem the study of the essences . . . and the things themselves reject and sigh over their own essences. . . . We *enjoy* ourselves and *glory* in the knowledge of that over which creation itself mourns" (emphasis added). Thus "is he not a madman who laughs at someone who is crying and lamenting. . . . laughing, they gather their knowledge with a marvelous display of power." In constructing the speculative Christianity, Inc. into which the philosophers retire, the "foolishness of the philosophers" is "content and at rest [*quiescit*] among these things, without care [*cura*] as to what the builder finally intends to make." Luther stresses that this aesthetic objectification of the *Deus absconditus* into a presence-before-the-hand is a "desire to dominate and master [*dominandi*]," for "they elevate their own opinion so high into the heavens that it is no longer difficult for them and no longer causes timidity for them to make judgments about God in the same way that a poor shoemaker makes a judgment about leather." The *theologia gloriae* "prefers works to suffering, glory to the cross, power to weakness, wisdom to foolishness."[11]

Just as Paul, Augustine, Pascal, and Kierkegaard understand metaphysics as a more sophisticated expression of "the world," the natural *concupiscentia oculorum, divertissement*, the "aesthetic" stage, so Luther takes the quietistic, ocular-aesthetic *gloriatio* of Greek philosophy and Scholasticism to be an expression of fallenness (the *status corruptionis* of original sin), which here means more specifically a falling away from the factical believer/God relation into the *superbia*, intoxication, sleep, and false *securitas* of speculative constructions. Because the self is "blocked" off from itself, "completely puffed up, blinded, and hardened," Luther calls for its *destructio*, following here the Pauline theme of the crucifixion and death of the old Adam:

> through the cross works are destroyed [*destruuntur*] and the old Adam, who has been built up [*aedificatur*] through works, is crucified. It is impossible for a person not to be puffed up by his good works unless he has first been deflated and destroyed [*destructus*] through suffering. . . . he who wishes to become wise does not seek wisdom by going forward, but becomes a fool by going backwards into seeking foolishness. . . . 'You must be born anew.' To be born anew one must first die. . . . To die, I say, means to feel death as present.

"A theologian of the cross (that is, one who speaks of the crucified and hidden God)," Luther also writes, "teaches that punishments, crosses, and death are the most precious treasury of all." He wants to return Christian experience to the facticity of a *Todesangst* in which we initially find "nothing in ourselves but sin, foolishness, death, and hell, according to that verse of the Apostle in 2 Cor. 6[:9–10]: 'As sorrowful, yet always rejoicing; as dying, and yet we live,' " that is, live reborn in faith. The enactment of this faith in the very midst of uncertainty, anxiety, and death is for Luther the only access to the *gloria Dei*. "Only he philosophizes well who is a fool, i.e., a Christian," that is, who philosophizes out of the historical facticity of the cross, suffering, and faith that is foolishness and a scandal to metaphysics. Commenting on Luther's notion of faith "in matters that we do not see," Heidegger's essay "Phenomenology and Theology" emphasized that "faith is not . . . a more or less modified type of knowing," and that "all theological knowledge is grounded in faith itself, it springs out of it and springs back into it." As Scheler and Heidegger noted, whereas Plato considered the "more being" (glorious presence) of reason that knows eternal objects to be ontolologically prior to the privative *me on* or "less being" of concrete human life, including unfulfilled care, death, and moods (with their variable objects), Paul, Luther, and other primal Christian thinkers affirm "*ta me onta* in order to bring to nothing *ta onta*" and thus make "an object which is *nothing*, i.e., the poor and needy person" prior ontologically. Metaphysical knowing, Aristotle said, is *theiotate kai timiotate*, the most divine and honorable, but he also said that it has little to do with living a human life (*anthropeuesthai*).[12]

In his early Freiburg period, Heidegger modeled his caustic destruction of metaphysics as the phantasy, myth, and masquerade of hyperbolic phantom life on the same kind of condemnations that he found in Luther and Kierkegaard especially. It is the language of this Christian *destructio* of the wisdom of the wise that Heidegger spoke when he referred to metaphysics as "ocular," "aesthetic," and "quietive," and as "absolute curiosity," "idle talk," "comfort," *securitas*, "self-satisfaction," "aestheticizing intoxication," a "soporific opiate."[13] We read that this "curiosity helps itself out so that, out of Dasein itself, it gets 'new food,' " and that in its fetish for absolute knowledge it functions as "the pimp for the public whore of the spirit, *fornicatio spiritus* (Luther)," the fornicating of the spirit (G63 63, 46). And in the style of Kierkegaard, Heidegger writes that "the high point of the comfort and bankruptcy of philosophy is when one pleads that the 'expression' ['life'] is not to be used. One pushes away the disturbing admonisher—and writes a system" (G61 89). The theme of the crucifixion of the *homo gloriens* of metaphysics and the rebirth of *homo crucis* that the young Heidegger found in Luther, Kierkegaard, and other Christian thinkers was for a time a model for his own attempt to drive a thorn into and destroy the traditional metaphysical concept of the self, and to find a new philosophical beginning that could conceive the personal relational sense of being *de profundis*, that is, as *homo absconditus* within the depths of an *ens absconditum*. This *ontologia crucis* was to have been a kind of philosophical Last Supper for the aestheticism of western metaphysics.

Kairological Time

To show that the believer/God relation in the New Testament is lived ultimately as authentic kairological time, Heidegger's WS 1920–21 course turned to an analysis of the notion of the Parousia of Christ within the Kairos, the eye-opening moment (*Augenblick*), as this is developed especially in the fourth and fifth chapters of 1 Thessalonians and the second chapter of 2 Thessalonians.[14] Heidegger showed how the "situation of historical enactment," the "context of enactment with God," in which the first Christians lived includes a dimension of "already having become," an "already having been" (*genesthai, Gewordensein*), or "now being" (*jetziges Sein*), which is disclosed in "remembering," "knowing," affectivity ("tribulation"), and "preaching." But this present perfect of "having been" is taken up into and shapes precisely the hopeful waiting toward the *Zukunft*, the future that comes toward one, which means here the *Second* Coming, the "thy Kingdom come!" Whereas in Greek philosophy *parousia* or *ousia* means constant presence, in the New Testament it means rather a futural "coming" that is just as much an *abousia*, the absence and mystery of the *Deus absconditus*.

This intertwining of having-been and futural coming in the believer/God relation is expressed in the following statement by Paul that Heidegger cited in WS 1920–21 and that is still another intimation of his notion of philosophical *Kehre*: "you *have turned to* God and *away from* idols in order . . . to *wait* for his son from heaven" (1 Thess. 1:9–10; emphasis added). The Coming will arrive only in the Kairos, the moment, "the fullness of time" (BZ 6). The time and content of this arrival are not objectively available in advance to be expected (*erwartet*), represented, and calculated, but rather are to be determined only out of the Kairos itself, which will happen with a "suddenness" and in "the twinkling of an eye" (1 Cor. 15:52). "Concerning the times and moments," says Paul, "we need not write to you, for you yourselves know that the Day of the Lord will come like a thief in the night" (1 Thess. 5:1–2). The situation of the parousio-kairological temporalizing of the believer/God relation is thus a futural Second Coming (*Wiederkunft*) that is textured by a having-been and that will be determined only out of the incalculable eye-opening moment of arrival.

The original Christians live in "a constant, essential, and necessary insecurity . . . a context of enacting one's life in uncertainty before the unseen God," in "daily doing and suffering." The temporal enactment of this fluid situation means a resolute and open *wachsam sein*, being-wakeful for the in-calculable Coming within the moment. Thus Paul writes, "But you are not in the darkness for that day to surprise you like a thief. For you are all children of the light and children of the day; we belong not to the night and the dark-ness. So then let us not sleep like the others, but rather remain wakeful, watch-ful, and sober. Sleepers sleep at night, and drunkards get drunk at night, but we who belong to the day wish to be sober" (1 Thess. 5:4–8). Heidegger pointed out that the words "day" and "light" in this passage mean both the "Day of the Lord" itself and also the light of self-comprehension, that is, the disclosedness or illumination of both God and the believer's own authentic self in the historical situation. Here factical life is not *in* time as an objective frame-work, but rather *is* and lives time itself (DMH 38).

Heidegger contrasted this authentic kairological time to inauthentic *chronological* time, that is, time-reckoning, calculating time. This is the time of those who await or expect the Coming by objectifying, representing, and calculating it in advance as an already-available, determined, and datable event, which is what happens especially in eschatological and apocalyptic speculations, visions, and prophesies about the coming of the last days (DMH 36). Heidegger showed how the Pauline notion of the Parousia within the Kai-ros differs radically from earlier Jewish prophecy and eschatology concerning the "Day of the Lord" and the coming of the "Messianic Man," as well as from Iranian-Babylonian notions of eschatology and even from the Synoptic teaching of the coming of the Kingdom of God. What one seeks in such chronological time is an escape from anxiety, insecurity, and difficulty into the security and comfort of an objective present-at-hand reality that can be ob-served and counted on. Heidegger pointed to Paul's statement that "when peo-ple say 'peace! security!' then suddenly destruction will come upon them as travail comes upon a woman with child, and there will be no escape" (1 Thess. 5:3). These people, says Paul, live in darkness, sleep, drunkenness. According to Heidegger, this means that they have fallen away from the historical situ-ation and from their authentic selves into the *present* world, they will be away when the Parousia arrives in the Kairos, they will go wrong and miss it, and they will be ruined.

Heidegger held that the understanding of time in primal Christianity was reawakened in such authors as Augustine, Luther, Pascal, and Kierkegaard. In SS 1921, he noted that the priority of temporal enactment-sense over content-sense was maintained in Augustine's discussion of the "will" in Book Ten of his *Confessions* (DMH 38). In his 1924 lecture "The Concept of Time," Heidegger began his discussion by introducing the objective concept of the "time of nature and world" in Aristotle and modern physics; this time appears as a series of homogeneous now-points that can be measured mathematically with clocks. But he then asked, "Am I myself the now and is my Dasein time?"

and translated from Book Eleven of Augustine's *Confessions*, "In you, my spirit, I measure times. . . . passing things that are encountered bring you into a moodful state [*affectio, Befindlichkeit*] which remains, whereas those things disappear. In present Dasein I measure the *Befindlichkeit*, not the things. . . . I measure my moodful finding-myself [*Mich-befinden*] when I measure time." Here Augustine dismisses the Greek concept of time as the motion of the *kosmos* and defines time rather as the *distentio animae*, the extension of the soul. The soul is not in time, but is time: "There are three times—a present of things past, a present of things present, and a present of things future. For these three exist in the soul . . . the present time of things past is memory; the present of things present is sight; the present of things futural is expectation." The remainder of Heidegger's lecture was precisely an exploration of this Augustinian thesis that "I am my time" (C 268, 272, 252/279, 281, 273; BZ 7-11, 27).

In WS 1929-30, Heidegger said that "what we mean here with the term 'moment' [*Augenblick*] is that which Kierkegaard conceptualized in philosophy for the first time—a conceptualizing with which, after antiquity, the *possibility* of a completely new epoch of philosophy begins" (G29/30 225). In SZ he referred the reader to Jaspers's long treatment in *Psychologie der Weltanschauungen* of Kierkegaard's concept of "temporality" and "the moment," as well as Kierkegaard's critique of the Greek and Hegelian concepts of time (SZ 447/388). Like Augustine, Kierkegaard takes authentic time to be not the "objective time" of the cosmos, but the "subjective" time of existing spirit. "Time has no significance at all for nature." Existential time is lived in the moment, which is not an abstract now-point in a series, but the synthesis of past and future. The human self is precisely this synthesis of past (necessity) and future (possibility) within the moment, the situation. Appropriating Aristotle's notion of *kinesis*, Kierkegaard sees time as the "transition from possibility [*dynamis*] to actuality [*energeia*]." This transition (*metabole*) is not a logical movement, but rather a qualitative "leap" of "historical freedom" that always brings something "new" into being within the moment (PDW 108-17, 419-32; COA 82-90).

The synthesis of the past and future in the moment can be seen in two basic Kierkegaardian concepts, namely, contemporaneity and repetition. The notion of contemporaneity is a rejection of the view of the past as a now that has flowed away into a fixed, objectified, and irrevocable past, which can be observed aesthetically or studied theoretically in historical disciplines. The contemporaneity of the past means that the past, e.g., the message of Socrates or Christ, persists as a futural possibility that is contemporaneous with the situation of any subsequent generation, and not just with Socrates's fellow Athenians or with the first generation of Christians. "Repetition" (*Wiederholung* in the German translations that Heidegger was reading) means thus that the past is repeated as futural possibility to be redecided and enacted in the moment. "The future is the whole of which the past is a part. . . . The past about which I am supposed to be anxious must stand in a relation of possibility to me. If I am anxious about a past misfortune, then this is not because it is in the past but because it may be repeated, i.e., become future." Whereas Plato taught that reality lies in a past eternity and is to be "repeated backwards" by "dying away" from existence, Kierkegaard sees repetition as a "recollecting forward" into the future and the moment. "When the Greeks said that all knowing is recollecting, they said that all existence that is has been; when one says that life is a repetition, one says: actuality that has been now comes into existence." "All life is repetition." Repetition is also distinct from mere "hope," insofar as the latter can involve futural possibilities having no basis in past actuality. Both recollection of the past and hope for the future are abstract, in that past and future are not synthesized in the moment. An example of repetition in the ethical sphere is marriage, which, unlike the fleeting love affair, involves the daily redecision and renewal of love. In the religious sphere, the paradigmatic stories are those of Job and Abraham, who suffer great loss, but will repetition through faith in God. In the religion of "the paradox," namely, Christianity, the synthesis of past and future through repetition in the moment takes place when the eternal breaks forth into time. Whereas Greek philosophy conceived of the eternal as something past to be recollected, and Judaism saw the eternal in a distant future to be anticipated, Christianity unites these two abstract factors in the notion of the Kairos of the Parousia, which is constantly taking place. "The pivotal concept in Christianity, that which made all things new, is the fullness of time [Gal. 4:4], but the fullness of time is the moment as the eternal, and yet this eternal is also the future and the past." For in the moment of the intersection of time and eternity, which for Kierkegaard is an ongoing matter, there is also a "repetition" of God's past incarnation in the world (COA 89–91; FTR 149, 131).

In referring to Paul's description of the *kairos* as "the twinkling of an eye," Kierkegaard notes that in the Danish *Øiblikket* and the German *Augenblick* the moment means literally a "blink or glance of the eye," i.e., a sudden eye-opening moment in which one catches sight of the situation. In his essay "The Lilies of the Field . . ." and in other texts, he lays out a number of characteristics of the moment, namely, keeping silent, hearkening, earnestness, suffering, and joy. He stresses that one does not await an objectified and available "tomorrow," rather one comports oneself in an anxious, wakeful keeping silent (*Schweigen*) and openness for the reality and requirements of the moment, which is always characterized by "the sudden" and the "new."

> From the lilies and the birds let us learn . . . *keeping silent*. . . . The bird lives in silence and waits: it knows . . . that everything occurs in its season. . . . it knows that it is not for it to know the time or the day, hence it keeps silent. . . . Then when the moment is come, the silent bird understands that it is the

moment, it employs it, and it is never put to shame. . . . only by keeping silent does one hit upon the moment.

Hearkening or obedience (*Gehorsam* in German translation) means that, in the moment, one is open for and chooses factical possibilities that are not arbitrary, but qualified by the necessity of the past. And when one "hits upon" the moment, one "understands that it is absolutely indifferent whether the spot be a dunghill" or a castle. "Only absolute obedience can with absolute accuracy hit 'the moment'; only absolute obedience can embrace the moment, absolutely undisturbed by the next moment." Thus the lily "was absolutely obedient, hence it became itself in its beauty, it became actually its whole possibility, undisturbed, absolutely undisturbed by the thought that the same moment was its death." Understanding and acting in the moment are also characterized by earnestness. Mere hope and Platonic recollection annul the seriousness of the moment for the sake of the seriousness of past and future. But earnestness understands that everything is constantly being redecided in the moment through repetition. "Repetition—that is actuality and the earnestness of existence." "Earnestness alone is capable of returning regularly every Sunday with the same originality to the same thing." Such existing is "suffering" in the sense of passionately enacting repetition within the moment in the face of the uncertainty of the future. "The bird is silent and suffers." Jaspers writes that, in the religious stage, "the consequence [of suffering] is a constant uncertainty in which the relation to the absolute is experienced and lived. . . . The religious person understands 'the secret of suffering [*Leiden*] as the form of the highest life' [Kierkegaard]." Despite this anxiety and suffering, Kierkegaard affirms that the moment is also characterized by joy. One is unambiguously "present to oneself" in the moment and does not suffer from that "unhappy consciousness" in which one is "always absent, never present to oneself," that is, living only in a remembered past or in a hoped-for future. " 'Behold the birds of the air . . . —unconcerned for the morrow. . . . Consider the grass of the field—which today is'. . . . the lilies and the birds are joy, because with silence and unconditional obedience they are entirely present to themselves in being today." Moreover, for Kierkegaard, the moment is that spot in which, as the "fullness of time," the eternal touches time, such that " 'even now today art thou in paradise.' " One who is open to the moment solves "the great riddle of living in eternity and yet hearing the hall clock strike."[15]

Kierkegaard contrasts the authentic moment with the inauthentic time that belongs to "worldliness" and the aesthetic stage of life. Since inauthentic time is dispersed and lost in the world, it practices not keeping silent, but "idle talk." It does not hearken obediently, but fails to listen and obey, shirking the factual demands of the moment. It does not know the joy of being unambiguously in the moment, but rather is constantly tormented with the anxiety of its worldly cares "for the morrow." Since it is always away from itself in the world, it is constantly deceiving itself and missing the moment. "While one is talking, though one says only a word, one misses the moment. . . . he cannot keep silent and wait, and perhaps this explains why he did not notice the moment when it came for him. For the moment . . . sends no messenger before it to announce its arrival, it comes too suddenly for that." The result is that one does not develop one's possibilities and falls into ruin. " 'To what purpose?' he would say, or 'Why?' he would say, or 'What is the use?' he would say—and so he did not unfold his whole possibility, but had his deserts, in that stunted and ill-formed he sank beforehand under the moment" (CD 324, 73–82, 325–26, 340). Kierkegaard shows how aesthetic "living in the moment" destroys the genuine moment. Here one moves from now to now in a disconnected series that does not involve the synthesis of past and future. Each now is simply aesthetically anticipated, tasted, and then abandoned into a remembered past that is not existentially repeated.

In SZ Heidegger wrote that, though Kierkegaard experienced it "in an existentiell manner," the moment "has not been made explicit existentially" here (SZ 447/388). Despite the questionable nature of this claim, what Heidegger attempted to do in the early twenties and in SZ was to conceptualize ontologically precisely the experience of kairological temporality in primal Christianity, which now became the paradigm of all experience for Heidegger. Here we come across the sources of many basic Heideggerian terms: for example, the "kairological characters" of experience, the moment (*Augenblick*), repetition (*Wiederholung*), "wakefulness," keeping silent (*Schweigen*), the passion (*Leidenschaft*) of temporal enactment, and the inauthentic time that involves idle talk and the calculative awaiting of a fixed future. As Heidegger himself later suggested, without this "theological origin," it is highly doubtful that he would have developed the question of "being and time."

In his course "Augustine and Neo-Platonism" and in his following courses, Heidegger argued that the eclipse of authentic kairological time by inauthentic chronological time is just what happened when Christian thinkers in the patristic period and in Scholasticism began to use the conceptuality of Greek and Roman philosophy to speak about New Testament experience. They fell into the Greek metaphysics of presence and began crying out, "peace! security!" Augustine's Neo-Platonic notion of the enjoyment of God means precisely speculation about *praesto habere*, a having present of God, who is *esse praesto*, a being present. In this quietistic vision of the *vita beata*, the absence, incalculability, and movement of the temporalizing of the believer/God relation is dehistoricized and mythologized into the dead eternity of a calculable presence. In a passage that Heidegger, drawing on his earlier studies, quoted in 1946, Augustine writes, "One who seeks what he cannot obtain suffers torment [*cruciatur*]. . . . For what do we call enjoyment but having present the objects we love? . . . The highest good must be in the condition of being present in our possession, if we think of living happily and blessedly." This highest good is that which "cannot be in a condition of being absent [*deesse*] while being loved. . . . what else but God is that eternal object which affects the soul with eternity?" This eternity is precisely a *nunc stans*, a standing now, the solidification of the present: "If the present were always present and did not go by into the past, it would not be time at all, but eternity."[16] From the standpoint of Pauline eschatology, this *fruitio Dei* amounts to falling away from the kairological temporalizing of the historical situation into the intoxication and sleep of the chronological time of speculative and apocalyptic visions. By adopting such foreign Greek conceptuality, Augustine obscured his own understanding of the kairological time that he expressed elsewhere in his writings.

Augustine thus prepares the way for the predominant Scholastic view of God as *substantia, ousia,* in its double sense of an objectified substance (thing) and presence given to contemplation in the blessed life. In WS 1925–26, Heidegger showed how, "in connection with Augustine," Thomas arrives at his position that "pure *visio Dei*, pure intuiting and the pure having present of God [is] the highest kind of being (*beatitudo*) that human being can have" (G21 114–23). In this "speculative thought," the desiderative comportment and motion toward God undergoes "complete fulfillment," whereas practical "willing" remains "unfulfilled" and burdened with the lack of the futural "not yet" of its ends. The metaphysics of presence is the death of desire. For Thomas, "the highest capacity of human being is knowing (that is utterly Greek) . . . 'whose highest object is the divine good.' . . . *speculativus intellectus* is also used for *theoretice*, i.e., it is the Greek *theorein*. . . . This *intelligere* is therefore defined: . . . 'the presence [*praesentia*] of the knowable in relation to knowing.' " Heidegger argued further that this *fruitio Dei*, with its fixation on the intuition of presence, reappeared in the concepts of "intuition" and being as presence that one finds in Descartes, Kant, Hegel, and Husserl.

In his WS 1920–21 lecture course, Heidegger claimed that "Luther *did* understand [the] basic experience of temporality [in Paul] and for that reason opposed Aristotelian philosophy so polemically" (IPR 322). In the young Luther, one finds an amazing critique of the *ontologia* and *theologia gloriae* as a metaphysics of presence. "A theologian of glory . . . does not know along with the Apostle the hidden and crucified God," but along with "the pagans" speaks of "how his invisible nature can be known from things visible and how he is present [*presentem*] and powerful in all things everywhere." *Gloria* means for Luther the Greek experience of the being of beings and the divine as radiant, exalted *presence* (WA I 614/XXXI 227). Heraclitus, for example, writes in fragment twenty-nine, "For the noblest choose one thing above all else: glory [*kleos*], everlastingly abiding over against mortal things."

Through Jaspers's *Psychologie der Weltanschauungen* and his own reading of *The Concept of Anxiety*, Heidegger was also familiar with Kierkegaard's criticism that the Greeks had reduced time abstractly to the present, and that their concept of being meant precisely a truncated presence. In his discussion of "the moment," Kierkegaard maintains that, in the Greek and Hegelian representation of time as "an infinite succession" of abstract now-points, time has been falsely "spatialized" and objectified. This series of nows is seen as running its course in an empty and indifferent present, which can be envisaged only through the "purely abstract exclusion of past and future." "As representation, the infinite succession is an infinitely contentless present." Plato in particular conceives of the moment or now of the present as "a silent atomistic abstraction" that in fact does not "occupy any time," even though it is supposed to be the transition point between rest and motion. Thus he and Parmenides can assert that "non-being is not" and that "only being is," i.e., only the "is" of an abstract present.

But this is nonsense for Kierkegaard, since the moment is precisely a *kinesis* from the nonbeing of futural possibility to the being of present actuality. He argues that, in the *Parmenides*, Plato equates the now of "present time," "being," and the idea of "the one": "The one must nevertheless be, so it is said, and then 'to be' is defined as follows: Participation in an essence or nature in the present time (*to de einai allo ti esti e methexis ousias meta chronou tou parontos*, 151e). . . . the present (*to nun*) vacillates between meaning the present, the eternal, and the moment." Kierkegaard notes that this equation turns up again in the "pure being" of Hegel: "In the most recent philosophy, abstraction culminates in pure being, but pure being is the most abstract expression for eternity, and again as 'nothing' it is precisely the moment." In the eternal now in which "ideas" are located, time and being are reduced to "the present in terms of an annulled succession. . . . in the eternal there is no division into the past and the future, because the present is posited as the annulled succession." Because they were lost in this abstract present, "the Greeks . . . did not in the deepest sense comprehend sensuousness and temporality." They failed to see the "historical presupposition," which involves precisely nonbeing and futurity. "This category is of utmost importance in maintaining the distinction between Christianity and pagan philosophy, as well as the equally pagan speculation in Christianity [Hegelianism]. . . . It is only with Christianity that sensuousness, temporality, and the moment can be properly understood." In the words of Jaspers's account of Kierkegaard, the aestheticism of the metaphysics of presence lacks the "secret of suffering," of life "hidden in suffering" (Luther) in the sense of the temporal enactment of being; it "suppresses the development of those capacities that seek the meaning of *Dasein* in the movement of the future and in self-chosen experience. This is replaced by the rest and repose of a transparent and complete world of eternally present meaning that comforts the soul" (COA 84–87; PDW 254–56).

In his 1515–16 *Lectures on Romans*, Luther comments on Paul's description of kairological time in Romans: "Our sufferings of the present moment [*tou nun kairou*] are not worth comparing to the coming futural glory [*ten mellousan doxan*] to be revealed to us. The expectation of creation waits anxiously. . . . we hope for the unseen. . . . And he who searches our hearts knows the *phronema* of the spirit" (Rom. 8:18–27). Here Luther performs a *destructio* of the metaphysics of presence practiced by *ontologia gloriae* in its doctrine of the categories of being. The metaphysicians "glory in the knowledge of that over which creation itself mourns," namely, the present. For Luther, the ocular-aesthetic quietism of Greek metaphysics and Scholasticism is intoxicated, "puffed up," and bloated with presence. It needs to be deflated and sobered up with a dose of Pauline eschatology. Luther amazingly suggests that Paul is the first "philosopher" to think the connection between being and historical time, and that his *theologia crucis* has made something like what Heidegger himself in 1921 calls a *Kehre* to a new postmetaphysical "genuine beginning":

> *The creation waits anxiously.* The Apostle philosophizes . . . in a different way than the philosophers and the metaphysicians do. . . . the philosophers so direct their eyes to the present state of things [*in presentiam rerum*] that they speculate only about essences and qualities of things. . . . the Apostle recalls our eyes away from the intuition and contemplation of the present, away from the essences and accidents of things, and directs us to the future. . . . in a new and amazing theological vocabulary he speaks of the "expectation of creation". . . . Therefore, you will be the best philosophers and the best speculators of things if you will learn from the Apostle to consider the creation as it waits, groans, and travails, that is, as it *turns away* in disgust from that which is and desires that which is not yet and in the future. . . .

In these lectures, Luther explores how kairological time characterizes not just the specific historical event of the Parousia, but all comportment to God. For, despite Augustine's speculations about *praesto habere*, "the condition of this life is not that of having God, but of questioning after and seeking God," who is hidden and absent. In the spirit of Kierkegaardian repetition, the believer is a constant beginner "who is always beginning, seeking, and renewing his questioning. . . . And he who does not renew his quest loses what he has found, since one cannot stand still on the way to God." And just as Kierkegaard appropriates basic concepts in Aristotle's practical philosophy and *Physics*, such as *kinesis*, to work out his ideas on the temporal nature of human existence, so Luther, in order to get at the sense of Pauline kairological time in Romans 8:24 ("hope that is seen is not hope"), again appeals in a highly creative manner to Aristotle's notion of *phronesis* (*prudentia* in Latin) as situational understanding within the *kairos*, the moment. "Hope transfers him into the unknown, the hidden and the dark shadows, so that he does not even know what he hopes for. . . . [W]e do not understand the work of God until it has been done." Thus "fools," those who lack prudence and fall prey to either excess or deficiency, "do not know how to greet God when they meet him, nor know how to receive the gifts he offers them." We have "the greatest need for prudence, so that we are not wise in things that are apparent . . . but rather in future and unknown things which do not appear. For this reason the Apostle in this passage uses a very significant word. . . . 'He knows what the prudence [*phronema*] of the spirit is.' " "But do we not preach the world . . . ?" Luther asks. "For we understand things metaphysically, that is . . . as things that are apparent and not hidden, although [God] has hidden his power under nothing but weakness, his wisdom under foolishness" (WA LVI 371–72, 239, 374–80/XXV 360–62, 225, 364–70).

Though in moments of excess Luther condemned Aristotle's entire corpus, he often expressed a great respect for Aristotle's practical writings, stating that "Aristotle is the best teacher one can have in moral philosophy." He maintained that the *Politics* "sketched out in the best way the essential characteristics of the state, the art of the administration of the state, and of justice." Likewise, Luther appreciated Aristotle's logical writings, *Rhetoric*, and *Poetics* because he thought that they provided practical training in the art of discourse and of "preaching" especially. For Luther, "it is not that philosophy is evil" in itself for the Christian, but rather its "misuse," which lies in replacing the New Testament with Aristotle instead of working from a position of faith and using what can be found in Aristotle's corpus to illuminate that faith as faith.

The Luther scholar Ebeling even argues that Luther defends the "true Aristotle" against Scholastic misinterpretations that miss both the dangers and the positive value of Aristotle's philosophy for Christian thought. "It is very doubtful whether the Latins comprehended the correct meaning of Aristotle," wrote the young Luther. What we find in his texts is that his destruction of Aristotle the metaphysician is complemented by a highly creative, non-Scholastic appropriation of those themes in Aristotle's practical philosophy and *Physics* that can be used to get at the nature of concrete historical existence. Luther uses the notions of *phronesis* and *kairos* in Aristotle's ethics to explore the meaning of not only the Parousia, but also the overcoming of the *gloria* and *superbia* of "the kingdom of the Law" through the Spirit of love that applies the Law interpretively and sometimes even "breaks the law" within the *kairos*. Luther writes in his *Commentary on Genesis*,

> In the fifth and most brilliant book of his Ethics Aristotle has a very fine passage about *epieikeia* [equity or justice in applying the law]. . . . Because there are innumerable occasions and countless dealings which, due to the diversity of circumstances, cannot all be included in a document and in laws,

and few men see clearly where the law should be properly and prudently mitigated, for this reason Aristotle has pointed out the best way. Thus he also adapts a definition of virtue to it when he says: "Virtue is a *habitus* regarding choice, consisting in holding to the mean relative to us [*pros hemas*], which is determined in a rule of thought and language and as the practically wise person [the *phronimos*] would determine it. [It is a mean between two vices, that of excess and that of deficiency.]" ... *epieikeia* breaks the law because of a sudden and unforeseen event.

Luther saw an analogy between Aristotle's anti-Platonic turn to a concrete historical *ethos* that interpretively applies ethical rules in situations and the Christian turn toward the Spirit (faith as *habitus*) that interpretively applies the Law within situations. "Aristotle explained how no work can be good unless it originates from correct insight [*phronesis*] and a good will [*ethos*]. . . . this view is irrefutable." But, for Luther's views on original sin, Aristotle's position is "a truth that in another manner is only properly valid in theology," for "good will and correct judgment . . . are to be sure meant as actualized through faith."[17]

Luther's *Lectures on Romans* also present a novel interpretation of Aristotle's *Physics* in order to work out the meaning of Paul's exhortation in Romans 12:2 to "those who have already begun to be Christians" that they "do not conform to the pattern of this age, but be transformed [*metamorphousthe*] by the renewing of your mind." He explains that the life of Christians is not a fall and coming to standstill in the world, the present age, but rather a constant circular *physis, kinesis,* and becoming (*genesthai*), since what one has become and is in present actuality (*energeia* and *eidos*) is never cut off from the lack, privation (*steresis, privatio*), not-yet, and nonbeing of futural possibility (*dynamis*), in terms of which one's life and "quest" on "the way to [the absent, hidden] God" are to be repeated and renewed from situation to situation. "Their life is not something in quiet rest and repose [*in quiescere*], but in movement from good to better," just as "in the case of the half-dead person who was taken into the care [*cura*] of the Samaritan":

> just as there are five stages in the case of the things of nature: non-being, becoming, being, action, passion, that is, privation, matter, form, operation, passion, according to Aristotle, so also with the spirit: non-being is a thing without a name and a person in sin; becoming is justification; being is righteousness; work is acting and living justly; passion is to be made perfect and complete. . . . through this new birth one moves from sin to righteousness, and thus from non-being through becoming to being. And when this has happened one acts justly. But from this new being, which is really a non-being, a human being proceeds and passes to another new being through passion, that is, through becoming new, one proceeds to a better being, and from this again into something new. Thus it is most correct to say that human being is always in privation, always in becoming or in potentiality, in

matter, and always in action. Aristotle philosophizes about such matters, and he does it well, but he is not understood in this sense. Human being is always in non-being. . . .

The Pauline and Lutheran destruction of the metaphysical *to on/me on* hierarchy amounts, then, to an affirmation of the ontological precedence of nonbeing over being, nonpresence over presence, mystery (*abscondere*) over evidence, privation (*steresis*) over form (*eidos*), the poor and needy over power and glory, situational difference over universality. "Only he is made rich who is poor," writes Luther and then refers to *Physics* I, 5–7 and to *De anima* III, 4. "As the philosophers say: a thing is not brought into form unless there is a lack [*steresis*] of form or a change of previous form; and the possible intellect does not receive a form unless it is in principle without form and like a *tabula rasa*. . . . God fills only those who are hungry and needy" (WA LVI 441–42, 218–19/XXV 433–35, 204; cf., 329–30/317). Human life, being, and God are for Luther "hidden in [the daily] suffering" (enactment) of a futural absence and mystery that are irreducible in this life and, if Heidegger is right, also in an afterlife.

Heidegger stated in his 1927 essay "Phenomenology and Theology" that, as that which defines "factical Dasein in its Christianness," "faith is a believing, understanding way of existing in the history revealed, i.e., happening, with the Crucified." "Therefore, theology, as the science of faith . . . is to the very core a *historical* science" (G9 54–55/PT 10–12). In his 1924 lecture "The Concept of Time," which was also delivered before the theologians, he stated that in faith's "relation to eternity," i.e., to God, "eternity [is] something other than empty being-always, the [Greek] *aei*" that was used to interpret God's eternity in Scholasticism (BZ 5–6). In SZ he explained that "the traditional concept of eternity in the sense of the 'standing now' (*nunc stans*) has been drawn from the ordinary [inauthentic] way of understanding time and has been limited to an orientation toward the idea of 'constant' presence-before-the-hand." In other words, Heidegger does not maintain only that "Christian faith [has] in itself a relation to something that happened in time"; rather, like Kierkegaard, for whom one does not cease "existing" in the afterlife, he held that "if God's eternity could be 'construed' philosophically, then it may be understood only as a more original and 'infinite' temporality" (SZ 564/479).

His destruction of the metaphysics of presence and his new beginning for the question of "being and time" were a radical ontologization of not only the mystical notion of "breakthrough," but also the Christian *destructio* of eschatological prophecy (Paul), the cosmological notion of time (Augustine), the truncated Greek view of time in terms of the present and of being as static presence (Luther, Kierkegaard), a critique which was then reasserted in the Lutheran philosophical tradition of the German Idealists, Nietzsche, and Dilthey.

If we stop for a moment and ask ourselves what it was that could have inspired the violent, explosive force of Heidegger's destruction of the concept of being as presence in the history of metaphysics (in Aristotle especially) and his thesis of the "forgetfulness of being," the answer can only be that it was his own passionately anti-Greek Christian heritage. Löwith, Gadamer, Pöggeler, Sheehan, and others have expressed this view for years. The reflections we have pursued here have only been an attempt to work out the details, regarding Luther especially, on the basis of more recent publications of Heidegger's texts. Heidegger himself later said that "without this theological origin I would never have come upon the path of thinking" (G12 92/10).

In 1520 Luther, colleagues, and students assembled before a bonfire outside the Elster Gate in Wittenberg and committed a number of Scholastic texts to the flames. Four hundred years later, the young Heidegger assembled colleagues and students for a farewell celebration on the eve of his departure to Marburg in 1923 and compressed the results of his early Freiburg period into the opening words of a rousing speech: "Be awake to the fire of the night. The Greeks . . . " (HW 96). The Greek question of being was to be destroyed and repeated in terms of the Pauline-Lutheran theme of remaining awake in the night of the world for the Parousia. Being comes like a thief in the night. Like Hegel's "way of the soul," Heidegger's *ontologia crucis*, which also contained strong elements of mysticism, wanted to conceive of the mystery of *ens absconditum* as enacted in and through the suffering and cross of history. In his SS 1923 lecture course "Ontology (Hermeneutics of Facticity)," a title that already gives the matter away, we find the following passage explaining his statement early on that "philosophy displays its corruption as the 'resurrection of metaphysics.' " It is an ontological reinscription of Christian kairological time and its critique of the chronological time of eschatological prophecy into a radical reformulation of the Greek question about being:

> Philosophy is what it can be only as philosophy of its "time." . . . As what being-here is encountered in being-wakeful . . . is not to be calculated in advance. . . . That such trivialities are today forgotten should not be surprising in the great industry of philosophy, where everything is geared to ensuring that one not arrive too late for the "resurrection of metaphysics" which, so one hears, is now beginning, where one knows only the single care of helping oneself and others to a friendship with the loving God that is imparted through essential intuition and as cheap, comfortable, and also profitably direct as possible. (G63 5, 19–20; cf., SZ 3/21)

9 | Husserl

In addition to his demythologizing of medieval Scholasticism, the young Heidegger also attempted to unmask the original kinetic-personal physiognomy of being behind the traditional guiding metaphysical question at work in Husserlian phenomenology. In this sense he approached Husserl as a paradigmatic representative of the modern epoch of transcendental "ego-metaphysics" (G61 173). One finds this historical situating in Husserl's own later *Krisis* and other contemporaneous writings, where he worked out systematically how his longstanding ideal of "rigorous science" fit into the history of metaphysics. He explained how the primal establishment (*Urstiftung*) of the ideal *telos* of "universal science" took place with the Greek philosophical turn to the intelligible *arche*, the origin/kingdom, of the *eidos*, which is universal and transtemporal. Here "metaphysics . . . was honored as the queen of the sciences."[1] The re-establishment (*Nachstiftung*) of this ideal in modernity began with Descartes's turn to subjectivity, which displaced both the Greek cosmos and the God of medieval thought as the *arche* of the universal, transtemporal *eidos*. With Descartes, writes Hegel, "we are at home, and like the mariner after a long voyage in a tempestuous sea, we may now hail the sight of land."[2]

The ultimate *telos* of the history of metaphysics is for Husserl the final establishment (*Endstiftung*), namely, the "infinite task" of his own phenomenological exploration of "the kingdom [*Reich*] of transcendental consciousness," which is "the kingdom of absolute being" (IRP1 159/194). Here Husserl casts himself in the role of an Old Testament prophet who, though certain of his mission to lead philosophy out of the exile, wilderness, and "crisis" of the contemporary loss of faith in metaphysics, nonetheless suffers from the "unhappy consciousness" of homesickness: "The author sees the infinite open country of the true philosophy, the 'promised land' on which he himself will never set foot" (IRP3 161/21). Similar to Derrida,[3] the young Heidegger, this hidden king, attempted to show precisely that Husserl's promised *ideal* of a universal, transtemporal eidetic kingdom of transcendental subjectivity was in principle unfulfillable through the praxis of *actual* phenomenological investigations and was exposed inevitably to deferral, exile, way, mourning. "Between the idea / And the reality / . . . Falls the Shadow / *For Thine is the Kingdom* / . . . For Thine is / Life is / For Thine is the."[4]

The Fundamental Book of Phenomenology

If Heidegger's new turn to Husserl's phenomenology around 1919 used phenomenological conceptuality in order to work out a phenomenology of primal Christianity, then conversely he simultaneously used the latter to effect a *destructio* and repetition of phenomenology, as well as of his own earlier phenomenological ontologic. He now wanted to push phenomenology in the direction of a more radical historical philosophy of that question about being he had discovered in Aristotelian Scholasticism, Brentano, and Braig during his student years. "The question about being," he wrote in SS 1925, "is sprung loose through the immanent critique of the natural trend of phenomenological research itself" (G20 124/91). If Husserl said, "you and I are phenomenology," Heidegger could well have replied, you and I—and Luther and Kierkegaard and Aristotle.

Here Heidegger focused on the Sixth Investigation in Husserl's *Logische Untersuchungen*. Because it dealt with intentionality as the "categorial intuition" of "being" and with the "truth" at work here, Heidegger, against the self-interpretation of the *mens auctoris*, preferred this early work to Husserl's later texts beginning with his 1913 *Ideen*, which announced a turn to transcendental idealism. Heidegger later reported in his "My Way in Phenomenology" that "the distinction worked out [in the Sixth Investigation] between sensory and categorial intuition revealed itself to me [after 1919] in its scope for the determination of the 'manifold meaning of being,' " a problem he had discovered in Brentano (SD 86–87/78–79). In a 1973 seminar devoted to the influence of the Sixth Investigation on his youthful thought, he said that the "essential discovery" and "burning point of Husserl's thinking" was the notion of the categorial intuition of being, which then became an "essential motivating force" and "basis" for Heidegger's own thought. For here Husserl "brushed against the question of being" (G15 373–78). In SS 1925, we thus find Heidegger stating that the *Logische Untersuchungen* is the "*fundamental book of phenomenology*," even though the later Husserl "no longer held his work in very high esteem." He saw Husserl's later transcendental "self-understanding" of phenomenology as a "fall" back into the prejudices of the ego-metaphysics of Descartes, German Idealism, and Neo-Kantianism (G20 124–28/91–93, 30/24, 188/139, 179/129).

Not only did Heidegger's lecture courses from KNS 1919 onward deal with phenomenology, but, as he later reported, "alongside my lecture courses and seminars I worked on the *Logical Investigations* weekly in special study groups with advanced students," though "Husserl watched . . . in disapproval." As Husserl's assistant, he held official and unofficial seminars on this text at least in WS 1921–22 (Vol. 2), SS 1922 (2nd Investigation), SS 1923 (Vol. 2), and WS 1923–24 (1st Investigation), holding a seminar on Husserl's *Ideen* (Vol. 1) in WS 1922–23. His SS 1923 lecture course began with a discussion of the concepts of intentionality, being, and ontology in Husserl, and in WS 1923–24, he provided a detailed discussion of the *Logische Untersuchungen*. In his 1925 Kassel lectures, he showed how Husserl's concept of intentionality in the Sixth Investigation provided the basis for understanding Dilthey and the question of the being of history. In his SS 1925 lecture course, which presented the results of his reading of Husserl in the early 1920s and is apparently the most sustained textual treatment, he delivered what eventually became "Division One" and the first third of "Division Two" of SZ as an "immanent critique" and "repetition" of the Sixth Investigation, which was the focal point of his almost two-hundred-page introductory discussion of Husserl's phenomenology. In his WS 1925–26 lecture course, which presented what eventually became Division Two of SZ, his discussion of temporality was preceded by an almost one-hundred-page discussion of Husserl's notion of "truth." When SZ appeared in 1927, it presented the systematic results but few historical details of Heidegger's appropriation of Husserl, though it acknowledged that "the basis" of this work had been prepared for by Husserl and, in the key discussions of truth and time, referred the reader to the Sixth Investigation.[5]

Heidegger claimed that a "fundamental critique of phenomenological inquiry" was needed. Beginning in KNS 1919, his destruction attempted to trace the founded, *theoretical* articulation of such Husserlian concepts as "intentionality," "content," "relation," "enactment," "temporalizing," "sense," "being," and "truth" back to the "genuine phenomenologically primordial stratum (*life in and for itself*)," which he was discovering first in primal Christianity and then in Aristotle's practical thought. These basic Husserlian concepts were to be repeated and rethought from out of their pretheoretical primal source (*Ursprung*). Heidegger's own historical ontology, that is, his fusion of Christianity and Greek philosophy, was simultaneously a "more radical internal development" of Husserl's phenomenology, an "ontological phenomenology," and indeed the "most radical phenomenology that *begins* in the genuine sense 'from below' " in the depths of *kinesis*. It was to be a new "genuine beginning" of phenomenology itself, which was understood not merely "in its *actuality* as a philosophical 'movement,' " but "as a possibility" of showing the things themselves. In SS 1925, Heidegger said that "even today I still consider myself a learner in relation to Husserl."[6]

In the remainder of this chapter, I outline how Heidegger's new beginning dismantled the intentional configuration of phenomenology and of his own earlier ontologic (logical sense/*noesis*/atemporal ideality) and reinscribed them from out of their own postmetaphysical ground-question. My interpretations of Husserl's Sixth Investigation follow the general directions of Heidegger's own readings, as they are given primarily in his 1925 Kassel lectures and then in a more detailed form in his SS 1925 lecture course.

The Phenomenon of Being

I begin with Heidegger's critical reinscription of Husserl's characterization of the intentional moment of content-sense. In Chapter Six ("Sensory and Categorial Intuitions") of his Sixth Investigation, Husserl oversteps the empiricist and Kantian restriction of intuition to sensory intuition of sensible objects. He shows how we are always performing acts of categorial intuition in which the categorial elements of perceptual expressions (e.g., the "this" and the "is" in "this paper is white") are brought to objective "givenness." Husserl explains that intuition in general is a fulfilling intention that fills an empty intention with the immediate givenness of the matter itself. For example, my imaginative intention of the white paper can be fulfilled by an immediate perception of the white paper (the perceived paper that is bodily there before my eyes). But Husserl insists that the empty meaning-intention in a linguistic expression of an object ("the paper is white," "the white paper") cannot be fulfilled merely through my sensory intuition. What I understand and express in my statement—"the paper-*being*-white," "the paper-*as*-white"—cannot be found in the sensuously intuited object, even though it is given "with" this object. "*Being is no real predicate* [Kant]. . . . I can see colour, but not *being*-coloured. I can feel smoothness, but not *being*-smooth. I can hear a sound, but not that something *is* sounding. Being is nothing *in* the object. . . . *being is absolutely imperceptible.*" Therefore, Husserl calls being an "excess [*Überschuss*] of meaning." Though in my statement "the paper is white," I say only what I see, what I see (in the wider sense of intuit) is also the *being*-white, the *as*-white, which exceeds the sensible aspect of the white paper. Husserl writes,

> I *see* white paper and *say* 'white paper,' thereby I express, with precise adequacy, only what I see. . . . We are not to let ourselves be led astray by such ways of speaking; they are in a certain manner correct, yet are readily misunderstood. . . . In *this* knowing another act is plainly present, which perhaps includes the former one, but is nonetheless different from it: the *paper* is known as white, or rather as a white thing, whenever we express our perception in the words 'white paper.' The intention of the word 'white' only partially coincides with the color-aspect of the appearing object; there remains an excess of meaning, a form, which finds nothing in the appearance to confirm it. White, i.e., *being* white paper.

In SS 1925, Heidegger commented on Husserl's meditations, " 'Being' is not a real moment in the chair like wood . . . [or] on the chair like upholstery and screws." Husserl maintains that, in an act of categorial intuition, I can bring what was emptily intended in "the little word 'is,' " e.g., the paper-being(as)-white, to an explicit self-givenness. "[The 'is'] is, however, *self-given* or at least presumably given in the *fulfillment* that under circumstances invests the judgment: in the *becoming aware* of the presumed state of affairs. Not only what is meant in the partial meaning *gold* itself appears, nor only what is meant in the partial meaning *yellow*, but also *gold-being-yellow* appears." For Husserl, the being (*Sein*) of a particular being (*das Seiende*) is able to appear, as it were, "before our eyes." In turn, my higher-level act of categorial intuition, which is still founded on sensory intuition, can become the basis for another type of categorial intuition, namely, "universal intuition" or "ideation" (what Husserl also later called intuition of essence [*Wesensschau*]). In this universal intuition, I no longer co-intend the founding sensible object (the white paper) of my categorial intuition, but rather abstractively intend its a priori categorial element (being-white, whiteness), which was previously only unthematically understood. The " 'as-what,' the universal character of house," Heidegger comments, "is itself not expressly apprehended in what it is, but is already co-apprehended in simple intuition as that which to some extent here illuminates what is given" (LU2 659–71, 690/775–85, 799; G20 78/58, 91/67).

Heidegger indicated that he found Husserl's notion of the categorial intuition of being significant for a number of reasons. First, being is presented as a phenomenon of lived experience, something that appears and "shows" itself. It is no longer—as it was in Heidegger's doctoral dissertation—confined to the function of the copula in judgments, i.e., the mere binding together of representations and concepts. Nor is being seen to be derived from reflection on inner sense (empiricism) or conceived as a subjective form with which sensuous material is ordered (Kant). Nor is it described as a real part of an object, a being, even though it is always the being of a being. Husserl's notion of being as an excess (*Überschuss*) of meaning is the precedent for Heidegger's interpretation of being as "transcendence," superabundance (*Überfülle*), and excess (*Übermass*) in the "ontological difference" between being and beings. We can likewise hear the Husserlian concept of the "givenness" of being behind Heidegger's description of the "nothing" of being, of which one can say not it "is," but rather only *es gibt*, it gives, it (is) given. For both Husserl and Heidegger, being is able to be brought to an "*originary self-giving* in corresponding acts of giving." Since being is a phenomenon, one can raise the question of the "sense" of this being, of what is *meant* by the word "being." Being is not a "mere *flatus vocis*" of speculative philosophy; rather, there can be a phenomenology of being.[7]

In 1973 Heidegger wrote that "Husserl's accomplishment consisted precisely in this making-present of being that is phenomenally present in the category. Through this accomplishment . . . I finally had a basis: 'being' is no mere concept, is no pure abstraction, which arises in the course of a derivation." Indeed we find Heidegger, in his 1925 Kassel lectures on Dilthey, stating clearly that phenomenology's two "decisive discoveries: intentionality and categorial intuition" made possible his question about the being of beings. In the "toward-upon-which [*Worauf*] of this directing-itself[-toward]" that characterizes intentionality," we "experience the meant in the determinations of its being-meant" and have "the possibility to interrogate the experienced world with a view to its being-here [*Dasein*]. We can learn to see beings in their being. Thus the scientific basis is won for the question about the being of beings." Heidegger continued, "We can touch briefly on the second decisive discovery, categorial intuition. We just distinguished beings and being. Being is not accessible to sensory intution, as beings are. But the sense of this being—that which is meant when I say 'is'—must be able to be shown somehow. The act that opens up access to it is categorial intuition." In its components, the term "phenomenology" thus means *logos* of that which "shows itself in itself" (*phainomenon*), namely, primarily the being of beings. In his SS 1925 lecture course, Heidegger explained also that Husserl's notion of categorial intuition as "universal intuition" provides the scientific methodological basis for investigating the categorial structures of being. Husserl showed how categorial-ontological structures can be brought to "evidential" givenness. An ontology of "being as such" and regional ontologies of the particular domains of being studied in the sciences become possible. Finally, by considering being as "objectivity," Husserl's phenomenology implicitly takes up the research of "ancient ontology," the question about being in Greek philosophy (G15 377–78; WDF 12–14; G63 67–77, 2).

But precisely how Heidegger appropriated Husserl's breakthroughs becomes clear only in the light of how he simultaneously traced them back into their pretheoretical primal source in factical life. He claimed to be doing nothing other than following up Dilthey's critical appropriation of phenomenology from the viewpoint of his own life-philosophy and "psychology as a descriptive science." In SS 1919, Heidegger wrote that "we are indebted to him for valuable intuitions about the idea of this science. . . . The secret longing of his life began to be fulfilled by phenomenology. . . . But he was no logician, and he saw immediately the significance of Husserl's *Logical Investigations* which were then hardly noticed and misunderstood." It was this work that Dilthey "called epoch-making and on which he held study sessions for years with his students." Heidegger followed Dilthey's attempt to use the *Logische Untersuchungen* not, as Husserl had sought to do, for the sake of a "pure logic," but rather for the sake of a "fundamental science of life." "Dilthey," Heidegger insisted, "was the first to understand the aims of phenomenology. . . . [T]he essential point here is not so much the conceptual penetration as the sheer disclosure of new horizons for the question of the being of acts and, in the broadest sense, the being of human being." Heidegger mentioned three horizons opened up by Dilthey, namely, "world" (content-sense), the "total person" (relational sense), and "historical context" (temporalizing-sense). Regarding content-sense, Dilthey maintained that "the person in his particular selfhood finds himself over against a world upon which he acts and which reacts upon him." "This whole context—self and world—is there in each moment."[8] Here Dilthey pushes Husserl's notion of intentional content out of the realm of logic and into the sphere of the lived experience of the practical and cultural world.

And how did Dilthey come upon his understanding of the factical life, in terms of which he was reinterpreting phenomenology? In his Kassel lectures, Heidegger made much of the fact that "Dilthey was at first a theologian, and herewith he was given a certain horizon and openness for Dasein which remained at work even later." Much like Heidegger himself, "Dilthey had planned a history of western Christianity, but during his study of the medieval era his plan fell apart along with his entire theological studies. . . . But from theology he took with him essential impulses for the understanding of human life and its history." Heidegger explained that this theological origin, including the "influence of Schleiermacher," is the real basis for Dilthey's appropriation of French positivism and for his positivistic "critique of metaphysics and emphasis of pure this-worldliness [*Diesseitigkeit*]."[9]

Heidegger argued that Husserl's characterization of being is taken from the specific way that it is experienced in theoretical thinking (*noesis*), the simple mental gazing upon the world that consummates itself in judgment and assertion, and for which the world, the *intentum*, appears as *noema*, the thought (to use the Greek terms Husserl introduced later in his 1913 *Ideen*). In his essay on Jaspers, Heidegger wrote,

> In the first breakthrough of phenomenology with its specific goal of originally appropriating anew the phenomena of *theoretical* experiencing and knowing (Logical Investigations, i.e., phenomenology of the theoretical *logos*), the goal of research was the winning of an unspoiled seeing of the sense of the objects experienced in such theoretical experiencing, i.e., of the how of its being experienced. . . . But the possibility of the radical understanding and genuine appropriation of phenomenological tendencies rests on the fact that . . . experiencing is seen in its authentically factical context of enactment in the historically existing self. . . .

Heidegger explained here that it is not enough that "the 'other' departmentalized 'spheres of experience' (the aesthetic, the ethical, the religious)" are researched in a manner "analogous" to the theoretical region, which would rather amount to their theorization. Instead, "the concrete self," which is revealed in these other spheres, "is to be taken up into the starting point of problems and brought to 'givenness' at the authentic, basic stratum of phenomenological interpretation, namely, one that remains related to the factical experience of life as such" (G20 61/45; G9 34-35; G56/57 87, 99-109).

"Phenomenology," Heidegger maintained, "is *unphenomenological!*" It does not get at the deepest sense of *die Sachen selbst*. As Husserl determines it theoretically, the basic sense of being is present-before-the-hand "thing," "object." This stratum of thinghood is supposed to function as "the fundament" for higher types of objects that have practical and aesthetic "value" in what Husserl calls the cultural environing world (*Umwelt*) (IRP1 56-61/91-96). Husserl thus theorizes, designifies, deworlds, "logicizes," and alienates the content-sense of being into the abstract "promised land" of logical sense. His account of the sense of being is still caught up in "the old mythology of an intellect that glues and rigs together the world's matter with forms." While being passionately committed to *die Sachen selbst*, he nonetheless naively takes over the traditional idea of being as present-at-hand thinghood (*res extensa*) from Descartes and ultimately from Greek philosophy. He fails to discuss "the question about the sense of being" explicitly. Heidegger was here also still following Lask, who, like Dilthey, was largely using the model of religious experience to rethink Husserl's phenomenology. Heidegger wrote in SS 1919 that Lask "discovered as ultimate lived experience *the* world," which is "not immaterial and extravagantly speculative, but rather factual." And elsewhere we find Heidegger appealing to Lask's interpretations of truth and categorial intuition in Husserl's Sixth Investigation.[10]

Heidegger thus renewed the *gigantomachia* about being that he had introduced in his student writings with the ontological alternative between the *Reich* of valid logical sense and historical particularity. He now comes down decisively on the side of the Heracliteans, St. Paul, and the historicists, and sympathizes with scepticism and psychologism. His courses of 1919 launched an all-out attack on the notion of logical sense in Neo-Kantianism and phenomenology. "Does [validity] correspond to a subject-correlate of an original kind," he asked, "or is it a founded, even extremely founded phenomenon?" (G56/57 50). In SS 1923, he called the philosophy of ideal validity a "Platonism of barbarians" (G63 42). Referring back to his "earlier investigation of the ontology of the Middles Ages," his WS 1925-26 lecture course argued that "this magical word 'validity' is at bottom a tangle of confusion, perplexity, and dogmatism" (G21 54, 64, 79). Here and in SZ, he asked regarding the *methexis* between the ideal kingdom and facticity, "Regarding the 'actual' judging of what is judged, is the separation of the real enactment [*Vollzug*] and ideal content [*Gehalt*] not altogether unjustified? Does not the actuality of knowing and judging get broken asunder into two ways of being and two 'strata,' whose piecing together never reaches the way of being that belongs to knowing?" And, "Is not psychologism right in holding out against this separation?" (SZ 287/259, §§33-34).

Following Dilthey, Lask, and then later Aristotle's practical thought, Heidegger's destruction sought to demythologize Husserl's theoretical concept of being by dismantling it back to and reinscribing it from out of the primal stratum of content-sense in the "lifeworld" and environing world (*Umwelt*). In 1926 Heidegger wrote to Jaspers that if "[SZ] is written 'against' someone, then against Husserl," and his marginal comments in SZ stated that the entire critique in Sections 18–21 of Descartes's view of the world as presence-at-hand was a "critique against Husserl's stratified construction [*Aufbau*] of 'ontologies.' " But this destructive repetition had been executed ever since Heidegger's first postwar course of KNS 1919. Here Husserl's notion of being as thinghood was rethought as the significance (*Bedeutung*) and lived "spatiality" of the "lifeworld," the "environing world," the "everyday" world. If Heidegger borrowed the terms *Lebenswelt* and *Umwelt* from Husserl, he nonetheless, unlike Husserl, took the practical sense immediately encountered here to be the primal stratum of lived experience. Taking up Dilthey's hermeneutics, Heidegger accordingly transformed Husserl's theoretical method of "universal intuition" or "ideation" into his own method of "hermeneutical intuition," the "lived experience of lived experience," "existentiell categorial interpretation," which interpretively explicates the factical preconception of being that belongs to factical life. "The phenomenological criterion," Heidegger wrote in SS 1919, "is solely the understanding evidence and the evidential understanding of lived experiences, of life in and for itself in its *eidos*." But he denied Husserl's claim that philosophy could arrive at transtemporal "essences" of being, to which an exact phenomenological terminology would ideally correspond. Taking up Husserl's own notion of the indication (*Anzeige*) of "occasional expressions" in the First Investigation, as well as his treatment of "generalization and formalization" in Chapter One of *Ideen* (G58 217; IRP1 31–33/64–66), Heidegger maintained that the concepts of philosophy are only "formal indications" that provisionally orient the search for the historical *Sache* of being. Husserl's recovery of Greek ontology was thus to be pushed in the direction of Heidegger's own "pretheoretical" "science of the primal source," a "phenomenological (existentiell, historical-cultural) 'ontology.' "[11]

Categorial Intuition and Truth

Heidegger also performed a destructive reinscription of the specific manner in which Husserl had worked out the relational sense of intentionality. This becomes visible when we consider Heidegger's reading of Husserl's discussion of "truth" in the *Logische Untersuchungen*. The question of categorial intuition in the Sixth Investigation involved for Husserl the issue of the truth present in the sphere of categorial intentions. He defines truth as the "synthesis of identification" achieved and experienced when the object gives itself immediately in my intuitive, fulfilling intention just as it was meant in the empty intention of my expression: "We experience how *the same* objective something which was 'merely thought' in a symbolic act is now intuitively presented in intuition, and that it is intuited as being precisely the determinate so-and-so that it was at first merely thought to be (merely signified)." He thus points out two meanings of the traditional Aristotelian and Scholastic notion of "being in the sense of truth" (*on hos alethes, ens tanquam verum*): first, being in the sense of the identification of the object as meant and object as intuited ("the paper [really] *is* white"); second, being in the sense of the "true-making thing," the intuited "being" that bestows fullness on my empty meaning-intention. Further, Husserl indicates that these two senses of truth underlie the standard definition of truth as the "correspondence of intellect and things," as the "correctness of our intention."

In the case of categorial intentions, truth is experienced as the synthesis of identification achieved when, in my fulfilling categorial intuition, the thing itself (paper-*being*-white, paper-*as*-white) "appears" in its "self-appearance" just as it was intended in my empty categorial meaning-intention. In Heidegger's reading in SS 1925, this means that "the founded acts *disclose* the simply given objects *anew*." "Categorial acts," he explained, "constitute a new objectivity. . . . [Constituting] means letting the being be seen in its objectivity." Husserl also maintains that, especially in those "static unions" of meant and intuited, which we have already achieved and in which we habitually live, we experience truth as identity without, however, thematically apprehending it. Heidegger's commentary on this theme runs as follows:

> In the coming into coincidence of the presumed with the intuited, I am solely and primarily directed toward the subject matter itself. . . . This is the phenomenological sense of saying that in evident perception I do not thematically study the truth of this perception itself, but rather live *in* the truth. Being-true is experienced as a distinctive *relation*, a *comportmental* relation between presumed and intuited specifically in the sense of identity.[12]

In my disclosive categorial intuition of the thing itself as-something (being), I focus intentionally on the thing itself without thematically considering my categorial meaning-intention, which remains in the background. It is only in a subsequent intentional act that I can make the truth as identity involved here into a thematic object or, further, thematize the operative a priori dimension of the categorial itself (ideation).

What captivated Heidegger's attention here was that truth was being investigated at a more basic level than its traditional definition as the mere correctness of propositions. In the first place, Husserl refers to being itself as "truth" in the sense of the appearance of beings in their being (the "true-making thing" that is disclosed), a notion which, according to Heidegger, is first found in the Greek meaning of truth as *aletheia*, unconcealment. "Truth here comes down to *being, being-real*. This is the concept of truth which also emerged very early in Greek philosophy." Moreover, Husserl's concept of truth as being-true (the synthetic act of identification) involves the intentional act of "disclosure," of "letting appear," which, according to Heidegger, is what Aristotle meant by *aletheuein*, unconcealing. In not confining truth to relational acts of predication in assertions, "phenomenology returns to the broad concept of truth whereby the Greeks (Aristotle) could call true even perception as such and the simple perception of something." Heidegger's new repetition of Husserl's concepts of intentionality and truth differed greatly from his earlier appropriation in his student writings, since it was now mediated through his closer identification with Dilthey and Lask. Dilthey approached phenomenology from the thesis that "the person, the total person, reacts [to the world], not simply in willing, feeling, and reflecting, but in all together always at the same time." And "insofar as life is living with others, the structures of living-with-others are also to be emphasized." Dilthey "wants to get at the totality of the subject which experiences the world and not to a bloodless thinking thing which merely intends and theoretically thinks the world."[13]

In his Kassel lectures, Heidegger thus maintained that "in its first breakthrough phenomenological research limited itself essentially to theoretical experience, to thinking. . . . Husserl misunderstood his own work" (WDF 14). Even when Husserl deals with "emotional experiences," "sense perception," and other practical comportments, he, like Descartes, models these types of intentionality on the attitude of "mere being-directed toward mere objects" that characterizes theoretical thinking (*noesis*) and its associated comportments of "intuition," "knowing," "judgment," and "assertion." "Every directing-itself-toward (fear, hope, love) has the feature of directing-itself-toward which Husserl calls *noesis*. Inasmuch as *noein* is taken from the sphere of theoretical knowing, any exposition of the practical here is drawn from the theoretical." Husserl fails to see that "the so-called logical comportments of thinking or objective theoretical knowing represent only a particular and narrow sphere within the domain of intentionality." Already in 1919, Heidegger charged that the "modification to the theoretical attitude" that Husserl's "mere being-directed toward" represents is a deliving of practical lived experience.[14]

Moreover, since Husserl describes human life, which has intentionality for its basic structure, as it is given to theoretical observation, the being of human life is delived into the present-at-hand being of an object. In Husserl's later transcendental self-interpretation under the influence of Neo-Kantianism and German Idealism, the person appears as a thinglike composite of a psychophysical animal and a pure transcendental ego. The latter is "the realm of absolute being" in relation to the contingent, founded being of the mundane empirical ego, which appears as " 'a real object like others in the natural world.' " Husserl's transcendental reduction to the "promised land" and "kingdom of transcendental consciousness" does indeed begin with a description of the "natural attitude" of everyday life, but this description is already colored by a very unnatural theoretical and objectifying attitude. "In the natural way of experience, do human beings experience themselves, to put it curtly, zoologically? Is this attitude a *natural attitude* or is it not? It is an experience which is totally *un*natural." Aggravating matters, Husserl then performs the reduction back to "an idealized absolute subject," which is "not human" and is in some sense eternal. Heidegger asked, Is this pure consciousness not "the old mythology" of "a *fantastically idealized* subject," a "phantasy of life and thinking," the hyperbolic "pure ghost" of ocular-aesthetic quietism, the "residues of [speculative] Christian theology," German Idealism, and Neo-Kantianism? He maintained that Husserl's concept of a pure intuitive consciousness stretches all the way back from Descartes's *intuitus* to the *gloria* of Thomas's *visio Dei* and Augustine's *fruitio Dei*, and finally to the Greek *theorein* with its associated notion of a pure, eternal *nous*. Like Jaspers, Husserl initiates his study of life within an "aesthetic ground-experience. This means that the authentic relational sense of the primary experience that puts forth the object 'life' in advance is an intuiting, a con-templating [*Be-trachten*] of something." Husserl's transcendental reduction and then his eidetic reduction to an "eidos-ego," that is, to the eidetic structures present in all egos, involve "giving up the ground upon which alone the question of the being of the intentional could be based," namely, factical life. He fails to raise the question of the "being of the human," "that of which intentionality is the structure." The question of the *sum* of the theoretically intentional *cogito* is left unasked. Because he sees neither the *sum moribundus* nor the pregiven I-am-with-the-Other as Other, Husserl begins with the *solus ipse* of the transcendental ego and attempts to explain the relational sense of intersubjectivity in terms of the attitude of "empathy" and analogical constitution (that is, as I am to myself as Other in self-consciousness, so I am to Others in intersubjective consciousness). But this cannot account for "the Other as Other" or for an "understanding of the stranger," since "the relationship of being to Others would then become a projection of one's own being toward oneself 'into an Other.' The Other would be a doublet of the self."[15]

Inspired by primal Christianity, Dilthey, and Aristotle's practical thought, Heidegger attempted to go back to the the original starting point of Husserl's reductions in the natural attitude and begin again with the investigation of the "being of the whole concrete human being." Here intentionality is not a present-at-hand "essence" (an eidetic "what") belonging to a thingly psychophysical subject (a "that") as its upper story, but rather the "how" of a "way to be" for a personal "who" characterized by "mineness" and the finitude of "awhileness." Accordingly, Heidegger's basic approach to the Husserlian theme of truth was to explore it not primarily as "the truth of theoretical knowing," but rather primarily as the truth of "practical insight," that is, of *phronesis*. Regarding Husserl's notion of "being in the sense of truth" as the "self-appearance" of beings in their objectivity (the disclosed "true-making thing"), Heidegger attempted to radicalize it into the notion of the "disclosedness" of the practical significance of ready-to-hand beings. Husserl's other sense of truth, namely, the intentional act of disclosing beings in the "identification" of the meant and the intuited, was transformed by Heidegger in a number of ways. In the first place, he placed Husserl's theoretically biased notion of intentionality back into its original setting of "being-in-a-world," where the basic character of this being-in is not "mere being-directed toward," but "caring," which involves practical understanding, mood, and language. Heidegger explained in WS 1921–22 that intentionality is something "ultimate," but this ultimate character has to be properly explained: "What has always disturbed me: did intentionality fall from heaven? If something ultimate: in which ultimacy is it to be taken? Certainly not secured in a specifically theoretical discovery and experience. . . . Accordingly, intentionality is the formal and basic structure for all categorial structures of facticity." And Heidegger's notes also read, "Caring is the basic sense of the relation of life. . . . Complete sense of *intentionality* in what is original!" In his 1922 essay on Aristotle, he wrote that "in its original intentionality concern is . . . related to its world," which is "the intentional toward-which of the tendency of caring." "Falling [in the world] is to be understood . . . as an intentional how." Thus

> full intentionality (the being-related to, the toward-which of the relation as such, the enactment of the self-relating, the temporalizing of the enactment, the preserving of the temporalizing) is none other than the intentionality of the object having the characteristic being of factical life. . . . intentionality is the first character able to be made to stand out immediately in the basic movement of life, that is, of caring.[16]

Heidegger also reinterpreted Husserl's notion of empty and habitual categorial meaning-intentions such that, at its deepest level, it now meant the unthematic, anticipatory "prestruction" or "preconception" of being that belongs to a markedly pretheoretical life. Husserl's notion was reinterpreted to mean the "familiar" disclosedness of the world of practical significance in which life "dwells." Heidegger's notes in WS 1921–22 read, "Prestruction . . . as an expression of intentionality: the formal primal structure of facticity (of the sense of the being of life)." In SS 1925, he wrote that "what is meant by intentionality—the bare and isolated directing-itself-toward—must still be set back into the unified and basic structure of being-ahead-of-itself-in-already-being-involved-in." Accordingly, he pushed Husserl's notion of the disclosing activity of categorial intuition, which fulfills the empty categorial meaning-intention (the enactment-sense of being-true), in the direction of his own theme of the "enacting" and "fulfilling" of the prior unthematic disclosedness of significance through the interpretive unconcealing (being-true) of beings in their "as-structure," significance, or being. In SZ Heidegger wrote that "Dasein only 'has' meaning insofar as the disclosedness of being-in-the-world can be 'fulfilled' through the beings which are discoverable in it." And later in his discussion of this fulfilling activity as "truth" (unconcealing), Heidegger referred the reader to the treatment of truth and categorial intuition in Husserl's Sixth Investigation.[17]

Husserl's static "apophantical 'as' " (the assertoric paper-as-white) was transformed into Heidegger's more situational and interpretive "hermeneutical 'as' " (the practical paper-as-for-writing, for instance). Whereas Husserl took a theorized type of sense perception to be the basic stratum on which categorial intentions (expressions) are founded, Heidegger himself wanted to make primary precisely the prior unthematic categorial "interpretedness" or "expressedness" of all experience in preconception, without which the sensed object would never have been accessible in the first place. What is primary is not sense perception but rather interpretation. Focusing on the way in which our immediate experience of things is articulated in advance in the public everyday understanding of the They, Heidegger wrote in SS 1925 that "our simplest perceptions and constitutive states are already *expressed*, even more, are *interpreted* in a certain way. . . . To put it more precisely: we do not say what we see, but rather the reverse, we see what *they say* about the matter." Thus, in Husserl's theme of the habitual, unthematic character of categorial meaning-intentions in the only "experienced" and not explicitly "known" identification of meant and intuited, Heidegger could also find his own theme of how factical life has the tendency to fall toward the beings in which its "care" is absorbed, such that the prior disclosedness of the world and itself in preconception remains unthematic. Factical life has the tendency to interpret itself solely in terms of beings. Thus, for Heidegger, the phenomenological "reduction" meant a going back not to the a priori of a transcendental-eidetic consciousness, but rather to the a priori operative within the preconception of factical life itself, which can be laid out through "hermeneutical intuition." His lecture notes for WS 1921–22 read, "The ruinant flight into the world; away from objects; positive meaning of Husserl's 're-duction.' "[18]

Making-Present

Heidegger also critically reinscribed Husserl's descriptions of the temporalizing-sense of intentional relation to being. In his *Logische Untersuchungen* and elsewhere, Husserl uses the terms temporalizing (*Zeitigung*), making-present (*Gegenwärtigen*), presenting (*Präsentieren*) to describe the temporal character of the fulfilling intentions in which an identification of the meant and the intuited, i.e., truth, is achieved. "The intentional character of perceiving . . . is making-present (presenting)," he writes. "The object is actually 'present' or 'given,' and present as just what we have intended it." As for categorical intuition specifically, it presents the sensuous object anew in its categorial structure and *"temporalizes [zeitigt]* a new consciousness of objectivity." The categorially structured object, the being in its being, becomes " 'present,' " is *"set before our eyes."* In the second volume of *Ideen,* to which Heidegger had access in the twenties before its publication, Husserl calls this making-present "appresentation." In his *Logische Untersuchungen,* he did not, however, systematically discuss the temporal character of intentionality. It was not until WS 1904–1905 that he began lecturing on the phenomenology of internal time-consciousness with its key themes of presentation, memory (retention), and expectation (protention). And though it was not until 1928 that the lectures between 1905 and 1910 were edited by Heidegger and published, Husserl did, as Heidegger notes, communicate important ideas from them in such published texts as the first volume of his *Ideen* (1913), and Heidegger, as Husserl's assistant between 1919 and 1923, may have had access to the manuscripts of these lectures much earlier than the late twenties.[19]

What attracted Heidegger was that, in Husserl's analyses, "being in the sense of truth" pointed in the direction of its basic meaning as time; that is, the disclosed "true-making thing" becomes present for the making-present of my disclosive fulfilling intention. But again his reinscription of these indications passed through the crucible of a destructive critique, which took up inter alia Dilthey's introduction of the theme of history into Husserl's phenomenology. In 1925 Heidegger wrote that, for Dilthey, "the structural context of life . . . is determined through its history," the "life-context of the person is in every situation one of development." And in his SZ, written the following year, Heidegger presented his analysis of history as an "appropriation of Dilthey's work" (WDF 11; G20 161–64/117–19; SZ 525/449).

He claimed that "phenomenology is distinguished by an ahistorical character and an animosity toward history because it believes that it is able to rid itself of the past as irrelevant and arrive at things from out of itself." He pointed out that, in his "critique of psychologism," Husserl draws the distinction "between the real being of the psychical and the ideal being of propositions in judgments—and moreover, between the temporal happening of the real and atemporal subsistence of the ideal." That is, he understands being and truth ultimately in terms of the eidetic "promised land" of the unchanging presence of ideal sense over against the temporal variance of intentional acts, subscribing to the traditional " 'couplets of opposition,' namely, real-ideal, sensible-nonsensible, beings–the valid, the historical–the transhistorical, the temporal–the atemporal." For Husserl, acts of making-present are thus at bottom individuating acts that instantiate ideal sense in the spatio-temporal world. Heidegger claimed that Husserl's speculative path toward a "chimerical trans-temporal in-itself" belongs to a *metaphysica gloriae* stretching back through the Neo-Kantian and Lotzean concept of validity, German Idealism, and Descartes to the *praesto habere* of the intelligible Kingdom of God in Thomas's *visio Dei* and Augustine's *fruitio Dei*, and finally to the Platonic-Aristotelian concept of being as the always-being (*aei on*) of the intellible *topos* of the universe. Husserl's notion of meaning as "immutable and invariant identity" is "identical with the discovery of the concept of being in Parmenides and in Plato." In an abrupt turn from his student years, Heidegger's WS 1925–26 lecture course called for a "critique of the critique of psychologism" and here took up ancient skepticism (Sextus Empiricus) and modern psychologism, since they called attention precisely to the problem of *methexis*, that is, "bridging the abyss between the real and the ideal." But already in his lecture courses of 1919 he pointed out that the ahistorical approaches of Neo-Kantianism and phenomenology lead to a dehistoricizing of historical time. "The pure ego," he said in a conversation in 1919, "would derive from the 'historical ego' via the repression of all historicity."[20]

Heidegger thus reinscribed Husserl's discussions of the temporal character of intentionality from the standpoint of the kairological time that he was discovering first in primal Christianity and Dilthey and then in Aristotle. He reinterpreted Husserl's notion of futural protention and his Platonic notion of the *a priori* (literally the "before," the "earlier") to mean the futural "not yet" and "horizon of expectation" (*Erwartung*) belonging to factical life. He also employed the Husserlian terms "temporalizing," "making-present," and "presenting" so that they no longer meant the instantiation of atemporal ideality, but rather the "temporalizing" of futural understanding (shaped by the retention of the past), which interpretively "makes-present," "presents," or "appresents" beings within the *kairos*, the situation. "The life-relation of the situational I," Heidegger wrote in SS 1919, "is no mere being-directed to mere objects. Every lived experience is intentional, it contains a 'view to' something or other (a loving, apprehending, perceiving, remembering view). The view has a 'quality' (quality of the act-character)." He used Husserl's temporal terminology throughout his lecture courses of SS 1923 (e.g., "presenting") and of SS 1925, which also used "appresenting" from the second volume of *Ideen*. For example, "Concern . . . has the mode of being of pure *letting-become-present*—a remarkable kind of being which is understood only when it is seen that this *making-present and appresenting is nothing other than time itself.*" "Interpretation appresents the *what-for* of a thing. . . . It brings to prominence '*as-what*' the encountered worldly thing is to be taken." Similarly, we read in SZ that "Husserl uses the expression 'making-present' to characterize sense perception. Cf. his *Logical Investigations.* . . . The *intentional* analysis of perception and intuition in general must have suggested this 'temporal' description of the phenomenon." Heidegger added, "That and how the intentionality of 'consciousness' is *grounded* in the ecstatical temporality of Dasein will be shown in the following [never published] section." In his review of Husserl's lectures on internal time-consciousness in SS 1928, he wrote, "That which Husserl still calls time-consciousness, i.e., consciousness of time, is precisely time itself in the primal sense. . . . Temporality in its temporalizing is the primally self-unifying unity of expecting, retaining, and making-present."[21]

Husserl himself acknowledged that phenomenology and the eidetic objects it investigates are caught up in internal time-consciousness and history, stressing that these objects are not "in a [Platonic] *topos ouranios* or in a divine Spirit" completely separate from history. Of his philosophizing, he wrote that it "does not speculate about a New Atlantis, but rather has actually wandered in the trackless wilderness of a new continent and undertaken bits of virgin cultivation." He insisted that there is "no '*Königsweg*,' 'royal road,' 'way of the king,' in phenomenology," but rather the laborious path of the "infinite task" of reduction to and surveying of the "promised land" of transcendental subjectivity, whose final establishment is a regulative Idea in the Kantian Sense. But Heidegger claimed that this "fantastic path to the transhistorical" was doomed not just in practice but rather in principle, since it ignored the a priori of temporality, historical difference, finitude, exile, way, nonarrival. He enjoyed telling the story in which, on the way to the Freiburg train station for a journey abroad, Husserl outlined for him how in a planned lecture he would show that the sciences could be grounded in his system of phenomenology. In being asked by Heidegger about the historical sciences, Husserl replied, "I forgot these."[22]

10 | Aristotle

Heidegger's Courses from SS 1921 to SS 1925

AROUND 1921 ANOTHER major influence entered the horizon of Heidegger's thinking and teaching, namely, an Aristotle who was very different from the Neo-Scholastic Aristotle of Heidegger's student years. From this point onward, there is a more complicated interweaving of Christianity, phenomenology, and Aristotle in the bricolage of Heidegger's texts. We see the intensity of this engagement with Aristotle in the record of Heidegger's courses and publication projects after his two religion courses. Already in SS 1921, while he was presenting his lecture course on Augustine, he also gave a seminar for "Beginners: In Connection with Aristotle's *De anima*." Then in WS 1921–22, he gave his first lecture course on Aristotle, which was titled "Phänomenologische Interpretationen zu Aristoteles. Einleitung" (Phenomenological Interpretations with respect to Aristotle: Introduction) (G61). In it he never really did get around to dealing with Aristotle's texts, but rather went through the history of the reception of Aristotle, dealt with the question of what philosophy is, explored the formally indicative nature of philosophical conceptuality, and gave a long preparatory analysis of the categories of being as they show themselves within factical life.

In the same semester, he held the seminar "Phänomenologische Übungen in Anschluss an Husserl, *Logische Untersuchungen*, II" (Phenomenological Exercises in Connection with Husserl's *Logical Investigations*, Vol. 2). It probably dealt with Husserl's first investigation on "Expression and Meaning," including the notion of "occasional expressions" and the important concept of indication (*Anzeige*), which we find Heidegger treating in depth in the first part of his lecture course in this semester. Then came a lecture course in SS 1922 with the same major title as the lecture course of WS 1921–22, but the different subtitle of "Ontologie und Logik" (Ontology and Logic) (G62). It proceeded by way of translating key terms and phrases from the first book of the *Metaphysics* and the opening chapters of the *Physics* (ML 25–26). Simultaneously he held a seminar on Husserl's "*Logical Investigations*, Vol. 2, Second Investigation."

Out of his two lecture courses on Aristotle, Heidegger composed in October 1922 a long introduction to a large projected work on Aristotle that had the same major title as his two Aristotle courses and was to have been published in the 1923 issue of Husserl's *Jahrbuch* (PIA). The introduction, titled "Anzeige der hermeneutischen Situation" (Indication of the Hermeneutical Situation), provided a preparatory ontological analysis of the categories of being found in factical life, as well as interpretations of the *Nicomachean Ethics*, *Metaphysics*, and *Physics*. The body of the work was to have provided expanded interpretations of Aristotle's texts, but it was never completed even though Heidegger worked on it until 1924 (ML 10).

For WS 1922–23, Heidegger scheduled the lecture course "Der Skeptizismus in der antiken Philosophie (Phän. Interp. zu Sextus Empiricus, *Hypotyposeon*, III)" (Skepticism in Ancient Philosophy [Phenomenological Interpretations with respect to Sextus Empiricus, *Hypotyposeon*, III]), but he did not hold it, due probably to the extra time needed for his book on Aristotle. In this semester, he gave only two seminars, one with the same major title as his Aristotle book (dealing with *Nicomachean Ethics* VI, *De anima*, and *Metaphysics* VIII) and the other for "Beginners: Husserl's *Ideas*, Vol. 1." Then in SS 1923 he held the lecture course "Ontologie (Hermeneutik der Faktizität)" (Ontology [Hermeneutics of Facticity]) (G63), which synthetically dealt with Husserl's phenomenology, Aristotle, and Christian thought in the systematic context of an investigation of being within factical life. Simultaneously he gave seminars on "Aristotle's *Nicomachean Ethics*" and "Husserl's *Logical Investigations*, Vol. 2," as well as holding his colloquium with Ebbinghaus on the Lutheran basis of Kant and German Idealism.

The first lecture course that Heidegger gave in Marburg in WS 1923–24 bore the title "Einführung in die phänomenologische Forschung" (Introduction in Phenomenological Research); it dealt with a clarification of Husserl's phenomenology via the texts of Aristotle, including *De anima* II (G17). He also held still another seminar on "*Logical Investigations*, Vol. 2, First Investigation." In SS 1924, we then find a lecture course on "Aristoteles, *Rhetorik* II" (G18), along with a seminar for the "Advanced: High-Scholasticism and Aristotle." In July of the same year, he went before the Protestant theology department in Marburg to deliver his lecture "Der Begriff der Zeit" (The Concept of Time), which contrasted categories of time in science and factical life (BZ). At the same time, he was working this manuscript up into a much longer journal article by the same title, which was also to have added an in-depth analysis of the concept of history in Dilthey and Count Yorck, but it was never published (G64) (WFD 3–22).

In WS 1924–25, Heidegger gave the lecture course "Interpretation Platonischer Dialoge (*Sophistes*)" (Interpretation of Platonic Dialogues [*Sophist*]), which placed Plato's question about being into the context of an introductory discussion, almost two hundred pages long, of Aristotle's concept of *aletheia* primarily in his practical writings (G19). Simultaneously he gave the seminar "Exercises in the Ontology of the Middle Ages." Upon the invitation of Scheler, he delivered on December 2, 1924 the lecture "Dasein und Wahrsein nach Aristoteles (Interpretationen von Buch VI Nik. *Ethik*)" (Being-here and Being-true According to Aristotle [Interpretations of Book VI, *Nicomachean Ethics*]) before the *Kant-Gesellschaft* in Cologne (DW; *Gesamtausgabe*, Division 3).

In SS 1925, he held the lecture course "Geschichte des Zeitbegriffs. Prolegomena zu einer Phänomenologie von Geschichte und Natur" (History of the Concept of Time: Prolegomena to a Phenomenology of History and Nature), which opened with a long reading of Husserl's phenomenology, including its relation to Aristotle, and then moved on to a systematic treatment of the question of being and time in pretheoretical life (G20 443/321). Simultaneously he held the seminar "Exercises in Descartes's *Meditations.*" Between April 16 and April 21, 1925 he gave a series of ten lectures in Kassel on "Wilhelm Diltheys Forschungsarbeit und der Kampf um eine historische Weltanschauung" (Wilhelm Dilthey's Research Work and the Struggle for a Historical Worldview) (WDF).

The Reception of Aristotle

Let us read again Heidegger's 1923 autobiographical statement that "companions in my searching were the young Luther and the paragon Aristotle, whom Luther hated. Kierkegaard gave impulses, and Husserl gave me my eyes." We can see how this context informed Heidegger's reading of Aristotle by looking at his treatment of "the reception of Aristotle" in the history of philosophy, which he provided in his lecture course of WS 1921–22 on Aristotle, in his 1922 introduction to a planned book on Aristotle, and in subsequent writings. He highlighted both the Christian reception and the late modern reception in the nineteeth century that culminated in Husserl's phenomenology. Let us begin with the latter.

With its key concept of intentionality, phenomenology was to provide Heidegger with the conceptuality with which to approach Aristotle's texts. He pointed out that the medieval concept of *intentio*, which was based on Aristotle, was picked up again in the nineteenth-century reception of Aristotle that began with Trendelenburg and passed to his students Brentano and Dilthey, to Brentano's student Husserl, and to James and Bergson. But if Aristotle's thought was to be interpreted in terms of Husserl's language of intentional content-, relational, and temporalizing-sense, then in turn these concepts were to be rethought and deepened within the context of Aristotle's practical philosophy. Heidegger actually saw the notion of intentionality as an implicit "return" to Aristotle's concept of *aletheia* in the *De anima* and Book Six of the *Nicomachean Ethics*. Thus he could say that "Aristotle [was] really in *De Anima* phenomenological (without the explicit reduction)." But Heidegger's primary concern was to explore this intentional *aletheia* as it functions not in Aristotle's *Metaphysics* but rather in the practical truth (*aletheia praktike*) of Aristotle's practical writings.[1]

This is why his writings on Aristotle also highlighted, as we have already seen, the Christian reception of Aristotle in medieval Aristotelian-Scholasticism, "Luther's religious and theological counterattack against Scholasticism," and Kierkegaard (G61 6–7; PIA 238–54). It is now clear that Heidegger's destructive repetition of Aristotle, illuminated by the conceptual "eyes" of phenomenology, also involved an ontological radicalization of the following themes in the Christian reception. First, Luther's *destructio* of the *theologia gloriae* of Aristotelian-Scholasticism and of Aristotle's ontotheological metaphysics itself. In his 1924 lecture "Dasein und Wahrsein," Heidegger concluded with the statement:

> All of the basic concepts of Greek ontology are concepts taken from the being of the world. When this fund entered into Christian theology and the being of God was to be determined with it, then what . . . lets itself be clarified in a radical critique is that here a reality is spoken of in categories which are all taken from a different reality, and are transferred to a being which, however, presumably has a different type of existence than the sun and the eternally revolving heavens. We are placed before the great task of developing an ontology of Dasein in contrast to the ontology of the world. . . . Thus a radical critique is required. . . . (DW)

And he added, "We today have the possibility for this basic type of philosophical research in phenomenology." Second, Heidegger radicalized Luther's and Kierkegaard's novel readings of key concepts in Aristotle's practical writings and *Physics* (for example, *physis, kinesis, ethos, phronesis, kairos*), which were undertaken in order to explain the kairological time of Christian life and ethical *Existenz*.

Heidegger was certainly aware of not only Luther's, but also Kierkegaard's positive appropriation of Aristotle. Not only did his first lecture course on Aristotle in WS 1921–22 open with two mottos from Kierkegaard, and not only was his reading here of the Platonic-Socratic quest for being organized around Kierkegaard's concept of "passion" and "subjective truth," but in SS 1923 he discussed Kierkegaard's appropriation of Aristotle through his "connection with Trendelenberg." Kierkegaard took his interpretation of *kinesis* in Aristotle from Trendelenberg and then, again following Trendelenberg, used it to criticize purely logical movement in Hegelian dialectics. Kierkegaard contrasts the anxious care (*orexis*) of Aristotelian praxis and its intention toward a futural end with the disinterest of *theoria*: "Abstract thought is disinterested, but for an existing individual, existence is the highest interest. An existing individual . . . has always a *telos*, and it is of this *telos* that Aristotle speaks when he says (*De anima*, III, 10, 2) that *nous theoretikos* differs from *nous praktikos to telei* [in its end]." The intentional movement toward the *telos* and its kairological enactment is what Aristotle meant by *kinesis* in human praxis: "The transition from possibility to actuality is, as Aristotle rightly expressed it, a *kinesis*. . . . When existence gives to the movement the requisite time, and I reflect this in my representation, the leap stands revealed in the only way possible: either that it must come, or that it has been." After showing that Scholasticism speaks in the "borrowed, alien categories" of Aristotle's metaphysics, Heidegger's 1922 essay on Aristotle added the following point: "That nonetheless precisely the Aristotelian ontology of soul helped in temporalizing a far-reaching and rich interpretation of the being of life within the Christian lifeworld is due to the fact that, with and precisely through the aspect of movement, the decisive phenomenal character of intentionality came into view." Heidegger surely had in mind here not only the medieval concept of intentionality, which originally had the narrower practical meaning of a practical "being out after something (*orexis*)," but also the interpretations of *kinesis* given by Luther and Kierkegaard.[2]

The Destruction of the Metaphysical Aristotle

Heidegger took the intentional configuration of Aristotle's guiding metaphysical question about being, namely, the present-at-hand categories of *ousia*/theory/presence (*aei on*), to be a deworlding, deliving, and dehistoricizing that masked, hyperbolically alienated, and mythologized the kinetic-personal physiognomy of the comportment to being in factical life. In 1922 he explained that, for Aristotle, being in the "genuine sense" is "finished-being," that is, *kinesis* that has "come to its end," which is thus a finished work (*energeia*) and substantial presence (*ousia*). Insofar as the movement of praxis is always a "being on the way" to the "not yet" of its intentional toward-which, "the highest idea of pure movement is satisfied only by *noesis* as pure *theorein*. The authentic being of human being temporalizes itself in the pure actualizing of *sophia* as the untroubled, time-passing (*schole* [leisure]), purely perceptual tarrying at home alongside the *archai* of that which ever is." This movement of the *manus mentis*, which has its end, i.e., eternal being, firmly in hand, maintains itself in the present perfect of having completely actualized itself, where "human life . . . has come to its end" and is in a certain *quies*. Preserving itself in the *gloria* of this activity of contemplating the divine *arche*, the origin/kingdom, life takes a holiday, as it were, from the toil and trouble of the incomplete *kinesis* of praxis. "Pure understanding [*sophia*] has its concrete possibility of actualization in being-free from the troubling concerns of performative dealings [in practical life]; it is the how in which life comes to a halt and takes up residence *(einen Aufenthalt nimmt)*" (PIA 268–69, 260–63). According to Aristotle, metaphysics, the king of the sciences, is that type of knowing which is "most exalted and honored," and *archiotate*, most royal and fit for ruling. For it is the ontotheological "science of the universal" and of the ultimate *arche*, governing principle/kingdom, which is God, the highest good as final cause. God is related to the cosmos in a way similar to that in which the "commander" orders the army, and thus those thinkers are wrong who "give us many governing principles. . . . the world refuses to be governed badly. 'The rule of many is not good; let there be one ruler, one king' [Homer, *Iliad* II, 204]" (Metaphysics 982a–83a, 1075a–76a).

What Heidegger thought was needed was a quasi-Lutheran destruction, unmasking, and demythologizing of this ocular-aesthetic quietism, not only in Aristotle's metaphysics but also in the entire western metaphysical tradition that consists of transformations *(Umbildungen)* and restructurings *(Neubildungen)* of the "very first beginning" in the Greek epoch. This *Abbauen*, dismantling, deconstructing, was to be a "regress to . . . Aristotle in order to see how something original came into a falling away and covering over and that we stand in this *falling away*." It took the form of tracing the key terms of Aristotle's metaphysical writings and the Latin translations back to their original meanings in the very prephilosophical life that Aristotle explored in his practical writings. Heidegger played the practical Aristotle off against the metaphysical Aristotle. For example, he pointed out that "*ousia* has the original meaning . . . of household, property, that which is environmentally available for use" (factical content-sense). Likewise, in his 1924 lecture "Dasein und Wahrsein" (DW), Heidegger wrote, "The etymology of *theorein*: the *theoros* is the visitor who goes to the festival and is all eyes." *Theoria* meant not only this sight-seeing, but also the sight of the artisan in *poiesis*, making; *eidos* meant the artisan's vision or plan, and *logos* meant "discourse, conversation" (relational sense). In this same lecture, Heidegger illustrated the meanings of *ousia*, *eidos*, *telos*, *arche*, and *hypokeimenon* with a simple example: "A shoemaker wants to make a shoe." Here and elsewhere, he pointed out further that *ousia* meant also presence (temporalizing-sense): "*Ousia* means simultaneously property, household, we translate best with present estate [*Anwesen*], thus a farmstead or the like that I have immediately available. . . . For the Greeks being means being present [*anwesend*]," namely, that which lies present around us in the great household and royal estate of the cosmos. "Thus the highest type of being lies in the purest presence [*Anwesenheit*]," that is, the ever-being *(aei on)* of the divine that makes up "the residence" in which *theorein* retires and dwells.[3]

It was from the vantage point of the practical Aristotle opened up through this destruction, an Aristotle very different from the Neo-Scholastic one

Heidegger learned in his student days, that Heidegger sought to reinscribe the Greek question about being from out of its ground question in his own new beginning. The being-question of the *Metaphysics* was dismantled into and remarked within the horizons of historical *bios praktikos* and *on hos pragma*, being as a practical matter, whose intentional configuration takes the form of *ethos/phronesis/kinesis* (*kairos*). Heidegger thus seems to have thought that his new beginning was already implicitly present in Aristotle himself and only had to be explicated and radicalized. In his 1921–22 lecture course on Aristotle, he wrote that modern thought has its "roots in *Greek philosophy*, and in such a way that in it both motives for beginning are alive (original explication of experience and categorial theoretical explication), and that the one simply got lost in the process of levelling what is original. (Cf. *ousia*, 'having,' 'household,' 'property.')" Anticipating Gadamer's notion of "fusion of horizons," Heidegger wrote regarding the destruction of Aristotle and the tradition based on him, "Corresponding to our position, the original position is to be again worked out anew, i.e., corresponding to our altered historical situation, it is something other and yet the same." The "effective possibility" of Aristotle's thought "for its future" was to be sprung loose through "repetition," in which it kairologically and "constantly becomes a new present." The young Heidegger, Gadamer reported, was an "Aristotle redivivus."[4] Though unpublished until recently, Heidegger's early courses on Aristotle effectively influenced generations of Aristotle scholars in Germany, including H.-G. Gadamer, Hannah Arendt, Helene Weiss, Walter Bröcker, and Ernst Tugendhat.[5]

Ethos, Oikos, Koinonia, Praxis

Heidegger actually modeled his destruction of Aristotle's metaphysics also on Aristotle's own attempt in the *Nicomachean Ethics* to destroy (*anairein*) Plato's science of a separate, universal, and timeless idea of the Good in a *topos ouranios*, a heavenly kingdom where the philosopher-king reigns over humanity (1096a). Practical philosophy must start not hyperbolically, not with "something magnificent and beyond [*hyper*]" the factual praxis of living as a human being (*ta anthropeuesthai*), but with the that (*to hoti*), i.e., the facticity of human life, and with *ta phainomena* here (1095a). "The *arche*, the starting point and guiding principle, is the that," the that-it-is of historical facticity, where life directed to the good shows itself not under the rule of a single *arche*-king, but in a highly differentiated manner with a great variety of historically changing principles of action (1095b).

In WS 1925–26, Heidegger defined Aristotle's ethics as "*episteme ethike*: science of *ethos*—of the self-having, the self-comportment of human being to other human beings and to itself: science of human being" (G21 1). This phenomenological ontology of the principles (*archai*) of the *kinesis* of practical human being (*anthropo onti*) is more particularly a hermeneutics (*hermeneneia*) of facticity (1178b; G63 9–11). Heidegger explained in his 1922 essay on Aristotle that, as *epagoge*, induction, this "*arche*-research" only draws out and explicates the understanding of the *archai* which is already operative in the that (*hexis, ethos*) of practical life, and which has already been expressed in statements (*legomenon*) and opinions (*endoxa*). The "hearer of lectures" "already has the *archai*" (1095b). Theoretical discussions are out of this factical life (*bios*) and about it (*hoi logoi d'ek touton kai peri touton*), a statement that Heidegger paraphrased as "Principial knowing that arises from such facticity and returns to this facticity" (1095a; G61 115). "*Epagoge* ('induction')," he wrote, is to be taken "in the purely literal sense of the word . . . as simple-direct leading-to . . . , letting-something-be-seen. . . . In *epagoge*, these *archai* are taken explicitly, as unveiled, into truthful sakekeeping" (PIA 259; G61 112). These principles are not free-floating structures, but are rather the essential possibilities of practical existence, which Heidegger himself called "principles," "existentiell" categories, and "existentials" (G61 86–88).

He showed how the three intentional moments of his notion of being-sense were also worked out after 1921 through creative repetitions of corresponding elements in Aristotle. His analysis of the content-sense of the environing world of ready-to-hand things, the social withworld, and the personal selfworld retrieved Aristotle's corresponding notions of the technical means-ends contexts of practical beings (*ta pragamta*) in the sphere of the household (*oikos*), the "being-with-one-another of humans" in the social-political community (*koinonia, polis*), and "*ethos*—self-having, self-comportment of humans to other humans and to oneself." Each of these worlds is, as both Aristotle and Heidegger put it, an expression of the for-the-sake-of-which (*hou heneka, das Weswegen, das Umwillen*) of human praxis. In "Dasein und Wahrsein," we read regarding the withworld that "the Greeks and above all Aristotle had a clear understanding for this basic phenomenon of everyday life, of speaking-with-one-another as being-with-one-another. . . . Aristotle's research on this basic phenomenon . . . is called Rhetoric." In SZ Heidegger said that the *Rhetoric* was "the first systematic hermeneutic of being-with-one-another."[6]

Regarding relational sense, Heidegger stated in 1924 that "Dasein means being in the world, this is the fundamental finding" of a reading of Aristotle's concept of *praxis*. Here he found a precedent for his concept of care in Aristotle's notions of *epimeleia*, care (1114a), and of *orexis*, which he translated as a "directed, caring 'being out after [*auf*] something,' " namely, after its intentional *Worauf*, its toward-which. He pointed out that the term "intentionality" "arose in the Middle Ages and has here a narrower sphere [than in Brentano]; it signifes voluntary being-out after something (*orexis*)." For Aristotle, "world . . . [is] immediately there in the dealings of *praxis*, of *caring* [*Besorgen*] in the widest sense." In his lecture course of SS 1925, Heidegger suggested that, as desiderative perception (*nous orektikos*), which has praxis itself and not the world as its primary end, *phronesis* (from *phren*, the heart) is self-care (*phrontis*) and thus echoes the concept of care in the New Testament (*merimna, phrontis*). And using Burdach's historical study of the concept of care, Heidegger also showed that "the New Testament term for 'care' (*sollicitudo* in the Vulgate), *merimna* (or as it probably was called, *phrontis*), was already a technical term in the moral philosophy of the Stoics." In his ninetieth letter, Seneca writes that "the good of the one, namely God, is fulfilled by his nature, but that of the other, the human being, is fulfilled by care [*cura*]." Likewise, Heidegger's concepts of mood, understanding, and discourse were developed through repetitions of Aristotle's corresponding interpretations of "*pathe* [passions] in the second book of his *Rhetoric*"; of *techne* and *phronesis*, which Heidegger translated respectively as a directional performative-productive procedure (*verrichtend-herstellendes Verfahren*) and solicitous circumspection (*fürsorgende Umsicht*); and of practical *logos* and *hermeneia*, which he translated as discourse (*Rede*) in the sense of an interpretive "discussing-as."[7]

Aletheia, Kinesis, Kairos

Heidegger took his understanding of these intentional comportments as truth in the sense of unconcealing (*aletheuein*) from Book Six of the *Nicomachean Ethics*, which examines the modes in which *he psyche aletheuei*, the soul trues, unconceals (namely, *nous, sophia, episteme, phronesis, techne*). "*Aletheuein* means . . . taking beings as unveiled into truthful safekeeping [*Verwahrung*]." Book Six is not mere "ethics" or "psychology," but studies the "intellectual virtues" as modes of the "enactment of the genuine truthful safekeeping of being." Being is the intentional toward-which of the modes of unconcealing and thus is *on hos alethes*. The latter means not "the being . . . of true judgments, but rather being itself in the how (*hos*) of its unveiled being-meant." Therefore, Heidegger stressed, the "connection . . . with the ontological problematic is clear." The "structural distinction between the two basic modes of perceiving" (*nous*), namely, *sophia* ("observational understanding") and *phronesis*, is organized precisely around the distinction between two types of being, namely, between the "authentic being" of the heavenly ever-being (*aei on*) and finished-being (*on energeia*) of the divine (fixed presence), on the one hand, and, on the other, the sublunar *on hos pragma*, being as that which can be other (*endechomenon allos echein*), alterity, unfinished historical being, which Aristotle calls a certain *me on* (nonpresence). Heidegger called it "factical being" and, like Paul, Luther, and Kierkegaard, approached this ontological alternative by dismantling Greek *ontos on* back to *me on*. Heidegger wrote, "Pure observational understanding brings into truthful safekeeping the being . . . [which] is in the manner that it necessarily and always is what it is. In contrast, solicitous-discursive circumspection brings into truthful safekeeping a being that in itself . . . can be other." Pure *nous*, *sophia*, and *episteme* ("authentic-seeing understanding") are intentionally correlated to the one type of being, whereas *techne* and *phronesis* unconceal the other type of being.[8]

But the latter modes of truth are also to be distinguished among themselves. The primary intentional end disclosed by the care and being-true of *phronesis* is not the artifact to be made, i.e., the world's being, as it is in *techne*, but rather practical human being itself in its moral ends. "*Phronesis* brings into truthful safekeeping the toward-which of the dealings [*Umgang*] of human life. . . . This dealing is *praxis*: action [*Behandlung*] with itself in the how of the dealing that does not produce, but rather in each case only precisely acts." As the conscience that cannot be forgotten and is thus a constant renewal of care, *phronesis* is "epitactical," ordering, commanding, not only because it "rules *techne*," but more specifically because it is a disclosive "looking *kata to sympheron pros to telos*," according to what is conducive to its end in the concrete situation. In interpretively concretizing moral ends, it discloses the "practical *aletheia*" of the *kairos* and simultaneously issues in a decision:

> The *aletheia praktike* is nothing other than the currently [*jeweils*] unveiled, full eye-opening moment [*Augenblick*] of factical life in the how of its decisional readiness in dealings with it itself, and this within a factical relation of concern to the world thus encountered. *Phronesis* is *epitactical*: it gives being in the character of that with which one is to be concerned, it brings and holds within this view each determination of the eye-opening moment— the current how, for-which, to-what-extent, and why. (PIA 259–60)

In WS 1924–25, Heidegger connected *kairos* in Aristotle with the Pauline theme of *kairos* as the "twinkling of an eye": "*Phronesis* is the glancing at the this-time, at the this-time-ness of the momentary situation. As *aisthesis*, it is the glance of the eye, the *Augen-blick*, toward the concrete at the particular time, which as such can always be other" (G19 163–64). In his 1924 lecture "Dasein und Wahrsein," he gave an example of *phronesis* that has a stronger ethical sense to it and relates to the role of *phronesis* in considerateness (*synesis*) and friendship, where it is also a matter of unconcealing the *kairos*, the situation, and the *agathon* of the Other. Here and in other writings, we also find Heidegger translating Aristotle's terms *bouleusis* (deliberation) and *prohairesis* (choice) into his terms *Umsicht* (circumspection) and *Entschluss* (resolve) or *Entscheidung* (choice):

> The object of *phronesis* is the *prakton* [the practical matter]. . . . In action, more exactly in the resolve, I anticipate the *arche* [the initiating end]. I resolve to bring some joy to my friend for his birthday, or to help him, in a matter that could not at all be something [merely] practical, and thus must be of an ethical nature. In deliberation, the *kairos* is made transparent. The

circumstances of action are uncovered in circumspection, which is guided by
the *agathon*, for which I am resolved. (DW)

What *phronesis* unconceals in the *kairos* is *to deon*, the fitting, e.g., the
fitting birthday gift. Because this lies as a mean between excess (*hyperbole*)
and deficiency (*elleipsis*), it is "difficult" to hit and "easy" to miss. In WS
1921–22, Heidegger quoted and translated *Nicomachean Ethics* (1106b28ff.)
as a source for his own concepts of the fitting (*das Gebührendes*), decision
(*Entscheidung*), "the difficult," "the easy," "missing," "the hyperbolic," and
"the elliptic." Surprisingly, this passage, the first of only two quotations of
Aristotle in the whole course, is back-to-back with the passage that, as we saw,
Luther quotes in his *Commentary on Genesis* in order to compare Aristotle's
concepts of *phronesis* and justice (*epieikeia*) with the New Testament theme of
the Spirit overcoming the Law (XLIV 703–705/VIII 171–72). "Further, missing [*hamartein, Verfehlen*] is manifold . . . but right action is of *one* kind [*monachos*]. (That is why the one is easy, the other difficult. Easy is it to miss the
mark, difficult to hit it.) And that is why excess [*hyperbole*] and holding back
[*elleipsis*] belong to badness, but holding-to-the-mean belongs to virtue."
Heidegger commented, "Hyperbolic Dasein shows itself simultaneously as elliptical: it gets out of the way of the difficult, that which is *monachos*, simple
(without beating around the bush); holds fast to no end; does not want to be
posed *toward* a primal decision and *in* it (repeating it)." Earlier he had written,
"In missing and overlooking itself . . . life mismeasures itself; it mistakes itself
in the measure fitting to it." In "Dasein und Wahrsein," Heidegger's Kierkegaardian reading even claimed that Aristotle's *Rhetoric* saw the phenomenon
of "idle talk" and *das Man* in its analysis of the discourse of the *hoi polloi*:
"The being-with-one-another of humans, the *koinonia* that is determined
through this speaking . . . is being-with-one-another in idle talk. They see,
they judge, they wish, they have needs, just as they say, as they speak. Therefore
the They" (G61 108–109, 103, 41, 62; G63 10).

Heidegger showed that Aristotle understood being in terms of *physis*
(*Vorkommen*, coming-forth) and *kinesis*, and attempted to trace this *kinesis* of
being all the way back to its temoralizing in practical life. His notes for his WS
1921–22 lecture course on Aristotle read, "The problem of beings and being
(*on—ousia—kinesis—physis*)." "The problem of facticity, the *kinesis*-prob-
lem." After citing the treatment of motion in Pascal's *Pensées*, Heidegger
noted, "Rest—unrest; phenomenon and motion (cf. the phenomenon of motion in Aristotle)." Thus he stressed that Aristotle's " 'ethics' is placed into the
ontological horizon" of the concept of *kinesis* in the *Physics, Metaphysics, De
anima*, and *De motu animalium*. Aristotle's ethics is "the explication of being
as human being, human life, the movement of life," "the categorial explication
of the sense of being of facticity," which Heidegger himself wanted to take up

and radicalize. The various modes of intentional *aletheuein* in Book Six are, at bottom, modes of *kinesis* in the direction of the toward-which of being (*telos*): "Being in the basic aspect of the being-moved of 'being out after something' is . . . the condition for being able to bring intentionality into relief." Whereas the intentional movement of *sophia* is that of a present perfect "finished-being," *phronesis* is an *energeia ateles*, an unfinished work and movement (*Bewegtheit*), an endless being on the way (*hodos, Unterwegsein*) from *dynamis* to *energeia* (G61 137–38, 112, 93, 117; PIA 267, 260).

Heidegger took this movement that concentrates itself at the extreme point (*eschaton*) of the *kairos* to be the kairological time that he had already discovered in Pauline eschatology:

> *Phronesis* is the illumination of dealings that temporalizes life in its *being*. The concrete interpretation shows how this being, *kairos*, is constituted. . . . It goes toward the *eschaton*, the extreme, in which the determinately seen concrete situation intensifies itself at the particular time. As the being that becomes unveiled and available in the *aletheuein* of *phronesis*, *the prakton* is something which is as *not yet* such and such being. As "not yet such and such" and indeed as the toward-which of a concern, it is simultaneously *already* such and such, as the toward-which of a concrete readiness for dealings, whose constitutive illumination is determined by *phronesis*.

Echoing his earlier treatment of New Testament *phronesis* and "being awake" for the unavailable, noncalculable (nontechnical) Parousia and Kairos, Heidegger also wrote that "as epitactical illumination, [*phronesis*] brings dealings into the basic stance of readiness to . . . , of breaking-forth toward. . . . " He also stressed the meaning of the term *steresis, privatio*: "The 'not yet' and the 'already' are to be understood in their 'unity'. . . . The concept of *steresis* is the category of the above-named *explicata*." In fact, "the 'fundamental category' of *steresis* . . . dominates Aristotelian ontology." *Steresis* is not only the loss of form and being that occurs in change, but the lack of possibility and futural not-yet that still pervades the already of being-in-work. As the way of *energeia ateles*, life is permeated by possible-being, nonbeing, not-yet-being, nonpresence (PIA 259–60, 266). Like Luther and Kierkegaard, Heidegger found in *steresis* an analogue of the concealment at work in the *Deus absconditus*, as well as in the *mysterium* of the mystics.

In Aristotle, *abscondere*, concealing, turned up for Heidegger as the *lethe*, concealment (*Verborgenheit*), which essentially defines *a-letheia praktike*. Like truth as unconcealment (*on hos alethes*), so too nontruth (*pseudos*) as concealing belongs not just to relational sense (*logos*), but also to the *Sache selbst* (*to pragma*) of the intentional toward-which, namely, being:

> As self-veiling, *pseudos* only has sense on the basis of the meaning of *alethes* [true/unconcealed] that is originally not *logos*-related: *doxa pseudes ege-*

neto, hote lathoi metapeson to pragma [opinion becomes false when, upon changing, the matter escapes notice, is concealed] (*De an.* 428b 8). *Remaining-concealed, being-veiled* is here decisively and expressly fixed as the sense of *pseudos* and therewith that of "truth." Aristotle sees being-concealed in itself positively, and it is no accident that the sense of "truth" for the Greeks is characterized privatively according to that sense—and not only grammatically. Being in the how of its possible "as-what-determinations" is not simply there, it is a "task." (PIA 255–57)

Aletheuein means "making that which was previously concealed, covered up to be as unconcealed, openly there, available" (G63 11). But in the task and work of practical truth, the concealment of being cannot in principle be exhausted and mastered, as it can be in the *aletheia theoretike* of *sophia*, which is correlated contemplatively and leisurely to the presence-before-the-hand of the ever-being that can never be other. Here the concealment of being is thought to be accidental, having to do with human shortcomings. The practical truth of *phronesis*, on the other hand, concerns the *on hos pragma* that can always be other and is essentially defined by the concealment and unavailability of the *steresis* of a futural not-yet. Here truth is in principle "privative": there will always be more being to unconceal in the temporal enactment (*Vollzug*) of praxis.

The task of practical truth can never be completed; it is an unceasing being-on-the-way toward, out of, and back into the concealment of being. This is exactly the point Heidegger made in his lecture "Dasein und Wahrsein" when, with a quote from the *Nicomachean Ethics*, he concluded his example of bringing the good of "some joy to my friend." Here again we hear echoes of "the unseen" in Pauline kairology: "The *agathos ou phainetai*, it [the good] does not show itself, it would then be for one who strives after it earnestly. Knowing, *episteme*, is [on the other hand] related to being that always is, and only when it can do this does there exist the possibility of knowing" (DW). My *Entschluss* (resolve) to bring the gift is not heroic resoluteness, but an *Entschluss*, a nonclosure, a not-being-blocked-off, a wakeful openness for what is concealed and deferred, namely, for the fitting gift that may or may not disclose (*erschliessen*) itself in the *kairos*, but in any case will have to repeated in the self-circling *kinesis* of practical life and friendship.

Aristotle said that there can be no royal science (*episteme*) of the practical good, which fails to appear in the universal form of the *eidos*, and Luther that there can be no *scientia gloriae* of the hidden God. The young Heidegger, speaking Husserl's phenomenological language, said that there can be no Husserlian rigorous science of the concealment and differentiation of the being of beings. In the WS 1921–22 lecture course, we sense all three influences woven together into Heidegger's formulation of the question about being through a Kierkegaardian reading of the Platonic Socrates. He first pointed out that, for

Plato, philosophy is "the enactment of the complete drawing around [*Umvoll-zug*] of the soul from a night-like day to the authentic day—the way up toward being as such" (*Republic* 521c). He then placed this way toward the content-sense of being in the context of his translation of the *Apology*, where we find an understanding of the philosphical way not as a mere body of doctrines called *philosophia*, but rather as "passionate" philosophizing (*philosophein*), as the personal "vocation" and "decision" of a practical way of life (*bios*) and quest of questioning after the questionableness of being (relational and temporalizing-sense):

> And I would be acting [*handeln*] in a manner absolutely worthy of damnation, if I now—God having ordered me (as I believed and confidently took upon myself) that I should live philosophically, questioning and examining myself and others—if now from fear of death or any trivial matter I wanted to abandon the direction, the direction of an enactment of life. (28e)

In another passage that took up Spengler's theme of "the decline of the west," that is, the *eschaton* of western culture and philosophy, and posed the possibility of a new beginning, Heidegger wrote that "if we 'go into decline,' then there again stands before us only *either*: . . . radical existentiell concern . . . *or*: degenerating into the gloss of mythical and theosophical metaphysics and mysticism, and into the dream-state of an occupation with sanctimony which one calls religion." And:

> In passionately taking up a position for and against *ahead of time*, what betrays itself is only the lack of genuine passion (which alone can provide the measure here), of the resolute openness [*Entschlossenheit*] of understanding, which is here all the more certain the less it breaks forth, but rather can keep silent and wait. Because we . . . in the mode of detective psychology and soul-snooping . . . want to have the business cleared up quickly in noisy zealousness, we fall toward the surrogates of spiritual advertisements or into an apparent, because eye-closing objectivity found in flight. (G61 49–50, 70–71)

Using Plato's dialogues, Heidegger explained that the question about being is a *taxis*, an order (*Ordnung*), a directive, a task. It is enacted in the "epitactical illumination" of a philosophical type of *phronesis*, which "questions kairological-critically 'in one's time.' " In his treatment of Aristotle's concept of *phronesis* later in this lecture course, Heidegger referred his students to the discussion of practical knowledge, the mean, excess, deficiency, and *kairos* in *Statesman* 284c–285b and *Protagoras* 356a. "We should divide the art of measurement into two parts . . . the other [nonquantitative] part comprises arts concerned with the suitable, the seemly, the moment [*ton kairon*], and the fitting [*to deon*], and all such standards situated in the mean between the extremes" (*Statesman* 284e). The temporal enactment-sense of philosophy's content-sense, namely, of being, is not the noninterpretive understanding of *techne*, which like *sophia* and *episteme* deals with the universal, unchanging *eidos*. Rather, this phronetic, kairological enactment is "analogous" to "artistic creation," where philosophizing has a sense similar, for example, to actual " 'music making' (cf. *Phaedo*) . . . playing music [*musizieren*] (remaining in the order, *taxis*!). . . . Playing music is here not a mere comportment to a possible 'business,' mastering a technique." Playing on the the word "music" and the Greek *mousike* (art, the arts), Heidegger also quoted *Phaedo* 61a: "Philosophy is the greatest *mousike*. *Phaedo* 61a . . . *mousike*, rhythmic 'educating/shaping' [*Bilden*] that holds itself in an inner ordering and enacts itself in it. Title for 'education,' *eukyklion paideia* [well-rounded education that moves well in a circle]. . . . Plato would never define philosophy as *techne*!" That honor, Heidegger indicated, was reserved for the Sophists, the "sham" philosophers who are hard to distinguish from the "genuine" ones (*Sophist* 216c) (G61 45–60, 41, 108).

In a passage from his SS 1923 lecture course, which clearly echoes Aristotle, we find Heidegger continuing to apply the notion of *phronesis* not only to philosophy, but also to the historical sciences and religion:

> Religion is misunderstood in the core of its Dasein when the history of religion today buys into the cheap game of sketching types, i.e., stylistic forms of piety in an entertaining table of pictures. The analogue counts also in economic history, the history of philosophy, and legal history. Possibilities . . . come into concrete Dasein . . . only insofar as at any time within [the respective] science the right man at the right place and at the right time decisively intervenes and takes hold. (G63 57)

In his WS 1923–24 lecture course, Heidegger "[urged] his students to adopt a more 'phronetic' approach toward their chosen science, contrary to the traditional equation of scientific comportment with *theorein*" (HA 395). In WS 1924–25, he opened his course with a long account of Aristotle's practical writings as the proper horizon for dealing with the pre-Socratic question of being in Plato's *Sophist*. Like his other courses on Greek metaphysics, it was an attempt to demythologize that being-question about which "each of them (the old philosophers of being) tells a *mython*" (G19 10ff.).

PART IV

New Beginnings

11 | The Questionableness of Being

Way-Traces

"ONE THING [is] certain," Heidegger wrote in WS 1921–22, "[thinking is] not at an end; therefore begin, *begin genuinely*, move toward the beginning." Heidegger added here that beginning has "its 'time' " and that "to begin for another time is senseless" (G61 186). How is the *kairos* of the young Heidegger's new beginning different from that of SZ and those in the later writings? If his demythologizing erased the hyperbolic inscriptions of the intentional configuration of being-sense in the ocular-aesthetic quietism of Greek, medieval, and modern metaphysics, how exactly did he retrace the *Sache* of the original kinetic-personal physiognomy of this configuration in his new beginnings, which took up the ground-question of metaphysics that he found already in primal Christianity, Dilthey's reading of Husserl, and Aristotle? If he thought he stood at the end of metaphysics, what was the *Kehre* to the new postmetaphysical type of thinking supposed to be? How far and how many were the first "youthful leaps" that he made into the primal anarchic source (*Ursprung*) of his lifelong *Sache*? In other words, in what novel ways did his youthful texts mark out the other two family resemblances that we find reiterated throughout his long career of thinking, namely, new beginning and constant beginning?

Concerning his youthful thoughtpaths, Heidegger later wrote, "I always followed only an unclear way-trace [*Wegspur*], but I followed. It was an almost imperceptible promise announcing a release into the open, now dark and confused, now lightning-sharp like a sudden insight, which then again for a long time withdrew from every attempt to say it" (G12 130/41; cf. 121/35, 87/6). He certainly had no apparently systematic work called *Sein und Zeit*. In the decade of silence between 1917 and 1926, he published nothing. Especially during the early Freiburg period, he was preoccupied more with the negative role of destroyer and demythologizer of metaphysics than with the positive task of working out a philosophy. He wrote to Löwith in 1921, "I am no philosopher," one who is working under the constant "danger of threshing empty straw" (BL 28, 30). The passionately antisystematic sentiments of his Kierkegaardian "skepticism" made him suspicious and hesitant about the very possibility of putting forward a philosophy, since he thought it would give the false impression of a direct answer and objectified result. His search for new beginnings did not know where it was going and aporetically experimented with many different way-traces.

On the basis of collaboration and correspondence in the early twenties, Löwith recounted regarding Heidegger's critique of philosophy and of the postwar cultural crisis in Germany that, "because of [his] negation in principle of everything in the status quo and also of all programs for its reform, Heidegger even protested against the misinterpretation and overevaluation of his own work which claimed that *he* had something 'positive' and 'new results' to offer." As late as 1924, Heidegger wrote to Löwith that "the illusion arises that through critique some content, corresponding to what has prevailed, is supposed to be put forth in opposition; and that my work is something for a school, a movement, continuation, completion." Löwith paraphrases the rest of Heidegger's letter: "However, it is *not* all this, but rather limits itself to a critical and conceptual destruction of the philosophical and theological tradition" (MLD 28–29). Heidegger told Löwith flatly in 1921, "I do not want to introduce a new movement in the history of philosophy" (BL 31). Let us read again his mediations on his new beginning around the same time: "No fantastic representation of new categories that comfortably lead us into a new kingdom. Existentielly it becomes more difficult" (G61 186). This hidden exiled king, who had lost the Aristotelian-Scholastic and Neo-Kantian *arche* of his students years, abdicated in principle the possibility of philosophical kingdoms.

As the previously given list of his youthful lecture courses, essays, and publication plans indicates, Heidegger's search for new beginnings makes up a long reproductive chain of textual traces and supplements, of differing/deferring drafts of a nonbook about the *Sache* "being and time" that, right up until his death in 1976, he kept trying to write, supplement, rewrite, retitle, and finally publish, but never really did (see SD 61/55). There never was *a* book called "Being and Time." Each of Heidegger's youthful texts was a highly creative and often idiosyncratic weaving of the being-question, phenomenology, primal Christianity, Aristotle, and other traditions into a *textum*, which momentarily presented his "darkly intimated" *Sache* until it eventually came apart at the seams and the remains were woven into the next draft of his planned book. As an *Anzeige*, an indicative trace of Heidegger's lethic *Sache*, each text was pursued for a while and then critically reinscribed in its successor, which thus was always also a multilayered palimpsest. When we sift through this literary "straw" and bricolage, we see that Heidegger's planned book had many different titles: for example, the Husserlian-Eckhartian draft called "The Idea of Philosophy and the Problem of Worldview" (KNS 1919), the Kierkegaardian-Jaspersian draft called "Comments on Karl Jaspers's *Psy-*

chology of Worldviews" (1919–21), the Pauline-Lutheran draft called "Introduction in the Phenomenology of Religion" (1920–21), the Aristotelian draft called "Phenomenological Interpretations with Respect to Aristotle" (1922), the Diltheyan-Yorckian draft called "The Concept of Time" (1924), the Husserlian-Diltheyan draft called "Time and Being" (1925) (TB 180–83), and the Kantian draft called *Being and Time* (1926).

Though each of the young Heidegger's drafts of his new beginning deserves a separate and detailed chronological treatment, Part Four of this study tries its own hand at Heideggerian bricolage and weaves these drafts together into a single cloth depicting his new beginning primarily in the early Freiburg period, which I call his anarchic kinetic-personalist thoughtpath. However, I do acknowledge the tears and seams between the different stages his thought went through after 1919. I also show more clearly how, using his readings of primal Christianity, Dilthey, Husserl, and Aristotle, Heidegger readdressed the ontological alternative he had posed in his student writings and performed destructive repetitions of the three "requirements" for the question about being he had put forward in the conclusion of his qualifying dissertation, namely, concrete categorial sense (content-sense), living spirit (relational sense), and history (temporalizing-sense). More particularly, I note how he now built on such earlier themes as being in the sense of the transcendental "something in any sense," heterothesis, the material determinateness and analogical differentiation of form, and haecceity. Moreover, I now bring into play his renewed appropriation of Christian mysticism in 1919–20 and show how it animated his development through the early 1920s, for it provides an important key for understanding how he was still concerned with the mysterious "depth dimension" of the being-question he had posed in his student writings.

The present chapter argues that he was not pursuing a mere philosophy of life, but rather was dealing with the question about being, that is, ultimately about the differentiated temporal giving of being in factical life. Chapters 12 and 13 then outline the intentional configuration of Heidegger's question, organizing their presentation around the terminology that he used in 1919, namely, "it worlds" (content-sense), "it worlds for me" (relational sense), and *Ereignis* (temporalizing-sense). Moreover, whereas in Chapter 7 I dealt with Heidegger's account of the hyperbolic, mythic understanding of being in the They of everyday life and in metaphysics, I now focus on the demythologized understanding of being, from which everyday life and metaphysics flee and to which they fail to own up in ownness (*Eigentlichkeit*) (G63 85). Chapter 14 proceeds to explain the continued influence of Christian mysticism on Heidegger and his understanding of the ontological "mystery . . . of all life." Chapter 15 outlines the role played by the method of "formal indication" in Heidegger's notion of constant beginning, and explores his indications here about the type of postmetaphysical ethics implied by his new beginning in ontology.

Chapter 16 returns to the issue of what new strategies for reading Heidegger's later thought are opened up by the rediscovery of his youthful writings in the "supplement" to his collected edition.

Vorhaben and *Kehre*

According to a common traditional view, Heidegger's philosophical biography shows the following development. His student writings worked out a mystical-theological metaphysics of being that was modeled on Franz Brentano's study of the Aristotelian being-question and on Meister Eckhart; then in an intermediate period during the early twenties, he became preoccupied with philosophy of life and with an existential-transcendental anthropologism in SZ (as Husserl, for instance, thought); and finally after 1930 he made a *Kehre* from this human-centered to a Being-centered philosophy. He made this turn, so this longstanding biography went, by returning to the deep being-question of his student years and pursuing it within the historical horizon that had been opened up through the analyses of the temporality of Dasein he had worked out in SZ. But, upon studying his youthful writings, we now know that his way-traces from his very first postwar course of KNS 1919 onward were already doing this.

As Heidegger later stated repeatedly, "the being-question . . . was set on the way" through the "preceding course of thinking" in the early twenties. He always stressed that "the question about being, aroused by Brentano's work, remained in view" (LR xii–xiii; cf., G1 56/R 21). His youthful destruction of the hyperbolic being-question was precisely an attempt to place it back into and repeat it (not dissolve it) within the "horizon" of the kairological temporality experienced in factical life. The goal of this "analysis of the temporality of Dasein" was to explore such a new, non-Aristotelian concept of time as "the horizon of the understanding of being." Within this horizon, being gives itself temporally as the *sense* of being, i.e., as the temporal content-sense of experience, which for its part temporally enacts this sense (G15 337–39).

Neither in his student period nor in the early twenties did Heidegger ever advocate a psychologistic, existentialist, or transcendental reduction of being-sense to the relational and enactment-sense of intending it. In fact, his thought in the early twenties was even less psychologistic than the critique of psychologism in his earlier pure logic. His major point was precisely that, given its mysterious character of futural not-yet and differentiation, as exemplifed in mysticism, the *theologia crucis* of the hidden God, and the *lethe* of *aletheia praktike*, being remains groundless, absence-permeated, unavailable, incalculable, and nonmasterable by intentional acts, whether by those of pure logic or religious speculation. As we have already begun to see, one can find in the young Heidegger a strong critique and demythologizing of modern "ego-meta-

phyics" and "technology," for which, as for eschatological religious speculation, being stands over against an autonomous ego as the *Reich* of a homogeneous presence-before-the-hand that is constantly available, calculable, and
controllable.

He took up precisely the "problem of the categories" of being and the mystical "depth dimension" of "the true actuality and the actual truth" that he
had explored in his student writings, and explicitly placed all this into the horizon of factical life and historical time that he was discovering in primal
Christianity, Dilthey, and Aristotle. That is why we now find him reading the
doctrine of the categories in Aristotle's *Metaphysics* and the transcendental
verum in Scholasticism from the vantage point of Luther's theology of the
cross, Kierkegaard, and Aristotle's own practical philosophy (reversing the latter's hierarchical ranking of *bios theoretikos* and *bios praktikos* in his ethics).
Similarly, we also find Heidegger interpreting the categorial intuition of being
in Husserl's Sixth Investigation in terms of Dilthey's analysis of historical life,
as well as synthesizing the *mysterium tremendum* of Eckhart with Luther's
theologia crucis into a kind of Lutheran mysticism and mystical Lutheranism.
He was so little a subjectivist or mere philosopher of life that he still understood himself as a Christian believer and a religious thinker until as late as at
least 1921. His letter of January 9, 1919 to Krebs stated that, in leaving the
Church, his Catholicism had not been replaced by "the angry and obscene po-
lemics of an apostate" (MH 107).

Accordingly, Heidegger's 1962 letter to Richardson repudiated the view
that there was a turn in his thought from a philosophy of life to a Being-centered philosophy (LR xiv–xvii, xxii–xxiii). He explained that on a certain
level there was indeed a bend or twist (*Wendung*) in his thought after 1930,
but that at a deeper level there was no real turn (*Kehre*) or, much less, a reversal
(*Umkehr*) from a "Heidegger I" of the twenties to a "Heidegger II" of his later
thought. For the *Vorhaben*, that is, the vague intention and forehaving of his
questioning toward which his way-traces traveled, remained roughly the same
from at least as early as 1919, through the early 1920s, and onwards into the
1930s and beyond. This *Vorhaben* was, as I pointed out earlier, never merely
the being of beings but rather the step-back and turn from being to the lethic
anarchic *Sache* of the differentiated temporal giving of being in and through
concrete life. The young Heidegger's inquiry into what he called the kairological questionableness of being (*Seinsfraglichkeit*) (G61 189) also makes questionable the claim that the ultimate goal of his questioning was ever simply
"being," which, even from a simple grammatical viewpoint (all nouns are
capitalized in German), has for years been mistakenly valorized in English
translation with a capital "B" as "Being," as if it were the capital, the *caput*,
as it were, of a kingdom, i.e., a super-entity (cf. "Supreme Being").

On the level of this *Vorhaben* toward the question of the temporal giving and differentiating of being, Heidegger explained that Heidegger II is already contained in Heidegger I, and Heidegger I is still contained in Heidegger II. The different thoughtpaths, way-traces, twists, turns, upsets, and "Heideggers" all come on the level of the analogical differentiation of his *Sache*, that is, on the level of the endless interpretive enacting, fulfilling (*Vollzug*), and temporalizing of this *Vorhaben*, though the latter also gets modified in the process. This supplementary chain of differing/deferring drafts of the topic of the factical life/temporal-giving-of-being relation runs its course from a mystical "transcendent relation of the soul to God" in 1915-16 to a quasi-mystical person/*Ereignis* relation in 1919, a quasi–New Testament wakeful life/kairological time relation in 1920-21, a Neo-Aristotelian practical life/*kinesis* relation in 1921-22, and a Neo-Neo-Kantian Dasein/temporal schematism relation in 1926-27, and then trails away into the many later thoughtpaths and even beyond into those that have been influenced by Heidegger. The longstanding view of the relation between "the early Heidegger" and "the later Heidegger" cannot see the *Sache* for all the thoughtpaths.

What often makes it seem that Heidegger's youthful writings are not pursuing the deep question about the giving of being is not only that he eventually in WS 1925-26 and in SZ misleadingly took up the transcendental language of Kant, but also that here and in his earlier courses the *actual* course of his analyses did not usually get beyond dealing with the "horizon" of temporality in factical life and to its ultimate *Vorhaben*, namely, an explicit treatment of how being is given and temporalized in this horizon. Thus Heidegger wrote to Löwith on August 20, 1927, "I am also convinced that ontology can be founded only ontically. . . . [In my Freiburg beginnings] I first had to begin with the fac*tic* [das Fak*tisch*] in an extreme manner in order even to gain fac*ticity* [die Fak*tizität*] as a problem" (BL 36-37). The existentialist or transcendental reading of Heidegger's youthful texts is bewitched by their surface and fails to see the depth of their *Vorhaben*, which often can be sounded out only by a sensitivity to the historical context in which Heidegger was working at the time (for example, his continued interest in mysticism into the early twenties).

Not only is Heidegger's single lifelong *Vorhaben* operative in his youthful period, but it was then that he made the first, decisive, and idyosyncratic turns *from* his earlier preoccupation with being as the static presence of valid logical sense and ultimately as the eternity of the absolute spirit of God *to* the temporal giving of being. This is the biographical sense of his talk about the end of philosophy and a new beginning. All this, as Gadamer has written, was "the turn before the turn" (DEW 15). The young Heidegger himself gave this step-back and *Kehre* to a new beginning a number of names: for example, breaking-through (*Einbruch*), a "going back always anew into the primal source," the leap (*Sprung*) into the primal source (*Ursprung*) (1919-20); "the regress into the primally-historical," a "complete turn-around" (*Umkehr*) and "complete transformation [*Umwandlung*] of philosophy" (1920–21); "a precautionary turning-forward" (*Vor-kehrung*), phenomenological "re-duction," "the other understanding" (1921–22) (G56/57 3, 214; G58 249; EPR; IPR 316–17; G61 39, 186).

After stating that, in its investigation of history, "philosophy springs out of the factical experience of life," Heidegger said in his lecture course of WS 1920–21 that "every way that leads out of the factical experience of life leads in fact only before the goal, not to the goal. A turning-around [*Umwendung*] is needed. And indeed not a 'turning of the gaze,' a changing of the direction of knowing toward qualitatively other spheres of objects, but rather this turning-around is better characterized as a transformation [*Umwandlung*]." "Philosophizing springs out of the factical experience of life and leaps—though after an essential turn-around [*Umkehr*]—back into it," that is, back into genuine historicity (EPR). In WS 1921–22, he introduced Plato's definition of philosophy as not "like the turning-around [*Umwenden*] of a potsherd, but rather the enactment of the complete drawing around [*Umvollzug, periagoge*] of the soul from a night-like day to the authentic day—the way up toward being as such." Accordingly, Heidegger himself defined philosophy as a "precautionary turning-forward" that constantly turns away from a fixed "content" (i.e., a fixed view of the being of beings) and turns back into the indicative "way" of the temporalizing of comportment to being. "Genuine *Vor-kehrung* is . . . genuine readiness to understand in a manner fitting to the situation," "to question kairological-critically" (G61 49, 41, 20, 32).

Picking up on his pursuit of the categories of being (of the "something in any sense") and the "metaphysical '*Ursprung*' " in his dissertation, Heidegger's KNS 1919 course likewise saw itself as a *"primal* science" (*Ur-wissenschaft*) of the categories of "the something in any sense," "the experienceable in any sense," or what he also called *das Ur-etwas*, the primal something. Philosophy is supposed to be a "science of the *Ursprung*," of the primal source of categorial sense in pretheoretical life. It is thus the heir of Greek *prote philosophia*, first philosophy, the science of the *archai*, the "ultimate 'origins' " or principles of beings, as this was initially pursued by "the old [pre-Socratic] philosophers of being" in the *gigantomachia peri tes ousias* and then less mythopoetically by Plato's dialectic and Aristotle's metaphysics (G56/57 68, 115, 96, 18–20). But we shall have to see how Heidegger's notion of *Ursprung*, a primal springing forth that is groundless, absence-permeated, and anarchically differentiated, is precisely an anarchic *arche* and does not mean the traditional notion of *arche*, i.e., a present homogeneous origin/kingdom.

Heidegger's WS 1921–22 course called this primal science an "ontology" that deals with being qua being (*Sein qua Sein*), "the questionableness of being," the worthiness of questioning about being (*Seinsfragwürdigkeit*). The "major *Sache*" of ontology—what is at issue, what it comes to (*worauf es an-kommt*)—is "not life, not world, but rather being, being-here [*Dasein*]." Being makes up the "principles" of beings, that which let them be as beings. "Principle is being (the sense of being) as the being of beings [*Seiendes*]." Thus "the object of the definition of philosophy is . . . defined: knowing comportment to beings as being." This "as" means that "that to which [ontology] comports itself must give itself in its genuine, ultimate, and characteristic principle: that which is [*das Seiende*], ultimately considered not in relation to something else that is, but rather in itself and as such." And "what is the principial for such beings in themselves? . . . Being or, more determinately, with regard to the way such 'being' is apprehensible: the 'sense of being'. . . . being, the sense of being, is the philosophically principial element of every being" (G61 49-61, 187-89).

Similarly, Heidegger's SS 1923 course "Ontology (Hermeneutics of Facticity)" opened with the point that he had been making ever since 1919, namely, that his philosophy is ontology. It is "a questioning and determining that aims at being as such. . . . With reference to the Greek word *on*, ontology means . . . questioning about being." Here he distinguished his ontology from the regional or "material ontologies" that investigate not the categories of beings as beings, but rather the categories of this or that kind of being (e.g., nature, culture). "With a view to consciousness of-, the *of-which*, i.e., the objective [categorial] characteristic as such of a being, is also and only thereby visible. And what concerns the ontologies is the objective characteristics of the respective region of being. And precisely not being as such, i.e., being that is free of the object" (G63 1-2).

In WS 1921-22, Heidegger explained further that philosophy is an intentional "comportment toward" (*Verhalten zu*) and that its content-sense (*Gehaltssinn*) is "beings as being," the sense of being. "The toward-which of the comportment is: the sense of being." Its relational sense is "knowing comportment." "Knowing is an apprehending of the object 'as' object and thus a determining. . . . the comportment holds [*hält*] itself in speaking at the object, be-speaks it, addresses it. . . . The relation is held by something as a being as be-ing and being such." The temporal enactment-sense of philosophy is "the having of the knowing comportment to beings as being" in the sense of the "passion of enacting" this intentional relation (as exemplified especially in the lives of Socrates and Kierkegaard). Heidegger specified this temporal enactment as phronetic "philosophizing" (analogous to "playing music") that "questions kairological-critically 'in one's time.' " This stands in sharp contrast to the *techne* of "studying philosophy," of the business (*Betrieb*) of learning and "falling toward" an "objectified" body of doctrines, which was exemplified in the Sophists and is to be found "at the universities" today (G61 45-60, 41).

However, the sense of being studied by philosophy is not only the content-sense of philosophy, but also philosophy's relational and temporalizing-senses. "The object towards which I comport myself determines the comportment itself with its own name. . . . The object of philosophy, beings as being, determines from itself (function of the principle) the comportment as well." Relational comportment and its enactment are also that which is, and thus there is a being of these, where being functions as their "principle." Being encompasses "the being of the having of the knowing comportment to beings as being. But the authentic having of a comportment as comportment is a how of enactment. Thus *the being of the enactment* (temporalizing, the historical) is decisive" (G61 60). The *Sache* of the sense of being is not a single element. It is articulated (*gegliedert*) and configured into its content-, relational, enactment-, and temporalizing-senses.

Earlier in his essay on Jaspers, Heidegger wrote that "the full sense of a phenomenon encompasses its intentional relational, content-, and enactment-character" (G9 22). Later in SZ, Heidegger thus stressed that the sense of being is not something "simple," but constituted by the "equiprimodiality" of these intentional moments. He wrote that the "underivability of something primordial and originary does not exclude a multiplicity of characteristics of being that may be constitutive for it. If these show themselves, then existentially they are equiprimordial." Traditionally, "the phenomenon of the *equiprimordiality* of constitutive moments has often been disregarded in ontology because of a methodologically unbridled tendency to establish the origin of everything and anything from a simple 'primal ground.' " The "idea of being in general is . . . far from being 'simple.' " The sense of being is rather worldly (content-sense), personal (relational sense), and temporal (temporalizing-sense) (SZ 175/170, 260/241, cf. 442/383).

The full definition of ontology in WS 1921-22 runs therefore as follows: "Philosophy is principially knowing comportment to beings as being (sense of being), and in such a manner that, in the comportment and for it, the issue is also decisively the being (sense of being) at the particular time of the having of the comportment." The "issue, what it comes to, is the sense of being of the having of the knowing comportment to [beings as being]." In other words, philosophy is "phenomenological (existentiell, historical-cultural) 'ontology' or *ontological phenomenology*" (G61 60-61). It is *phenomenological* ontology because it studies being as it *appears* historically to intentional experience, and it is *ontological* phenomenology because it also studies the *being* of the intentional relation to *being*. The question about being has to question after the being of that being which questions being, philosophy has to philosophize also about the philosopher, ontology has to ontologize also about this ontological entity. And this is not for the sake of a mere philosophy of life and much less in order to dissolve everything into subjectivism, but rather for the sake of gaining access to the manifold intentional senses of being.

Factical Life in the University

To explore the being of the philosophical comportment-to-being, Heidegger's WS 1921–22 course proceeded in a very prosaic manner with how this usually shows itself, namely, as a "university." If the philosopher is Da-sein in the sense of a here (*da*) of being, then today this intentional here usually takes the form—Nietzsche aside—of "research," "study," "courses, seminars," conferences, writing books, applying for grants. The university with its lecture halls and seminar rooms filled with students and teachers—where "philosophy is supposed to be, here [*hier*] and now"—is a personal and communal site of being. "We designate this closest, withworldly and environmentally definable (selfworldly) situation and the context of life that prevails and lives genuinely in it with the title *university*." Heidegger's key move here was to point out that, for those who work there, the university is not something external to their own being, but is built on and is "our own historical factical life," which includes the historical world that one has brought along from outside the university. "What is going on in this 'living' at and in a university? Going to university and experiencing it? And simultaneously this question should indeed only be posed concretely—how we go to it today, here and now, how we live it. We live it just as we ourselves are—out of and in our *factical Dasein*" (G61 63–78).

As Heidegger put this in KNS 1919 (when he was also thinking about "university reform"), academic life is a historical "context of motivations," the "habitus of personal Dasein," a "lifeworld" that is built out of the initial "context of the natural consciousness of life." He wrote, "Every Dasein of personal life has—in each of its moments within its specific prevailing lifeworld—a relation to the world, to the motivational values of the environing world, of the things on its life-horizon, of fellow human beings, of society." And it is this historical being in the world that comes to be shaped in academic life, art, politics, religion: "These life-relations can be permeated . . . by a genuine form of activity and life, e.g., the scientific, the religious, the artistic, the political." The specific activity of "the scientific human being" is *Forschung*, research, which is not usually "isolated," but rather in the social context of "scientific academies and universities" (G56/57 3–4).

Heidegger's point was that, if you want to get at the being of the philosophical comportment to being, you must explore "the sense of the being of factical life" that philosophy and "university philosophy" in particular presuppose. This means, first, an ontological analysis of the comportment to being in pretheoretical life on which philosophy and the sciences are based. In KNS 1919, Heidegger's way of talking about this "phenomenological (existentiell, historical-cultural) ontology" was to say that "there must be a pre-theoretical or transtheoretical, in any case a nontheoretical science, a genuine *primal* science, out of which the theoretical itself has its primal source." This science studies the primal intentional structure of "I comport myself to" something (being), "the lived experience of something," with regard to the pretheoretical "sense" of its "content," "relation," and "temporality." It is a pretheoretical science in the double sense that it describes the "primal stratum" of "the essentially atheoretical sphere" of "life in and for itself" and also avoids misdescribing it from the way it is seen in the special objectifying attitude of theory. "The primacy of the theoretical must be broken. . . . The theoretical itself and as such refers back to the pretheoretical" as its "primal source" (G56/57 96, 66–69, 121, 89, 59).

Heidegger began using the term "facticity" around the time of his WS 1919–20 course (G58 80ff.), and by the time that he gave his SS 1923 course "Ontologie (Hermeneutik der Faktizität)," he was saying that ontology must also be a "hermeneutics of facticity." In "ancient ontology ('metaphysics')" and "modern ontology," the "question—from which field of being the decisive sense of being guiding all problematics should be drawn?—is in no way posed." Rather they simply begin with "*object*-being, the objectivity of definite objects" and, moreover, with the "object for indifferent theoretical thinking." Thereby they "mislay access to the being that is decisive within the philosophical problematic: the *Dasein* out of which and for which philosophy 'is'. . . . Thus the title [of the course] reads rather: *Hermeneutics of Facticity*." Ontology is "*principial knowing* that springs forth from and goes back into this facticity." More specifically, it is hermeneutical-phenomenological ontology because it interpretively radicalizes, lays out, and describes the ways of intentional comportment to being already operative in the "everydayness" of factical life, that is, the ways in which the sense of being comes to language and shows itself in factical life. "The task: to make [the being-character of being] into a phenomenon. . . . The hermeneutics of facticity attempts to go along this path." Heidegger's hermeneutics was not just philosophical anthropology, but rather the *euangelion* of this Neo-Greco-Christian "hermeneutics is the proclaiming of the being of a being in its being to-(me)," in its to-me-being (*Mir-Sein*) (G63 2–3, 85, 76, 10; G61 115, 138).

In 1921 Heidegger threw out in class an enigmatic and unexplained formula to indicate that he was not pursuing only a philosophy of life: *Leben = Dasein, in und durch Leben* "Sein." Life = Dasein, being-here, in and through life "*being*." This felicitous ontological rune captures the spirit of his anarchic kinetic-personalist thoughtpath toward being-in-and-through-life in his youthful Freiburg period (cf. DEW 14–15), where "anarchic" and "kinetic" refer to the deep temporalizing-sense of being that radically differentiates itself, and "personalist" indicates its relational and enactment-senses. Heidegger's rune can thus be interpreted to mean: my life is literally Da-sein (being-here) in the sense that the temporal giving of being (temporalizing-sense) is "in" this life (relational sense) and "through" it (temporal enactment-sense). Earlier in the course, Heidegger had similarly told his students that "what is at issue, what it comes to, is being, i.e., that it 'is,' the *sense of being*, that being 'is,' i.e., as being is *here* [*da*] (*in* the phenomenon). . . . What it comes to is that it comes to 'being,' that it stands *in* our exertion. . . . It is indeed the being of the comportment [to being], i.e., here [*hier*] (phenomenologically) *through* comportment; its temporalizing" (emphasis added). And again later, "Here [*hier*] and now we live in [philosophical comportment to being] and indeed in this place [*Ort*], in this lecture hall. You before me, I before you, we with each other." Heidegger similarly described the being of the world as "in and for a caring." Finally, "Not life, not world, but rather being, Dasein. . . . Da-sein, being-here: hearing lectures, seminars, interest in education; which being hereby [*dabei*], which possibilities and omissions?" In KNS 1919, we find an isomorphic formula, but it is used to describe and criticize that Neo-Kantian idealism which exaggerates and misconstrues the nature of personal enactment-sense: "being is only in and through thinking" (G61 85, 61, 63, 91, 187; G56/57 83).

The investigation of "the sense of the being of factical life" with which "phenomenological (existentiell, historical-cultural) ontology" begins involves "existentiell categorial interpretation" of the basic "categories" of life. "The categories," Heidegger wrote, "are nothing contrived or a society of logical schemata for themselves, a 'grid,' but rather in an original manner they are *living in life itself*" (*im Leben selbst am Leben*), "living in one's own concrete life." In 1919 his primal science of the "phenomenological disclosure of the sphere of lived experience" called these categories "principles": "The issue is the principles of all spiritual life. . . . [The] goal is the seeing and bringing-into-view of the genuine, truthful sources of any spiritual life whatsoever" (G56/57 109, 127). In 1923, the task of the hermeneutics of facticity was said to be "the clarification of the *basic phenomenon of the 'here'* and the categorial-ontological description of Da-*sein*, *being*-here." And around this time Heidegger also sometimes referred to "the categories of Dasein . . . as existentials [*Existenzialien*]." Regarding the basic category, Heidegger wrote that "intentionality [is] the formally primal structure of facticity (of the sense of being of life)." Or, as he also put this, "Dasein (factical life) is being in a world." "Factical life (Dasein) means: being in a world." But this basic category contains a multiplicity of other categories that are equiprimordial. "What is meant with 'world,' what does 'in' a world mean, how does 'being' in a world appear? The phenomenon Dasein is not to be built up from these determinations, but rather the emphasis at any time of *one* term of the indication should always be only a possible view of the same unified, basic phenomenon." The basic categories of being-in-a-world, as comportment to being, are the content-sense of world, the relational sense of being-in (care), and the enactment- and temporalizing-senses of the be-ing this relation (G61 88, 99, 131, 52–53; G63 66, 80, 85; G58 260–61).

In the following two chapters, I outline these intentional categorial senses and show how each in turn contains its own categorial multiplicity. But note that, though Heidegger used the intentional concepts of "content," "relation," "enactment," and "temporalizing" from his student writings until his very latest writings, he used the more specific compound terms of "content-sense," "relational sense," "enactment-sense," and "temporalizing-sense" mainly from WS 1919–20 to 1922 and only sparingly afterward. But, just as Chapter 2 used these terms to get at the family resemblances in Heidegger's later thoughtpaths, so I use these terms again to get at the familial style of his whole early Freiburg period and the first part of his Marburg period.

12 | It Worlds for Me

THE PRESENT CHAPTER sketches how the young Heidegger's kinetic-personalist thoughtpath explored the demythologized content-sense of the being-question as an "it worlds" and described its relational sense in personalist terms as the "Dasein of personal life." Though it was only in his lecture course of KNS 1919 that he actually spoke of these intentional senses as an "it worlds for me," I show that this notion of worlding-for-me was also operative throughout his early Freiburg period. I begin with his treatment of the it-worlds and its regional categories of the environing world, withworld, and selfworld. I then survey his descriptions of the basic categories of personal relational sense, namely, care, understanding, mood, language, and interpretation. I illustrate these categories through Heidegger's own phenomenological "exercises" of describing such everyday phenomena as the lectern at which he is speaking and the seats in which his students are sitting, the sunrises experienced by hikers and by Theban elders in Hölderlin's translation of Sophocles's *Antigone*, the table in his own home at which his family has its evening meal together, and the toys of his childhood.

Phenomenological Kindergarten

In WS 1921–22, Heidegger defined the content-sense of intentional comportment in the following way: "The relation of comportment is a relation to something; the comportment to . . . holds itself at something. . . . The upon-which and to-which [*Worauf und Wozu*] of the relation is the *content*. . . . Every object has its specific *content-sense*." To get at the primal sense of this content, as well as of the other intentional moments, he entered into a linguistic analysis of "the verb 'to live' " as the basic sense of comportment. "The intransitive-verbal meaning of 'to live' explicates itself . . . always as living 'in' something, living 'out of' something, living 'for' something, living 'with' something, living 'against,' living 'towards' something, living 'from' something. We define the 'something' . . . with the term '*world*.' " Thus "with the phenomenological category of 'world' we speak of . . . *what* is lived, that by which life is held, that at which it holds itself. . . . [W]orld is the basic category of what has content-sense in the phenomenon of life." My previously expressed suspicion that in 1921 Heidegger already used the term Dasein in the sense of a site of being (as in the formula "life = Dasein, being-here, in and through life *'being'* ") is also confirmed by the fact that in the same year and especially in 1923 Heidegger clarified that " 'Dasein' designates equally the being of the world as the being of human life." The world and each worldly thing in it are a topological *Da* (here) of being, such that Heidegger talked about the "Dasein of the world," the "Dasein of this table," of a "broken toy," "a pair of old skis standing in a corner of the basement," a "book," or a "library." Thus, if we want to get at the content-sense of world, "the basic task that is posed [is] to grasp ontologically-categorially the immediate closeness of beings which are here [*Daseiendes*]" in the world (G61 53, 85–86, 91; G63 86–99). Here Heidegger took up and fulfilled the first "requirement" for rethinking the categories of being that he had expresssed in the conclusion of his qualifying dissertation, namely, displacing categorial sense from the realm of valid logical sense into the depth-dimension of historical worldview as this is exemplified especially in medieval mysticism.

The phenomenological analyses pursued in his youthful lecture courses exercised a quaint and magical power of conjuring up the phenomena before the eyes of his students. As the numerous anecdotal reports by his early students attest, Husserl's "phenomenological child" had a real knack for philosophizing with "things," inviting the students into his wondrous "phenomenological kindergarten" (G15 288) of colorful examples, exercises, thoughtpaths, and outings into *die Sachen selbst*, which they were supposed to learn to see as if for the first time. His courses display a style of thinking and lecturing that he himself in 1921 called "questioning kairological-critically," that is, philosophizing in the *kairos*, the critical moment, the "here and now . . . in this place, in this lecture hall. You before me, I before you, we with each other." These courses are themselves performative illustrations of the indexical meaning of Da-sein, here-being!, insofar as they point to being in and through "my lectern," "your seats," the "janitor" over there, the "toy" in the basement, your kitchen "table" at home.

In KNS 1919, Heidegger's investigation of the different intentional senses of comportment-to-something (being) was organized around a peculiar exercise of "phenomenological seeing." He asked the students to consider their experience of " 'seeing your seat' " when they come into the lecture hall each week for his class; or, alternatively, "you can at least enact my own perspective: walking into the lecture hall, I see the lectern." This "phenomenological seeing," Heidegger said, requires that we "radically suspend [*ausschalten*] all relativities (that are essentially theoretical presuppositions)" and let the lived experience be seen as it is prior to theorizing about it. "I cannot clarify this meaningfully sensuous phenomenon of the lived experience of the environing world in such a manner that I destroy its essential character, annul it in its sense and project a theory. . . . If I attempt to clarify the world theoretically, then it collapses into itself." We must follow the Husserlian " 'principle of principles,' " thanks to which " 'no conceivable theory [can] lead us astray,' " namely, "everything that presents itself originally . . . [is] simply to be taken as what it gives itself to be" (G56/57 70-71, 109-11, 98, 86). The proper attitude of the phenomenologist must be that of devotion (*Hingabe*) to and immersion (*Versenkung*) in pretheoretical experience, an attitude that Heidegger modeled on the mystical experience of Eckhartian *Gelassenheit*.

In Heidegger's analysis of comportment-to-something (being), his own "lived experience of his lectern" was contrasted with "the lived experience of the [philosophical] question" *gibt es etwas*, is there something given? "Let us," Heidegger prompted, "enact it in its full vivacity, and let us follow its sense and look upon it." "Questioning: *gibt es etwas?*, I comport myself by positing, and indeed by positing something in any sense as questionable. . . . This 'living towards' [*auf hin*] is a 'questioning living towards something.' " The intentional content of this comportment is the *es-geben*, the there-is-ing/it-giving of the something (being): "The questioning has a specific content: whether 'there is/it gives' a something. . . . not whether something exists, whether something values [*wertet*], or whether something oughts [*soll*] is asked, but whether *there is/it gives* something. What does 'there is/it gives' mean?" Or the question can take a more determinate form, *gibt es eine Aussenwelt*, is there (given) an external world? In both questions, the motivational content-sense of the "something" that "is" or "is given" is *Real-sein*, real-being, *Gegenstandsein*, object-being, *Dinghaftigkeit*, thingliness. Here, the *es gibt* of the something means being a "datum" in the sense of "the mere thing," "the object" (G56/57 77, 66-67, 73, 89).

More specifically and especially in the question of the external world, the givenness of the "something" is taken as "the Dasein of sense data" or "impressions." As Heidegger knew from firsthand experience, for both the "critical realism" of "Aristotelian-Scholastic philosophy" and the "critical-transcendental idealism" of Neo-Kantianism, the "common point of departure" is that "sense data are given." What distinguishes them is only that one does and the other does not think that we can "get out of the 'subjective sphere' of sense data and to the external world of knowledge." Realism sees the something (being) as the "thing in itself" that consists only of the quantitative "primary qualities" studied in mathematical physics. This naked thing is, however, seen to be built up into the actual, subjectively experienced object through a "context of founding," whereby the thing comes to be experienced as possessing "secondary qualities" through its "stimulation" of the "sense organs" and the "nervous system." The stratification of founding perceptions of, for example, the lectern is thus supposed to run in a "series" something like: "thing," "wood," "brown-colored," "box," "lectern." Neo-Kantian idealism appeals to something like the same series of founding perceptions, except that it starts not from the thing in itself, but from "a thinking that enacts itself . . . through reshaping sense data with the help of logical forms, of categories. . . . all being is only in and through thinking." These valid categories make up a "multiplicity of forms of thingliness" that have their unity precisely in the understanding of the something (being) as thingliness (G56/57 80–84, 89–90).

Because this "objectifying" comportment acknowledges only the barren presence of physical and psychical "things" (*Sachen*), its "psychology without the soul" creates a kind of "desert" in which there are no nonobjectified selves who are experiencing these things and, for this very reason, actually no things that could be *given*. And so "we stand," Heidegger said, "at the methodological crossroads that decides the life or death of philosophy in general—at an abyss: either into the nothing, i.e., absolute thingliness, or we succeed with the leap into an *other world*, or more precisely: into the world for the very first time." In other words, he was now ready to take his first "youthful leap" (*Sprung*) into the atheoretical primal source (*Ur-sprung*) of the "worlding" of the world for nonobjectifiable personal experience, which is the "genesis" of all knowing. And here again he appealed to his Judeo-Christian roots by actually quoting from Chapter 2 of *Genesis*: "We have entered into the wretchedness of the desert and wait *in order to understand by seeing* and to see by understanding, rather than to *know* things eternally. ' . . . and the Lord God let spring forth . . . *the tree of life in the middle of the garden*—and the tree of knowledge of good and evil' (Genesis 2:9)" (G56/57 63–65, 88).

If metaphysics defines the content-sense of comportment-to-something as object-being, as the "theoretical something," then one must leap back into what Heidegger's extemporizations recorded in the student transcripts referred to as "the pretheoretical something" or primal something (*Ur-etwas*), which gives itself as a worldish something (*welthaftes Etwas*), and whose sense is a significant "worlding" (DK 107, 122). Heidegger contrasted the theoretical question, "Is there something?," with the lived experience of his students— "each individuated I-myself who sits here"—in "seeing *your* seat" when you "come as usual [*wie gewöhnlich*] into this lecture hall," as well as with his own experience of "walking into the lecture hall, I see the lectern." And here he pushed to the extreme the principle of the a priori "material determinateness of form" that he had introduced in his qualifying dissertation in connection with Lask's thought. "What do 'I' see?," he asked. "Brown surfaces that intersect at right angles? No, I see something else. A box, and indeed a larger one with a smaller one built on top of it? Absolutely not, I see the lectern at which I will speak, you see the lectern from which you will be addressed, at which I have already spoken. . . . I see the lectern all in one stroke, as it were." And again, "Immediately, the lectern is given to me. . . . I see this as such and do not see something like impressions and sense data; I have no consciousness of impressions whatsoever." The something that immediately gives itself is not a brute and irrational sense datum, but rather "this object that we all perceive here somehow has the specific significance 'lectern,' " is "laden with a significance," is immediately seen "*as* lectern." Nor do I first see a naked thing and then build it up into the full-blown implement, namely, academic lectern, by attaching this practical significance to it through acts of positing. There is "no—as one says—context of founding, as if I first saw brown intersecting surfaces, which then give themselves to me as box, then as a desk, further as a desk for academic speeches, as lectern, such that I, as it were, affixed the character of lectern to the box like a label. All this is bad, misinterpreted interpretation, a deflection from the pure gaze into lived experience" (G56/57 71, 85).

In order to get at the immediate and significant "worldly something" of the environing world, the world around us (*Umwelt*), Heidegger told his students that it can be called an *es gibt sich mir unmittelbar*, there is/it gives itself to me immediately; an *es bedeutet mir*, it signifies to me; and, most significantly, an *es weltet für mich*, it worlds for me, and *es ereignet sich*, it events/enowns itself.

> In the lived experience of seeing the lectern, something gives itself *to me* out of an immediate environing world. The environmental (lectern, book, blackboard, notebook, fountain pen, janitor, student in the duelling corps, streetcar, automobile, etc., etc.) are not things along with a specific character of significance, objects, and in addition to this also grasped as signifying this and that, but rather that which is significant is primal, gives itself to me immediately, without any mental detour via a grasping of things [*Sacherfassen*]. Living in a world around me, it signifies to me everywhere and always, it is everywhere worldish [*welthaft*], "*it worlds*," which does not coincide with "it values."

The around (*um*) of the world is a primal element of sense in which I am always already immersed, live, move, and have my being. "In the lived experience of the world around us," Heidegger wrote, "there lies absolutely no *theoretical positing* [*Setzung*]. The 'it worlds' is not theoretically established [*festgestellt*], but rather experientially lived 'as worlding.' " Lectern, seats, books, pens world immediately for the teacher and students who walk through the lecture hall door. Similarly, "there is/it gives [*es gibt*] triangles, there is/it gives Rembrandt's paintings, there is/it gives U-boats," as well as "chairs," "tables," "houses," "trees," "Mozart's sonatas." Heidegger's attempt to get at the immediate and ultimately temporal sense of the something (being) traced "genealogically" the Neo-Kantian impersonal *es gilt*, it validates, through a series of increasingly more primal impersonals: *es soll*, it oughts; *es wertet für mich*, it values for me; it gives; and finally, it signifies, it worlds, and it events/enowns.

Following his own lead in verbalizing the substantive "world," as well as the tendency in the German language itself to verbalize substantives (cf. *es herbstet schon*, it autumns/it is autumn already; *es wintert schon*, it winters; *es nachtet*, it nights; *es weihnactet sehr*, it really Christmases/it's really Christmasy), we could also use the following poetic phrases to get at the immediate signifying of worldly things: it lecterns, it chairs, it books (G56/57 88, 72–75, 94, 67).

Heidegger continued with this type of phenomenological exercise in his courses after 1919, and one can imagine that there was a lot of it going on in his seminars, many of which have the main title "Phenomenological Exercises" (*Übungen*). In WS 1921–22, his key meditation concerning comportment to being is again being "here and now . . . in this lecture hall," as well as the everyday experience of "being anxious for one's 'daily bread.' " Though his impersonals *es weltet* and *es ereignet sich* disappear after KNS 1919 and resurface only after SZ, his WS 1921–22 course expressed the same idea with the notion of immediate encounter (*Begegnis*) of its *happening* to be encountered by me. "It is thus not the case that objects are at first here [*da*] as naked realities . . . which then, in the course of experiencing, get dressed up with a *value-character* so that they do not have to run around so naked." In SS 1923, his analysis is centered on the phenomenological example of "the Da-sein of this table" in his own home. "We will," he announced, "call on the purest everydayness: dwelling at home, being-in-the-room [*Im-Zimmer-sein*] where something such as a 'table' happens to be encountered!" What better way to get at being-in-the-world than by focusing on being-in-the-house, especially since Da-sein means generally "dwelling, not running away, *here*-at-home [*Dabei*], Da-sein" (G63 7; cf. SZ 73/80). His description of family meals at the table even reminds one of his later meditations on worlding and *Ereignis* in connection with a line from Georg Trakl's poem "A Winter Evening": "There lie, in limpid brightness shown, upon the table bread and wine." Back in SS 1923, he gave still more illustrations from the world of the household: "Concernful being-in discovers the world thus, grows right into this world: table, jug, plough, saw, house, garden, field, village, path. . . . Grain, flour, bread." With such homey meditations on *die Sachen selbst* Heidegger attempted to bring home to his students the deepest meaning of the venerable ontology that had been initiated by the Greeks. He emphasized again and again that the Greek word *ousia*, being, substance, originally meant "household," and pointed out that the basic concept in ethics, namely, *ethos*, originally meant "home," "dwelling place" (G63 88, 112; G61 90–92). His illustration of the sense of being through the table in his own home was not arbitrary.

As in KNS 1919, Heidegger started in SS 1923 with the traditional "faulty description" of the "being-here of the world." "As what is [the Dasein of the table] encountered? A thing in space; as a spatial thing it is also a material thing. It is so and so heavy, so and so colored, formed in such a way, with rectangular or round wood; so high, so wide, with a smooth or rough surface. . . . The authentic being of the table is: spatial thing." To this he contrasted his own more faithful and "devout" phenomenological description:

> Nothing of what was mentioned in the first description is to be found in the concrete dealings [*Umgang*] that dwell [at home with the table]. . . . In *the* room here [*da*] it is *the* table here [*da*] (not 'a' table alongside many others in other rooms and houses) at which one sits *in order to* write, to eat, to sew, to play. You can—e.g., while visiting—immediately tell by looking at it: it is a writing table, dinner table, sewing table; primally, it is so encountered in itself. The character of 'in order to do something' is not foisted on it. . . . Its standing-here in the room means: to play this role in such and such characterized usage. . . .

With the same immediacy as the lectern in KNS 1919, the table "in-dicatively signi-fies [*be-deutet*] itself into the 'here' of a whiling [*Verweilen*] and situation of everydayness. . . . [C]orresponding to its awhileness [*Jeweiligkeit*], it *tarries* throughout it in this being-here" (G63 88–90, 95). It worlds, it homes, it tables, it jugs, as it were—without the need for any act of thinking or positing. As Heidegger put this point much later in his lecture "The Thing," "The jug is a thing insofar as it things. Out of the thinging of the thing events/enowns . . . the presencing of what presences in the manner of a jug." "The thing whiles [*verweilt*] the fourfold. The thing things world." "The world presences by worlding" (VA 170–73/PLT 177–81).

Heidegger did not deny that one *can* see the lectern and the table as mere spatio-temporal objects with logical meaning and value externally attached to them, but only maintained that this is a basic modification of how we primally see them, namely, as practically significant. "I can of course," he wrote in KNS 1919, "look away from all that belongs to the lectern, delete everything down to the mere impression of brown. . . . [But] does it world in the brown [of the lectern] as such and grasped as datum? . . . The impression is itself here, but only through my having destroyed the environmental, having deleted, looked away, . . . and pursued theory, primarily *in* the theoretical attitude." "The something in any sense, after whose 'there-is-ing/it-giving' [*es-geben*] we questioned, does not world. The worldish is extinguished." This modifying is what Heidegger called the "objectifying" and "theorizing" of the world. Regarding worldly content-sense, it has the form of a designifying or deworlding of the significant worlding of the world. "The 'it worlds' is already extinguished in [thingliness]. The thing is merely still here as such a thing, i.e., it is real, it exists. . . . What is significant is de-signified down to the remnant: real-being" (G56/57 85, 73, 89–91).

In its "origination out of the lived experience of the environing world," the "process of theorizing" undergoes "various levels," which can be traced in a "genealogy." The initial "*step into the theoretical* that determines everything else" in both Aristotelian-Scholastic realism and Neo-Kantian transcendental idealism is simply to take the world to be "given," as in the questions, "Is there something given?" "Is there given an external world?" In the experience of "a *given* environing world," the " 'it worlds' is already no longer primal. 'Given' is already a quiet, still inconspicuous, and yet indeed actual theoretical reflection on it. . . . 'Givenness' signifies the first objectifying encroachment." From this theoretical *es gibt* one must, of course, distinguish Heidegger's own operative nontheoretical notion of it as equivalent to it-worlds. For example, "what is significant . . . gives itself to me immediately. . . . '*it worlds*.' " The next level of theorizing involves taking the reflectively given lectern or table as a "thing": "If now the authentic sense of the environmental, its character of significance, is at it were raided and robbed, then what was already posited as given is dimmed down into a mere thing." This leads to the "extinguishing of the context of the situation" that lends "unity" to environmental beings, e.g., "the objects on my writing table build a situation." "I do not see [the lectern] merely isolated. . . . I see the lectern in an orientation, illumination, a background." Or in experiencing a "sunrise" on top of a mountain, there is a unified context of "the sun's halo, the clouds, the masses of rock." "On the other hand, a pure theoretical objectivity is possible. The objects are no longer held together through the situation; they are isolated. . . . The situational character disappears. The unity of the situation explodes." The things "stand here merely as facts." Another level of theorizing occurs with "the designifying of the secondary sensuous qualities (colors, tones) into physicalistic invariants," the so-called primary quantitative qualities that are then reduced to mathematical values (G56/57 87–90, 71–73, 205–206, 209).

Further, "this datum [the thing] is taken as something psychical," a sense datum "*in* my consciousness," so that we now have the " 'burning' problem of the reality of the external world" that is answered in different ways by realism and idealism. But "the question, 'Is this lectern (just as I experience in the environing world) real?,' is an *absurd* question" because, as an intentional disclosure, the very question "distorts the sense" of "my environing world" by asking about a "de-signified derivative," and also because "the environmental has its genuine self-showing in itself. The genuine solution of the problem of the reality of the external world lies in the insight that it is not at all a problem, but rather an absurdity." Finally, the "absolutizing of the theoretical and the logical" takes place in Neo-Kantianism (especially Natorp) where the sense datum is "suspended" and taken as a brute irrational "X" that "acquires meaning in any sense only in the context of theoretical objectification" through formal logical categories (G56/57 78–87, 91–92, 108).

The being-here of world can generally be characterized as the *Umwelt*, the environing world, since world is precisely "around" us as a dynamic element of sense in which we are immersed like life "in God" or the mystic in *unio mystica.* The worldly spheres of implements, others, and even myself are different spheres of the topological here or around of world. But Heidegger reserves the term *Umwelt* to describe the sphere of implements, using withworld (*Mitwelt*) and selfworld (*Selbstwelt*) for the other spheres. In the flow of experience we are always oriented primarily to one of these "worlds of caring," while the other two are there in the background. "That in which a factical life is caringly immersed [*aufgeht*], that from which it lives, is always in one of the basic highlightable worlds that we characterize as the *environing world*, the *withworld*, and the *selfworld*" (G56/57 72; G61 130, 94; G63 102; G58 33–46).

Environing World

Heidegger explained in SS 1923 that the being-here of beings within the world is a significant "being-here-to-hand" (*Zu-handen-da-sein*) for our *Umgang*, our dealings, going around, playing around. "The character of the being-here of the world is terminologically fixed as *significance*. Significant means: being, being-here in the manner of a specifically encountered signifying." There is an ontological difference to be observed here between the practically "to-hand" being that is significant and significance (being), between the disclosed being and its disclosedness (*Erschlossenheit*). "Significance is not a thingly characteristic, but rather a characteristic of being." "Significance is a categorial determination of world; the objects in a world, the worldly, worldish objects are lived in the character of significance." Our dealings are usually turned directly toward worldish things as opposed to the worldly significance itself, which is a background of interpretedness (*Ausgelegtheit*) upon which we can understand things "as" this or that and thus deal with them. "The object of care is not significance as a categorial characteristic, but rather in each case something worldly. . . . Significance is not as such expressly experienced; but it can be experienced" (G63 93–96; G61 90–93).

Things are *bedeutsam*, significant in the literal sense of being the dynamic (worlding) sites of a *Be-deuten*, a significant pointing and indicative signi-fy-ing. "Significant means: being, being-here in the how of a specific *Be-deuten*." In the phenomenological tradition out of which Heidegger was working (compare the "doctrine of *Bedeutung*" in his qualifying dissertation), the term *Bedeutung* usually means the noetic meaning-intention that animates the flesh of our verbal or written signs, but Heidegger extended the activity of signifying to the things themselves in the environing world. It is not only we who mean something in our speaking and writing, but rather things, too, far from being brute irrational objects, are themselves intentional environmental marks or signs that gesture and signify. The flesh of the world itself is always already ensouled, animated, alive with significance. In their it-worlds and it-signifies, the lectern, classroom, table, house are woven into contexts of sigificance, which, as the quasi-texts of a kind of primal writing, can be read and interpreted. Heidegger here took up the theory of signs in Husserl's First Investigation and collapsed its division of signs into the nonsignificant "indications" of things and the "significations" of discourse, such that indicative things are seen to be significant and significant discourse is seen to be indicative (becoming "formal indication" in philosophy). Referring to the First Investigation, he wrote in SZ that "being-a-sign-for can itself be formalized into a *universal kind of relation* so that the sign-structure itself provides an ontological clue for 'characterizing' all beings in any sense" (G63 93; SZ 103/108–109, 220/209).

Signifying is more specifically a "signifying that *verweist*," ap-points, assigns, de-signates, that is, refers a to-hand thing to that with which it is contextually involved. One type of assignment is the from-which (*das Woraus*), that from which a to-hand thing has come to be. For example, Heidegger's notes read, "made out of-, the from-which itself; wood, to order [it for the table]. Wheat, flour, bread." Another assigment is the to-which (*Wozu*) or the for-which (*Wofür*) the to-hand thing is marked, understood, and used. "Something [is] in use for something." "That which is encountered 'worldishly' . . . indicates itself as being useful to-, used to-, no longer really suited for-, no longer used to-; its being-here is being-*here-for*. 'To-this' means: to-hand for *being-occupied with*-, for a dwelling at-home with [*bei*] it." The table is that "at which one sits down *to* write, to eat, to sew, to play." "The to-which and for-which [are] . . . the daily meal, the customary [*gewöhnliche*] writing and working, the sewing from time to time, playing" (G63 98–99, 112, 93, 90).

Through these types of assignments, a thing signi-fies (worlds) itself within, out of, and into the being-here of the contextual whole of assignments into which it is inscribed. "The phenomenal whole of disclosedness, out of which something factically encountered indicatively signi-fies itself into its here, is itself a characteristic context of assignment": for example, the "unitary context of significance" of the university classroom in which Heidegger's lectern of KNS 1919 belongs, or the context of the domestic world of "jug, plough, saw, house, garden, field, village, path" in which the table belongs. Likewise, the spatiality of the "around" of the environing world has to be understood out of and as a context of assignments of places to others places, and not as consisting of brute spatial points and distances. "Factical spatiality . . . has its distances, as here is: too far, nearby, through the street, through the kitchen, a stone's throw, back of the cathedral, and the like. A familiarity with its assignments at a particular time lies in this spatiality." And already in KNS 1919, Heidegger wrote, "On a hiking trip I come to Freiburg for the first time and, entering the city, ask: 'Where is the quickest path to Münster?' This spatial orienting has nothing to do with a geometrical spatial orientation as such" (G63 99, 95–96, 101–102, 86, 112; G56/57 86).

The text of the world is a context, a shifting quasi-sign system in which any single thing is what it is only by its signi-fying and as-signing to other things and activities. The table is "as" a table, the jug is "as" jug on the basis of its relations to other articles in the house and the activities here. There is no such thing as a coffee spoon apart from the rest of the cutlery, or "right- and left-handed hammers." As Heidegger will say in SZ, while taking up his old example of the table, "*an* implement never 'is.'" In KNS 1919, he performs the following thought-experiment: "Let us imagine a Senegalese negro suddenly transplanted here out of his hut." Would this individual see the thing Heidegger is standing at "as" a "lectern"? Dwelling within a different "worldview" and context of significance, he would rather see "perhaps something that has to do with magic, or something behind which one could find good protection against arrows and stones." There are no nonrelational substances in the world—only insubstantial contextualized sites of an ecstatic worlding, signifying, and referral that is simultaneously deferral into a futural for-which that never gets completely fulfilled. What will one put on "the table" for dinner tomorrow? What will one say at "the lectern" during the next class (SZ 145/143, 92/97; G56/57 71-72)?

Withworld

In SS 1919, Heidegger stressed that "the practical-historical I is necessarily of a *social* nature, it stands in a context of life with other Ies [*Iche*]." In the previous semester, he had already indicated that the immediate worlding of the environing world lights up not only things such as the lectern and the sunrise, but also the "Others" who are or could be woven into the "context of the situation": for example, the students with their "notebooks," the "janitor," the "student in the duelling corps," the "farmer from the far regions of the Black Forest," the "Senegalese negro" who might visit the class. In WS 1919-20, he gave more examples of "our withworld—parents, brothers and sisters, acquaintances . . . strangers . . . the man with the crutch . . . the little girl here with her doll." He contrasted this view with that of the traditional problem of other minds, in which it is a question of the "very fuddled process" of inferring and positing other subjectivities from one's sense impressions of their bodily expressions: "Even [other human beings] are given to me at first through sense impressions . . . that are produced by psychical processes; I grasp this psychical connection in a unified manner as soul, subject, an other I" (G56/57 210, 78, 81-82; G58 33). But in the lived experience of the lecture hall, the world of Others "gives itself to me immediately, without any mental detour via a grasping of things." Taking up Heidegger's term "withworld" after 1919 for this social aspect of the immediate worlding and eventing of the world, we could by right again use poetic language here: it withworlds, it students, it janitors.

In WS 1921–22 and SS 1923, he explained that, though the content-sense of the being-here and the around of the world includes Others, these with-worldly Others are "here" in such a way that, unlike the lectern and the table, they also intentionally have and share the content-sense of the world "with" me. We are not merely "in front" of but also "alongside" one another. Personal relational sense is interwoven in the withworldly content-sense of interpersonal interrelational sense. "This *disclosedness* [of signi-fying]," Heidegger wrote, "shows itself in two characters: 1) in the character of the before-the-hand-availability [*Vorhandenheit*] [of what is to-hand]; 2) in withworldly *Vor-schein*, ap-pearance, shining forth, showing up, turning up (i.e., in bringing-to-ap-pearance the withwordly [Others], holding the withworldly [Others] in appear-ance)." Others are also inscribed in the contextual whole of as-signments, such that things in one's environing world signify the "other lives . . . one 'has to do' with, with whom one works, plans something," just as in turn Others and I myself are referentially directed to the environmental things and activities with them. "In its being-*here*, the here that is available-before-the-hand brings to appearance 'the Others,' a specific circle . . . of those who live-with . . . he who gave the book; the carpenter who made the table; or he who has a better library." Things signify and world not only other things but also the somewhat ghostly being-here of Others, who always show up "here" in thingly traces even though they may be absent or deceased, or the "Other" may be one's childhood that appears in a broken toy from days past. Others haunt things. The types of signification at work here are a "for whom," "from whom," or some variant of "with whom." These significations are here even when we come across completely strange items: for example, those that the previous ten-ants, "the strangers," left behind. "Even where *something alien* penetrates into our closest world and we take exception to it, precisely here the character of disclosedness [of Others] announces itself in our dwelling on it, searching around. . . . For whom is it? What is it supposed to be? Who made it?" (G63 94–95, 99).

Heidegger's key illustration here was again "the Da-sein of this table" in his own home with his wife and two *Buben*, boys, who were born in 1919 and 1920. It is the table for the family's "daily meal," for the wife's "sewing," for the "playing" of the boys, for the father/husband's "writing," and for the friend's "visit." His letters to Blochmann offer us a window into this domestic world of Heidegger the young husand and father. For example, on May 1, 1919, he wrote to her that "my life is quiet but rich and has a beautiful *imme-diacy* in Elfride and the little farmer [Jörg]. And what I can give and receive in friendship is for me an enhancement of my life" (emphasis added). Heidegger's phenomenological meditation in 1923 took up precisely the "immediacy" expressed here:

> Here and there [the table] shows lines—the boys like to busy themselves at the table; these lines are not mere interruptions in the paint, but rather: that was the boys, and they are still that. This side is not the eastward side, and this narrow side so many cm. shorter than the other, but rather it is the side at which my wife sits in the evening when she wishes to stay up and read; here at the table that time we had such and such discussion; here this decision was made that time with a *friend*, here at one time that *work* was written, that *holiday* celebrated.

The table is "like other 'things' [in the house], for example, a toy, worn out and almost unrecognizable—it is my childhood. In a corner of the basement stands a pair of old skis; the one is broken in half; what stands here is . . . the skier of that time, of that daredevil trip with so and so." Likewise, "this book here is a gift from X; this one here was bound by such and such bookbinder . . . this library is not as good an A's, far better than B's. . . . These are characters of encounter. What needs to be questioned now is how they make up the being-here of the world." In the table's being-here, there also worlds the presence and absence of friend, wife, husband, child, bookseller: "That which is encountered is what it is and how it is as "*the* table here" at which *we* . . . eat our daily meal, at which . . . that game was played in which these specific human beings *were here*-at-our-house, i.e., *are* still here with us in the being-here of the table. . . . The Others are here in that which is so encountered in everydayness" (HB 16, 13; G63 90–91, 98).

Selfworld

The disclosed context of assignments that makes up the being-here of the world includes also the personal selfworld. "In the most immediate everyday dealings, the environing world is always also here as the withworld and the selfworld." The environing world and withworld signi-fy "for me" such that the type of as-signment operative here is this "for" or "for the sake of" (*umwillen*). And if the world is also its relation to me, then in turn I myself am referentially directed to the world. My relations to these things and to these Others—that is my self: teacher at the lectern, husband, friend, child. My self is being-in-a-world: in-the-house, in-the-family, in-the-classroom. I am in the world like the mystic is "in God" as participating in God. My self is woven into and mediated by the topological here of the environing world and withworld—a textured self contextualized in the text of the world. Thus in my "self-having," I have myself as a personal worldly content-sense: "I en-counter myself in the world in which I live, to which I give myself over and concern myself [*abgebe*] . . . in my surroundings, in my environing world, in my withworld." My self-having is precisely my "having of . . . comportment [to the world]." When I am concerned about myself, I am concerned about my environmental withworldly self: "[Life] cares for [*besorgt*] itself insofar as it meets up with itself in a worldly manner in the here that happens to be encountered by it [*im begegenden Da*]." "As selfworld, the 'me' for which I care is experienced in specific significances that are wrapped up [*aufgeht*] with the complete lifeworld in which the environing world and withworld are always also here with the selfworld" (G63 102, 94; G9 29; G61 94–95).

It is for these reasons and not because he was pursuing an existentialized transcendental solipsism that Heidegger said that I am the world and that the world is a "category" of factical life. The "world," he wrote, "happens to be encountered [*begegnet*] as *that-which-is-cared-for*. . . . [Being 'in'] is that which the world en-counters, and in such a way that it is in this world as that which is cared for, the world-being-here. . . . it 'is' its world that happens to be encountered by it." Heidegger decentered and desubstantialized the self, letting it be seen not as a worldless I, a self-conscious transcendental ego, a subject capable of existing on its own, but rather as a project that is ecstatically related to other selves and things. "The *selfworld* may not first of all be identified with the 'I.' " The selfworld is not "the subjective isolation of a liberated ego. . . . Selfwordly experience has nothing to do with psychological and indeed theoretical-psychological reflection, inner perception of psychic experiences, processes, and acts" (G63 86; G61 94–95). The self does not have to transcend the alleged empty container of consciousness to make contact with the world, but rather, as with the other spheres of world, there is an immediate worlding of the fully environmental withworldly selfworld, such that again one can poetically say of the self that, as it were, it husbands, it wifes, it friends.

The disclosed context of assignments making up the fabric of environing world, withworld, and selfworld "is encountered with the trait of *familiarity* [*Vertrautheit*] at a particular time. . . . that which is encountered is well-known (*hexis, aletheia*) . . . as the where-in [*Worin*] one knows one's way around." In other words, "the multiplicity of assignments is nothing other than that wherein concern *sich aufhält*, holds itself, dwells, takes up residence." The sense of the content (*Gehalt*) of world provides intentional comportment (*Verhalten*) with the toward-upon-which (*Worauf*) of a *Halt*, a hold, something to hold and hang onto. The being-here of the world provides this having of it (*Haben, hexis, habitus*), and this dwelling and whiling at-home in it (*Verweilen bei*), with the familiarity and awhileness (*Jeweiligkeit*) of its *Aufenthalt*, abode; its *Habe*, household; its *Gewohnheit*, habitation—in short, with its *ethos*, home. To be in a world is to in-habit the habitat of a world or, better, worlds. "*Gewöhnlich, Gewohnheit*, habitation," Heidegger wrote, "present basic categories of life in its facticity." It worlds, it homes (G63 99–103, 87, 109; G56/57 4; G61 92, 18, 64, 96).

The Dasein of Personal Life

Heidegger's qualifying dissertation had also expressed a second requirement for rethinking the question about being, namely, "the insertion of the
problem of the categories into the problem of . . . the subject." Heidegger now
made the decisive move in fulfilling this requirement. In 1921–22, he defined
relational sense as a "comporting oneself to . . . , standing in relation to . . . ,
having a relation. . . . [Comportment] is graspable in view of the relation, is to
be interrogated on the basis of its sense in the direction of the relation: *relational sense.*" Whereas the accusative terminus of the verb "to live" expresses
the content-sense of comportment, its "intransitive-verbal meaning" expresses
relational sense. "To live as intransitive: to be alive, someone lives (in the sense:
he lives intensely); 'he lives dissolutely'; 'he lives withdrawn'; 'he lives only
halfway'; 'one lives thus' " (G61 52–53, 82).

Under the influence of Schleiermacher, Kierkegaard, Luther, Pascal, Nietzsche, Dilthey, Scheler, and Bergson, Heidegger radicalized his earlier theme of
a pretheoretical "living spirit" modeled on the "historical personality" of the
"inward Dasein" of medieval mysticism and continued to speak in distinctively
personalist terms: for example, "your personal Dasein," "one's ownmost personality," "the most personal experience" (1918); "each Dasein of personal
life," the "genuineness of your personal being," "personal *Existenz*," "my personal rhythmic," "my I," the "historical I" (1919–20); "my concrete factical
life," my "I am," the "having-me-myself" that possesses an irreducible "(I)
'am'-sense" (1920–22); " 'our' 'own' Dasein" (1923); "*my* Dasein" (1924)
(HB 7–14; G56/57 4; G58 197, 33; G61 174, 80; G9 29; G63 7; BZ 13). Such
is the tenor of the young Heidegger's personalist formulation of the question
about being, which gives, worlds, events itself "in and through [my personal]
life," my "personal Da-sein." Here "in this place, in this lecture hall," at this
kitchen table, before this sunrise—"you before me, I before you, we with each
other."

In order to get at the personal relational sense of comportment-to-something, Heidegger's KNS 1919 course showed that the pretheoretical "primal
something" (being) takes the form of a "something gives itself *to me*," of an
"it worlds for me." He invited his students to perform the phenomenological
exercise of describing their lived experience of " 'seeing your seat' " when each
one walks into the lecture hall:

> *I* bring to givenness to myself a new lived experience not only for myself, but
> ask you all, each individuated I-myself who sits here, to do the same. . . .
> You come as usual [*wie gewöhnlich*] into this lecture hall at the usual [*ge-
> wohnte*] hour and go to *your* usual seat. Concentrate on this lived experience
> of 'seeing your seat'. . . .

Heidegger showed the same point with his own experience of "walking into the lecture hall, I see the lectern" and, as a very short man, having to make do with the high lectern: "I see it not merely isolated, I see the desk placed too high for me. I immediately see a book lying on it as annoying me." That *"my* seeing [the lectern, etc.] is something individual in the highest degree" applies equally to the unique experience of the students, the "janitor," the "student in the duelling corps," the "farmer from the far regions of the Black Forest," the "Senegalese negro," or whoever else might enter the lecture hall. "*My* I goes completely out of itself, swings *along* and resonates [*schwingt mit*] in this 'seeing' [of the lectern], just as what is peculiar to the negro in question simultaneously reverberates [*mitanklingt*] in his experience of the 'something with which *he* does not know where to begin.'" And the same holds for all the different personal Daseins around "the table" in Heidegger's house: father/professor, wife/mother, the boys, the friend, the stranger. "Only in this simultaneous reverberation of one's own I at the particular time is something experienced environmentally, does it world, and where and when it worlds for me *I* am one way or the other completely here [*dabei*]" (G56/57 70–73).

Heidegger contrasted this immediate personal experience with theoretical experience and with the description of the human being in traditional theory. In the question, "Is there something given?," or "Is there (given) an external world?," what gets suppressed in the experience of the "worldish something" is the "given for *me*"—this unique human being here and now. The world is objectively experienced as a "desert" of "absolute thingliness" in which no experiencing persons appear to whom these things are given:

> Let us immerse ourselves again in the experience [of the question]. Is there in it something like the meaningful pointing back to me, who stands here at the lectern, with this name and at this age? Check it for yourselves by all of you asking: does there lie in the question, "Is there something given?," a for me (Fräulein Arts Candidate), a for me (Herrn Dr. X), a for me (Herrn Law student)? Obviously not.

My theoretical experience of the objectivist question shuts down the worlding of the world "for me" and prevents my I from going forth and resonating in the experience. Just as Heidegger himself had previously done in his dissertations, in the objectivist question I have "struck out, disregarded, suspended [*ausschaltete*] my historical I and pursued theory":

> The something in general, about whose "there-is-ing/it-giving" we asked, does not world. . . . This grasping and establishing [*Fest-stellung*] as object in general lives at the expense of pushing back my own I. In the sense of the something in general lies the fact that *I* do *not* simultaneously resonate in the establishing of it as such, but rather this co-resonating, this co-going-forth of mine is suppressed. Object-being, standing-over-against-being as such

does not concern *me*. . . . The objective, the known [*Er-kannte*] is as such dis-tanced, lifted out of genuine living experience. (G56/57 68, 85, 73)

All that remains of personal relational sense is the residue of an anonymous and deathly theoretical I. "It is the essence of a thing and a thingly context to give itself only in theoretical comportment and for the theoretical I. . . . [Here] I am directed to something, but *I* do not live (as a historical I) towards this or that worldish [being]." In the mode of the theoretical I, the person has been reduced to a bloodless knower that lacks all emotional and practical relations to the world. "Theoretical comportment places itself out of the experience of life in that it directs itself extensively to pure states of affairs in which all emotional relation is suppressed." Insofar as the modification from the pretheoretical primal source to the level of "theorizing" also suppresses the concrete personal I for whom the world worlds, Heidegger referred to this theorizing not only as designifying, but also as *Entleben*, deliving. This is the desert where the "tree of life" withers and "one runs out of breath and cannot live":

> Lived experience of the environing world is de-lived to the residue: knowing something real as such. . . . Thing-experience [*Erfahrung*] is undoubtedly lived experience [*Erlebnis*], but understood in terms of its origination out of the lived experience of the environing world it is already de-living, un-life [*Ent-lebnis*]. (G56/57 74, 211, 112, 89–90)

The delived relational sense effected by traditional philosophy appears not only as "knowing," but also as a "reified" and depersonalized ego. According to the objectifying attitude of modern psychologism and Neo-Kantian logical theory, the self is a "complex of [psychical] processes." Or it is taken to be the factual instantiation of a universal and impersonal rational ego, as in the question, "Is there something given?": "Just through the fact that the sense of the question is in general related to an I, it is not related to my *I*. . . . The 'is there/does it give' is a 'there-is-ing/it-giving' for an I—and yet it is not *I* for *whom*, to *whom* the sense of the question has a relation." Drawing on his earlier investigations of the haecceity of "individual-being," Heidegger objected that originally one "does not experience the 'I' as standing in a region, as the individuation of a 'universal,' as a *case* of—but rather experiencing is the experiencing of the 'I' as self." "Factical Dasein is what it is always only as one's own Dasein, not as the Dasein in general of some universal humanity." Similarly, the traditional definition of human being as *zoon logon echon*, the living being having reason, *animal rationale*, the rational animal, places the human being "in the order of things that is indicated through the objective series: plant, animal, human being, demon, God." More specifically, here "it is a question of specifying the endowments [reason] to a pregiven thing [animal], which, on the basis of these, is then accredited subsequently with a determinate mode of being and is left indifferently within the realm of real-being" (G56/57 61, 68–70; G9 29; PIA 239; G63 21).

In his formula *cogito sum*, Descartes indeed pointed beyond this traditional reification in that he concentrated on the "I am," but he also aggravated matters in that he determined the "I am" precisely as the "I think," as the substantial being of the "thinking thing," and thereby inspired the "metaphysics of the I and egoist idealism" in "Kantian theory of knowledge" and "absolute idealism":

> The "*sum*" is indeed first also for Descartes, but precisely here already lies the mistake: he does not remain here and has already the preconception of its sense of being in the mode of a mere conclusion [*Feststellung*]. . . . the "*sum*," its being and its categorial structure, became in no way problematical for him, but rather the meaning of the word "*sum*" was intended in an indifferent, formally objective sense. . . .

In light of this crossroads in Descartes, "what is important is precisely to pursue the sense of the '*sum*' in the '*cogito-sum*' in a more original problematic." One needs to get at the primal "(I) 'am'-sense" of "the full concrete historically factical self," of "my concrete factical life" (G9 29–30; G61 173–74). The self is not a thing, an assemblage of thingly parts, or an instance of a universal, but rather a nonobjectified, unique, unitary, personal, self-caring, and ultimately temporal site of the historical worlding of being.

Taking up the concept of *privatio* in Luther and *steresis* in Aristotle, Heidegger told his students in 1921–22 that, "in its relational sense taken in the widest sense, life is: caring for, being anxious for [*sorgen um*] one's 'daily bread.' 'To go hungry,' 'to be needy' [*Darbung*] (*privatio* [deprivation], *carentia* [going without, lack]) is the basic how of the sense of being of life regarding its relationality and enactment." Life is always the "factically hungry life" of an intentional "being out after something." "The basic sense of the factical movement of life is *caring (curare)*," a position that derives not only from Heidegger's readings of the New Testament and Aristotle's ethics, but simultaneously from his reworking the definition of teleological "living spirit" as "drive," "life-will," and mystical "love" in his qualifying dissertation. Insofar as it is defined by the absence, scarcity, and hunger of a "not" (*Nicht*), a "not yet," and a "being-possible," the person/world relation is encountered in "questionableness." "Being itself [is] never a possible object of having, insofar as what comes toward it as an issue is it itself, *being, to be*." Factical life is not arrival, but perpetual Parousia and the pilgrimmage of "the on-the-way of itself to itself" (G61 90, 155, 148, 185; PIA 240; G20 408/295; G63 17, 7).

I am not "in possession" of my life as an "object" that is present-before-the-hand and available "like jewels on a platter." Where it looks like people are leading an "objective life" that is secure (literally, without care), satisfied, and full, then it is only that the hunger "secretly eats itself into and has eaten itself into" their hearts. "Secure objectivity is insecure flight in the face of facticity." Our primal relation to ourselves and the world is then hardly an objective theoretical "knowing," but rather "caring for the morrow," restlessness (*Unruhe*), and "worry [*Bekümmerung*] of the self for itself." "Existence-sense is precisely *the* sense of being that can be gained not from the 'is' . . . that objectifies, but rather from the basic experience of *worried* having of itself." I do not have myself in the same way that things have properties. Since that about which the self cares is itself precisely as being-in-a-world, caring entails a transitive concern (*Besorgen*) about one's environing world and solicitude for one's withworld. "Being-in-the-world does not mean occurring among other things, but rather: dwelling at-home in the around of the encountered world about which one is concerned. The genuine way of being in a world is itself *caring*, as ordering, performing, taking into possession, preventing, guarding against loss, etc." "In the here about which one is concerned, the withworld . . . is [also] that about which one is concerned." Self-care thus means care for its caring relation to world. "Caring always cares for itself in some way. . . . It cares for itself in that it finds itself in a worldly manner in the here that is encountered" (G9 38, 32, 30; G61 90; G63 102).

The significance of the world is a "here" of illumination (*Erhellung*), relucence (*Reluzenz*), "disclosedness," or unconcealment (*aletheia*). This "disclosedness stands in *care* at a particular time. The multiplicity of assignments is nothing other than that wherein concern resides." As being-in and dwelling at-home in the luminous here of its world, caring has the corresponding role of "letting be encountered," "illuminating," unconcealing (*aletheuein*), "disclosing," or announcing (*Melden*) (G61 128, 152, 185, 138; G63 99, 101, 96). This disclosive role of caring has the three characters of affect (mood), interpretedness (understanding), and discourse. These aspects of being-in-the-world are also radicalizations of the pretheoretical *modus significandi, modus intelligendi*, and "absolute devotion and temperamental immersion" that Heidegger found in his earlier investigations of the medieval mystical experience of being "in God."

"Affect" illuminates world in the character of its "to-me-being," its mattering to me. In moods, the world announces itself as something that "pesters" or "plagues" me, "gnaws" and "eats at" my "factically hungry life," such that "day and night [it] does not let me come to rest." I toss and turn in "restlessness." "If factical life is wholly in anxious concern [*Besorgnis*], then such a thing as that which plagues (plaguing [*Quälen*]), a gnawing, or boring can be factically encountered." Thus it is incorrect "to characterize these (formal) characters simply as 'feelings.' 'Feeling' is a psychological category" that points only to interior processes. But moods also disclose the world. It is in announcing the world in its "to-me-being" that affect discloses the "me" to whom the world matters. "In the manner of plaguing, something announces itself that eats at life. . . . a *coming forth* in facticity (the 'eating away,' gnawing) announces itself, wherein the 'at-which' of the eating comes forth: 'life itself.' " This "to me" is illuminated in an exemplary manner in the particular affect of "horrescence" or "anxiety." The "special announcement-sense" of affect is not on the level of "directives forward and backward (which provide knowledge) or reports." Rather, world and self are announced simply as *befindlich*, as affectively found and situated in this or that mood. There is "no theoretical context of founding" where we would first know and then be affected by the world, but rather a primal "context of enactment, *adfectus*—being to me!" Philosophical interpretation thus amounts to an explicit "apprehension of the factical that is already 'found' [*befindlich*] in an inconspicuous having" (G61 137–38, 195, 180; G63 17; G56/57 211).

Affect works hand in hand with pretheoretical understanding. If affect makes up one's moodful prehaving (*Vorhaben*) of world and self, it is understanding or interpretedness (*Ausgelegtheit*) that makes up one's preconception (*Vorgriff*). The disclosedness of worldly significance as a whole of assignments is held within the "preunderstanding" of interpretedness, such that in our dealings we "know our way around" in the world. There is always "a determinate preunderstanding that Dasein has of itself: the guiding 'as what' in which it addresses 'itself.' " This interpretedness is articulated in advance also in the preconception of discourse (*Rede*), which is not ruled by logical "grammar," but by the "the immanent speaking of life itself." The translation, "a being endowed with reason," does "not touch the decisive sense of *zoon logon echon*. In the classical scientific philosophy of the Greeks (Aristotle), *logos* never means 'reason,' but rather discourse, conversation; therefore, the human being is a being that has its world in the manner of something addressed." "It is the achievement of discourse to make something accessible as openly here. . . . As such, *logos* has the exemplary possibility of the performance of *aletheuein* (making what was previously concealed, covered up to be as unconcealed, openly here, available)." The prior illumination of world through the prehaving and preconception of affect, understanding, and discourse is precisely the "pre-care" and "pre-encountering" that guides the more concrete care of our everyday dealings (G63 15–16, 31, 21, 27, 11, 98; G56/57 116; G61 83).

As care, mood, understanding, and language, factical life is that in and through which world worlds. Does not this worlding-for-me already suggest the time of an *Er-eignis* for me?

13 | *Ereignis*

Uɴᴛɪʟ ʀᴇᴄᴇɴᴛʟʏ ᴡᴇ had always thought that the terms it-worlds, *Es gibt* (there is/it gives), and *Ereignis* (event/enownment) belonged only to the lexicon of Heidegger's later thought. Here, I discuss how the young Heidegger already described the temporalizing-sense of the being-question as *Es gibt* and *Ereignis*. Though the term *Ereignis* disappeared after 1919 and resurfaced again only in the 1930s, I show that, like the term it-worlds, it continued to be operative in Heidegger's early Freiburg period when he began to speak of temporalizing-sense as kairological time (1920–21) and as *kinesis* (1921–23). The present chapter thus pursues the following course of analysis. I begin by focusing on the nonpersonal depth-dimension of *Ereignis* and showing how, in continuity with Heidegger's earlier concepts of haecceity and analogy in the heterology of his qualifying dissertation, this *Ereignis* is conceived of as an an-archic differentiation of being into the alterity of historical periods, societies, and individual personalities. I then examine how after 1919 Heidegger continued to explore and deepen this basic insight under the new rubrics of kairological time and *kinesis*, which stress how the absent, nonobjectifiable, noncalculable depth-dimension of the futurity of being is temporalized and individuated in unique situations. Finally, I emphasize the profoundly personal aspect of *Ereignis*, show how this continues to be operative in the development of Heidegger's early Freiburg period, and argue that it entails both a personalist thoughtpath and a fundamental critique of the modern metaphysics of subjectivity. I illustrate these points by again taking up Heidegger's own phenomenological exercises of describing concrete phenomena such as the lectern, sunrises in the Black Forest and in Sophocles's *Antigone*, and the table in his own home.

It Events/Enowns

In WS 1921–22, Heidegger defined the sense of the enactment of the person/world relation as follows: "Comporting oneself is also definable as a how of formal happening, proceeding—in view of how it acts, i.e., is enacted, as enactment, according to its *enactment-sense*." *Vollzug*, enactment, means the way that the intentional relation literally pulls or draws (*zieht*) from the source of possibility into full (*voll*) actuality, and can therefore also be translated as fulfillment, carrying out, or performance. " 'Life' and 'world' are not two objects subsisting in themselves like a table to which the chair standing before it is spatially related. The relationality is that of a relation, i.e., is *enacted*, lived." Enactment is the transitive sense of the verb "to live," where the object here is life itself in relation to world: "To live in the transitive sense: 'to live life,' 'to live one's work'; here mostly in compounds: 'to live through this and that'; 'to live out one's years.' " Enactment is, however, dependent upon its deeper historical sense as temporalizing. Heidegger's notes read, "But, furthermore, this [comportment] particularly as to how the enactment as enactment becomes in and for a situation, how it 'temporalizes' itself. Temporalizing is to be interpreted on the basis of *temporalizing-sense*." "The how of being-related-to-world and the world itself are in factical temporalizing." By showing that "temporality" is "the basic phenomenon of facticity," Heidegger endeavored to revive ontology from "the old metaphysics" that was fixated naively on being as unchanging presence (*Präsenz*): "It shall be shown 'in time' precisely that fundamental tasks also lie in ontology!" (G61 53, 86, 82, 97, 176; G63 31, 65, 43, 79, 3).

Beginning with his courses in 1919, Heidegger thus took up the third requirement for rethinking the question about being that he had put forward in his qualifying dissertation, namely, "history . . . must become a meaning-determining element for the problem of the categories" of being in the sense of the "something in any sense." He also continued the analysis of historical time initiated in his 1915–16 essay on history, which defined time as the "effective context" of a unique historical *Ereignis* that involves a circular movement of past, future, and present. Similarly, his KNS 1919 lecture course explored the "*Ereignis*-character" of the primal something (being) that worlds and e-vents/en-owns (*er-eignet*) for me, and in which I e-vent/en-own it to myself. Life, he explained, is always a "situation in the context of life" and "the I is itself a situation-I; the I is histor'ical,' " a "historical I." Intentionality is not only horizontally directed to the worlding of the world, but also vertically extended through the historicity of situations that build on and "permeate each other." Heidegger provided an example by recalling his own wartime experience in the previous year: "Their durations do not exclude each other (e.g., a year in the field, a semester: no objective time-concept). . . . The intentionality of all lived experiences of a situation has a definite character that springs from the whole situation. Example of a situation: 'Going through the course.' " The intentionality of the situation involves a protentional "tendency" toward something futural that is guided by a retentional "motivation" from past situations. Life is "forward-reaching [*vorgreifend*] and backward-reaching [*rückgreifend*], i.e., . . . motivated tendency or, alternatively, tendential motivation."

Thus, more formally, the "sight" and the concept (*Begriff*) of a situation involve both a preconception or precept (*Vorgriff*) and a recept (*Rückgriff*) (G56/57 205–207, 74, 116–17).

In order to illustrate *Ereignis* as the temporal sense of comportment-to-the-primal-something (it-worlds-for-me) and as the temporalizing of situations, Heidegger's lecture course of KNS 1919 set up still another contrast in his phenomenological kindergarten. He first described the theoretical experience of a sunrise in astronomy. Next to this he held up the experience of sunrise from a mountain top (for example, in an outing in "the 'free-German youth movement' ") and after a battle in Friedrich Hölderlin's translation of Sophocles's *Antigone*:

> Let us transplant ourselves into the comportment of astronomers who in astrophysics investigate the phenomenon of the sunrise as a mere process [*Vorgang*] in nature and, indifferently comporting themselves to it, merely let it run its course before them. And let us hold up beside this the lived experience of the chorus of Theban elders in Sophocles's *Antigone* who, on the first friendly morning after the victorious counteroffensive, look toward the rising sun . . . O glance of the sun, you most beautiful one, who / upon seven-throned Thebes / ever shine . . .

In the theoretical experience of the sunrise, whether in astronomy or traditional philosophy, the pretheoretical *Ereignis* of the it-worlds/breaks-forth-for-me is objectified into a *Vor-gang*, a pro-cess. Theory thereby dehistoricizes (*entgeschichtlicht*) it in two basic ways. First, not only are the worlding of the world and the personal I designified and delived into naked and discrete "things," but simultaneously their flowing circular *Ereignis* out of an unavailable future is "reified" into a "thing-time," into the static *presence* of an available pro-cess that runs its course before one's all-seeing gaze. "[The situation] contains no static moments, but rather '*Ereignisse*,' " events/enownments. The happening of the situation is no 'process'—as this is observed, for instance, in the physicist's laboratory in a theoretical attitude, e.g., an electrical discharge" (G56/57 74, 205–208, 65–66, 89).

The second way in which theory dehistoricizes the *Ereignis* of the it-worlds-for-me is by obliterating it as a personal *Ereignis* "for me." When, as a theoretically disinterested astronomer, I observe and objectify the sunrise, it now appears as a pro-cess (*Vor-gang*) that impersonally runs its course in front of me. "It simply goes-by-before [*vor-bei*], before my knowing I, has only the relation of being-known to this I, this paled I-relatedness reduced to a minimum of living experience. . . . I am directed to something, but *I* do not live (as historical I)." Thus, Heidegger concluded, "the historical I is de-historicized to the remnant of a specific I-hood as the correlate of thinghood." Not only is the *Ereignis* of the sunrise no longer uniquely for the personal I, but this I has also been broken out of the *Ereignis*, reified and depersonalized into a present-at-hand ego, and thus deprived of its historical *Ereignis*-character. "The character of the situation disappears. The unity of the situation is exploded. . . . Thereby, the situation-I, the 'historical' I, is simultaneously *driven away*. The 'dehistoricizing of the I' steps in. Suppression of the living relation of the I to a situation." The full sense of the dehistoricized temporalizing-sense effected by metaphysics is thus the static and impersonal presence of an objective something (being) over against a present-at-hand I. Here the something, being, does not event/enown for me. As another counterexample to the theoretical experience of the sunrise as process, Heidegger also dealt with the *Ereignis* of his "seeing the lectern":

> But something indeed happens [*es geschieht etwas*] [in seeing the lectern]. . . .
> The living experiencing [*Er-leben*] does not merely go by before me like a thing that I posit as object, but rather I myself e-vent/en-own it to myself [*ich selbst er-eignet es mir*], and it e-vents/en-owns itself according to its essential presencing [*es er-eignet sich seinem Wesen nach*]. (G56/57 205–206, 74–75, 89)

There is much to digest in this passage. Let us begin by noting that the *Er-eignis* of lived experience has a doubled aspect of content/relation, depth/surface, nonpersonal/personal in accord with the doubled aspect of the intentional configuration of I-comport-myself-to-something. Let us first focus more on the deep, nonpersonal temporalizing-sense of the *Ereignis* of the primal something (being) that "e-vents/en-owns itself according to its essential presencing."

What is the sense of this *es geschieht etwas*, something/it happens? Later we are told that "the sense of the something means precisely: 'what is experienceable in any sense.'" Heidegger was here critically deepening the historical heterology of being that he had developed in his qualifying dissertation and in his 1915–16 essay on history. It was then that he had first equated the "primal category" and "primal element" of being (*ens*) with "the something in any sense," "what is experienceable in any sense," and "givenness." The upshot of our analysis of Heidegger's heterology was the following: The indifference of the something (being) is marked by a transcendental inclination into heterothesis (alterity, difference) and haecceity (historical such-here-now-ness, individual-being). The givenness or "there is/it is given" (*es gibt*) of real being means that it is given as an Other that is historically such-here-now, at this particular time (*jeweilig*). In relation to its enactment by historical consciousness, the something is a futural *telos* of noematic sense and value that intentionally points into its fulfillment and analogical differentiation within the alterity and haecceity of historical being (the *Umwelt*, individual persons, groups, institutions, cultural worldviews, epochs, historical *Ereignisse* such as the birth of Christ, famines, wars). The something is a dynamic analogical identity-in-difference similar to "a bundle of rays flowing together in a single point." But we must also be aware that, by sharply distinguishing the pretheoretical something from the theoretical logical something, Heidegger's KNS 1919 course criticized the metaphysical elements in his earlier treatment of the something, namely, its identification with "object in any sense" and ultimately with atemporal "validity" and "value," as well as the characterization of its enactments in history as "objectifications." All this still involved the theorization that leads to deworlding, deliving, and dehistoricizing. Regarding the notion of validity, Heidegger asked: "Is this a founded, even extremely founded phenomenon? . . . Validity is ultimately a phenomenon constituted by its subject matter, presupposing not only intersubjectivity but further historical consciousness as such!" (G56/57 115, 50–51; G1 214–17, 318).

He pointed out that the primal something is precisely the futural "not-yet" and "preworldly something" of the situation. As such, it makes up the toward-which or upon-which (*Worauf*) of tendency, of "living toward something" (*auf etwas zu*). Insofar as this primal something has always already been fulfilled and differentiated in the "worldish something" of "lifeworlds" and "specific spheres of lived experience" (e.g., "aesthetic," "religious," "political" experience), the tendency toward the primal something is always "motivated" by this dimension of having-been. Of the primal something, Heidegger wrote, "Its sense rests in the fullness of life itself and means precisely that this has not yet marked-out [*ausgeprägt*] a genuinely worldish characterizing, but that such no doubt motivationally lives in life. It is the 'not-yet,' i.e., that which has not yet broken-forth into a genuine life, it is the essentially preworldly" (G56/57 68, 115–16, 4).

As such a preworldly future, the Ur-etwas is an "index" or pointing into its breaking-forth and fulfillment in the different lifeworlds and experiences of the "worldish something." "It is the index for the highest potentiality of life. . . . there lies in the sense of the something as the experienceable the moment of the 'out towards' [*das 'Auf zu'*], of the 'direction out towards,' of the '*into* a (specific) world'—and indeed in its undiminished 'centrifugal force of life' [*Lebensschwungkraft*]." The out-toward of the primal something into specific worlds is what Heidegger meant by *Ereignis*. The "worldish something" of the ancient Greek sunrise or of the twentieth-century lectern "e-vents/en-owns itself according to its essential presencing." The student transcripts of this course describe the *Ereignis* of the primal preworldly something as a "to world-out [*auszuwelten*] into specific lifeworlds" (DK 113). This *Ereignis* of being is also described as a temporal there is/it gives worlds. In the phrase "it e-vents/en-owns itself," the nonpersonal "it" that encompasses the personal I is precisely the *Ereignis* of the *primal something*, of being, of worlds. Heidegger's primal science is focused precisely on this Ur-etwas as an *Ursprung*, a primal source from which worlds spring forth (*ent-springt*). "Everything flows," having its "primal source from the in-itself of the streaming experience of life," from "the flowing stream" of the *Ereignis* of life. The world is not made up of frozen and static "things," but is the rhythm of swinging (*Schwingung*) and swaying (*Entschwebung*). "The environing world does not stand there with a fixed index of existence, but rather sways in lived experiencing, carries in itself the rhythm of lived experiences and can be experienced only as this rhythmic." Like a primal breathing or tidal movement, *Ereignis* is the circular in-and-out rhythm from the futural primal something into the "centrifugal force of life" toward particular lifeworlds and back again (G56/57 115–16, 171, 100, 98).

Heidegger stressed that there is an "indifference lying in the something in any sense over against every genuine worldishness," such that the *Ereignis* of this something is precisely an anarchic *differentiation* into the alterity of lifeworlds and worldish beings. In the following passages on the "there is/it gives something," we can hear distinctive echoes of Heidegger's earlier idea that being is an analogical identity-in-difference:

> What does this mean: "*es gibt*," "there is/it gives"? *Es gibt* numbers, *es gibt* triangles, *es gibt* the paintings of Rembrandt, *es gibt* U-boats; I say: *Es gibt* rain again today, *es gibt* roast veal tomorrow. Manifold "there is/it gives[s]," and at each particular time [*jeweils*] it has a different sense and yet again each also has an identical moment of signification that is found in each. Precisely because of its simplicity, even this completely dimmed, mere "*es gibt*" emptied, as it were, of specific significations has its manifold enigmas.

Heidegger called this necessary differentiation of the "index" of the primal something its *Angewiesensein*, its "being-assigned" in the sense of being always already and continually "submitted" or "allotted" to a differentiated concretion. "When we try to apprehend the sense of the something in any sense, we reach back to individual objects with specific concrete content. . . . Ultimately, there indeed lies in the something in any sense the fact that it is somehow assigned to [*angewiesen auf*] a concretion." We always find the "there is/it gives something" differentiated into "there is/it gives tables and chairs, houses and trees, Mozart's sonatas and religious powers." "Every worldish being (be it of, e.g., an aesthetic or religious or social type) is something. Everything experienceable in any sense is a possible something, regardless of its genuine world-character." All these "somethings" are the effects of the differentiating *Ereignis* of the primal something. As Heidegger already suggested in his 1915–16 essay on history, the very term *Ereignis* means an "event" or "happening," which is unique, unrepeatable, special. For example, *das ist wirklich ein Ereignis*, it's quite an event; *in Belfast ereignen sich Dinge*, things are happening in Belfast. Every *Ereignis* is an *Er-eignis* in that it "lives *aus dem Eigenen*," out of the own, the peculiar, the idiosyncratic (G56/57 115, 67–68, 75). Every experience of something is in some sense a "special event," a "special time." Like the demonstrative "it" in "it worlds," the term *Ereignis* is what Husserl called an "occasional expression," since its meaning is specified only within the unique occasions in which it is employed.

Given its "*Ereignis*-character," the "indifference" in the formal category of the preworldly primal something is to be sharply distinguished from the empty objectified "something" in the theoretical question, "Is there something?," or in any traditional theoretical treatment of the category of being.

> The indifference over against every genuine worldishness . . . is in no way identical with delivedness [*Entlebtheit*] or indeed with the highest stage of this, with the most sublime theorization. It does not mean the absolute interruption of the relation to life, the unwinding of deliving, the theoretical establishment and cold-clocking of something experienced.

The contrast can be summarized in the following way. The indifferent formal category of the primal something is originally the futural moment of pretheoretical life itself and, as a differentiating *Ereignis*, worlds-out into a "worldly something" that is "for me." But the empty generality of the traditional notion of the something (being) theorizes and reifies the primal something, so that it now amounts to the identical presence (dehistoricizing) of universal "real-being" (designifying) that is impersonally present for a cognitive ego (deliving). "The something in general, about whose 'there-is-ing/it-giving' we questioned, does not world," does not e-vent/en-own for me. The intentional content/relation/temporalizing configuration of primal being is world/person/eventing (differentiating), whereas that of theorized being is thinghood/knowing/presence (identity). In fact, Heidegger maintained here that, given the derivative status of the theorized something of "real-being," its appearance is just one more, albeit derivative differentiation of the primal something, of "the experienceable [*Erlebbares*] in any sense." For "the environmental is something; the valued is something; the valid is something" (G56/57 115, 73).

In order to get at this aspect of differentiation, Heidegger's courses of 1919 again mentioned his earlier Neo-Kantian and Diltheyan notions of "heterothesis," "heterogeneity," "otherness," and "unsurveyable multiplicity" within historical reality. Here we see more clearly the an-archic character of the *Ereignis* of the primal something, an anarchic *arche*, which means that no one differentiation and effect of it, that is, a particular lifeworld, can be raised to the level of a universal *arche*, principle/kingdom, and privileged over other effects, except at the cost of becoming an ideological myth and principle of ontological violence. In Heidegger's SS 1919 lecture course, we read, "Every reality exhibits its own, peculiar, individual mark [*Gepräge*]. There is nothing absolutely homogeneous; everything is other, *everything actual is an heterogeneity.*" Reminiscent of his earlier Scotist notion of haecceity, such-here-nowness, Heidegger's essay on Karl Jaspers spoke of the "*hic et nunc*" of the historical "situation" and again took up the old adage that "*individuum est ineffabile*," the individual is inexpressible, that is, cannot be reduced to essential or universal moments. But now all these earlier and still residually "theoretical" concepts were stripped of any reference to "objects" or "objectifications." In and after 1919, Heidegger was thinking rather of a heterothesis of the *Ereignis* and worlding-out of non-objectified historical lifeworlds, whose "contexts" or "situations" are characterized by "the unique, particular, and individual." The closing comments of his treatment of the primal something in KNS 1919 referred to both heterothesis and haecceity: "Problem of heterothesis, negation. . . . Life is historical; no dismemberment into essential elements, but rather context" (G56/57 171–73, 165, 117, 123, 209; G9 32, 39).

In the background of the notion of *Ereignis*, we also find Heidegger's old interest in the "historical consciousness" and worldview-orientation of the German Romantics (Novalis, Schlegel), Hegel, and Dilthey. In SS 1919, Heidegger contrasted these figures with the project of the eighteenth-century Enlightenment (G56/57 129–36). The latter was guided by "a universal idea of history," namely, the progress of "civilization," over against particular peoples (*Völker*) and "nations," especially so-called "primitive peoples" and "barbarism." This idea of universal history was "grounded in the absolute dominion [*Herrschaft*] of mathematical natural science and of rational thinking in general at the time," in the "triumph of pure thinking." It was expressed in, for example, Kant's notion of history as the "development and fulfillment of rational determinations, rules, and ends of humanity." And it was articulated in a cruder form by Turgot and then later by Comte in "the law of the three stages [of human development]: the theological-mythical, the metaphysical, and the positive stages."

But this view thereby "dissolved all historical happening [*Geschehen*] into conceptual connections, causes and purposes, and conceptually clear goals, treating the individual (the unit of historical happening) not as individuality, but as a particular case of the genus, as a historical atom, if you will." Here Heidegger made a comment that relates to his use of "the sunrise" in Sophocles's *Antigone* as an example of the notion of *Ereignis*, as well as to his interest in Hölderlin and the Romantic poets: "Thus the poets were not valued as creative shapers within a genuine world of lived experience, but rather as perfecters of language, which in its refinement and polish brought social and public life to an elevated stage." In his courses of 1919, Heidegger mentioned repeatedly that the distinctive and irreducible types of lifeworld in which one finds the worlding-out of the primal something include the artistic, the religious, the political, and the scientific. The artistic and the religious spheres are not inferior or antiquated such that in the march of progress they need yield to the positivist's theorized world of "things" and "facts."

If, according to Heidegger, France and England were the primary exponents of the Enlightenment, "technology," "naturalism," and "materialism," the "German movement" in the eighteenth and nineteenth centuries brought about a "reversal" vis-à-vis the Enlightenment project. Starting with Herder, the focus now became historicity (*Geschichtlichkeit*), "historical conscious-ness," "historical Dasein." This received "a decisive clarification" especially through the category of *Eigenheit*, ownness or peculiarity, in which we should hear resonances of the terms *Ereignis* and haecceity:

> Under the influence of Hamann, [Herder] saw historical actuality in its manifold and irrational fullness and above all acknowledged the inde-pendent ownmost value [*Eigenwert*] of each nation, each age, and each his-torical appearance in any sense. Historical actuality was no longer seen ex-clusively within a schematically rule-oriented and rationalistically linear direction of progress. . . . There awakens an understanding for individual, qualitatively original effective centers and effective contexts; the category of "ownness" becomes meaningful and related to all shapes of life, i.e., *this category* becomes visible for the very first time.

In the work of Herder, Schlegel, and others, the historical lifeworlds of peoples were explored through their expressions in literature, myths, sagas, folksongs, political and legal history, and so on. "Schleiermacher saw for the first time the ownmost being [*Eigensein*] and ownmost value [*Eigenwert*] of the community and of life in the community, as well as the peculiarities [*das Eigentümliche*] of the Christian community." Heidegger expressed his high regard for the Ro-mantics in the statement to Blochmann in 1918 that "these romantic figures were indeed eminent philosophical figures" (HB 11).

This movement underwent a "deepening" in the German idealism of Fichte, Schelling, and Hegel. Schleiermacher's discovery of "primal Christian-ity" "influenced decisively Hegel's youthful writings on the history of religion and indirectly the whole of Hegel's specifically philosophical systematic, in which the decisive ideas of the German movement in general condensed as their high point." Heidegger was thinking here of Hegel's "(phenomenology) of spirit and of the historical dialectic of reason." With reference to his lectures from the previous semester, he added that "Hegel's so-called pan-logic has its origin out of historical consciousness and is not merely the consequence of a radical theorizing of the theoretical!" Indeed, in KNS 1919, he had told his students that, once "the idea of the system" is seen to be "illusory," "we stand facing Hegel, i.e., before one of the most difficult confrontations" (G56/57 97). He was thereby renewing his earlier call in 1915–16 for a "confrontation with [Hegel's] system of historical worldview."

Heidegger explained further that Dilthey then "tackled the problem of a critique of historical reason . . . in continuity with the German movement (with Schleiermacher above all) and the development of historical conscious-ness." "Dilthey already (1883) saw clearly the significance of the singular and the unique in historical actuality. . . . In [the natural sciences] this is only a 'means,' a passageway to be transcended in analytical generalization; in history it is the 'aim' and goal." And, near the end of his life, he "saw the significance of Husserl's *Logische Untersuchungen*" for a descriptive psychology of historical consciousness. Finally, the problem of history was taken up in Neo-Kantian "value-philosophy," where we find, for example, Rickert's notion of the "unsurveyable multiplicity" and "heterogeneity" of "actuality in its individuality and uniqueness." Here we also find Heidegger describing Windelband's notion of the historical human sciences as "*Ereignis*-sciences," which are "oriented to the happening of a unique, temporally demarcated actuality and its exhaustive presentation. Shapes of human life—heroes and peoples, languages, religions, legal systems, literatures, art, sciences—are supposed to be presented in their 'unique actuality.' " Whereas the natural sciences are "nomothetic," i.e., oriented to universal laws, the historical sciences are "idiographic," i.e., oriented to *to idion, das Eigene*, what is own, the peculiar, the idiosyncratic in the *Ereignisse* of history (G56/57 163–73).

Kairological Time and *Kinesis*

Turning from his studies of mysticism to those of Pauline, Lutheran, and Kierkegaardian kairology and of Aristotle's kinetics, Heidegger's courses after 1919 found new ways to explore the notions of the anarchically differentiating *Ereignis* of being, the it worlds-out, the *es gibt*, and the ryhthmic of "the flowing stream." The "it e-vents/en-owns" and "it worlds" was displaced by talk about how it temporalizes, it comes forth, it flows, it happens to be encountered, it whiles. Instead of speaking of the "*Ereignis*-character" of being, Heidegger now spoke of its "kairological character," "temporalizing-character," "movement-characters," "encounter-character," and "kairological moments." For example, regarding the encounter-character (*Begegnischarakter*) of "the being-here of the world," he said that "world is that which happens to be encountered [*begegnet*]." "[Worldly] objects happen to be encountered, and caring is an experiencing of these objects in their happening to be encountered at the particular time [*in ihrer jeweiligen Begegnung*]. Encounter characterizes the basic way of the being-here of worldly objects." Likewise, the term "temporalizing" turned up in Heidegger's writings. In colloquial German, *Zeitigung* has the sense of the Greek *genesthai* (becoming, birthing) and *phyein* (bringing forth, producing), and thus means bearing (fruit), ripening, unfolding *pros kairon*, in its own time and season. Time is "kairological." In the same spirit, we find Heidegger also using the term *Vorkommen*, coming forth, to describe the temporalizing out of the future that comes toward us (*Zukunft*) (G61 137, 97, 114, 90–91; G63 101, 86, 32, 94, 100).

It was around 1920–21 that Heidegger started calling this temporalizing "the kairological—'time' ":

every manner of coming forth has its definite (factical) *kairological character* (*kairos*—time), its definite relation to time, i.e., to *its* time, which lies in the sense of the context of the enactment of facticity. The kairological, therefore, encompasses categorial determinations. . . . The question is how life as such announces itself (comes forth) and can announce itself (come forth) in a kairological respect in anxious concern.

Kairos, the kairological, means not just the critical eye-opening moment (*Augenblick*), but rather this moment in the sense of the circular movement of the "context" of the "whole situation" that includes past and future. In 1923 Heidegger wrote regarding the being-here of the person/world relation: "Being-here has its own *temporality*. That about which one is concerned is here as not yet, only to-, as already, as nearly, as until now, as for the moment, as finally. These are to be characterized as *kairological* moments of being-here." The *kairos*, "the time," "its time," is not a punctual instant, but the temporal spacing of an intentional stretching along (*Erstreckung*) from the past through the future and into the moment. At any particular time (*jeweils*), Dasein is this stretch, tract, or spacing of time and the circular being-on-the-way along it from the cradle to the grave. In his WS 1921–22 lecture course, Heidegger took this stretching along of the situation as the first of three basic characteristics of the temporal meaning of the term "life": "1. life in the sense of the *unity of the course and temporalizing* of both previously mentioned [intransitive and transitive] modes of [the verb] 'to live,' this unity in its total or in each case limited stretching along, in its complete or partial multiplicity of enactments." This theme of a primal *distentio animae* that Heidegger took from his reading of Augustine's *Confessions* is what his SS 1923 course then called "the stretching along of awhileness" (*Jeweiligkeit*), where the temporalizing of the situation takes the form of the whiling (*Verweilen*) of a while (*Weile*) (G61 137–39, 35, 41, 84; G63 101, 87).

The second temporal meaning of the term "life" that Heidegger specifies in WS 1921–22 is the stretching along of care into the not-yet and absence of futural possibility. "2. Life . . . now with the meaning of something that in a specific sense bears *possibilities* in itself, ones that are to some extent temporally unfolded in it itself and for it. Life, of which we say—what can bring everything that is incalculable, unpredictable. . . . it itself [is] as possibility." Similar to the New Testament concept of the Parousia that arrives within the *kairos* "like a thief in the night," the future is generally a *Zu-kunft*, a coming toward that is unavailable in advance, nonobjectifiable, and thus unable to be calculated, predicted (*unberechenbar*), closed off:

[Being-here] is not to be calculated in advance and is nothing for universal humanity, nothing for a public, but rather it is the definite, decisive possibility of concrete facticity in each case. . . . As historical *possibility* . . . existence is already ruined as what it is when one suggests that it be present [*präsent*] in advance for a philosophical curiosity that pictures it. It is never an 'object'. (G61 84; G63 19, 100)

The third temporal meaning of "life" is stretching along in the "actuality" of our having-been (*das Gewesene*), into which life constantly falls and with which the future becomes weighted down. "3. Life understood in a meaning in which 1. and 2. are intertwined: the unity of stretching along in possibility and as possibility—fallen [*verfallen*] into possibility, loaded with possibility and loading itself, cultivating possibilities—and this whole taken as actuality." Even if we do not fall passively into "tradition," tradition still maintains itself as a facticity that guides our futural possiblities, which would otherwise be completely imaginary and arbitrary. "But our time is simultaneously always expressly from yesterday as well . . . with the yesterday we still have yesterday's seeing and having. . . . [W]e 'are' in it, and being itself, our being, cannot be sublated" (G61 84 73, 65).

But of the three moments of future, past, and present, "the basic phenomenon of time is the future." Thus the temporalizing of these temporal modes is circular because the past is not only behind one, as it were, but also in front as something that has always already circled back into the future in terms of the possibilities that are bound up with it. One's having-been is not a finished product for theoretical observation, but is rather still open, unfinished, on the way, an *energeia ateles*. Thus to retain and stretch along into the past is actually to stretch beyond it into the horizon of its unfinished and unpredictable business, toward which one futurally lives. "[The enactment of experience] has its authentic historical stretching along into the past of the 'I,' which past is (for this I itself) not a piece of baggage dragged along, but is experienced in the I's horizon of expectation that is placed in advance of itself." History as a "phenomena of *historical-enactment*" has to be distinguised from "an objective-historical phenomenon" studied in the science of history, which sees the past as a finished objectified present. "The 'historical' is not the correlate of an objective-historical, theoretical observation, but rather the content . . . *and* the how of worry of the self about itself. Having-oneself arises from . . . *worry*, in which the specific past of the self, the present, and the future are experienced" (BZ 19; G9 31–33). No matter how often it has eaten, as it were, life cannot escape the "hunger," the "being anxious for one's 'daily bread,' " the "care for the morrow" that gnaws at the hole of futural absence in its being.

When the circular movement of temporality has been taken up actively in one's life, Heidegger calls this *Wiederholung*, repetition, retrieval of one's having-been. " 'Repetition': everything hangs upon its sense." "In being-futural, Dasein is its past; it comes back toward it in its how. . . . Only the how is repeatable." Repetition means not mere duplication or application of a past actuality in the present, which is what Heidegger's *Der Akademiker* articles seemed to be suggesting in reviving the medieval worldview. Rather, repetition means fetching back the how of the open-ended "questionableness" and incalculable possibility that the past retains within the futural horizon of one's own contemporary situation. In repetition, the point is "to overcome the yesterday radically" by subjecting it to "the most radical critique" and only then performing an appropriation (*Aneignung*) of it within one's own situation. Understanding the past "does not mean merely becoming informed through observation, but rather primally repeating that which is understood within the sense of one's ownmost situation and for it." The past should "constantly become a new present." Moreover, what is repeated is not just the questionableness of this or that specific past, but the essential condition of questionableness itself that is constantly being forgotten. This repetition constitutes *Eigentlichkeit*, authenticity, ownness, owning-up, where what is one's own is the insurmountable questionableness of what is one's own. History, Heidegger wrote, is "objectively there in a relevant sense then and only then . . . when it gives out . . . *what is worthy of thought [Denkwürdigkeiten]* in a radically simple manner and thus . . . throws [present understanding] back on itself in order to intensify questionableness" (G61 80, 109, 190, 65; BZ 25; PIA 238–39).

Around 1921 Heidegger began pursuing temporalizing-sense in terms of a Pascalian, Lutheran, and Kierkegaardian reading of Aristotle's notion of *physis* and *kinesis* in practical life. This temporal movement is an unending on-the-way (*Unterwegs*) of movement (*Bewegtheit*) from the not-yet of possibility to enactment, a movement that always circles back into the inexhaustible lack and absence (*steresis*) characteristic of possibility. " '*Time*' [is to be] understood . . . as a specific *how of movement*," Heidegger told his students in 1921–22, and thus "the movement of factical life can be interpreted and described in advance as *restlessness*. . . . cf. the phenomenon of motion in Aristotle." He had already in 1919 referred to time as a Bergsonian *élan vital* and "flowing stream," and he pursued the same imagery in 1921–22 with the concept of " 'motion' ('process', 'stream', 'flux', the happening of life, context of enactment, temporal unfolding)." And again, "One speaks elsewhere of process, stream, the flux-character of life. . . . we take this as an indication for the pursuit of the basic structures of *life as motions*. . . . Facticity (the being-sense of life) is co-determined out of movements." Just as he had previously talked about the "rhythmic" of the world, so now he spoke about its swimmableness (*Verschimmbarkeit*). "What belongs more or less in the environing world modifies itself constantly. . . . This swimmableness of the lifeworld, this unbroken shiftability of its extent . . . is based in the character of temporalizing" (G61 112, 139, 93, 80, 102, 114, 96; G63 17, 65, 109; HB 14).

After 1919 Heidegger also pursued in new ways the notion of the *Er-eignis* of being as the indexicality and movement of differentiation into alterity, uniqueness, and "ownness." Leaping ahead first to his 1924 talk "The Concept of Time," we find him returning to his 1915-16 essay on history and taking up the contrast there between homogeneity and heterogeneity in the mathematical and the historical concepts of time. Whereas the former involves "the homogenization [of time] into now-points," the genuine concept of temporalizing in pretheoretical life is precisely the "principle of the individuation" of being and time. "The basic assertion: *time is timely* [*zeitlich*], is thus its most authentic definition—and it is no tautology, because the being of temporality means dissimilar actuality. . . . there are/it gives [*es gibt*] many times. *The* time is meaningless; time is timely. . . . Time is the proper *principium individuationis*" (BZ 23-26).

Between 1919 and 1926, Heideigger developed a long chain of associated terms to express the differentiation and individuation of being, each of which was a predecessor also to his even earlier concept of haecceity defined as "individual-being" and "such-here-now"-being. Take Heidegger's term for time around 1921-22, namely, *kairos*. He understood it as "the time" or "its time" in the sense of, for example, "everything in its own time" (*zu seiner Zeit*), "Lincoln's time," "medieval times," "one's own time." "Factical life has its time." Heidegger called both being and time "kairological" in the sense that both are always "timely," "at the time." *Kairos* is thus the unique "situation" in its "*hic et nunc*," its "now-being": for example, the situation of the first Christians, or the fact that back in WS 1921-22 Heidegger and his students "live here and now . . . at this place, in this lecture hall." Following St. Paul, as well as Aristotle, Heidegger stressed that particular *kairoi*, situations, are always "new creations" that come "like a thief in the night." As the temporalizing of the situation "in its *own time,*" *kairos* thus means the same as *Er-eignis*, the ownmost event of the unique situation. Back in 1919, Heidegger had clearly said that "every situation is an '*Ereignis*'." Likewise, the term "Dasein," being-here, means that being is always *hic et nunc*; when we search for being itself we find only this and that differentiated and unique "being-here" (for example, that of "the table," "the skis," "the library," and these at different "times"). Still another term that Heidegger used to express differentiation into uniqueness was that of the "facticity" of the "sense of being of life." "The being of life [is] as its 'facticity' " (G61 41, 137-39, 114; IPR 320; G56/57 206).

Finally, we need to consider the all-important term *Jeweiligkeit*, awhileness or temporal particularity. This term recieved much attention in Heidegger's SS 1923 lecture course and in his 1924 talk "The Concept of Time," where we read that time is "the *principium individuationis*, i.e., that from which Dasein is in awhileness." *Jeweiligkeit* expresses the fact that the being-here of a situation is *jeweilig*, at the (particular) time, for a while. *Der jeweilige König*, for example, means "the king at the time," the king who was for a while. A situation has its particular and finite *Weile*, while. "Awhileness means a bounded situation in which everydayness finds itself, bounded by a proximity for a while at the particular time [*ein jeweiliges Zunächst*], which is here [*da*] in a whiling and dwelling at-home at it [*Verweilen bei ihm*]." The "being-here of the world," which Heidegger will later call the "*topos*," "illuminated clearing," and "*ethos*" of being, has a stretch or span (*Erstreckung*) of time in which it whiles, abides, tarries. Thus he referred to this awhileness as an *Aufenthalt*, an abode at which one sojourns (*sich aufhalten bei*) for a while. Thus there is, for example, "the Greek abode and its doctrine of being." "This *whiling* at- has its while, the sojourn-character [*Aufenthaltsmässiges*] of the *temporality* of everydayness, a whiling at- in a drawing-out of temporality" (BZ 26; G63 87, 108–109). And given that "*the* time" does not exist, there are of course many different time-lines, whiles, lifelines, abodes and homes (*ethoi*).

Heidegger illustrated this point with the being-here of "table, jug, plough, saw, house, garden, field, village, path." The table has its "*jeweiligen 'Da,'*" its here for a while at the particular time. It is "*the* table here (not 'a' table alongside many others in other rooms and houses)." It has its own time-line of awhileness, such that "corresponding to the awhileness, it *tarries* throughout it in this being-here." "As the something of concern, the encountered being-here has its own *temporality*." That is, the while of its being-here is stretched along through the three "kairological moments" and "encounter-characters" of the "not yet" (the for- or to-which), the "already," and the "at" (*bei*) or "for the moment."

> In such being-here-to-hand itself as such, the *to-which* is here as familiar and disclosed; and this to-which in the type of being of a specific everyday being-*thus*—e.g., to eat (this alone or with specific Others, at the times of the day). Even *this specific everydayness and temporality* is therefore *extant* [*vorhanden*]. Already having-been-here thus and being here thus in becoming. Past and future [are] specific horizons that in each case determine the present; pressing forth into the here out of past and future. Temporality: from that time, for, at, here for-the-sake-of.

As this passage indicates, the table is a site, a here of the temporalizing of its being. The circular temporalizing of this extended while of the table's being-here is an ongoing "movement," "becoming," or "whiling" from the past-textured future into the present, which Heidegger would have earlier called *Ereignis*, worlding-out, and there is/it gives. He stressed that dwelling at the table is not something static, but rather, as his lecture notes read, " 'whiling at' [is] a way of enactment and temporalizing" that involves the "questionableness" and "incalculability" of an absent futural not-yet. The "genuine abode" is in fact the "movement" of temporalizing itself. Thus it is that, similar to the Parousia of St. Paul's "thief in the night," "something like 'the strange' can come forth in the proximity of the worldly here; it is the not-familiar. . . . The usually-always-somehow-other permeates the encountering of the world; it is comparative: other than—one thought, planned, etc." Given the mystical and Pauline overtones that are still present in Heidegger's writings around 1923, one can say that the here of the table is parousio-kairological, that is, it is the on-the-way of an incalculable coming-forth (*parousia*), illumination (*Erhellung*), revelation (*aletheia*), announcing (*Meldung*), and *hermeneia* (interpretation) in the sense of the "tidings [*Kundgabe*] of the being of a being in its being to—(me)" (G63 29, 94–95, 100–101, 108, 10).

The awhileness of the table consists not only in that it is "*the* table," the unique table in Heidegger's house with its own history, but also in that it is itself an open-ended process of differentiation into the unique whiles, stretches of time, or situations that come forth, linger for a while, and then pass away in the span of the table's life from the carpenter's workshop to the clutter (*Gerümpel*) into which it will eventually turn. The table is kairological; it is here as this for a while, and here as that for another while. For example, one finds these whiles during "the times of the day," week, and year at which the table was "here" for the family's "daily meals," the philosopher's writing of "that work," the wife/mother's "reading" and "sewing from time to time," the "playing" of boys, the showing up of "a friend," the celebration of "that holiday." All "this," Heidegger wrote poignantly, "is *the* table, thus is it here in the temporality of everydayness, and thus will it perhaps be encountered again after many years when it is found folded down and unusable on the floor, just like other 'things,' e.g., a toy worn out and almost unrecognizable—it is my childhood" (G63 90–91). Each while belonging to the table, the toy, and the broken "pair of old skis" was a different and unique *kairos*, *Er-eignis*, worlding-out, there is/it gives. Every supper with its "care for the 'daily bread' " had the eschatological character of a last supper. Bread and wine, "in limpid brightness shown," worlded and whiled, and then were gone.

I Event/Enown It

Our treatment of Heidegger's concept of *Ereignis* emphasized its nonpersonal depth-dimension, that is, the *Ereignis* of the primal something (the content-sense of being), which "e-vents/en-owns itself according to its essential presencing." But for Heidegger, *Ereignis* meant more precisely the happening of "the lived experience" in the intentional sense of the whole configuration of I-comport-myself-to-something. Thus it includes an "I myself e-vent/en-own it to myself," that is, the temporalizing-sense of the personal I:

> But something indeed happens. In seeing the lectern I am also here with my full I, it swings along and resonates [*schwingt mit*], as we said, it is a lived experience specifically [*eigens*] for me, and I also see it thus; however, it is no process, but rather an *Ereignis*. . . . The living experiencing [*Er-leben*] does not merely go by before me like a thing that I posit as object, but rather *I*

myself e-vent/en-own it to myself, and it e-vents/en-owns itself according to its essential presencing. (G56/57 75; emphasis added)

There are a number of important points in this passage regarding the personal sense of *Ereignis*. First, it tells us that the "historical I" is the personal, differentiating site of the *Ereignis* of the primal something. "*I* am one way or another completely hereby [*dabei*]"; I am the situated unique here of being. The happening of the primal something (e.g., the lectern, "your seats," the sunrise) is always a unique, individuated " 'something' . . . for me (Fräulein Arts Candidate), for me (Herrn Dr. X), for me (Herrn Law student)." The *nonpersonal* depth-dimension of *Ereignis* is not the theorized and delived *impersonal* something that merely "goes by before" me as an objective pro-cess, as an absolute in-itself. Rather, "*Ereignisse* 'happen to me.' " The stem *eigen* (own) in the term *Er-eignis* expresses not only the *ipseity* of the nonpersonal worlding-out of the primal something, and not only its differentiation and individuation into the *ownness* (*Eigenheit*) of the content-sense of communal lifeworlds (worldviews). Rather, it also expresses the fact that the terminus of this worlding-out of the primal something is ultimately an anarchic differentiation and individuation into a "to me" and "my own" in unique personal experience. The *Ereignis* of the primal something is always also a personal *Ereignis*, an enownment, an event that is my own (*eigen*), an e-vent that is an ad-vent (*par-ousia*) for the personal I. "Lived experiences are *Er-eignisse*, insofar as they live out of what is own [*aus dem Eigenen*] and life only thus lives." Likewise, "the 'is there/does it give' is a 'there-is-ing/it-giving' [*es geben*] for an I." All this is a welcome supplement to Heidegger's later almost exclusive stress on the nonpersonal cosmic aspect of *Ereignis*. Whereas the later Heidegger focused on such things as the sun, stars, deities, bridges, as elements in the *Ereignis* of "the fourfold" of earth and sky, gods and mortals, and virtually left it at that, the young Heidegger also stressed the personal aspect of these worldly events. We find, for example, still another description of a sunrise in 1919; this time it is not a Greek, but a German sunrise, one that seems to be associated with an outing in "the 'free-German youth movement' " (cf. HB 127):

> For example, mountain climbing to see the sunrise up there. One has made it to the top, and each waits in silence. One is completely abandoned in the *Ereignis*, one sees the sun's halo, the clouds, the masses of rock. . . . Here the I nonetheless remains existing. . . . Every situation is an *Ereignis* and not a 'process'. That which happens has a relation to me; it streams [*strahlt*] into one's own I. (G56/57 73–75, 68–69, 205–208)

A second basic point is that the personal historical I co-temporalizes the worlding-out of the primal something. The latter does not, as it were, wash over a purely passive I and sweep it along at the mercy of its flux. Rather, it "e-vents/en-owns itself," and I "e-vent/en-own it to myself." I make it my own, appropriate (*aneignen*) it (G58 208). It temporalizes (*zeitigt*, brings forth, births) by coming toward me as a future, and I co-temporalize it in the sense of a co-bearing, a co-birthing. This is the temporal sense of my *Vollzug* of it, that is, my drawing it into the fullness of the present. There is here both an it-gives and an I-receive. After 1919, Heidegger went on to explore how the authentic temporal enactment of *Ereignis*, of what he now called kairological time and *kinesis*, involves the fitting, conscience, wakefulness, resolute openness, having-time, waiting, keeping silent, making-it-difficult, and decision. He explained that, if factical life is characterized by the not-having-time of ruinant movement away from the factical situation into the hyperbolic abstractions of the everyday and the philosophical They, it is also equally characterized by a "counter-ruinant movement," that is, "the tendency toward the possible *appropriation of the 'before'* and therewith of that which life authentically holds before itself in the 'before'." It is conscience as the "historically directed renewal of worry" that calls one back from falling into "responsibility" for one's historical situation and thus for the "temporal unfolding of an authentic *coming-forth* of life." Heidegger wrote that, "according to its basic sense, 'conscience'—here understood as the enactment of conscience, not as occasionally having a conscience (*conscientia*)—is a historically characterized how of self-experiencing." The mark at which one aims in the futural repetition of the past within the eye-opening moment (*Augenblick*) is the fitting. For factical life in general as for the kairologically oriented definition of philosophy, "the *situation*, fitting which understanding has to enact itself, itself arrives in the understanding glance [*Blick*]. What is at issue must come 'to the light of day'. . . . The problematic shifts ever more sharply and adamantly into the conscience" (G61 106, 62; G9 33).

Authentic "hungry life" has the character of waiting kairologically for its "daily bread": "Caring—waiting; the 'not'. . . . Waiting provides the basic historical sense of facticity; in the 'toward' of the specific world- and object-relation. And simultaneously the character of going-hungry: in waiting: *not yet*." Unlike the idle talk that calculates the future as a ready-made, objective set of possibilities, authentic waiting involves "wakefulness" and "passion . . . the resolute openness of understanding that . . . can keep silent and wait." Thus one "has time" in the double sense of attentively having time for one's time and thus having one's time: "The kairological—'time'. Sitting still, being able to wait, i.e., 'giving it time' in the world and its history. Factical life *has its time*; 'time', what is entrusted to it, which it can 'have' in various ways: keeping in expectation, preserving." Though this temporalizing issues in decision, it can never find rest and ease in the results of its decisions, but must constantly practice repetition. One is "posed *toward* a primal decision and *in* it (repeating it)." This what Heidegger called taking the difficulty of life seriously and actively making-it-difficult so that it does not fall into the easy and the comfortable. "The most unmistakable manifestation of this [difficulty] is the tendency of factical life to making-it-easy-for-itself. . . . When it authentically is what it is in this being-heavy and being-difficult, then . . . the mode of truthfully safekeeping it can only consist in a making-it-difficult." Thus conscience is not a one-time thing, but a constant vigilance and countermovement that is ever pulling life back from falling into fixed results and the abstractions of the They. The "genuine abode" (*Aufenthalt*) is not retirement in the static presence of the social They or the They of metaphysical theories, but an "abode *before* the *possible* leap of worried decision" that is simultaneously an abstentious holding oneself away (*Enthalten*) from falling. Heidegger's notes read, "Abiding at life itself, at its object- and being-sense: facticity. Holding oneself away from ruinous movement, i.e., taking the difficulty seriously, enacting the thereby *wakeful* making-it-difficult, truthfully safekeeping" (G61 184–85, 71, 139, 109; G63 15–16, 109; PIA 238).

A third point we can gather from Heidegger's descriptions in 1919 of the "I myself e-vent/en-own it to myself" is that "one is completely abandoned [*hingegeben*] in the *Ereignis*." Just as the primal something is a moment of the *Ereignis* and is not a process separate from me, so I, too, am a moment therein and am not a worldless ego separate from the primal something. Thus I event/enown the *Ereignis* not from a position outside it, but from within it:

> Just as little as a type of thing do I see an objectified thingly sphere, a being [*Sein*], neither physical nor psychical being. Simply understanding the lived experience, I see nothing psychical. *Er-eignis* also does not mean that I appropriate [*an-eignen*] to myself the lived experience [*Er-lebnis*] from outside or from somewhere; "outside" and "inside" have here as little sense as "physical" and "psychical."

The I is characterized by an *Unabgehobenheit*, which has a first, more literal meaning of "not-being-lifted-out" of the event and a second consequential meaning of "inconspicuousness" within the event. Heidegger's notes read, "The *Unabgehobenheit* of the I in the situation. The I does not need to be in view, it swims along [*schwimmt mit*] in the situation." Situations, which encompass the intentional doublet of person/world, are a "flowing stream" in which we are immersed up to our necks. This unbroken medium of *Ereignis* is also expressed in Heidegger's description of the temporalizing of the situation as an elemental "rhythmic," "swaying," "swinging," "ringing," and "springing forth." Situations tremble, vibrate, flow. This is due to a great extent to the fact that a situation is not a theoretically known object, but an emotionally charged and attuned milieu. Heidegger described the "abandonment" of the historical I in the situation as a "swimming along with," a "ringing along with" or "reverberating" (*Mitanklingen*), and a "swinging along with" or "resonating" (*Mitschwingung*) with the worlding of the world and the world-ing-out of *Ereignis*. The I is no more separate from the situation than the ringing from the bell, the dancer from the music, the swimmer from the stream, the mystic from the *unio mystica*, or the sun-worshiper from the sunrise. *Mit-anklingen* and *Mitschwingung* are harbingers of Heidegger's later notions of correspondence (*Entsprechung*) with being and attunement (*Be-stimmung*) by being. Back in 1919, he emphasized, however, that the situation is nothing like "an electrical discharge," the personal I does not drown in the flux of *kinesis*. The situation does have its nonpersonal moment, but it is also a "personal life-stream." In his descriptions after 1919 of the flowing stream of *kinesis* and kairological time, Heidegger continued to make the point that "factical life is caringly absorbed [*aufgeht*]" in situations. "Living and caring in the selfworld is not and rests upon no *self-reflection*. . . . I encounter myself in the world in which I live, with which I concern myself and give myself over [*womit ich mich abgebe*]" (G56/57 75, 206, 211, 73; HB 14; G61 94–95).

The Abandonment of the Transcendental Ego

Heidegger's insistence in 1919 that in the *Ereignis* of the I-comport-my-self-to-something there is neither a subjective "inside" nor an objective "out-side" and his use of impersonal verbs with the indefinite pronoun "it" ("it e-vents/en-owns," "it gives," "it worlds"): all this suggests that there is no sub-stantive subject, agent, cause, or ground that is the giver, worlder, or eventor. At the deepest level of *Ereignis*, there is neither an object acting on a subject nor a subject acting on an object, neither a cosmological ground nor a tran-scendental subject. Rather, there is only the immediate and unified pure verb and action of the giving, worlding-out, and e-venting/en-owning of the I-ex-perience-something. The deepest depth-dimension of *Ereignis* is neither the personal I nor the primal something (being), but the abyss of the temporal giv-ing of being to the personal I. The indefinite "it" of "it e-vents/en-owns" has the purely indicative and evocative function of pointing to the mysterious "in-dex" and "breaking forth" of the person/being relation out of the absence of a nonobjectifiable and incalculable future (G56/57 115).

Here Heidegger had already made the *Kehre* from the modern metaphysics of subjectivity to his lifelong topic of the differentiated temporal giving of be-ing to human being. The first turn in his thought was a turn from the residual transcendental Neo-Kantianism of his own student period. Gadamer writes: " 'It worlds.' Even this was the turn before the turn. In this expression no ego ap-pears and no subject and no consciousness."

What then remains of the transcendental ego? . . . Ten years before Heideg-ger overcame his own transcendental self-interpretation and his patterning himself on Husserl [in SZ], he had found a first word in which the point of departure was neither the subject nor "consciousness in general." Rather, the event of the "clearing" expressed itself in "it worlds" like a harbinger.

The basic point here is that the I is "completely abandoned in the *Ereignis*," such that there is no worldless substantial ego outside of this *Ereignis* that posits, re-presents, or ob-jectifies it before itself as a pro-cess, something present-before-the-hand. We do not "grasp these [lived experiences] as pro-cesses, as objects that are represented, established [*vor-, festgestellt*]. . . . The living experiencing does not merely go by before me like a thing that I posit [*hinstelle*] as object. . . . I understand it . . . rather as . . . an *Ereignis*." Heidegger wanted to have nothing to do with "critical-transcendental idealism" and its central concept of "a thinking that is enacted . . . through reshaping sense-data with the help of logical forms, the categories. . . . All being is only in and through a thinking." If being is "in and through" the temporal enactment of factical life, then it is equally true that this life is in and through the *Ereignis* of being (DEW 14-15; HW 141; G56/57 75, 94, 80-83).

Though after 1919 Heidegger replaced the terms *Ereignis* and worlding-out with such terms as kairological time, coming forth, *kinesis*, and whiling, his *Kehre* from transcendental subjectivity was still operative. For example, we find him in WS 1921-22 criticizing the whole modern tradition of "ego-meta-physics" and "egoistic idealism" from Descartes to Neo-Kantianism and Husserl. What it "cannot at all allow to arise [is] the question of the *sense of the '[I] am'* ":

> —not the I as source and agent of a specifically formulated transcendental-relative or absolute-idealistic problematic of constitution; the idea of constitution, and indeed of phenomenological constitution, is not necessarily tied to the transcendental question, the idea of the constitutively seen generation of the world and positing out of the I or consciousness and in it. (G61 173)

The sense of the "I am" is precisely to be absorbed in the dynamism of temporalizing that encompasses both the I and the world. Regarding his statement that "the how of being-related-to-world and the world itself are in factical temporalizing," Heidegger underlined that here "one should not in an 'ideal-ist' or any other theoretical-epistemological manner represent to oneself a solitary production of the world. In temporalizing, the encounter [*Begegnis*] with a world, with a world-object is just as relevant as the encountering" (G61 97). Gadamer reports a 1924 conversation with Heidegger in which the latter again referred back to his notion of *Ereignis*: "We asked Heidegger what the ontological difference was really all about? . . . Heidegger answered: We do not make the difference. . . . The difference is that in which we happen. So the turn was there in 1924 in conversation" (DEW 14-15).

Recall that in 1919 Heidegger said that "the pure ego would derive from the 'historical ego' via the repression of all historicity." The concept of an autonomous pure ego is an "alienated" false consciousness that arises through deliving and mythologizing the factical *Ereignis*-"abandoned" personal I into a hyperbolic "pure ghost," a "contortion of spirit, the phantasy of life and thinking that has been elevated into a principle" (G61 81, 99). Heidegger's youthful thought is neither transcendental philosophy nor any version of subjective personalism, existentialism, or philosophy of life. For he saw the personal I as enveloped and sustained by at least two depth-dimensions, namely, the primal something (being) and groundless *Ereignis*, which, though nonpersonal (*nicht-personal*), are not for that reason impersonal (G56/57 78). The "Dasein of *personal* life" is haunted by the "it" of an "it signifies," "it worlds," "there is/it gives," "it events/enowns." The personal I gets its own depth from living *de profundis*, out of and in these depth-dimensions in the same way that the mystic lives "in God." *Ereignis* is that in which we live and move and have our personal being.

Heidegger's Personalist Thoughtpath

Even though he abandoned the transcendental ego, the young Heidegger still put a profoundly personal face on the cold stare of Greek *ousia*. Aristotle's question *ti to on*, what is being?, suddenly became simultaneously the question: "Am I?" "Am I my time?" (G61 174; BZ 27). Given Heidegger's intense identification with the personalism of the Judeo-Christian tradition at this point in his life, he was closer than he would ever be to a figure such as Levinas, who maintains that the sense of being, the divine, and the ethical "opens forth from the human face" (TI 78). In WS 1951–52, Heidegger did call the human being "the *persona*, the mask, of being," though without stressing the personal dimension at work here and more often than not talking about the epochal face (*Antlitz*) of the *Ereignis* of being. Already in 1919, Heidegger seems to have been playing on the original meaning of the term *persona* as that through which (*per*) something sounds (*sonare*), such that this term originally meant the face-mask through which the actor speaks. For example, in his letter to Blochmann on "the mystery . . . of all life," he told her that it is a misunderstanding of "personal [*personalen*] life" to expect it always "to resonate [*schwingen*] with the same broad and tonally rich [*klangreich*] amplitudes with which it wells forth" in a moment of unusual intensity. Why does Heidegger, who always used language with great sensitivity, avoid the German adjective for "personal," namely, *persönlich*, and instead apparently coin the adjective *personal*? Similarly, we read in KNS 1919 that "*my* I" "swings *along* and resonates [*schwingt mit*] in this 'seeing' [of the lectern], just as what is peculiar [*das Eigene*] to the negro in question simultaneously reverberates [*mitanklingt*]." *Anklingen* means here "to be discernible," but Heidegger is certainly playing on its original meaning: namely, to sound-, ring-, reverberate-at (WHD 28/62; G15 369; HB 14; G56/57 73).

All this suggests that, as Heidegger put the matter in 1921–22, being is " *'being'* in and through [per-sonal] life." There is no being without the physiognomy and personality of being, that is, without its coming forth (*phyein*) and sounding forth (*sonare*) through (*per*) the personal relational sense that has it and through the temporal enactment-sense that enacts it. Persons are onto-personal animals, per-sonifications of being, through whom the differentiated and individuated senses of being sound forth *de profundis*, from the depths of *Ereignis*. The Dasein of personal life is the look or face (*eidos*) of being, that through which it surfaces, where face (*facies*) hearkens back to its original sense of "appearance" on the stage of things. Since for Heidegger persons do not exist outside of the historical *Ereignis* of being, the term "person" cannot mean anything like Boethius's classical definition of person as an "individual substance of a rational nature" (*persona est naturae rationabilis individua substantia*) (G63 22). Rather, Heidegger in effect gave an ontological rendition of the original sense of "person" as *dramatis persona*, so that it now meant the mask/face and role played in the drama of *Ereignis*.

Heidegger's lecture course of WS 1919–20 focused on the "concentration [*Zugespitztheit*] of life on/toward [*auf*] the selfworld," as this had been stressed especially in primal Christianity. "Factical life can be lived, experienced, and accordingly also historically understood in a noteworthy concentration on the selfworld." "Not only in significant personalities does the selfworld have this special functional tendency, but rather *every* psychical life lives in some manner centered in a self—even if in an unemphatic way" (G58 59, 206). *Spitzen, zuspitzen* means to make pointed, sharpen, intensify, concentrate, focus, gather, as when one *die Lippen spitzt*, puckers one's lips, or *die Ohren spitzt*, pricks up one's ears. *Spitze* thus means gathering point, culminating point, climax, extreme, aim, end, the intentional point, toward which everything is gathered, con-centrated, intensified, brought to a head. It can mean the point of a spear or the tip of somebody's nose. *Ich sehe es dir an der Nasenspitze* means "I can see it written all over your face."

Heidegger used this term *Spitze* again in a 1953 essay that questioned after the site (*Ort*) of Georg Trakl's poetry: "Originally the word 'site' meant the point [*Spitze*] of a spear. In it everything flows together. The site gathers unto itself into the highest and the most extreme" (G12 33/159). Whereas this later usage aimed ultimately at the epochal site and gathering point of being, his earlier usage was focusing on "the selfworld, the 'toward-which of the point [*Spitze*],'" that is, situated personal Da-sein, the individuated here of being (G58 85). It focused, for example, on the way in which the significant context of the *Ereignis* of the sunrise is concentrated and gathered in the situational selfworld of Sophocles's Theban Elders, or the way in which the relation of

faith to God is concentrated intensely and dramatically in Kierkegaardian secret inwardness and passion. In introducing this concept of "concentration" in
WS 1919–20, Heidegger had in mind not only the example of such mystical
notions as Theresa's "interior castle" and Eckhart's "little castle" of the soul
(for Heidegger, the mystics stressed both the deep *mysterium tremendum* and
the concentration on the selfworld) (G58 205, 212). He also appealed generally to the tradition of religious "autobiography," "the confessions of a selfworld" (e.g., Augustine's *Confessions*), because it is here that the concentration
can become "emphatic" in a transparent "authentic" manner:

> It is self-meditation in the specific form of religious reflection on destiny and
> the effective, hindering and helping, punishing and gladdening powers of the
> world. It is enacted always in forms of wisdom-teachings, maxims, 'apho-
> risms'. . . . The forms of shaping and expressing such inward experiences are
> summed up under the title 'autobiography'. According to its structure, they
> can be very different: soliloquy, factual reports, fabricated legal speeches,
> rhetorical declamations, literary portraits, memoirs, diaries. (G58 57–62)

The sense of this "concentration" is ultimately temporal. For the gathering
point, the site, of being is the personal, unique, historical situation of Dasein,
in which being is *vollzogen*, drawn together, toward the self, and into completion "here and now . . . at this site [*Ort*]. You before me, I before you, we with
each other." "What does this concentration mean? It [is] 'seen,' lived, and [is]
living in a basic situation. The self lives in situations which are ever new, penetrate anew, and cannot be lost for those that follow." "This accentuation of the
selfworld is such . . . in specifically accented, here-and-now *enactment*" (G58
62, 58). In Aristotelian language, the gathering point is the *eschaton* (the extreme point) of the individual's *kairos*, the mark at which the pointed arrow of
phronesis aims. The "ends" of practical being are sharpened and individualized into a *pros hemas*, a toward and in relation to us, that is, each individual.

In Christian terms, the gathering point is the *eschaton* of the Parousia, the
Kerygma, the Logos that is always differentiated kairologically *pro nobis* and
in nobis, toward us, in us, and for us. Heidegger's translation of *pros hemas*
and *pro nobis* is to-me-being (Mir-Sein), the "being of beings in its being to-
(me)" (G61 138; G63 10). The point of being, the terminus of its anarchic
differentiation, is the selfworld. Persons are personifications of being, in and
through whom the intentional rays of the worlding and *Ereignis* of the world
refract and intensify into a myriad of eye-opening moments, twinklings-of-an-
eye, looks, expressions, styles, facets, as in the different "viewpoints of a spatial thing" or of a "concert" (G58 206–207). Being is written all over this
personal *facies*. For the young Heidegger, the *Spitze*, the ultimate gathering
point, of the *Er-eignis* of being is not merely its epochal constellations and
faces, nor is it a mere epochal "mask" worn by individual Dasein. Rather, it is

the per-sonalization and individuation of being, the unique individual's relation to and enactment of it.

Heidegger's heterology of the nonpersonal depth-dimension of *Ereignis* is simultaneously a profoundly *per-sonalist* ontology. We find him saying that "philosophy is one way or another concerned ultimately with [the] self," that "science evolves simultaneously into the habitus of a personal Dasein," that the "selfworld" is "the sphere of the primal source of phenomenology," and that "I take the person to be of decisive importance" (G9 35; G56/57 4; EBF 105; BL 30). But this personalist thoughtpath is situated before and beyond the opposition between sentimental personalism and cosmological impersonalism, for its topic is the dynamic relation of being *and* personal life that Heidegger expressed in his unique use of the term *Ereignis*. The young Heidegger can be called an ontological personalist and a personalist ontologist, since he fused the Greek question of being with Judeo-Christian personalism. One can speak of a distinctive personalist thoughtpath here because, even though many key terms such as *Ereignis*, worlding, and *es gibt* will turn up again publicly in his later philosophy, they have a peculiarly personal aspect in his early Freiburg period that is not evident in the later writings.

14 | The Mystery of All Life

THE MODEL FOR Heidegger's notion of *Ereignis* was hardly transcendental idealism, but rather his own phenomenology of religion and, more specifically, medieval mysticism and the Romantic mysticism of Schleiermacher's free Christianity, which he understood as reassertions of primal New Testament Christianity against its Hellenization. Accordingly, he planned to give his course on "The Philosophical Foundations of Medieval Mysticism" in WS 1919–20. But his courses of KNS and SS 1919 had already taken up not only his former historical heterology of "the something" (being), but also the ultimate sense of this, namely, a mystical-personalist heterology that was influenced especially by Eckhart, but also by the mystical strains in Novalis, Schlegel, and Hegel. However, here he gave up his former identification of philosophy with "the true [religious] worldview" and now used the lifeworld of Christian mysticism as an ontic model for gleaning general ontological insights, just as he applied the same strategy to the lifeworld of art in Sophocles, Hölderlin, and Schlegel in 1919, to the religious lifeworld of Pauline kairology around 1920–21, and to the moral lifeworld and technical work-world of Aristotle's ethics in 1921–23.

In 1919, he was working mainly with an analogy between the ontic (Christian mystical experience) and the ontological (experience in any sense), which concerns not merely proportionality (similarity of proportions or structure), but rather something like synecdoche (similarity of an exemplary part and the whole). The medieval mystic's *unio mystica* and abandonment (*Hingabe*) in the *mysterium tremendum* of the analogical efflux of the Divine Life also tells us something about the way that all experience is abandoned in the mysterious depth-dimension of the differentiating *Ereignis* of being, just as do Schleiermacher's "feeling of [the] absolute dependence" of finite particularity on the divine infinite universe, the artist's ecstatic releasement and abandon in creative work, the trusting "surrender" of Pauline-Lutheran faith to the kairological Parousia of the *Deus absconditus*, the earnest absorption of Aristotelian practical wisdom in the *lethe* and kairological *kinesis* of futural moral ends, the Aristotelian artisan's dedication to a craft, the mountaineer's abandonment in the sunrise, or the family's heartfelt surrender to the "evening meal."

The analogy between mystical experience and experience in any sense can be expressed more precisely in terms of the similarity of two intentional configurations. On the one hand, we have the religious configuration of Heidegger's Eckhartian model from 1915–16 and of his own modern reformulation of medieval mysticism during those years, which took the following shape: the undifferentiated unity of the Godhead (content-sense); the soul's self-surrendering devotion (*Hingabe*) to God (relational sense); and the differentiating emanation of the divine efflux (temporalizing-sense). On the other hand, we have Heidegger's ontological configuration of 1919, namely, the indifference of the primal something or being (content-sense); the personal I's self-surrendering abandonment in and devotion to (*Hingabe*) being (relational-sense); and the differentiation of *Ereignis* (temporalizing-sense). Indeed, we already find Heidegger referring in 1919 to this configuration as "the mystery . . . of all life," that is, to a concept of ontological mystery that will later turn up again as the "mystery of being" in his publications after 1930. Though he apparently used the term "mystery" to describe *Ereignis* only in his letter of May 1, 1919 to Blochmann, the concept is nonetheless *operative* in his courses of the same year and in those following.

The present chapter thus examines, one by one, the intentional moments of this analogy to Christian mysticism in Heidegger's concept of ontological mystery, beginning with content-sense, turning then to temporalizing-sense, and finally dealing with relational sense and enactment-sense. I also show that this ontological reinscription of mysticism continued to be effective in Heidegger's subsequent attempts to model his new beginning on a more direct return via Luther and Kierkegaard to the kairological time of the New Testament, and on his Christianized reading of Aristotle's notion of *aletheia praktike*. I argue that, influenced by Schleiermacher's mystical Protestantism and Natorp's synthesis of Eckhart and Luther, Heidegger's phenomenology of religion around 1920–21 was in fact developing a kind of Lutheran mysticism and mystical Lutheranism. I stress that, though modeled on the ontic sphere of Christian experience, the young Heidegger's concept of ontological mystery is not restricted to either the Christian lifeworld or "mystical experience" in any religious sense. Rather, it applies to both non-Christian religious experience and such nonreligious lifeworlds as poetry, philosophy, and the domestic, institutional, and recreational spheres that Heidegger illustrated with his descriptions of "the lectern," "the sunrise," the skiing "trip," the "toy," and "dwelling at home" around "the table." "The original region of philosophy is . . . nothing mystical (i.e., something only experienced in religion)," wrote Heidegger in the WS 1919–20 lecture course that replaced his originally planned course on mysticism (G58 203). Though very interested in applying his new "atheistic" ontology to a phenomenology of the Christian religion, he was by no means attempting to reduce it to "true worldview" of the Kingdom of God.

Abousiology

If, in the Eckhartian model used by Heidegger's qualifying dissertation, the content-sense of the Godhead is the *mysterium tremendum* of an undifferentiated simplicity, abyss, and wasteland, an "emotional nothing," then we find in the Heidegger of KNS 1919 the similar notion that the primal something, being, is likewise the "enigma" of an "indifference" and simplicity (*Einfachheit*). Though in a different manner than the theoretical something, even the pretheoretical *preworldly* something ("empty" of all worldly content) is a "nothing" (not-yet) and "abyss" that leads us into "the wretchedness of the desert," a phrase that reminds us of "the gray desert of a great simplicity [*Einfalt*]" in Heidegger's 1916 poem "Nightfall on Reichenau" (G56/57 115, 67, 112, 63, 65). Heidegger explicitly took up this analogy between "the 'something' of factical experience" and "the 'something' in the *mysterium tremendum*" also in WS 1919–20:

> Even the 'something' that I experience, that I experience as indeterminate, vague, undefined, *is experienced in the indeterminateness of a determinate context of significance*—an "inexplicable" sound in the room ("it is something not right," "it is something eerie"). . . . the pretheoretical something bears the highest, potential, and utter uncanny not-being-at-home [*Unheimlichkeit*] of life and indeed of its obscure but living contexts of expectation, without precisely the least explicitness of the style of the world and the experience being present. — [The 'something' in the *mysterium tremendum*.]

And again later in this course Heidegger wrote that, since it is a "pure something in the sense of the not-yet," "the something is fulfilled as the indeterminate in a context of significance, is charged with life, such that it can take on an impending character that engenders anxiety" (G58 107, 125, 217). Similarly, in SS 1921 he said that the anxiety of Augustine's "pure fear" before the *Deus absconditus* encounters this God as an everlasting "*mysterium tremendum et fascinans*" (G60; HBC).

We can already see that there is also an analogy here regarding temporalizing-sense, which is based on the absence-permeated, incalculable, and differentiating "not yet" of the future. For Eckhart, the efflux of the undifferentiated Godhead is analogical differentiation into the multiplicity of the created world. Likewise, the modern reformulation of medieval mysticism in Heidegger's dissertation, which aimed at a "breakthrough" into the "depth-dimension" of "true actuality and actual truth," spoke of "the absolute spirit of God" as a primal source (*Ursprung*) analogically differentiating itself in the haecceity and alterity of historical *Ereignisse*, worldviews, and personal experience. According to this view, being is thus an identity-in-difference.

Similarly, the Heidegger of 1919 spoke of the *Ereignis* of the primal something as a worlding-out from the "preworldly" not-yet of the future into the multiplicity and ownness of historical lifeworlds. Already in his qualifying dissertation, he had introduced Eckhart's notion that God *west*, essences/presences. Again in 1919, the Eckhartian phrase "it essences/presences" served as an important precedent for Heidegger's impersonal phrases of "it values," "it gives," "it worlds," "it e-vents/en-owns," for not only did Heidegger's KNS 1919 course use the term *Wesen* in a verbal sense (for example, "even *Wesen* [essencing] can found *Sollen* [oughting]"), but in his transcript of this course Oskar Becker "adds a footnote to *es wertet* [it values]: 'Compare *es west* in Eckhart' " (G56/57 48; WSH). This is why we have translated Heidegger's phrase *es er-eignet sich seinem Wesen nach* as "it e-vents/en-owns itself according to its essential presencing."

In using "the category of 'ownness' " (*Eigenheit*) in the religious Romanticism of Schlegel and Schleiermacher to flesh out his own notion of *Er-eignis*, Heidegger was again moving in the sphere of mystical thought. Schlegel, to whom Heidegger had already appealed in his qualifying dissertation, took the historical development of linguistically unique nations and the creativity of artistic genius to be symbolic expressions of a relation to the divine Godhead. Likewise, for his friend Schleiermacher, the "God-consciousness" of the "feeling of dependence" immediately intuits itself and its world as being unique and finite historical manifestations of the undifferentiated unity of the infinite universe. "Religion wishes to see the infinite, its imprint and manifestation, in humanity no less than in all other individual and finite forms." "In religion . . . only the particular is true" (OR 102, 107). Against the rationalism of the Enlightenment, Schleiermacher maintains that there is no free-floating universal humanity or universal religion, but rather only "the ownmost being" of particular, historically conditioned societies, institutions, and religious communities, all of which are different manifestations of the infinite.

But Heidegger was working with a notion of "the mystical" in the wide ontological sense of the mysterious character of *Ereignis*. As Kisiel puts the analogy here between the mystical in the religious and the nonreligious senses, "there is an analogy of ineffabilities upon which the Young Heidegger draws: As the mystic is related to the influx of the Divine Life, so am I immediately related to my own life in its unfathomable nearness and inaccessibility" (GBT 30). Heidegger himself wrote that, "just as a great reserve allows the religious person to keep silent [*schweigen*] before his ultimate mystery [*Geheimnis*], just as the genuine artist only lives in that he creates and does not talk and hates all gossipy chatter about art, so the scientific person works only through the vivacity of genuine research" (G56/57 5). This passage begs to be compared to Heidegger's description of the experience of the sunrise: "each waits in silence [*schweigend*]. One is completely abandoned in the *Ereignis*." In a remarkable letter to Blochmann two weeks after his KNS 1919 course closed with its culminating discussion of the *Ereignis* of the primal something, Heidegger applied many of the basic concepts of this course to a discussion of "the mystery . . . of all life," of the intensity of its welling forth (*Aufquellen*) kairologically in certain eye-opening moments, and of how we must learn to repeat and live within this stream that flows mysteriously toward us out of the future. All this echoes the Eckhartian theme of the Divine Life spilling over into the life of the soul, if not also Luther's juxtaposition of contemplative "enjoyment" and the constant kinetic-kairological renewal of *theologia crucis*:

> It is a rationalistic misunderstanding of the essential presencing [*Wesen*] of the flowing stream of personal life when one believes and demands that it must resonate [*schwingen*] with the same broad and tonally rich amplitudes with which it wells forth in the graced eye-opening moment [*Augenblick*]. Such claims stem from a lack of inner humility in the face of the mystery [*Geheimnis*] and grace-character of all life. We must be able to wait for the highly charged intensities of meaningful life—and we must remain in continuity with these moments—not so much enjoy them—as rather build them into our life—take them along in the forward movement of living and draw them into the rhythmic of all coming life. (HB 14)

One can find a number of themes in Heidegger's courses of 1919 and the following years that would have led him to speak of "the mystery . . . of all life" in this letter. First, similar to the nonpersonal Godhead that precedes all "names," including the persons of the Trinity, the "it worlds" and "it events" is at it deepest level subjectless and groundless; the "it" points not to an agent or cause, but to the mystery of sheer *Ereignis*. Heidegger's treatment of the latter was quite similar to Eckhart's notion of the Divine Life of the Godhead and our participation in it as life "without why." Eckhart's statement that "life lives out of its own ground and wells forth out of what is its own [*aus seinem Eigenen*], thus it lives without why," is surprisingly similar to Heidegger's statement that "lived experiences are *Er-eignisse*, insofar as they live out of what is own [*aus dem Eigenen*] and life only thus lives." Eckhart's statement is actually quoted in Natorp's *Deutscher Weltberuf*, which Heidegger was reading around 1919 (DW2 74; WFH 73).

Moreover, like the *mysterium tremendum* of mysticism, the *Deus absconditus* of Pauline parousio-kairology, and the *lethe, steresis*, and nonbeing operative in Aristotelian moral life, the futural not-yet character of what Heidegger first called *Ereignis* and then kairological time and *kinesis* is an unavailable absence and concealment that can never be fully drawn into the present, objectified, and brought to closure. Like the mystical emanationist view of the world as a book of divine writing filled with signatures and traces pointing backward and forward into the dark absence of the *mysterium tremendum*, Heidegger's ontology in 1919 saw every present "worldly something" as a differentiated effect and trace of the *Ereignis* of the primal something, which always retains its not-yet and indifferent character. The temporal worlding and signi-fying of such things as the lectern, the sunrise, the table, and the broken toy and skis is precisely a pointing into the absence of the horizonal contexts of other things and persons, into the absence of the having-been of "my child-hood," of "that decision with a friend," and most importantly into the absence of the futural to-which and ultimately into the darkness of death.

In SS 1925, Heidegger gave a fitting example: "The umbrella is forgotten by someone. . . . The empty place [at the dining table at home] appresents co-Dasein to me in terms of the absence of Others" (G20 329/239). Given the inexhaustible futurity of things, their referral is a constant deferral into a "to-morrow and tomorrow." No matter how closely and firmly we try to hold onto things and our own lives, they are always haunted by these kinds of ghostly absences. Like Derrida's notion of the differing/deferring of arche-writing, which was heavily influenced by Heidegger's notion of temporalizing, the pri-mal spacing of temporal stretching-along is made up of ecstatic horizons of traces/tracks (*Spuren*) that carry us away into absence. Life is the movement of being ever on-the-way in these horizons, without ever fully arriving or ever really knowing for sure where we are going. It is a "wakefulness" and "wait-ing" for a coming that never fully comes, an openness for an opening that never fully opens up, a "being anxious for one's 'daily bread' " that always "goes hungry" and is left waiting at the table of factical life. As Heidegger put this point in SZ, when we live genuinely in the nonpresent horizons of tem-poralizing, then this brings about "a depresenting [*Entgegenwärtigung*] of the today," a weaning and exiling (*Entwöhnung*) from the pretense of being at home in a realm of fixed presence. And here "the *enigma* [*Rätsel*] of *being* and . . . of *motion* haunts everything" (SZ 517/444, cf. 514/441).

The "mystery . . . of all life" can also be found in the fact that, like the Eckhartian birth of the Logos in the soul, like the Pauline Parousia that "comes like a thief in the night," and like the kairological *kinesis* of Aristote-lian moral life, the absent not-yet of all life is also characterized by the "incal-culability" of its arrival in the present. The future is not fully available, at the disposal of the *manus mentis*, and under its control. We are never sure of the exact times, places, and shape of the concealed future coming toward us, and must live in wakefulness and openness. Finally, the *Ereignis* of the primal something, kairological time, *kinesis*, and whiling all entail differentiation and individuation into unique ownness. As Aristotle asserted, historical being is "that which can always be other." This multiplicity and alterity can never be either empirically surveyed or known through universal reason. *Individuum est ineffabile*, the individual is inexpressible.

The "primal source" studied by Heidegger's pretheoretical science in 1919 is a subjectless, absence-permeated, incalculable, and anarchically differentiat-ing *Ereignis*. Here *Ursprung*, primal source, does not mean the classical *arche*, principle/kingdom, but rather an anarchic *arche*, that is, the an-archic spring-ing forth (*Ur-sprung*) of an alterity of lifeworlds, realms, Eckhartian "little castles." "I can go back from that which has sprung forth [*das Ent-sprun-genen*] to the primal source, the primal spring [*Ur-sprung*]. (Because the flow-ing river is a river, I can go back to its wellspring [*Quelle*].)" Heidegger's SS 1919 lecture notes on this regress stress that the primal source is not a fixed origin: "The requirement of the 'eternal youth' of the theoretical human being. Always going back anew into the primal source, the first spontaneity. From this stems an oscillation [*Schwanken*] between worldly environmental and theoretical life and a suffering under its opposition" (G56/57 24, 5, 214). The term *Schwanken*, oscillation, swaying, swinging, hearkens back to Heidegger's use in the previous semester of the terms *Schwingung*, swinging, and *Entschwe-bung*, swaying.

All three terms suggest the circular rhythm of *Ereignis* from the indiffer-ence of the primal preworldly something to the worlding-out of different life-worlds, from futural absence to worldly presence, from the middle voice of agentlessness to the activity and passivity of world and I, from the incalculable to the calculable, from breakthrough to forgetfulness. This is the circle of suf-fering and repetition in which the thinker, a perpetual beginner, is ever on the way, constantly re-turning *in a new way* to the inexhaustible and ultimately impenetrable primal fountain of philosophical youth, only to lose it still again. One year earlier, Heidegger wrote to Blochmann that "where, with inner truthfulness, a personal life is on the *way* to fulfillment—and we are indeed *essentially on the way*—here there necessarily belongs to one the bitterness of a split-being, of relapses and new beginnings, unbearable suffering under that which is problematic and worthy of questioning [*das Fragwürdige*]" (HB 7).

All this is undoubtedly the fruit of Heidegger's germinal thoughts in 1915–16 about philosophy being haunted by a "depth-dimension" of conceal-ment that can never be mastered. Recall his statements to Ochsner in 1916, and note their marked similarity to his above-quoted statement from SS 1919: "The immanent structure of philosophy is a back-and-forth between sense and being. In this duality lies the tragedy of the philosopher." "Searching for one-self and not being able to find oneself is the innermost rhythm of philosophy." And whereas in 1916 he had quoted the statement from the mystical poet No-valis that "everywhere we seek *das Unbedingte*, the unconditioned, and always find only *Dinge*, things," in KNS 1919 he himself wrote that "when we try to apprehend the sense of the something in any sense, we reach back to individual objects with specific concrete content," such that "the sense of the 'it gives' [something] has its manifold enigmas precisely because of its simplicity."

Heidegger went on after 1919 to exploit the symmetry between the inten-tional configuration of especially Eckhartian mysticism (*mysterium tremen-dum*/the birth of the Logos in the soul/differentiating emanation) and the original Christian configuration of Pauline-Lutheran parousio-kairology (*Deus absconditus*/faith as rebirth/historical-situational revelation). "Only from [the history of the reassertion of ancient Christianity]," he wrote, "is medieval mysticism to be understood" (G58 205). Recall his point in SS 1921 that, in Augustine's understanding of authentic kairological time, the *Deus absconditus* of the New Testament is experienced by "pure fear" precisely as a *mysterium tremendum et fascinans*. He then explored the symmetry between these two configurations and the configuration of Aristotle's practical philosophy (*ethos*/*phronesis*/the *steresis* of *a-letheia*). All three thoughtpaths can be called an abousiology, letheology, and mysteriology, that is, a discourse on absence (*abousia*), concealment (*lethe*), and on a being-closed (*myein*) that, as it were, closes the eyes of theory's view toward pure presence. If it is still phenomenology, it can be called a hyper-phenomenology and a-phenomenology of the disappearance (*aphaneia*) that exceeds appearance, of the absence exceeding presence—a parousiology of that which never fully arrives, a kairology of that which is never fully on time.

Even SZ still belongs to the effective history of the young Heidegger's concept of ontological mystery, as does his use of the concept of the "mystery of being" in the thirties and forties. In October of 1926, when he had just composed SZ, Heidegger again wrote to his friend Blochmann in a spirit similar to the letter of 1919 that spoke of "the mystery . . . of all life." "The owl of Minerva, Hegel says somewhere, begins its flight only in the night. Everything positive lifts itself out of the darkness of the nothing. It is plenty dark in the pages [on my desk]. Whether the owl has even taken wing, one will never oneself want to decide" (HB 16). SZ is so little merely a philosophy of existentialized transcendental subjectivity that, in its descriptions of truth as un-concealment, of the "nothing" of anxiety and possibility, and of time as an unavailable and noncalculable futural coming to which we authentically comport ourselves in the "call" of conscience, resolute openness, and keeping silent, we can still hear echoes of Heidegger's earlier analogy to the mystical and Pauline *Deus absconditus*, though they have been muffled by his Aristotelian and Kantian-transcendental terminology.

The concept of *Entschlossenheit*, resolute openness (often mistakenly translated merely as "resoluteness"), is not the noisy power and *gloria* of decisionism, but the poverty (*privatio, carentia*) of going-hungry, being anxious for one's daily bread, and taking up the difficulty of one's cross (*an sich selbst schwer Tragen*) (PIA 238). As being-true, it is keeping silent, openness, letting-be, and unconcealing of futurally concealed being in the *kairos*. Whereas "for the They the situation is essentially closed off," "*Entschlossenheit*, resolute openness, is a distinctive mode of the *Erschlossenheit*, disclosedness, of being-here." We also read, "The situation cannot be calculated in advance. . . . It is disclosed only in a free open resolving. . . . in accord with its own sense as disclosure, the resolve [*Entschluss*] must hold itself free and *open* for factical possibility at the particular time."

Like Heidegger's earlier courses, SZ is so scattered with references and allusions to, and terminological borrowings from, Christian kairology and mysticism that, were it not especially for the overlayings of Aristotelian and Kantian terminology, as well as the shortcomings of translations, it would be hard to see how anyone could have missed its mystical overtones and conceived of it as mere decisionistic existentialism. Not only is SZ still working with the idea of being as an analogical category that differentiates itself into the ownness of being-here, but we also find Heidegger still speaking of one's "reflectionless being devoted and abandoned [*Hingegebensein*]" to worldly situations in moods, though this is now also modeled on the devotion of the Aristotelian artisan and moral individual to the worlds of work and moral ends. As thrownness that is disclosed in the attunement of moods, care is an absorption that is "surrendered [*ausgeliefert*] to the world of its concern (thrownness)." "Attunement befalls us," wrote Heidegger. "It comes neither from 'outside' nor from 'inside,' but rises forth as a way of in-the-world-being."

Here too, then, we find traces of his old idea of the mysterious agentless "it" of "it events" that is neither inside a solipsistic ego nor outside in an objective world. In his analysis of the thrownness disclosed through mood, he wrote that "the pure 'that it is' shows itself, but the whence and the whither remain in darkness"; the former "stares [Dasein] in the face with inexorable mysteriousness [*Rätselhaftigkeit*]." "*That* it is, [is] concealed as regards the *why*" (an echo of Eckhart's "without why"). It is the futural "nothing," the "uncanny not-being-at-home" (*Unheimlichkeit*), and the "anxiety" of this dark "it" of thrownness that makes up "the 'it' that calls" in the conscience and brings one back from fallenness. " 'It' calls, against our expectations and even against our will. . . . The call comes *from out of* me and yet *from beyond* me" (SZ 393–407/343–55, 179–82/173–76, 264/243, 365–67/320–21). We must recall here that Heidegger originally used the concepts of *Unheimlichkeit* and "anxiety" in the analogy he discussed in WS 1919–20 between "the 'something' of factical experience" and "the 'something' in the *mysterium tremendum*," as well as in his treatment of Augustine's "pure fear" before the *mysterium tremendum et fascinans* (G58 107, 217).

Hingabe

Do we also find in Heidegger's courses of 1919 an analogy in relational sense between mystical experience and experience in any sense? According to his earlier "philosophy of . . . God-intimacy" (*Gottinnigkeit*), God is the deep teleological value toward and into which the soul is ecstatically stretched and "submerged" in an attitude of "absolute *Hingabe*, devotion, abandonment, and temperamental immersion," of noematically oriented and "moodful self-surrendering." The soul "participates" and lives "in God." We find Heidegger, still following in the footsteps of Lask, employing the term *Hingabe* again in 1919 (and equivalent terms in his following courses) to talk about how "one is completely abandoned [*hingegeben*] in the *Ereignis*." "*My* I goes fully out of itself and swings *along in this 'seeing'* " of the lectern or the sunrise, for example. Intentionality is a moodful and ecstatic "tendency" that stretches toward and into its toward-which in the depths of the situation. It is "no mere being-directed toward mere objects," but rather a "loving" (*liebend*) "view toward" its world. The artist (Sophocles), the politician, the researcher (Heidegger at his lectern), the mountaineers and Theban elders at sunrise, the family having its evening meal at "the table," and the child playing with a "toy" are all pre-reflectively "abandoned" in the flowing depths of the *Ereignis* of their life-worlds, in a manner similar to the mystic abandoned "in God," in the *mysterium tremendum* of the efflux of the Divine Life (G56/57 73, 206–207).

Heidegger's use of the term *Hingabe*, especially regarding its emotive aspect, is also influenced by the mystical overtones of Schleiermacher's notion of an "immediate self-consciousness" and "God-consciousness" in the "*feeling* of dependence." For one thing, this "intuition" is for Schleiermacher not an accidental or occasional feeling, but rather the essential emotional tone of our total existence, pervading all of our experience, including the most mundane affairs of everyday life. Moreover, like philosophy and ethics, it has the universe as its object, but, unlike them, it is an immediate, precognitive, and prevoluntary "feeling" of dependence on the infinite universe that is God. In 1918 Heidegger wrote to Blochmann (whom he was tutoring on Schleiermacher right into 1919), "You have the right *feeling* for Schleiermacher—I am convinced that his personality can only be wholly and *immediately* grasped by a woman." On another occasion he told her that "in moments where we *immediately feel* ourselves and the direction in which we vitally belong . . . this understandingly having-oneself is . . . simultaneously a being, a to-be [*ein Sein*]" (HB 10, 14; emphasis added).

Heidegger also modeled phenomenological "intution" and "seeing" on the mystical sense of *Hingabe* and on Schleiermacher's notion of "intuition" and "feeling." Insofar as it must avoid deliving and dehistoricizing lived experience, phenomenological method cannot be merely the mental seeing expressed in Husserl's "principle of principles." Rather, "[the principle of principles] is the primal intention of truthful life in general, the primal attitude of lived experience and life as such, absolute *life-sympathy* that is identical with lived experience itself." Heidegger described this life-sympathy as "hermeneutical intuition" in the sense of the "lived experiencing of lived experiencing"—a "total intuition," as he said in a letter to Blochmann (HB 15). Like the mystic's intuitive immersion in the depths of the flowing stream of the Divine Life, and like Schleiermacher's "God-consciousness" in the immediate *"feeling* of dependence," phenomenology too must start from an immersion (*Versenkung*) in the flowing stream of life and an affective "living into" life's own *Hingabe* in *Ereignis*. "Let us," Heidegger prompted his students almost in the attitude of religious prayer and meditation, "remain in the lived experience of the lectern. . . . Let us once again live into its life"; "let us immerse ourselves again in the lived experience." And later he told them that, in these exercises, "we surrendered and devoted ourselves [*sich hingaben*] purely to a sphere of our own." Phenomenology is "absolute surrender and devotedness to the topic [*Sachhingegebenheit*], truthfulness," just as the same attitude of *Hingabe* "allows the religious person to keep silent before his ultimate mystery" (G56/57 110, 117, 88, 68, 79, 212–13, cf. 61, 65).

As in his qualifying dissertation, Heidegger's primary model in 1919 for the destruction of philosophy and *Kehre* to a new postmetaphysical beginning was not yet Luther and Kierkegaard, but rather the *via negativa* of the *unio mystica* and Schleiermacher's regress to the feeling of absolute dependence. The notes for Heidegger's canceled WS 1919–20 course indicate that he planned to deal with how mysticism " 'is centered on the movement of a conative experience which is detaching itself in the process of finding God.' He accordingly plans to map the entire gamut of negative and positive movements of religious life, beginning with the repulsiveness of a corrupt world, around Eckhart's master concept of 'detachment' (*Abgeschiedenheit*)." The latter is "oriented toward not a theoretical but rather an 'emotional nothing,' 'the God-ignited emptiness of form' reached by way of a progressive suspension of all multiplicity, particularity and specificity." Devotional manuals such as Francis of Assisi's *Fioretti*, Theresa's *Interior Castle*, and Eckhart's popular sermons were intended to give practical guidance precisely in this *via negativa, reductio, Kehre* and constant *itinerarium* from the fallen world back to the *mysterium tremendum* of the Divine Life (HBC).

One finds this same point in the courses Heidegger held in 1919. He explained that the "natural attitude" of "life-experience" that is absorbed in its environing world is defined by Christianity, Plato, and German idealism as *Leiblichkeit*, corporeality, and *Sinnlichkeit*, sensousness, sensuality. "All living experience is 'burdened' with this basic stratum, but there are forms of liberation and transformation. Francis of Assisi: All natural life-experience is integrated into a new sense and can be understood only from out of this in religious human beings." The introduction to Heidegger's KNS 1919 course expressed this mystical regress also with a quotation from the Eckhartian mystic Angelus Silesius: " 'Man, become essential!' (Angelus Silesius)" (G56/57 210–11, 5).

One is immediately struck especially by an analogy here between Eckhart and Heidegger. On the one hand, we have the Eckhartian *unio mystica* that involves both the *via negativa* of detachment from falling into the world and *Gelassenheit*, releasement and abandonment into the indifferent "emotional nothing" of the Godhead. And we have, on the other hand, Heidegger's phenomenological "science of the primal source" that involves both the methodological "path" of a "breaking loose" from the "natural attitude" and the "regress" to the indifference of the primal preworldly something. In a passage that reminds one of his 1919 letter to Blochmann about "the mystery . . . of all life" that wells forth in "moments" of "highly charged intensities," Heidegger wrote in his KNS 1919 course:

> [The preworldly something] is a ground-phenomenon that can be experienced understandingly, e.g., in the experiential situation of passage from one experiential world to another genuine one, or in moments of especially intensive life; precisely not or seldom in such types of experience that are caught fast and spellbound in a world *without* attaining, precisely therein, a highly increased life-intensity.

"Phenomenological life in its increasing intensification of itself" is an "upswing" into and "habitus" of "inner truthfulness," an "awakening and elevation," a "rebirth." In other words, "genuine insights are to be gained only through a genuine . . . immersion in the genuineness of . . . personal life" (DK 107). Heidegger's 1919 letter to Blochmann about "the mystery . . . of all life" continued with similar overtones of Eckhartian *Gelassenheit*: "It is thus that I think of your clear attachment [*Verhaftetsein*] to scientific work—out of the total genuineness of your personal being [*Personsein*]—without any forced idealizations—but rather with the uninhibited *Freiwerdenlassen*, releasement, letting-become-free, of the feminine soul." And in 1918, discussing the same theme, he had written to her that "each accomplishment [in academic life] gains a character of finality in the sense of genuineness, i.e., of inner belonging to the central I and its God-directed purposeful striving" (G56/57 210–13, 115, 4–5, 110; HB 14, 7).

We also find Heidegger continuing to appeal to Eckhart's notion of *Gelassenheit* as a breakthrough (*Durchbruch*). For example, philosophy is supposed to "mean for immediate life-consciousness a transformative intervention in it," a "breaking-through [*Einbruch*] . . . the context of natural life-consciousness." It "brings with it a transition into a new attitude of consciousness and therewith a unique form of the movement of the life of spirit." Like the mystic's breakthrough to the silent flowing depths of the Divine Life, so "phenomenological life" makes a breakthrough into the depths of pretheoretical life. In 1923 Heidegger was still telling his students that "the tendency of philosophy of life must indeed be taken in a positive sense as the breakthrough [*Durchbruch*] of a radical tendency of philosophizing" (G56/57 3; G63 69).

Lutheran Mysticism and Mystical Lutheranism

Finally, there is also an analogy between the temporal enactment-sense of Heidegger's personal I and that of the soul in mysticism. Let us begin by recalling that, according to the Eckhartian model with which Heidegger was working around 1915–16, the deep "ground" and "little castle" of the soul are the "co-bearing" site of the personal birth and analogical differentiation of the divine Logos in the soul. The Logos thus manifests itself in an analogical community of persons that is an identity-in-difference. According to the language of Heidegger's own mystical-personalist heterology at that time, God is the milieu of sense that is analogically differentiated into the heterogeneity and haecceity of "inward Dasein," of "the immanent personal life of the individual." We again meet up with Eckhart's notion of the "little spark" in Natorp's *Deutscher Weltberuf*, which Heidegger was drawing from in 1919 and afterward, so much so that in 1922 Natorp was "almost shocked" to learn of "how closely" Heidegger's views resembled his own in this work (ML 14; for the following, see DW1 79–85; DW2 50–52, 97–108; WFH 71–73; HA 394).

A major theme in Natorp's *Deutscher Weltberuf* is his Eckhartian-Lutheran view of history as an "eternal ground" (Eckhart's "dark primal ground of the 'Godhead' ") that is "a having-become" in the world (the Incarnation), but indeed one still "temporally open" and thus constantly manifesting itself in the divine trace (*Spur*), the "divine spark, the mystical *scintilla*" of the individual soul. Natorp argues here for a synthesis of the Catholic medieval tradition (that is, the mystical stress on the deep Godhead, sacramental symbolism, and the orientation to "universality" and community) with the emphasis on "individuality," "creative personality," and individual "appropriation" in the modern Protestant tradition from Luther through to Kant, Schleiermacher, and Dilthey. "It is never the case that we are pure spirits; spirit requires a body not merely as symbol, but as an implement, as a basis for making good and true in creating and working." Eckhart without Luther is empty, just as Luther without Eckhart is blind.

Natorp argues in fact that Eckhart and Luther were, each with his own emphasis, talking about the same issue, namely, the differentiation of the Godhead in the individual. He claims that Luther's *theologia crucis* stood squarely in the tradition of medieval mysticism and that Luther's theme of the death and "rebirth" of the soul through self-surrendering faith in God has the same "fundamental content" as the Eckhartian mystical themes of *Gelassenheit* and the "birth of God" in the soul. For both figures, this birth and differentiation of a "transpersonal source" in the soul make up the soul's "ownmost own" (*eigenstes Eigen*). Thus we find Natorp talking about a kind of Lutheran mysticism and mystical Lutheranism:

Luther stands . . . completely on the basis of the Eckhartian requirement to 'surrender' [*lassen*] one's self, the whole of one's own will, and all one's speculation . . . and to trust and hold steady only to God's working, the divine light that shines and burns in us. . . . They certainly find this in one's own soul, in the innermost ground of the soul . . . in something of which, as their ownmost own [*eigenstes Eigen*], they are conscious. . . . it is, according to Eckhart's simple and clear word, the 'birth of God' in the soul. . . . [Likewise, for Luther,] faith is 'a living spiritual flame, whereby the heart is enkindled by the holy spirit, born anew, and converted' . . . 'a divine work in us that tranforms us and gives birth to us anew out of God.'

According to Eckhart's notion of the birth of the Logos in the soul, which uses the terminology of Aristotelian physics, the little spark and castle of the soul are matter that receives, is "formed over" into, and analogically differentiates the form of the Logos. We do find in his *Lectures on Romans*, as we have already seen, that Luther also uses this Aristotelian terminology to talk about how faith is a "rebirth" and constantly "new birth" (WA LVI 441–42/XXV 433–34). He sees the soul as a circular *phyein* (birthing) and *kinesis* in which the form of the Logos is constantly coming to be, passing away, and being repeated within the double neediness (*privatio*), *steresis*, and nonbeing of the soul's matter and potentiality, that is, within its constant futural lack of form and its loss of form into the past. Luther writes, "It is necessary that the wisdom of the flesh be changed and give up its form and take on the form of the Word. This happens when it gives itself up to faith, destroys itself, and conforms itself to the Word. . . . Thus 'the Word was made flesh' [John 1:14] and 'took on the form of a servant' [Phil. 2:7]" (WA LVI 329–30/XXV 317, cf. 218–19/204). Whereas Eckhart talks about the birth of the Logos as the historical efflux of analogical differentiation, Luther speaks of the *kinesis* of a historical-situational revelation. In both we find reassertions of the New Testament theme of the kairological Parousia and Incarnation of the *Deus absconditus*.

Natorp explains that, unlike Greek philosophy, Christianity is oriented not to "a timeless idea that is in itself" and then subsequently instantiated in the world, but rather to "the fulfilled actuality of an enacted fact [*Tatsache*]," that is, the Incarnation and its ongoing movement in history. The "lived experiencing" of this historical manifestation of God in the individual takes place "neither in knowing nor in willing," but in the Eckhartian-Lutheran "ground of the soul," the "little spark" of the "conscience." According to Natorp, "already Eckhart and then later Luther call [the 'little spark'] 'conscience.' " He continues,

Conscience [*Gewissen*] in distinction from science [*Wissen*] (*conscientia* versus *scientia, syneidenai* vs *eidenai*) is nothing other than that ultimate ground of certainty, which no longer has to do with truths, principles, subject-object-connections that are universal, or specific, or valid for individual cases, but rather goes back to the ultimate and original unity of self-consciousness, which is not "a" truth but the wellspring of all truth. This is the 'light that shines in the darkness.' . . . 'History,' that means here the eternal ground of a temporally open having-become. . . .

Conscience is not merely consciousness, but the "self-consciousness" and "self-certainty" of "inwardness" that is aware of the Incarnation and of itself as the ongoing historical manifestation and "birth" of God, of the "dark primal ground of the 'Godhead'." For both Eckhart and Luther, the spark of conscience is the point of direct historical contact between God and the soul, which does not have to be mediated by the institutional Church. Natorp is here perhaps thinking of the origins of both Eckhart's "little spark" and Luther's "conscience" in the patristic, Scholastic, and mystical term for the conscience, namely, *synteresis*, which was described as a *lumen naturale* and *scintilla*, and which, similar to Aristotle's self-directed *phronesis*, meant an unforgettable vigilance toward and truthful preservation (*aletheuein*) of inborn divine ends that are applied and enacted in situations. Luther himself still uses the term *synteresis* in his *Lectures on Romans* and elsewhere to discuss the phronetic understanding of God in historical situations (WA LVI 177, 237ff., 275/XXV 157, 222ff., 262).

According to Natorp, one finds this unifying theme of self-consciousness that is historical God-consciousness in "the 'I think' (*cogito*)" of Augustine's *Confessions*, "in the whole of Christian mysticism, especially German mysticism from Eckhart to the *German Theology*, later in Jakob Böhme, Angelus Silesius, and many others, and truly in Luther," as well as in the notion of self-consciousness in Kant, German idealism, and Schleiermacher. A basic insight that Natorp gleans from this tradition is that, as the finite manifestation of the infinite Godhead, the divine "spark" and the conscience contain a "twofold," namely, "genuine individuity" (*Individuität*) and "its precise counterplay: genuine university [*Universität*] (literally, directedness-to-one, Kant's unconditioned totality, wholeness), which has left behind all merely relative, delimited generality, just as full individuity overcomes merely conditioned separateness (particularity)." "University" means here a regulative Kantian idea of infinite totality that functions as an inexhaustible horizon of possible manifestations and experiences of the divine in individual consciences. An individual conscience is precisely a circular "living from the inward to the outward, out of the center to the circumference, out of the Godhead into the world." This circular experience is thus "from the start related and finally oriented to its ultimate ideal center, and to its ultimate ideal circumference, in a twofold inner and outer infinity."

Natorp's concept of conscience and his synthesis of mysticism and the Protestant concept of conscience remind one especially of Schleiermacher's notion of self-consciousness as a "feeling of dependence." On the one hand, this feeling is precisely the awareness of oneself as having a unique identity characterized by what Schleiermacher calls *Eigentümlichkeit*, ownness, peculiarity, particularity. But, like Natorp's Eckhartian-Lutheran concept of a conscience knowing its "ownmost own" and "individuity" as the differentiating birth of God in it, Schleiermacher's notion of the self-consciousness of one's ownness is simultaneously a "feeling of dependence" and "God-consciousness," since here the self is aware that its unique identity or unity is effected by God, that its ownness is a particular finite manifestation of the infinite divine universe. But, against the Romantic overemphasis on individuality, Schleiermacher stressed that individual persons have and can cultivate their uniqueness only within a historical community. Here we find the idea of a community of personal sites of differentiation, such that this community of persons is an analogical identity-in-difference, an analogical community. We have already seen this notion in Natorp's idea of the mystical interplay of "individuity" and "university," and in Eckhart's idea that we are sons and daughters of God "by analogy" in the mystical body of the Logos.

Similar to Natorp's synthesis and to the Romantic mystical Protestantism of Schleiermacher, Heidegger's religious turn from Catholicism to free Protestantism in the war years led him in the direction of this kind of free Lutheran mysticism. He wanted to place his earlier Catholic Eckhartian-Hegelian concern with the deep mysterious temporalizing-sense of the "the absolute spirit of God," the nonpersonal "emotional nothing," into the horizon of that "concentration of life on its selfworld," namely, in personal enactment-sense, which he had already found in the medieval doctrine of analogical differentiation, but which he now explored more intensely in the Protestant figures of Luther, Schleiermacher, Kierkegaard, and Dilthey, as well as in Paul and Augustine and then later even in Aristotle's practical philosophy. His earlier emphasis on the personal "God-intimacy" of the "transcendent relation of the soul to God" in the Middle Ages was now concentrated into an exploration of the relational and enactment-sense of sin, death, anxiety, the going-hungry of care, conscience, faith, waiting, wakefulness, resolute openness, keeping silent, passion, choice, repetition, and everyday life. This was not an abandonment of his earlier mystical orientation, but an attempt at "making-it-difficult," just as analogously his attempt to put the being-question into the horizon of its personal enactment-sense was not subjectivism. In his 1927 lecture "Phenomenology and Theology," Heidegger said that theology cannot "make the acceptance of faith easier. . . . Theology can only make faith more difficult." Following Overbeck's Christian skepticism and Luther's position that this life is not a "having" but a questioning after a hidden God, Heidegger stressed around 1921 that one must start from the absent "away" of God and enact a constant being-on-the-way to God. This is what he also meant with his statement that philosophy must be "a-theistic." That is, if "I as a philosopher" want also to be "a religious human being," then I must begin philosophically not with "mythical and theosophical metaphysics and mysticism," but rather with the "a-" ("without") *theos* (God) and thereby bring myself into "the situation of a religious decision":

> "But the art lies here": to philosophize and simultaneously to be genuinely religious, i.e., to take up factically one's worldly, historical task in philosophizing, in action and in a concrete world of action, not in religious ideology and phantasy. . . . philosophy must in principle be *a-theistic*. It cannot presume [*vermessen*] to have and to define God. The more radical it is, the more definitely is it an away from him, the more therefore is it—precisely in the radical enactment of this "away"—precisely an ownmost difficult 'with' [*bei*] him. For the rest, it may not on that account ruin itself through speculation [*sich verspekulieren*], but rather has its work [*ihr' Sach'*] to do. (G9 56/PT 12, cf. BZ 6; G61 70, 197; cf. PIA 246)

One can see Heidegger's synthesis of the Catholic-mystical and Protestant traditions in his various accounts of the history of Christianity, for here he placed "medieval mysticism and Luther" side-by-side as reassertions of the factical life and kairological time of the New Testament (G56/57 18; G58 61–62, 205, 212; G61 7). In WS 1921–22, he wrote that "Luther's religious and theological counter-attack now enacted itself against the Scholasticism that . . . had been loosened up in its vivacity of experience through the mysticism of Tauler," who was a follower and perhaps an actual student of Meister Eckhart. These two traditions revive roughly the same intentional configuration of the original New Testament Christianity, namely, the mysterious hidden God/surrender/time, but the one often emphasizes deep nonpersonal temporalizing-sense, whereas the other often emphasizes personal enactment sense.

In his explorations of the history of Christianity that were guided by Dilthey and Natorp, Heidegger was fully aware aware that, in the key themes of the personal birth of the Logos, an institutionally unmediated relation to God, sanctity through not works but inwardness, and the fulfillment of faith through works in contrast to monastic and speculative quietism, Eckhart and the tradition of Rhineland mysticism he inspired anticipated Protestantism and the personalist orientation of Kant, the idealists, and German Romanticism (cf. TME 102ff.). Heidegger wrote that "[the new significance of the selfworld] showed itself in Augustine (*Confessiones* among other works) and further in the Middle Ages, especially in medieval *mysticism*" (G58 212). It was this personal enactment-sense that he found expressed in the mystical notion of the "interior castle" and "little spark" of the soul, and generally in the practical devotional manuals of Eckhart, Bernard, Theresa, Francis of Assisi, and Thomas à Kempis that he was studying around 1919 for his planned course on mysticism (HBC). As far back as 1915, he was planning this study of "mystical, moral-theological, and ascetic literature."

He was also surely aware of the extent to which Luther's "new position," similar to Descartes's allegedly new rationalistic beginning, still stood on the basis of not only Augustine, but also aspects of medieval Scholasticism and Rhineland mysticism. If Eckhart was already a modern personalist, Luther was still a medieval thinker of the deep mystery of God. Despite the prevelant opinion that Luther dimissed the mystical tradition, he was in fact, as Natorp rightly points out, deeply influenced at an early date by its devotional simplicity and its theme of personal rebirth after the self-despair and surrender of "the dark of the night of the soul." In 1516 he studied and annonated with great enthusiasm an edition of the sermons of the Eckhartian mystic Tauler. In the same year he discovered an anonymous mystical text, which originated from the Eckhartian group called "The Friends of God," and stressed simple surrender to the mystery of God. Luther, who thought that the author belonged to Tauler's school, published an edition of this work in 1516 and a second more complete edition two years later under the title *Ein deutsch Theologie*, which is known to us today as the *Theologia Germanica*. Luther wrote in his preface, "To boast with my old fool [namely, Paul], no book except the Bible and Augustine has come to my attention from which I have learned more about God, Christ, human life, and all things" (WA I 378–89/XXXI 73–76; English edition of Luther's works, XLVIII 36). One hears these mystical overtones in the Protestant tradition not only when Heidegger stresses Luther's understanding of God as the *Deus absconditus*, but also when he takes up Kierkegaard's notion of "keeping silent" before the intersection of time and eternity in the eye-opening moment.

As indicated by the interests of his phenomenology of religion, Heidegger's religious thinking pointed in the direction of not only a Lutheran mysticism that could read Eckhart through Luther and Kierkegaard, but also a mystical Lutheranism that could read Luther, Kierkegaard, and even Aristotle's concept of *aletheia* through Eckhart. For example, his description of Lutheran Christianity in his lecture "Phenomenology and Theology" sounds distinctively like a type of mystical Lutheranism, since it uses the quasi-mystical vocabulary from his courses of 1919, namely, *es gibt, Ereignis,* and *Hingabe.* Here he described Christian existence as "participation in" the ongoing "primally historical *Ereignis*" and "revelation" of the Crucifixion. But "this parti-*cipating,* which is enacted [*vollgezogen*] only in existing, is as such always *given* only as faith through faith." Faith is the *gift* of "rebirth" and as such is taken up as a "manner of the historical existing of factical believing Dasein." Summing up this definition of faith and stressing that this participation is not a "type of knowing," Heidegger wrote, "Luther says: 'Faith means surrendering oneself [*Sichgefangengeben*] to matters that cannot be seen' " (G9 52–53/PT 9–10).

Heidegger had found this mystical Lutheranism, this synthesis of Eckhart and Luther, of medieval mysticism's depth-dimension and Protestant personalism, not only in his reading of Natorp around 1919, but also in his enthusiasm for the Romantic Protestant mysticism of Schleiermacher, which stressed that the free development of unique personality is permeated by the ineffable ground-feeling of absolute dependence on the undifferentiated infinity of God.

The Anarchic Community of Persons

The ontological analogues of this religious synthesis of Eckhart and Luther are the young Heidegger's unique doubled-sided notions of the *Er-eig-nis* of the primal something, the parousio-kairological time of being, and the *kinesis* of being, which express both the mysterious depth-dimenison of a subjectless, absence-permeated, incalculable, anarchically differentiating temporalizing-sense and the highly personal, individuated enactment-sense of surrender, conscience, resolute openness, keeping silent, wakefulness, and choice.

More specifically, Heidegger worked out an ontological analogue in temporal enactment-sense to the Eckhartian, Schleiermachean, and Natorpian notion of an analogical religious community of unique and free persons. For Da-sein is not just the personal, co-temporalizing, and self-surrendering *site* of the *Ereignis* of being. It is not a mere instantiation of being. Rather, like Eckhart's idea that the efflux out of the mysterious depths of the Divine Life of the Godhead is a constantly flowing *analogical* birth of the Logos in the co-bearing "little castle," Dasein is for Heidegger also the site of an analogical *personalized differentiation* of the mysterious *Ereignis* of the primal something (being). There are in fact a number of interwoven sites of differentiation: the being-here of communal lifeworlds (worldviews) and institutions (e.g., "the university"); of persons; and of things (e.g., "*the* table"), plants, and animals. Like Schleiermacher, Heidegger underlined that "every Dasein of personal life" is in a historically unique environing world and society (*Gesellschaft*). "It stands in a context of life with other I's [*Iche*]," with "fellow human beings" (G56/57 4, 210).

But the *Ereignis* of the primal something is differentiation not just into the ownness of worldviews, societies, and institutions, but further into the personal *Er-eignisse*, e-vents/en-ownments, for each of the Ies that live in communities. *Ereignis* is not just "for us" and not just "to me," but also uniquely "for me," and this differentiation is irreducibly *eigen*, my own, shared by no one else. The terminus of differentation is a "concentration . . . on/toward the selfworld." *Ereignis* is inherently open and pluralist, other and an-archic. There is no such thing as *the Ereignis*, but rather *Ereignisse*. Just as Eckhart emphasizes that the Logos is like a light or a face refracted infinitely in a mirror, Heidegger stressed an an-archic community of persons, each of whom is the site of localized personal *Ereignisse*. For example, "my seeing [of the lectern] and that of a Senegalese negro are indeed basically different. They have only the common moment that in both cases something is seen. *My* seeing is an individual seeing in the highest degree." Everyone, including students, janitor, farmer, sees the lectern in the lecture hall, but differently, just as the sunrise is a unique *Er-eignis* for each of the mountain climbers, and the table in Heidegger's house appears differently in each *kairos* and "while" for those who are "whiling at-home," namely, husband, wife, boys, friend, stranger. Heidegger wrote in KNS 1919, "However the lived experiences of other subjects in general may have reality, then indeed only as *Er-eignisse*, and they are such and can be evident only as *Er-eignisse*, as own-ed [*ge-eignet*] by a historical I. For me they are not *Ereignisse*, for essentially they are indeed precisely only as for an Other." And he immediately added, "Moreover, this concerns not only the reality of individualized I's, but also that of groups, communities, societies, church, state" (G56/57 72, 78).

In contrast to his later tendency to emphasize the mystery of *Ereignis* and the worlding of the world as given in extra-ordinary meditative and poetic experiences, in 1919 Heidegger thought that not only a glorious dawn after a great battle or seen from a mountain top, but rather any personal everyday situation is an *Ereignis* and worlding-out of the world. "Every situation is an '*Ereignis*' and not a 'process'." In his phenomenological exercises, he repeatedly stated that "any lived experience" can be "taken as an example" of worlding and *Ereignis*. He alluded to, for example, a year in the field, a semester, seeing the lectern, seeing your seat as you walk into the classroom, the things on your desk, walking down the street, taking a ride in a car. "*Es gibt* rain again today . . . roast veal tomorrow. . . . tables and chairs, houses and trees, Mozart's sonatas and religious powers" (G56/57 67–75, 205). And we find the same orientation in SS 1923 regarding the incalculable parousio-kairological whiling of "toy," "table, jug, plough, saw, house, garden, field, village, path." The intimate domestic realm of the family's daily meals at the table, the wife's sewing, the philosopher's writing, the boys' playing, the friend's arrival, the holiday—in 1919 Heidegger would have said that each of these is a personal "it worlds" and *Er-eignis*. We hear echoes here not merely of Aristotle's world of *techne* and praxis (which in fact only begins to be a model for Heidegger around 1921), but also of the love of the commonplace and the diminutive that is found in the tradition of Rhineland mysticism, especially in Meister Eckhart, who teaches that one must learn to find the mystery of the Divine Life in everyday things (TME 136–38). It is clear that Heidegger was still reading Eckhart into the 1920s, for Gadamer reports that "I myself experienced with what enthusiasm he reacted in 1923 to the publication of the *Opus tripartitum* of Meister Eckhart" (DEW 18).

In his discussion of time as the *principium individuationis* in 1924,

Heidegger asked, "But to what extent is time, as own-ish [*eigentlich*] time, the principle of individuation, i.e., that out of which Dasein is in awhileness, temporal particularity?" He answered that "in the futural being of anticipation [of especially its death] . . . [Dasein] becomes visible as the unique this-time of its unique fate in the possibility of its unique no-longer." Time is "in each case mine-ish [*meinig*] time." "I *am* never the Other," just as Heidegger had earlier said that the *individuum est ineffabile*, the individual is ineffable. But this "individuation" of being and time in my life is individuation within the analogical category of a *condition humaine*, which is an identity-in-difference. Thus Heidegger wrote, "This individuation has the peculiarity that it does not allow Dasein to come to an individuation in the sense of a fantastic development of exceptional existences; it lays low every making-an-exception-of-oneself. It individuates such that it makes all alike and equal [*gleich*]." Particularly "in connection with death, each is brought into the how that each can be in equal measure [*gleichmässig*]; into a possibility in relation to which no one is exceptional; into a how in which every what is dispersed." Thus the posing of Augustine's question about time must pass first from a "what" to a "who" and then from a "we" to an "I": "What is time? has become the question: who is time? Better: are we ourselves time? Or better yet: Am I my time?" One year earlier, Heidegger had made the same point that "facticity" means not pure relativism, but rather differentiation into the haecceity of ownness (*Eigenheit*): "As in each case my own, Dasein does not mean an isolating relativization into externally viewed individuals and so the individual (*solus ipse* [myself alone]), but rather 'ownness' is a how of being" (BZ 26–28, 16; G63 7).

In all this, we hear echoes of Heidegger's position in his qualifying dissertation that, because being contains right within itself the category of haecceity, it entails neither a genus nor a pure nominalistic particularity, neither a monism (univocity) nor a pure pluralism (equivocity), but rather an identity-in-difference and a difference-in-identity (analogy). It is clear that into the twenties Heidegger continued to be preoccupied with this problem of the analogical sense of being that he had inherited from medieval Scholasticism and mysticism. For example, he had chosen Thomas's *De ente et essentia* (On Being and Essence) for his SS 1924 seminar on "High Scholasticism and Aristotle," but as soon as he found out that the edition chosen by Gadamer contained Cajetan's *De nominum analogia* (On the Analogy of Names) as an appendix, he responded by saying "that's a nut!" and devoted the entire semester to it instead. And near the end of the course, he finally dropped the question on his students, "Now then, gentlemen, what does this really mean—'being'?" (EMH 111; EHA 25–26).

Writing to Löwith in 1927, Heidegger highlighted the continuity between his qualifying dissertation and SZ: "I am also convinced that ontology can be founded only ontically. . . . The problems of facticity continue to exist for me just as in my Freiburg beginnings. . . . That I constantly preoccupied myself with Duns Scotus and the Middle Ages and then, further back, with Aristotle is surely no accident" (BL 36–37). In SZ Heidegger introduced the question of being in the context of the "darkness" surrounding the "problem of the unity of being over against the multiplicity [*Mannigfaltigkeit*] of material categories" in Aristotle and in "the Thomist and Scotist schools," including Cajetan's work on analogy, which Heidegger cited later on in SZ. We read that "being is not a genus" (Aristotle), that it is what the medieval thinkers call a "transcendental," and that as such it has only a "unity of analogy" over against its differentiated senses. According to Scholastic ontology, "between both beings [namely, God and world] there exists an *infinite difference* precisely of being" (emphasis added). Thus "Scholasticism understands the positive sense of the signifying of 'being' as an 'analogous' signifying in opposition to one that is univocal or merely homonymous." Moreover, the Scholastics maintain that "truth" was a transcendental convertible with being, where truth means the knowability of beings. And this means that the "the soul" is seen here as a "distinctive being" among all other beings since, possessing the *lumen naturale* of understanding, it is "the being whose nature it is to meet up with all other beings" (Thomas). As Aristotle put this, "the soul is in a way all beings," for it has the possiblity of *aletheuein*, unconcealing (SZ 4–5/22–23, 124–25/126, 16–19/32–34).

Heidegger presented this "truth" as the historical precedent of the notion of the "ontic priority" of Dasein over all other beings: "Understanding of being is itself a definite characteristic of Dasein's being." Dasein, being-here, is the topological here and lighted clearing (*lumen, Lichtung*) of being. But being is given always to a radically individuated, personal being-here, which is defined by "mineness" and is "never to be taken as a case or example of a genus." Using Scholastic Latin, Heidegger here referred to being as a *transcendens* that is "individuated" within the temporal particularity and mineness of Dasein:

> *Being is the* transcendens *pure and simple.* And the transcendence of the being of Dasein is distinctive insofar as there lies in it the possibility and necessity of the most radical individuation. . . . Phenomenological truth (disclosedness of being) is *veritas transcendentalis.* . . . The question about the sense of being is the most universal and emptiest of questions, but in it lies simultaneously the possibility of the extremest individuation into Dasein at any particular time [*auf das jeweilige Dasein*].

In a marginal note to this passage, made at a later date in his own copy of SZ, Heidegger indicated what we have been surmising here all along, namely, that this passage is an echo of his earlier concept of the differentiating *Ereignis* of the primal something: "But transcendence from the truth of being: *Ereignis*." And his gloss on the term Dasein, being-here, in the same passage reads:

"Ownmostly [*eigentlich*]: enactment [*Vollzug*] of in-stance in the here" (SZ 176–77/170–71, 284ff./257ff., 51–57/62–68).

The terminus and major focus of the young Heidegger's thinking, especially in his early Freiburg period, were neither the *Ereignis* of epochal constellations hovering over us as a cosmic *arche*, nor the *Ereignis* of a homogeneous *Volk*, which is the impression one often receives in his writings of the thirties and thereafter. Rather, without falling into either metaphysical subjectivism or asocial individualism, the young Heidegger stressed a free, an-archic, and analogical community of persons, each of whom is a site of a differentiated personal *Ereignis* of being, epochal worldview, and community. His anarchic *arche* is a divided kingdom, a radically ontological version of Kant's "kingdom of ends." On whatever scale, a community of persons is neither a pure identity nor a pure difference, neither Enlightenment universalism nor psychological atomism and anarchistic individualism, but rather an analogical identity-in-difference, which is like "a bundle of rays flowing together in a single point."

The *condition humaine*, society, state, church, the family having its evening meal at the table, the group of mountain climbers, the Theban elders, "you before me, I before you, we with each other" in the lecture hall—each of these is a refracted analogical identity-in-difference. This an-archic predicament is modeled not on political anarchism or subjectivistic existentialism, but rather on the medieval-mystical doctrine of analogy and emanation, as well as on the tradition of Christian personalism in such figures as Eckhart, Schlegel, Schleiermacher, Natorp, Augustine, Luther, and Kierkegaard. To understand Heidegger's ontological notion of individuality, one should look especially to Eckhart's religious notion of an analogical multiplicity of "little castles," that is, personal sites, in the mystical body of the Logos, as well as to his reading of "Adolf Deissmann's studies on Pauline mysticism and the grammatically oriented question of what it means to be 'in' . . . regarding the Biblical formula 'Christ in me, I in Christ' " (DK 109–10). If we explore the Eckhartian sense of this formula, we arrive at the following analogy in Heidegger's thinking: As the Logos is in me and I am in the Logos analogically, so being is in me and I am in being analogically. Likewise, I am in a community, family, etc. and the community, family, etc. is in me analogically.

The linguistic precedents for Heidegger's use of the adjective "own" (*eigen*), for his concept of a personal *Er-eignis*, and for his notions of "mineness" and *eigentlich* (own-ish, authentic) are to be found not in the troubled waters of subjectivism or decisionism, but rather in Scotist "haecceity," Eckhartian life that lives "out of its own," Schleiermachean "ownness," and the "ownmost own" of "individuity" that Natorp finds in the mystical tradition. For example, in his SS 1923 statement that, "as in each case my own, Dasein does not mean an isolating relativization . . . but rather 'ownness' [*Eigenheit*] is a how of being," one finds Heidegger still using the old Schleier-

318 | *New Beginnings*

machean term *Eigenheit* that he had introduced back in SS 1919 (G63 7, 85). When, in his 1924 lecture "The Concept of Time" and elsewhere, he said that death is not merely a biological process or a public fact, but rather that own-most (*eigenste*) possibility which individuates Dasein and frees Dasein for its *Eigentlichkeit*, own-ishness, authenticity, he was still thinking about *Er-eignis* with all its mystical overtones, even though he was no longer using precisely this term (BZ 15–16). Being anxious for my daily bread, daily dying my own death—that, too, is *Ereignis*.

15 | Indications of Ethics

HEIDEGGER CALLED HIS "authentic beginning" of philosophy "the most radical phenomenology that *begins* 'from below' " in the midst of *kinesis* and not from some mythological high-ground above factical life (G61 195). There is a double sense of "radical" at work here. It suggests the depth-dimension of the primal source (*radix*) of *Ereignis* and *kinesis* that produces being as an effect, as well as the profoundly ethical significance of a stress on the alterity and ownness into which this depth-dimension becomes anarchically differentiated. Here Heidegger contrasted openness toward the cultural, social, personal, and philosophical Other with being closed off (*Abreigelung, Verschlossenheit*) to the Other. In other words, he contrasted "humility before the mystery and grace-character of all life" with the fallenness, hyperbolic presumption (*Vermessen*), and pride of metaphysics, which exhibits the attitude of "a logical tyrant" (G58 263). The original model for Heidegger's notion of ontological humility and openness was actually the religious contrast between humility and pride before the *mysterium tremendum* of God, between *theologia crucis* and *theologia gloriae*. Chronologically, Heidegger's models were, first, Eckhartian letting-be of the mystery of the flux of the Divine Life and Schleiermachean mutual respect within free sociality (1917–20); then, the wakefulness toward incalculable Parousia, toward kairological alterity, and toward the unique situation of the individual, which are found in Paul, Luther, and Kierkegaard (1920–21); and, eventually, also the resolute openness toward being as "that which can be other" in Aristotle's kairological ethics and its critique of the Platonic Idea of the Good and philosophical kingship (1921–22).

I examine the following themes in the young Heidegger's thought, which indicate the ethical significance of his new beginnings for the question about being: (1) unmasking the illusions of homogeneity and calculative control in the technology and worldview-ideology of metaphysics; (2) formal indication as the type of postmetaphysical discourse that cultivates openness to and constant beginning within the mystery of the anarchic differentiation of *Ereignis*; (3) the influence of Eckhart's attitude of letting-be and Schleiermacher's notion of free sociality on Heidegger around 1917 through 1920; (4) Heidegger's sketches in WS 1921–22 for a kairological ethics based on Kierkegaard, Jaspers, and Aristotle; (5) cultural and universal reform; and (6) Dasein and *Geschlecht.*

Unmasking Technology and Worldview-Ideology

Heidegger's "completely new concept of philosophy" and "genuine beginning" mean precisely a humility and openness toward the topic of the primal flowing source that is ultimately groundless, absence-permeated, incalculable, differentiated into ownness, and therefore an-archic and nonmasterable. His notion of the "end of philosophy," on the other hand, means precisely the end of the traditional "kingly vocation" from the Greeks to modernity that lies in searching for a metaphysical *arche*, principle/kingdom, which would be fully present, calculable, identical and universal, and thus available to and masterable by the *manus mentis* of the knowing subject. For example, his KNS 1919 course noted that, for Plato, "dialectic is the only way [*methodos*] that advances in this manner . . . up to *ten archen*, the principle/kingdom itself, in order to find certainty," the "fixed secure element of *logos*." This "upward path of the soul to the *noeton topon*, the intelligible place," is "the making explicit of the valid ideas that provide an ultimate grounding" (*Republic* 517b, 533c). But in erecting its principles, metaphysics performs a violent act of de-historicizing, deworlding, and deliving through its "theoretical fixation and cold-clocking" of the "stream of lived experience," its "objectifying and still-ing" of the an-archic flux of *Ereignis*. "We make a grab [*Griff*], as it were, into the flowing stream of lived experiences and seize out one or more, i.e., we 'still the stream' " and "destroy" it. The ocular-aesthetic quietism of metaphysics wants objectification, totalization, homogeneity, mastery, and *securitas* in the sense of the carefreeness that is no longer anxious for its daily bread. It wants to be "secure absolute science" (G56/57 11, 20, 115, 100, 86; DK 107; G61 56).

In fact, Heidegger already understood modern culture and philosophy as "technology" that seeks to master the unruly abousiological and heterological character of life by turning it into a presence that can be calculated according to rules. Recall that his qualifying dissertation had already characterized the modern in contrast to the medieval worldview as "the will to power" of both the " 'natural-scientific worldview' " and the general "consciousness of methods" in philosophy that seeks the "constant control of every step of thinking" (G1 198, 415). In SS 1919, he suggested that especially the rationalism of the modern Enlightenment with its "schematically rule-oriented" approach played a key role in preparing for the distinctive stamp (*Gepräge*) of the late nineteenth and early twentieth centuries, namely, "the development of technology in the widest sense." "One speaks of the natural-scientific age, of the century of technology." "An age that is seized by this consciousness sees its own purpose of life in forward-striving work on the real itself, on real being. Its mastery in knowledge of every kind and praxis of every form makes one at times undemanding for transcendent philosophical 'phantasies' " (G56/57 130–36). Heidegger was here probably already drawing his observations on modern technology from Spengler, for he discussed Spengler's *Decline of the West* (1918) in WS 1919–20 and SS 1920. In April of 1920, he presented lectures on "Oswald Spengler and His Work *The Decline of the West*" in Wiesbaden. His WS 1921–22 course discussed Spengler's theme of "technization" and "decline" in modern culture, and Spengler turned up again as a key figure also in SS 1923 (G58 3ff.; HJ 15; G61 26, 68–76; G63 37, 55; cf. HCM 21–33).

According to Heidegger, the hyperbolic presumptuousness of the They in prephilosophical life is characterized by a tendency to technization and ideological dictatorship, to the substitution of *techne* for *phronesis*. It is this tendency that he thought had become aggravated specifically in the realm of modern technology. Thus, as became evident especially in his later thinking, his account of the category of the They is very much bound up with a historical critique of modern technological culture (cf. HCM 21–33). Not only are his descriptions of the They oriented to modern mass culture, but he stated explicitly in SZ that "the forcefulness and explicitness of [the They's] dominion and mastery [*Herrschaft*] can change in the course of history" (SZ 172/167). The They operates with "authoritative" public "rules," "standards," "norms," and "calculable maxims" that regulate all spheres of life. These rules, which express a universal *eidos*, are noninterpretively applied to Dasein as an object of concernful *techne*, that is, as a *poioumenon*, a produced manipulable being. Dasein is not approached as a "practical affair" in which *phronesis* interpretively concretizes moral ends in unique personal situations. As Heidegger wrote, it is "as if Dasein were a household." "Everydayness takes Dasein as something ready-to-hand to be concerned with, that is, managed and reckoned up. 'Life' is a 'business' " (SZ 329/292, 355/312, 382–89/334–40; G61 25–26; PIA 253).

Controlled by the "prescription" of these public rules and ideologies, Dasein becomes a slave to this dictatorship and exists in a condition of "alienation" from its own individual unique being: "Dasein stands in subjection to the Others. . . . [T]he Others have taken its being away from it. . . . What is decisive is just the inconspicuous mastery by Others. . . . One belongs to the Others oneself and solidifies their power [*Macht*]. . . . the real dictatorship [*Diktatur*] of the They unfolds itself." This dictatorship is "the dominion of public interpretedness," i.e., of the interpretive sense of being regarding its worldly content, its relational sense, and its temporalizing-sense. "Publicness proximally regulates and controls all interpreting of world and Dasein," and this disclosedness (truth) operates precisely by simultaneously closing-off and distorting everything that is different. "The They prescribes one's moodful state of mind, and it decides what and how one 'sees,' " as well as how one "talks" and "writes." This "idle talk discusses everything in a curious insensitivity to difference" (G63 31). Like speculative eschatology in the New Testament, the dictatorship of calculative "public time" decides what will happen, how and when it will happen, and to whom it will happen. The "different time" of one's own time is "suppressed." In the face of this "levelling" of difference into "averageness" and of incalculable, absence-permeated kairological time into the static calculable presence of "the today," "everything original becomes handy and manipulable [*handlich*]." And "every mystery [*Geheimnis*] loses its force." But Dasein can never completely escape this "dominion" of the They into, as it were, the "free and open country of a 'world' in itself" (SZ 168–72/164–67, 224–31/212–18).

Just as Heidegger thought that the masquerade and hyperbolic phantom life of the They is taken up and amplified in metaphysical myths, so he thought that, especially in the modern age of technology, its tendency to technization and ideology is raised to the second power in metaphysics. Throughout the early twenties, he warned that philosophy must resist its own tendency to technization, that is, its reduction to a "method" in the sense of a "technique" and business (*Betrieb*) consisting of rules that can be mastered. In WS 1921–22, he argued that, like playing music, philosophy "is not a mere comportment to a possible 'business' [*Betrieb*], mastering a technique." "Plato would never have defined philosophy as *techne*! . . . We say . . . 'to study philosophy.' 'Philosophy' must here be taken in the modern sense where it means a context of knowledge, something like 'science', objectified, distanced . . . a cultural object, educational object," a "developed doctrine" that is given out at the universities. In SS 1923, he accused contemporary historical science and philosophy of reducing being to a "presence" that is "calculated" by the classifying methods of history and by the Neo-Kantian method of filing and ordering particular historical realities away into a logical system of timeless universal truths. And in WS 1925–26, he called the whole of modern calculative, rule-oriented logic from Descartes to Neo-Kantianism the "technique or, better, technology of correct thinking" (G9 9; G61 115, 48, 50; G63 52–65; G21 37).

In its drive toward totalization, homogenization, and technization, metaphysics not only levels differences, but rather, like the popular They, actually winds up bringing the flux of *Ereignis* to closure in one of its particular effects and falling into a worldview-ideology, including "objectified significance (personality, an ideal of humanity)" and "religious ideology and phantasy." It elevates a historically conditioned perspective to the privileged standpoint of a timeless universal truth and "absolute ethics," and thereby suppresses and "alienates" historical periods, societies, and individuals that are different. We have already seen this in Heidegger's critique of the Eurocentric "heavenly city" of the Enlightenment,[1] which tended to dismiss what did not fit into its vision of "universal history" (indigenous cultures, the lifeworlds of poetry and religion) as "barbarism, superstition, illusion, and disorder." Heidegger made similar charges against the purportedly universal and timeless "values" put forward in Neo-Kantian value-philosophy. Likewise, the "great business of philosophy" in modernity is generally marked by the drive "to calculate [being] in advance" for all ages and all humanity; it "steals away artificially from its own time and is capable of making an 'effect' only in this form. (Business, propaganda, proselytizing, cliquey setup, intellectual wangling.)" Heidegger cited the following description of traditional philosophy given by contemporary worldview-philosophy, but unlike the latter he wanted precisely to criticize it: "The view of the great philosophies moves towards something ultimate, universal, and universally valid in every sense. The inner struggle with the mysteries of life and world seeks to come to rest in the fixation of something conclusive. . . . every great philosophy completes itself in a worldview . . . every philosophy is a metaphysics" (G9 34; G61 197, 165; G56/57 132, 8; G63 18–20).

Heidegger had clearly given up his former position that philosophy should provide "the true worldview," namely, the epochal "Catholic worldview" of the Middle Ages and modern Neo-Scholasticism. This hidden, self-exiled king now asserted a "radical separation" of worldview and philosophy. In order to avoid putting forward a worldview-ideology, philosophy must stand "beyond every relation to the ultimate questions of human life" and must abdicate "its most ancestral privileges, its superior kingly vocation." Heidegger now practiced a kind of ontologically emancipatory critique of all such pretensions and the marginalizing effects of their hierarchical claims. "Philosophy," he insisted, "has no mission to take care of universal humanity and culture and indeed to take away from coming generations and races [*Geschlechter*] once and for all the concern for questioning or even merely to interfere with them through topsy-turvy claims to validity." "Philosophy is not art (poetry), not life-wisdom (practical supplying of rules)," not "absolutism," "absolute ethics," or a "solid ground" of any kind that provides reassuring universal solutions, answers, and techniques. It is, moreover, "atheistic" in the sense of being neutral over against every particular religious worldview. In contrast to his later statements in his rectorial address of 1933, the exiled king of the early 1920s underscored that philosophy must proceed "without prophecy and the affectations of Führers," philosopher-kings, and prophets who offer grandiose heavenly or epochal visions of the kingdom of truth, destiny, and salvation. "Philosophy is not supposed to give a worldview. . . . It is not destined to save or lead [*führen*] its age" (PAA July 26, 1920). Its role is not to flaunt "prophetic pageantry that brings world-historical salvation." It has no "cultural mission" and does not "put up bail for coming cultural periods and destinies of humanity." There is no *Heilsweg*, no way of salvation. The philosopher is not a privileged world-historical know-it-all, "philosophical medicine-man," or Führer who can legislate a timeless universal truth and concept of the good. As "skepticism," philosophy practices this abdication and asceticism not out of indifference, but rather due to the demand that it remain nonideologically "open" to and respectful of the concretion and differentiation of being in *all* historical periods, societies, religious and aristic lifeworlds, and individual worldviews. For "the farmer in the Black Forest has his worldview . . . the factory worker has his worldview . . . the educated person has his worldview; political parties have their worldview. There is even talk about the contrast between the English-American and the German worldview." Ontology cannot privilege any one of these to the exclusion of the others. The young Heidegger's "phenomenological critique" (1919), "destruction" (1920), and unmasking (1921–22) of the "masks" of "reification," "alienation," and "worldview"-ideology perpetrated by metaphysics has definite similarities with the critique of ideology in the Young Hegelians and contemporary Neo-Marxism.[2]

Formal Indication and Constant Beginning

Heidegger later reported that the *Sache* of his new beginning in the early Freiburg period continually "withdrew from every attempt to say it" as he searched for a new type of nonobjectifying language (what he later called an "other language") and accordingly experimented with various "way-traces" (G12 130/41; cf. G12 151). But the message we get from these youthful texts themselves is that this new language cannot ever transcend such way-traces into the self-withdrawing topic. The young Heidegger was preoccupied precisely with the "methodological problem" (G56/57 110) of finding a type of nonobjectifying philosophical language that would allow one to speak about and yet precisely preserve the prereflective nonmasterable "mystery" and movement of the subjectless, absence-permeated, incalculable, and anarchically differentiating *Sache* of his thought. It was to replace the hubris of traditional objectifying language that leads to the violent dehistoricizing, depersonalizing, technization, and ideologization of the *Ereignis* of being into statically present, calculable, and homogeneous metaphysical principles and worldviews. What kind of language could alternatively remain open to and encourage the concealment and anarchic differentiation of *Ereignis* in the manifold ways of different philosophies, historical eras, cultures, societies, and personal lives? What was "the word" that could constantly call thinking to and preserve it within the movement of being-on-the-way and openness to these Others?

Religiously, Heidegger's linguistic problem was the traditional mystical problem of saying the unsayable (cf. HA 390; EBF 98ff.), as well as the Lutheran "task . . . to find the word that is able to call one to faith and preserve one in faith" against the objectifying Hellenization of historical Christian ex-

perience. According to Luther, there can be no science of the historical enactment of faith's surrender to and constant "questioning after" the *Deus absconditus*. According to the *via negativa* of the mystical tradition, the *unio mystica*
with the *mysterium tremendum* is ineffable, nameless. For Schleiermacher the
prereflective "feeling" of absolute dependence is not accessible to conceptual
thinking, and for Kierkegaard's "Concluding *Unscientific* Postscript" the individual's relation to God is the "secret" of inwardness. Similarly, the essentialist
onto-logical tradition initiated by the Greeks maintained that the individual is
alogon, inexpressible. There can be *logos* and science only of the *eidos*, the
universal form, such that Aristotle maintained that there can be no science of
the good in practical life.

On an ontological level, Heidegger, too, thought that there can be no rigorous science and transcendental logic of his *Sache*, but he wanted nonetheless
to find a new *logos* to talk about it. "It is easy to run away from the university," he wrote (G61 66). He attempted to create an opening within academic
discourse for precisely those concerns that traditionally had been considered
beyond its reach. Without this new language, he would have been literally at
the end of philosophy, at pure *aporia*, the total absence of ways. With regard
to his own new beginning, it was a matter of preventing its closure by articu-
lating it within a language open to constantly beginning anew in different
thoughtpaths and way-traces toward the *Sache*. The problem of method was
literally the task of preserving thinking within its essential character of *methodos*, way-toward. In 1919, Heidegger expressed this constant beginning as the
"requirement of 'eternal youth'. . . . Always turning back anew into the primal
source" (G56/57 214). In WS 1921–22, he said that "the philosopher . . . is
precisely the genuine and constant 'beginner'." As "kairological-critical" questioning, "beginning has its 'time'. To begin for another time is senseless" (G61
13, 186).

In 1919 Heidegger adressed his linguistic methodological problem by taking up Natorp's twofold criticism of Husserl's phenomenological method of
reflective description. In the first place, its objectifying intuition "stills the
stream" of lived experience. Second, the "grasping-in-words" of conceptual
expression "generalizes," homogenizes, and dissolves the particularity of lived
experience into "generalities." If all discourse is of this nature, "it is therefore
hopeless to try to avoid theorization if one wants to make lived experiences
into the object of a science." But what underlies this objection is the "unproven
prejudice" that "all language is in itself already objectifying" and "generalizing" (G56/57 100–111). In his essay on Jaspers, Heidegger hearkened back to
his treatment of haecceity in his qualifying dissertation and again addressed
the traditional problem of "the inexpressability of the soul," "the impossibility
of completely grasping the individual," that is, "factical life-experience that is
lived *hic et nunc* . . . in this historical situation." But "instead of always repeat-

ing anew the often expressed '*individuum est ineffabile*,' it should be about time to ask which meaning the '*fari*' should actually have here" (G9 32, 39–40). In SS 1920, Heidegger again addressed this problem in his lecture course titled "Phenomenology of Intuition and Expression: Theory of Philosophical Concept-Formation."

In WS 1921–22, he argued that, on the one hand, philosophy has to avoid its "overestimation" as "a secure absolute science," "absolutism," whose "logic" offers a "universal definition" of philosophy under which all historical philosophies could be subsumed as particular cases. This approach reduces philosophy to a *techne* that realizes an unchanging universal *eidos* in various historical instantiations. On the other hand, one has to avoid simultaneously the "underestimation" of philosophy, which takes the forms of "relativism" and "lazy and tired skepticism"; the view that philosophy is not system-building but "concrete work" on particular problems; and the Romantic enthusiasm and rapture (*Schwärmerei*) which maintains that "philosophy . . . can only be 'experienced in life.' " It is a "private" "lived experience" of the "felt 'depths' of life," and therefore is not science and cannot even be defined. A "genuine intention" lies in both the overestimation and the underestimation of philosophy. The overestimation is oriented to principles in the sense of basic starting points and, as science, does not perpetrate ideological worldviews. The underestimation is oriented to concreteness and to personal "passionate" "philosophizing" in one's historical situation. But in synthesizing these two intentions, Heidegger wanted to step outside of the either/or of "absolutism" and "its counterparts: relativism and skepticism," the either/or of pure identity and pure difference, by working out a new "genuine 'logic'," an "existentiell logic" in which "philosophizing can 'come to language.' " He called this postmetaphysical type of speaking and writing "formal indication" and devoted the entire first half of this lecture course to its explication. But he had already introduced it in his WS 1919–20 and SS 1920 lecture courses, and then extensively in the opening of his WS 1920–21 lecture course, as the methodological requisite for dealing with Pauline kairological experience of the *Deus absconditus*, which he treated in the second part of the course.[3]

In 1919 Heidegger modeled his new indicative language on the Idea in the Kantian Sense, the mystical *via negativa*, and the individualizing science of Dilthey and the Neo-Kantians. Thereafter he also took up Kierkegaard's method of "indirect communication" that he found laid out in Jaspers's *Psychologie der Weltanschauungen*, which itself took up this method in its ontology of the "principles and categories" of "what human being is," that is, of the limit-situations. "Regarding Kierkegaard," Heidegger wrote in his essay on Jaspers, "it must indeed be pointed out that it is not often that in philosophy or theology (where is here indifferent) such a height of rigorous consciousness of method has been achieved as it was precisely by him." Not only did Heidegger quote Kierkegaard's statement that philosophy can only "point [*hinweisen*] human beings (individual human beings) to the ethical, the religious, the existential" as a motto for his WS 1921–22 lecture course, but he used extensively Kierkegaard's description of indirect communication as *aufmerksam machen*, calling attention to, making take note of, making remark by giving a mark, a sign, a *Merkmal, nota* (G9 6, 28, 42; G61 180, 169, 185; G63 18). He explained that, as *hermeneia*, that is, as the "communication" and intimative announcing (*Kundgabe*) to others, one's philosophical "concept-formation means not putting forth a theoretical theme with a merely theoretical aim," but rather the attempt "to call attention to a *way*" that is to be enacted "passionately" in one's own historical situation. "The withworldly intimative announcing, the communication of philosophy to others, the suggestive idea that one puts to others with this indicative professing . . . must have an understandability and one which lays itself precisely before withworldly decision in a definite situation" (G63 10, 14; G9 41, 27; G61 182, 167, 36).

The indirect and direct modes of communication are for Kierkegaard the modes of writing and authorship corresponding to objective and subjective truth. Since objective truth is thought to be objectively present and universal, one attempts to convey it to the reader in the "direct communication" of objectifying and impersonal scientific discourse, logic, doctrine, the textbook, the encyclopedic system. But, according to Kierkegaard, subjective truth is "absent," "hidden," a "secret" that consists in (1) a nonobjective content (e.g., the futural hiddenness of ethical ends and the paradoxical "mystery" of the infinite hidden in the human figure of Jesus); (2) the hidden inwardness of the individual's unique relation to and enactment of that content; and (3) the dialectical synthesis of these first two moments in the interpretive manifestation of moral ends or God in one's historical situation, that is, the "contradiction that the universal is posited as the individual." Because this truth is inexpressible directly, it can be intimated to the individual reader only by "pointing" at and "calling attention" to it in the nonobjectifying and personally oriented "indirect communication" of an "unscientific" writing, which makes use of such literary devices as pseudonyms, epigrams, anecdotes, thought-experiments, the subjunctive, *aporia*, and irony. According to Jaspers, philosophers can be classified either as "prophets of indirect communication" (e.g., Socrates, Kant, Kierkegaard) or as "teachers of determinate principles" and "the totality of life" (e.g., Thomas, Hegel). The pointing of indirect communication is supposed to lead the readers to the subjective truth that is to be found in the their own historical situations. Here there is both a negative repellent moment of pointing-away and a positive directive moment of pointing-to. Communicating is in the first place "the art of taking away," similar to when "a man has his mouth so full of food that he is prevented from eating." The emetic moment in communication consists in repelling reliance on the *mens auctoris* of

328 | *New Beginnings*

the writer and the direct content of the communication (CUP 232, 73, 245–46; TC 134). In Jaspers's words, indirect communicators "refuse to be prophets," a "superior" "Führer and Master" with a "following" and "school." The content of the communication must be "no fixed doctrine" and "nothing 'positive' " that makes it "easy" to understand, but rather it has to throw individuals back into the "difficulty" of finding and enacting the truth in their own existence. As Heidegger stressed, for Jaspers this means that his indirectly communicative ontology of the limit-situations "should, however, develop and impose no positive worldview." Jaspers insists that one must not pursue "prophetic philosophy," which preaches "tables of values" and "what we should live for and how we should live, what we should do." As Heidegger also pointed out, Jaspers grafts onto Kierkegaard Max Weber's "separation of scientific observation and worldview valuing" in academic life (PDW 376–79, 3; G9 2, 40).

According to Kierkegaard, the positive moment of indirect communication consists in the fact that its "philosophical scraps," its "scrapings and parings of systematic thought," are "signs" pointing out the direction toward "personal appropriation" and concretion. Indirect communication of the truth "acknowledges the given independence in every human being" and gives "an impulse to go precisely one's own way." "Truth consists in personal appropriation. . . . it is not the truth but the way which is the truth" (CUP 2, 557, 71–72, 232, 247; TC 124ff.). As Heidegger noted, for Jaspers this means that philosophy "should provide 'clarifications and possibilities as means to [worldview] self-reflection' " (G9 2). Indirect communicators "appeal to the life that is in the Other," "the concrete decisions of personal destiny," "free spiritual intellectuality." "They love freedom in the Other." They do not rule and "manage life" as philosopher-kings; rather, like the "maieutic art" of the barren Socrates, they "only help" Others bring forth subjective situational truth in their own lives (PDW vii, 377).

Long before Derrida's *Speech and Phenomena* developed an initial formulation of "deconstruction" by generalizing Husserl's regional concept of "indicative" signs and reinscribing it as "arche-trace" and "arche-writing," the young Heidegger was setting a precedent for this, though it was not until later that he started calling "indication" by the name of *Spur*, trace.[4] In developing his notion of "formal indication," Heidegger took the term *Anzeige*, indication, from the theory of signs in Husserl's First Investigation, "Expression and Meaning," on which he held formal and informal seminars in the early twenties. Thus we find Günther Stern, a participant, submitting to Husserl in 1924 a dissertation on "The Role of the Category of the Situation in 'Logical Propositions,' " in which he took up Heidegger's reading of Husserl's concept of indication in "occasional expressions."[5]

In Chapter Three of his First Investigation, Husserl juxtaposes two types of expressive signs in speaking and writing, namely, the *"objective* expressions" of science and the *"essentially subjective and occasional* expressions" of "ordinary life," which are essentially "indicative" expressions. This distinction is very similar to the Kierkegaardian distinction between the modes of direct and indirect communication that correspond to the two modes of objective and subjective situational truth. A nonindicative objective expression in science, logic, or mathematics, e.g., "there are [*es gibt*] regular solids," can be understood "without necessarily requiring a view toward [*Hinblick auf*] the person uttering it, or to the circumstances of the utterance." The meaning-content is (1) nonsituational and atemporal; (2) always identical in different acts of intending it; and (3) fully present.

However, for a nonobjective occasional expression, e.g., *"es gibt* cakes" or "I forgot my umbrella," it is "essential for it to orient its here-and-now meaning at each particular time [*seine jeweils aktuelle Bedeutung*] to the occasion, to the speaking person and the situation." This nonobjectifiable meaning-content (1) is bound up with the situation of the subject; (2) "fluctuates" in the different situations of the speakers and writers; and (3) is thus never completely present in intuition. Here, as Derrida writes, "the thing itself always escapes" and "there never was any 'perception' " in the classical sense of full presence.[6] There is/it gives only the indicative sign, the way-trace. In fact, the nonpresence of the meaning-content of these expressions is aggravated when it concerns their function of indicatively intimating (*Kundgabe*) the subjective intentional acts of the speaker or writer to others, since this subjectivity is, for Husserl as for Kiekegaard and the young Heidegger, an essentially nonpresent and nonintuitable Other for the audience. It can only be "appresented" on the basis of the indications of spoken or written expressions, facial expressions, and gestures. For all these reasons, occasional expressions are similar to *nonexpressive* indications such as facial expressions, memorials, and the shadowed profiles (*Abschattungen*) of an intended object, though Husserl maintains that these indicate not a meaning, but only a particular, variable, and nonpresent existent. Types of occasional expressions are personal pronouns ("I," "you," "we"), personal possessive adjectives ("my," "your"), demonstratives ("this lamp"), the definite article ("the Kaiser" in the sense of "the present German Kaiser"), "subject-bound" spatial and temporal expressions ("here," "over there," "now," "tomorrow"), all expressions for "beliefs, doubts, wishes, fears, and commands" ("it might snow"), impersonalia (*"es gibt* cakes"), enthymematic expressions ("but my dear!"), and the vague morphological expressions of everyday life ("shrub," "black," "a long walk").

The indicative meaning of occasional expressions is marked by two intentional moments, namely, "a universally operative indication" (the empty indicating meaning) and "the singular presentation" (the fulfilling indicated meaning). The former is, for example, the purely formal "meaning-me-myself" "at the particular time" that operates in the word "I," or the meaning-here-and-now-where-I-am that operates in the word "here." Unlike the material generic term "lion" that can "directly" give rise to an intuition of its meaning, the "universally indicative function" in occasional expressions has no concrete content and does not have, for example, "the power to arouse the specific I-presentation." It is only an empty, indexical toward-which that "indirectly" points out a "direction" in which to look and find its concrete fulfillment in the "singular presentation," which is the "geunine aim" and "genuine meaning" (LU2 557–58/686–87). When the speaker says "I," the "indicating function mediates, calling, as it were, to the listener: Your vis-à-vis means himself/herself." One must actually look toward the situated Other. That is, one must "enact [*vollziehen*] the indicative function in here-and-now presentation" of "what is meant *hic et nunc*" in the unique situation. This fulfilling intention, Husserl says, is *augenblicklich*, momentary, kairological. "The word 'I' names a different person from case to case, and does so by way of an always new meaning."

According to the Heideggerian interpretation given by Stern in his 1924 dissertation, an occasional expression is an interplay between empty categorial meaning-intention (the indicating meaning) and fulfilling categorial intuition (the indicated meaning), which intends "being-sense" in the indexical category of a "there is/it gives here" for me and "being-here-now" for me, that is, in "the category of the situation," haecceity, temporal particularity (*Jeweiligkeit*). "Almost every '*es gibt*' is an '*es gibt* here,' '*il y a*.' It is related . . . to *my* existence. . . . With the sentence 'S is here' is expressed . . . its 'being-here-now,' its being-graspable, its 'standing-available' (Heidegger)." For example, "a pencil in a coal-box is not 'here'; it is 'here' on the desk and in writing (Heidegger). . . . the being-here is here somewhere . . . alongside [*bei*] someone. . . . 'S is here' means 'I have S.' " In the statement "there is/it gives S," the real subject is not S, "the given," but the "it" that gives, "the 'giving,' " the happening of the situation. Thus the statement means " 'there is/it gives also S' . . . from out of and in . . . the situation." The categorial form in which being is experienced and expressed is ultimately a "temporal form": "The 'is' of the ultimate existential-judgments is a *present-ish* [*präsentisches*] and also therefore a *temporal* 'is.' But if the object of logic can be a temporal form, it is not understandable why it cannot with equal right likewise be the other temporal forms (the 'was,' the 'been,' etc.)."[7]

Heidegger's impersonals of 1919, namely, "there is/it gives," "it worlds," "it e-vents/en-owns," are precisely occasional expressions operating with the indexical temporal category of "the situation." Husserl himself shows this with his example of "there are/it gives cakes": "In the first place we do not mean that absolutely and in general there are/it gives cakes, but that *here and now—for coffee—there are/it gives cakes. It's raining* does not mean that it's raining in general, but rather that it's raining *now, outside.*" Appropriately, the everyday term *Anzeige* means "notice" or "announcement" of a unique *Ereignis* (e.g., birth, marriage, party, funeral) in a newspaper, card, letter. Heidegger's writings on "the something," the "it," "being-*here*," "mineness," "facticity," "awhileness" consist not of objective, but rather of occasional expressions whose indicative function is simply being held in unfulfilled suspension. All the while, he was using everyday examples of occasional expression in his courses to show the nonobjective, situational understanding of being: for example, "the shortest way to Münster," "a stone's throw," " 'no longer' useful ... 'in the way,' clutter," "the hammer is too heavy," which have little to do with the objective concepts of space and time in natural science (G56/57 86; G63 101, 94; G20 §25b; SZ 209/200).

"Actually since Aristotle's time," Heidegger wrote in WS 1921–22, "philosophy has no longer understood the problem of genuine logic." He noted that, according to Aristotle, the nature of a discipline's *methodos,* its way-to-ward the subject matter, and its rigor have to be determined out of the matter itself, and that it is the mark of education to accept that amount of exactitude (*akribeia*) that the matter itself affords (G61 21; BZ 27; G61 111; G63 71–72). Aristotle's *Nicomachean Ethics* contrasts the methods of metaphysics and practical philosophy, just as Kierkegaard contrasted direct and indirect communication and Husserl juxtaposed objective and occasional expressions. Corresponding to the universality and fixed presence of ever-being, to that which cannot be other, is the method of contemplative science and its *logos* of demonstration (*apodeixis*), which affords a degree of exactitude that is similar to that available in mathematics. But there can be neither an exact science, nor a *techne,* nor a philosopher-king in the sphere of human praxis and its goods, since that sphere does not display the *arche,* the principle/kingdom, of a universal *eidos.* Aristotle's ontology of practical human existence has a quite different method. Corresponding to the being that can be other, namely, the highly particular, *lethe-permeated* historical being of the *kairos,* is the open-ended method whose *logos* is only that of indication (*endeixis*), of "indicating the truth roughly and in outline [*typo*]" (1094b, 1104a, 1140a). *Typon* means mark, print, outline, sketch, draft. This descriptive phenomenological method of *typo legein,* discoursing in outline, is also called *perigraphein,* inscribing, writing, sketching in outline the typical characteristics of praxis (1098a).

The existentiell principles (*archai*) of the basic characteristic of motion-for-the-sake-of (*kinesis heneka tou*), which Aristotle's method inductively transcribes from concrete practical life, are supposed to be seen neither as Platonic forms (essentialism) nor as particular goods (ideology), but rather as the analogical similarities displayed immanently by different historical shapes of practical life, though Aristotle does inconsistently mix this analogical inquiry with the historical value-system of Athenian patriarchy and religion (1096b–

1097a). The anti-Platonic gesture that Aristotle makes in Book One of his *Nicomachean Ethics* with his critique of the Platonic Idea of the Good is that one should distance the inquiry of practical life from the *pros hen* analogy of attribution, which establishes a hierarchico-teleological relationship either between different structural characteristics (reductionism) or between different historical visions of the good (hegemony), though again in tension with this approach he does end his *Nicomachean Ethics* with an account of the heavenly realm of the divine *arche*-king as the highest good.[8]

In the anti-Platonic Book One of his work, he subscribes to the analogy of proportionality, which concerns similarity of proportions or relations and has the following form: as A is to B, C is to D. The best example of relational similarity between historical shapes of praxis, which may be radically different on the level of their actual content, is the means-end relationship. But induction also draws out and formalizes similarities in the functional relationships between all other equiprimordial characteristics of the content-, relational, and temporalizing-senses of praxis: for example, deliberation, choice, passion, *phronesis, aletheia, kairos*. Even arts such as strategics and medicine are guided by the category of *kairos*, but the contents here are quite different: "There are many skills even of the things that fall under one category, e.g., that of *kairos*, for *kairos* in war comes under strategics and in disease under medicine" (1096a).

Aristotle's rough draft outlines the *archai* in the double sense of the analogical principles/starting-points of both action itself and ontological inquiry, which as such indicate a *methodos* toward their enactment in the historical being that can be other. The *typon*, outline, of practical philosophy is also a kind of tympan (*tympanon*) and urging forward (*protreptikon*) that announces and calls attention (*hermeneia*) to a way, which the hearer (*akroates*) or reader of Aristotle's lectures is supposed to take up and enact (1095a, 1179b). "The beginnings/principles have great importance for what follows. For the beginning/principle seems to be more than half of the whole" (1098b). In the first place, the philosophical draft of the *archai* is incomplete and requires redrafting, reinscribing, filling out (*anagraphe*) (1098a). Second, this ontology of human existence must be concretized interpretively in the particular practical disciplines and arts (1096a–1097a). Finally, practical philosophy is from out of and back into actual praxis, that is, "the end is not knowing but praxis" (1095a).

Praxis is an "aiming at that which is in relation to the *kairos*," and this comes "under no *techne* or instruction." But though Aristotle's rough descriptive draft renounces the superior prophetic role of Platonic kingship that offers a prescriptive technical program for life and usurps the autonomy of different historical communities and individuals, it can "still try to be of help" (1104a). Aristotle's metaphor here is that, like rough guidelines in archery, his rough philosophical indications can help actual praxis to aim at and hit its shifting *kairos* by making it more aware of the types of things to be aware of, though the indications cannot legislate the concrete historical content of the target and alleviate the difficulty of hitting it (1094a). The indications have to be interpretively enacted and fulfilled by the individuals themselves in the diverse particularity of their practical lives.

In Aristotle's indicative draft of analogical beginnings/principles, Heidegger found a prototype that he reinscribed in the formally indicative method of his own new beginning, which dealt similarly with the analogical principles of the temporalizing of being. In the notes for his planned book on Aristotle, he wrote that "these pages are in no sense a 'program,' but a pointing to principles, a pointing in the direction in which the end of the guiding themes, along which our 'course' should go, is made fast. And who really 'has' the rigor, i.e., has understood it and in this understanding has appropriated it, he has 'already more than half the whole.' " And then he quoted Aristotle: "For the beginning/principle seems to be more than half of the whole." "The *guidelines*," he also wrote, "are not a fixed framework; precisely not the framework, but rather something much more decisive, out of which developing the problematic has first to be enacted, and this 'always anew.' " The guidelines must be open to and "fitting to the situation." It is not the role of the philosopher to "write a system," "propaganda," or prophetic "brochures" and "programs" for the concrete living of life or for such things as cultural and "university reform," a piece of advice Heidegger later apparently forgot in his 1933 rectorial address (G61 192–94, 70–71, 112, 89; G63 19; G56/57 4).

To understand Heidegger's method of formal indication, it is also important to begin with his insight that form, indication, and *methodos* belong originally to the *Sache* itself as it is experienced in pretheoretical life. As he explained in 1919 and the early 1920s, the form, category, or principle of the primal something (being) is an "index," a primal sign, a primal signi-fying (*Be-deuten*). As a motivational recept (*Rückgriff*), it points retentionally back to the having-been of its being-assigned (*Angewiesensein*) to an individuated "concretion" in historical life. As the preworldly something, futural not-yet, and tendential precept (*Vorgriff*), it points protentionally into the "direction out toward" and way (*methodos*) of its ongoing repetitive worlding-out, differentiating *Ereignis*, and fulfilling enactment in the alterity and haecceity of concrete worldly somethings, namely, those of historical ages, communities, selfworlds, philosophies. Though it includes all intentional moments, the indexicality of being is primarily its temporalizing- and enactment-senses. Thus Heidegger called this indexicality the "*Ereignis*-character" of being.

The kinetic-kairological temporalizing of the ascriptive-prescriptive trace/track (*Spur*) of the primal something is a kind of primal method, indication, and inscription, which Heidegger referred to as "characterizing" and

Ausprägung, express marking-out, stamping, imprinting in the sphere of the worldly something (G56/57 115–16). Already in his dissertation on the Scotist theory of signs, he had maintained that, especially as signitive meaning intended in the *modus significandi*, the teleological categorial sense of the "something in any sense" is an "indicating" "sign" of and directedness to objects, which, on the one hand, is always already materially fulfilled, determined, and analogically differentiated in historical *Ereignisse* by the "individualizing function" of meaning, and which, on the other hand, still points forward into the future of ongoing repeated fulfillment.

In 1919 Heidegger maintained that the pretheoretical meaning-intentions and "linguistic expression," to which the index of the primal something is given as recept and precept, are *not*, as Natorp claimed, objectifying and universalizing, but rather express "*Ereignis*-characters" and work in the "individualizing function" of meaning. Natorp fails to see that individual life is not a brute ineffable "irrational" to which general concepts and words are subsequently applied. Rather, as Dilthey saw, life is already laden with self-expressed meaning. "Thus meaning [*Bedeutungsmässiges*], linguistic expression, need not without further ado mean in a theoretical or indeed an object-like manner, but rather is primally experiential, *preworldish* and *worldish*. The preworldish and worldish functions of meaning have the essential characteristic in themselves of expressing *Ereignis*-characters." These meaning-functions "are preceptual and simultaneously receptual, i.e., they express life in its motivated tendency and its tendential motivation." To work out a nonobjectifying language and so avoid Natorp's objections concerning description of factical life, the concept-formation of Heidegger's hermeneutics of facticity and its self-expression simply inductively transcribes this expression of the indexicality of being into a rough sketch of philosophical concepts. "Hermeneutical intuition" is an "originary phenomenological recept- and precept-formation, from which all theoretical-objectifying and also transcendent positing drops out" (G56/57 116–17).

Heidegger explained what he meant here with a diagram on the blackboard, which is recorded in the student transcripts (DK 122). Taking up Husserl's distinction between generalization and formalization (G58 217), it showed how the two moments of "the pretheoretical something," namely, (1) the "preworldly something" and (2) the "worldly something" of specific experiential spheres and lifeworlds, motivate the two corresponding moments of "the theoretical something," namely, (1) the "formal-logical objective [*gegenständlich*] something" and (2) the "object-like and object-specific [*objektartig*] something." In the formal-logical something, one formalizes the preworldly something, whereas in "the object-like and object-specific something" one transforms the preworldly something into "genus-concepts" or concepts limited to specific lifeworlds. One formalizes the preworldly something in that one loosens it from its concretion in the pretheoretical sphere of the worldly some-thing and especially from its concretion in the dehistoricizing philosophical moment of the object-like and object-specific something (the something as "thing" grasped in genus-species concepts).

Thus Heidegger wrote, later in WS 1921–22, that "being, being-sense, is the philosophically principial element of every being; but it is not their 'univer-sal', their highest genus, what would have beings under it as special cases" (G61 58; G58 216–17). In formalizing, one transforms the recept and precept of the pretheoretical something into the concept (*Begriff*) of the formal-logical something, since the fulfillment of the pointing backward and forward into specific lifeworlds is held in abeyance and these indicative *Ereignis*-characters are retained only as an empty, ontically noncommittal, and open-ended point-ing. We read, "*Only* the formal objective *something of knowability* is moti-vated out of this preworldly something of life. . . . The tendency into a world can be deflected theoretically *before* it is expressly marked-out [*vor ihrer Aus-prägung*]. Thus the universality of the formally objective is proper [*eignet*] to its primal source out of the in-itself of the flowing experience of life," that is, out of the *Er-eignis* of being. Unlike the "object-like and object-specific some-thing," which deworlds, delives, and dehistoricizes the pretheoretical some-thing, the formal-logical something (though it is theoretical) still "points *back* into a basic level of life in and for itself," namely, into *Er-eignis* (G56/57 111, 116).

Taking up Husserl's adoption and Natorp's mystically oriented use of the regulative Ideas of Reason in Kant's First Critique, Heidegger maintained that the indexicality of being is transcribed into an Idea in the Kantian Sense and, specifically, into philosophy as such an Idea. Philosophy is the science of the *Ursprung* in the double sense of the primal source (that is, *Ereignis* of being) and the starting point (*Anfanghaftes*) for thinking. In the regulative Idea of the primal source, which provides the starting point of philosophy, "the possible direction of the idea-determination is already positively sketched out in ad-vance [*vorgezeichnet*]." This "direction is method (*methodos*), the *way*" to-ward determining the *Ereignis* of being and determining philosophy as the study of this *Ereignis*, that is, determining and concretizing them within his-torical situations. But right in its positive determinate moment, the Idea con-tains also an indeterminate "*negative* moment." It is not a Platonic *eidos*, be-cause "it does not give something, namely: does not give its object in complete adequacy, in a closed [*abgeschlossen*] full determination." The "object remains ever undetermined," since, as Husserl put it, the object is an infinitely open horizon of different shadowed profiles which can never be totalized. In its "in-finite task" of exploring this historical horizon, philosophy is exiled to wander endlessly in the varied shadows of the object, namely, the *Ereignis* of being, without ever reaching the Husserlian "promised land" of a completed, unified science. The Idea of the primal source, of the anarchic *arche*, has always already lost it, in such a manner that this re- and pre-ceptual Concept expresses a regulative *telos* that is ever deferred, an unfulfilled signitive meaning-intention, an empty concept without a full intuition. The negative indeterminate moment of the Idea also means that, as science, philosophy renounces its "kingly vocation" and does not attempt ideologically to enclose the Idea or its object, the *Ereignis* of the primal something, within a particular determinate "worldly something," namely, a *material* worldview that makes universal and transhistorical claims about the ultimate questions of life. This "negative, suspending delimitation" means that "philosophy is not art (poetry), not life-wisdom (giving of practical rules)." The Idea gives only determinate "motivations for the determinability of the never completely determined object of the Idea." Nor should philosophy bring the Idea of the *Ereignis* of the primal something to closure in a particular *formal*-philosophical articulation of it; rather, "the possibility remains *open* that new characteristic moments will emerge, that new moments will be initiated on those already gained and will modify them" (emphasis added). The Idea provides the principial point of beginning and setting-forth, that is, the *Ur-sprung*, which both demands and holds open "the living enactment of the motivations." This enactment means the constant beginning anew of philosophy, concretion of the Idea in the "individual sciences," and ultimately constantly "leaping" back "*into* a (determinate) world" or, better, worlds, that is, back into "the flowing stream of the lived experiences" of pretheoretical life itself, from which philosophy's method of inductive formalization begins (G56/57 13–14, 23–24, 210, 63, 115).

In 1919 Heidegger's models for this enactment were still, as they were in his qualifying dissertation, the analogical differentiation of the divine *telos* in religious (especially mystical) life, and the "individualizing concept-formation" of Dilthey and the Neo-Kantians, including especially the "idiographic" "*Ereignis*-sciences" of which Windelband spoke. Moreover, the models in the background of his "negative" indicative Idea of the depth-dimension of the subjectless, absence-permeated *Ereignis* of being are not only Husserl's and Natorp's use of the Idea in the Kantian Sense, but also what is itself effective in Kant's and Natorp's use of the regulative idea of God, namely, the mystical *via negativa* for which the *mysterium tremendum* of the Divine Life is approached through traces and signatures in the Book of the World (G56/57 30, 165–73).

In the following year and especially in his lecture course of WS 1920–21, Heidegger began to speak of how the "principles" and existentiell "categories" of being are "lifted out" of factical life and transcribed into "formal indications." These categories, which include content-, relational, enactment-, and temporalizing-sense, are in turn taken up into Heidegger's formally indicative definition of philosophy as "knowing comportment to beings as being (sense of being), and in such a manner that . . . the issue is also decisively the being (sense of being) at the particular time of the having of the comportment." Heidegger's notes regarding this definition read, "*Formale Anzeige:* 'being' is that which is indicatively formal-empty, and yet firmly determining the starting point for the direction of understanding." The indicative definition provides the starting points of a way: " 'Formal', the 'formal' is a content in such a manner that the indication points into a direction, sketches out the way in advance." The indicators present the "task" of passionately "appropriating," "temporalizing," and "concretizing" them in a way that is "fitting to the situation" in which one finds oneself: "In [formal indication] it is said that I stand at the . . . *direction for beginning,* that—should it come to what is genuine—it gives only the way for making the most out of, tasting to the full [*auszukosten*], and fulfilling what is non-genuinely indicated, i.e., for following the way" (G61 80ff., 61, 33–34, 114, 20).

Formal indication has both a positive directive moment and a negative "repellent" or "prohibitive" moment. "Along with its pointing character, formal indication has simultaneously in itself a *prohibitive* (shooing, repellent) *character.*" As an indirectly communicative calling attention to the way of philosophizing, formal indications repel the individual from "falling toward" their immediate "content" by making it the direct "theme." Moreover, "nothing is factically 'said' with [formal indication] regarding the concrete movements of factical life, but rather they give precisely only the direction of the view." It "prevents falling uncritically into a specific conception of existence" and "setting up an ontological metaphysics of life" (for example, in the "Christian" sense of "Scheler and Bergson"). Rather, formal indication remains ontically "non-committal" and nonideologically open for being kairologically fulfilled and an-archically differentiated into an alterity of principles, historical ages, philosophies, worldviews, societies, institutions, and personal selfworlds, including " 'non-Christian' life." The reign of these *archai* is not philosophical kingship that leaps in and chooses for individuals. Rather, in an Aristotelian spirit, "the 'formal' is not autonomous, but only a worldly discharge and relief." Finally, formal indication repels the tendency to take the indicated principles or categories to be free-floating structures, essences, or a Kantian "society of logical schemata for themselves, a 'framework'," which is supposed to be instantiated in particular Daseins. In the term "formal indication," "formal is not the same as eidetic" in Husserl's sense. The categories, which are existentiell possibilities and ways to be, "can never (and thank God never) be freed from [factical possibilities]." "Formal" means rather an inductive formalizing of the existentiell categories, which demands its own "deformalization" and "concretion." " 'Formal' gives the 'beginning-character' of the enactment of the temporalizing of the fulfillment of what is indicated."[9]

The negative and positive moments of formal indication are at play in

Heidegger's title of "skepticism" for his new beginning. For it is, on the one hand, a deconstructive suspicion about all prophetic claims regarding the royal "place" of a single privileged meaning of being and, on the other, an endless questioning and situational search (*skepsis*) for being in the face of its questionableness. Heidegger wrote concerning his "formally indicative definition" of philosophy,

> By indicatively stressing the becoming-decisive of the being-sense (at the particular time) of each knowing comportment [to being], one (*negatively*) repels the possibility of talking about philosophy in such a general, indefinite manner. . . . It repels precisely that one should be able to preach philosophy from some elevated but basically indefinable place, as if it could put up bail for coming cultural periods and destinies [*Schicksale*] of humanity, such that one does not know who speaks for whom and for what, and what is the point of these prophecies and schools of wisdom, and who has assigned them such a cultural mission. There is no such thing as *the* philosophy—in such universality, in comfortable timelessness. . . .

But Heidegger immediately noted that "simultaneously the directive is (*positively*) given to develop the problematic with a view to the basic sense of the situation (at the particular time) of the comportment at the particular time." And this means openness and letting-be of such diverse enactment:

> It lies in the sense of the definition that it *lets* possiblities remain *open* [*offen lässt*], but just as much gives the directive to "look" precisely toward the one coming into question at the particular time. . . . The definition is essentially a task. . . . The indication stresses precisely that it should remain *open* for other contexts of life to be able to temporalize their approach to philosophy and enactment of philosophizing. (G61 66–67; emphasis added)

The positive directive toward the things themselves provides way-traces for independent "questioning and establishing kairological-critically 'in one's time,' " "here and now . . . in this place. . . . You before me, I before you." Heidegger's new beginning provides only the "situation of the point of departure for enactive movement in the direction of the full appropriation of the object." Similar to his later statement that "the sail of thinking keeps trimmed hard to the wind of the *Sache*," he said in WS 1921–22 that his indicative "guidelines" do not provide, as it were, a comfortable metaphysical fortress high above the flux, but rather are only like rough provisional maps that make the individual thinker ready to leap (*auf dem Sprung*) passionately and Odysseus-like into the "speeding boat" of "philosophizing" on the open waters and unknown horizons of *kinesis*. Heidegger's formal indications are really questions indirectly communicated to others for their own quests and adventures toward the ever-elusive things themselves:

This situation is not the saving coast, but rather the leap into a speeding boat, and now everything depends on getting the rope for the sail into one's hand and looking to the wind. One has to see precisely the difficulties. . . . To steer into absolute questionableness and to have it in sight, this means taking hold of philosophy authentically. The solid ground (ground something that always only temporalizes itself, just as appropriation does) lies in taking hold of questionableness, i.e., in the *radical temporalizing of questioning*. . . . This "passion" (real) as the only way of philosophizing is something that for a long time has no longer been recognized. (G61 34, 37)

Independent enactment of the way means that the rough indicative sketch of Heidegger's new beginning is itself subject to the deconstructive repetition of constantly beginning anew, reinscription, redrafting. "No result in an external sense is to be expected, the draft [*Entwurf*] of a system, the sketching out [*Auszeichnung*] of grand perspectives, glowing description [*Umschreibung*] of a standpoint," or "a 'program.' " Rather "that towards which philosophy, as knowing comportment [to being] directs itself, must again and again be drafted up [*entworfen*], caught sight of anew, and in such a way that one searches in different directions." We have already seen this constant beginning anew in the young Heidegger's own chain of differing/deferring drafts, but, like the fragments of the pre-Socratics, these drafts are not only retentional traces of how the *Sache* showed itself in his thought, but also protentional tracks into independent critical repetition and reinscription. To prevent his readers from falling passively toward and objectifying his formal indications into fixed results, he emphasized in the spirit of Socratic-Kierkegaardian maieutics that the indications are supposed to repel individual readers from the direct communicative content of his texts and from the *mens auctoris*, and should throw them back upon their own critical enactment of the way-markers toward the topic itself, so that in the end they can find their own way. "The Other is ruthlessly driven into reflection." "Who . . . does not himself dig in, to him must be said that he has not understood what is authentic. . . . I must step back and declare that, even if a quality of research has been given to me, I can make for no one the discovery of 'what the issue is,' 'what it comes to.' " As Löwith emphasized, the young Heidegger did not want to provide "something positive," to teach directly, to preach, to lead, to be a philosopher-king. Concerning his new beginning he wrote, "No fantastic representation of new categories that lead us comfortably into a new Reich/Kingdom. Existentielly it becomes more difficult." Regarding the question, What is philosophy?, one should "not lazily call upon crown authorities [*Kronzeugen*], but rather understand it radically!" The indications are not to be dehistoricized and mythologized into speculative or scholarly objects for quietistic ocular-aesthetic contemplation: "Formal indication is always misunderstood when it is taken as a fixed, general proposition . . . and fantasized." Philosophy involves a constantly vigilant demythologizing of the ruinous tendency to turn the indicators into doctrines and myths about a privileged sense of being outside the flux of life (G61 39–41, 56, 191, 186, 153; G9 42; G63 80).

The negative, repellent moment of formal indication is precisely the moment of the constant critical destruction of these indications on the way to the elusive things themselves. "Formal indication is to be clarified concretely . . . in connection with phenomenological destruction." The "appropriation of the concrete situation of enacting philosophizing is enacted in the manner of a destruction." In the first instance, this destruction is simply the de-construction and reinscription of the indicative "prestruction" in order to get at *die Sache selbst* in one's own historical situation. But since, as a starting point that only guides the questioning, it does not give the matter itself fully and "authentically," the formally indicative preconception of the matter has the status of a "presupposition" and "prejudice" that is characterized by a certain "evidencelessness" and "questionableness." Its "commensurateness is absolutely *questionable*." The "eventuality of its going wrong is a fundamental one that belongs to its own being." Thus one must prevent formal indications from "drifting away into autonomous blind dogmatic fixations of categorial sense that have been cut loose from the presupposition, the preconception, the context, and the time of the interpretation." The "answers" one gives must not lose their character of continuing to be "questions." The judging of the preconception (*Vorgriffsdijudikation*) is always required. "The preconception is not non-discussable and dogmatic," but rather demands "skepticism" and "critique." "The point of departure must be enacted critically in a radical manner" on "the path of the deconstruction [*Abbau*] of critically detected concealments." This is exactly what the young Heidegger was doing with the indicators provided by Plato, Aristotle, and Jaspers. And he claimed that Jaspers's indirect communicative method went wrong precisely in failing to see that its traditional basic concepts (which prejudged life as presence-at-hand) required not only application, but also critique in order to accomplish the task of freeing the individual for independent reflection. Philosophy must be "the 'infinite process' of radical questioning that holds itself in questioning" and "destructively self-renewing appropriation."[10]

But repetition and constant beginning of the formal indications of Heidegger's ontology mean also concretizing them in individual sciences such as "ethics," "art," and "theology." He himself did this concretizing not only in his remarks on "ethics," but also especially in his 1927 lecture "Phenomenology and Theology," in which he argued that "philosophy is the possible, formally indicative corrective of the ontic and indeed pre-Christian content of basic theological concepts." Ontology cannot indeed provide the ontic content and enactment of Christian faith, but its indications are capable of indirectly "leading into the situation of religious decision." And it was precisely in a formally indicative *theological* language modeled on Kierkegaardian indirect communication that Heidegger was searching for "the word that is able to call one to faith and preserve one in faith" (G61 15, 54–58, 197; G9 61–67/PT 17–21).

Finally, constant beginning means the ongoing concretization of formal indication in the lives of individuals. Heidegger told his students that, because of the personal relational and enactment-sense in the categories of factical life and in the definition of philosophy, the formal indications here and the questionableness they entail are ultimately to be interpretively concretized and re-inscribed as questions about one's own life. The formalizing method of formal indication "springs from" and "goes back to" "one's own concrete life." "The going back is left to the individual." The indicative question about being is enacted as the question about "being to-(me)," "to-me-being." The concept of world means: How does it world for me? The question, "What is time?, becomes the question: Who is time? Better: Are we ourselves time? Or better yet: Am I my time? . . . Such questioning is therefore the most appropriate mode of access to and treatment of time as in each case my time" (BZ 27–28). Likewise, "the formal indication 'I am,' which guides the problematic of the being-sense of factical life, becomes methodically effective in the sense that it . . . is enacted as the concrete historical question: '*am I?*,' whereby the 'I' is to be taken merely in the sense of a pointing toward my concrete factical life . . . in its situational possibility." The concepts of care, mood, and death really mean the questions: How do I care? How do I feel? Am I dying? As Heidegger repeated later in SZ, "the word 'I' may be understood only in the sense of a non-committal *formal indication*," as an occasional expression (SZ 155/151–52). In WS 1921–22, he explained what "non-comittal" meant here. It "remains undetermined and questionable and uncertain what 'I' and 'mine' are supposed actually to say. . . . This indeterminateness of the object 'my life' is methodically no deficiency, but rather it guarantees precisely the *free* and always new possibility of access in the ongoing temporalizing of factical life" (emphasis added). As "withworldly intimative announcing, the communication of philosophy to others," the formal indication "I am" can only point into the nonpresence and "hidden inwardness" (Kierkegaard) of the situations of Others. With Kierkegaard's and Jaspers's method of indirect communication, Heidegger concurred that, though philosophy can give the "means to self-reflection," it should not "impose a doctrine of life" and must attempt to "attain the highest measure of non-interference in personal decision-making and thus set the individual free for self-reflection." However, Jaspers's failure to subject his basic concepts to critique led him into "imposing a *specific* world-view" on "the Other" (G61 169, 134, 174–75, 36; G9 8, 42).

Gelassenheit, Free Sociality, Free Christianity

The young Heidegger's indicative method and its an-archic style of thought also provide indications of the ethical significance of his ontology, which centers around the theme of openness to philosophical, historical, social, and personal otherness. We can follow up these indications chronologically by first looking more closely at how, in the years 1917 through 1920, this attitude of openness is modeled on Eckhartian *Gelassenheit*, letting-be, and Schleiermacher's notion of "free sociality."

Let us first note the connection Heidegger made in 1919 between *es wertet*, it worths, it values, and the "mystery" of differentiating *Ereignis*. Being, philosophy, humanity, an age, a society, a university, a religion, a family, or an implement like a table are subject to *Ereignis* and differentiation not only into ownness of being, but also into ownmost value (*Eigenwert*). The latter notion and that of the "it values" recall Heidegger's 1915–16 concerns with the transcendental *bonum* that is convertible with *ens*, being, the something. His Neo-Kantian position back then was that atemporally valid values are differentiated into the haecceity of the qualitative "significance" of history and personal life.

But in 1919 he took the notion of value out of this theorized Neo-Kantian context and acknowledged it as a nontheoretical moment of "life in and for itself." More specifically, value is the sphere of the "good and beautiful," the "ethical and aesthetic." Though Heidegger stressed that the "it worlds" does "not coincide with the '*es wertet*,' it values, it worths," he did indicate that it would be the task of an "eidetic genealogy" to show that there is a "connection" between them consisting in the fact that the "it worlds" is that which gives rise to the "it values." Similar to his earlier position that the *bonum* and the other transcendentals are based on the *ens*, so in 1919 he suggested that value is founded in the pretheoretical primal something (being) and its worlding-out into the practical "significance" of lifeworlds. For value means "something has significance," being "historically significant." In the worlding of the lectern for the "Senegalese negro," for example, the lectern "has a significance for him," namely, "protection against arrows and stones," whereas for the German professor it has the practical significance of "the place for the teacher." The differentiating *Er-eignis* of the primal something into lifeworlds is also an e-venting/en-owning into the *Eigen-wert*, the ownmost value, of these worlds. "It events" is simultaneously an "it signifies," "it values," "it worths" (G56/57 38, 145, 71–73, 47, 49).

That the "it values" is founded in the "it worlds" does *not*, therefore, mean that it is to be equated with the theoretical notion of "value" in Neo-Kantianism, where it is supposed to be externally imposed upon brute sense-data through subjective acts. Rather, the impersonal "it values" or "it worths" (the latter deflects the subjectivist connotation Heidegger wants to avoid) means precisely that, like the worldish something in which it is based, "the value-ish [*das Werthafte*] as such gives itself to me" immediately without a "detour" through a "positing" and "representing." Heidegger's example again concerns the significant *Ereignis* of the sun, "I step into the study in the morning; sunlight lies on the books, and so on; I am pleased. . . . The 'pleasant' as such gives itself to me [*gibt sich mir*]. . . . The value *is* not, but rather it 'values'. . . . In taking-in-value 'it values' for me, for the value-experiencing subject." Bathed in sunlight, the study itself worths, pleasants, gladdens for Heidegger personally, just as the significant *Ereignis* of the sunrise, of "the glance of the sun, you most beautiful one," does for the "loving . . . glance" of the Theban elders and the German mountaineers. Whereas taking-in-value (*Wertnehmen*) is an "originary phenomenon of the primal source and constitutes life in and for itself," explaining-as-value (*Für-Wert-Erklären*) is a "derived phenomenon that is founded in the theoretical and is itself theoretical." Heidegger here already alluded to the Greek definition of "being-true" as "*a-letheia*," un-concealment, in order to make the point that value has its own nontheoretical illumination: "Being-true (*a-letheia*) as such does not 'value'. . . . In taking-in-value the 'it values' does something *for me*, it penetrates into me. . . . In taking-in-value lies nothing theoretical; it has its own 'light', spreads its own luminosity: '*lumen gloriae*' [the limelight of fame]" (G56/57 46–49).

Neo-Kantian value-philosophy takes itself to be "transcendental value-philosophy, 'critical science of universally valid values' " (Windelband). However, because the eventing/enowning of being is precisely differentiation and individuation into ownmost value, "value-*theory* and even more so every value-*system* . . . is illusory." What is required is rather "a critical-positive, phenomenological overcoming of value-philosophy." Taking up the method of "individualizing science" in Dilthey and the Neo-Kantians themselves, the positive aspect of Heidegger's critique entails the *ideal* of openness to and respect for the ownmost value of differences, even though his own stereotyping descriptions of the "Senegalese negro" *in fact* smacks of ethnocentrism, as does his stereotyped contrast of "the German movement" with the "materialism" of "England and France" and "the English-American worldview." Against the Enlightenment's marginalizing of the different as "barbarism, superstition, illusion, and disorder," Heidegger followed Herder's and Schleiermacher's affirmation of "the independent ownmost value of each nation, each age, and each historical appearance in any sense." Here the "goal of progress is also no longer an abstract, rational happiness and virtue, but rather 'each nation has the center of its happiness in itself, just as each ball its center of gravity' [Herder]." There is no central ruling *arche*, principle/kingdom, but rather many "individual, qualitatively original effective centers." Heidegger likewise recommended Schleiermacher's stress on the "ownmost value ... of [individual] life in the community." Similarly in Kant, Fichte, Schelling, and Hegel, "the historical in its individual multiplicity and ownness [*Eigenartigkeit*] is now seen from the creative activity of the subject—the selfworth of the person," which in Kant's theory of "practical reason" is expressed in the notion of the "kingdom of ends" (G56/57 146, 97, 141, 127, 132–34; G61 164). Accordingly, in ontologizing this tradition of Christian personalism, Heidegger affirmed the inherently open and pluralistic character of the differentiating *Ereignis* of being, historical ages, and social realities into personal sites of ownmost value. To bring in Heidegger's terminology from 1924, there is/it gives being to each "in equal measure." *Er-eignis* "makes all alike and equal" (BZ 27).

In this attitude of openness and respect for ownmost value, we also again detect Heidegger's analogy between mystical experience and experience in any sense, that is, between Eckartian letting-be (*Gelassenheit*) and the general attitude of surrender (*Hingabe*) and openness. In 1915–16 Heidegger's position, based on medieval mysticism, was that God is telelogical value that, like the sun in Heidegger's courses of 1919, emanates analogically and sacramentally into a great treasury of "manifold differentiations of value" in history and personal life, similar to "a bundle of rays flowing together in a single point." The analogical doctrine of categories in Scholastic philosophy was geared to preserving precisely the living experience of mystical emanationism and differentiation in medieval culture. Heidegger himself used this doctrine as a model for his own attempt to formulate a doctrine of categories that would be capable of an "openness [*Aufgeschlossenheit*] of empathetic understanding and ... philosophically oriented valuing" vis-à-vis the haecceity of "individual epochs" and historical life in general (G1 408).

Similarly, in 1919, when he dealt with the "negative" regulative Idea of the *Ereignis* of the primal something, which is never "closed" but always "remains open," Heidegger's model was to a great extent still this mystical and Scholastic tradition of analogicity. In his synthesis of Eckhart and Luther, Natorp used the Idea in the Kantian Sense to express the infinite horizon of the analogically differentiating birth of the divine Logos in the "little castle" of individual consciences, each of which has distinctive "selfworth," as one also sees in the Kantian analogue of "the kingdom of ends." Similarly for Heidegger, the Idea (like its terminological successor "formal indication") can only point into and hold itself open for the mysterious horizon of the subjectless, absence-permeated, incalculable, and anarchic *Ereignis* of the primal something, which differentiates itself in the "ownmost value" of "personal Dasein" (HB 8).

At the close of his KNS 1919 course, Heidegger made a comment, recorded in the student notes, that clearly expressed his Eckhartian model of surrender and letting-be of the mystery of the efflux of the Divine Life into lifeworlds. "Despite the appearance of a philosophy of life, it is really the opposite of a worldview. A worldview is an objectifying and stilling of life at a certain point in the life of culture. In contrast, phenomenology is never closed off [*abgeschlossen*], it is always provisional in the absolute immersion [*Versenkung*] in life as such" (DK 106). Similarly, in WS 1919–20, he wrote that "this primacy of the scientifically *researching* tendency is in itself a letting-be-open [*Offen-lassen*] of the perpective and of the constantly new-beginning. All 'completion' is relative." He equated this attitude with "love," "life-sympathy," and "surrender": "The true philosophical attitude is never that of a logical tyrant who, through staring at life, alarms it. Rather, it is Plato's *eros*. . . . philosophy demands letting-oneself-go [*Sich-Loslassen*] into life . . . submerging the self into its primal source." "Understanding is found in *love*, in surrender [*Hingabe*] . . . loving the near and drawing all . . . nearness out of distance and so coming into genuine distance of the primal source" (G58 25, 263, 168; G56/57 110).

As Heidegger's 1919 letter to Blochmann indicated, the attempt to "still the stream" and bring *Ereignis* to closure in a fully present, calculable objectification is "a rationalistic misunderstanding . . . of the flowing stream" and its character of "mystery" and "grace." Heidegger's letter then made a .comment to Blochmann with strong overtones of Eckhartian *Gelassenheit*: "So I think about your clear devotion [*Verhaftetsein*] to scientific work—out of the total genuinenesss of your personal being—without forced idealizations—but rather with the uninhibited letting-become-free [*Freiwerdenlassen*] of the feminine soul." In the same spirit are his earlier comments to her about "one's ownmost personality and the fulfillment of its value," "the selfworth of one's own vocation," becoming "inwardly free," "openness for the goods of personal life" (HB 7–14). Like his use of the mystics, Heidegger will later also appeal to Luther's critique of metaphysics as the prideful *theologia gloriae* that wants to objectify and have power over the *Deus absconditus*.

According to Natorp, the Eckhartian-Lutheran notion of the birth of the Logos in the self-worth of individual conscience also expresses itself in Schleiermacher's notions of "the feeling of dependence" and the value of free creative personality (DW2 108). Thus it is relevant to look more closely at the influence of Schleiermacher's idea of free sociality (*Geselligkeit*) and "free Christianity" on Heidegger around the years 1917 through 1920, when the latter underwent his confessional conversion to a free Protestantism. For Schleiermacher, the individual's ownness or particularity, which lies in being a unique manifestation of the infinite, means that the individual has a unique moral and religious vocation to be cultivated through education and other cultural activities. The goal is to become a fully and harmoniously developed moral and religious personality. But individual life is always "life in the community."

Schleiermacher insists that one intuits oneself as a unique being only *within* a historical community of other individual personalities, which community in turn possesses its own uniqueness vis-à-vis other communities. As Heidegger put this in 1919, "Schleiermacher saw for the first time the ownmost being and ownmost value of the community and of living in the community" (G56/57 134). Schleiermacher qualifies the Romantic overemphasis on individuality through the position that a person "exists only in relation to Others," as a member of a community and institutions such as family, education, state, and church. These are or ought to be defined by the free sociality of mutual acknowledgment, communication, dialogue, and respect. It is only in the presence of Others that the individual can come to self-knowledge, self-expression, and fulfillment of his or her unique moral and religious vocation. Since the religious consciousness of the feeling of absolute dependence on God is the highest aspect of the individual's ownness and vocation, free society entails especially religious freedom of conscience. Unique personality presupposes moral-religious community, and the community in turn presupposes the differences between persons, such that there is something like an analogical community of identity-in-difference at work here, one that has its ultimate basis in the differentiating activity of the infinite universe of God.

Heidegger's correspondence with Blochmann and his courses of 1919 show the influence of Schleiermacher's social and religious liberalism on his own ideas about religious freedom, the social and educational rebuilding of Germany after the First World War, university reform, and the role of women in education (HB 7–16). In fact, it appears that the "doctoral plan" on which Blochmann was being intimately counseled by Heidegger had something to do with Schleiermacher's "political theory," for in November of 1918 Heidegger wrote to her that she must avoid "submitting a standard type of dissertation consisting of citations and passages in which Schl[eiermacher] speaks of politics." And in his next letter of January 1919 he sent along a reference found while "rummaging" in the library, namely, "H. Reuter, *Schleiermachers Stellung zur Idee der Nation und der nationalen Staates.*"

Both in the Blochmann correspondence and in his courses of 1919, one of Heidegger's key terms was that of *Geist*, spirit. The term carries overtones of his earlier notion of "living spirit," his subsequent study of Schleiermacher, and other religious sources. Though, as Derrida points out, this "spirit" will appear in all its fury in Heidegger's later writings, including those on National Socialism, it is in Heidegger's youthful period a friendlier, more personal, liberal, and anarchic spirit.[11] Its militancy is more that of a fierce ethical, religious, and academic individualism. Though in his qualifying dissertation, Heidegger often used the singular term "the spirit," which suggests the *Heilige*

Geist of the New Testament and the "absolute spirit of God," he was now working strictly with a notion of analogical differentiation into the ownness and uniqueness of personal life. It is Schleiermacher's idea that God is found only in the self-consciousness (conscience) of the feeling of absolute dependence. Here there is in effect no "Spirit" with a capital "S" over and above this and that spiritual individual. Concerning spirit, Heidegger urged Blochmann to "go with much trust, with quiet humility before the spirit." "Just as you hold yourself inwardly free, joyful and willing [*freudig*], so will the spirit seize [*befallen*] you." "You have faith in the spirit. And that it is working in you is shown by your 'confession'—what you search for, you find in yourself." But this "spirit is only at work as *life*," as "one's ownmost personality," as "your personal Dasein."

Also similar to Schleiermacher is the stress that Heidegger's letters to Blochmann place on the "selfworth of one's own vocation" (*Bestimmung*) and calling (*Berufung*), one's "personal destiny" (*Schicksal*), to which in 1924 he refers again as one's "unique destiny" (BZ 27; cf. G61 84). The sense we get from these letters and from his courses of 1919 is that the goal of all religious, academic, popular-educational, artistic, and social life is the development of this personal vocation, which development Heidegger described not only as "letting-become-free" and becoming "inwardly free," but also as the "movement" of "the personal stream of life" in the face of "the mystery and grace-character of all life," "fulfillment," "becoming," working (*Wirken*), "inner growth," "becoming-ripe," "the habitus of spiritual Dasein," "inner truthfulness," "genuineness."

He likewise seems to have been taking up Scheleiermacher's idea of living in a free community (*Gemeinschaft*) of dialogue and mutual respect. It has to be remembered here that he is writing to Blochmann during the collapse of the German *Kaiserreich* at the end of the First World War. For example, a letter from the front reads, "How life will ever take shape after the end (this had to come and is our only rescue) is uncertain." It is in view of the "new life" to come and, more particularly, the rebuilding and reform of Germany's educational institutions that he wrote to her about "the giving [*schenkend*] and *taking* entry into the new communities" (*Gemeinschaften*), recommending "openness for the goods of personal life and of working in society," and talking about his "constant learning in community with Husserl." Regarding Blochmann's "membership in our circle," Heidegger advised her that she must follow "the will to unconditional discussion and to removing every conventional barrier and elaborateness. . . . it should be a duty among us to express what we experience in ourselves in inner truthfulness," for all this is "the possibility of giving and of taking." "What I can give and take in friendship," he also wrote, "is for me an elevation of life." In fact there is much in these letters on the nature on friendship. The theme turns up again in 1926: "And just as the innermost energy lies in *presupposing* that one is loved by the Other, so genuine friendship lives out of the same basis." And early in 1928: "*Volo ut sis*, I will that you should see—Augustine once interpreted love thus. And he understood it as the innermost freedom of one toward the Other" (HB 17, 23).

Later, in the thirties and forties, Heidegger's Schleiermachean notion of a society of free individuals will appear to be almost dissolved into a hyperreality called *das Volk*, Spirit, or Being, which speaks through philosophical, political, and artistic Führers. But given his idea of a free society of mutually respecting individuals, each pursuing her or his unique vocation, it seems impossible, as we have seen, for the young Heidegger to advocate the role of autocratic Führers and institutions, whether in religion or in academic life. As Heidegger will put the matter in SZ, solicitous being-with-Others should not take the form of "leaping in and dominating," but rather "leaping ahead and freeing," that is, liberating the Other for his or her own possibilities and self-development (SZ 164/159). In his discussion of Jaspers's method of indirect communication, he wrote that "one can impel someone into reflection, call something to someone's attention, only in such a way that one goes in advance along the path itself for a stretch" (G9 42).

Heidegger's way of expressing this point in 1918–19 is to say that one cannot "supply rules" and "programs" for the Other, but rather can only *vorleben*, that is, live ahead as an example and model of what it means to take hold of one's own possibilities (G56/57 5). Any notion of "duty" thus derives in the end from the "conscience" of the individual: "The valuing of spiritual realities, a sense of duty, and the will to its fulfillment are produced as the fruit of inner growth that is so nourished." This *Vorleben*, which is exemplified not only in the relation of teacher and student, but to one degree or another in all social relations, is precisely a being-for-one-another that does not take away the freedom of the Other: "Because the spirit is only at work as *life*, living *being*-for-one-another can work such wonders. But it places on the existence of one's ownmost personality and its fulfillment of value the great demand of innermost energy [*Tatkraft*] and being-grounded in oneself." In light of Heidegger's appropriation of Schleiermacher, Kierkegaard, Dilthey, Aristotle's practical philosophy, and other sources (in the later twenties Heidegger's model will focus on Kant's concepts of "respect" and the "kingdom of ends"),[12] we can thus find in his early Freiburg period an ontological reading of many of the focal points of traditional Greco-Christian humanism, namely, the uniqueness, dignity, integrity (wholeness), freedom (agency), and development of individual persons living in free society.

We can see Schleiermacher's influence also on Heidegger's confessional turn from the conservative Catholicism of his student years (especially from its lack of historical consciousness, overbearing papal authority, hierarchy, antimodernism, and antiliberalism) to the type of "free Christianity" that he found around 1917 expressed in Hermann Süskind's *Christentum und Ge-schichte bei Schleiermacher*, which he was not only reading, but also enthusi-astically giving away as an Easter gift to his friends. Heidegger's critique of philosophical "Führers" and "prophets" ran parallel to his critique of institu-tional religious authority (the latter could for him only take the form of *Vor-leben*). Recall that in his 1912 *Der Akademiker* article he had actually spoken critically of "subjective religious experience" in "modern Protestant theology that is oriented toward Kant, Schleiermacher, and Ritschl." But by 1914 he was already privately dissociating himself from the very extreme antimod-ernist program of Pope Pius X, writing to Father Krebs about a recently issued papal document (*motu proprio*) in which certain teaching restrictions for Catholic theology schools in Italy were laid out: "We still don't have the *motu proprio* on philosophy. . . . all who succumb to having independent thoughts could have their brains taken out and replaced with spaghetti. Philosophical demand could be met by setting up vending machines in the train station (free of charge for the poor)." In his letter of January 9, 1919 to Krebs, in which he announced his confessional turn, Heidegger began by stressing his need for "freedom of conviction and teaching" and ended with an appeal to his own "inner calling" (*Beruf*), to "justifying my very Dasein and activity before God." It was an appeal to the Lutheran theme of a personal God-relationship that is not in the first place mediated by the Church, but rather takes place in the call of conscience, that is, in the Eckhartian "little spark" and Schleier-macher's "self-consciousness" that is a "God-consciousness" (DMH 326; CA 504–505; HL 113; MH 106–108).

That Heidegger had in mind the kind of free Christianity and liberal the-ology advocated by Schleiermacher is also indicated by the remark of his wife to Krebs that "both of us now think in a Protestant manner—i.e., without a fixed dogmatic tie . . . without Protestant or Catholic orthodoxy." Before it became the theme of his phenomenology of religion, Heidegger was actually attempting to live the personal and historical primal Christianity of the first Christian communities, Augustine, and the mystics that he thought Schleier-macher had rediscovered. In one of his 1918 letters on Schleiermacher to Blochmann he wrote, regarding her religious interests and her "confession," that "what you search for you find in yourself, there is a path from primal religious experience to theology, but it *need not* lead from theology to religious consciousness," though it can. In the synthesis of Eckhartian mysticism and Luther effected in his *Deutscher Weltberuf*, Natorp attempted to synthesize Catholic Eckhartian mysticism with the Protestant "emphasis on the right and duty of individuality," on "the 'self-worth' . . . of the free creative personal-ity," and on "free individual conviction and appropriation" of the Christian faith, which was affirmed by Luther, Kant, Fichte, Schleiermacher, and Dilthey. "Luther's 'freedom of the Christian person,' Kant's autonomy of the ethical:

that can ever be surrendered." "The soul is not under the dominion of the emperor" (DW2 106–107, 100). What we find here in Natorp, in Schleiermacher's feeling of absolute dependence, and in Heidegger's appropriation of these figures is, then, what can be called either a free mystical Lutheranism or free Lutheran mysticism. The unique individual believer is always anchored in a mystical depth-dimension, which in turn has always differentiated itself in the freedom of personal life and conscience. This is the theological counterpart to Heidegger's ontological personalism and personalist ontology: personal Dasein is always anchored in the mysterious depth-dimension of *Ereignis* of being, which in turn is always differentiated in personal Dasein.

Kairological Ethics

After 1919 Heidegger's models of openness to alterity became the kairology of Paul, of Kierkegaardian and Jaspersian indirect communication, of Socratic midwifery, and of Aristotle's practical philosophy, all of which are oriented to the Good as "that which can be other" in the unique *kairos* of the individual. Heidegger's mystical language of *Gelassenheit* and *Hingabe* was replaced by talk of how philosophy must "remain open" for "other contexts of life" and the "ownness" of individual being-here, "set the individual free for his self-reflection," and cultivate resolute phronetic openness, wakefulness, and keeping-silent in the face of the flux of being. It is not only one's own *kairos* but also the an-archic differentiation of being in the *kairos* of the Other that cannot be objectified, rendered present, calculated, technized, and mastered. Moreover, Heidegger's concept of *Vorleben* was now worked out anew not only with the ethical approaches of Kierkegaard's indirect communication and Aristotle's "rough outline," but also with Aristotle's account, in Book Six of the *Nicomachean Ethics*, of those modes of other-directed *phronesis* which are oriented to the *kairos* of the Other, and which are operative in all spheres of being with (*syn-*) Others, including friendship, giving advice, and the equitable or just application of the law.

In SZ's analysis of the type of "sight" or understanding that belongs to "leaping ahead" and "freeing" the Other, the German terms *Rücksicht* (the sight of considerate understanding) and *Nachsicht* (the sight of patience and leniency) seem to be translations of Aristotle's terms *synesis* (understanding with and toward others) and *syngnome* (sympathy, forgiveness) (SZ 164/159). For example, as Luther suggested in his analogy between Aristotelian ethics and the Spirit's overcoming of "the kingdom of the Law" in the New Testament, and as Derrida has suggested recently, equity or justice (*epieikeia*) to the situation of the Other involves constant transgressive interpretation of the law and can even lead to "breaking the law" in the name of justice.[13] The interpretive application of the law and of all ethical ends always trembles in the tension of its *pro me*, toward me. Kairological ethics means openness to the Other of universalistic legal, moral, and philosophical systems.

In WS 1921–22, Heidegger thus played the kairological ethics of Aristotle and Kierkegaard off against "absolute ethics" in Platonism, Neo-Kantian transcendental philosophy of value, and the drive to "technization" in modern culture. He took ethical systems to be an instance of Aristotle's notion of hyberbolic excess that elliptically misses the fitting measure of unique historical situations. His motto from Kierkegaard reads, "The whole of modern philosophy is, both ethically and Christianly, based on easygoingness." And here he also suggested how the formal indications of his ontology could be concretized in a kairological ethics. The first thing that is needed is a destruction of the pretensions of absolutist ethical theories:

> One can draw up an absolute *system of ethicalness* [*Sittlichkeit*], of ethical values and value-relations that are valid in themselves and can meanwhile—I am not saying: be a bad person; this argument is immediately out of place here. But precisely with and through these absolute relations of validity and laws, one can be blind to objects and relations that are accustomed to coming forth at particular times in living ethicalness, i.e., in facticity as the how of its possible sense of being and enactment. . . . one is an undisturbed advocate of an absolute ethics.

Such ethical systems fail to see the phronetic, kairological character of practical life and attempt to bring it under a technique of inflexible calculable rules. The "tyranny" of this ethical They "leaps in" and "dominates" the Other, usurping the role of individual "conscience." As Heidegger wrote in SZ, such systems arise out of the everyday inauthentic "expectation of currently useful instruction about available, calculable, and secure possibilities of 'action'." One "forces Dasein's existing to be subsumed under the idea of a regulated business procedure" (SZ 390/340). In WS 1921–22, Heidegger recommended that ethics be rethought out of the differentiated and situational character of factical life, which had been stressed by Aristotle, Kierkegaard, and others:

> Prior to all comfortable calculations in advance about validity and objectivity for humanity stands the reflection on what we actually [*eigentlich*] have and can have before us [*vorhaben*], on the available ways of enacting this; and further that one stays free from all wide-ranging exaggerations, with whose novelty one musters oneself, if need be, to an exceptional paragraph . . . but nothing otherwise. (G61 108–109, 103, 182, 164–65)

But just as Heidegger did not himself work out in detail his indications for rethinking Christian theology (this was done in certain directions by Bultmann and others), so he did not himself follow up on his indications for rethinking ethics along Aristotelian and Kierkegaardian lines, even though he maintained in SZ that the ontological analysis of Dasein laid bare "the condition of the possibility . . . of morality in general" (SZ 380/332). Instead, his ethical and political reflections led him eventually in the catastrophic direction toward the policies of the German National Socialist Movement and its Führer Adolf Hitler. One cannot help but wonder about what would have happened—and not happened—if Heidegger had instead stuck with his Schleiermacher, Kierkegaard, and Aristotle. However, his early Kierkegaardian interpretations of Aristotle's practical writings, in which the notion of *phronesis* played such a key role, provided many basic insights that were developed in certain directions in the so-called "rehabilitation of practical philosophy" effected by such figures as Hannah Arendt, Hans-Georg Gadamer, Jürgen Habermas, and even Richard Rorty.[14] More recently, John Caputo and David Krell have pursued the ethical significance of Heidegger's youthful way-traces along different paths that lead not just back to Aristotle, the New Testament, Eckhart, Kierkegaard, Kant, and Marx, but also forward to such figures as Levinas, Derrida, Foucault, Lyotard, and Irigaray.[15]

Cultural and University Reform

One finds Heidegger applying first his mystical Schleiermachean terminology (spirit, personal vocation, development, free community, *Vorleben*) and then later his Aristotelian-Kierkgaardian terminology to the reflections on the student-teacher relationship and postwar university reform that he pursued in his courses and in his correspondence with Blochmann and Löwith. We have already seen that he defined philosophy not only as comportment to being, but as the personal and situational having of this comportment as well (i.e., philosophy is passionate philosophizing in one's own situation), and that accordingly he saw the university as a "context of life" that is lived "out of and in our factical Dasein." In KNS 1919, he told his students that types of "scientific consciousness" are genuine only "where they grow out of an inner vocation at a particular time," immediately quoting the Eckhartian mystic Angelus Silesius and the Gospel of Matthew: " 'Man, become essential!' (Angelus Silesius)—'He who can understand it, let him understand it' (Matt. 19:12)." And, like his letters to Blochmann, Heidegger's courses of 1919 stressed that the goal here is the cultivation of one's ownmost vocation, that is, the "working out of originally motivated personal-impersonal *being*," "becoming ripe," "phenomenological life in its growing intensification of itself," "inner truthfulness." Thus science is simultaneously "the habitus of a personal Dasein" (G56/57 3-5, 213).

In WS 1921-22, Heidegger expressed this point by saying that "philosophical research" is the "working out of the specific existence of concrete researching-questioning being," namely, "one's own facticity in one's own life." In SS 1923, he called this personally based research the "hermeneutics of facticity," the wakeful and interpretive laying out of one's factical understanding of being. What he wanted to avoid was precisely the deliving and dehistoricizing of philosophy that are effected by disconnecting it from "the genuineness of personal life" in which it is differentiated. For there is no such thing as *"the* philosophy." For Heidegger, there can be no strict "objectivity" in philosophy and in the university, since his definition of philosophy is precisely an "indicative stress on the becoming-decisive of the being-sense (at the particular time) of each knowing comportment [to being]." Philosophy is always kairologically and phronetically "fitting to the situation," to different historical periods, cultures, university arrangements, and ultimately to different philosophizing individuals (G61 169, 66, 71).

Heidegger also emphasized in KNS 1919 that the scientist and the philosopher are not "isolated," but rather "bound to a community [*Gemeinschaft*] of similarly striving researchers—with these rich relations to students. The life-context of scientific consciousness works itself out in an objective form and organization in scientific academies and universities." Within this community, however, "the theoretical sphere is the sphere of absolute *freedom*" (G56/57 4–5, 213). Similarly the "relations to students" can only take the form of a *vorbildliches Vorleben*, a living ahead as a model and example, which forces students back on their own existences. One "frees the individual for his self-reflection" through the Socratic and Kierkegaardian maieutic method of indirect communication, in which "the Other is in a definite manner ruthlessly driven into reflection such that he understands that . . . to the matters [*Sachen*] of philosophy also belongs philosophizing itself and (its) notorious wretchedness" (G9 42).

One sees Gadamer's point that Heidegger was essentially "student-less" especially in Heidegger's letter of August 19, 1921 to Löwith, in which he clarified his relation to his students (EMH 111; BL 27–32). He explained that "you and Becker stand similarly at a *distance* from me," and that this is how it always has to be since one always philosophizes out of one's own factical origin and provenance (*Herkunft*): "I work concretely and factically out of my 'I am'—out of my intellectual [*geistig*] and utterly factical origin—milieu—contexts of life. . . . I live the inner duties of my facticity. . . . To this my facticity belongs—which I mention in brief—that I am a 'Christian theo*logian.*' " Philosophical "rigor" cannot mean strict objectivity (*Objektivität*), but rather only *Sachlichkeit*, fittingness to the matter, since the latter is always on the move and historically differentiated within facticity. "Even in destruction," Heidegger wrote, "I do not want and I do not dream about an in-itself-objectivity; it is one's own facticity that gets 'pushed underneath'—if you will." "The objectivity of philosophy . . . is something that is one's own. . . . I am a *dogmatic* subjective relativist, i.e., I fight to get my 'position' through—and am 'unfair' to Others in the knowledge that I myself am 'relative'." He thus underscored here that "I do not want to introduce a new position in the history of philosophy." Even though he acknowledged "a *certain* guidance" to be his "duty" as a teacher, he insisted on the necessity of Löwith's critical independence, of "your position (completely freed from me). . . . I cannot say that I ever regarded you primarily and actually as my '*Doktorandus*' [doctoral student]. . . . I have tried to influence you as little as I have Becker." In the teacher-student relation, Heidegger wants no direct leadership (*Führung*) and following: "I cannot circulate with human beings. And 'leadership' always becomes awkward; I have even nothing to say to you."

The university, this communal site (Dasein) of being, can only be an analogical identity-in-difference in which there are many different ways into the same topics: "According to 'system', 'doctrine', 'position', we are perhaps far apart—but just so *together* in the only way that human beings can genuinely be together: in existence." The university is not a universality, but is refracted into "how each understands the *unum necessarium*." It is a free community in which "we live here and now . . . you before me, I before you, we with each other." Heidegger's youthful Freiburg period presents us with what Kisiel has called "an an-archic sense of the philosophical community," a view that is closer to Derrida's conception of the university than to Heidegger's own later views in his 1933 rectorial address.[16]

These reflections put us in a position to understand the sense of Heidegger's early thoughts on university reform and on the cultural-educational reform of postwar Germany as a whole. With the collapse of the German *Kaiserreich* at the end of the First World War, discussions and plans were everywhere for the reform of Germany's educational system, including the creation of a new type of adult-education school (*Volkshochschule*) that would assist in the social and political rebuilding of the country (HB 137). Heidegger seems to have had an opportunity to work on committees for these new schools, for he told Blochmann in 1919 that "I have declined collaboration—we have in our own house enough to turn around and to take care of through positive work so that the universities do not become intellectual dunghills." Like his letters to Blochmann, which abound in thoughts on "the new communities" and "the new life that we want," the opening of Heidegger's KNS 1919 course dealt with university reform, and one of his SS 1919 courses was actually titled "On the Essence of the University and Academic Studies" (HB 15–16). He also treated this topic in his WS 1921–22 course, discussing a current view at the time that the university was an "institution whose Dasein has perhaps precisely today been brought to an end." "Today one refers noisily and often to the notorious barrenness and 'cultural' unfitness of ossified and specialist philosophy at the universities" (G61 65, 68). Jaspers recounted that during these years they shared a "vague certainty that something like a reversal was necessary within the context of professorial philosophy" (PA 94).

Heidegger's views on educational reform had certainly advanced on the program he expressed in his *Der Akademiker* article "On a Philosophical Orientation for Academics," as well as in his other student publications. This conservative program was centered around a return to the lost *arche*, origin/kingdom, of the medieval Catholic worldview. It understood the modern liberal culture of "free-thinking" and "individualistic ethics" to be a fall from "the ancient wisdom of the Christian tradition," from its "sources of religious-ethical authority," and ultimately from the teleological depth-dimension of God. In the midst of this crisis and danger, it issued a militant call for a revolutionary retrieval of the Christian heritage that would be achieved through *Kampf*, struggle. Let us compare this program with Heidegger's views on reform in the late teens and early twenties, when he had given up the identification of philosophy with religious worldview.

He did in fact still express the opinion that modern rationalism and technization in academic life and in culture in general were a falling away, but now this fall meant not so much the loss of a particular religious worldview as rather the eclipse of the original questionableness and differentiation of the *Ereignis* of being, in which there can be nothing like a true worldview. It is the fall out of the speeding boat of *kinesis*, not out of the solid ground of the medieval worldview. In WS 1921–22, Heidegger continued with his reflections on "the century of technology," which he had begun to discuss in SS 1919: "One can say that there never was such an 'unphilosophical' time as today. . . . The talk about a falling away, technization (Bergson, Spengler) is muddled so long as the phenomena are not converted positively into the problem of in whom, for whom, and with whom the falling away is enacted." Later in the course, he again both adopted Spengler's "perspective of decline" and criticized it for not being radical enough. Specifically regarding academic life, Heidegger explained that this decline into technization takes the form of approaching philosophy as an "educational object" and "technique": " 'Philosophy' characterizes also and immediately a developed doctrine . . . just as we see it today, as it gives itself out at the university" (G61 26, 74, 50). Heidegger's point was that, in both academic life and other forms of cultural life, decline meant the fall *into* the vision of a static, homogeneous, and impersonal world that can be calculated and mastered, and thus a fall *away from* the differentiating temporalizing-sense and personal enactment-sense in the definition of philosophy and in life itself.

What then did the concepts of "return" and "revolutionizing" mean for the young Heidegger in the context of university reform? They meant an instituting of the end of philosophy and the new beginning in which there is effectively no such thing as "*the* philosophy" or *the* origin. Institutional reform was to have the sense of an institutional destruction of the old metaphysical concept of the university back to the type of analogical and anarchic philosophical community about which Heidegger told Löwith. He wanted to put the university back into the questionableness of the happening of being within personal academic life. The primal source to which he wanted to return was neither a worldview nor any homogeneous reality; rather, it was seen to be pluralized into the localized factical origins of the philosophizing individuals that make up the university. There are only primal situational sources (*Situationsursprünge*). This is the sense of his statement to Löwith that "I work concretely and factically . . . out of my intellectual [*geistig*] and utterly factical origin [*Herkunft*]. . . . And I am this in the life-context of the university." Thus,

> One can overcome the old university . . . [only] such that, in contemporary facticity, one goes back into the primal enactment-sources [*Vollzugsursprünge*] of what survives and decides on one's own what one can do. . . . [T]he one [university] we do have lies in our hands, whether we agonize away in the moods of opinion and ponder about possible primal cultures, or whether we *sacrifice* ourselves and find our way back to ourselves in *existentiell* limitation and facticity, instead of reflecting ourselves away into programs and universal problems. (BL 29, 31; G61 67)

"The new life that we will, or that wills us," Heidegger wrote to Blochmann in 1919, "has renounced being universal." He had one recurrent complaint about the reform plans that were being put forward in postwar times: they were symptoms of the very problem, namely, technization and falling away into static and impersonal universality. He stated in KNS 1919 that "the much-discussed university reform is completely misguided and a total misunderstanding of all genuine revolutionizing of spirit when it spreads itself in appeals, protest meetings, programs, orders and associations." For such reform can only take place through the development of a whole generation of individuals, each with his or her ownmost vocation:

> We are today not ripe for *genuine* reforms in the realm of the university. And becoming ripe for this is a matter of an *entire generation*. Renewal of the university means rebirth of genuine scientific consciousness and life-context. But life-relations renew themselves only in a regress to the genuine primal sources of spirit; as historical phenomena, they require the repose and certainty of genetic self-reinforcement, in other words: the inner truthfulness of value-replete life that builds upon itself. Only life, not the noise of overhasty cultural programs, makes 'epochs'.

In the previous year Heidegger had actually written to Blochmann about this very theme of university reform, stressing that it takes place through the development of personal vocations as opposed to universal visions:

> Spiritual life must become again a truly *actual* life in us—it must take on a momentum born out of the personal, one that 'overturns' and compels to genuine uprise. . . . This simple composed way of spiritual being and life has

been lost in our universities—whoever has seen this . . . sees also, however, only the same confusion in the programmatic reform proposals and theories about 'the essence of the university.' (HB 7, 15; G56/57 4–5)

Heidegger insisted here and in his KNS 1919 course that, in the university, "intellectual life can only be *lived* and shaped as an example [*vorgelebt*], such that those who are to participate in it are grasped and stirred by it in their ownmost existence." Thus in WS 1921–22, he stated flatly that this means that there is no role here for prophets or Führers with their abstract visions: "These discussions about reform . . . are all uncritical; they overlook the question of competence and forget the question about the suitable [*geeignet*] time. For us here it is a matter of philosophically seeing the actual [*eigentlich*] situation without prophecy and the affectations of Führers. (One writes today about the Führer-problem!)" About such "psychological technique," Heidegger also wrote, "No big reform plans, claims, noisy demands before one actually 'is there'. . . . humanity is called without human beings." The option that he put forward was precisely the choice between personal existentiell experience and the illusions of universal programs: "And if we 'go into decline,' then there again stands before us only *either*: . . . radical existentiell concern . . . *or*: degenerating into the padding of mythical and theosophical metaphysics." Not only, as Löwith reported, did Heidegger have no "positive" plan for reform of either philosophy, the university, or postwar German culture, but he seemed to be in principle against the very idea of a universal "program" and "movement," since this type of approach does not spring from and return to one's own personal existence. This hidden king, who shunned the public light of reform discussions, did not—or, rather, did not yet—want to be a philosopher-king in a new Platonic Academy (HB 7; G61 69–70, 187–88; MLD 28–29).

Dasein and *Geschlecht*

One also finds the ethical implications of Heidegger's ontology pointing in the direction of question of "woman." In SS 1923, he wrote that, "in the indicative definition of the theme of hermeneutics: facticity = our own Dasein at any particular time, the expression 'human' [*menschlich*] Dasein or 'being of humanity/man' [*des Menschen*] is avoided." And in SZ, "spirit" is added to the list of inappropriate terms, though—like the above terms—it turns up again with a fury in Heidegger's later writings. Why are these masculine terms to be avoided? In addition to suggesting a present-at-hand substance, they bias the analysis of "Dasein" (an ontically noncommittal indicator) to some particular differentiation of being and marginalize other differentiations. Heidegger showed this with the gendered theological definitions of Dasein in passages from Paul's letters: "For a man [*aner*] ought not to cover his head, since he is the image and glory of God [but woman is the glory of man. (For man was not made from woman, but woman from man. Neither was man created for woman, but woman for man)]. . . . Problem: what is woman?" (1 Cor. 11:7-9; cf. 2 Cor. 3:18, Rom. 8:29). Heidegger's gesture toward "woman" and the ideal of letting-be that it expresses goes back to his correspondence with Blochmann, who as a student of pedagogy was especially concerned with the role of women in education. In 1918 we find Heidegger replying to her concerns: "The academic Dasein—or more precisely the 'intellectual' [*geistig*] existence of woman was for me at no moment an impossible problem. . . . when intellectual women actually strive for a meaning and importance, then their ownmost character [*Eigenart*] expresses itself in an especially strong manner." Regarding Blochmann's planned dissertation on Schleiermacher, Heidegger emphasized that, just as it was women in Schleiermacher's intellectual circles that "understood and valued him in the deepest and most immediate manner, so today also women will be able to make a decisive contribution to the elucidation of his being." "I am convinced that his personality can be grasped completely and immediately only by a woman." And it was in 1919 that he wrote to her in Eckhartian language about "the uninhibited letting-become-free of the feminine soul" (G63 21-22; SZ 62/72; HB 10-11, 14).

The theme of "woman" turned up again in Heidegger's lecture course of SS 1928. Again he stated that the masculine term *Mensch*, human being, man, must be avoided in favor of "the neutral term *Dasein*," which expresses an indifferent "primal source, the not-yet of factical dissemination" [*Zerstreutheit*], which is open to being "differentiated," "disseminated," and "individuated" in every possible concretion of humanity. "Neutrality is not the voidness of an abstraction, but precisely the potency of the *primal source* that bears in itself the intrinsic possibility of every concrete factual humanity," including "the possibility for being disseminated into bodiliness and thus into sexuality," into "the two genders" (*Geschlechter*).[17] Given the openness of the "transcendental dissemination" of Dasein, Heidegger here expressed the *ideal* of "neutrality," that is, the analysis of Dasein should be "prior to all prophesying and heralding of worldviews," whether these may be "male" or "female," European or non-European, etc. (though in SS 1923, for example, he *actually* presented woman in the patriarchal stereotype of wife and mother) (G26 §10). As Heidegger had stated earlier, philosophy has "no mission . . . to interfere with [coming *Geschlectern*]," where the latter ambiguous term can be construed to mean either "generations," "races," or "genders" (G63 18).

Geschlecht means not only the or a "human race," but also any race or genus of living things. Surprisingly, not only did Heidegger speak of "the Dasein of this table," of the "toy," "jug," "house, garden, field," "nature" (G63 112), but he even acknowledged the sentient "Dasein" of "the animal" and its sentient "being-in-the-world." In his 1925 Kassel lectures on Dilthey, he explained that, unlike "a chair," for example, "the Dasein of life" is "in" its world as a here [*da*] that is disclosed (*erschlossen*) "for it." The term "Dasein of life" encompasses both the disclosedness of world for human animals and its sentient disclosedness for nonhuman animals:

> The primal givenness of Dasein is that it is in a world. . . . Every living being has its environing world as something that is not present-to-hand next to it, but rather is here [*da*] disclosed, uncovered for it. This world can be very simple for a primitive animal. . . . Such knowledge is gradually beginning to be advanced also in biology. . . . the animal has a world. In the same way we ourselves are also always in a world such that it is disclosed for us. . . . all life is here [*da*] in such a way that a world is also here [*da*] for it. (WDF 15–16)

In his SS lecture course of the same year, Heidegger gave a phenomenological analysis of the "being-in-the-world" of a "snail in its house," its shell. This is "a being to which we must likewise attribute (in a formal manner) the kind of being of Dasein—'life'." Heidegger compared the container-like view of the human mind in modern epistemology with the snail in its house, in order to turn the comparison around and show that, like the knowing subject, the snail is always already a being-in-the-world. The snail stretches itself out of its house "toward something. . . . Does the snail thereby first enter into a relation of being with the world? No! Its crawling out is but a local modification of its already-being-in-the-world." It is because the world is always already disclosed to the snail that it can crawl out and touch something: "It does not first add a world to itself by touching; rather, it touches because its being means nothing other than to be in a world. This applies similarly to a subject to which knowing is ascribed" (G20 223–24/165–66).

In Heidegger's youthful writings, we find the original questionableness of being differentiated into an alterity of sites (Da-sein) of *Ereignis*, each with its *own* value: things, implements, architecture, plants, animals, communities, and persons. The realm of persons is exemplified through the rich array of figures turning up in Heidegger's phenomenological exercises: woman, man, child, friend, stranger, janitor, factory worker, farmer, non-European, ancient Greek. The admirable *ideal* that one finds expressed here is that of noninterference and letting-be, even if the young Heidegger himself did not always actually measure up to it in his phenomenological descriptions (e.g., of the "Senegalese negro," the "wife"), even if there are elements in his thought that will later get out of control and be put in the service of totalitarian politics (e.g., militaristic imagery, German nationalism, romanticism, the language of origins, and an ethics of *Kampf*, struggle[18]), and even if, as John Caputo has argued, Heidegger's emphasis on the passionate *Kampf* of the individual for inner truthfulness allows letting-be to obscure helping-be and the other "categories of the heart" that were missed in his reading of the New Testament (flesh, pain, disease, mercy). But if the young Heidegger did not hear Levinas's "call of the 'widow, the orphan and the stranger,' "[19] if his analyses of the relational and enactment-senses of personal life need to be supplemented by an investigation of what might be called inter-relational, inter-personal, inter-active, and compassionate sense, one can still learn from his writings something important about the ethical that is not found in the later writings.

In the interim between his two nostalgic quests for the kingdom of a homogeneous origin, namely, the medieval Catholic worldview of his student years and the Greco-Germanic worldview of the history of being in his later writings, this hidden exiled king without a kingdom affirmed an anarchic community of free, personal, and local origins, and he did so under the impetus of his own attempt to free himself from the perceived constraints of his Catholic and Neo-Scholastic beginnings. The young Heidegger of the early Freiburg period was more a negative Socratic, Pyrrhonian, and Kierkegaardian thinker than a positive thinker, more a deconstructive than a constructive philosopher. The passion moving his thought was romantic rebellion against naive tradition and authority, the project of ushering in the end of philosophy, caustic demythologizing of all speculative system-building and cultural "programs," and defending the right of historical individuality and difference. He was a Christian without a confession, a philosopher without a philosophy.

It is true that the terminology of his cultural critique in his student years (namely, origin, fall, crisis and danger, a call to return, revolution, and militant struggle) turned up again in his early Freiburg period, especially in his thoughts on university reform. But this terminology was now used in the new context of his confessional and philosophical conversions and his project of the end of philosophy. These terms have to be understood in relation to his central theme of the questionableness of being and its radical differentiation into particularity. It is the falling away from this that leads to crisis, the call to origins, revolution, and struggle. The young Heidegger's *Kampf* was primarily a struggle for academic, religious, moral, and cultural individualism and self-development. For example, in his 1919 letter to Krebs, announcing his philosophical and confessional independence, he wrote that "inner truthfulness regarding oneself . . . demands sacrifices and renunciations and struggles [*Kämpfe*]." In WS 1921–22, he spoke of the constant "*struggle [Kampf]* of philosophically factical interpretation *against its own factical ruinance*," i.e., against falling away out of situational questionableness into ahistorical, impersonal visions of universality and objectivity (MH 107, cf. HB 10, 12; G61 153).

The young Heidegger of the early Freibrug period had lost—and actively renounced—his origin, his worldview, and his leaders, but sometime around the late twenties he would, in a move that betrayed a loss of both nerve and humility, start looking for replacements in the notion of a fated history of being and in a metaphysical interpretation of National Socialism. He would put the rhetoric of primal source, fall, crisis, return, revolution, and struggle in the service of these replacements, and allow the nationalistic, militaristic, and romantic elements of his thought to gain the upper hand over the liberal spirit he once advocated under the influence of such figures as Schleiermacher and Kierkegaard. He would again give a lecture course on "Introduction in Academic Studies" in SS 1929 and a seminar on "Folk and Science" in WS 1933–34. But here and in his 1933 rectorial address, his model becomes Plato's authoritarian *Republic*, whereas earlier it had rather been Schleiermacher's free sociality and the Socrates of the *Apology*, who is sentenced to death for his free-thinking. And it is here in the early Freiburg period, in this twilight period between a no-longer and a not-yet, that we find a decisive direction in Heidegger's thought itself to play off against, among other things, his failure of nerve and humility in WS 1929–30 when he forgot his earlier warning about the *gloria*, pride, and "affectations of Führers," and called for "the governor [*Verwalter*] of the inner grandeur of Dasein" (G61 49–50; G29/30 244; cf. HCM 33). The hidden king had come out of exile.

16 | Reinscribing Heidegger

Heidegger proved indeed to be a "constant beginner." His subsequent drafts of of "Being and Time" from SZ onward reinscribed the seminal way-traces of his new beginning, and effected a remarkable filling out and deepening of his earlier rough sketches, which also brought many new themes. We certainly do not find in the young Heidegger everything that we find in the later Heidegger. We only have to consider the later Heidegger's rich analyses of the end of philosophy, new beginning, and the way-character of constant beginning with their themes of being-in-the-world, *Kehre*, indication and the trace, the anarchic play of the *Ereignis* of being, *Es gibt, aletheia*, the worlding of the fourfold, mystery, the divine, the thinging of things, poetic dwelling, meditative Eckhartian *Gelassenheit*, the originary ethics of "homecoming," language, poetry, contemporary cultural crisis, the kairological history of being from the pre-Socratics through to Hölderlin, Nietzsche, and modern technology, as well as even the Eastern experience of being. But, instead of exploring further this continuity, enrichment, and novelty, which we have already glimpsed in Chapter 2, I want now to deal instead with the longstanding concern over serious problems in Heidegger's later reinscriptions, which has been spurred on recently by Farias's and Ott's new disclosures of the extent and depth of Heidegger's involvement with National Socialism. Thus, unlike Chapter 2, which dealt with the ambiguous genitive case of the phrase *die Sache des Denkens* mainly in terms of "the *subject matter* of the thinking," the present chapter deals with it mainly in terms of "the matter, the affair, the controversy, the court case of *the (Heidegger's) thinking*," that is, *l'affaire Heidegger*.

Diverse figures such as Jacques Derrida, Emmanuel Levinas, Jürgen Habermas, Theodor Adorno, Herbert Marcuse, Richard Bernstein, Richard Rorty, feminist theorists, Werner Marx, John Caputo, Thomas Sheehan, Theodore Kisiel, Michael Zimmerman, David Krell, and others have all in their own ways suggested that strong metaphysical and ideological traces of essentialism, mythopoetic speculation, ethnocentrism, genderism, anthropocentrism, authoritarianism, and political ideology are still at work right within Heidegger's postmetaphysical formulations of the being-question, which therefore need to be deconstructed and "demythologized"[1] at the same time that they are appropriated. In the following, I show how the dangerous "supplement" of Heidegger's youthful writings in his collected edition and especially their method of demythologizing can (1) aid in identifying and sketching these metaphysical traces *genealogically*; (2) add another strategy for deconstructing them; and therefore (3) add also another strategy for helping us to get on with the task of that independent critical appropriation and reinscription of Heidegger's thought that he himself always recommended. In other words, I combine in a single ambiguous gesture a radical critique and an equally radical defense of this great thinker, taking the *via media* between the abstract extremes of complete rejection and complete acceptance.

I argue that, in the palimpsests of his later drafts of "Being and Time," Heidegger *simultaneously* inscribed into his previously demythologized question about being certain traits of deworlding, deliving, and dehistoricizing, that is, remythologizing tendencies, which hyperbolically masked and effaced the anarchic kinetic-personal physiognomy of being that he had sketched out earlier. Some of these tendencies were already at work in his thought from the very beginning, but they became increasingly aggravated as his thought developed. I am not attempting to reduce Heidegger's later writings to these tendencies, since they are, as we have seen in Chapters 1 and 2, ambiguously accompanied by equally strong postmetaphysical countertendencies. To unlock the sense of these mythologizing tendencies, I present a number of rough sketches of how they took the form of reconfigurations or reconsignments of the content-, relational, enactment-, and temporalizing-characters of the intentional relation to being. More specifically, this application of Heidegger's youthful project of demythologizing to his later writings pursues the following course of analysis: (1) the transcendental reconfiguration in the Kantian draft of "Being and Time" in SZ; (2) Heidegger's post-SZ turn as a reinscriptive re-turn to his early Freiburg period; (3) the deliving reconfigurations in the later Heidegger's mythopoetic drafts (namely, primitivistic, antihumanist, essentialist, and speculative configurations); (4) the dehistoricizing reconfigurations in these later drafts (namely, Helleno-Germanic, religious, gendered, anthropocentric, and authoritarian configurations); and (5) the prospect of independent critical reinscription of Heidegger's thought.

The Kantian Draft of "Being and Time":
The Existential-Transcendental Configuration

Around WS 1925–26, a fourth major and renewed influence entered Heidegger's thinking, namely, Kant and German Idealism.[2] This was the very time when in 1926 he was finally compelled, under the pressure of the academic politics of publish-or-perish (SD 87–88/80; TB 180–83), hastily to finish weaving the bricolage of his lecture course manuscripts and unpublished essays into a publishable text, which was a much later Kantian draft that he called *Sein und Zeit*. In place of his earlier planned book on Aristotle, it was published in the 1927 issue of Husserl's journal, and thereafter fatefully became known as Heidegger's magnum opus. This fact makes it almost seem as if the Heidegger of 1926 is already "the later Heidegger" and SZ one of "the later writings," and thus forces us to start rethinking the longstanding chronology of Heidegger's development. As Gadamer has written, in light of the nontranscendental character of the young Heidegger's concepts of "it worlds" and *Ereignis*, "the epoch of *Sein und Zeit* is pushed aside into a certain relativity" (MV 230).

The record of Heidegger's courses indicates clearly his turn to Kant. During WS 1925–26, he was holding seminars on "Phenomenological Exercises (Kant, *Critique of Pure Reason*)" and "Phenomenological Exercises (Hegel, *Logic*, I)." He wrote to Jaspers, on December 12, that "the nicest thing is that I am beginning *actually to like Kant*" and, on December 16, that "I . . . feel traces of the world-spirit in the neighborhood of both of them [Kant and Hegel]" (HJ 57, 59). This turn to Kant explains why, even though Heidegger's lecture course of WS 1925–26, "Logik" (Logic), had originally planned to deal with the concept of truth in Husserl and Aristotle, it abruptly deviated from the original plan after the Christmas break and entered headlong into an intense analysis of especially the doctrine of schematism in Kant's First Critique (G21). Here Heidegger worked out much of his analysis of time in Part One, Division Two, of SZ. In SS 1926, he delivered the lecture course "Die Grundbegriffe der antiken Philosophie" (The Basic Concepts of Ancient Philosophy) (G22), as well as the seminar "Exercises in History and Historical Knowledge in Connection with J. B. Droysen, *Grundriss der Historik*." In WS 1926–27, he lectured on "Geschichte der Philosophie von Thomas v. Aquin bis Kant" (History of Philosophy from Thomas Aquinas to Kant) (G23), and held the seminar "Selected Problems of Logic (Concept and Concept-Formation)."

In SS 1927, we find the lecture course "Die Grundprobleme der Phänomenologie" (The Basic Problems of Phenomenology) (G24), in which Heidegger delivered a reworked version of major unpublished portions of SZ, namely, Division Three ("Time and Being") of Part One, as well as Division Two (the concept of *cogito* in Descartes and Kant) and Division Three (Aristotle's concept of time) of Part Two (the destruction of the history of ontology). Simultaneously he held a seminar on "The Ontology of Aristotle and Hegel's *Logic*." In WS 1927–28, he delivered the lecture course "Phänomenologische Interpretation von Kants *Kritik der reinen Vernunft*" (Phenomenological Interpretation of Kant's *Critique of Pure Reason*) (G25), holding seminars on "Concept and Concept-Formation" and "Schelling, *On the Essence of Human Freedom*." During the lecture course, he told his students that, "when I began again to study Kant's *Critique of Pure Reason* a few years ago and read it, as it were, against the background of Husserl's phenomenology, it was as if the blinders fell from my eyes, and Kant became for me the confirmation of the correctness of the way for which I was searching" (G25 431). In WS 1928-29, he held the seminar "Phenomenological Exercises for Advanced Students: Kant, *Groundwork of the Metaphysics of Morals.*" In 1929 he gathered together his lecture courses on Kant and published the book *Kant und das Problem der Metaphysik* (Kant and the Problem of Metaphysics) (G3), which presented a reworked version of the unpublished Division One (Kant's doctrine of schematism) of Part Two of SZ.

In 1925-26 Heidegger had found in Kant's transcendental doctrine of schematism a new linguistic model for talking about the *Sache* of "Being and Time" (SZ 31/45). Thus, his earlier experimentation with a plethora of different thoughtpaths narrowed and hardened for a time into a quasi-Kantian transcendental self-interpretation, which also included an affiliation with the concept of transcendental "constitution" in Husserl's phenomenology (cf. VZB 600-602/118-21). In SZ Heidegger effected a reconfiguration of his earlier articulation of the intentional senses of being. Here the "it worlds" of content-sense, the "Dasein of personal life," and the freewheeling *Ereignis* and *kinesis* of temporalizing-sense came to be reinscribed respectively as the existential-transcendental "structures" of the "worldhood" of the world, of the "existentiality" of Dasein, and of the "schemata" of temporality (SZ 17/33, 482-83/416). Combining the medieval theory of transcendentals with Kant, Heidegger wrote that time is "the transcendental horizon for the question about being" (SZ 53/63).

As Becker, Jaspers, Gadamer, Marcuse, and others saw, the static transcendental language of SZ brought about a certain deliving and dehistoricizing of the concreteness of Heidegger's earlier kinetic-personalist drafts. Similarly, William Barrett reported how, after teaching SZ for years, he "woke up one morning with a very disturbing feeling" that "Dasein has no soul."[3] Due to their traditional theological and substantialist connotations, Heidegger hastily abandoned the terms "person" and "life" as central terms around SS 1923, eclipsing them with the key term "Dasein," which ironically turned out to have an even more static meaning for his readers (G63 21). The "transcendental knowledge" and "absolute science of being" claimed by the "fundamental ontology" of SZ generated the misleading impression of atemporal eidetic "structures," that is, "existentialia," which are instantiated in each particular Dasein (SZ 51/62, 304/272; G24 15/11). By the time Heidegger published his Kantbook in 1929, he was already talking about "the Dasein *in* human being," as if it were a historicized Aristotelian *nous poietikos* incarnated in the Kierkegaardian individual (G3 §41). What also aggravated this transcendental reading of SZ was the fact that, though Heidegger still used the term "formal indication" throughout the published portion of the text, its apparently planned explanation in a chapter on "concept-formation" and "grammar" in Division Three of Part One was never published (see SZ, English tr., p. 401, n. xiii; cf. SZ 52/63, 220/209, 8/26). In August of 1927 he wrote to Löwith that "formal indication . . . is still there for me, even if I do not talk about it" (BL 37).

Under the influence of Kierkegaard, as well as Dilthey's critique of Hegelian essentialism and Kantian logicism, Heidegger had actually warned around 1920 about the inadequacy of the abstract term "schematism" that he took up in SZ. "The past, present, and future of the self are experienced not as a time-schema for an objective ordering of things, but rather in the non-schematic sense of worry that concerns the enactment of experience" (G9 33; cf. G56/57 133). Discussing "the empty schematism of transcendental philosophy" and, more specifically, Natorp's theory of the constitution of experience in terms of a "basic schema" of a priori categories, Heidegger also wrote in SS 1920 that "a schema cannot and should not be given for [concrete, here-and-now, selfworldly Dasein and indeed in its individuation]" (PAA July 1, 12, 19). And in WS 1921–22 and SS 1923, he reaffirmed that "the categories are . . . not a society of logical schemata" and that " 'concept' is no schema, but rather a possibility of being, of the eye-opening moment" (G61 88, 139; G63 16). A category, a concept, is originally the factical "index" of the *Ereignis* of historical sense which is enacted kairologically in individual life. Only subsequently is it inductively lifted out, formalized into formally indicative concepts, or alternatively hardened into the illusion of a universal, static "schema," even if it is thought to be "temporal" in character.

Simultaneously with his turn to Kant's transcendental language, Heidegger began using a heavily "existential" terminology (e.g., "existence," "existential," "existentialia," "existentiality," "ecstasis") (OWB 197). The palimpsest SZ obscured the earlier mystical, kairological-Christian, and Aristotelian drafts over which it had been written, and gave the misleading impression of advocating a subjectivist philosophy of human Dasein as an existentialized transcendental subjectivity, which "constitutes" the world through the activity of schematizing. The Kantian strains of SZ evoked "the old mythology of an intellect which glues and rigs together the world's matter with its own forms." Like Becker, who saw that SZ was "no longer the original Heidegger," Heidegger soon realized that this draft "carried with it inadequate readings of my own intention," and withheld publication of the remaining divisions of the text (DMH 351; LR xiv–xv). In the margin of his Kant-book Heidegger later wrote, "Relapsed totally into the standpoint of transcendental questioning" (HW 111; cf. SD 47/44; G9 357/BW 235; G15 335, 345).

In SS 1939, Heidegger leveled criticism at the notion of "schematism" in Kant and Nietzsche, thus in effect picking up his critique from the early 1920s (N1 551–77/NIII 68–89). It was more this transcendental thoughtpath of SZ, and not his preceeding "youthful leaps" themselves, that amounted to the real

Abweg of his early thinking. It was a partially aberrant enactment of his earlier intention to make the *Kehre* from being to the differentiated temporal giving of being, an intention that had been articulated in the preconception of formally indicative starting points in his youthful writings. SZ had originally become known somewhat misleadingly as Heidegger's magnum opus, but now that we are able to contextualize and relativize this text within the comet's tail of drafts stretching back into the early Freiburg period and beyond, we see that it, too, was neither a teleological necessity nor even a completed work, but a contingent way-trace in the reproductive chain of differing/deferring drafts of the nonbook about the *Sache* of "Being and Time" that he went on reinscribing in many different ways.

Re-Turn and Mythopoetic Configuration

In order to effect the "bend" in his thinking after SZ, which would bring about a more adequate fulfillment of his intention toward *Kehre*, Heidegger's turn returned creatively to the terminology of his youthful drafts and reinscribed it in novel ways. Among the first signs of this return is his lecture course of SS 1928, "Logik" (Logic) (G26). Shortly after its completion in August, while he was preparing for his return from Marburg to take over Husserl's chair in Freiburg, Heidegger wrote to Blochmann that he was "laying down new tasks or, rather, slowly venturing into something which was still inaccessible to me in my first Freiburg period. And so it will . . . become for me something completely new. Already the last Marburg course this summer was a new way or, rather, a following of paths which for a long time I still believed myself able to intimate only" (HB 24).

Near the close of the course, Heidegger had actually indicated that he was now rethinking Division Three ("Time and Being") of Part One of SZ (G26 268/208). Here, at a time when he was still in the midst of finishing up his readings of Kant, he no longer used the Kantian term "schema," but in fact set about reinscribing the notion of "temporality" back into the very quasi-mystical terminology of KNS 1919, and thereby freeing the suppressed subtext of SZ. He explained that the "ecstatic" temporalizing of transcendence is a "primal source," an originary nothing (*nihil originarium*), an "abyss," a "concealment," a "not-yet of factical dissemination," out of which factical worlds "spring forth" (G26 172/137, 234/182, 268–74/208–12, 281/217). "The ecstematic temporalizes itself, oscillating and resonating [*schwingend*], as a worlding." "Time . . . is essentially a self-opening and expanding into a world." In using the term "to world" to explain the experience of *kosmos* in Parmenides and Heraclitus, Heidegger told his students that this term was used "already in my early Freiburg lecture courses" (219/171). Since it is not a being, world is "nothing that is and yet something that there is/it gives. The 'it' that here gives this not-being is itself not in being, but rather is self-temporalizing temporality." As worlding, temporalizing is the *Ereignis* of "primal history": "The *Ereignis* of the world-entry of beings is the primal *Ereignis* and is, in its essential presencing [*Wesen*], temporalizing." As the *principium individuationis*, this temporalizing "differentiates," "individuates," and "disseminates" itself into historical worlds and into the mineness of Dasein. Heidegger's model here is no longer Eckhart's "little castle," but Leibniz's concept of the "monad" as a "unique" "microcosm," a "little world," a house with "no windows" in which the universe undergoes "mirroring" and "perspectival refraction" (118–20/96–97).

In the fall of 1928, Heidegger was working simultaneously on his essay "Vom Wesen des Grundes" and on his inaugural lecture "Was ist Metaphysik?," in which he again wrote of "primal source," "the nothing," *Schwingung*, and the "primal happening" of world. "World never *is*, but rather *worlds*." After this, "worlding" was reiterated as a central term especially in Heidegger's later essays on poetic dwelling in the fourfold of earth and sky, gods and mortals. In the seminar that he held in SS 1928, namely, "Phenomenological Exercises: Interpretation of Aristotle, *Physics* II," he again used the term *Ereignis*, translating *dynamis* (possibility) as *Eignung* ("suitability," but literally "owning") and *kinesis* as *Ereignen*, eventing/enowning. This retracing of the 1919 term *Ereignis*, in which it was grafted onto Heidegger's subsequent reading of Aristotle, was meant to describe the circular movement of being from the *steresis, lethe*, and absence of *dynamis* into the unconcealment of presence.[4]

By the time Heidegger wrote in 1936–38 his unpublished *Beiträge zur Philosophie (Vom Ereignis)*, which was to be a rewriting of SZ and a kind of second magnum opus, he had completed the translation of "temporality" in SZ back into the central term of his KNS 1919 course, namely, *Ereignis* (see G65 §42 "From *Sein und Zeit* to '*Ereignis*' "). Here, as in such works as his 1946 "Brief über den Humanismus" and in his later marginal notes to SZ, we find a rethinking of many of the major concepts of SZ in connection with time as *Ereignis*. As a synonym of *Ereignis*, *Es gibt* also turned up again as a major term, along with reflections on the mysterious character of the "it" that gives (see G9 334–36/BW 214–16 and Heidegger's 1962 seminar "Zeit und Sein," which bears the very same title as the unpublished Division Three of Part One of SZ [SD 1–60/1–54]). But already in SS 1928, Heidegger had quoted Heraclitus's fragment that "*physis* loves to hide," in order to get at the "concealment" of the primal source out of which worlding happens (G26 281/217). And then his earlier concept of ontological "mystery" actually resurfaced in his 1930 lecture "Vom Wesen der Wahrheit," which maintained that the *lethe* in the Greek concept of *aletheia* is not just "concealment," but also "mystery." "The concealing of beings as a whole events/enowns itself in the ek-sistent freedom of being-here. . . . The mystery (the concealing of the concealed) as such reigns throughout the being-here of humanity" (G9 193–94/BW 132–33). In his *Beiträge*, Heidegger referred to this mystery as "the mystery of eventing/enowning" (G65 408).

Likewise, the young Heidegger's notion of *Kehre*, as a constant turning and being on the way into the temporal happening of being, made its appearance again. In his SS 1928 lecture course, he stated that the "finitude of philosophy," of ontology, has to be expressed in a "metontology," which is a constant turn (*Kehre*), "overturning," "transformation," and "concretion" back into the historical happening of Dasein. It "demands again and again a new awakening," a constant beginning anew. Thus "philosophy . . . is more original than every science" and "every worldview." Reverting back to his language of WS 1920–21 and WS 1921–22, he insisted that philosophy is rather "philosophizing" that "transforms everything in us," since it is an "existing out of the ground," an "oscillating and resonating in the upswing, in that which carries us away and gives us distance" (G26 198–201/156–58, 285/xv). In his very first lecture course back in Freiburg, namely, his WS 1928–29 "Einleitung in die Philosophie" (Introduction in Philosophy) (G27), where, as he told Blochmann, he would continue pursuing "something completely new," Heidegger again maintained that philosophy could not be a "science." Rather, it "springs out of the always overflowing happening of Dasein" and is always "a 'leap into' the historicity of its Dasein," an "explicit letting-happen of the happening of Dasein" (EBF 119; DK 106).

Heidegger thus also focused again on his earlier notion of formal indication in his WS 1929–30 lecture course, "Die Grundbegriffe der Metaphysik (der Weltbegriff)" (The Basic Concepts of Metaphysics [The World-Concept]) (G29/30), about which he wrote to Blochmann in September of 1929 that "in my metaphysics-course in the winter I will succeed with a completely new beginning" (HB 33). Taking up the unpublished chapter on concept-formation in Division Three of Part One of SZ, he explained regarding the basic concepts of SZ (e.g., death, resolute openness, history, existence, world) that "all philosophical concepts are *formally indicative*" and point into the "eye-opening moment." He noted, as he had in KNS 1919, that these concepts have the character of an Idea in the Kantian Sense which never gives its matter as fully present in intuition. "The meaning-content of these concepts," he wrote, "does not mean and say directly that toward which they are related, it gives only an indication, a directive that the one who understands this context of concepts is to enact a transformation of himself into the Dasein [in him]." "Insofar as one takes these concepts free from indication like a scientific concept," that is, takes them as "meaning the properties . . . of something present-at-hand," "something ultimate and universal," one "falls victim to the primal metaphysical illusion" to which Kant had pointed in his notion of "the dialectical illusion of reason." Thus there can be "no system of Dasein" for "philosophical speculation" (G29/30 421–32). After taking up his youthful notions of *Anzeige* and "leap" again in his *Beiträge* (see G65 §218 "The *Anzeige* of the Essential Presencing of Truth"), Heidegger went on to explore formal indication, as well as the notion of "way" and constant beginning, with such terms as "trace," *Wink*, "way-marker," and "forest-path."

But we must not fail to emphasize that the young Heidegger's concern with cultural crisis, technology, and cultural and university reform also resurfaced in new ways after SZ, as we see, for example, in the development of Heidegger's continued correspondence with Blochmann from 1929 onward (HB 31ff.). In his WS 1929–30 lecture course, Heidegger again treated Spengler's work on "technization" and "the decline of the west," as well as the cultural critiques given by Scheler and others, in order to explore the cultural crisis in the modern technological era with its "basic mood" of "deep boredom" and "homesickness" (cf. HCM 26–33). Under the influence of Ernst Jünger especially, Heidegger treated this theme regularly in his subsequent courses and essays under the rubrics of the "world night" and "wasteland" of the technological era. Regarding university reform, Heidegger's model eventually ceased to be the free-thinking Socrates of the *Apology* and the liberalism of Schleiermacher, and became in a certain way the doctrines of truth, education, and the tripartite structure of society in Plato's *Republic*. In 1930 Heidegger wrote to Blochmann that, regarding university reform and "the coming world-age," "we must also abstain from renewing the stale and now alien idealisms from the time of Humboldt, Schleiermacher, and Schelling" (HB 38).

Carrying forward his reflections on the university in his 1929 lecture "What is Metaphysics?," Heidegger's SS 1929 lecture course on "Einführung in das akademische Studium" (Introduction in Academic Studies) treated Plato's Allegory of the Cave. So did subsequent lecture courses, namely, his WS 1931–32 "Vom Wesen der Wahrheit ('Höhlengleichnis' und *Theätet*, über *pseudos*)" (On the Essence of Truth ["Allegory of the Cave" and *Theaetetus* on *pseudos*]) (G34), his SS 1933 "Die Grundfrage der Philosophie (Wesen der Wahrheit: 'Höhlengleichnis')" (The Basic Question of Philosophy [The Essence of Truth: "Allegory of the Cave"]) (G36/37), and his WS 1933–34 "Vom Wesen der Wahrheit" (On the Essence of Truth) (G36/37). In WS 1933–34, he also gave the "well-attended seminar" "Volk und Wissenschaft" (Folk and Science), and continued thereafter to treat the theme of the university in his courses and lectures. (Regarding SS 1929 and WS 1933–34, see SDU 22/482; HEL 26; HA 396–97.)

In May of 1933, he presented his inaugural rectorial address as the new National Socialist rector of the university, namely, "The Self-Assertion of the German University," in which he called for a radical program of university reform in step with his own ontological interpretation of the deepest goals of Hitler's National Socialist State. The core of this program was the quasi-Platonic notion of university life not as decadent "academic freedom," but as a tripartite "service of labor," "military service," and "service of science," each of which was to be in its own way the enactment and being-in-work (*energeia*) of the truth (*aletheia*) of the historical destiny of being (SDU 12–16/472–77).

All the while, as we saw in Chapter 2, Heidegger was also reinscribing in his *Beiträge* and other texts his earlier concepts of *Verhalten, Gehalt, Bezug, Vollzug, Zeitigung, Seinssinn, aletheia*, the first beginning, the history of metaphysics, the end of philosophy, and the new beginning (cf. G65 §85). Here the tendency was to reinscribe the intentional configuration of being-sense into mythopoetic drafts of "Being and Time." In his SS 1928 lecture course, Heidegger stated that, as primal history, the *Ereignis* and worlding of world out of the abysmal primal source (as seen in the New Testament and pre-Socratic thinking) points precisely to the reality and the problem of "the mythic." "From out of this primal history a region of problems must be uncoiled . . . : namely, the mythic. The metaphysics of mythos must be understood out of this primal history." As Heidegger mentioned here, the point of transition between his Kantian transcendental model and this new mythopoetic model was Kant's "doctrine of the transcendental productive imagination," which performs the activity of temporal schematism. However, Kant did not succeed in working out "the radical consequences" of his own doctrine, in which for the very first time "metaphysics endeavored to liberate itself from logic" (G26 270–72/209–11, 219–20/171–72).

This liberation led Heidegger rather to the appropriation of Kant's transcendental imagination in the later Schelling's Romantic "philosophy of mythology" and Cassirer's treatment of "mythic Dasein" in his "philosophy of symbolic forms." Already in WS 1927–28, Heidegger held a seminar on "Schelling, *On the Essence of Human Freedom.*" And in SS 1929, while lecturing on "Der Deutsche Idealismus (Fichte, Hegel, Schelling) und die philosophische Problemlage der Gegenwart" (German Idealism [Fichte, Hegel, Schelling] and the Present Situation of Philosophical Problems) (G28), he wrote to Jaspers that "I am lecturing for the first time on Fichte, Hegel, Schelling—and a world is dawning for me again" (HJ 123). In SS 1930, he held the lecture course "Einleitung in die Philosophie (*Über das Wesen der menschlichen Freiheit*)" (Introduction in Philosophy [*On the Essence of Human Freedom*]) (G31), and in WS 1930–31 he gave another lecture course on "Hegel's *Phenomenology of Spirit*" (G32).

Heidegger had appealed in SZ to Cassirer's study of mythic "primitive Dasein" in his *Philosophy of Symbolic Forms*, Volume 2: *Mythical Thinking*. For, as in the Greco-Roman "fable of *Cura*," "primitive Dasein often speaks more directly out of an original absorption [*Aufgehen*] in the 'phenomena' " (SZ 68–69/76, 261/241, 415/361). In 1928 Heidegger published a review of Cassirer's work, in which he stressed that Cassirer was taking up Schelling's insight that "myth," "the mythical understanding of being," is "a unique possibility of human Dasein which has its own kind of truth." "Myth [is] the destiny of a people (Schelling)." According to Heidegger, Cassirer sketches out the content-sense of "mythic life" as the world of "mana," which is "not a being among beings but . . . the 'how' of all mythic actualities [earth, sky, day, night, totemic relations, the seasons, the gods], i.e., the being of beings" as the overpowering (*Übermächtigkeit*) of "the holy." The relational sense of "mythic Dasein" has the character of "thrownness" and "care" in the specific experience of "being-delivered-over to," "overpowered," and "captivated" by the "magical power" of "the overpowering." In this premodern mythic experience, as in medieval Christian life, the " 'subject' as such remains concealed." Likewise, temporalizing- and enactment-sense is here "far removed from a mere reckoning." The "ordering of time is, as the ordering of destiny, a cosmic power and reveals in its lawfulness an obligation which pervades and binds all human deeds." But this "mana-ish actuality announces itself in each case precisely in a specific 'eye-opening momentariness' [*Augenblicklichkeit*]." As Heidegger suggested in his SS 1928 lecture course, such a mythic history that binds a people and culture together is an ontic worldview-manifestation of the "transcendence of Dasein," i.e., of the *Ereignis* and worlding of the world. Again appealing to Kant's transcendental imagination (*Einbildungskraft*), Heidegger's review explained that this historical experience imaginatively enacts, expresses, and develops (*ausbildet*) itself as "cult and ritual" and "mythical narrative" (MD 1000–1011/PT 32–45).

One also sees Schelling's influence in Heidegger's letter of September 12, 1929 to Blochmann. Here he rendered their experience of the office of matins at the Beuron monastery into a "symbol" of the experience of the dark "depths" of being, which is needed in order to effect the "turn of the age." "In the matins there is still the primal mythical and metaphysical force of the night, which we must constantly break through [*durchbrechen*] in order to exist truthfully. For the good is only the good of evil." We must cultivate "daily readiness for [the Night]," since "[the essential] flourishes only when we *completely*, i.e., in the face of night and evil, live according to our hearts. This primally powerful *negative* is decisive" (HB 31–32).

Here Heidegger reinscribed precisely the old quasi-mystical and quasi-Pauline terminology from earlier correspondence with Blochmann into his new Schellingian mythopoetic model. According to Schelling's *On the Essence of Human Freedom*, which was heavily influenced by the mysticism of Jakob Böhme, the divine is an interplay of the darkness of the impersonal abyss of the Godhead (the principle of evil) and the light of its manifestation in the personal loving God, an interplay that is mirrored in the human personality, where it takes the imperfect form of the strife between good and evil. "All birth," Schelling wrote, "is out of darkness into light," and thus "the good must be brought out of darkness."[5] The last phase of Schelling's thought, namely, his philosophy of mythology and revelation, was precisely an attempt to document the historical manifestation of the divine ground in the myths of Western and Eastern cultures.

Eventually the major models in Heidegger's mythopoetic drafts became Hölderlin's poetry, the "poetic thinking" of the pre-Socratics (G40 153/144), the Greek tragedians, and Nietzsche's Dionysian thinking. Between SS 1932 and WS 1944–45, Heidegger gave, in addition to numerous talks, at least three lecture courses on Hölderlin, five lecture courses on the pre-Socratics, and five lecture courses on Nietzsche. In his WS 1951–52 lecture course, Heidegger explained that the *mythos* of the pre-Socratics and Hölderlin is the unconcealment of the being of beings: "*Mythos* is essential presencing in its saga—that which shines forth in the unconcealment of its appeal" (WHD 6/10). During his analysis of Sophocles's *Antigone* in his SS 1935 lecture course, Heidegger said that "knowledge of primal history" is "mythology" and "poetry" (G40 164–65/155, 112/105). In the mythopoetic reconfiguration of being-sense that Heidegger worked out in his Schellingian, Hölderlinian, pre-Socratic, and Nietzschean drafts of "Being and Time," his youthful theme of the "it worlds" of content-sense was reinscribed as the worlding of the fourfold of earth and sky, mortals and gods. The "Dasein of personal life" and the "dwelling" belonging to relational sense were restamped into the poetic dwelling of mortals. And the *Ereignis, Es gibt,* kairological time, and *kinesis* of temporalizing-sense were rewritten as the *Ereignis, physis, a-letheia,* and mysterious "giving" of epochs in the destined history of being.

Heidegger's model for *Hingabe* in the *Ereignis* of being was no longer the *unio mystica,* Pauline surrender to the hidden God, or the Aristotelian artisan's absorption in work, but rather, as he put it in his 1928 essay on Cassirer, the pretheoretical mythopoetic experience of being-delivered-over to the mana, the holy, of the world and its historical happening. But even the turn to this new model was in a way a return to his early Freiburg period and the Romantic mysticism of his qualifying dissertation. In KNS 1919 and WS 1919–20, he had used as a model for *Ereignis* also Hölderlin's translation of Sophocles's *Antigone,* the German Romantic poets, and in general the "lived experiential character" of the "art work," that is, the "lifeworld" of the "artist" and "the poets" as creative "shapers" of a people's worldview. Against Comte's dismissal of the first "theological-mythical stage" of human history in favor of the scientific-technological stage of the modern Enlightenment, Heidegger insisted on the "ownmost value" of "primitive peoples" and the historical "beginnings of peoples," which had been reaffirmed by such figures as Herder and Schlegel in their "study of myths and sagas" (G56/57 207, 132–34; G58 111; cf. G20 375–76/272). And here Heidegger saw the world of art, including the art of Shakespeare, Dostoyevsky, Stefan George, Rembrandt, and Bach, as "concentrated on the selfworld." "An original context of expressing the selfworld exists in *art*" (G58 32, 65, 69, 76, 205, 85, 58).

But Heidegger later often forgot his earlier sober warnings against "telling a *mython*," a metaphysical story. For his return to and reinscription of the terminology of his earlier poetic, mystical, kairological, and Aristotelian models effected not only a deepening and advance, but simultaneously and ambiguously a *mythologizing* in the young Heidegger's very specific sense of this term. The later mythopoetic drafts of "Being and Time" contain simultaneously *mythic* drafts. When the young Heidegger spoke negatively of "myth," this term meant the eclipse of personal relational sense (deliving), concrete content-sense (designifying), and anarchic temporalizing-sense (dehistoricizing), which could in principle take place in either philosophical, religious, or mythopoetic thinking. In this sense, the mythopoetic experience of the *Ereignis* of the sunrise in Sophocles's *Antigone*, as described in KNS 1919, is not "myth," but the concept of a transcendental ego, eschatological religious speculation, or, as I shall argue, *some* aspects of the later Heidegger's recycling of this very Sophoclean example of a sunrise in SS 1935 are myth. "Let us think of the sun," he wrote in 1935. "Only a very few astronomers, physicists, and philosophers . . . experience this matter . . . as motion of the earth around the sun. . . . This shining appearance [of the sun] is historical and history, uncovered and grounded in poetry and saga" (G40 112/105). According to the young Heidegger, the counterconcept of myth is not a nonpoetic and nonreligious *logos*, but rather a hermeneutics (whether philosophical, religious, or poetic) of facticity. In an undecidable play of countertendencies, the later Heidegger's hybrid mythopoetic-philosophical hermeneutics of facticity in his post-SZ "bend," attempting to effect a more adequate fulfillment of his youthful intention toward *Kehre*, nonetheless brought with it *also* certain hyperbolic mythologizing "bents" toward deliving, designifying, and dehistoricizing his youthful sketches of the personal-anarchic physiognomy of being.

In other words, Heidegger exhibited tendencies toward mythologizing his topic into a highly historicized *arche*, that is, into a grounding origin/kingdom, which is marked by a historicized hyperbolic character, presence, and homogeneity. We find this ambiguity graphically expressed in the image of the "kingly child" at the close of Heidegger's WS 1955–56 lecture course "The Principle of Ground." In order to evoke the groundless, agentless play of the historical sendings of the being of beings, that is, the sendings of the various historical principles and grounds of beings, he nonetheless took up Heraclitus's poetic notion of *arche* as "kingship" and "kingly child," rendering it into an explicitly historical *arche*. He explained that the kingly child is the *aion*, that is, the "world that worlds and temporalizes," the "fated sending of being," which in the "mildness of its play" governs the realm of being. He translated fragment 52, "The fated sending of being [*aion*], it is a child, playing, playing a board-game; a child's is the kingship [*Königtum*]—i.e, the *arche*, the founding governing [*verwaltende*] grounding, the being, for beings" (SG 187–88). But does this notion of kingship, of an anarchic *arche*, simultaneously contain a number of residual metaphysical principles and grounds? Did Heidegger forget his earlier warnings against the hubris of prophetic claims about "categories that lead us comfortably into a new kingdom"?

Löwith suggested that, in his so-called " 'turn' to a self-giving being" and in his reversion to the Greek origin of the being-question, Heidegger now found a *Boden*, a grounding soil and native land, to replace the Neo-Scholastic metaphysical origin of his student years that he, a hidden exiled king, had lost and renounced during the "intermediate stage" of his early Freiburg period. In fact, Löwith maintained that "Heidegger's 'turn' to a self-giving being was a return to his theological origin" in his student years. Though the later Heidegger also reinscribed many nonmetaphysical themes from his student years, this return looks simultaneously like a king coming out of exile to reclaim his lost kingdom, his royal "house of being." As we have seen, the later Heidegger's own autobiographies, playing down his antispeculative thought in the early twenties, continually stressed this connection with his early "speculative-theological thinking" about the "metaphysical 'origin'," which had been inspired by Braig, Brentano, Hegel, Scotus, Eckhart, and the Romantics. This origin was first seen to be the "kingdom of validity," the "Dasein" and "logical place" of sense, but ultimately was interpreted as the transcendent "depth-dimension" of the "true reality and real truth" of "the absolute spirit of God," the kingdom of God, which manifests itself teleologically in the ancient, medieval, and modern worldviews. Thus Löwith wrote,

> If one translates "true reality" and "real truth" with "truth of being" and "being of truth," the dimension of "spiritual life" reaching into the transcendent with "ex-istence," "God" with "being," and the "self-loss" of contemporary humanity in the "content of the breadth of the sensuous world" with the fall into the world and the forgetfulness of being, one can thus recognize the later Heidegger already in his qualifying dissertation. (MLD 27–42; HDZ 20–21)

Caputo, taking up the later Heidegger's own indication of the structural analogy of proportionality between the being/Dasein relation and the Godhead/soul relation in medieval mysticism, has concluded similarly that "a study of [the qualifying dissertation], then, reveals a remarkable thing about Heidegger's development: Heidegger's later thought is not so much a 'reversal' as it is a return to his earlier interests in medieval life and thought in general and in medieval mysticism in particular" (PMG 116–17). We can recognize in

Heidegger's student writings not only the appellations of his later thought-paths (namely, the "sense," "truth," "lighted clearing," and "place" of being) and his notion of the history of the epochs of being, but also anticipations of how in the later writings these regal topics effected a speculative eclipse of personal relational and enactment-sense, as well as of anarchic temporalizing-sense, that is, a disastrous confusion of ontology with cultural and religious worldview.

Ontologia Gloriae

Let us begin with sketches of the later Heidegger's hyperbolic reconfigurations of being-sense, which involve primarily deliving, alienating, and depersonalizing his earlier notion of the factical *Ereignis* of persons. Here we can refer to Heidegger's primitivistic, antihumanist, essentialist, and speculative drafts of "Being and Time," in which he seems to have forgotten his earlier ideal of humility and Luther's and Kierkegaard's warnings against the hubris of speculative *theologia* and *philosophia gloriae*. These and the other configurations I sketch below are effective throughout the development of Heidegger's later thought, but, of course, to different degrees and with different nuances at each of its waystations. Detailed chronological analyses, which I cannot provide here, are thus needed to fill out my rough sketches. But a precedent for them can be found in Heidegger's own fragmentary "Sketches for a History of Being as Metaphysics" (N2 458/EP 55).

The Primitivistic Configuration

We have already glimpsed this hyperbolic redrafting of "Being and Time" clearly in Heidegger's 1929 letter to Blochmann about "the primal mythical . . . force of the night" and the good that is "the good of evil." Here the signifying and worlding of content-sense was restamped in the shape of the worlding of the fourfold of earth and sky, mortals and gods, along with technological enframing as its inverted, daemonic, and fated "photographic negative," as it were (G15 366). The *Ereignis* of temporalizing-sense was reinscribed as a dark, capricious, and impersonal force that, in fatefully sending the epochs, oscillates between an abysmal nothing and being, *lethe* and *aletheia*, darkness and light, malice and the holy, evil and good, the daemonic power of technological enframing and the poetic beauty of the fourfold (G9 359/BW 237). The concrete *Ereignis* of personal relational sense was superscribed, delived, and masked into the hyperbolic phantom of a transcendental-poetic site and plaything of these impersonal cosmic forces. The enactment-sense of our proper response to these forces was described as a fatalistic "corresponding" and uncritical primitivistic awe (*Scheu*), which, especially in the thirties and forties, also includes shock (*Erschrecken*), terror (*Entsetzen*), horror (*Schrecken*), "danger," *Kampf*, "violence," "honor," and "grandeur" (G40 66–67/61–63, 153–73/144–65; G65 §§5–6, 249, 269). "The *mystery* is missing in our Dasein," Heidegger wrote in WS 1929–30, "and thereby there stays away the inner terror which every mystery bears within itself and which gives to Dasein its grandeur" (G29/30 244). All this is what Levinas criticizes as Heidegger's "philosophy of the Neuter," of "pre-technological powers," the "mythical format of the element," the "mythical facelessness" and "horror" of the "impersonal *there is*" (the French *il y a*; the German *es gibt*), in which the ethical sphere of the personal "face to face" is dissolved (TI 46–47, 77–79, 140–42, 189–90, 298–99).[6]

The Antihumanist Configuration

In this antihumanist draft of "Being and Time," temporalizing-sense surfaced as an *Ereignis* of the worldly epochs of being that possesses the following table of virtues: *freedom* (nonlimitation by historical laws); *uniqueness* (each epoch is unique); *dignity* (the ultimate for-the-sake-of-which); *integrity* or wholeness (affirmation of all epochal sendings); and *development* (the anarchic unfolding and self-accomplishing of epochal sending). Whereas his youthful period involved a creative ontological appropriation of traditional humanism and personalism, as well as an affirmation of the "equiprimordiality" of the different intentional senses of being, Heidegger later reinscribed and delived relational sense such that the above list of virtues was ascribed to the *Ereignis* of persons only in a secondary hierarchical-teleological sense and was even sometimes apparently withdrawn from persons. The latter thus seem to lack *uniqueness* (because reduced to a homogeneous epochal "essence of human being"); *dignity* in the Kantian sense of an end-in-itself (because for the sake of the dignity of being); the *freedom* and responsibility of enactment-sense (because determined by destiny); the *integrity* or wholeness of concrete embodiment (because modeled on a quasi-contemplative "thinking" and "poetizing"); and the active *development* of *humanitas* (because entangled in technological will-to-power and summoned to "wait" upon the development of the truth of being, even though it withholds itself and abandons us to the epochal "world-night," "wasteland," and "destitution" of modern technology, where "only a god can save us").[7]

"Even this [attending to the dimension of the truth of being]," Heidegger wrote in his "Letter on Humanism," "could take place only for the dignity and honor [*Würde*] of being and for the benefit of the being-here [*Da-sein*] that humanity eksistingly sustains, not for the sake of humanity, so that through its creativity civilization and culture might assert their validity" (G9 329/BW 209). In his *Beiträge* and others texts, Heidegger dissociated *Ereignis* completely from his earlier personalist lexicon of "lived experience," "life," "person," "personality," and identified that lexicon as an expression of the "forgetfulness of being," "nihilism," and representational technological thinking (G65 §§61–72, 153–54, 212).[8]

But can we really overcome technological anthropocentrism simply by reversing it into its immanent opposite, namely, ontocentrism, as Heidegger does with Sartre's statement that "there are only human beings," such that we are left "in a situation where there is principally being" (G9 334/BW 214)? Can we transcend the abstract exaggeration of relational sense by replacing it with an equally abstract elephantiasis of the deep temporality of content-sense? Is it not basically the same monistic eclipse of the equiprimordiality of the contextualized intentional senses of being, the same "unbridled tendency to establish ... from a simple 'primal ground,' " the same master/slave relation, whether humanity is depicted as the technological "tyrant of being," or whether it is depicted as an abject "shepherd of being" (G9 330–31/BW 210)? Is it not the same technical, manipulative relation?

For example, drawing on his early Freiburg period, Heidegger's 1946 essay on Anaximander reversed the meaning of Augustine's term "enjoyment" as "having present," such that it no longer meant "a form of human behavior" (*fruitio Dei*), but rather the fact that "being uses [*uti*] the essential presencing of humanity" in the sense of giving, sending, having, and enjoying this presencing. "Usage" here translated Anaximander's term *to chreon*, which "suggests *he cheir*, the hand"—not the hand of the artisan God in the Book of Genesis, but the hand of being. " 'To use' ... *frui* ... means: to hand something over to its own essential presencing and to hold it in hand preservingly" (G5 366–73/EGT 51–58). Here Heidegger's bend from SZ to the later writings often looks like what he insisted it should not be taken to be, namely, a mere reversal (*Umkehr*). We read in the *Beiträge* that "talk of the relation to beon [*Seyn*, the archaic spelling of *Sein*, being] expresses what is actually to be thought into its opposite [*Gegenteil*]. For the relation to beon is in truth beon, which as *Ereignis* moves humanity into his relation" (LR xvi–xvii; G65 490).

The Essentialist Configuration

The young Heidegger's notion of relational and enactment-sense as an anarchic differentiated community of unique persons was reinscribed and eclipsed, first, into the hyperbolic They of the collectivist "Dasein of the [German] Folk" and the "Dasein of the [National Socialist] State." As rector of the university, Heidegger wrote to a colleague in December 1933 that "the individual, wherever he stands, counts for nothing. The destiny of our people in its State is everything" (MH 229). The "Dasein of personal life" was also superscribed into the phantom-like Dasein of the "essence [*Wesen*] of humanity," a homogeneous and epochal essential-presencing, which is sent by the *Ereignis* of being. According to Heidegger, this essence takes the historical shape of an ek-sistence or in-stance "in the truth of being," and individual human beings participate in and "endure" it. Though nothing in principle stopped him, Heidegger now did not stress, as he once had, the differentiation and individuation of Dasein into the *Ereignis* of the personal I. "Beon . . . events/enowns Da-sein," he explained in the *Beiträge*, but this being-here, which makes up "selfhood," "can be conceived neither as 'subject' nor indeed as 'I' or as 'personality' " (G65 483, 489). The "*who?* or the *what?*" are both inappropriately applied to Dasein and ek-sistence as "essence." For "the personal no less than the objective misses and misconstrues the essential presencing of ek-sistence in the history of being" (G9 327/BW 207).

Heidegger's retrospective marginal note on his statement in SZ that "Dasein exists as it itself" was, "But not as subject and individual or as person" (SZ 194/186). Moreover, "the essence of humanity is essential to the truth of being in such a way that the human being is thus not—simply as such—what matters" (G9 345/BW 224). What happened to the young Heidegger's insistence upon not just the "it e-vents/en-owns itself according to its essential presencing," but also and equiprimordially the "I e-vent/en-own it to myself"? In its extreme form, Heidegger's essentialist draft of "Being and Time" gives the impression of an almost complete "masking" ("larvance") of the concrete individual, insofar as the latter is seen to wear the ghostly "*persona,* the mask, of being." The concrete individual looks like an ontological mouthpiece, which is "used" by the address (*Anspruch*) of being, and which thus itself speaks only in that it *ent-spricht,* speaks-out the language of being (WHD 28/62; G12 30/PLT 210).

Rather than, after SZ, simultaneously exploring the historical facticity of *both* the depth-dimension of *Ereignis* and its differentiation into the "Dasein of personal life," the later Heidegger often aggravated the abstract structuralism of SZ by pushing it in the direction of historicized cosmological structures such as the "lighted clearing" and "topos" of being, as well as historicized transcendental-poetic essences such as the essence of humanity, technology, evil, poetic dwelling, mortality, homelessness, pain, and National Socialism.[9] This hyperbolic attitude is indifferent to, misses, and reductively dissolves the concrete manifestation of these realities in embodied factical life. Here we can apply to Heidegger his early categories of "presumptuous mismeasuring" (*Vermessen*), "blinding," the "elliptic," "missing," and "going wrong," as well as his later concept of the "forgetfulness of [concrete] being."

One sees these categories at work not only in the fact that the foolish eschatological speculation of Heidegger's ontologized and romanticized *mythos* of the "glory and grandeur" (SDU 19/480) of the National Socialist Revolution (supposedly the Kairos of the Second Coming of the *arche*, the origin/kingdom, of being) blindly "went wrong" regarding the *Realpolitik* of the third Reich/Kingdom and thus aided one of the most horrifying acts of evil in Western history. One sees them at work also in his continued indifference to the factical mortality, pain, homelessness, and evil caused by Nazism and other forces of twentieth-century technology. For example, in his *Beiträge* he wrote that "the *essential* sign of 'nihilism' is not whether churches and monasteries are destroyed and human beings are murdered" (G65 139; emphasis added). In a quasi-revisionist statement made during a series of public lectures in 1949 (which included the later published essays "The Thing," "The Question Concerning Technology," and "The Turning"), Heidegger claimed that the "millions of impoverished people" "perishing" from hunger "in China" were not really "dying," and that millions of Jewish persons did not really "die" in Nazi death camps since their mechanized biological perishing was not in accord with the "essence" of death (while elderly Schwabian peasants in the romantic setting of the Black Forest around Todtnauberg, on the other hand, were presumably really "dying" [see G13 9–13]). "Hundreds of thousands die en masse. "Do they *die*? They succumb. . . . They are liquidated inconspicuously in extermination camps. . . . But to die is to endure death in its *essence*" (emphasis added). In the same lecture series, he maintained that, in light of the "essence of technology," the "motorized food-industry" of "agriculture" is, "*in essence, the same* as the manufacturing of corpses in gas chambers and extermination camps" (HN 41–42; emphasis added). Here Levinas has asked, "Doesn't this silence, in the time of peace, on the gas chambers and death camps . . . reveal a soul completely cut off from any sensitivity, in which can be perceived a kind of consent to horror?"[10]

Caputo has called this essentialism in Heidegger a "phainesthetics" of the shining fourfold of earth and sky, gods and mortals, which is simultaneously an "anesthesia" toward the suffering flesh of factical life.[11] Insofar as it emphasizes a historical Platonic *eidos* and as such affirms the "grandeur," "power," and "dignity and honor of being," this essentialist phainesthetics alerts us to the fact that, here and in the later Heidegger's other metaphysical tendencies, we find a sophisticated reversion to the Hellenic *theologia gloria* (Luther) and speculative aestheticism (Kierkegaard) which, "puffed up, blinded, and hardened," looks down indifferently from the speculative heights of *ontos on* (e.g., the essence of death) at the *me on* of "suffering and the cross" (e.g., the death camps).

Examine closely Heidegger's vision of the destiny of being in which the transition from technology to the new beginning may very well occur apparently in an apocalyptic nuclear holocaust: "Before being can event [*ereignen*] in its original truth, being as the will must be broken, the world *must* be forced to collapse and the earth must be driven to devastation. . . . The laboring animal *is* abandoned to the giddy whirl of its products so that it may tear itself to pieces and annihilate itself in empty nothingness" (VA 69/EP 86–87; emphasis added). This *theoria* strikes one as a historicized version of the very ocular-aesthetic quietism that Heidegger had so virulently deconstructed in his youthful period (the categories of "the tranquillizing," "taking-it-easy," "the alienating," and the "annihilating" also apply here). And his "original ethics," which focuses on the epochal *topos* of being, looks much like a historicized version of the Platonic "absolute ethics" that his kairological ethics criticized in the twenties.

The later Heidegger not only resurrected Augustine's *fruitio Dei* to describe the relation of being to human being, but also took up, as a model, the pre-Socratic and Greek poetical experience of the unconcealment and "radiance of being" in its "look [*Ansehen, eidos*] as glory [*Ruhm, doxa, gloria*]." The poet's *logos* has the sense of "glorifying," "placing into the light" the glorious shining "look" of the hero, "the gods and the state," "the temples," "the games," the "earth," the "sunrise," all of which is "myth." "For the Greeks *on* [being] and *kalon* [beauty] meant the same thing (presencing was pure radiance)." Heidegger contrasted this sense of *doxa* ("the look as glory") with its later sense as mere subjective "opinion" in Plato and the Sophists, as well as with its sense among us trivial "moderns," for whom "art is a matter for pastry cooks" and "glory has long been nothing more than celebrity . . . almost the opposite of being" (G40 105–15, 140/98–108, 131–32).

The Speculative Configuration

In its most aggravated form, the later Heidegger's essentialist bent led to a superscription of temporalizing-sense in the hyperbolic Beyond of a hypostatized, quasi-absolute, cosmological *Ereignis* and there-is/it-gives, an ultimate "impersonal *there is*" (Levinas), which hands out the epochs of being. "In [the essay] 'Time and Being,' however," he said, "the *relation* of the Appropriation [*Ereignis*] and the human being of mortals is consciously excluded" (EP xii; emphasis added). What was suspended and completely effaced here was his youthful theme of *Mir-Sein*, to-me-being, and *Mir-Ereignen*, eventing/enowning to myself, that is, my personal co-temporalizing, enactment, and appropriating of the *Ereignis* of the world as *pro me* in my concrete unique situations. For the later Heidegger's speculative depth-hermeneutics, *Ereignis* suddenly no longer included the *Ereignis* of the "Dasein of personal life" in any sense. His exploration of the ultimate "it" of temporalizing-sense went so deep that he also suspended the factical content-sense of world. "In glancing through authentic time," he wrote in "Time and Being," "it has been our task to think being in what is its own—out of *Ereignis*—without a view to the *relation* of being to beings" (SD 25/24; emphasis added). But in attempting this abstract thinking of the quasi-objective "truth" of "being itself," Heidegger forgot his earlier Kierkegaardian warning against "the illusion that human beings could, as one prosaically says, speculate themselves out of their own good skin and into pure light."[12]

Stories of Being

Let us turn now to sketches of the later Heidegger's reconfigurations which involved primarily dehistoricizing the temporalizing-sense of being, that is, the mystery of the anarchically differentiating *Ereignis* of being. To these Hellenic, Germanic, religious, gendered, anthropocentric, and authoritarian drafts of "Being and Time," one needs to apply the young Heidegger's categories of "presumptuous mismeasuring," "effacing time," "not having time," "the quietive," "ruinance," "obstruction," "alienation," "annihilating," and myth as worldview-"ideology." Heidegger often displayed tendencies toward a hierarchical-teleological privileging of some supposedly proper epochal sense, site, or reading of being, such that the incalculable mystery of the anarchic differentiation of being is violently rendered into a historically calculable *arche* that can be brought to closure in the *manus mentis* of a thinker. This sometimes implicit and sometimes explicit privileging leads to "objectifying and stilling" the *kinesis* of being into one of its effects, thereby "alienating" and marginalizing the haecceity, alterity, and "ownmost value" of other worldviews, historical periods, readings, societies, and personal selfworlds. Mythologizing here takes the form of ideologizing the being-question.

The later Heidegger often fell short of his own ontological-ethical ideal of humility, openness, and letting-be, an ideal modeled originally, in his early Freiburg period, on Eckhartian mysticism, Schleiermacher, Kierkegaard, Jaspers, and Aristotle, and which expressed itself in his method of ontically noncommittal formal indication, his sketches for a kairological ethics, and his reflections on such matters as university reform and *Geschlecht*. He often forgot his earlier warnings against presumptuous claims to a "new kingdom," "fantastic world-history," "destinies of humanity," "cultural missions," "world-historical salvation," "ideology and phantasy," "prophecy," and "Führers." In short, he forgot his warning that we should not "tell a *mython*," a story in the sense of an ideological meta-narrative about being, as if it were a present homogeneous object. The hidden king often later came out of exile to claim the mythical dominion of a homogeneous historicized *arche*, thereby "presumptuously mismeasuring," "missing," and "going wrong" in the differentiated kairological character of " '*being*' in and through [factical] life."

We first find the narrative of origin, fall, crisis, danger, *Kampf*, revolutionary return, and second coming of the *arche*/kingdom in the teleological Christian worldview-metaphysics of Heidegger's *Der Akademiker* articles and qualifying dissertation. These writings issued a militant self-righteous call for radical critique of the decadent fallenness of modernity and for the *Kampf* of a revolutionary return to the medieval worldview and its forgotten "metaphysical 'origin'," namely, the kingdom-come of the "absolute spirit of God." After Heidegger left behind his liberal ontology of the early twenties, he in effect returned to the meta-narrative of Western history he had worked out in his student period, historicized it in a radical manner, and reinscribed it in the notion of "the history of being" that he began to develop in the late twenties and early thirties.

For example, in his letter of September 12, 1929 to Blochmann about "the primal mythical . . . force of the night," he stressed that "the contemporary," including the "abomination" of "contemporary Catholicism" and "Protestantism," had fallen away from "the power and nativeness of what is great in history." Thus what was needed was a "turn [*Wende*] of the age out of the depths." The turn, he explained, was to be a "return," but "this return is no taking over what has been, but its transformation." Reinscribing his old eschato-parousiological model of the Pauline "thief in the night," he stressed that this revolutionary return is a waiting for the "day and the hour" of "destiny" and a "daily readiness" for "the primal mythical . . . force of the night," which we must "break through." "[Inner truthfulness] requires its day and hour. . . . our heart must be held open for grace. God—or as you name it— calls each with a different voice."

During the correspondence of 1930–33, this narrative gains in vehemence and recalls the reactionary antimodernism of Heidegger's *Der Akademiker* articles. He warned that one must not become a "fool of fortuitous modernity" and its "celebrated tolerance" and "liberalism," but must "renounce all claims of renewing the stale and now foreign idealisms from the time of Humboldt, Schleiermacher, and Schelling." For modernity has fallen away from "the great beginning with the Greeks," which is our "foundation" and "origin," and "must become present for us once again" in the "revolution" of "the coming world-age." We must make a revolutionary return to "the Greeks, to whom Nietzsche said the Germans alone are equal." For it is in connection with this tradition that one finds "those forces . . . which have the will for fruitfully shaping the 'Reich'/'Kingdom' and its spiritual world." Early in 1933, Blochmann considers "breaking off the 'intensity' of the correspondence" (HB 31– 62).

In the later thirties, forties, and fifties, this *mythos* of origin, fall, and second coming of the *arche*/kingdom-come was worked out in other versions of Heidegger's notion of the destined "history of being." Though it was a reinscription of his earlier model of Christian parousiology and kairology, Heidegger's account of this history nonetheless often seems to fly in the face of his early warnings against eschatological speculation. According to this *Geschichte*, this history/story, which Heidegger constantly revised right into the sixties and seventies, the first beginning (*erstes Anfang*) and first arrival (*parousia, Anwesen*) of the poetic truth of being took place with the pre-Socratics and the Greek tragedians, who at least implicitly experienced it. The falling away from this original dawn into the "western land of evening" (*Abendland*), which has its Lutheran analogue in the *status corruptionis* of original sin, began with Plato and unfolded in the long history of the "oblivion of being," culminating in the "world-night" of the departure of the gods and the "wasteland" of the epoch of modern technology. In this ongoing night of "homelessness," where we are "too late for the gods and too early for beon," "commemorative thinking" must "wait" for the uncertain *Eschaton* of the technological epoch and for the the address of the second arrival of being in the other beginning (*anderes Anfang*), which will come incalculatively like a thief in the night, releasing the "saving power" of poetic dwelling in the fourfold and the "arrival of the [new] god" (G12 76/PLT 4; NG 209/58).

Though many have been tempted to reduce this *grand récit* completely to a kind of quasi-religious fanaticism (as Walter Kaufmann tended to do in his essay "Heidegger's Castle"),[13] there lies in it perhaps the most ingenious account of "the history of ideas" and culture that has ever been put forth. And yet, in addition to the tendencies toward deliving that we examined above, this meta-narrative also contains a number of dehistoricizing and ideological tendencies that bring to closure the anarchically differentiating *Ereignis* of being, which Heidegger first articulated in his early Freiburg period but continued to express ambiguously also in his later writings.

The Hellenic and Germanic Configurations

In the configuration of being-sense with which Heidegger's narrative of the history of being worked, his earlier expression of relational and content-sense as ontically noncommittal formal indicators was reinscribed ontically in terms of the worldview of the ancient Greek experience of *aletheia* and the fourfold of earth and sky, gods and mortals. Temporalizing-sense was restamped in the ontic shape of the eschatological second arrival of the first Hellenic *arche*/kingdom in a new Neo-Hellenic beginning for the West. According to Heidegger, the spiritual heirs of this Hellenic configuration are the Germans as "the people of poets and thinkers," who have an exemplary relationship to the question about being. The term "spirit" now turned up again in Heidegger's writings, and it had become a decisively militant German *Geist*. Löwith maintained rightly that this amounted to a "translation of [the neutral, formally indicative phrase] 'Dasein that is in each case mine' into 'German Dasein,' " as well as an ideological reinscription and centralization of the "formal sketch" of all the other formally indicative "categories" of being from Heidegger's youthful period into the worldview of this Helleno-Germanic being. In SS 1935, Heidegger stressed the "assumption of the historical mission of our people at the center of the west" (G40 53/50). In the thirties, Heidegger seems to have thought that the kingdom-come of the second arrival of being was at hand in the "private National Socialism" of his metaphysically inter-preted third Reich (SDU 30/490). Using the exact phrase that he warned against in WS 1921–22, namely, a "new Reich/Kingdom," Heidegger opened his 1933 Heidelberg lecture on "The University in the New Reich/Kingdom" with the statement that "we have the new Reich/Kingdom and the university which must take its tasks from the Reich's/Kingdom's will to Dasein" (NH 74).

Then, after the "glory and grandeur" of National Socialism "went wrong," the second arrival along the Greek-German axis was deferred to the utopia of a distant future for which one must "wait" and "prepare." "The Germans and they alone can save the West," he stated in his course of SS 1943 on Heraclitus (G55 108). He maintained some version of this view right up until his 1966 interview in *Der Spiegel*, in which he insisted upon the "special task" of Ger-mans that lies in "the inner kinship between the German language and the language and thought of the Greeks. . . . When [the French] begin to think, they speak German. They assure [me] that they do not succeed with their own language" (NG 217/62; cf. G40 61/57). Tell that to Levinas or Derrida. Heidegger accordingly aligned other countries such as "America" and "Rus-sia" with "the forgetfulness of being" (G40 40/37; NG 214/61). "Bolshe-vism," he wrote in his *Beiträge*, "is in fact Jewish" (G65 54). It was also this narrative of the history of being that lay beneath such paranoid anti-Semitic statements by Heidegger as his 1929 warning that one must not "abandon [our German spirit] to the growing Jewification" and his assertion to Jaspers around 1933 that "there is a dangerous international alliance of Jews."[14]

Is it not possible to acknowledge the decisiveness of Greek and German thought in the formation of Western culture, but without Heidegger's baffling hierarchical-teleological exclusion of other decisive contributions? His concen-tration on the Helleno-Germanic configuration in his later reinscription of the being-question suggests a *prescriptive*, ethnocentric marginalizing of the ep-ochal and cultural Other. This Helleno-Germanic draft of "Being and Time" eclipses the roles and contributions of other cultures both in the genealogy of the West and in the future of the pluralistic, multicultural, and ecumenical "house of being" that we are attempting to build in the late twentieth century. What about the role here of the "commemorative thinking" of other peoples such as the Jewish people, including Holocaust survivors? Or Russian being, French and Swedish fourfolds, Celtic relational sense, American-Indian and Zen Buddhist poetic dwelling, African and Oriental temporalizing-senses? What happened to the humility of the young Heidegger's culturally neutral formal indications, his kairological ethics, and his stress on the *Ereignis* of be-ing into "the independent ownmost value of each nation, each age, and each historical appearance," where "each nation has the center of its happiness in itself"? Do we not need to rethink the sense of the later Heidegger's notions of the first beginning and the other beginning in this more open manner?

The Helleno-Christian Religious Configuration

After the loss of his Christian faith, Heidegger came to identify with Hölderlin's and Nietzsche's modern experience of "the time of the departed gods and of the coming god" (Hölderlin), who would be a rebirth of the divine from the Hellenic world. The motto that Heidegger wrote for the section called "The Last God" in his *Beiträge* was, "The completely other in contrast to the past, especially against the Christian one" (G65 403). He thereby inscribed into his earlier religiously neutral formal indications of the intentional configuration of being and the mystery of being the prescription of a particular religious worldview. Content-sense was restamped ontically in the shape of the divine as it appears in his quasi-Hellenic fourfold of earth and sky, mortals and gods, where Christ is seen to be the last Greek god in the Hellenic pantheon, who announces the departure of the gods from the world and the approaching world-night. Relational sense was reinscribed not as Lutheran existential faith, but as what Luther would surely have called a sophisticated *theologia gloriae*, one focused on the shining play of the "glorious manifestation" and concealment of the gods. Dealing with the Greek temple in his essay on "The Origin of the Work of Art," for example, Heidegger wrote that "to dedication belongs glorifying [*Rühmen*] as honoring the dignity and shining splendour [*Glanz*] of the god. . . . in this shining splendour the god presences" (G5 30/PLT 44). Temporalizing-sense was rewritten as a quasi-Pauline eschatological destiny of being that offers the possibility of the Parousia, the second coming, of Hellenic divinity in the Kairos of the birth of a new god in the midst of the world-night of technology.

What happened to the young Heidegger's insistence, partially under the influence of Schleiermacher's liberal theology, that the formal indications of ontology are "atheistic," that is, are not biased toward any particular religious worldview and do not practice "religious ideology" (G61 197), but rather remain "open" for concretion in all religious lifeworlds? The later Heidegger's Hellenic-religious draft of "Being and Time" effects a certain marginalizing of the non-Helleno-Christian religious Other. But can even Christians recognize themselves in Heidegger's later theology per se?

The Gendered Configuration

In contrast to his earlier insistence upon avoiding such terms as human being/man (*der Mensch*) and "spirit" in favor of the less substantialist and more gender-neutral formal indication "Dasein" (and even before this the feminine noun *die Person*, the person), which would not exclude "woman" and "the academic Dasein . . . the 'intellectual' existence of woman," Heidegger began in the thirties reinscribing gender into the configuration of being. The term "spirit" that he repatriated here is not only Helleno-Germanic, but a decidely masculine *Geschlecht*. In his rectorial address, Heidegger maintained that "spirit is attuned, knowing, resolute openness to the essential presencing of being," and that this spirit must take the form of a spiritualized Teutonic "battle-community of students and professors," which is entrusted with the destiny of being and the Fatherland. This destiny requires "the hardest clarity of the highest, widest, and richest knowledge." "Young students, who at an early age have ventured into manhood [*Mannheit*] and who extend their willing to the future destiny of the nation, force themselves to serve this knowing" (SDU 14–18/474–79).

In his lecture "The University in the National Socialist State," given in Tübingen a few months later, this reference to "manhood" took the form of the statement that "we need a hard race/gender [*Geschlecht*]. . . . we fight heart to heart, man to man [*Mann bei Mann*]" (MH 231). And in his Heidelberg lecture on the same topic, he stated that "the battle will be fought with the forces of the new Reich/Kingdom, which Chancellor Hitler will bring to actuality. A hard race/gender must wage it. The battle is over the image of the teacher and the Führer in the university" (NH 75). After the thirties, Heidegger continued to use more subtle versions of this masculine draft of "Being and Time," for example, "the essence of humanity/man [*des Menschen*]," and "the herdsman [*der Hirt*] of being." In a sentence from his "Letter on Humanism," which takes up his youthful terminology of content-, relational, and temporalizing-sense, we read that "thinking enacts the relation of being to the essential presencing of humanity/man" (G9 331, 313/BW 210, 193). The enactment-sense of acting out this man/being relation suggests a marginalization of feminine being.[15]

The Anthropocentric Configuration

In contrast to his earlier willingness to say that "the animal has a world," "Dasein," and "being-in-the-world" (even acknowledging the "Dasein" of things and the plant world), Heidegger insisted later in WS 1929–30 that "the animal is world-poor," suggesting that the human *Geschlecht* is not merely one differentiated *Ereignis* of being, but rather the measure of the *Ereignis* of non-human life (G29/30 388). The relational sense of being was now inscribed exclusively as *human* Dasein, insofar as—and Heidegger stressed this already in SZ—we humans are characterized by an "ontic priority"; that is, we are the only being with an understanding of the being of beings (SZ 15–20/32–35, 66–67/75, 78/84, 457/396). Similar to the traditional Christian view of the centrality of the human species as *imago Dei*, the chosen site of the revealed truth of God and the custodian of creation, Heidegger's later position was that, as bearers of Da-sein, we are the privileged site of the truth of being and must take on the caring role of shepherds. "I name the standing in the light of being the ek-sistence of humanity. This way to be is proper only to human being." On the other hand, "living beings are as they are without standing in the truth of being. . . . they are separated from our ek-sistent essence by an abyss" (G9 323-26/BW 204-206). Thus the content-sense of the fourfold and its temporalizing-sense mean the happening of "earth and sky" exclusively for human animals. Though involving the benevolent role of caretaker, Heidegger's anthropocentric draft of "Being and Time" suggests a marginalizing of the sentient and living Dasein of nonhuman Others, that is, a kind of apparently friendly speciesism. His antihumanism turns out to be simultaneously very humanistic, if not anthropomorphic.[16]

The Authoritarian Configuration

In contrast to his earlier restrained position that one cannot "leap in" to play the role of philosopher-king, prophet, and Führer for others, but can only "live ahead," "leap ahead," and communicate indirectly in formal indications to the conscience of others, Heidegger later tended to presume a certain elitism, prophecy, hegemony, and authoritarianism, which underwent different versions as his thought developed. This tendency exaggerated his early distinction between "inauthenticity" and "authenticity," as well as the role of the genius, the master, and the teacher, who, according to Kierkegaard, Jaspers, and the young Heidegger, can only use noncoercive indirect communication to inspire others to take up their own unique free relationship to the topic under consideration. Due greatly to his perception of the crisis of the times, Heidegger later came to the conclusion that there is only a very small number of authentic privileged recipients, custodians, and Führers for the second arrival of the "saving power" of being along the Greek-German axis. Already in WS 1929-30, he called for a "governor of the inner grandeur of Dasein" (G29/30 244), and in the *Beiträge* he underlined that the thinking directed to the second arrival is "for the few—for the rare," who, like prophetic heralds, are the "futural ones," "witnesses," and "staff-holders of the truth of beon," those spokesmen who are claimed by the address, the *euangelion*, the good news, of the second arrival, and who correspondingly speak-out (*entspricht*) its truth to the others. "The essence of the folk," he wrote, "is its 'voice'. . . . The *voice* of the people speaks rarely and only in the few" (G65 11, 395, 319). Accordingly, Heidegger was apparently fond of quoting Homer's *Iliad* II, 204: "The rule of the many is not good; let there be one leader, one king" (HN 38).

In his SS 1935 lecture course, Heidegger quoted fragment 53 of Heraclitus, which names the struggle (*polemos, Kampf*) between unconcealment and concealment as that which "reigns" over being, and which is thus closely related to fragment 52 ("Time is a child playing . . . a child's is the kingship—

i.e., the *arche* . . . the being for beings"): "Struggle is . . . the king of all things. . . . it creates some as slaves, some as free." Heidegger then explained that this "struggle is sustained by creators, poets, thinkers, and statesmen [*Staatsmänner*]," those rare leaders and "violent ones" who contend for leadership and whose *Kampf* carries out the unconcealed truth of being into the work (*energeia*) of the artwork, philosophy, and the state (G40 66–67/61–62). During the early thirties, when his hegemonic attitude led to applying the "Führerprinciple" to all sectors of the new state of the Third Reich/Kingdom, Heidegger had in mind with these "poets, thinkers, and statesmen" primarily the 3-H Club of the poet laureate Hölderlin, the political dictator Adolf Hitler (whom Heidegger supported at least until 1936), and Heidegger himself as a kind of aspiring philosopher-king for reforming the German universities.

As the National Socialist rector of the university, Heidegger announced in 1933 that "the much celebrated 'academic freedom' is banished from the German university," and that the university would be subjected to the "Führerprinciple," militarized, and directed according to the goals of the National Socialist State (SDU 15/475). "Doctrines and 'ideas' shall not rule your being. The Führer [Adolf Hitler] himself and alone," Heidegger proclaimed, "is German reality and its law, today and for the future. . . . Heil Hitler! Martin Heidegger, Rector" (NH 136). He supported or, at the least, was willing to acquiesce in Hitler's suspension of civil rights and constitutional democratic government, the application of "cleansing" laws to Jewish university students, Germany's withdrawal from the League of Nations, and its militarism and annexationist policies.

While the Second World War raged on, Heidegger even provided from his classroom lectern ontological interpretations and justifications of major battles and events (e.g., the defeat of France, America's entry into the war, the campaign against Russia) in terms of the history of being. Short of the death camps and political assassinations such as those perpetrated in the Night of the Long Knives, Heidegger seems to have generally consented to Hitler's tactics. Apparently until the day he died, he did not once directly and clearly state that these methods were wrong, but only explained that they were misdirected into an erroneous biological and technological interpretation of the "inner truth and grandeur of National Socialism." As late as 1966 he stated that he did not know which "political system" was best suited for overcoming the "epoch of technology," but was still "not convinced that it is democracy" with the "halfway measures" of its "system of constitutionally guaranteed citizens's rights." Rather, only "the inner truth and grandeur" of National Socialism "went in this direction" of combating techology. In fact, Heidegger wrote to Heinrich Petzt in 1974 that "our Europe is being ruined from below with 'democracy' "[17] (HN 38–45). In his 1966 *Der Spiegel* interview, he still maintained that "very few people can have the [necessary] insights," and emphasized again in a subtler form the Greek-German axis, the centrality of Hölderlin's poetry for the arrival of a new god, and the need for a "thinker who would be 'great' enough" (NG 201-19/55-65).

In this authoritarian draft of "Being and Time," which is offset by equally strong insistences upon independent thinking (cf. LR viii-ix), the sense of being was reconfigured into the moments of a highly localized address (temporalizing-sense), prophetic individuals and Führers (relational sense), and the inscription of this address in sacralized texts (content-sense). As in his closure of *Ereignis* within the historicized *arche* of a Helleno-Germanic, religious, gendered, and anthropomorphic worldview, Heidegger's "hand" accordingly makes an appearance also as a hegemonic hand that wants to lead others along this *Heilsweg*. Jaspers, on whose reading of Kierkegaard Heidegger had once modeled his notion of formal indication, could say, though somewhat reductionistically, that "Heidegger's manner of thinking . . . appears to me to be in its essence unfree, dictatorial, uncommunicative" (MH 316; cf. PA 92-111; MLD 42-45).

What happened to the young Heidegger's sober Kierkegaardian insistence, often repeated also but far less insistently in the later Heidegger, that the being-question is open to anarchic differentiation into a plurality of unique paths, that formal indication has the repellent function of throwing "individuals" back upon their own existences and "freeing" them, that the teacher/student relationship is a completely noncoercive one, that "philosophy is not supposed to save or lead [*führen*] its age," that it is not "prophetic pageantry which brings world-historical salvation," that philosophers are not supposed to "lead us comfortably into a new Reich/Kingdom," but rather should practice "non-interference in personal decision"? The later Heidegger would have done well to remember his personal confession to Löwith in 1921 that "I am a *dogmatic* subjective relativist, i.e., I fight to get my 'position' through—and am 'unfair' to Others in the knowledge that I myself am 'relative.' "

The later Heidegger's prophetic, authoritarian tendency involved the exclusionary gesture that, due to the "forgetfulness of being," no one before the thinker Martin Heidegger had really thought the question concerning being. Dolf Sternberger recounted how the later Heidegger once made the "conceitedly superhuman" claim that SZ "posed and developed 'for the first time in the history of philosophy' the question regarding the sense of being" (MHG 42). When he was asked in 1958 whether "Martin Luther was an exception to this charge" of the forgetfulness of being, Heidegger answered, "Would you care to guess how many Catholics ask me the same thing about Thomas Aquinas?"[18] In 1943 Heidegger, who had once modeled his interpretation of Aristotle on Kierkegaard's own reading, said that "Kierkegaard remains essentially remote from Aristotle. . . . For Kierkegaard is not a thinker but a religious writer" (G5 249/QCT 94).

Heidegger's own rich array of mystical, Lutheran-Kierkegaardian, Aristotelian, Husserlian, and Diltheyan drafts of "Being and Time" in his early Freiburg period had worked, however, precisely on the assumption that the new postmetaphysical beginning was already implicitly effective in such traditions. But, scandalously reluctant to acknowledge his original indebtedness to these traditions, the later Heidegger instead progressively marked them as "metaphysics" within the history of the forgetfulness of being and placed them in a hierarchical-teleological relation to his own later thoughtpaths. For example, to his statement in SZ that "the tendency toward an understanding of the being of Dasein lies unexpressed in . . . [Dilthey's] 'philosophy of life,' " he later added the marginal note: "No!" (SZ 62 n. a/72). He wrote in the *Beiträge* that "Dilthey, as well as Jaspers, [are] without any idea of . . . the other beginning" (G65 337–38; regarding Kierkegaard, see N2 476–80/EP 70–74). What suggests that these gestures are a reductionistic suppression of the free proliferation of thoughtpaths is the fact that the historical figures on whom the young Heidegger drew are still alive and well in current "postmodern" discussions (for example, Derrida's ongoing readings of Husserl, the renewed interest in Kierkegaard, the effective history of Aristotle's *phronesis*).

In placing also his own youthful writings into a teleological relation to his later thought, consequently excluding the former from his collected edition, and in practicing autobiographical revisionism, Heidegger elevated his authorial self-interpretation to an authoritative status. In this author-itarian draft of "Being and Time," the configuration of being was retraced as address (temporalizing-sense), its inscription in Heidegger's later texts and his collected edition (content-sense), and the effective principle of the *mens auctoris* (relational sense). This has played right into the hands of a growing Heidegger, Inc. and a "last/ultimate hand edition," which intimidate the hermeneutical Other, the "heretic," who has an apocryphal reading of the texts. Here, as Foucault maintained, "the author is an ideological product" that discourages the "proliferation of meaning" in the "free composition, decomposition, and recomposition" of texts. What happened to the young Heidegger's insistence, repeated often enough later, that the formal indication of his texts is not a direct content "before the hand," but is rather supposed to repel the reader from reliance upon the mind of the author, prevent the founding of a "school," and encourage also critical non-Heideggerian readings of Heidegger?

What It Comes To

What Heidegger has bequeathed in his texts is the preconception of indicative starting points and traces that sketch out in advance a way of enactment toward the "turn" to another beginning of poetic dwelling beyond the present age of technology. In his 1964 essay "The End of Philosophy and the

Task of Thinking" and in his 1966 *Der Spiegel* interview, he stressed that to-day the "task is only of a preparatory . . . character. It is content with awaken-ing a readiness in humanity for a possibility whose sketch remains dark, whose coming remains uncertain." Appealing once again to Aristotle's method of "rough outline," he said that thinking can offer only a *Wegweiser*, a way-pointer, a signpost (SD 66–67, 80/59–61, 72). But, as he stressed back in WS 1921–22, in these indications "the object [is] signified 'emptily': and yet deci-sively! Not arbitrarily . . . but rather . . . determining, indicating, binding the direction" (G61 33). Indications always consist of "presupposition" and "preju-dice" that are "questionable" and "evidenceless."

So we can ask roughly what, according to the later Heidegger's prepara-tory sketches and drafts, is supposed to be coming in this second coming? Are we simply to call out: *Komm, Viens,* Come! Thy kingdom come, Thy will be done? The problem is that, to one degree or another, right up until the end of Heidegger's life's work, ideological tendencies (ethnocentrism, religious world-view, genderism, anthropomorphism, authoritarianism) and hyperbolic ten-dencies (primitivism, antihumanism, essentialism, speculation) were inscribed right within the indicative starting points of his sketches, and thus are inter-woven undecidably right within the countertendencies that made Heidegger the great thinker that he "is."

This is why many serious, dedicated Heidegger-scholars have maintained that Heidegger's question concerning being "is" in itself already metaphysical "nazism" in the wider sense of an ideological totalizing gesture. (The same would have to be said about, for example, Plato.) It is too simplistic to say that it became "Nazism" externally and momentarily through a mere "applica-tion" for a few years to the National Socialism of Adolf Hitler. This was in-deed the first "enactment" or, better, acting out of the intention (*Vorhaben*) and preconception of the "turn" to a new beginning that underlay it. This concrete enactment-sense involved Heidegger's "program" of *Kampf* for "mo-bilizing," politicizing, and militarizing the German universities. We read in the rectorial address about "the march which our people has begun into its future history," that "Germany's student body is on the march" (SDU 14/475). But this enactment also included the lengthy list of Heidegger's tasteless and dis-criminatory actions before, during, and after his rectorship (combined ambigu-ously with acts of kindness and generosity) that has been compiled by Farias, Ott, Sheehan, and others. When conducted rightly, this historical research is thus not mere ad hominem argumentation, but shows within the workings of practical reason the logical consequences of the ideological tendencies in Heidegger's ontology itself and alerts us to the need to criticize his "ideas."

While in Rome in 1936 to deliver his lecture "Hölderlin and the Essence of Poetry," which was published in *Das Innere Reich* (The Inner Reich/King-dom), Heidegger, wearing a swastika pin in the presence of his exiled Jewish

student Karl Löwith, told the latter that "his partisanship for National Socialism lay in the essence of his philosophy," explaining that "his concept of 'historicity' was the basis for his political 'engagement.' " Heidegger still "left no
doubt about his belief in Hitler. . . . He was convinced just as before that National Socialism was the prescribed [*vorgezeichnet*] path for Germany; one
simply had to 'hold on' long enough." As when he resigned his rectorship in
1934, Heidegger's disagreement seemed to have been basically with those
around Hitler who, so Heidegger thought, had usurped and corrupted the direction of National Socialism into a biological and technological movement.
He still retained the hope that Hitler would see the light of Heidegger's own
ontological version of the movement (MLD 57). Until the end of his life,
Heidegger seemed to subscribe to a distinction between inauthentic "bad Nazism" and the authentic "good Nazism" of his ontological "private National
Socialism," thus still maintaining in 1966 that, unlike communism and liberal
democracy, "the inner truth and grandeur of National Socialism," i.e., its "essence," lay in its attempt to "achieve a satisfactory relationship to the essence
of technology" (HN 42; NG 209–14/55–61).

Heidegger finally realized that Hitler too was a "bad Nazi," that his own
eschatological speculation about the *euangelion* of the new beginning "went
wrong," and that his identification with the movement "carried with it inadequate readings of my own intention" and was, as he confided in a friend, "the
greatest stupidity of his life." After this disillusionment, his colleague Schade-
waldt sarcastically asked him the following question in reference to Plato's attempt to establish an authoritarian state in Syracuse which would be ruled by
a philosopher-king: "Well, back from Syracuse, Herr Heidegger?"[19] Heidegger
henceforth withdrew even further into intellectual exile to rethink things in
lonely and prophetic dialogue with Hölderlin, Nietzsche, and the early Greek
thinkers (cf. G65).

However, much of the underlying intention toward the "turn" that had
originally been acted out in his political engagement remained operative, only
its indications were now held in abeyance, subjected to critical reflection and
reinscription, enacted in new thoughtpaths, and postponed to the "right moment" of a distant future. Heidegger now engaged in that preparatory thinking that waits for "a possibility whose sketch remains dark, whose coming
remains uncertain" after the world-night of technology. What exactly did the
following types of statements that Heidegger made at the end of the war mean?
"Everybody is now thinking of decline. We Germans cannot go into decline
because we have not at all yet risen and must first travel through the night."
"Despite groundlessness and exile, it is not as if nothing happens [*ereignet*] in
this *homelessness; an Advent conceals itself* therein" (MH 157, 30; cf. HN
45).

What is coming in this uncertain Advent? Who is this thief in the night?

Who is the coming god? *Worauf kommt es an?* What does it all come to? Still working with his model of Pauline parousiology, Heidegger wrote in 1947 that "thinking is *une aventur* [an ad-venture] not only as searching and questioning forth into the unthought. . . . Thinking is related to being as that which comes, the comely [*das Ankommende*] (*l'avenant*). Thinking as such is bound . . . to being as advent" (G9 363/BW 240–41). Accordingly, Heidegger had a star placed on his gravestone presumably in reference also to his following poetic image of thinking: "To head toward a star . . . " (G13 76/PLT 4). Is this the star over a new Bethlehem, over the kingdom of the children of a new god? Or do we need to listen to W. B. Yeats's foreboding in his "The Second Coming"? "Surely some revelation is at hand; / Surely the Second Coming is at hand. . . . / And what rough beast, its hour come at last, / Slouches towards Bethlehem to be born?"[20]

At the close of his television interview with Richard Wisser in 1969, Heidegger quoted Heinrich von Kleist in order to express his relation to the type of "future thinker" for which he, now near the end of his own life's work, was preparing, "I step back before one who is not yet here and bow a millenium ahead of him, before his *spirit*" (MHG 77; emphasis added). What is the proper name of this millenial spirit: *psyche, Geist, esprit, larva*? What is calling in the address, the *euangelion*, of being? We read from 1949, "The address of the pathway," which "speaks abandonment into the same" and "makes us be at home in a long provenance" before "the two world-wars," "now points clearly. Is the soul speaking? Is the world speaking? Is God speaking?" (G13 90/PW 39). What or who is really there on the other end of this distant call? If the enactment of the indicative waymarkers is a "leap into the speeding boat," would it come to the arrival of a saving ark after the great flood of technology, or the blessing of another fleet of U-boats? Would the acting out of the indications come to still more nazisms of varied kinds, or to idylls of poetic dwelling? Or both?

We do not know what this thief in the night "is," and that is an uncanny thing. The "is" in the question, "What is Heidegger's thought?," trembles in dangerous undecidability because it is caught up in an irreducible interplay of countertendencies and ambidexterities. On the one hand, Heidegger's thought "is" in itself nazism, and, on the other, it "is not" nazism. But would not the passive enactment- and fulfillment-sense of the ideological tendencies that are there lead us, perhaps not to another National Socialism, but to other concrete nazisms of ethnocentrism, religious parochialism, genderism, speciesism, authoritarianism? Derrida has written, "I believe in the necessity of showing— without limit, if possible—the profound attachment of Heidegger's texts (writings and deeds) to the possibility and reality of all nazisms" (HN 47). Are we to be the passive kairological "staff-holder" and "shepherd" of these aspects of the "truth of beon"?

Thus I am recommending that we apply to Heidegger himself, both the later Heidegger and the young Heidegger, his own advice from WS 1921-22 that, because the "commensurateness" of a philosopher's indicative sketches is always "absolutely questionable" in relation to the *Sache*, these starting points must be subjected to the adventure of "questioning kairological-critically" and "enacted critically in a radical manner" toward the topic itself (G61 41, 34). We must not make these indicative traces into the direct theme of inquiry and allow them to harden into "answers" and "blind dogmatic fixations" of a Heidegger, Inc. We should practice "skepticism" upon them in the twofold sense of critical suspicion and the search for different ways to continue, as he himself constantly did, critically reinscribing and proliferating these drafts of the *Sache* of "Being and Time" in different situations. This adventure is not "the saving coast" of a Heidegger, Inc., but getting "the rope for the sail into one's hand and looking towards the wind." Heidegger later often repeated this demand.

We read in his essay "The End of Philosophy and the Task of Thinking" that "thinking must first learn what remains pre-served and held open for it to let itself get involved in, and in this learning it prepares for its own transformation" (SD 66/60). A great thinker "will bow to the necessity of later being understood differently than he meant himself to be understood" (G9 ix). Emphasizing "the almost insurmountable problem of communication," he wrote to Richardson that the "indications [are to be] taken up as a directive to put oneself on the way of thinking independently toward the indicated topic itself" (LR viii-ix). "I cannot help you. . . . Well, I can't" (NG 213/60). This last statement from 1966 echoes Heidegger's WS 1921-22 course, "I can make the discovery of 'what it comes to' for no one" (G61 191). At his best moments, he always, in the manner of indirect communication, repelled his readers from the *mens auctoris* and back into their own adventure with the topic itself.

What, then, does it come to? As we have already begun to do here in our reading of the "supplement" to Heidegger's collected edition, one important thing that we can do is to apply the young Heidegger's warning against "telling a myth" and his project of demythologizing and unmasking to the residual hyperbolic, ideological, and autobiographical myths in the *gigantomachia peri tes ousias* of the later Heidegger, this twentieth-century Father Parmenides of "postmodern" thinking. Such a deconstruction means allowing these myths and the young Heidegger's own myths to crumble back into the flux of the anarchic kinetic-personal physiognomy of being.

Taking up Plato's theme in the *Sophist* of parricide against the pre-Socratic Fathers and their mythopoetic thinking, Heidegger apparently told his students in WS 1924-25 that "the philosopher must dare to become a father-killer."[21] But this radicality was repeated later in such statements as that "questions . . . must stab themselves in the heart, not that thinking should die from it, but rather live transformed" (G9 417/QB 95). But this philosophical parricide opens up the way to repetition and reinscription. For the young Heidegger alerts us to what his later mythopoetic drafts always simultaneously and ambiguously affirmed, namely, that the *Ereignis* of being is a mysterious anarchic play in contrast to the totalizing claims of metaphysics and technology, that *Ereignis* always entails the *Ereignis* of personal being, and that the role of philosopher-king in the "house of being" never really suited him. The rediscovery of his youthful writings can help to give cultural, religious, and philosophical difference full play in the later Heidegger's notion of the *Ereignis* of earth and sky, gods and mortals; to welcome into this pluralized poetic "house of being" not just gods and jugs and trees, but also the mystery of the *Ereignis* of persons, feminine being, and the sentient being of animals; and to explore and outline the *ethos* of a postmetaphysical "originary ethics" of ecumenical difference and attunement to "suffering and the cross." In his 1956 essay "Hebel—the Housefriend," Heidegger said that we are still looking for "the friend[s] for the house of the world" (G13 133-50/HFH 89-101). Can we draw inspiration here from the notion of anarchic community and the kairological ethics of *Gelassenheit* and free sociality in Heidegger's early Freiburg period?

Using these youthful writings as an archive of supplementary Rosetta stones, as it were, we now have the opportunity of grafting and reinscribing the later Heidegger's explorations of the end of philosophy, *Kehre*, the other beginning, the way-character of thinking, trace, *Ereignis*, *Es gibt*, *aletheia*, worlding, Sophocles's *Antigone*, mystery, the divine, the significant thinging of things, dwelling, *Gelassenheit*, originary ethics, Hölderlin's poetry, the pre-Socratics, technology, and cultural crisis onto the corresponding explorations in his youthful writings, as well as to read, deepen, and criticize the young Heidegger through the texts of the later Heidegger.[22]

This proposal joins the choreography of other strategies that are currently being ventured for supplementing, demythologizing, repeating, and reinscribing Heidegger by grafting him onto the bricolage of other lexicons, in order to pursue the *Sache* of thinking in new drafts of "Being and Time," in new thoughtpaths that no longer bear Heidegger's seal, and, in general, in what Foucault called the "free circulation," "free composition, decomposition, and recomposition" of texts. Here, to get on with the task of thinking after the recent preoccupation with the serious problems in Heidegger's thought, especially his allegiance to National Socialism, we can use not only his youthful writings, which have their own problems,[23] but also, as is already being done, everything from the countertendencies in Heidegger's later thought itself, Derridean deconstruction, feminist theory, Foucault's genealogical thinking, critical theory, Gadamerian hermeneutics, phenomenology, Levinas, Wittgenstein, American neo-pragmatism, literature, Luther's *theologia crucis*, the New

Testament, and whatever else works. Dispersing the hyperbolic, ideological gestures of the Heideggerian *manus mentis*, we need to proliferate the reproductive supplementary chain of differing/deferring way-traces and drafts of "Being and Time," lending our voices to the "rumor of the hidden king" and allowing it to continue to echo kairologically "here and now . . . in this place," in a way similar to how Derrida has encouraged us, regarding Husserl, "to make our voices *resonate* throughout the corridors in order to *supplement* the breakup of presence."[24]

Wakeful guardianship of the topic of thinking can never be equated with protecting a present-at-hand treasure in the king's castle from thieves in the night. It always abdicates such a presumptuous office. The later Heidegger said that (VA 177/PLT 184). Truth (*a-letheia*), including the truth of Heidegger's topic and texts, is "at any particular time, as it were, a *robbery*" that wrests the matter kairologically from concealment into unconcealment (SZ 294/265). Heidegger, Inc. can be built only on this dangerous truth—a philosophical burglary waiting to happen. The good news is that what guardianship comes to is rather the very ambiguous apo-logia of adventurous thieves in the night working right inside Heidegger's own ambiguous Corporation.

Notes

1. Heidegger's Autobiographies

1. Hannah Arendt, "Martin Heidegger at Eighty," in Michael Murray (ed.), *Heidegger and Modern Philosophy* (New Haven: Yale University Press, 1978), p. 293; HW 82, 61; Hans-Georg Gadamer, *Die Idee des Guten zwischen Plato und Aristoteles* (Heidelberg: Carl Winter, 1978), p. 6; Karl Löwith, "Karl Löwith," in MHG 38-40 and HDZ 20-21, 106–107; Wilhelm Szilasi, *Macht und Ohnmacht des Geistes* (Freiburg: Karl Alber, 1946), pp. 7–9, and his "Interpretation und Geschichte der Philosophie," in *Martin Heideggers Einfluss auf die Wissenschaften* (Bern: A. Franke, 1949), pp. 75–77; Leo Strauss, "An Introduction to Heideggerian Existentialism," in Thomas L. Pangle (ed.), *The Rebirth of Classical Political Rationalism: An Introduction to the Thought of Leo Strauss* (Chicago: University of Chicago Press, 1989), pp. 27–28; Helene Weiss, *Kausalität und Zufall in der Philosophie des Aristoteles* (Basel: Verlags Haus zum Falken, 1942), pp. 6, 52, 100.

2. See John D. Caputo, RH and his *Demythologizing Heidegger* (Bloomington: Indiana University Press, 1993); David Farrell Krell, *Daimon Life: Heidegger and Life-Philosophy* (Bloomington: Indiana University Press, 1992).

3. Otto Pöggeler, "Heideggers Begegnung mit Dilthey," *Dilthey-Jahrbuch* 4 (1986–87): 126.

4. See Christoph von Wolzogen, "Nicht Leben oder Welt, sondern Dasein: Heidegger—alte Fragen, alte Quellen," *Frankfurter Allgemeine Zeitung*, no. 258, November 6, 1985: 36; Philipp W. Rosemann, "Langgehütetes Werk: Warum die erste Fassung von Heideggers 'Sein und Zeit' 1925 nicht erscheinen konnte," *Frankfurter Allgemeine Zeitung*, no. 194, August 23, 1989: N 3.

5. SZ 8/26; G15 334-39, 372-400; LR viii–xv; UZP; SD 81-90/74-82; G12 81-146/1-54; G1 55-57/R 21-22; G13 87-90/PW 32-39; V 303-304.

6. G15 337; G12 121/34; SD 87/79-80; LR xii–xiii; G1 55; DMH 351.

7. G12 88-91/7-10, 121/35; SZ 72/102, 268/313; G26 220/171.

8. SD 87/79; G12 91/10, 130/41; LR x–xi; G1 56/R 21.

9. G12 87/6; G1 56/R 21; VA 177/PLT 185; G5 preface.

10. G12 87/6, 121/35, 130/41; LR x–xi; G9 284-85/BCP 256-57.

11. G5 preface; G13 91, 254; G15 366; VA 7; SZ vii/17; G9 343/BW 222.

12. Jacques Derrida, "Geschlecht II: Heidegger's Hand," in John Sallis (ed.), *Deconstruction and Philosophy: The Texts of Jacques Derrida* (Chicago: University of Chicago Press, 1987), pp. 161-96. For the notion of Heidegger's "two hands" cited below, see also Derrida's *Margins of Philosophy*, tr. Alan Bass (Chicago, University of Chicago Press, 1982), p. 65.

13. PIA 258; G56/57 116, 100; G61 35, 37, 67, 175; G9 4, 38; TK 40/QCT 40; G9 313/BW 194; G15 399.

14. Jacques Taminiaux, *Heidegger and the Project of Fundamental Ontology*, tr. Michael Gendre (Albany: State University of New York, 1991), p. i.

15. G1 55, 57/R 21–22; G9 ix; G5 26/PLT 40; Friedrich-Wilhelm von Herrmann, "Die Edition der Vorlesungen Heideggers in seiner Gesamtausgabe letzter Hand," *Heidegger Studies* 2 (1986): 165.

16. Regarding Aristotle, see OWE 135; Jacques Taminiaux, "Poiesis and Praxis in Fundamental Ontology," *Research in Phenomenology* 17 (1987): 137–69; and Manfred Riedel, "Zwischen Plato und Aristoteles: Heideggers doppelte Exposition der Seinsfrage und der Ansatz von Gadamers hermeneutischer Gesprächsdialektik," *Allgemeine Zeitschrift* 19 (1986): 1–28. Regarding Husserl, see Jacques Taminiaux, "Heidegger and Husserl's *Logical Investigations*: In Remembrance of Heidegger's Last Seminar (Zähringen)," in John Sallis (ed.), *Radical Phenomenology* (Atlantic Highlands: Humanities Press, 1978), pp. 58–83. Regarding Kierkegaard, see RH Chaps. 1, 3; and George Stack, *Kierkegaard's Existential Ethics* (University Park: University of Alabama Press, 1977).

17. VVU 663–65; G12 86/5, 121–23/34–36, 129/41, 90/9; PAA July 19; G56/57 117; MH 85.

18. See also the invaluable study by Kisiel, "Edition und Übersetzung" (EU). I am grateful to Professor Kisiel for generously providing information on the publisher's prospectuses, as well as his unpublished paper "The Genesis of *Being and Time*: Its Doxographical Surface and Hermeneutic Depth," from which I have also benefited greatly in my discussion of Heidegger's collected edition.

19. Prospectus of June 1987, p. 7; BZ 29; Frithjof Rodi, "Die Bedeutung Diltheys für die Konzeption von 'Sein und Zeit.' Zum Umfeld von Heideggers Kasseler Vorträgen (1925)," *Dilthey-Jahrbuch* 4 (1986–87): 166; G56/57 215; von Herrmann, "Die Edition der Vorlesungen Heideggers," p. 154, as well as the original version of his essay in *Freiburg Universitätsblätter* 78 (December 1982): 85. I am indebted to Theodore Kisiel for information concerning the course "Aristoteles, *Rhetorik*, II." For the Derridean sense of "dangerous supplement" to which I am appealing, see Jacques Derrida, *Of Grammatology*, tr. Gayatri Chakravorty Spivak (Baltimore: Johns Hopkins University Press, 1976), pp. 141ff.

20. Von Herrmann, "Die Edition der Vorlesungen Heideggers," p. 155.

21. Jacques Derrida, *Limited Inc* (Evanston: Northwestern University Press, 1988); "Otobiographies: The Teaching of Nietzsche and the Politics of the Proper Name," tr. Avital Ronell, in Christie MacDonald (ed.), *The Ear of the Other* (Lincoln: University of Nebraska Press, 1985), pp. 1–38; and especially "Interpreting Signatures (Nietzsche/Heidegger): Two Questions," in Diane P. Michelfelder and Richard E. Palmer (eds.), *Dialogue and Deconstruction: The Gadamer-Derrida Encounter* (Albany: State University of New York, 1989), pp. 58–71, where Derrida criticizes Heidegger's interpretive attempts to see unity in the names "Nietzsche" and "Heidegger" and does not take "the risk of seeing the name dismembered and multiplied in masks and similitudes."

22. For these "names," see William J. Richardson, *Heidegger: Through Phenomenology to Thought* (The Hague: Martinus Nijhoff, 1963); Theodore Kisiel, "Heidegger (1907–1927): The Transformation of the Categorial," in Hugh J. Silverman et al. (eds.), *Continental Philosophy in America* (Pittsburgh: Duquesne University Press, 1983), p. 166.

23. PA 100; HAN 192, 161, 119; EMH 155; MH 71, 89; HL 105; HJ 38.

24. Jacques Derrida, *Speech and Phenomena And Other Essays on Husserl's Theory of Signs*, tr. David B. Allison (Evanston: Northwestern University Press, 1973), p. 104.

25. Derrida, *Limited Inc*, pp. 19–21, 31, 108.

26. Derrida, *Limited Inc*, p. 20.

27. Roland Barthes, "The Death of the Author," in his *Image-Music-Text* (New York: Hill and Wang, 1977), p. 146.

28. Von Herrmann, "Die Edition der Vorlesungen Heideggers," pp. 165–71.

29. Michel Foucault, "What Is an Author?" in Paul Rabinow (ed.), *The Foucault Reader* (New York: Pantheon Books, 1984), pp. 103, 118–19.
30. Barthes, "The Death of the Author," p. 146–47.
31. Foucault, "What Is an Author?", p. 113–17.
32. Derrida, *Limited Inc*, p. 31.
33. Ulrich Sieg, " 'Die Verjudung des deutschen Geistes,' " *Die Zeit*, no. 52, December 29, 1989: 19; MH 187; NH 144, 154, 215.
34. Hannah Arendt, "Martin Heidegger ist achtzig Jahre alt," *Merkur* 10 (1969): 895, 900–902.
35. Jacques Derrida, "Différance," in his *Margins of Philosophy*, p. 22.

2. Figuring the Matter Out

1. N1 456/NII 191. For the notions of deconstruction, first beginning, guiding question, the history of metaphysics, fundamental metaphysical positions, the forgetfulness of being, nihilism, and the end of philosophy, as well as those of repetition, ground question, and other beginning, see especially SZ §§2, 6; N1 79–81/NI 67–68; N1 448–62/NII 184–97; N2 335–98/NIV 197–250; N2 399–480/EP 1–74; G65 pts. II–IV; SD 1–80/1–73; G15 326–71.
2. G65 415, 489, 452, and §§134–35; G12 118/32; G15 370–71; WHD 73/79; G9 313, 352, 356/BW 193, 231, 235; N2 207/NIV 153; SZ 226/214; cf. SZ §§4, 44a.
3. Arendt, "Martin Heidegger at Eighty," pp. 295–301; *Republic* 592a.
4. G9 313/BW 193; G15 345; SZ 209/200, 57/68, 64/73; G65 31–33, 239. For *Vollzug* and *Zeitigung*, cf. SZ §§10, 13, 32, 44a, and Division Two; G65 §§34, 98, 122, 139, 238–42; N1 448–62/NII 184–97.
5. N2 389–90, 397/NII 243–44, 250; SD 46/43; G15 365–66, 20/HS 8; Thomas Sheehan, "Introduction: Heidegger, the Project and the Fulfillment," in Thomas Sheehan (ed.), *Heidegger: The Man and the Thinker* (Chicago: Precedent Publishing, 1981), p. vii; RH 85.
6. See RH Chaps. VI–VII and IX, from which I have drawn in the following. See also Reiner Schürmann's important study: *Heidegger on Being and Acting: From Principles to Anarchy* (Bloomington: Indiana University Press, 1987).
7. G29/30 421–35; G65 344, 7; VA 7, 253/EGT 106; G13 78/PLT 6; G9 344/BW 224.
8. LR viii–ix; G1 438; EMH 111, 202; Walter Biemel, "Erinnerungen an Heidegger," *Allgemeine Zeitschrift für Philosophie* 1 (1977): 2; WHD 160/158.
9. Cf. "By Way of Introduction," *Heidegger Studies* 1 (1985).
10. Jürgen Busche, "Wie lesbar darf ein Philosoph sein?" *Frankfurter Allgemeine Zeitung*, no. 233, October 21, 1978; Thomas J. Sheehan, "Caveat Lector: The New Heidegger," *New York Review of Books*, December 4, 1980: 40.

3. Curricula Vitae

1. For the following, see HL 77–137, MH 45–105, MHT 534–41, which also contain Heidegger's university transcripts from 1909 to 1913 and other important texts.
2. Franz Brentano, *Von der mannigfachen Bedeutung des Seienden nach Aristoteles* (Freiburg: Herder, 1896; repr., Hildesheim: Georg Olms Verlagsbuchhandlung, 1960); LR x–xi; G12 88/7; SD 81/74.
3. SD 81/74; Carl Braig, *Vom Sein. Abriss der Ontologie* (Freiburg: Herder, 1896), p.

v; John D. Caputo, *Heidegger and Aquinas: An Essay on Overcoming Metaphysics* (New York: Fordham University Press, 1982), pp. 45–55.

4. SD 81–82/74–75; HL 116, 79; Herbert Spiegelberg, *The Phenomenological Movement* (The Hague: Martinus Nijhoff, 1982), p. 340.

5. G1 56/R 22; SD 83/76. Regarding the importance of Lask's influence on Heidegger, as well as other themes that I discuss (namely, the material determinateness and analogical differentiation of form, the "heterothesis" of being, mysticism, the role of religious *Hingabe*, and the continuity of these concepts with Heidegger's treatment of the "primal something" in his courses of 1919), I have benefited greatly from the series of ground-breaking essays by Theodore Kisiel which are referred to in my List of Abbreviations and in endnotes, and which the author has gathered together in his *The Genesis of Heidegger's Being and Time* (Berkley: University of California Press, 1993). I have also found helpful John Caputo's *The Mystical Element in Heidegger's Thought* (TME) and his *Heidegger and Aquinas*, as well as Otto Pöggeler's classical study *Der Denkweg Martin Heideggers* (DMH).

7. Demythologizing Metaphysics

1. G56/57 11–12, 125–31; BL 28; G61 35, 186, 182; Thomas Sheehan, "The 'Original Form' of *Sein und Zeit*: Heidegger's *Der Begriff der Zeit*," *Journal of the British Society for Phenomenology* 10 (1979): 82.

2. G56/57 11; Immanuel Kant, *Kritik der reinen Verunuft* (Stuttgart: Philipp Reclam, 1966), p. 865/Immanuel Kant, *Critique of Pure Reason*, tr. Norman Kemp Smith (London: MacMillan, 1978), pp. 7–8; G61 184, 70, 36–37, 99; G63 41–42.

3. G61 70, 99, 163–64, 197, 182; BZ 25; G58 203; G20 45/35, 96/70; G56/57 19; G19 §64; SZ 8/26; G63 65.

4. I have borrowed this fitting translation of *Sturz* as "crash" from David Krell's *Daimon Life*, p. 49.

5. G61 26, 111, 81, 163–64, 182, 192; G63 61–63, 19, 42, 103; PIA 238.

6. Rudolf Bultmann, *New Testament and Mythology: and Other Basic Writings*, tr. Schubert M. Ogden (Philadelphia: Fortress Press, 1984).

7. G1 191; MH 96–104, 114–15; SD 85/78; HB 12, 16; Thomas Sheehan, "Heidegger's Early Years: Fragments for a Philosophical Biography," *Listening* 12 (1977): 7; PA 92; Dorion Cairns, *Conversations with Husserl and Fink*, ed. Richard M. Zaner (The Hague: Martinus Nijhoff, 1976), p. 9; G63 5.

8. LG 104; Sheehan, *Heidegger: The Man and the Thinker*, p. 25; MH 106; HB 16.

9. G58 205, 61–62; DMH 327–28; G61 7. For the influence of Dilthey and Natorp on Heidegger's phenomenology of religion, see EBF 104–105; ML 14; WFH 68–72; CEM 250–67; DW1, DW2. For Scheler's influence, see G20 180/130, 418/302; G26 169/134; LE 5–28.

10. DK 109–10; HL 94; HBC; G58 62, 205; MLD 29; G56/57 211, 5, 18; DW2 Chap. 3; G61 7. In 1930 Heidegger provided Blochmann with a bibliography on medieval mysticism that may provide further clues to what Heidegger was reading around 1919; he mentions inter alia Francis of Assisi, *Opera omnia* and the *Theologia Germanica* (HB 36).

11. DW2 Chap. 4; PA 93; ML 14, 25; HJ 15, 222; Julius Ebbinghaus, "Julius Ebbinghaus," in Ludwig J. Pongratz (ed.), *Philosophie in Selbstdarstellungen*, Vol. 3 (Hamburg: Felix Meiner, 1977), p. 33; WFD 5.

12. Otto Pöggeler, *Neue Wege mit Heidegger* (Freiburg: Karl Alber, 1992), pp. 466–67.

13. Otto Pöggeler, "Zeit und Sein bei Heidegger," *Phänomenologische Forschung* 14 (1983): 164; EMH 219, 157, 51; Herbert Spiegelberg, "Husserl to Heidegger: From a 1928 Freiburg Diary by W. R. Boyce Gibson," *Journal of the British Society for Phenomenology* 2

(1971): 74; Gerhard Wolfgang Ittel, "Der Einfluss der Philosophie M. Heideggers auf die Theologie R. Bultmanns," *Kerygma und Dogma* 2 (1956): 92; HW 131; WT 6; Gerhard Ebeling, *Lutherstudien*, Vol. 2: *Disputatio de Homine, 1. Teil, Text und Traditionshintergrund* (Tübingen: J. C. B. Mohr, 1977), p. ix.

14. SZ 252–53/235, 313/278; G61 7; PIA 250; G63 24–26; *Briefwechsel zwischen Wilhelm Dilthey und dem Grafen Paul Yorck von Wartenburg 1877–1897* (Halle, 1923), pp. 154, 158.

15. Rudolf Bultmann, "New Testament and Mythology," in Hans Werner Bartsch (ed.), *Kerygma and Myth*, tr. Reginald H. Fuller (London: S.P.C.K., 1953), p. 23; G56/57 7–12; PIA 246; G61 197.

16. PAA June 24ff.; G61 9, 135; G20 28/23; WDF 9; WSH.

17. Christoph von Wolzogen, " 'Es gibt': Heidegger und Natorps 'Praktische Philosophie,' " in A. Gethmann-Siefert and O. Pöggeler (ed.), *Heidegger und die praktische Philosophie* (Frankfurt: Suhrkamp, 1988), p. 321, n. 38.

18. István M. Fehér, "Heidegger and Lukács: Eine Hundertjahresbilanz," in Fehér (ed.), *Wege und Irrwege des neueren Umganges mit Heideggers Werk* (Berlin: Duncker & Humblot, 1991), pp. 43–70.

19. HW 142; G56/57 18; G61 7; PIA 250; G63 41–42; DMH 41, 34; SZ 63/72; 278/253.

20. I have drawn the list of courses given here and in subsequent chapters from VVU 663–71 and from later extensive corrections of it in HEL 23–29; ML 23; OWB 196; OWE 134. My listing of Heidegger's seminars on Husserl's *Logische Untersuchungen* is based on written communication from Theodore Kisiel (September 27, 1990).

21. G9 47–67/PT 5–21; G9 482; WFH 74–75; HW 29, 147; HB 25–26; G65 Division VII, "Der Letzte Gott."

8. Primal Christianity

1. G61 6; DMH 39–42; Augustine, *De doctrina christiana*, I, 4–5, in *Corpus Christianorum*, Vol. 32 (Turnholti: Typographi Brepols Editores Pontificii, mcmlxxv), pp. 8–9/*On Christian Doctrine*, tr. D. W. Robertson (Indianapolis: Bobbs-Merrill, 1958), p. 10.

2. LA 3–4, 19, 37–38; WA *Breifwechsel* I 359, 88/XLVIII 112, 38; WA VI 458/XLIV 201; Peter Peterson, *Geschichte der aristotelischen Philosophie im protestantischen Deutschland* (Leipzig: Felix Meiner, 1921) p. 34.

3. Sheehan, "Heidegger's Early Years," p. 11.

4. WA *Deutsche Bibel* VII 23–25/C. S. Anderson (ed.), *Reading in Luther* (Minneapolis: Augsburg Publishing, 1967), pp. 211–12.

5. G56/57 134–35; G. W. F. Hegel, *Phänomenologie des Geistes, Gesammelte Werke*, Vol. 9 (Hamburg: Felix Meiner, 1980), pp. 18, 27, 48, 55, 434; G9 6; G61 36; VA 177/PLT 185; SD 1/1.

6. 1 Cor. 7:32–33, cf. 12:25; Tit. 3:8; Phil. 2:20. See the article by Konrad Burdach, to which Heidegger often refers (G20 419/303; SZ 262–64/242–43): "Faust und die Sorge," *Deutsche Vierteljahrschrift für Literaturwissenschaft und Geistesgeschichte* 1 (1923): 46–49.

7. LE 5, 24–28; G20 222/165; SZ 185/178; PO 123–35/"On the Passion of Love," in *The Miscellaneous Writings of Pascal*, tr. M. P. Faugère (London: Longman, 1849), pp. 129–44.

8. SZ 185/178; BZ 11; Augustine, *Contra Faustum*, lib. 32, cap. 18, in *CORPVS CHRISTIANORVM*, Vol. 25 (Pragae: F. Tempsky, 1891), p. 779/*Reply to Faustus the Manichean*, in Marcus Dods (ed.), *The Works of Aurelius Augustine*, Vol. 5, *Writings in Connec-*

tion with the Manichean Heresy, tr. Richard Stothert (Edinburgh: T. & T. Clark, 1872), p. 545; C Book 11, Chap. 27.

9. PO 458/PK 154; PO 185/"On the Art of Persuasion," in *The Miscellaneous Writings of Pascal*, p. 150; SZ 185/178.

10. G20 404/292; SZ 252/235; WA XLII 127–34/I 170–80; cf. *Heidelberg Disputation*, theses 4, 7–12, 17–18.

11. WA LVI 371–72/XXV 360–62; I 362–63/XXXI 53–54; Martin Luther, *Theologie des Kreuzes*, ed. Georg Helbig (Leipzig: Alfred Kroner, 1933), p. 247.

12. WA I 362–65, 357, 613/XXXI 53–57, 44, 225; PPT 34–35; G9 53, 61/PT 10, 16; LE 8–9; G20 353/256; SZ 183/177; *Republic* 585d; *Metaphysics* 983a; *Nicomachean Ethics* 1178b.

13. G63 54–62; SZ 528/451; G9 23, 37, 39–40; G61 111, 140.

14. IPR 317–22. I have borrowed this translation of *Augenblick* as "eye-opening moment" from Th. C. W. Oudemans's essay "Heidegger: Reading against the Grain," in RHS.

15. COA 87–88, 149; CD 325, 339–40, 347–55; FTR 133; PDW 254–56; EO 220.

16. DMH 41–42; Augustine, *De moribus ecclesiae catholicae*, I, c. 3, in B. Roland-Gosselin (ed.), *Oeuvres de Saint Augustin* (Paris: Desclée, De Brouwer et Cie, 1949), pp. 142–44/*On the Morals of the Catholic Church*, tr. R. Stothert, in *Basic Writings of Augustine*, Vol. 1, ed. W. J. Oates (New York: Random House, 1948), p. 321; G5 367/EGT 53; DQ 51–52/65–66; C 238/268.

17. LA 28–33, 39; WA I 363, 226/XXXI 55, 12; XLIV 703–705/VIII 171–72; PPT 34–35; Gerhard Ebeling, *Luther*, tr. R. A. Wilson (Philadelphia: Fortress Press, 1970), p. 89.

9. Husserl

1. Edmund Husserl, *Die Krisis der Europäischen Wissenschaften und die Transzendentale Phänomenologie* (Husserliana VI) (The Hague: Martinus Nijhoff, 1954), pp. 7, 71–74/*The Crisis of European Sciences and Transcendental Phenomenology*, tr. David Carr (Evanston: Northwestern University Press, 1970), pp. 9, 71–72.

2. G. W. F. Hegel, *Lectures on the History of Philosophy*, tr. E. S. Haldane and Frances H. Simson, Vol. 3 (London: Routledge and Kegan Paul, 1974), p. 217.

3. See Derrida's *Edmund Husserl's Origin of Geometry: An Introduction*, tr. John P. Leavey (Lincoln: University of Nebraska Press, 1989) and " 'Genesis and Structure' and Phenomenology," in his *Writing and Difference*, tr. Alan Bass (Chicago: University of Chicago Press), pp. 154–68, as well as his essays on Hebraic "unhappy consciousness" in ibid., pp. 64–78, 294–300.

4. T. S. Eliot, "The Hollow Men," in Gary Geddes (ed.), *20th-Century Poetry and Poetics*, 2d ed. (Toronto: Oxford University Press, 1973), pp. 86–87.

5. SD 87/79; G12 86/5; G63 1–3; OWB 196; G20 420/303; SZ 51/62, 124/91, 289/261, 480/414.

6. G20 62–63/46–47, 184/136, 168/121, 420/304; G61 60, 195; SZ 51/63; G56/57 110, 121.

7. G20 72–80/54–60, 93–103/68–75, 193/143; G24 §§2, 7–9, 16–18; G15 331, 334; G40 36–39/33–36; SD 3/3.

8. G56/57 164–65; G20 30/24, 161–64/116–19; G61 80. Cf. Otto Pöggeler, "Heideggers Begegnung mit Dilthey," *Dilthey-Jahrbuch* 4 (1986–87): 121–60.

9. WDF 4–7, 10; see Georg Misch's overview of Dilthey's theological heritage in the latter's *Gesammelte Schriften*, Vol. 5: *Die Geistige Welt, Einleitung in die Philosophie des Lebens* (Leipzig: B. G. Teubner, 1924), pp. xxii–xxvii.

10. G61 91; G20 178–79/128–29, 83/61, 165/119, 301/219, 94–96/69–70, 139/101; SZ 289/261.

11. HJ 71; SZ 132, 63; G56/57 4, 70–73, 86, 110, 117, 126, 13–15, 96; G63 85, 93–101, 13–14, 16, 71; G61 88, 34–35, 47, 60.

12. LU2 566/694, 651–52/765–66, 569–70/697; G20 84/62, 97/71, 69–70/52.

13. G20 71–74/53–55, 163–64/118–19, 302/220; G21 169–182; WDF 10–11.

14. G56/57 206–207; G20 246–47/182, 219/163, 61/45, 106–107/78, 124/91.

15. G20 172–73/124–25, 131/96, 148–57/108–14, 62–63/46–47; SZ 303/272, 166–67/162–63; G61 47, 81, 99, 173; G21 §§9–10; G9 23, 4–5. See also Heidegger's 1927 letter to Husserl concerning "the transcendental ego" (VZB 600–602/118–21).

16. G20 148–52/107–10, 205–207/152–54, 173/125, 420/303–304; G21 8; G63 93, 102; G9 22; G61 131, 98; PIA 242, 247.

17. G61 131; G63 97; G20 349/253, 420/303–304, 226/167, 328/238, 73/54; SZ 201/193, 289/261.

18. SZ 210/201; G21 135–61; G20 74–75/56, 65/48, 372/270, 416/300; G61 39.

19. LU2 646–47/761–62, 670–75/784–87; G20 85–90/63–66, 96–97/70–71, 168/121, 126/92; IRP2 161–69; *Vorlesungen zur Phänomenologie des inneren Zeitbewusstseins* (Husserliana X) (The Hague: Martinus Nijhoff, 1964)/*The Phenomenology of Internal Time-Consciousness*, tr. James S. Churchill (Bloomington: Indiana University Press, 1964).

20. WDF 28; G20 92/68, 102/75; G9 4–5; G63 75, 83, 43, 65; G21 50–54, 87–93; English translation of UZP, p. 199.

21. G56/57 115, 206–207; G20 99/72–73, 292/213–14, 359/261; G9 22; G63 55–56, 79; G21 192; SZ 480/414; G26 264/204.

22. LU1 106/330; IRP3 154/15; IRP1 223/259; Otto Pöggeler, "Zum Tode Martin Heideggers," in John Sallis (ed.), *Radical Phenomenology* (New Jersey: Humanities Press, 1978), p. 34.

10. Aristotle

1. G63 5, 67–77; G61 8–9; G20 23–35/19–28, 73/55; G21 93–96, 7–8; Herbert Spiegelberg, "Husserl to Heidegger," p. 73.

2. G63 41–42, 70; CUP 100, 278, 306; PIA 263, 267. For Kierkegaard's reading of Aristotle, cf. Stack, *Kierkegaard's Existential Ethics*; RH 11–35.

3. PIA 249, 253; G63 76, 10, 21; G61 48–49; G9 4; G19 §7.

4. PIA 268, 260, 238; G61 92; G63 76; Hans-Georg Gadamer, *Hermeneutik II: Wahrheit und Methode, Ergänzungen, Register, Gesammelte Werke*, Vol. 2 (Tübingen: J. C. B. Mohr, 1986), p. 486.

5. See OWE 136, n. 11; Franco Volpi, "Heidegger in Marburg: Die Auseinandersetzung mit Aristoteles," *Philosophischer Literaturanzeiger* 37 (1984): 173, n. 3. See especially three early studies that, on the basis of attendance of Heidegger's courses, work out many details of his reading of Aristotle's practical philosophy: Hans-Georg Gadamer, "Praktisches Wissen" (written 1930), in his *Griechische Philosophie I, Gesammelte Werke*, Vol. 5 (Tübingen: J. C. B. Mohr, 1985), pp. 230–48; Helene Weiss, *Kausalität und Zufall in der Philosophie des Aristoteles* (Darmstadt: Wissenschaftliche Buchgesellschaft, 1967; unaltered reprint of the 1942 Basel edition), Chap. 3, "Menschliches Dasein—*praxis* (Nikomachische Ethik)"; Wilhelm Szilasi, *Macht und Ohnmacht des Geistes* (Freiburg: Karl Alber, 1946), Chap. 2, "Betrachtung über das Dasein: Aristoteles, Nikomachische Ethik."

6. PIA 253–61, 267–68; DW; G63 94; G21 1–2; G20 250/185, 364–65/264, 394/285; SZ 92/96, 184/178.

7. DW; PIA 240, 255–59; G63 70, 27, 10; G19 §§7–8, 19–24; G20 380/275, 393/284, 419/303; Sheehan, "Caveat Lector," p. 40; SZ 227/215, 184/178.

8. PIA 254–68; G63 11; G19 §§3–9, 18–19, 23; G21 127–95; SZ 298/268.

15. Indications of Ethics

1. Carl L. Becker, *The Heavenly City of the Eighteenth-Century Philosophers* (New Haven: Yale University Press, 1979).

2. G61 36–37, 66–70, 162; G56/57 7–11, 24, 127; G63 15–20; G9 6. See Jean Grondin's important essays: "Die Hermeneutik der Faktizität als ontologische Destruktion und Ideologiekritik," in Dietrich Papenfuss und Otto Pöggeler (eds.), *Zur philosophischen Aktualität Heideggers*, Vol. 2: *Im Gespräch der Zeit* (Frankfurt: Klostermann, 1990), pp. 163–78; "The Ethical and Young Hegelian Motives in Heidegger's Hermeneutics of Facticity," in RHS.

3. G61 162–64, 13–39, 196–97, 56, 183; G58 85, 198, 248. Regarding "formal indication," cf. Th. C. W. Oudemans, "Heideggers 'logische Untersuchungen,' " *Heidegger Studies* 6 (1990): 85–105; DEW 23–25.

4. See Otto Pöggeler, *Neue Wege mit Heidegger* (Munich: Karl Alber, 1992), pp. 317–39.

5. Günther Stern, *Die Rolle der Situationskategorie bei den 'Logischen Sätzen'*, Doctoral Dissertation, Albert-Ludwigs-Universität, Freiburg, 1924. A shortened, revised version appears as Chapter 7, "Satz und Situation," in Stern's *Über das Haben: Sieben Kapitel zur Ontologie der Erkenntnis* (Bonn: Friedrich Cohen, 1928). I am grateful to Theodore Kisiel for alerting me to this work and for information about Stern's participation in Heidegger's seminars. See also the references in SZ 103/108, 220/209 to the theory of signs in Husserl's First Investigation. For the following, see LU1 85–97/313–22.

6. Derrida, *Speech and Phenomena*, pp. 103–104.

7. Stern, *Über das Haben*, pp. 167–71.

8. *Metaphysics* 1076a. Gadamer has explored this tension in his *Die Idee des Guten zwischen Platon und Aristoteles*, pp. 77–103.

9. G61 32–33, 141–42, 154, 88, 99, 145; G9 10–11, 42; G63 18; G21 410–14.

10. G61 141, 67, 34–35, 159–62, 153, 180; G63 76, 16; G9 7–9, 22, 42–43, 4.

11. Jacques Derrida, *Of Spirit: Heidegger and the Question*, tr. Geoffrey Bennington and Rachel Bowlby (Chicago: University of Chicago Press, 1989).

12. See Frank Schalow, *The Renewal of the Heidegger-Kant Dialogue: Action, Thought, and Responsibility* (Albany: State University of New York Press, 1992).

13. Jacques Derrida, "Force of Law: The 'Mystical Foundation of Authority,' " in Drucilla Cornell et al. (eds.), *Deconstruction and the Possibility of Justice* (New York: Routledge, 1992), pp. 3–67.

14. See Manfred Riedel (ed.), *Rehabilitierung der praktischen Philosophie*, 2 Vols. (Freiburg: Rombach, 1972, 1974); Hans-Georg Gadamer, *Truth and Method* (New York: Continuum, 1975), pp. 278–305, 489; Hannah Arendt, *The Human Condition* (Chicago: University of Chicago Press, 1958); Jürgen Habermas, *Theory and Praxis*, tr. J. Viertel (Boston: Beacon Press, 1973), p. 42, n. 4; Richard Rorty, *Philosophy and the Mirror of Nature* (Princeton: Princeton University Press, 1980), p. 319; Richard J. Bernstein, *Beyond Objectivism and Relativism* (Philadelphia: University of Pennsylvania Press, 1983), pp. 109–69.

15. RH 236–67; Caputo, *Demythologizing Heidegger*; Krell, *Daimon Life*.

16. Kisiel, "The Genesis of Being and Time: Its Doxographic Surface and Hermeneutic Depth"; Jacques Derrida, "The Principle of Reason: The University in the Eyes of Its Pupils," *Diacritics* 13 (1983): 3–20.

17. Cf. Jacques Derrida, "Geschlecht: Sexual Difference, Ontological Difference," *Research in Phenomenology* 13 (1983): 65–83.

18. See HA 390–95 and John D. Caputo, "Heidegger's *Kampf*: The Difficulty of Life," *Graduate Faculty Philosophy Journal* 14–15 (1991): 61–83.

19. John D. Caputo, "*Sorge* and *Kardia*: The Hermeneutics of Factical Life and the Categories of the Heart," in RHS.

16. Reinscribing Heidegger

1. See Caputo, *Demythologizing Heidegger* and RH Chap. 6; HN 47; Jürgen Habermas, "Hans-Georg Gadamer: Urbanizing the Heideggerian Province," in his *Philosophical-Political Profiles*, tr. Frederick G. Lawrence (Cambridge: MIT Press, 1983), pp. 191–99; and my "Persons, *Kinesis*, Demythologizing," in Roy Martinez (ed.), *Hermeneutics after Gadamer* (forthcoming).

2. For details of Heidegger's interpretations of Kant, as well as for a positive appreciation of his readings of such Kantian themes as "imagination" and the ethics of "respect," see Frank Schalow, "The Kantian Schema of Heidegger's Late Marburg Period," and Daniel O. Dahlstrom, "Heidegger's Kant-Courses at Marburg" in RHS; Schalow, *The Renewal of the Heidegger-Kant Dialogue*; John Sallis, *Echoes: After Heidegger* (Bloomington: Indiana University Press, 1990); Daniel O. Dahlstrom, "Heideggers Kant-Kommentar, 1925–36," *Philosophisches Jahrbuch* 96 (1989): 343–66; Charles Sherover, *Heidegger, Kant, and Time* (Bloomington: Indiana University Press, 1971).

3. PA 98–99; EMH 162; William Barrett, *The Illusion of Technique* (New York: Doubleday, 1978), p. 234; Theodor W. Adorno, *The Jargon of Authenticity*, tr. Knut Tarnowski and Frederic Will (Evanston: Northwestern University Press, 1973).

4. HB 27; G9 103–22/BW 95–112; G9 123, 164, 173–75/ER 3, 103, 127–31; Thomas Sheehan, "On Movement and the Destruction of Ontology," *Monist* 64 (1981): 537; OWE 136ff.

5. Schelling, *Werke*, ed. Manfred Schröter, vol. 4 (Munich: C. H. Beck'sche Verlagsbuchhandlung, 1927), pp. 252, 296.

6. Cf. Werner Marx, *Heidegger and the Tradition*, tr. Theodore Kisiel and Murray Greene (Evanston: Northwestern University Press, 1971), pp. 243–56 and *Gibt es auf Erden ein Mass? Grundbestimmungen einer nichtmetaphysischen Ethik* (Hamburg: Felix Meiner, 1983), pp. 1–60; Jürgen Habermas, *The Philosophical Discourse of Modernity: Twelve Lectures*, tr. Frederick Lawrence (Cambridge: MIT Press, 1987), pp. 131–60; Caputo, "Heidegger's *Kampf*," pp. 72–77.

7. G9 313–64/BW 193–242; G5 269–320/PLT 91–142; G5 321–73/EGT 13–58; NG 193–219/45–67.

8. Cf. Richard Bernstein, "Heidegger on Humanism," in his *Philosophical Profiles* (Philadelphia: University of Philadelphia Press, 1986), pp. 197–220; Murray Miles, "Heidegger and the Question of Humanism," *Man and World* 22 (1989): 427–51; HCM 255–68.

9. Cf. Jürgen Habermas, "The Great Effect," in his *Philosophical-Political Profiles*, pp. 58–59; Adorno, *The Jargon of Authenticity*; Herbert Marcuse, "Heidegger's Politics: An Interview with Herbert Marcuse by Frederick Olafson," *Graduate Faculty Philosophy Journal* 6 (1977): 28–40, and "Enttäuschung" in EMH 162; John D. Caputo, "Thinking, Poetry and Pain," *The Southern Journal of Philosophy* 28 (1989): 155–81.

10. Emmanuel Levinas, "As If Consenting to Horror," tr. Paula Wissing, *Critical Inquiry* 15 (1989): 487.

11. Caputo, "Thinking, Poetry and Pain," pp. 155–81.

12. Cf. Thomas Sheehan, "Heidegger's Philosophy of Mind," in G. Fløistad (ed.), *Con-*

temporary Philosophy: A New Survey, Vol. 4: *Philosophy of Mind* (Hague: Martinus Nijhoff, 1983), pp. 287, 304, 309, and "On Movement and the Destruction of Ontology," pp. 535–36.

13. Walter Kaufmann, *From Shakespeare to Existentialism* (New York: Doubleday, 1960), pp. 339–69.

14. Sieg, " 'Die Verjudung des deutschen Geistes,' " p. 19; PA 101. Regarding Heidegger's Helleno-Germanic bias and his involvement with National Socialism, cf. RH Chap. 6; HN 38–47; Derrida, *Of Spirit: Heidegger and the Question*; HA 363–404; Richard Rorty, "Taking Philosophy Seriously," *The New Republic*, April 11, 1989: 31–34; Jürgen Habermas, "Work and Weltanschauung: The Heidegger Controversy from a German Perspective," tr. John McCumber, *Critical Inquiry* 15 (1989): 431–45.

15. Cf. HCM 268–71; Krell, *Daimon Life*; Derrida, "Geschlecht: Sexual Difference, Ontological Difference," pp. 65–83; "*Geschlecht* II: Heidegger's Hand," 161–96; *Spurs: Nietzsche's Styles,* tr. Barbara Harlow (Chicago and London: University of Chicago Press, 1978).

16. Cf. Krell, *Daimon Life*; HCM 191–97, 241–44; RH 153–54, 205, n. 16, 288; Derrida, *Of Spirit*, pp. 47–57; "*Geschlecht* II: Heidegger's Hand," pp. 161–96; John Llewelyn, *The Middle Voice of Ecological Conscience* (London: Macmillan, 1991).

17. Heinrich Petzt, *Auf einen Stern zu gehen* (Frankfurt: Societät, 1983), p. 232.

18. Sheehan, "Introduction: Heidegger, the Project and the Fulfillment," p. viii.

19. Petzt, *Auf einen Stern zu gehen,* p. 43; cf. Hans-Georg Gadamer, "Back from Syracuse?," *Critical Inquiry* 15 (1989): 427–30.

20. Geddes, *20th-Century Poetry and Poetics,* p. 7.

21. Hans-Georg Gadamer, "Auf dem Rückgang zum Anfang," in his *Neuere Philosophie, I: Hegel, Husserl, Heidegger, Gesammelte Werke,* Vol. 3 (Tübingen: J. C. B Mohr, 1987), p. 406.

22. See, for example, Krell, *Daimon Life*; Caputo, *Demythologizing Heidegger* and RH; and my Chapter 2.

23. Cf. HA 390–97; Caputo, "Heidegger's *Kampf*," pp. 61–83; and my "Persons, *Kinesis, Demythologizing.*"

24. Derrida, *Speech and Phenomena,* p. 104.

Index

JOHN VAN BUREN is Assistant Professor of Philosophy at Fordham University. He is coeditor of *Reading Heidegger from the Start: Essays in His Earliest Thought* and translator of *Ontology (Hermeneutics of Facticity)* by Martin Heidegger.